W9-CCU-883

BOOKS BY LADISLAS FARAGO

The Game of the Foxes
The Broken Seal
It's Your Money
Patton: Ordeal and Triumph
Strictly from Hungary
The Tenth Fleet
Burn After Reading
War of Wits
Behind Closed Doors
Secret Missions
Axis Grand Strategy
German Psychological Warfare
The Riddle of Arabia
Palestine at the Crossroads
Abyssinian Stop Press
Abyssinia on the Eve

Classified

The Japanese: His Character and Morale
History of Propaganda in World War II
Propaganda and Psychological Warfare
Morale and Its Maintenance in the German Navy

Aftermath

Martin Bormann and the Fourth Reich

BY

LADISLAS FARAGO

Simon and Schuster
NEW YORK

PUBLISHED BY SIMON AND SCHUSTER
ROCKEFELLER CENTER, 630 FIFTH AVENUE
NEW YORK, NEW YORK 10020

SBN 671-21676-7
LIBRARY OF CONGRESS CATALOGUE CARD NUMBER: 73-22782
DESIGNED BY IRVING PERKINS
MANUFACTURED IN THE UNITED STATES OF AMERICA
BY AMERICAN BOOK-STRATFORD PRESS, INC.

1 2 3 4 5 6 7 8 9 10

For
Professor Robert M. W. Kempner,
with a profound sense of admiration and gratitude,
and my wife,
again and forever

Contents

Part Four: Trouble in the Fourth Reich

Part Five: Contours of the Third World

"I have no premonition of death; on the contrary, my burning desire is to live."

—Martin Bormann *to his wife, on February 19, 1945*

"The Führer is dead! Every man for himself!"

—Sergeant Tornow, *kennelman in the Führerbunker, upon hearing of Hitler's suicide on April 30, 1945*

Martin Bormann, former Reichsleiter, head of the Nazi Party chancery and secretary of the Führer, survived World War II and managed to escape to Argentina in 1948, with the help of the Perón regime.

When I was in contact with him in February 1973, he had just moved from Chile to southern Bolivia. A very sick man, he was cared for by four German nursing sisters of the Redemptorist Order in their convent near Tupiza, a remote region of Potosí Province in the Andes.

Until recently, Bormann was in Argentina, again enjoying the hospitality and protection of the man he called his "great benefactor," the late President Juan Domingo Perón.

He was living on a secluded estate of friends just north of the General Paz Speedway, overlooking the Rio de la Plata. He was as well and as comfortable as a man of his age could be—he celebrated his 74th birthday on June 17, 1974.

Introduction

The Search for Martin Bormann and the Mystery of His Death in Berlin

1

On August 11, 1973, a military court in Minsk in Byelorussia sentenced to death by firing squad four native Nazis for their participation, as members of the 57th [German] Police Battalion commanded by an SS thug named Hans Ziegland, in the shooting of Jews and partisans in a cowshed near the village of Soligorsk. Retribution thus came to them twenty-eight years after the war, at a time when the prosecution of Nazi criminals had become a rarity.

The trial rekindled the gruesome memories of the Nazi era with the by now familiar drama of such proceedings. A witness shook an accusing fist at the prisoners in the dock as he described how, in February 1943, Ziegland's men shot him with a group of fellow captives. He was only wounded, but he feigned death, then crawled out from among the corpses and escaped to the nearby woods. He survived both the war and his own execution to bear witness now against the killers.

A few days before, at Kennedy Airport in New York, a woman was placed on a plane and flown to Düsseldorf to stand trial for the murder of inmates at the Ravensbrück concentration camp, where she had been stationed during the war with an SS squad of female guards. Almost three decades had elapsed before she was finally brought to justice. She had married an American and settled in Queens, a New York borough populated largely by the conservative middle class, where her neighbors grew to like her for what they described as her kindness to stray dogs. Then, abruptly, her case was revived by the American authorities, who shipped her back to Germany where she was wanted for murder.

At about the same time, the governments of France and Peru petitioned Bolivia to extradite a man going by the name of Klaus Altmann. For some twenty years, Altmann had lived in comfort and affluence in La Paz, managing a prosperous maritime company, supported by the admiral in command of landlocked Bolivia's little "navy" of gunboats. Then it was discovered that this portly pillar of the community was, in fact, the notorious Nazi Klaus Barbie. He was wanted in Lyons, France, where, during World War II as a Gestapo commander, he had ordered the torture-murder of forty-one-year-old Jean Moulin, former prefect of Eure-et-Loir, who became a legendary French resistance hero; Obersturmführer Barbie had also sent a thousand children of Lyons to their death in an extermination camp.

For well over a year after he had been unmasked, Barbie-alias-Altmann fought off retribution with the help of his powerful Bolivian friends. Then suddenly they seemed to have abandoned him. Barbie was sent to prison in La Paz pending the outcome of a series of extradition hearings in various Bolivian courts. He had been sentenced to death in France *in absentia* more than a quarter century before.*

Almost overnight in early 1973, long-delayed trials of war criminals were placed on the calendars of courts in Germany, Poland, the Soviet Union and Yugoslavia. Nazis confidently expecting to escape revenge after all these years were caught in a new dragnet. Others who had been released from custody were rearrested to be tried at last. The delayed-action justice reached high up into the ranks of prominent Nazis who had faded quietly into the postwar world and became convinced that they would never be called to answer for their old crimes.

* In the end, both extradition attempts failed. The pro-Nazi Bolivian regime of Colonel Hugo Banzer Suárez not only refused to abide by the decision of its own courts to extradite Barbie, but vowed to "protect" him, as President Banzer put it, "from any attempt to kidnap him by former members of the French resistance movement." In Peru, Altmann-Barbie was formerly charged (in his absence) on December 6, 1973, with being one of the leaders of an international currency smuggling ring. For the strange case of Altmann-Barbie, and of Banzer's Bolivia as one of the last havens of Nazi fugitives in the world, see page 408. Incidentally, in a book (*S.O.E. in France*) Professor M. R. D. Foot claimed Barbie was "in Westphalia," adding the gratuitous anti-American slant: "The French tracked him down there after the war, but could not persuade the Americans to extradite him."

In Argentina, the odious case of Dr. Josef Mengele, the infamous "angel of death" in the Auschwitz-Birkenau murder camps, was suddenly revived by a federal judge in the District Court of San Martin. Nazis throughout South America lived in fear for their future as the tolerance of the authorities in Brazil, Peru and Paraguay showed signs of ending.

Even in the United States, which appeared to be most remote from the problem (but was not, in fact, for many Nazi criminals had succeeded in submerging here), a sudden stirring propelled the issue to the front page of *The New York Times.* Under a three-column headline ("U. S. Opens New Drive on Former Nazis"), Ralph Blumenthal wrote on December 30, 1973: "Immigration investigators here have been put in charge of a new countrywide effort to resolve the long-dormant cases of suspected Nazi war criminals living in the United States." District Director Sol Marks of the Immigration and Naturalization Service confirmed that thirty-eight persons were "under investigation"—all that was left of sixty-five suspects whose cases had been allowed to remain dormant for years.

During those years, nine of them died, seventeen vanished without a trace, one left the country on his own. Twenty-five of the remaining thirty-eight managed to become citizens in the meantime, among them Bishop Valerian D. Trifa, of the Rumanian Orthodox Church in Michigan, who was naturalized in 1957. Bishop Trifa is wanted in Rumania to serve a life sentence imposed *in absentia* for his alleged leadership, as the Führer of pro-Nazi Iron Guard students in Bucharest, of a bloody uprising in 1941. Another member of this Nazi group, a carpenter living in the New York suburb of Mineola on Long Island, was sentenced to death by a Soviet war crime tribunal in 1965.

According to two Immigration Department officials—Vincent A. Schiano, the former chief trial attorney in New York, and Investigator Anthony J. DeVito—their pursuit of the Nazi criminals who are left at large in the United States, from coast to coast, had been "hampered by political pressures from Washington." As a result, they complained, "only a handful of suspected Nazi war criminals had ever been prosecuted" in the United States—that is, until recently.*

* The most notorious case of a suspected war criminal residing unmolested in the United States is that of Dr. Andrija Artukovic, who was Minister of the Interior and later Minister of Justice in the bloody Pavelic government in Croatia that, if possible, outdid even the German Nazis in the persecution of Jews. The Croats contributed to the extermination of 25,000 out of a Jewish population of 30,000, the five thousand

I would like to think that I have made a contribution to this sudden change in the international attitude toward these criminals.

It was, indeed, one of my hopes when embarking on this project that I might be able to rekindle the worldwide dormant conscience. But frankly, this was not the basic purpose of my endeavor. I was not motivated by any sanguinary thirst for punitive reprisal, nor was I imbued with the missionary zeal of men like Simon Wiesenthal and Tuvia Friedmann, who seek to pursue the fugitive Nazis to the end of the world to prevent us from ever forgetting the holocaust.

I have long been intrigued by the moral issue of responsibility in public life, that people, no matter how high or low, are liable for their actions. I became interested specifically in the difference between collective and individual responsibilities. I was troubled by the consequences of situations in which a single individual or a small, privileged group of powerful individuals takes on *collective* responsibility for all acts of the state, thereby absolving of *individual* responsibility the executors of their decisions and orders. This was the case in the closed society of the League of Assassins, a secret order of extremist Shiites that flourished in Syria in the eleventh century. Unquestioning obedience from its members was demanded by superiors, who regarded their retainers—called "the Uninitiated"—as mere instruments of murder.

The worst example of such phenomena in civilized society occurred in Germany during the Hitler regime, between 1933 and 1945. The omnipotent, hypnotic Führer arrogated to himself total and personal responsibility for everything that went on in the Third Reich and thus made possible the perpetration of the most horrendous crimes, leading to war and to the deliberate murder of millions.

But then one morning in the spring of 1945, his followers woke up to find that their Führer was no longer there to assume responsibility for their deeds. Overnight, the collective responsibility had dissolved. *Responsibility shifted to the individual.* Moreover, in the

---

escaping only because they lived in the Italian zone and the Italians refused to surrender them. The three Croatian ringleaders escaped after the war, President Ante Pavelic to Spain and Argentina, Gestapo chief Eugene Kvaternik to Argentina, and Artukovic to the United States, where he arrived in 1948 on a visitor's visa. Pavelic was shot in Buenos Aires and later died of his wounds in Spain; Kvaternik was assassinated in Argentina. But deportation proceedings, pending before a federal court in Los Angeles since 1959, have failed to uproot Dr. Artukovic and return him to Yugoslavia, where he is wanted for mass murder.

person of the victors, an authority suddenly appeared in the lives of these forsaken people to actually make them personally responsible for their acts. I decided to examine how this sudden challenge to thousands of individuals was met.

I found that some could not cope with it and committed suicide. A few were so overcome by feelings of personal guilt that they denounced themselves, though not always succeeding in drawing attention to themselves or getting the punishment they craved. Still others, if only a relative handful, have paid the penalty for their crimes under sentences imposed by Allied and German courts. Others still—indeed, the majority of those criminally involved—sought to escape their responsibility by submerging in the postwar world, often with counterfeit identities.

Statistics prepared by the Ludwigsburg Center for the Investigation of Nazi War Crimes, a German government agency of admirable intentions with about a hundred employees headed by forty-nine-year-old, Munich-born Dr. Adalbert Rückerl, show that a total of 100,000 German nationals and so-called *Volksdeutsche,* nationals of other countries of German extraction, were directly involved in the murder of innocent people as members of various execution teams. According to Dr. Rückerl, the Allies succeeded in arresting only 50,000 of them to face trials on various war-crime charges. But only 5,025 of those ultimately tried were convicted, and of the 818 sentenced to death, only 489 were executed.

As far as the Germans' own prosecution of Nazi criminals is concerned, exact statistics are difficult to come by.* When the so-called Auschwitz trial of but twenty-two of the camp's hundreds of guards opened on December 20, 1963, Gerd Wilcke of *The New York Times* regarded it as a reminder for many Germans that they

* "The Germans as a group," wrote Gerd Wilcke in 1963, "are widely split over the need of war-crimes trials nearly two decades after the crimes were committed. The older generation, perhaps because of its direct involvement, tends to favor the quick end of the proceedings. Younger people, backed by most members of the Government [of Christian Democrats], argue that no matter what the cost and effort, a law-abiding nation cannot afford to let matters rest until offenders are punished." Although written ten years ago, Wilcke's observation is still remarkably accurate for today's Germany. Strange as it may seem, the Christian Democrats under Adenauer, Erhard and even Kiesinger were far more energetic in pursuing the criminal elements among the overseas remnants of Nazism than were the Socialists and Free Democrats of the Brandt coalition. In Argentina, for instance, I was told on high authority that no inquiry involving Bormann had been received from the Brandt-Scheel government, whereas such inquiries used to be quite frequent, especially during the long regime of Konrad Adenauer.

had a long way to go before the last known Nazi criminal would be brought to justice. Today, ten years later, no German in authority would even attempt to predict when the books will be closed.*

The prosecution of Nazi crimes is not a federal responsibility in West Germany. In 1958, when the Ludwigsburg Center was originally set up (proceeding against a mere 590 "primary" suspects during the first five years of its existence), Bonn farmed out the delicate and unpopular task of homemade retribution to the eleven *Länder,* the states which together constitute the Federal Republic, each of which is sovereign in juridical matters. Some, like the State of Hesse, handle celebrities of the Bormann and Mengele brand. Most of them deal perfunctorily with the small fry in more or less obscure proceedings.

The Germans of today are as anti-Nazi as any people in the world. Yet the manner in which the job is handled in both Germanys, East and West, is little short of farcical. A whole book could (and should) be written about the rather odd judicial process and convoluted legal machinery of which the main beneficiaries are former Nazis with criminal records. Such a book would be comic were its theme not so tragic.

In early 1973, meeting on West German soil for the first time, the International Committee of the Survivors of Auschwitz deplored the fact that twenty-eight years after the war, innumerable Nazi criminals still remained at large, due mainly to infinite postponement of proceedings against them. The Auschwitz committee cited "four big Nazi criminals" by name, living free despite their well-documented murderous past: Horst Wagner, the Foreign Ministry's liaison man to Adolf Eichmann, Dr. Horst Schumann, a Luftwaffe medical officer engaged in experiments for the mass sterilization of inmates in concentration camps, Johannes Thümmler, a Gestapo "judge" in Katowice who was personally responsible for the murder of 658 Poles, and Theodor Albert Ganzenmüller, the under-secretary in the Nazis' Transportation Ministry who saw to it that the death trains to Auschwitz ran on time.

West German justice grinds slowly for such key Nazis. In most states the courts proceed so casually, and at such a leisurely pace,

* On May 5, 1955, the Allies, both tired of and embarrassed by what used to be their lofty and determined anti-Nazi stance, abdicated their responsibility of punishing the criminals of the Hitler era, leaving the task entirely to the West German authorities. The Soviet Union was not a party to this Anglo-American surrender of an unfinished business to hands which are unlikely ever to finish it.

that only two trial days per week are usually held in cases involving Nazi criminals.

The dilatory tactics of the judicial process reflect the general attitude of the public to the prosecution of the Nazi criminals. What Alexander Mitscherlich called "corrupted apperception" *(korrumpiertes Bewusstsein)* of the Nazi past, including its blatantly criminal aspects, remains widespread among the Germans whose own repudiation of Hitler and anti-Nazi measures had left much to be desired. Hitler and his Nazis were eventually evicted, not by the Germans in a mighty rising against evil, but by the Allies and the Soviet Union with the sacrifice of their own sons.

"Germany," wrote Mitscherlich in his gripping introduction to the record of the murderous doctors' trial in Nuremberg,

> this classic land of revolutions which do not take place, will now be compelled, after stubborn resistance, to come to grips with that crucial showdown that anywhere else would produce a revolutionary process: the violent and emancipatory reaction against the unbearable burden of "Führers" who have so deeply entangled themselves and the country in their guilt. We staged no revolution after 1945. During that critical period, when a revolutionary period of transition would have brought a purgative relief, the Allies coddled us. The trials of Nuremberg, the denazification process did not stem from German initiative.

Mitscherlich spoke of *verdrängte Schuld*—repressed guilt—which emerges but somnambulantly, still not certain whether it will ever penetrate into the consciousness of the Germans. "Only time will show," he wrote, "whether progress has been made and maturity reached, by recognizing and ingesting our guilt."

The redeeming concept of Hitler's blanket responsibility for the deeds of the individual was shattered in the dock at Nuremberg, of all places, by Dr. Hans Frank, of all men, who was once Hitler's own defense attorney, then became the Nazi despot of Poland under whose rule millions died. "I myself," he said, "have never installed an extermination camp for Jews or promoted the existence of such camps; but if Adolf Hitler personally laid that dreadful responsibility on his people, then it is mine too. . . . A thousand years will pass and still this guilt of Germany will not have been erased." It was the pathetic cry of a single man. It had no echo outside the courtroom.

Cases that are featured prominently abroad receive but scant attention in the German press. In a typical example on July 16, 1964, D.P.A., the German press association, reported the aborted trial of SS Hauptsturmführer Otto Hunsche, one of Eichmann's chief henchmen at large, in an item of forty-six words. It took up exactly one inch in the newspapers that deemed the news that the man charged with personal responsibility for the murder of 1,200 Hungarian Jews had been declared unfit to stand trial important enough to print.

The story of the Auschwitz committee's convention in Düsseldorf was played down in the German news media. Its statement pinpointing the four key Nazi criminals attracted little attention and evoked no indignation.

Any Nazi criminal who is able to afford one of the shrewd attorneys specializing in the defense of these people (such as Dr. Fritz Steinacker of Frankfurt who represents Dr. Josef Mengele) is given broad opportunity to take the fullest advantage of the innumerable loopholes in the laws. Since most of the accused Nazis assure their continued freedom or escape prosecution by pretending to be so ill that they cannot stand trial or even undergo preliminary questioning, Dr. Robert M. W. Kempner, the American dean of the prosecution of Nazi criminals, a hale and vigorous septuagenarian, unforgetting and unforgiving, who is still pursuing them relentlessly, recently proposed that a free nursing home be set up to restore the failing health of the remaining unpunished major Nazi criminals. It might be sufficient to put an end to what is a transparent subterfuge.

Because of the decentralization, there are no comprehensive (or, for that matter, reliable) records kept in Germany on the exact number of Germans tried for war crimes in German courts. Between 1945 and 1963, the German judicial authorities investigated approximately 30,000 cases, producing 12,846 indictments. However, only 5,426 convictions were obtained. In answer to a resolution of the United Nations General Assembly of 1969, the Federal Republic of Germany stated on July 7, 1970, that a total of 6,215 Nazi criminals had been "sentenced to varying terms of imprisonment" under German jurisdiction as of that date. A mere 403 of the defendants had been convicted of premeditated murder, which in these cases invariably meant mass murder. The West German authorities executed only three of the twelve convicted Nazis doomed before the abolition of capital punishment in 1949. Significantly, 90 percent of all convictions were obtained prior to 1954, which may be a reflection of the more lenient attitude adopted by the German courts as the memories of the Nazi past recede into limbo.

These statistics show that at least half of those guilty of mass murder during the Hitler regime have never been found or touched (the Poles alone have a waiting list of 15,000 Germans wanted for murder and plunder). Moreover, only about 20 percent of those apprehended have been brought to justice thus far. Professor Kempner has written:

> Even today many of the murders committed by members of the SS remain unatoned. In the [series of] Nuremberg trials, only five high SS-officers and seven SS-doctors had been executed, aside from [SS-Obergruppenführer] Ernst Kaltenbrunner who had been sentenced to death by the International Military Tribunal. The other SS-leaders convicted in Nuremberg on charges of murder have been prematurely pardoned and freed, as a result of strong pressure by certain, partly still anonymous *Hintermänner* (sponsors).

In the early fifties, the Allies magnanimously amnestied thousands of Nazi criminals, the exact circumstances of which represent a festering but carefully concealed scandal. As the Cold War was heating up, in a process begun in 1946 by Secretary of State James F. Byrnes and inspired by Dean Acheson, the United States shifted its traditional alignment in Europe from Britain and France to the renascent Germany of Konrad Adenauer. The great pied piper of Bonn (whose own chief aide was a former Nazi official who had drafted the lethal anti-Jewish laws) promoted the idea, at first subtly, then vigorously, that the wholesale prosecution of the Nazis was putting "a heavy psychological burden on the rearmament problem" in the course of West Germany's rehabilitation for its role in the "defense of Western Europe."

On June 6, 1949, and July 21, 1950, jurisdiction in the prosecution of Nazi criminals was transferred by two executive orders from the military to the civilian United States High Commissioner, John J. McCloy. Mr. McCloy, a pioneer among the eloquent and effective anti-Nazis in the United States, was now turning *Realpolitiker*.

Although in uniform, the American judges and prosecutors in Nuremberg were distinguished lawyers in civilian life. "They had not come," Raul Hilberg wrote, "to exonerate or to convict. They were impressed with their task, and they approached it with much experience in the law and little anticipation of the facts." But the climate of Washington was becoming the atmosphere of Nuremberg. "We have to worry about the Russians now," James Morris told Josiah DuBois, judge and prosecutor respectively in the I. G. Farben trial. Brigadier General Telford Taylor, the brilliant New York attorney who had succeeded Supreme Court Justice Robert H. Jackson as the senior American prosecutor, was forced to write in his final report that, on the whole, "the sentences became lighter as time went on."

The whole structure was then gradually liquidated when Mr. McCloy took over. There was nothing sinister about the change, but its long-range implications became painfully obvious only much later in hindsight. Quietly in April 1950, a three-member Clemency Board, consisting of a New York Supreme Court judge, the chairman of the New York Board of Parole, and a State Department lawyer, arrived in Germany and recommended that the whole system be overhauled from top to bottom. Individual sentences were to be revised downward. In case of variations in sentences for similar offenses the most lenient was to be adopted henceforth. Imprisonment before and during trial was to be counted as time served. Sentences were to be cut by one third for "good behavior."

On January 9, 1951, a bipartisan German delegation led by the president of the Bundestag met with Mr. McCloy behind closed doors, urging him to adopt the recommendations of his Clemency Board. The prison doors opened, the cells emptied. By January 31, when Mr. McCloy announced as his future policy and practice the recommendations of the Board, he had commuted most of the death sentences and freed about half of the convicted Nazis. Among those promptly released were *all* the imprisoned industrialists, urgently needed for the impending German *Wirtschaftswunder,* the economic miracle. The background of McCloy's decision and the shape of things yet to come were spelled out succinctly by Dr. Fritz Ter Meer, one of the major defendants in the I. G. Farben case, charged with abusing inmates of concentration camps in forced labor. "Now," he said in the summer of 1950, walking out of jail in the company of eighteen of his freed colleagues, "that they have Korea on their hands, the Americans are a lot more friendly."

Emboldened by their success, the Germans intensified the pressure on McCloy, and he commuted the sentences of twenty-one of twenty-eight SS murderers awaiting execution at Landsberg. But when he refused to relent in the cases of the remaining seven—leaders of the killer-commandos and Oswald Pohl, the SS economic tsar who managed the loot of the extermination camps—a chorus of German politicians led by Vice Chancellor Franz Blücher vehemently criticized him. The seven were eventually executed on June 7, 1951.

On May 5, 1955, in a formal agreement called *Überleitungsvertrag* (a convoluted term in German meaning a "treaty of transfer"), the Allies abdicated their responsibility in this field and charged the Germans with it for the future. By then, the number of perpetrators still in American and British prisons in Germany had shrunk to about two dozen. Their exact number could not be determined because the Allied authorities refused to release any information on this score, in accordance with a directive of March 1954, under which the United States discontinued announcements involving the premature freeing of its Nazi prisoners.

2

Although the vast majority of Nazi criminals live in Germany (some of them once holding official jobs, others prospering in the private sector), my interest was pre-empted by those who chose to escape and start a new life. There are among these fugitives, living mostly in South America, a number of major war criminals missed by the Allied roundup and the German dragnet.

Among them I found Klaus Barbie in Bolivia, Heinrich Müller in Argentina, Josef Mengele in Paraguay, Walter Rauff in Chile, and Friedrich Schwend in Peru. I claim no discovery in unearthing them. They were uncovered by previous inquiries, especially those conducted by Simon Wiesenthal and Dr. Michael Bar-Zohar.

Only one man at the very top remained shrouded in mystery. He was, of course, Martin Bormann.

At the beginning of my inquiry, I was not particularly curious about Bormann and I did not single him out for special scrutiny. All I hoped to do was to establish, once and for all, whether he had really died on his flight from the Führerbunker, or had succeeded in surviving the war.

The scope of my inquiry broadened as my probe progressed. In the end, Martin Bormann became the center of my study. He loomed larger than the rest, for he is after all the highest-ranking survivor of Nazism and the most elusive of the fugitives.

This book is not meant to be either recriminatory or accusatory. It is written rather to raise another issue, which our generation is inclined, if not eager, to overlook. My original attitude toward the project and my understanding of the problem changed radically one afternoon in Lima, Peru, when I listened to an impassioned discourse by Albert Chambon, the French ambassador to Peru, shortly after the unmasking of Klaus Barbie. During World War II, Chambon was a member of the resistance, and he was inmate No. 81490 at the Buchenwald and Annen-Witten concentration camps. The old number is still indelibly tattooed on his wrist.

> The survival of Nazi criminals with impunity in the postwar world [he told me] is not a political issue. Neither is their apprehension a mere matter of criminology. It is clearly a moral issue that weighs heavily on the conscience of mankind and pollutes the climate of our own days. No passage of time, no statutes of limitation can expiate their crimes or make us forget these criminals.
>
> To those who glibly say that they ought to be left alone so many years after the end of the Second World War, I say this: Jesus was crucified by the Romans almost two thousand years ago. Yet the Jews have been made accountable and were persecuted at various times for the murder of this one man.

He spoke with passion and looked at me with tears in his eyes.

> I am a diplomat [he said], a professional victim of compromise and equivocation. For years, I myself was inclined to dismiss the often hysterical charge that these Nazi murderers remain at large among us. But the case of Barbie has brought home to me the tragic truth of this charge and demonstrated the danger these fugitives represent.
>
> Not until all these killers are made to pay the forfeit for their terrible deeds can the world come to peace—to peace with itself.

3

The true purpose of this book may seem to have been somewhat marred by the series of articles that I wrote about Bormann in November 1972. There was a rather bizarre sequel to the publication of the articles. A few days after their appearance in the London *Daily Express,* the authorities of the State of Hesse, who had searched for Bormann on and off, but completely in vain since 1960, announced that they had suddenly found what they suspected to be his skull and some of his bones.

The discovery was said to have been made entirely by accident, but in the exact spot in West Berlin where a deliberate and elaborate search for Bormann's remains produced absolutely no results seven years before. Assuming that the finding of the skull and bones at this particular time was purely accidental, as Procurator Joachim Richter asserted afterwards, it was an amazing coincidence.

I have authoritative proof that Bormann survived the war and went to Argentina in 1948; and obviously he could not have made the trip without his skull and bones. However I feel that a few remarks may be in order here, to set the record straight.

Not a single governmental agency supposedly interested in Bormann and presumably looking for him thought it necessary to contact me, interrogate me, and ask me to produce my documentation. Authorities of the United States, France, and Soviet Union—three members of the Big Four of World War II—remained aloof. The Foreign Office in London dismissed my story with one of those supercilious but basically ephemeral comments that are typical for diplomats in general and for British diplomacy in particular.

The Germans were no exception. If anything, they tried, on the official level, to discredit my material with condescending statements, while the mass-circulation magazines, such as *Stern* and *Der Spiegel,* mounted a campaign of slander, printing a set of mendacious articles and doctored documents.

Even so, I decided to aid the floundering German search for Bormann by submitting to the Hessian authorities my evidence and volunteering my collaboration in the hope that my help, unsolicited as it was, might lead to Bormann's apprehension, in which, I was made to believe, the Germans were genuinely interested. During two visits to the office of the Hessian procurators in Frankfurt—on December 4, 1972, and January 10, 1973—I left with Oberstaatsanwalt (Senior Procurator) Wilhelm Metzner and Staatsanwalt (Procurator) Joachim Richter copies of the key documents in my collection. Moreover, I offered to give them copies of *all* documents in my possession and the names and addresses of South American contacts who could confirm their authenticity. I also suggested that I prepare a list of reputable and competent witnesses (including judges in Argentina, Paraguay and Peru) who could and would testify—under oath if desired—that Bormann had gone to Argentina in 1948 and was still living in South America in 1973.

When the articles first appeared, Herr Metzner promptly joined the chorus of skeptics, expressing no faith in their veracity. However, when he was interviewed by David Binder of *The New York Times* after my first visit to his office, Metzner changed his tune. He told Binder that he had seen some of my documents, they had made a "credible impression" on him, and he had under consideration the immediate reopening of the proceedings as a means of attaining Bormann's extradition.

Before my second visit, at a time when the alleged Bormann skull began to figure prominently in the picture, Richter promised that a "final determination" of the Bormann case would be made on January 15, by which time, he said, the matter of the skeleton would be cleared up conclusively one way or another. Now, however, apparently impressed with my presentation, Herr Metzner overruled his assistant and decided to postpone the "final determination," to give his office time, as he put it, to check out my documentation with the Argentine authorities through the Foreign Ministry in Bonn and the German embassy in Buenos Aires.

The fact that I had to make two visits to Frankfurt (all the way from the United States, at my expense) to confer with these people sheds an interesting and perhaps significant light on the handling of the Bormann search by the German authorities. The impression is widespread, and is shrewdly promoted by German public relations, that while it lasted, the Bormann search was an elaborate effort, presumably conducted by a large team of prosecutors, magistrates and special investigators. In actual fact it was, until 1968, the more or less personal project of the late Procurator General Dr. Fritz Bauer. He was aided in the pursuit of the Bormann search far more energetically by outsiders, like Dr. Kempner and Simon Wiesenthal, than by members of his own staff.

After Bauer's death (which occurred suddenly under somewhat mysterious circumstances), the Bormann case was assigned to an investigating magistrate, Horst von Glasenapp, and Assistant Procurator Joachim Richter. The latter was the very man on Bauer's staff who had consistently refused to share his chief's belief that Bormann was alive. Richter built his case on the premise, promoted by *Stern* magazine for reasons of its own, that the Reichsleiter had died in Berlin on his flight from the Führerbunker.

When Herr von Glasenapp withdrew from the case on December 13, 1971, Richter remained the only official anywhere in West Germany in charge of a search that was purely bureaucratic, using none of the simplest methods and techniques of modern criminal investigation. In other words, what is still believed to have been a broad-based, energetic and competent manhunt for the number-one fugitive of Nazism was in fact a one-man effort, conducted on a shoestring by an elderly, ailing minor official from a cubbyhole in Frankfurt. Moreover, the Germans' sole Bormann hunter proceeded from the preconceived notion that Bormann was dead and the search, inspired by Dr. Bauer, was a waste of time and money.

When I first visited him, Herr Metzner candidly told me that although he was the head of the Office of the Procurator at the Higher Land Court in Frankfurt under State Procurator General Horst Gauf (who had his office in Wiesbaden), neither Herr Gauf nor he himself was directly involved in the Bormann case. They had, as he assured me, only very scant knowledge of the details of the investigation. He asked me, therefore, to come back in January when Procurator Richter, the only member of his staff assigned to and familiar with the case, would return from what Metzner described as an extended sick leave.

I was back in Frankfurt on January 6, 1973, then waited a few days for Herr Richter's return. We had our meeting at last on the tenth in Metzner's office, and I not only produced additional documentation but also submitted a long prepared statement in which I wrote, among other things:

> For all I know, the skeleton recently found in the Invalidenstrasse in Berlin may be that of Bormann. However, no such definitive determination can be made, even on the basis of the best available forensic opinion, without subjecting my documentation to the most meticulous scrutiny in Argentina.
>
> Bormann could not have met two fates after the war—he could not have died in Berlin in 1945 and then come to life in South America three years later. Only one of these two possibilities can correspond to the actual facts.
>
> It is neither my duty nor my intention to pursue the Bormann matter beyond the evidence contained in my documenta-

tion. . . . The final determination of Martin Bormann's fate is a problem only the proper authorities can resolve, by reviewing *all* evidence on hand with equal care and objectivity.

In the end, Gauf and Metzner (who admittedly knew little of the case) accepted Richter's recommendation to reject my offer of collaboration and ignore my documentation. They dismissed the latter out of hand in favor of the fragments of an obscure carcass the Berlin police had tagged *vermutlich Martin Bormann* ("presumably Martin Bormann").*

4

It must be made absolutely clear that, contrary to the widespread belief assiduously cultivated by the German authorities and erroneously reported by the media, the death of Martin Bormann was never definitively established and confirmed, nor was it ever explicitly certified, either by the prosecutors in charge of the *Fahndung* ("search") or by any of the courts to which the case had been submitted by them.

In fact, the German authorities in general and the Hessian authorities in particular showed a strange reluctance to make Bormann's alleged death *official.* He was proclaimed dead, so to speak, not by due judicial process or proper legal determination, but in an arbitrary statement during a show-business-type press conference staged with considerable ballyhoo in Frankfurt, on April 11, 1973.

In that press conference, it was stated that Dr. Hans Jürgen Spengler, a medical examiner of the City of West Berlin (whose office, by another coincidence, was also in the Invalidenstrasse, not far from the spot where the skull and bones were found), had iden-

* This *dénouement,* then still in the making, was obvious to me during my conference with Herr Richter. In its immediate wake, I wrote privately to Mr. Binder, then the Bonn correspondent of *The New York Times:* "Richter tried to bully me into withdrawing my claim. He suggested that I be a good sport and concede that my documents are forgeries. Since I have every reason to believe . . . that my documents are genuine, I did not budge. This confronted Richter with a dilemma. On the one hand, he would like to close the case as conclusively proven that Bormann is dead, basing his conclusion on the forensic evidence from Berlin. On the other hand, I will continue to insist that Bormann survived the war. Metzner is in the middle and, if anything, seems to be leaning slightly towards me." On April 27, 1973, after I had called his attention to certain glaring incongruities and obvious errors in the forensic evidence on the basis of which he had made his final determination, Richter informed me that since he had closed the case (*"das Verfahren von mir abgeschlossen ist"*) he would henceforth ignore my intervention and refrain from answering my letters.

tified "the skeleton" as that of a man, approximately between 1.6 and 1.7 meters (5 feet 4 inches and 5 feet 8 inches) tall, who must have been between thirty and forty years old at the time of his death. Dr. Spengler, whose duties include the testing of drunken drivers and the preparation of blood tests in paternity cases, had "practically no doubt," as it was put, that the skull and the fragments of the skeleton were the remains of Martin Bormann.*

Dr. Spengler's tentative identification seemed to be borne out by an improvised dental chart that Dr. Hugo Johannes Blaschke, Bormann's dentist, had drawn from memory, after the Reichsleiter's alleged death, for the benefit of his Allied interrogators in Nuremberg. Although Dr. Blaschke died a few years after the war and was not around to comment on the contrived chart in 1973, the accuracy of his memory was attested to by one Fritz Echtmann, a dental technician, also from memory. In actual fact, Echtmann never met Bormann and, consequently, never had an opportunity of looking into his mouth. He asserted, however, that once he had made a bridge for a patient he assumed was Bormann, on orders and specifications he had received from Dr. Blaschke.

All the other evidence on which Dr. Spengler based his expert opinion was either conjectural or mere hearsay. No medical charts or X rays of Bormann were available to permit comparisons or to make the identification even nearly as plausible as possible in forensic medicine, which is as much an art as it is an exact science.†

On the basis of this evidence Procurator General Horst Gauf proclaimed peremptorily that "*Bormann ist tot,*" then repeated for greater emphasis and for the benefit of the English-speaking correspondents in the room, "Bormann is dead."

According to Herr Gauf, Bormann died on May 2, 1945, between 1 and 3 A.M., by biting into a glass capsule containing what was described as *Blausäure,* or prussic acid. It was supposedly one of the 850 vials that had been manufactured for the Abwehr, the German military secret service, by the Schering pharmaceutical company, for espionage operatives on perilous missions. Some of

* Bormann would have been a few weeks short of forty-five years old on May 2, 1945. According to his personnel record on file at the Berlin Document Center, his height was 1.65 meters (5 feet 6 inches).

† Bormann's medical chart is on file at the Policlinica Ciancaglini in San Isidro, Argentina (see page 416). According to the best medico-legal opinion I could procure (see page 443), a court pathologist or medical examiner is not qualified to identify a cadaver from random bones found in an old grave. Only an experienced, imaginative forensic anthropologist is competent to make a satisfactory skeletal identification and, as far as I know, no such expert aided Dr. Spengler in his Bormann work.

these capsules, containing *Zyankali* (cyanide of potassium), came into the hands of high officials of the Nazi regime during the final days of the Third Reich and were used by Heinrich Himmler and Hermann Göring to commit suicide.*

The dental picture, which is usually decisive in post-mortem identifications by medical examiners, was of extraordinary interest in this particular case. It added considerably to the confusion regarding the skull that the procurators of Hesse (and, of course, the editors of *Stern*) insisted was that of Martin Bormann.† Missing for some time after the war, because it had been misfiled in the National Archives in Washington, D.C., a set of five head X rays of Adolf Hitler, made in July 1944, had been discovered by Professor Reidar F. Sognnaes of the University of California's School of Dentistry in Los Angeles. The discovery enabled Dr. Sognnaes, whose specialty is oral biology and anatomy, to resolve once and for all the lingering mystery of Hitler's death, obscured by both the Russians and certain German historians, for reasons of their own. With Dr. Blaschke's dental charts now supported by the X rays, Dr. Sognnaes established definitively that the badly charred body that the Russians found in the courtyard of the Reich Chancellery in May 1945 was Hitler's.‡

As soon as photographs of what was alleged to be Bormann's skull appeared in the press, Professor Sognnaes—who had a copy of Dr. Blaschke's memorized dental chart of Bormann and had spent some time previously trying to evaluate it—expressed doubt that the skull found in the Invalidenstrasse was really Bormann's. In actual fact, a series of photographs was issued between December 8, 1972,

* The claim that Bormann committed suicide by biting into one of these Schering capsules was also circumstantial. No chemical analysis was made, for no traces of the *Zyankali* had been found in the skull. Moreover, the procurators failed to develop evidence to support their contention that Bormann had such a vial in his possession. The data they used in putting forward their assertion were obtained *sub rosa* from the Berlin Document Center, the supersecret American depository of captured Nazi documents. The information supplied by the Americans in this matter did not involve Bormann. It was a description of the Schering vial, based on an unpublished report about the investigation of Göring's suicide.

† On December 13, 1972, Inspector Böhme of the West Berlin police, who was in charge of the case, explicitly stated that "preliminary reports show no connection" between "the skull uncovered last week near a spot where some witnesses said Martin Bormann . . . was last seen in 1945" and the missing Reichsleiter. He declined to elaborate on this statement or to change it one way or another when I discussed the matter with him in West Berlin, on November 20, 1973.

‡ The discoveries were, in fact, not as new, and as personal to Dr. Sognnaes, as this might suggest. In the third (1956) edition of *The Last Days of Hitler,* and all subsequent editions of the book, Professor Trevor-Roper had the "lost" X-ray photographs of Hitler's head, and had interpreted them, with the aid of an English dentist, long before their discovery and interpretation by Dr. Sognnaes.

and April 12, 1973, showing what appeared to be *four distinctly different skulls,* each allegedly belonging to the same Bormann.

Skull number one, a formless earthen clod whose picture was published on December 8, 1972, showed only fragments of three or four teeth in the left lower jaw. The second photograph, published two days later, showed a slightly different skull with six distinctly and two vaguely visible teeth in the same area. A third picture, dated December 13, presented *an entirely different skull,* which in the meantime had grown an almost full set of teeth—but still not enough to satisfy Professor Sognnaes.

He found that apart from other apparent discrepancies, and even though the spot where it should have been had been filled with other teeth, a bridge consisting of three teeth was missing from the neatly tidied and liberally betoothed skull number three. Dr. Sognnaes called this to the attention of the German authorities in a letter addressed to Chancellor Willy Brandt, in the mistaken belief that the federal government was involved in the search for Bormann. In the same letter, Professor Sognnaes also asked the Chancellor that he be allowed to examine the skull, since, in the meantime, as he put it, he had "gathered extensive odontological data, including dental crowns, bridges, fillings, missing teeth, as well as the color of the teeth present in . . . Martin Bormann as these conditions existed in 1945."

His letter to Chancellor Brandt, dated January 9, 1973, was forwarded to the Hessian Ministry of Justice, to the attention of Minister Hemfler (a total stranger to the case), only seven weeks later, arriving in Wiesbaden on February 27, 1973. It reached Procurator Richter in Frankfurt on March 2, a Friday, after his office had closed down for the weekend.

Now another astounding coincidence took place. By some miracle for which not even Richter has a convincing explanation, the missing three teeth were suddenly found, allegedly in the vicinity of the spot where, over three months before, the first skull had been discovered. When Professor Sognnaes subsequently heard of the finding of the bridge exactly ten days after his letter of January 9 had reached Herr Richter with a delay of two months, he remarked:

"I wonder whether those three teeth had been dug up with a bulldozer or a teaspoon."

The bridge was then placed in the skull, first in the lower jaw (mistakenly, as it turned out, for Bormann already had a partial bridge, called *Fensterkronenbrücke* there). It was then moved to the upper jaw where it eventually appeared in the photograph of skull number four, what could be called Bormann's "last-but-not-least" skull, as presented at the press conference.*

The request of Professor Sognnaes, who had expressed purely scientific interest in the case, citing his long preoccupation with Hitler's and Bormann's dentistry, that he be permitted to be of help in the dental identification of the controversial skull, was gruffly declined by Richter. He told Dr. Sognnaes that "the German dentists involved in the case . . . do not need his assistance."

Interviewed by the British Broadcasting Corporation on April 12, 1973, Professor Sognnaes stated bluntly that while he regarded his dental identification of Hitler as conclusive, he could not say the same as far as Bormann's identification from his teeth was concerned. After having practically lived with the case for four months, and having prepared his own charts and models of Bormann's dentistry (which differed in important respects from the odontological picture presented by the four successive skulls), Dr. Sognnaes told me in no uncertain terms that he did not believe that the skull found in the Invalidenstrasse was the skull of Bormann. Moreover, he said that by this time (in April) there would be no purpose in his examining the skull, for it had been obviously doctored in the course of tidying it up for presentation at the press conference.

It was a strange press conference, to say the least. The day before, when it was suddenly announced that it would be held, it was too late for me to attend it. I phoned the Procurator's office in Frankfurt from my home in Connecticut. Herr Metzner accepted the call and I asked him whether any reference would be made to the Argentinian papers I had left with him.

"No," he said, "none whatever."

To my next question whether my documents had been considered in the final determination of the case and checked out, he replied that no effort had been made to authenticate any part of my material, implying that the Foreign Ministry in Bonn refused to cooperate by making the necessary inquiries in Argentina. Metzner then said that they would convey to the press their conclusion that Bormann was dead, based entirely on the findings of Dr. Spengler and the opinion of a woman doctor named Matschke.

* How Dental Technician Echtmann could recognize a bridge as his own two months before it was found is another intriguing question to which I could obtain no clarification from Herr Richter.

Although it featured a bust of Bormann especially prepared for the occasion by a Bavarian police officer named Moritz Furtmayr (whose hobby is the making of such "reconstructions" by some pseudo-scientific method said to have been invented by a Russian criminologist), the press conference was anticlimactic. It had been scooped by *Stern* magazine, which printed the facts leaked to it by the Procurator's office and pictures of Furtmayr's bogus bust in its issue dated April 12, which was already on the newsstands on the tenth.

Simon Wiesenthal had bought a copy of *Stern* No. 16, containing the premature revelation of Herr Richter's big secret in Vienna, on his way to Frankfurt to attend the press conference scheduled for the next morning. At the conference he then raised the issue of this gross indiscretion, if not premeditated collusion, with the one German publication that had a professional stake in making Bormann's death official at last. Way back in 1965, *Stern* had assured its readers unequivocally that Bormann had died in Berlin during his flight from the bunker. It was now fighting to vindicate its old and bruised scoop in the light of my revelations.

Richter rose with face flushed and righteous indignation in the tone of his voice, not to deny the fact of his collaboration with *Stern*, but to censure Herr Wiesenthal for his complaint.

"You have given us," he told Wiesenthal testily, "only vague information without any specific names, addresses and dates—tips, in fact, which proved useless in our investigation. On the other hand, Herr Jochen von Lang of *Stern* magazine cooperated with us closely and was instrumental in aiding our determination of the case with invaluable factual data."

As the *Frankfurter Rundschau* pointed out the morning after, Jochen von Lang, the *Stern*'s Bormann expert responsible for its 1965 "scoop" (who was also the source of recurring claims that Bormann and Heinrich Müller were dead), had become the "respected assistant [*Hilfsbeamte*] of the Procurator's office" and Herr Richter's chief aid in the solution of the case. He was, therefore, entitled to a break in a story which, in the final analysis, was his scoop anyway, perhaps even more than the independent product of the official investigators.

When the correspondent of a London newspaper called attention to several glaring discrepancies in the forensic evidence on the basis of which the procurators had made their "final determination of the Bormann case," Richter conceded that they existed, indeed.

But he insisted that such discrepancies occur in any evidence, and the Bormann case was not different from others in which several experts of divers opinion were involved. When he was asked how he explained the accident of finding the skull and bones just when my articles appeared, he shrugged a shoulder and said that it was "pure coincidence."

Richter denied that the determination of the case was a foregone conclusion long before the experts' opinions were in. He disputed this in the face of the fact brought out by Wiesenthal and other correspondents that he had cooperated with *Stern* through the period of suspended activity (December 7, 1972, to April 11, 1973), and enabled the magazine not merely to write its story of the impending press conference well in advance, but also to commission Inspector Furtmayr to create his bust. Moreover, thanks to this close collaboration, *Stern* had ample time to make a documentary motion picture in anticipation of the outcome of which Herr von Lang was never left in any doubt. The crude bust was ready to be featured as the prime exhibit at a press conference. So was the documentary film, which was briskly peddled by *Stern* salesmen to potential buyers at the session.

Allegedly, no official minutes of the conference were made. None of the experts' documents supporting the procurators' conclusion was made available. They are still held closely by Richter. My own efforts to obtain copies of them drew an annoyed reply from Frankfurt, dated December 13, 1973. Writing with what he described as the explicit approval of his superiors (Gauf and Metzner), Richter categorically refused to give me access to any of his documentation, on the grounds that I was not a party to the proceedings and, therefore, was not authorized to see his evidence. He reiterated in his letter that "the relevant decisions of the courts had not been made public" and, therefore, their exact wording cannot be divulged to an outsider like me. As a parting shot, he refused my offer to send him a complimentary copy of this book upon publication and told me that he does not want to hear from me in the future.

The press conference was inconclusive. It settled nothing. In spite of what Messrs. Gauf, Metzner and Richter evidently regarded as definitive forensic proof to support their dramatic resolution of the long-simmering case, they apparently lacked the courage of their conviction since they refrained from declaring Bormann legally dead right then and there. They would rather submit the evidence, they said, to a Hessian court with the motion that it pronounce Bormann dead, thus endorsing the prosecution's preconceived but "inoperative" decision to close the case.*

This was what actually happened. The case was submitted to Strafkammer 3 (the Third Chamber of the Criminal Court in Frankfurt) with a motion that included certain recommendations which were nothing short of outrageous. Messrs. Gauf, Metzner and Richter asked the court to permit them to deliver the alleged remains of the supposed Reichsleiter to the Bormann family for what was called a decent Christian burial. This was in violation if not in open defiance of the will of the victorious Allies. Bormann had been sentenced to death *in absentia* by the International Military Tribunal in Nuremberg, a sentence which is still fully valid and with which the Germans are not permitted to tamper. By the decision of the Allied Control Council, Bormann would, like all the other war criminals who died on the gallows, have to be cremated, to prevent the development of a legend or a movement around their graves that could become Nazi shrines. Moreover, the motion the Hessian procurators submitted to the Strafkammer proposed that the controversial estate of Bormann be settled, allowing his heirs to benefit from his criminally acquired wealth.

The Strafkammer (under Presiding Judge Arnold Schmidt) categorically refused to act on the motion, or even as much as accept the case. The whole matter was returned to the procurators, leaving it to them to make their own determination. "Contrary to what the public was made to believe," wrote Joachim Neander, Frankfurt correspondent of *Die Welt* on July 8, 1973 (three months after the spectacular press conference in which Bormann had been proclaimed dead),

> the case against Martin Bormann is by no means closed. Even the warrant for the arrest of the man who was Adolf Hitler's deputy at the end of the war is still in force.

* To understand what follows, the juridical apparatus of the State of Hesse involved in the Bormann investigation needs to be explained, especially since it is so different from the Anglo-Saxon legal machinery. A lower court called Amtsgericht (in Frankfurt) was the competent juridical forum to issue the original warrant, signed by a judge named Opper, for Bormann's arrest. A state court, or assize, called Landgericht, also in Frankfurt, ordered the so-called *Voruntersuchung,* or preliminary investigation, conducted by a judge in his capacity of investigating magistrate. It was this court that the procurators initially asked to make Bormann's death legal and official. A superior court called Oberlandesgericht was the authority to which the procurators complained when the state court refused to act upon their motion. The Bormann case was dealt with by their criminal divisions, called Strafkammer in the lower and Strafsenat in the higher court. Both the Landgericht and the Oberlandesgericht consist of three judges sitting in cases which come before them.

> Although Procurator Richter, the official in charge at the office of the Hessian Procurator General, had—on the basis of a thorough examination of the skull found in Berlin—announced that the investigation of Bormann had been terminated, it remained concealed from the public that the Procurator General had not marked the case closed, as is the usual practice and procedure, but passed the buck to the Third Criminal Court, the so-called *Beschlusskammer* ["chamber of decision"] to make the juridical determination of the case and cancel the arrest warrant currently in force against Martin Bormann.

"A formal decision has to be made," Richter had said, "in order to cancel the warrant or else any demented police officer could arrest anybody who resembles Bormann or goes by his name." In his eagerness to have the warrant lifted, the fact that "anybody" who looked like Bormann or bore his name actually might be Bormann did not seem to occur to Herr Richter.

Since there were no grounds to *appeal* to a higher court (for no decision had been rendered one way or another), the baffled prosecutors decided to enter what they called a *Beschwerde* (complaint) with another court, hoping to persuade its justices to give them what they wanted. They again failed in their efforts to obtain—this time from the Third Senate of the Criminal Court (under Chief Judge Kiessling)—the verdict that Bormann was dead. *However, they succeeded in persuading the judges to cancel the warrant for his arrest.*

The Bormann case thus took on a strange new complexion. It was only in 1960 that Martin Bormann had become the subject of German investigation. Thanks to the initiative and influence of the late Dr. Fritz Bauer, Herr Gauf's predecessor as Hessian Procurator General, a *Haftbefehl* was issued for Bormann on July 6, 1961, to launch the process called *Fahndung,* a kind of search warrant under the circumstances, rather than a regular warrant for his arrest.

The Strafsenat's verdict (which was met with complete silence in the world press) was, of course, the scandalous compromise in a matter which the court itself had decided to leave basically open and unresolved. The lifting of the warrant, for all practical purposes, sets Bormann free, wherever he may be, to do as he pleases. As it was interpreted by Gauf and his associates, rather than as explicitly designed by the court, it is tantamount to squashing once and for all even the halfhearted German investigation of Bormann, and to terminating the *Fahndung.*

In its broader ramification, even if only by inference, the decision of Judge Kiessling and his colleagues casts a shadow on the validity of the death sentence meted out by the International Military Tribunal. As Herr Richter perceives it, Bormann is now a free man both *de jure* and *de facto*—in a sense also freed of the stigma of guilt as stipulated in the verdict of the International Military Tribunal. As far as the Germans are concerned, his status as a fugitive is over. "For all practical purposes," a distinguished German judge told me, "he could come home and nothing would happen to him." In spite of the fact that no authority—in Germany or elsewhere—had declared Bormann dead and had formally closed his case, Joachim Richter's withdrawal from the investigation left nobody in charge of the matter, thus indicating that the German authorities in Frankfurt are neither interested in looking for Bormann nor really anxious to find him.

5

In November 1972 I became the center of an international Bormann sensation because of my articles in the *Daily Express*. From all over the world, newspapers rushed scores of special correspondents to Buenos Aires with explicit instructions to discredit me by punching holes into my story. It proved a futile assignment. There was hardly a line, in the 25,000 words I had published, that they could deny, discredit or expose.*

To the contrary, confirmation of my story arrived promptly on the wires of Reuters. Although it became merely a brief flash of

* A couple of photographs that the *Daily Express* printed with the first article of the series purported to show a confrontation in Mendoza between Juan José Velasco, an Argentine intelligence agent, and a man who called himself Ricardo Bauer but whom Velasco believed to be Martin Bormann. The stranger turned out to be a highly respected Buenos Aires schoolteacher named Nicolas Siri whose resemblance to Bormann was, in fact, uncanny. As for my part in the publication of those photographs, I have in my possession Velasco's affidavit stating that his confrontation of the man was a case of mistaken identification on the part of one of Velasco's colleagues who took the pictures in Buenos Aires; and the affidavit of Siri confirming in no uncertain terms that I had nothing whatever to do with the photographs or even with the incident that resulted in the confrontation and the taking of the pictures. Incidentally, in a press conference at Kennedy Airport in New York upon my return from London on December 4, 1972, I explicitly disavowed those photographs, stating that the alleged confrontation in Mendoza had not been verified by me and, therefore, I had no reason to believe that the man in the photographs was in fact Martin Bormann. As it turned out, I was right on both scores. Unfortunately, I was not successful in conveying my misgivings to the *Daily Express*.

triumph, it remains one of the most authoritative corroborations that Bormann survived the war and migrated to South America.

With the dateline "Buenos Aires, Nov. 27," *The New York Times* printed the Reuters dispatch on the morning of the twenty-eighth. It read:

> Argentine secret service sources said today that Martin Bormann was sheltered in this country after World War II, but could not confirm reports that he still lived there.
>
> Sources in Salta confirmed that the ranch where Bormann was said to have lived was owned by German industrialists.
>
> The intelligence sources said other Nazis arrived in Argentina with Bormann and were sheltered there, particularly by Vittorio Mussolini, son of the Italian dictator.

The dispatch, of which this was a brief excerpt, originated with Latin, Reuters' South American associate, the most reliable and responsible, influential and respected press association throughout South America. The report was written by Jorge Rocha. Enrique Jari, the distinguished newspaperman who is editor in chief of Latin, personally queried the Argentine authorities about my claim and received confirmation from Colonel Miguel Eduardo Grivas, director of Coordinación Federal. The accuracy of my story was confirmed also by Commissioner Pablo Messore, spokesman of Policia Federal, serving under Brigadier General Alberto Samuel Caceres, who was the author of the crucial top secret report about Bormann to the President of the Republic in 1963.*

Today I know that the great Bormann mystery was never really a mystery at all. His survival was known to the governments of countries in whose territories he lived with impunity since 1948.

This knowledge, however, remained the best-kept secret of the world, even in countries where secrets are rarely kept. It was by penetrating the confidential files of Argentina, Chile, Brazil, Paraguay, Bolivia and Peru, where Martin Bormann lived and moved, that I was able to solve the mystery, and write this book.

* For details of the Caceres report, which is one of the keys unlocking the Bormann mystery, see pages 94-96.

PART ONE

On the Bormann Trail

Chapter One

"Re: Martin Bormann, War Criminal"— The F.B.I. File

Around eleven o'clock at night on May 1, 1945, Reichsleiter Martin Bormann, one of the most powerful yet most obscure men at the apex of the Nazi hierarchy, vanished from the Führerbunker, the crammed, labyrinthine command post on the grounds of the Reich Chancellery where Adolf Hitler and the remnants of his once glittering staff had holed up while Berlin was burning.

One by one, during the last days of the Third Reich, the top leaders of the defunct regime were caught in the Allied and Soviet dragnets. It was a strange collapse of individual resistance amidst the final disaster of Nazi Germany; the highest-ranking members of history's most sinister criminal conspiracy gave themselves up meekly. It was an astounding spectacle, this mass surrender of the once powerful leaders of the Hitler regime. For all their immense power and efficiency during their halcyon days, they had failed to make provisions for this eventuality. Now they found but two ways to end their agony: to commit suicide or go into captivity.

By the end of May, when the great roundup in the wake of Germany's surrender was concluded, they were either dead, as were Hitler and Goebbels, or squatting helplessly, a bedraggled lot, in the cages of British, American, Soviet and French prison camps.

Martin Bormann, head of the Party bureaucracy and secretary of the Führer, seemed to be the sole exception. Having grown omnipotent during the *Götterdämmerung* of the Thousand-Year Reich —which lasted exactly twelve years, three months and eight days— he somehow succeeded, either by chance or by design, in escaping the tightening noose. It was established with certainty by Major Hugh R. Trevor-Roper, the brilliant young Oxford historian who traced the escape routes and tracked down the fugitives almost single-handed for British Intelligence, that Bormann had left the Führerbunker with a desperate group of survivors. But Trevor-Roper could follow him only as far as the Weidendammer Bridge in the heart of downtown Berlin. There he lost the enigmatic Reichsleiter, never to find him again.

Almost instantly, strange stories about Bormann began cropping up, and rumors began to spread about this most wanted fugitive. On May 4, only four days before the formal surrender, he was reported to be in Prague, "trying to hold the Czechoslovak pocket together and possibly . . . to fight it out."

Two days later, a Prague radio station still in German hands announced that Bormann had died during the Red Army's attack on the Reich Chancellery, together with Goebbels and Werner Naumann, the Propaganda Minister's deputy. The station cited as its authority "the Supreme Command of the German troops in Bohemia and Moravia."

On May 10, a member of the Allied War Crimes Commission announced the capture of Reichsmarschall Hermann Göring, and added that "the Russians have established to a fair degree of certainty" that one of the bodies they found in Berlin had been identified as that of Martin Bormann.

On June 12, *The New York Times* reported in a dispatch based on an item broadcast by the Soviet-controlled Berlin radio that Martin Bormann had been arrested, presumably by the Russians.

On August 2, word came from London that, according to war crimes investigators, "secret evidence" had been uncovered that Martin Bormann "may still be alive" and may be a "prisoner of the Russians."

On September 1, *The New York Times* reported Bormann's arrest by the Russians. At the same time, an Associated Press correspondent accredited to the headquarters of Field Marshal Sir Bernard Montgomery asserted that according to British Intelligence circles, Martin Bormann, "once reported to have died at Hitler's side in the ruins of the Reich Chancellery in Berlin," had been seen in a Hamburg suburb on the night of May 1 by "an anti-Nazi German physician who had been acquainted with him."

On November 1, the British confirmed officially in a long and dramatic report written by Trevor-Roper that Hitler had ended his life in the Berlin bunker. The same report mentioned in passing that Bormann "was killed while trying to escape from the bunker . . . on the day after Hitler had died."

Bormann's death was seemingly corroborated when his name next appeared in the news, on December 5. An aviator named Hanna Reitsch, who had volunteered to fly the Führer out of Berlin at dawn on April 30, spoke of a suicide pact in which Bormann had joined. But she was not sure the Reichsleiter had abided by it. "When I last saw him," she said, "he was sitting at his desk recording the momentous events in the bunker for posterity, while Hitler raved."*

The contradictory stories continued unabated. On December 31, *The New York Times* published a Reuters dispatch reporting from Czechoslovakia that Bormann had been arrested, this time by the British, somewhere in Germany. British Intelligence responded promptly, denying Bormann's arrest, but qualifying the disclaimer by adding "in the light of our present knowledge."

The next day, however, it was announced that Bormann had been arrested, even as Reuters had claimed, on a farm near Neumünster in Schleswig-Holstein, twenty miles west of Plön, where Grand Admiral Karl Doenitz briefly had his government as Hitler's heir. "He is being intensively questioned and investigated," the report added, quoting a spokesman at headquarters of the British Eighth Corps in Plön, "to establish or disprove his identity as Bormann."

The result of the investigation proved anticlimactic. The arrested man turned out to be a Neumünster farmer named Marius who strongly resembled Bormann but was not he. Yet there are still today British Intelligence officers who claim that "Marius" was Bormann after all and that the British slipped up badly when they set the man free and thus let the fugitive Reichsleiter continue his flight.

In February 1946, a report placed Bormann in Spain, supposedly hiding in a village near Salamanca. Then, on the sixth, a clandestine radio calling itself "The Voice of Argentina" and operated by anti-Perón exiles in Montevideo asserted that he had

* This tale of Bormann's alleged manuscript survived for twenty-seven years, mostly in the form of vague claims that the Russians had possession of it. But in late 1972, the Soviet authorities, in a long-overdue letter to Judge Horst von Glasenapp, the former investigating magistrate of the Bormann case, disclaimed any knowledge of such a record and denied categorically that they had it in their Bormann file.

been taken to Argentina aboard a German submarine and had gone ashore near Rawson, 700 miles southwest of Buenos Aires. According to the broadcast, which was traced to two Argentine refugees, José Gabriel and Guillermo Korn, the U-boat was scuttled by her crew. But Bormann succeeded in making his way to a safe haven in the north and was staying on a farm owned by a German Evangelical minister named Hoppe at Obera, in the Province of Misiones.

This particular report, in a garbled version, appeared in the *Chicago Tribune,* with a Montevideo dateline and the by-line of Vicente de Pascal, the paper's correspondent in Uruguay. Pascal was the author of several such stories, some even claiming that Hitler himself was in Argentina.

An inquiry was made by the so-called legal attaché of the American embassy in Montevideo—actually the representative of the Federal Bureau of Investigation—but it produced no evidence to bear out Pascal's story. However, as we shall see, both the report placing Bormann in Spain and the one reporting him in Argentina had some grains of truth in them.

Then, on July 3, came what appeared to be the first conclusive proof that Martin Bormann was dead after all. Questioned by American Prosecutor Thomas Dodd in Nuremberg before the International Military Tribunal trying twenty-one top Nazis, with Bormann among them, Erich Kempka, Hitler's chauffeur, testified that he had seen Bormann die from a bazooka blast in the streets of Berlin. Appearing as a defense witness for Bormann, Kempka said that the Reichsleiter, trying to sneak to freedom shielded by a tank moving toward the Weidendammer Bridge, had been killed when the tank was hit "with such force that it was impossible for him to survive."

Although Kempka conceded later that he himself had been blinded by the bazooka blast and could not actually observe the death of Bormann, his testimony endured more or less unquestioned for years and became one of the main sources of claims of Bormann's death in Berlin. This despite the fact that the Tribunal itself discounted Kempka's testimony, especially when, only twenty-three days later, information reached the prosecutors that Bormann had been seen alive riding in a car through the streets of Munich.

The information was of the utmost importance, if only because it stemmed from a man who knew Bormann well. He was Jakob Glas, the Reichsleiter's former driver. Glas's intervention triggered a furious investigation in Germany, the manhunt in Munich culminating in an exhaustive house-to-house search in the area where Glas allegedly had seen his former boss. But Bormann was not found.

In September, Allied listening posts in Germany picked up "strong rumors" that Bormann was in the Brenner district in Austria. Although he was ill, the rumors averred, he was preparing to make a dramatic comeback by broadcasting on a clandestine Alpine radio, accepting leadership of a neo-Nazi resistance movement. But in December, a report from Stockholm that seemed to have originated with the Swedish intelligence establishment had him back in South America, this time allegedly with Scandinavian credentials.

So it went, month after month, Martin Bormann was rumored to be, and sometimes even was sighted, in a number of places—in Germany and Austria, in Italy, in Spain, in South America. But none of the sighting reports could be confirmed, nor could Bormann be tracked down on the basis of the rumors.

Was Bormann alive or dead?

The International Military Tribunal of Nuremberg, sifting carefully all available evidence of both Bormann's survival and his death, resolved to regard him as living. It refused to heed the plea and act upon the motion of Dr. Friedrich Bergold, Bormann's court-appointed defense counsel, to declare him dead and dismiss the case. In its verdict, reached on September 30 and pronounced in open session on October 1, 1946, the Tribunal sentenced Martin Bormann *in absentia* to death by hanging "when and if apprehended." The sentence still stands.*

* On December 4, 1972, persuaded of the authenticity of my documentation, Dr. Robert M. W. Kempner, former deputy chief counsel for the United States at the war-crimes trials of Nazi leaders in Nuremberg, filed arguments with the American embassy in Bonn, also for transmission to the British, French and Soviet embassies, that the Four Powers reopen the Bormann case within the framework of the International Military Tribunal. Although the Allied machinery of retribution has been disbanded and the Nazi crimes left over from the series of Nuremberg trials are now prosecuted by the State courts of West Germany, the Allied Control Council is still operative in Spandau where it administers the prison in which Rudolf Hess is kept. It would have to be to Spandau, rather than into German hands, that Bormann would have to be delivered when caught, under the I.M.T. decision of October 18, 1945, which stipulated as follows: "Should [Bormann] be found guilty, and as soon as he is found, the verdict will be carried out without any further proceedings, in accordance with the instructions of the Allied Control Council." The verdict, of course, was *Tod durch den Strang* ("death by hanging"). Dr. Kempner was advised, however, that the reopening of the Bormann case would be "impractical, if not impossible," if only because it would be difficult to reconstitute the I.M.T. to hear the case and the Allied Control Council to carry out the execution.

In the wake of Bormann's death sentence, efforts were made by several American and British intelligence organizations—such as the C.I.C. of the American Army and MI.5, the British counterintelligence agency—to find the man and bring him to justice.

Two reports reached American Intelligence in April 1947, both attributed to "anonymous but reliable sources." According to one, Bormann was in Italy; according to the other, he was in Spain. The second report went so far as to claim that he had broadcast on a secret Spanish radio station to assure his followers that he was alive and working on the revival of Nazism, true to the mandate he had received from Hitler in the Führer's will, a copy of which—the one copy that is still missing and is presumed to be in Bormann's possession—he had with him.

In March 1947, the Allies were alerted to Bormann—and to the danger he represented—by a strange article that appeared in the *Aargauer Tageblatt,* a Swiss newspaper; it sounded like the manifesto of a powerful neo-Nazi movement with its center in the Bayreuth area. As an American intelligence report summarized it, "the article set out that the Germans are in the last depths of oppression; the Moscow Conference will end the occupation of Germany because a war will result between the U.S. and the U.S.S.R.; the outcome of this war will leave Germany the only strong nation in the world; Germany will then begin warfare against the present allies" and *"the head of the German government will be Martin Bormann, who presently is reportedly hiding in the Swiss Alps."*

The Allied intelligence organs were confused by both the quantity and the quality of the contradictory reports that kept pouring in from "sources of diverse reliability."

In August 1947, a report described in great detail the existence and activities of a German organization with headquarters at San Sebastian in Spain and branches in Sweden and Norway. It asserted that the organization, composed of former Nazis, was engaged "in the smuggling of prominent German individuals." As part of this report, a Swedish informant told the American consul in Bilbao, Spain, that Bormann was "in friendly hands in Spain," hinting rather broadly that he was enjoying the hospitality of the Franco regime and the protection of the Falange.* But a report dated November

* Spanish authorities I consulted conceded that "it was possible that Bormann [had] spent some time in Spain during this period." But they insisted that it was without the knowledge of the Franco regime. He was supposedly hidden, probably around Madrid and Seville, by Léon Degrelle, the Fascist leader under death sentence in and wanted by Belgium.

10, 1947, stated bluntly that "the ubiquitous Martin Bormann, until recently hiding in Berlin, is now in the Soviet Union."

The records of the search show that the Allied efforts to find Bormann were halfhearted and amateurish. Thanks to inefficiency and a lack of direction, the tracks of Bormann were lost.

Then, in the spring of 1948, a man arrived in Washington, D.C., from Montevideo with the startling information that Bormann was indeed alive. Bormann was living in Argentina, he said, shielded by a group of Nazis joined together in a vast and well-financed conspiracy to build a Fourth Reich on the ruins of the Third.

The man himself survives only as a shadowy figure in the Bormann saga. He was John F. Griffiths, a reputable, responsible and reliable American in the export-import business in Uruguay. He also had an official status that added weight to his sensational testimony. For some time until about the middle of 1946, he had been employed in the Cultural Department of the American embassy in Buenos Aires, dealing mostly with labor matters.

Griffiths was an idealistic liberal, strongly opposed to Juan Perón, the best friend the Nazis had in Argentina, an attitude that did not aid his career in the Foreign Service. In 1946, he was dismissed on orders from the State Department, and then, in April 1948, he was expelled from Argentina. He moved to Uruguay whence he continued his fight against the Perón regime.

Now, in May 1948, Griffiths went to Washington on a secret mission, at his own expense on borrowed money, seeking neither reward nor publicity for his information. In Washington, he sought out the man who, he assumed, had the greatest interest in Bormann —Associate Justice Robert H. Jackson of the Supreme Court. In Nuremberg, Mr. Jackson, as chief counsel of the American team, had led the prosecution of the major war criminals.

The Justice agreed to see Griffiths in his chambers in the Supreme Court Building and a meeting was arranged for May 6. By coincidence, just when Griffiths had one of his sessions with Mr. Jackson, Bormann showed up again in print, even if only by proxy, in an item in the Washington *Times-Herald*. It reported that his eighteen-year-old son, Adolf Martin Bormann, had been discovered in the seminary at Ingolstadt, Germany, studying for the priesthood in the Roman Catholic Church, which his father had loathed and reviled throughout his career as a Nazi.

Behind closed doors, Griffiths treated Justice Jackson to a fantastic tale of adventure and intrigue, with Bormann gradually dominating the drama. The information had been obtained, Griffiths said, from a friend of his, an Argentine official named Juan Serrino of Quilmes, a suburb of Buenos Aires.

Serrino, it seemed, had been for many years a key employee of the port authorities of Buenos Aires. In the course of his official business with German vessels, he had become friendly over mugs of beer with a man he knew only as "Otto." Quite early in World War II, his drinking companion dropped his mask and confided to Serrino that he was a member of the sprawling German intelligence and sabotage contingent in Argentina. He then invited his friend to smuggle explosives, which he would procure, onto British and American ships passing through Argentine ports.

Serrino insisted that he had steadfastly refused to go along with the proposition. But he conceded that he remained on friendly terms with Otto and, through him, had met other members of the Nazi spy colony, who apparently thought that he was, as Serrino put it, "favorably disposed toward Germany in general and the Nazis in particular."

In June 1945, in a tavern at Quilmes, Otto introduced Serrino to a man called "Alfredo"—actually Alfred Müller, a veteran German spymaster with an extensive career in the Argentine underworld of espionage. Müller was a brilliant organizer, an inspiring leader, a sober, hard-working Nazi. Expelled in 1940 from Argentina for his involvement in what became known as the Patagonia plot, Müller was mysteriously active in Lisbon during the war, directing from Portugal some of the German operations on the other side of the South Atlantic.

He returned to Argentina after the war and resumed his subversive activities. Conspiracy seemed to be his sideline, for he was active in the steel business in partnership with another German and financed his plots from his own funds.

After the encounter in the saloon, Müller replaced Otto as Serrino's contact with the postwar Nazi conspiracy. A man of obvious authority and Prussian callousness, Müller wasted no time in discussions or amenities. He told Serrino he would be asking him for "small favors from time to time," and Serrino agreed to do what he could.

Not long after this initial contact, Serrino learned from his German friends that two U-boats had come to Argentina and surrendered to the authorities, but only after they had put ashore a number of crates marked "top secret" and an unspecified number of passengers.* Without ever confirming the arrival of these U-boats, Müller asked Serrino to make travel arrangements for "some important Germans" who had just arrived in Argentina and to do certain odd jobs for the newcomers.

Before acceding to Müller's request, Serrino had a change of heart. Suspicious of Müller and his crowd, he consulted one of his German friends, an anti-Nazi journalist named Naumann, at La Plata. Naumann advised him to get in touch with Ambassador Spruille Braden of the United States, but Serrino could not arrange a meeting with the ambassador. Naumann then suggested that he see John Griffiths, one of the few embassy officials keenly interested in the growing activities of the Nazis in Argentina.

Serrino made contact with Griffiths and, at his recommendation, deepened his relation with Müller, now in an effort to penetrate the conspiracy. Still in mid-1945, he was able to pinpoint some of the information he had given Griffiths, if only because Müller had begun to call on him to do more and more of those "small favors." In August, for example, he asked Serrino to accompany him to an *estancia* at Caleta Olivia in the Province of Santa Cruz, in the far south of Argentina. There he met the manager of the *estancia,* a man named Schulz,† and a number of newcomers from Germany, many of whom seemed to be scientists.

In the middle of 1946, at the request of Schulz, Serrino went by boat to Asunción, Paraguay, and then was taken by car to a spot in the country, a two-hour drive from the capital. It turned out to be an *estancia* among orange groves and was populated by some of the Germans he had previously met at Caleta Olivia. The dean of the colony was a stocky man in his middle forties, called "Don

* In point of fact, two German submarines did put into an Argentine port in June 1945 and surrendered after disabling their engines. Extensive investigation by British and American naval authorities at that time failed to produce any evidence that any Germans other than the crews had been carried by these U-boats. But rumors were widespread even then that "prominent Nazis" had come in these vessels and managed to escape into the interior of Argentina with the help of local agents.

† In the Argentine documents, I found references to two Germans called Schulz, both apparently involved in operations affecting Bormann. One was Martin Alfred Schulz, supposedly a former sailor from the scuttled pocket battleship *Graf Spee,* aiding, as an intelligence report stated, in the unloading of U-530 and U-977, on July 10 and August 17, 1945. The other "Schulz" was a senior intelligence agent of the Abwehr, actually named Ludwig Schultz-Hausmann. He was living in Argentina underground after his *pro forma* expulsion in 1941 as an unmasked spy. My own investigation indicates that the Schulz mentioned by Serrino was the *Graf Spee* man, who, I believe, is still living in Argentina.

Martin" and treated deferentially by the other Germans. Serrino learned from Schulz that this "Don Martin" had been "one of the most important members of the Nazi leadership in Germany" and was commuting between South America and Spain, assisted in his travels by a foreign power, which Serrino thought could have been the Soviet Union.

Serrino continued to do those "small favors" until July 1947, when Schulz asked him to go to Fray Bentos, a port in western Uruguay, to meet "Don Martin," who had just come back from Europe on another of his frequent trips, bringing along several crates and a couple of suitcases with what Schulz described as "important documents." On this occasion, at a luncheon, Serrino was introduced to "Don Martin" himself, whom he later identified as Martin Bormann from photographs Griffiths and Naumann had given him.

The purpose of the lunch was to persuade Serrino to assist "Don Martin" with the shipment of the crates and suitcases to Argentina and Paraguay. He was assured that he would be aided by two influential persons, later identified as a Uruguayan Senator named Alfredo Haedo and "a prominent German-Argentine banker well-known as an aide of the Nazis both during and after the war," in fact, Ludovico (Ludwig) Freude. Moreover, Serrino was told explicitly that his activities had the support of President Perón himself, so that he had nothing to fear in carrying out these transactions.

This was the information that Griffiths gave Justice Jackson. Although the evidence it produced was circumstantial, based entirely on data supplied by Serrino, Justice Jackson regarded it as important enough to warrant immediate action. At first he thought of introducing Griffiths to F.B.I. Director J. Edgar Hoover, with whom he was on excellent terms from his tenure as Attorney General. But Griffiths balked. He told Justice Jackson that the F.B.I. was conducting the manhunt spasmodically, and that he had no confidence in Mr. Hoover's willingness to follow down the lead, unless he was ordered to do so by President Truman himself. Impressed with Griffiths' sincerity and eloquence, Justice Jackson decided to take up the case with the President, determined to persuade him to authorize Director Hoover to pursue the case.

Truman had a high opinion of Jackson. He not only regarded him as "one of the country's most eminent jurists," but liked him personally as well. When he was to be sworn in on April 12, 1945, following Franklin D. Roosevelt's sudden death, Truman asked Attorney General Francis Biddle to call Chief Justice Harlan F. Stone to administer the oath, adding that "if he couldn't get the Chief Justice to get Mr. Justice Jackson to come." On May 2, 1945, he chose Jackson to serve as chief counsel of the United States at Nuremberg.

He had been enormously impressed with Jackson's performance, not merely with the way he had carried the main burden of the prosecution, but especially with his ability to create a smooth coalition atmosphere at Nuremberg. Thanks to his legal skill and innate talent for diplomacy, the trial was held without the bickering of the Cold War intruding on this historic experiment in international criminal law.

When Jackson presented the case to the President, Truman showed only mild interest, probably because the name Martin Bormann meant little to him. But the Justice had come well prepared. He brought along a memo outlining the biography of the former Reichsleiter, summarizing the text of his Nuremberg indictment and of the verdict, and describing the propaganda implications of a top Nazi left at large. Shrewdly Jackson's memo touched upon the threat that Bormann's presence in South America—or, for that matter, anywhere in the world—represented to the West in the context of the Cold War.

Even so, the first session remained inconclusive. The President asked for more information before he would agree to involve the F.B.I. in the manhunt. It was supplied by Jackson in a letter dated June 16, in which he wrote to Truman:

> Circumstantial evidence indicates that Bormann probably is dead. But the uncertainty as to whether he may have escaped was enough so that we [at Nuremberg] considered it wise to indict and convict him in absentia. Many rumors that he has appeared in various parts of the world have proved false. Griffiths' evidence depends on a native informant who, of course, neither I nor the FBI have interviewed. This informant is now said to have identified the person he suspects from a photograph of Bormann. Identification, however, is not easy, for Bormann was the least photographed of the Nazi high officials.*

* This, of course, was not quite correct. An examination of the Hoffmann Archives, left behind by Hitler's court photographer and now administered by his son, shows that Bormann was one of the most photographed among the top Nazis, if only because he appeared in most of the innumerable group pictures taken with the Führer. However, he was rarely identified in the captions. As a result, the Germans were fairly familiar with his face, but few of them knew the name or the function of this man who was Hitler's constant shadow.

> A complete investigation would be extensive in time and cost [the Justice continued]. In addition, it would not be possible to apprehend or interrogate suspects or witnesses without the cooperation of the governments involved. Informed opinion of the FBI is to the effect that if Bormann is in the Argentine, it must be with the connivance of the Argentine government. Obviously, the situation requires discreet handling.

He then added important arguments in favor of the investigation:

> On the other hand, to neglect entirely to investigate this lead has two dangers. First, it is possible that Bormann is there. Second, even if he is not, publicity might be given to the fact that this information was laid before United States officials who did nothing and therefore are charged to be, in effect, protecting him. This claim would have propaganda value to Russia, for Bormann in the Eastern countries was one of the most hated of the Nazis.

Justice Jackson concluded his long letter with a firm recommendation:

> My suggestion, therefore, is that the FBI be authorized to pursue thoroughly discreet inquiries of a preliminary nature in South America and to encourage and cooperate with Griffiths in developing his sources of information, to check those sources as to their probable reliability and accuracy, and to determine on the basis of the preliminary investigation whether a more thorough and full-scale investigation should be undertaken, perhaps after communication with any government affected.

Upon receipt of the letter, Truman telephoned Jackson and asked him two questions. "Do you really think," was one, "that this sonuvabitch is really worth the effort?" The other was: "Is your man Griffiths on the level?" The Justice answered both questions firmly in the affirmative. On June 21, "pursuant to the request of Mr. Justice Robert H. Jackson," as the President phrased it, Truman authorized the F.B.I. to undertake immediately "a preliminary investigation of a report from one John Griffiths, that Martin Bormann, Adolph Hitler's deputy fuehrer, is in the River Plate area of Latin America."

Mr. Hoover, to say the least, was not elated by the "authorization," which was tantamount to a presidential order. For one thing, he was feuding with Mr. Truman over the activities of the F.B.I. in South and Central America. Extremely active and effective during the war, with scores of agents stationed throughout South America, the F.B.I. had been virtually banned from the area after the war. In fact, the President had humiliated Hoover by peremptorily withdrawing from the F.B.I. "the authority it had possessed for seven years in counterespionage work throughout Central and South America."

For another thing, the capacity of the Bureau had been stretched to the breaking point under an avalanche of new responsibilities. It was now playing a major part in the Loyalty Program, checking out thousands of government employees and investigating job applications for a number of such sensitive agencies as the Atomic Energy Commission and even the Voice of America.

Moreover, the F.B.I. was no longer interested even in the remnants of Nazism. It was busy with Communist agents who had infiltrated the American government since the thirties. Evidence of a vast Soviet espionage effort in North America was accumulating in the wake of the defection of Igor Guzenko, a Soviet code clerk stationed in Ottawa, who exposed a huge Russian spy ring fishing for atomic secrets in Canada and the United States. More and more informants came out of the shadows—like Elizabeth Bentley and Whittaker Chambers—to provide hard intelligence from their own experience about an intricate Communist conspiracy that involved some of the most trusted officials of the Treasury and State departments. As Mr. Hoover saw it, Soviet spies were more active and probably more dangerous in the United States than Nazi agents had ever been before and during World War II.

But Hoover could not ignore Truman's order. To familiarize himself with the case, he asked for the Bureau's own Bormann file. It turned out to be a bulging dossier containing the fascinating record of Trevor-Roper's independent investigation and a copy of his famous book *The Last Days of Hitler,* which had been published in 1947 and had numerous references to the Reichsleiter (including a brief account of his escape from the Führerbunker and what Trevor-Roper assumed was "his fate"); several intelligence reports from C.I.C., MI.5, Scotland Yard and other Allied agencies contradicting one another; some captured German documents of peripheral interest; but mostly newspaper clippings which confused rather than clarified the issue.

From the material in the dossier, a summary of the case was prepared for Hoover. It was a most impressive document of seven pages of closely typed text crammed with data. It survives as one of the best studies of the Bormann case ever written, including a brilliant review of this obscure man's career.

Mr. Hoover forwarded a copy of the study to Justice Jackson and advised him that he would send a special agent—all he could spare at this time—to Buenos Aires, to undertake what he explicitly limited to "a preliminary investigation." He then chose Special Agent Francis E. Crosby to make the trip, more because he happened to be available at the moment than for any real qualifications Crosby had for such a delicate and intricate mission.

He was a veteran G-man, had some knowledge of South America and spoke a little Spanish. But he seemed totally unfamiliar with the complex web of Nazism in the postwar world and apparently did not properly fathom—either intellectually or even from a purely investigative point of view—the broader implications of his mission. Moreover, he was a pedantic sleuth, going by the book instead of using the initiative and imagination required by the situation.

Crosby's instructions were to conduct the preliminary investigation even as Justice Jackson himself had suggested and as Mr. Hoover preferred to regard the unsolicited assignment. The agent interpreted his mission in still narrower terms. He resolved to limit himself to checking out Griffiths and Serrino rather than to use the lead they had provided to find Bormann.

Crosby left Washington on July 3, then commuted between Buenos Aires (where Serrino was) and Montevideo (where Griffiths now lived) between July 7 and August 23. He thus spent all but seven weeks of the mission waiting for Serrino. The Crosby mission never really began to be effective, even within the narrow confines of his own interpretation. For one thing, seven weeks in the field by a single agent operating on a limited budget were insufficient to make an investigation in depth, even if the search had been conducted with zeal. For another, Crosby instantly disliked Griffiths. This bias spoiled their relations from the outset. His first meeting with Serrino, on July 10 in Buenos Aires, was brief and perfunctory. It turned out to be their only encounter. Crosby treated the seventy-four-year-old informant, who was understandably uneasy about this surreptitious contact with an American agent and needed reassurance to allay his apprehension, with such condescension and distrust that Serrino decided to have nothing more to do with him.

A second interview was arranged for the nineteenth, but the Argentine official had been so disgusted by the high-handed manner in which Crosby treated him and so intimidated by the G-man's bluntly hostile attitude and lack of tact that he became afraid to have any more contacts with him on Argentine soil, and failed to appear at the appointment. Griffiths then arranged for Serrino to go to Montevideo and there submit to a thorough interrogation, but the plans failed, because by then Serrino had come to fear Perón more than he could trust Crosby.

As Crosby later reported to Hoover, "In the one interview I had with him, the informant talked in very general terms, and furnished no fact susceptible of independent verification." He offered neither an explanation nor an apology for his failure to interrogate the very man he had been sent to Buenos Aires to question.

As for Griffiths, Crosby conceded that, to be sure, he was "a highly intelligent man." But he then proceeded to demolish him as a trustworthy source. "He seems to have a detective complex in exaggerated form," the American agent wrote. "It apparently never occurred to Griffiths that among all the allegations and reports he had received and in turn furnished, there was not one single specific fact which could be verified independently." As we have seen, this statement was patently untrue. Griffiths had furnished hard intelligence with names, places and dates. Special Agent Cosby preferred to ignore his data.

Aside from Griffiths and Serrino, Crosby made no effort to develop sources of his own to broaden the search. He interviewed only one other person, a Julio Genoves Garcia, who had been introduced to him by Griffiths. A respected Argentine journalist in his forties, with live lines to the Nazi underground in South America, Genoves could have been an important and useful link in the chain of surveillance, had he been properly handled. He had valuable information of his own about the mysterious "Don Martin," whose identity as Martin Bormann he claimed to have positively ascertained by his own means and contacts.

But by this time, Crosby had concluded that this whole Griffiths affair was merely a plot to embarrass Juan Perón. He therefore dismissed Genoves out of hand. "This individual," he wrote, "a newspaperman and attorney at Buenos Aires, is apparently a rabid anti-Peronista who inspires Griffiths' complete confidence. He was the intermediary at Buenos Aires between Griffiths at Montevideo and the informant at Quilmes."

With Perón foremost in Crosby's mind, Bormann receded into the background as far as Crosby was concerned. Indicative of his whole attitude toward his mission and of the scope of his investigation was an aside in his report. It went far to show how superficially and, indeed, stingily the matter was handled.

"It should be mentioned," Crosby wrote, "that a total of 325 Uruguayan Pesos were furnished to Griffiths between July 10 and August 23, travel expenses for Genoves Garcia and Juan Serrino." These disbursements amounted to the formidable sum of $420, but it seemed enough to induce Crosby to add: "It was not felt that the circumstances justified any additional outlay of funds."

After, as he put it, "no developments of a concrete nature had taken place," Crosby returned to Washington on August 23. He reported to Director Hoover categorically that "Griffiths' report was without substance."

He based his conclusion not on anything he had discovered by his own efforts or had found out from Serrino, but "on the behavior of Griffiths and Serrino." He concluded his report by discrediting Serrino as a reliable informant if only because, as he phrased it, "experience has indicated that where they have reliable elements available, the Germans do not give employment of so delicate a nature to casual acquaintance and Serrino is both casual and improbable."

Mr. Hoover forwarded Crosby's negative findings to Justice Jackson with a letter that reflected the agent's arbitrary and patently wrong conclusions without any qualifications. "In spite of the circumstance," Hoover wrote in a letter dated September 8, 1948, "that a Bureau Agent spent in excess of seven weeks in Montevideo in constant contact with John F. Griffiths, no fact was forthcoming from Griffiths or the original informant, one Juan Serrino, who is allegedly in touch with some Germans, which could be verified by investigation. The Agent observed a reluctance on the part of Serrino to be interviewed.

"It does not appear from the memorandum that any facts were furnished which could serve as a basis for further investigation of the report that Bormann and certain unidentified documents are in the River Plate area of Latin America."

The case was closed. Martin Bormann was safe from the F.B.I.

In 1949, there was a sequel to the Crosby mission, in a confidential report to the State Department from Ambassador James Bruce in Buenos Aires, dated January 21. It somehow summarizes the mission and explains why it failed. The ambassador had been left out of the melodrama. He had been totally unaware of the F.B.I. agent's presence in Argentina and, of course, knew nothing of the nature of his assignment.

The Crosby mission occurred during a thaw in the relations of the United States with Argentina and Perón's moral rehabilitation by Washington. Ambassador Bruce, a hardheaded businessman, was sent to Buenos Aires to "repair the damage" done by his predecessor, Spruille Braden, who had inspired the publication of the State Department *Blue Book.* It was designed to aid Perón's defeat during the 1946 elections by documenting his pro-Axis activities during World War II and his close personal and business association with leading Nazis.

Now, only two years later, the Nazi issue was dropped and Ambassador Bruce called Perón "the great leader of a great nation," in a Cold War demonstration of Pan-American solidarity in the face of increasing Soviet penetration of the Hemisphere. Crosby's sojourn also coincided with the closing of the biggest postwar deal in Buenos Aires by George E. Allen, former close associate of President Truman, on behalf of a Cleveland company, with a concern represented by Ricardo Staudt. Since Staudt was the number-two Nazi listed by Braden in the *Blue Book* (and, as we shall see, was in fact one of Bormann's trustees at this time) it was luminously apparent where things stood and why the finding of Bormann—or even a really energetic search for him—would have been embarrassing to the State Department.

The motto of its new Argentine policy was, "the war is over and finished." A scandal, like the uncovering of Bormann in Perón's Argentina, could have jeopardized Argentina's ratification of the Treaty of Rio de Janeiro, which was calculated to present a united front to the Russians.

Ambassador Bruce learned about the Crosby mission only secondhand and reported it to the State Department in rather caustic terms, reflecting some skepticism and quite a bit of criticism of Crosby's handling of the case. The report is so unusual, especially for the normally pro-Perón Mr. Bruce, and it is so illuminating as regards the F.B.I.'s involvement in the Bormann hunt, that it deserves to be quoted in full.

Sent as a radiogram under No. A-37, it read as follows:

> The following would seem fantastic and unworthy of credence if it had not come from a source from which we have received from time to time very valuable information, all of which has been substantiated and found correct. We are very anxious for the Department to help us out in the determination of whether or not there is any substance whatsoever to this matter. It is as follows:
>
> When John Griffiths was expelled from Argentina, instead of going to Miami and staying there a few days, borrowing some money from a friend and returning to Montevideo, he proceeded to Washington where he had an interview with Mr. Justice Robert Jackson. In the course of this, he told Justice Jackson that he was in a position to uncover certain Nazi criminals who were hiding in South America, among them Martin Bormann, that he needed some help, and that these men were all sufficient criminals to have been tried at Nuremberg if they had been apprehended and caught in Germany.
>
> The story runs that Justice Jackson spoke to President Truman about the matter, and that the President suggested that it be taken up with J. Edgar Hoover. It was explained to Hoover, and after Griffiths proceeded to Montevideo, Hoover sent an FBI agent to assist Griffiths in uncovering these Nazis.
>
> The FBI agent was not very discreet and it soon became known what his mission was, and particularly to some of the ex-Nazis on this side of the river, whereupon they concocted the idea of using Perón as somewhat of a sucker in the performance and producing the assassination plot, which to some extent actually had already been in the making.
>
> Of course the whole thing was done with the idea that Griffiths would become involved and that they would start anti-United States feeling here, which they certainly did. Immediately when the agitation started over the plot every effort was made to get hold of John Griffiths and bring him back here. The Uruguayan Government was afraid he might be hit over the head and shanghaied, which would have caused an unpleasant incident from their standpoint, and have had him reasonably heavily guarded ever since. The result of the matter, as told to us, was that the traces of the criminal Nazis have all disappeared and that all the leads which John Griffiths had to their whereabouts have been dissipated.

As for Bormann, it was a close call. He was in Argentina when Special Agent Crosby was looking for him. Had the search been handled with greater finesse; had Crosby conducted himself with more attention to the psychology of Latin Americans, Juan Serrino, for all his reticence and fears, could have led the F.B.I. to the fugitive Reichsleiter.

The Federal Bureau of Investigation never again picked up Martin Bormann's trail.

It cannot be said that John Edgar Hoover put his best foot forward in trying to find Bormann on John Griffiths' promising tip. In a letter closing the case, Hoover assured Justice Jackson that the agent he had sent to South America had "made a thorough, intelligent and adequate preliminary investigation." He endorsed his man's conclusion that "no full-scale investigation would be justified at this time . . . in the light of the information we have." Justice Jackson accepted Hoover's verdict.

The record shows, however, that for all his apparent indifference, Hoover was neither pleased nor completely satisfied with Crosby's inconclusive inquiry. Strange as it may seem, he continued to be preoccupied with the case, but now it was on a purely personal and, so to speak, sporting basis.

What intrigued him then was exactly what continued to puzzle the world for so many years afterward. It had been irrefutably established that Bormann had made a determined attempt to escape. His movements had been reconstructed in the immediate wake of his departure from the Führerbunker. After that everything was hearsay.

Whatever *evidence* there was of Bormann's death was presumptive at best, certainly to an experienced criminologist like Hoover. Was it possible, he asked himself in effect, to resolve the mystery with the methods of criminal investigation as perfected by the Bureau under his leadership? The answer to this largely hypothetical question, as he posed it, first merely interested, then fascinated him. In the end, the solution of the mystery, as if it were a complicated jigsaw puzzle, became a hobby with him.

He issued an order to route to his personal attention every scrap of information about Bormann that would reach the Bureau. Much of what he then received was rubbish. But once in a while, there would come to his desk a piece of intelligence that had to be taken seriously.

Shortly after Crosby's return from Uruguay, for example, the

Bureau's representative in London was informed by MI.5 that, according to a Scotland Yard inspector stationed in northern Italy, Bormann was at large there.

> It is an undisputed fact [the report from Britain stated] that subject Bormann's wife died in Southern Tyrol and that she is buried in or near Bolzano, Venezia, Italy; and that the exact position of her grave is presumably known to Intelligence Authorities in the district. Further information furnished was to the effect that Bormann has three children, and that these children were seen by this member of British Intelligence in Bolzano in February 1948. Information was also given that the true identity of the children is generally known to all residents in the Bolzano district and presumably to the Intelligence authorities there.

As for Bormann himself, the Scotland Yard inspector voiced the "belief" that he was "hiding in Southern Tyrol, which is exceedingly rugged country and very suitable for being used as a hideout." Finding him was difficult, the report went on, partly because "the Italian Police Officials in that part of the country are reported to be very corrupt and uncooperative."

Hoover was impressed with the report, but left it to the British authorities to track it down. His interest in Bormann had become purely vicarious. But from reports like this, and others that he would read, he was coming closer to answering the basic question that intrigued him—did Bormann die during his flight in Berlin or did he manage to escape to a safe haven? This was the extent of his interest in the matter. He did not care where Bormann was, if indeed he had survived. He had no intention of using the Bureau to find him. But his formidable investigative imagination was at work. Gradually he formed an opinion, nothing more—but it was a definitive answer to the question. It was spelled out in a stray sentence I found in another F.B.I. report. "*It must be acknowledged,*" it read, "*that there is no evidence on the question of Bormann's death.*"

Chapter Two

A Matter of Life or Death

Exactly twenty-four years after the F.B.I. had undertaken its futile search, I succeeded in establishing that Martin Bormann had been in Argentina when Agent Francis Crosby was vainly looking for him.

Late at night on September 12, 1972, in a "safe house" secured for me in the elegant River Park residential district of Buenos Aires, I was handed a pink folder marked "Dirección Coordinación Federal —División Delitos Federales."* It contained documents "borrowed" for me from the closely guarded archives of the Argentine's top intelligence agency, now called Seguridad Federal, but still using leftover folders bearing its former official designation.

The folder had been removed surreptitiously from its filing cabinet at the end of this workday, and I was told that it had to be returned first thing next morning before its brief absence could be discovered. I thus had only what was left of the night to examine the contents of the folder and make copies of those documents that

* In literal translation, "Directorate of Federal Coordination—Federal Criminal Division." In the vast intelligence and security establishment of Argentina, Coordinación Federal (now renamed Seguridad Federal) represents a combination of our Federal Bureau of Investigation and Central Intelligence Agency, performing certain functions of both. It serves as an umbrella organization of the federal government to coordinate the various nonmilitary intelligence and security agencies (including the Alien Control Bureau), and as a clearinghouse for documentation, the only Argentine bureau where the enormous paperwork of the intelligence community is centrally filed and is easily accessible. Its archives include documents from Secretaría de Informaciones de Estado (or S.I.D.E. for short), a special bureau collating and orchestrating all high-level intelligence data for the information of the President of the Republic. Its reports are either summaries of material collected by the scattered intelligence and security agencies or comparable to the so-called "National Estimates," special reports the C.I.A. prepares for the President of the United States on important issues or events.

had a bearing on my search, which was not basically different from that of Agent Crosby. I, too, was looking for evidence that would solve the mystery of Martin Bormann's fate after World War II.

The folder contained forty-one separate papers. Most were reports of secret agents typed on the official forms of various security organs, supplying accounts of their own observations or summarizing data they had received from informants, with the name "Martin Bormann" recurring frequently in all of them. Also included in the folder were two longer documents, both captioned "Martin Bormann," one with the photograph of the former Reichsleiter at the top of the first page.

The documents I had before me exposed the secret of a fantastic venture; they told in detail one of the greatest and strangest escape stories of all time and solved, apparently conclusively, what was hitherto the mystery of Martin Bormann's postwar fate. They contained firsthand evidence that the Reichsleiter had survived the war and succeeded in escaping to Argentina. It was attested by the Argentine authorities themselves, in highly classified intelligence reports and position papers drawn up for their own secret and official use.

I had no reason to question the authenticity of the documents. Martin Bormann was a controversial figure, running away from the death sentence that the International Military Tribunal had meted out to him in Nuremberg.

Why, I asked myself, should the Argentine authorities concede in so many words that he had entered their territory and found there the haven he desperately needed? This was not a matter to brag about or even to record, except in documents whose secrecy and security were believed to be inviolable.

Contrary to the widespread belief that several governments were engaged in a global hunt for the former Reichsleiter, I found that, in actual fact, none was interested in and seriously looking for him. The former Allies (the United States, Britain and France) and the U.S.S.R., whose joint military tribunal had sentenced Bormann to death, made no effort whatever to find and apprehend him—"it would only complicate matters," an American diplomat told me in Asunción.

The Germans' search was as superficially laborious as it was nebulous. It consisted of a strictly bureaucratic investigation confined to the indiscriminate interrogation of random witnesses and the collection of files in which quantity triumphed over quality. As a matter of fact, neither the magistrate in charge of the preliminary investigation until the end of 1971 nor the lonely procurator who handled the case for a decade ever visited South America in search of the fugitive, although they made frequent trips to places in Europe where they knew Bormann would not be found.

But what about Israel? Were not the Jews in general and the Israelis in particular interested in Bormann, who was, after all, the biggest game in the unending Nazi hunt? This question raises a complicated and delicate issue. For, in fact, Israel's pursuit of Nazi criminals burned out with the capture of Adolf Eichmann and is today a matter of theory rather than practice—a problem, indeed, the Israelis' solution of which requires compassionate understanding.

Although the State of Israel maintains the Yad Vashem, a huge national institution founded in 1955, both as "a memorial of the Jewish victims of Nazism and a documentation center on Nazi crimes," the government of Israel is no longer actively pursuing Nazi criminals either overtly or covertly. Gone from the scene are the shirt-sleeved, swarthy, sullen-looking young men—members of the scattered commando teams of the Israeli Secret Service, whose very shadow drove terror into the hearts of Nazi fugitives.

One of the reasons for this development may be found in the natural evolution of Israel from a free-wheeling, adventure-prone young country into a responsible, mature state. It is beset by more pressing immediate problems than the sentimental preoccupation with the tragic past, and it is committed to the strict observance of international law and protocol in foreign relations.

The reaction to the abduction of Adolf Eichmann in 1960 persuaded even Prime Minister David Ben-Gurion, the great mentor of the Avengers, that such a state-sponsored adventure must be an isolated incident, that it would redound to Israel's lasting disadvantage if repeated. As a matter of policy, Israel was never after Nazi criminals pursued by other legitimate agencies of retribution. Its authorities sought only those in whose punishment nobody else seemed to be interested or the handful who, like Eichmann, managed to fool the hunters.

As far as Bormann was concerned, the Israelis never evinced any great or direct interest in him. He had been tried by the I.M.T.

in Nuremberg and sentenced to death. It was, therefore, in the opinion of the Israelis, incumbent upon his Allied prosecutors to find him and get him into the gallows. It was in 1967 when the Israeli government last intervened—and most secretly at that—in a matter involving a Nazi fugitive, but only to assure the punishment of Franz Paul Stangl, former commandant of the Treblinka extermination camp. He had been arrested in Brazil, but his extradition either to Germany or to Poland was hitting a succession of snags, until an Israeli agent "expedited things," as it was put.*

In 1968, it became the top-secret official policy of the Israeli government to refrain even from such indirect interventions, mainly to avoid frictions with sensitive South American governments, whose good will was becoming absolutely essential for Israel. The chief agent of the Israeli Secret Service specializing in Nazi criminals at large in South America was relieved of this duty and moved from Rio de Janeiro to Quito, assigned to a bona fide diplomatic post as ambassador to Ecuador.

When too, in 1968, diplomatic relations were normalized with Paraguay, the most notorious haven of Nazi fugitives, harboring and protecting Dr. Mengele, Benjamin Varon, the newly appointed Israeli ambassador, had explicit instructions to assure President Alfredo Stroessner that he would not raise the issue of Nazi criminals supposedly hiding in the country. As a result, Ambassador Varon became the most popular foreign envoy in Asunción. Thanks to his efforts (or nonefforts, as the case may be), Israel was assured of treatment as a most-favored nation. Paraguay became its stanch and steady champion in the United Nations, one of only seven countries which never cast their vote against Israel.†

Cynical though such "arrangements" may appear against the gruesome reality of the holocaust, they are an inevitable ingredient of the *Realpolitik* that Israel must pursue—even more than other states—in its precarious existence in a generally hostile world.

* For details of this "intervention," see page 379.

† During his four years in Paraguay, Ambassador Varon received innumerable tips about Mengele in particular, some true, some false, but several pinpointing his movements accurately and at least two betraying his hiding places. The ambassador ignored these tips. Once he told his friend Under-Secretary of State Alberto Nogues of the Foreign Ministry that if by some perverse chance Mengele himself would show up in his embassy *applying* for a visa to Israel, he would have to deny it to him, under his standing instruction to ignore the doctor's presence in the country and never to let the thorny problem of Nazi criminals disturb Israel's friendly relations with Paraguay.

My own acquisition of the Bormann documents was no accidental discovery, no windfall. It was rather the not unexpected result of an arduous ten-month quest at the end of an odyssey that had taken me to the jungles of Brazil and Paraguay, to Peru, Bolivia and Chile, and eventually to Argentina on a tip that it was in Buenos Aires that I would find what could be called the "final solution" of the Bormann mystery.

J. Edgar Hoover's random conclusion that no evidence was on hand supporting the assumption that Bormann was dead did not mean, of course, that he had any proof that the former Reichsleiter was alive. For me, however, the mere fact of Mr. Hoover's preoccupation with the Bormann mystery attained a special significance. I regarded his interest in Bormann and his probing of Bormann's postwar fate as a challenge, and decided to conduct my own investigation in an effort either to confirm that he was dead or to find whatever evidence I could to prove that he had survived the war and probably was alive.

By the fall of 1971, when I became involved in the solution of the problem, there was a veritable worldwide industry flourishing in the enduring Bormann mystery. A former British intelligence agent, Roland Gray, for example, peddled the story that Bormann was definitely dead. He had no doubt, since he himself had killed him, Gray claimed, while the defunct Reichsleiter was trying to escape in the chaotic wake of Germany's defeat.

Erich Karl Wiedwald, a dark-haired, pudgy-faced ex-corporal allegedly in the Waffen SS, was just as positive that Bormann was alive. He knew for sure, Wiedwald insisted, for it was he who had smuggled him across the Atlantic into South America. Two competing German illustrated weeklies published simultaneously in 1965 conflicting articles on the topic, presenting what each purported to be convincing evidence—*Bunte* of Munich claiming that Bormann was alive, *Stern* of Hamburg insisting that he had perished in Berlin in 1945.

Wiedwald's tale was echoed by Anthony Terry, Bonn correspondent of the *Sunday Times* of London (in a series of articles confidently titled "The Hiding Place of Martin Bormann"), while his colleague, the Bonn correspondent of the London *Daily Express*, featured the *Stern* claim. At the same time, Herbert John, the South

American correspondent of *Der Spiegel,* and one of the most resourceful and courageous reporters on the trail of fugitive Nazis, insisted that Bormann was living in Bolivia, and rather gregariously at that. John supported his claim by producing a photograph that, he said, showed a broadly smiling Bormann leaving a Rotary Club luncheon at La Paz in the summer of 1958.

The two best books on Bormann, one by the German historian Josef Wulf and the other by James McGovern, a former American intelligence officer who, during his years in the C.I.A., was the agency's Bormann specialist, foundered in their vague conclusions. McGovern in particular was overcautious in his attempt at resolving the issue. He drew up a series of what he called "scenarios," each describing a different account of Bormann's postwar fate, speculating what could have happened to the man in imaginative monographs based on the contradictory information he was able to gather.

When I met McGovern, hoping to persuade him to elaborate on his "scenarios" and give me some data that security considerations had prevented him from divulging in his book published in 1968, he proved evasive. As far as he was concerned, he said, Bormann was "dead," if only because he himself had lost interest in him.

I tapped contacts I had inside the British Secret Intelligence Service and the American Central Intelligence Agency. My friends in S.I.S. expressed the opinion that Bormann may have survived the war but hastened to add that they could not care less whether he now was alive or dead. I was told by one of the highest-ranking British intelligence officers that in the immediate wake of the war, when rumors were abroad that Bormann had managed to escape to South America aboard a U-boat, the Naval Intelligence Division had made an effort to get to the bottom of these tales. But they were more interested in the wayward U-boat than in its notorious passenger. The perfunctory investigation produced no definitive results, and the search was abandoned, closing the Bormann case once and for all as far as the British were concerned.

A contact inside the C.I.A. proved more productive. He told me that subsequent to the inconclusive McGovern investigation, which harked back to the early fifties, the agency received information that tended to prove that Bormann was alive, living somewhere in South America. C.I.A. stations in Brazil and Argentina would report from time to time that Bormann had been sighted—in São Paulo, for instance, and repeatedly in Bariloche, the Argentine mountain-resort region, which seemed to be (and, as it turned out, actually *was*) his favorite place of relaxation on his constant wanderings. The C.I.A. man in Asunción was said to be especially eloquent in his coverage of Bormann whenever the fugitive was alleged to have been in Paraguay.

But while the C.I.A. thus seemed to be persuaded that Bormann was alive, and concluded that he was living in South America, the reports were filed and forgotten. There was no interest in Bormann anywhere in the American government to trigger or justify a serious and probably costly effort on the C.I.A.'s part.

In my initial endeavors I focused on three major authorities who had a professional interest in Bormann. One was Dr. Fritz Bauer, the highly respected Procurator General of the State of Hesse, in whose jurisdiction rested the German search for the missing man. Dr. Bauer was *positive* that Bormann was alive, and he worked passionately and indefatigably until his death in 1968 to find him.

My second authority was Simon Wiesenthal, a native of Poland and an engineer by profession, who blossomed after the war as the world's foremost authority on missing Nazis, leading a global search for them from his small office in Vienna. Wiesenthal had in his archives hundreds of letters and other private reports about the fugitive Reichsleiter, their contents boiled down to two paragraphs in his book, *The Murderers Among Us*.

> Suppose [they read] I can provide evidence that Bormann lives at a certain address in Curitiba—what will happen? Twenty-four hours later he would disappear. He can easily submerge in South America. He has money and a network of fanatically devoted helpers.
>
> Many countries are interested in Bormann, but no country is *really* interested. Fritz Bauer, prosecutor in Frankfurt, doubts whether any South American country would extradite him. The mystery of Martin Bormann—most probably now living near the frontier of Argentina and Chile as I write this, early in 1966—will degenerate into a simple biological equation. He is well protected. No country will want to attempt a second Eichmann case. Bormann will come to his end some day, and the reward of 100,000 marks will never be paid.

Wiesenthal concluded this summary of his knowledge of Bormann's postwar fate with a bit of philosophical musing. "Death," he wrote, "needs no money."*

My third authority was Dr. Michael Bar-Zohar, a former Israeli government official, now the enterprising author of a number of excellent books about the Israeli Secret Service and the Nazi scene in the postwar world. In one, called *The Avengers* (1967), he described in broad strokes the global search for Hitler's missing minions. Bar-Zohar too was positive that Martin Bormann was alive.

> The statements of Bormann's associates [he wrote], the reports of various secret services, and the files of press agencies contain a mass of contradictory information on what happened to Bormann when he left the bunker. . . . One thing only is certain—he was not killed in Berlin. His presumed death was carefully planned. . . .

Basing his conclusion on information he received from "a secret agent with great experience dealing with Nazis"—presumably his friend Isser Harel, diminutive former chief of the Israeli Secret Service, who plotted and directed Eichmann's abduction—Bar-Zohar placed Bormann in the Mato Grosso, a vast swampy jungle in Brazil "crossed by only two roads, often made impassable by torrential rains." Bormann was well protected, Bar-Zohar concluded his report, "aided by the physical features of the Mato Grosso and by the solidarity of the outlaws who have found refuge there."

So it went to and fro, pro and con. While still trying to resolve the mystery within the narrow confines of my library in Connecticut, I prepared a big wall chart, listing in separate columns those who claimed that Bormann was dead and those who insisted that he was alive. The chart proved nothing. For instance, I had in one column Arthur Axmann, the former Reich Youth leader, who was regarded by Professor Trevor-Roper as a reliable witness, insisting that he himself had seen the body of Bormann in the rubble of

* On March 27, 1967, in a press conference promoting his book in New York, Wiesenthal left no margin for error. Bormann was alive, he stated without qualification, adding the new twist that the Reichsleiter was "using five or six names" and "utilizing a double" to evade the authorities. Described as the man "who has tracked down 1,000 Nazi war criminals, including Adolf Eichmann," Wiesenthal told Irving Spiegel of *The New York Times:* "Bormann travels freely through Chile, Paraguay and Brazil. He has a strong organization [and plenty of money] dedicated to aiding other Nazi war criminals." Incidentally, Mr. Wiesenthal's 1967 book was republished in 1973 in a paperback edition, without any revisions or additions.

Berlin during his own flight from the Führerbunker. In the other column I had the distinguished Dr. Fritz Bauer, who had gone to considerable lengths to check out Axmann's testimony and found it wanting. He insisted, on the basis of his own elaborate investigation and information given him by witnesses he regarded as reliable, that Bormann was alive.

Baffled by such contradictions in the available evidence and discouraged by the apparent impossibility of resolving the case, I was about to ignore Bormann and concentrate my efforts on those Nazis whose survival in South America was not subject to doubt. But in the midst of my vague pursuit of the elusive Reichsleiter, two incidents occurred in the early fall of 1971 that brought the man back into sharper focus.

A friend of mine, a young British historian, confided to me that Professor Trevor-Roper, to whom he was close, had had a strange experience in 1960 that caused him to revise his earlier conclusion, based on the testimony of Arthur Axmann, that Bormann had died in Berlin. According to my friend, Trevor-Roper was now inclined to believe, with only some reservations, that Bormann had survived and managed to escape, first to northern Italy and then to South America.

It then developed that in the mid-sixties, during the investigation of the Bormann case by Judge von Glasenapp, Trevor-Roper had given him a deposition in London, relating all he apparently knew of the case.

In his deposition he retreated from his previous conclusion that Bormann was dead, mainly because he had since learned that the fugitive Reichsleiter had been spotted in Bolzano, Italy, in early 1948, by a woman named Thalheimer. This could not have been a case of mistaken identification. The widow of a Bavarian physician who had once treated Bormann, she had seen the Reichsleiter in her husband's office in Munich.

The recognition in Bolzano, Frau Thalheimer insisted, was instant, unmistakable and mutual. When Bormann bumped into her, he panicked and ran into a nearby house, to which the woman did not dare follow him. Although this was the extent of this particular bit of evidence, Trevor-Roper accepted it at face value and so informed the German investigator, assuring him that he regarded Frau Thalheimer as a trustworthy observer and reliable informant.

Then, in September 1971, a news report by Henry Raymont in

The New York Times disclosed that General Reinhard Gehlen, former intelligence chief of the German Army General Staff on the eastern front, and postwar head of the senior branch of the German secret-service combine, would solve the Bormann mystery once and for all with a categorical statement in his forthcoming memoirs.

According to Gehlen, Bormann had been a traitor and a spy, using a clandestine radio transmitter to send invaluable intelligence to the Soviet Union. In a single paragraph on page 48 of the original German edition of his book, Gehlen went on to add that though he himself was unable to investigate Bormann's disappearance until 1946, Admiral Wilhelm Canaris, wartime chief of the Abwehr, and two anonymous informants had told him that the man had been alive in the 1950s and lived "undercover" in the Soviet Union until his death in the late 1960s.

I myself was skeptical of Gehlen's claim and was further told by several reliable informants that the Bundesnachrichtendienst, Gehlen's own organization at Pullach, had information on file that was quite different from what the general wrote in his memoirs. Certain people in the BND even told me that Gehlen himself had authorized a search for Bormann in the 1960s, and that, in its course, a member of his secret service, going under the name of Horst von Westernhagen, had been sent to Brazil on the Bormann trail.

This emissary died under mysterious circumstances shortly after his arrival in Rio de Janeiro. He had allegedly been murdered in gangster fashion by the Nazis, who had been tipped off, presumably from Pullach, about Westernhagen's special mission involving the Reichsleiter. But other Gehlen agents more fortunate than Major von Westernhagen provided ample hard intelligence to persuade the BND that Bormann, far from having died in the U.S.S.R. after an ignoble career as a Soviet spy, had managed to escape to South America, where he was still living at the time of General Gehlen's sensational claim.

Even Gehlen could not sustain his version of the Bormann story and was obliged to disavow it. The two German officials in charge of the Bormann case—Judge von Glasenapp and Prosecutor Richter—called on him, at his retreat at Berg on Lake Starnberg, to demand that he divulge to them whatever evidence he had to support his assertion. The outcome of their visit on September 21, 1971, was a sworn deposition (marked "Confidential") in which Gehlen insisted that he had deliberately refrained from involving his agency in the worldwide search for the missing Reichsleiter. He declined to reveal the identity of the "two friends" who had given him the information, justifying his refusal to cooperate on the somewhat doubtful moral grounds that security is more important than truth.

"I refuse," he said, "to disclose the two [living] sources of my information whose veracity I do not question, even though I am aware of my duties as a witness. I am convinced that I am acting in the spirit of the law when I give priority to considerations of security over the obligation to tell the whole truth."

Did he think, his interrogators asked Gehlen, that Bormann was alive or dead?

"It goes without saying," the general replied, "that over a period of time the Secret Service received numerous reports about the supposed whereabouts of Bormann. I treated—and still treat—these reports with skepticism, mainly because I was never satisfied with the reliability of the informants. . . . On my part I believe that Bormann, with probability bordering on certainty, has died. However," he added, disavowing blandly his own Bormann story, "I never claimed that I ever had any even approximately positive source of information to bear out this belief."

Chapter Three

The Pursuit of a Shadow

Although General Gehlen's sensational revelation turned out to be just another dud, it revived interest everywhere in the elusive Bormann. It also changed my original concept of this project and shifted the emphasis of my research.

Simon Wiesenthal once claimed that he had a "private list" of 22,000 Nazi war criminals and estimated that 16,000 of them were still living "either openly or in hiding in various parts of the world." This was a lot of people to keep tabs on. Wisely (and economically), Wiesenthal concentrates on a few of the criminals at large at any one time. In 1967, for example, his targets were Martin Bormann, former Gestapo chief Heinrich Müller and Gruppenführer Richard Glücks, the inspector general of all concentration camps.*

* Wiesenthal's enduring interest in Glücks shows how steadfast he is in his pursuit of Nazi criminals. Hospitalized in Flensburg with terminal cancer, Glücks committed suicide on May 10, 1945. Although his death was subsequently certified by the British authorities, Wiesenthal refused to believe that the notorious Gruppenführer was really dead. His stubborn unlaid ghost remained on Wiesenthal's most-wanted list for over twenty years. The dean, and unquestionably most resourceful and dedicated of Nazi hunters, Wiesenthal is one of the busiest men in the world. He is running his Jewish Documentation Center with an iron hand, raising funds in personal efforts which range from Vienna to Johannesburg and Los Angeles, and is spending much of his time on lecture tours or on TV talk shows. For relaxation, he is engaged in proving that Christopher Columbus was a Jew; and for a hobby, probably to relieve the dreadful gloom of his main pursuit, he is collecting Jewish jokes for a book he is planning to write one of these days. Incidentally, he was never directly involved in the tracing or capturing of Eichmann; and of the 16,000 Nazi criminals on his private list, he was personally responsible for the eventual downfall of only two, Franz Paul Stangl, former commandant of the Treblinka death camp (see page 380), and an Austrian named Erich Rajakowitsch, one of Eichmann's representatives in Holland (see page 194). The invaluable service he is rendering to the cause is in his missionary zeal, selfless dedication and, in the final analysis, publicity savvy, which combine to prevent us from ever forgetting these fugitives and to prod the authorities, frequently against their will or better judgment, to keep after them.

Later his chief targets were Bormann and Dr. Josef Mengele, then Bormann and Obersturmbannführer Walter Rauff, manager of the SS motor pool of gassing vans (see page 199). But whoever appeared in second or third place on Wiesenthal's most-wanted list, Bormann was the permanent fixture as Number One.

At the outset, I had no such special villains on my roster of Nazi rogues. Interested in the fugitives as a more or less homogeneous group, I was trying not to track down individuals, but to establish how successful they were in reviving and perpetuating Nazism in exile and how much of a threat their amorphous Fourth Reich represented to the stability and tranquillity of the world.

But, what with all the telltale clues about Bormann littering my trail—and the consensus of such experts as Dr. Bauer, Professor Kempner, Wiesenthal and Dr. Bar-Zohar that he was alive—I decided to make a stab of my own at clearing up the mystery. In the midst of the furor stirred up by the Gehlen story, I broadened my investigation of Nazi fugitives and joined the Bormann hunters in earnest.

To begin with, I turned to the National Archives and Records Center in Washington, D.C., and to the closely guarded Berlin Document Center, expecting to find in their huge collection of captured German and Nazi papers (the Document Center alone has forty-four million pieces of them) some promising leads to start off my investigation.

I was not disappointed. At these two major sources, I was rewarded with some 12,000 sheets of Bormann papers. Among them I discovered what appeared to be the last letter Bormann dictated to Else Krüger, his secretary, and signed himself while still holed up in the Führerbunker. It encouraged me, at the very outset of my quest, to pursue the search.

Dated April 5, 1945, the three-page typewritten letter was addressed to Dr. Ernst Kaltenbrunner, chief of the Main Security Office, Himmler's deputy at the head of the terror machine that was, in its last throes, to frighten the Germans into fighting their lost battle. The caustic letter was commenting on an SS report that Kaltenbrunner had handed to Bormann earlier in the day, containing information on certain high-ranking Nazis who were said to be making wholesale attempts to escape. It made Bormann furious. "As far as the report you gave me today is concerned," he wrote, "it is the *typical* SS report."

He went on to reprimand Kaltenbrunner for taking seriously

such "hogwash" and to censure him for objecting to the escape attempts of certain of the Nazi leaders. "The author of your report," he wrote, "must be oblivious to the conditions as they exist, or else he would not have made these totally unwarranted accusations." He singled out for special comment the exodus of the Nazi leadership from the Saar region and Pomerania, crass cases that figured prominently in the indignant SS report. "Do you mean," he wrote to Kaltenbrunner, "to make me personally responsible or blame the gauleiters for the sudden collapse of the fronts as a result of which hundreds of thousands are liable to fall into the hands of the enemy?"

To my great surprise, Bormann appeared to be in favor of *escaping in time* rather than fighting for a lost cause to the bitter end. This was what Hitler called "defeatism" and was punishing with summary sentences of death. Was Bormann defying his Führer's order "to stand fast with our unshakable faith in [our] ultimate victory"? The letter was the missing link I needed to persuade me that Martin Bormann, well-nigh alone among the top leaders of Nazism, was a "defeatist" at heart, as Hitler would have viewed it, and a supreme realist in his own mind. He was, it seemed, wholeheartedly in favor of saving his own skin, even as he condoned and advocated the escape attempts of his gauleiters.

I found among the documents many other clues that indicated that Bormann was not a man who, like Goebbels, was determined to perish with the Third Reich; nor was he eager, it seemed, to commit suicide. In another document he expressed the opinion that he was probably the least tainted among the Nazis in the Führer's immediate circle and would therefore be acceptable not only to Hitler's successors, but even to the victorious Allies, much in the manner in which former Fascist functionaries had been utilized in conquered Italy.

After examining thousands of his personal papers and reading everything I could find written about Bormann, I felt that I had done my homework and was adequately briefed to continue my search in the field. All signs pointed to Brazil and Paraguay as Bormann's most likely hiding places—Paraná and Mato Grosso in western Brazil and certain more or less inaccessible areas in southern and eastern Paraguay. There was no shortage of seemingly positive clues firmly offered about his whereabouts by people I came to call Bormanniacs—otherwise sane and sound men whose imagination had been ignited by the romance inherent in the Bormann saga and what they had read about Nazis on the run.*

According to one of my early informants, Bormann was living in "a heavily fortified island called El Dorado in the Paraná river in southern Paraguay, guarded day and night by thirty members of his own SS guard, who shoot and kill every trespasser without challenging him." Another contact, a Viennese vagabond turned soldier of fortune in South America, now living in Canada in what he somewhat loosely describes as "political exile," placed him in an uncharted region in eastern Paraguay near the Brazilian border, allegedly called "Waldner 555." There, too, Bormann was supposed to be occupying a fortress in a clearing in the jungle, protected by five blockhouses surrounding it, and guarded by a detachment of General Stroessner's soldiers changed every twenty days.

On March 3, 1972, I made my first excursion into their wild blue yonder, followed by several exploratory trips between April and August. I flew to São Paulo and Curitiba in Brazil, my bases of operation, then went by chartered planes to the general areas where Bormann was supposed to be hiding.† I needed only a few weeks to establish that, by this time, he had no fortified island anywhere in the Paraná nor a stronghold in the Paraguayan jungle. As a matter of fact, he was nowhere near El Dorado (which, incidentally, turned out to be a lively marketplace of some 2,500 souls, not in Paraguay, but in Misiones National Territory in Argentina) nor in "Waldner 555." The latter was, in fact, Military District X in eastern Paraguay, closed for certain obscure strategic reasons (in anticipation, as I was told, of an unlikely war with Brazil) and not to conceal Bormann at the time of my visit.

Yet the trips were by no means wasted. El Dorado lived up to

* There are, of course, also a handful of con men and black-marketeers who peddle their own Bormann confections simply to make money. Most notorious among these peddlers is the self-styled "Brazilian cop" who has a single story to sell—that he had personally killed Mengele in an eyeball to eyeball confrontation at the Paraguayan border. He managed to sell it over and over again to several news media, practically living off this figment of his colorful imagination.

† The romance of the venture was its own reward. For example, when looking for the stronghold in "Waldner 555," I had to follow instructions that read: "Proceed to Foz do Iguaçu, where the frontiers of Brazil, Argentina and Paraguay converge, and look for a pilot named Mario. Tell him Erico sent you. Hire his air taxi, then fly across the Paraná river due west from the airport of Foz to about three miles inside Paraguay, turn sharp north, continue at thirty degrees in a straight line, fly for exactly 20 minutes and 21 seconds at a speed of 320 km per hour, and you'll see Bormann's house below." It was a thrill by itself, irrespective of the outcome, to follow instructions like these.

its reputation, as found by explorers like Gonzalo Pizarro and Jiménez de Quesada, and held none of the secrets they and I had come to find. "Waldner 555" also failed to yield the fugitive. But I found many traces of Martin Bormann in this remote region. Although, of course, no plaques commemorated anywhere that Bormann had slept here or there (as, for example, in the Hotel Vienna in Tirol, a resort town twelve miles west of Encarnación, and in the Hotel Tyrol in Foz, where, I later found out, he actually had stayed), I found much evidence that he had been in the region repeatedly, moving from spot to spot, country to country, in his peripatetic exile.

Major Costa, who had commanded a battalion of Paraguayan soldiers in the area and was the *de facto* military governor of the region (but had been exiled to Argentina for his participation in a stillborn rebellion against General Stroessner), was certain that Bormann had lived in District X briefly in 1960, when the abduction of Adolf Eichmann made it advisable for him to go deeper underground. Captain McEwan, a former American service attaché accredited to Argentina and Paraguay, who had reconnoitered the area from the air on a number of flights in his U.S. Navy plane from Buenos Aires to Asunción, told me that he had seen the compound and had taken photographs of the place for an American intelligence agency, which, however, chose to ignore his lead. He was convinced, the officer assured me, that either Bormann himself or some other important Nazi fugitive was the tenant of the jungle-enshrouded *estancia.**

I met scores of responsible and reliable people in the area who conceded (or even boasted) that they had seen Bormann, had spoken with him, or even sheltered him briefly on various trips. Although he used a variety of aliases, these people had no reason to question his true identity. Bormann's survival may remain a controversial issue everywhere else, but there is nothing dubious or mysterious about it as one gets closer to the places where he has lived since 1948. As Judge Luis Carnero Checa, a distinguished Peruvian magistrate indirectly involved in the Bormann case, told me in Lima, "It is beyond the shadow of a doubt, and proved by innumerable pieces of persuasive evidence, that Martin Bormann

* By the time I flew over it, at some peril of being shot down by Paraguayan Air Force patrols, the only "*estancia*" I could see far and wide was a battered old farmhouse, badly whitewashed with its grayish paint peeling, its windows wide open, their glass panes all broken, letting the wind blow through. The place appeared to be completely deserted, but I saw some activity nearby, a couple of roads being built through the dense jungle by army engineers.

came to South America. I myself have proof that he has been in Peru as late as 1971." The judge gave me a deposition attesting to these facts.

Moreover, I found many signs of neo-Nazi activities in the regions densely populated by Germans. In Paraguay, their hub was Encarnación, the country's second-largest city, surrounded by many prosperous colonies of German and Italian immigrants in whose mind memories of World War II still shimmer. The city itself was headquarters of a firm operated partly as a front for fugitive Nazis and Fascists. Also in Encarnación, running a parquet-flooring factory, was a brother of Josef Mengele, whom the doctor visited from time to time.

In Cambirela, some twelve miles from Encarnación, I picked up another clue that Bormann was alive, this one from a former SS lieutenant named Detlev Somemburg, who professed to be a friend of the younger Mengele. During a clandestine meeting arranged by a go-between, he insisted that he himself had seen the fugitive Reichsleiter and heard Mengele addressing him deferentially as "Herr Bormann" at a meeting held in a hotel in nearby Tirol. This was the vacation resort in a secluded wooded area to which Bormann traveled by way of Posadas under the pseudonym of "Ricardo Bauer," Mengele using the alias "Dr. Gregor."

It was my first opportunity to see for myself that the existence of a kind of "Fourth Reich" was not the mere pipe dream of the Nazi hunters and to convince myself that these remote, landlocked regions were the favorite hiding places of many Germans with a dubious political and criminal past.

The center of neo-Nazism was the town of Marechal Candido Rondon, named for a Brazilian military hero, now infested with some of the most vicious and cunning specimens of an era we think has passed and a regime we would like to believe has been eradicated.

I found the town, on the westernmost edge of the state of Paraná, a veritable microcosm of Nazism. Its mayor at the time of my visits was a handsome young Brazilian of German parentage, Werner Wanderer. A bitter anti-Nazi, he did whatever he could to curb the activities of these "Germans" who chose his city as their haven, probably because it provided the ideal refuge for people whose very survival depended on their concealment.

Even a brief stay revealed the pall of fear that hung over Rondon. The Nazis of the town terrorized their fellow inhabitants, native Brazilians and bona fide German immigrants alike, and blackmailed them into tolerating this obnoxious crowd. Among the refugees at Rondon I met a former Luftwaffe doctor who had participated in the fatal medical experiments for which inmates of concentration camps were used as guinea pigs. His wife, rated as a celebrity among the fugitives, was often described as the "First Lady of Nazism" in South America. Known by her maiden name, Ingrud Klagges, she was the daughter of Dietrich Klagges, the first Nazi to seize power in a state, Braunschweig. Using his powers, he enabled Hitler, an Austrian citizen, to participate in German politics and run for the presidency against Hindenburg by conferring German citizenship on him.

The former Fräulein Klagges remembers the Führer with undimmed adoration. "He loved children," she told me, "and I, a little girl then, was his favorite. My God," she added, her eyes brightening with the cherished memories, "how wonderful it was when he had me on his knees and petted me fondly, our Führer, the greatest man in all history."

I found others like this unreformed couple in and around Rondon, all of them gathered about a strangely dashing man in his early fifties, with a passion for anonymity. He was (and may still be) one of the most dangerous Nazis on the run, although no roster of war criminals lists him and he is not wanted anywhere for any known crimes.

He goes by the name of Herbert von Gaza, and though he is reputed to be an exceptionally competent nuclear physicist, he is satisfied with living the humdrum life of an oculist. It is a tenuous cover by any standards, for he consistently neglects his business, which is hopelessly unlucrative anyway in a region where hardly anybody wears eyeglasses. It does not explain his ability to live in the big, fortresslike house, which he built from funds of obscure origin.

Herbert von Gaza is dangerous because he is smart, one of the handful of men among the refugees with brains. Too young in the forties to hold any important position under Hitler, he chose to escape when he was barely twenty-five years old and on the threshold of a brilliant scientific career only because he could not bear the downfall of the beloved leader, to whom he was fanatically devoted.

He came into his own in his chosen exile when he began to make himself useful from his power base at Rondon in aiding the escape of war criminals, in supporting them from a mysterious fund entrusted to his hands by anonymous donors and, eventually, in organizing the most diehard and trustworthy among his wards into a neo-Nazi movement that he calls the "Ultras." It is probably the most insidious such group in the Western Hemisphere, with tentacles reaching to Chile's neo-Nazi movement called "Das Reich," and to scattered colonies of unreformed Hitlerites elsewhere.

Herbert von Gaza is both the ideologue and the iron-fisted manager of Nazism surviving in this part of South America, holding absolute sway by virtue of his control of those mysterious funds and the unquestioned superiority of his searching mind.

Although mystery thus surrounds him, Gaza was willing to receive me and submit to an interview. But he stipulated that it had to be conducted in front of his thick-walled, windowless house, whose hospitality he brusquely denied to me. He spoke freely and candidly, admitting the existence of his Ultras, even conceding that he still had in fairly good repair the SS uniform he used to wear back in Nazi Germany. I asked him to pose for a picture wearing it, but he declined with a bemused smile.

"It's too early," he said in a low voice, leaving me to wonder whether he was referring to the time of day—it was ten o'clock in the morning—or to the stage in the evolution of his movement.

After three trips to western Brazil and a clandestine journey to southern Paraguay—finding a number of Nazis, to be sure, but only traces of Martin Bormann—I returned to São Paulo, so disillusioned and downhearted that I was prepared to abandon the search for Bormann. But my ordeal was not yet over. A new lead was waiting for me in Rio, to usher in the most romantic and potentially most dangerous phase of my venture. Another contact had developed during my absence, a formidable and colorful character, as he turned out to be. He oozed confidence with his categorical statements and tolerated no contradictions.

He was a smuggler by profession, a native of Bolivia who operated out of Paraguay on the Asunción–São Paulo circuit, flying contraband Scotch whisky, American cigarettes and Japanese electronic gadgets to the many hidden airstrips in Brazil.*

* Smuggling is Paraguay's major national industry and the source of the revenue of its armed forces. It was quite quaint to find that the best-selling Scotch whisky consumed within the land is Old Smuggler, bright neon lights advertising it (as well as the country's big business) on rooftops in Asunción.

I met him through a Brazilian magazine editor of impeccable credentials and excellent connections, to whom the man had offered Bormann for a price. The editor decided not to buy—Bormann is not big news in South America. But he thought I might be interested in sizing up the man and making one more attempt at getting to my elusive quarry.

The smuggler was restive. Fearing that his presence in São Paulo had been discovered by the authorities and he was in danger of being arrested if he stayed, he had made his arrangements to return to Paraguay at once. In great hurry, a meeting was set up in a room at the Othon Palace Hotel. I went there with instructions from my friend to call the man I was to meet "Alfredo" and ask no questions.

The smuggler turned out to be a tall, debonair, professional-looking man, broad-shouldered, who spoke good English in a low, husky voice. The deal he offered me was simple and straightforward; he was able, he said, to take me to Bormann. But the means by which I would gain this end sounded complicated. Alfredo also claimed that Bormann was staying "somewhere" in District X. The price he asked for his efforts was $10,000, which seemed to be the going rate for such services rendered.

I was to go to Foz, then take an air taxi to Cascavel, some eighty miles northeast, where a limousine would be waiting for me, with a driver called "Jipinho" by his nickname, who would take me to the Paraná river for the crossing into Paraguay. Over there, Alfredo himself would be waiting for me in the Volkswagen and drive me to Bormann, who, he assured me, was willing to see me as a special favor to his friends.

"But you must have the money on you in cash," Alfredo warned me, "all of it in fifty-dollar bills. No money, no Bormann. This is the deal."

It was a strange proposition, fraught with danger, going into the wilderness carrying $10,000. But Alfredo had made a good impression, and moreover, I was so eager to stay on the trail that I decided to take the risk and make a last try.

I followed Alfredo's instructions, except for one important detail. I decided not to take the money with me. It struck me as patently absurd to travel through the jungle with such a small fortune in cash. I hoped that when the time came, Alfredo would accept my check.

I reached Cascavel, met Jipinho, and though he had been hired for the trip by Alfredo, he turned out to be no friend of his. He drove me on the bumpy roads toward the river, passing through the town of Marechal Rondon, a familiar sight from my previous trip. But when we reached the other side of the town, where the Foz–Guayra road appeared in the distance, he stopped the car to talk to me in German.

"Don't go on, senhor," he said, obviously ending a long spell of silent contemplation about whether he should speak up. "This is just a trick to get your money." His face darkened as he told me in an ominous voice: "They'll kill you if you go. There is no Bormann at the end of this rainbow."

I sobered up with a jolt, and felt embarrassed and foolish as this simple stranger placed the whole inane adventure in the light in which I should have seen it from the outset. But what should I do?

Jipinho must have guessed my thoughts, for now he said: "Instead of taking you to the river, I'll drive you back to Foz. It's now four o'clock in the afternoon. You'll be back at the Cataratas by eight. Then get out of Foz as fast as you can if you know what's good for you. Strong-arm men like Alfredo have very long arms."

Although I stood up Alfredo at the water's edge and perhaps missed a chance to find Bormann, the experience somehow invigorated me. For one thing, my faith in humanity in South America had been restored by meeting a completely honest man, Jipinho, my driver, who probably risked his own life in acting to save mine.

For another, Paraguay now had a peculiar fascination for me. In every report I collected about Bormann's presumed hiding place, Paraguay invariably showed up. In some of them it loomed enormously, in others it appeared merely in passing, but it was always there, either as the permanent residence of the famous fugitive or as a stopping point when he was moving about in his furtive but remarkably successful efforts to evade his pursuers.

The benign treatment of Nazis by the Stroessner dictatorship, attributed to General Alfredo Stroessner's German descent and totalitarian sympathies, and his regime's stubborn refusal to apprehend even as notorious a criminal as Dr. Josef Mengele have pinpointed Paraguay as the most likely of all South American countries to afford a safe haven for the only surviving member of the Nazi leadership.

Paraguay always attracted the imagination of the Nazi-hunters, both professionals like Simon Wiesenthal (who never ventured even near to its borders but watched it from the safe distance of Vienna) and amateurs like reckless young Jews from Brazil and Argentina, members of groups calling themselves *Al Tishkakh* ("We Will Never Forget") and "Commando Isaac."

Strange stories were rife about goings-on in this landlocked, primitive land as far as its Nazi guests and their postwar enemies were concerned. I was told repeatedly the story of two Americans—variously described as C.I.A. agents and F.B.I. men—who had gone to Paraguay to look for Bormann. According to this tale, they went to the cinema in the sumptuous Guarani Hotel in the center of Asunción to see a film during a break in their search but were found dead in their seats when the lights went on at the end of the performance. Stories of similar incidents ending in homicide abound in the lore of the Nazi-hunters. There is documentary evidence that the plane crash in which Colonel Arganas, Bormann's friend and Mengele's protector, perished in 1965 had been an act of sabotage, perpetrated by Jewish agents to avenge the murder of two of their brothers. En route to find Bormann and kill Mengele, the two Jewish agents were intercepted by Arganas' thugs, and their throats were slashed from ear to ear. Then their bodies were thrown into the Paraná river and floated downstream with outstretched arms, to deter others from coming on such missions.

Most of the Nazi hunts in South America ended abruptly at the Paraguayan border. Yet now in my utter frustration, as I contemplated my future course on the terrace of the Hotel das Cataratas in Foz to the accompaniment of the thunder of the nearby Iguassú Falls, I became determined to enter Paraguay at whatever risk, for there, I thought, was hidden the key that would unlock the Bormann mystery. After a sleepless night during which I weighed all the pros and cons, I decided to abandon my indirect approach and go directly to Asunción to make my own on-the-spot search.

I spent the whole of a Saturday in May 1972 in my hotel room, writing up the story of my Bormann hunt as far as it went, then composed a farewell note to my wife, Liesel, preparing her for any eventuality. "This letter may sound somewhat melodramatic," I wrote, "but it doesn't matter, for by the time you receive it, I'll be either dead or safely back in Brazil."

Asunción received me with open arms at the international airport named, as everything else in this country, for General Stroessner. I found all the quaint color of this strange little country crammed into the few square yards of the big front hall of the terminal building. The big three-cornered entry stamp of Immigration went into my passport without any questions asked. My luggage was released by the customs inspector without a single piece being opened. A friendly lady from the National Tourist Bureau officially cautioned me not to exchange my dollars at a bank but sell them on the flourishing black market on a street called Palma, where I would get much more favorable rates of exchange.

I made the long trip to the inner city in a 1946 Dodge with a solicitous driver who never stopped apologizing for shaking me up, a welcome change from all the efforts at shaking me down without any apologies. As the clamor and commotion of the airport receded, I found Asunción deserted and serene on this Sunday afternoon, with only a few cars, but many cows and donkeys, on the well-paved road.

I checked into the magnificent new Hotel Guarani, then ventured out into the hostile city, fully expecting to be shadowed by Nazi agents and trailed by native gumshoes. I was alone, however, left entirely to my own resources. Not even a uniformed cop was in sight as I walked, past the movie house in which the American agents had allegedly met their sudden death, out into the big square on which the hotel fronted, called the Plaza de los Heroes for the little domed Pantheon at its southern end, in which is displayed the sarcophagus of Marshal Francisco Lopez, the mad Napoleon who had waged endless and inane wars with Argentina, Brazil and Chile and decimated Paraguay's male population in the process.

The serene calm ended dramatically next day, at lunch in the hotel's dining room. As I was seated, I discovered to my horror that sitting but two tables from me was Alfredo, the suave smuggler I had stood up a week before. All of a sudden, I felt terror in the pit of my stomach. He recognized me, of course, and beckoned to me to join him where he was sitting with two companions clad in what I recognized as the uniform of these smugglers, $250 suits from Rattner's of Miami Beach.

"What's cooking?" he asked me in the American idiom he acquired on his frequent flying trips to Florida, the northern terminus of his beat, where he picks up his merchandise.

"I really don't know," I said sheepishly. "I'm here as an ordinary tourist, just trying to get the feel of this place."

"Are you still interested in Bormann?" he asked.

"I am," I heard myself say, against my better judgment.

"He's here in Asunción, you know," he said in a businesslike voice but, as it turned out, with no business in mind. Then in a sudden burst of philanthropy, he said: "I can show you where he hides."

I was back in the old Grand Guignol, up to my neck, filled with forebodings when he volunteered to drive me to the "hideout" in his car. Was he planning to take me for a ride? I could not know, but I could not say no, so I meekly followed him out of the dining room, down to the hotel's covered driveway, and climbed into his big Plymouth, at whose wheel was a sullen-faced, pock-marked, burly young man, not unlike the junior *mafiosi* who drive the death cars in *The Godfather*.

He said something in Spanish to the driver and off we went, driving down on Avenida Pettirossi through the New City, to a big, exquisitely landscaped square, at the far end of which stood a huge yellow-painted building. As the car stopped, Alfredo invited me to get out and then, almost in the singsong of a sightseeing guide, he said: "This is the Central Military Hospital. Up there on the second floor, behind the first three windows on the left, is Martin Bormann. He was brought here a few days ago from his country place on the Rio Itaimbey where I was planning to take you to meet him. He has cancer, but *they* are taking good care of him up there. As a matter of fact, he's attended by Dr. Hugo de Jesus Araujo, the President's own physician."

How much more specific could one get? This was the culmination of my search. And I got it casually and free of charge, for Alfredo drove me back to the hotel and bid me goodbye, without ever mentioning the $10,000 fee we had agreed upon.

But the triumph was not destined to last. The momentous secret of my knowledge of Bormann's terminal hideout dissolved in less than twenty-four hours—the next morning, in fact, when I kept an appointment at the Foreign Ministry with Dr. Alberto Nogues, Under-Secretary of State for External Affairs.

A former lawyer at the Bank of Development, one of the Stroessner regime's key institutions, Dr. Nogues was a polished diplomat. I found him a highly cultured, open-minded man, not unwilling to discuss frankly and objectively the painful subject of the Nazis in Paraguay, including the case of Dr. Mengele.

"You know," he said in his fluent English, "our problem as far as these Nazis are concerned can be summed up in one word—Wiesenthal. It's his business to keep tabs on them and chase them down, and he stays in business by hunting for the big game among these fugitives in the full glare of worldwide publicity. Our trouble is that whenever he loses one or another of his suspects, or doesn't know where a certain missing Nazi actually is, he claims that he's hiding in Paraguay.

"Contrary to the widespread belief," Dr. Nogues went on, "that we *protect* this Mengele, I can tell you that we loathe him as much as anyone familiar with his crimes." Suddenly a subtle sarcasm seeped into his voice. "We hate him even more," he said, "because he let this Wiesenthal get out of Auschwitz to plague us with his venomous publicity."*

It was a plain statement, rather crude for a diplomat. But it reflected the Paraguayan government's bitterness in the face of the widespread charges that the country was the last refuge of these fugitives. Encouraged by the Secretary's bluntness in discussing with me what is regarded as a delicate topic in General Stroessner's entourage, I decided to take Dr. Nogues into my confidence and tell him of my recent experience with Alfredo. He listened quietly as I related to him the story of my original deal and its astounding denouement the day before, when Alfredo showed me what he claimed was Bormann's hiding place behind those three windows of the Central Military Hospital.

Without uttering a word in rebuttal, Dr. Nogues pushed a button on his desk and spoke to an earnest young man in a white shirt who responded to the call in Spanish. Then he turned back to me.

"This is one of my secretaries," he said. "He will take you in my car to the hospital right away. You have my permission to inspect it without any restriction. If you find Bormann behind those three windows, or for that matter, anywhere in Asunción or in the whole of Paraguay, please let me know, and we will give him to you with our compliments."

* Dr. Nogues was wrong about Auschwitz. Wiesenthal was fortunate in that he escaped that Nazi death trap. Arrested on July 6, 1941, by a Yiddish-speaking Ukrainian policeman at his home in Lvov, the Galician province of Poland, he was taken to Brigidki Prison in the city, then transferred to the nearby Janowska concentration camp, from which he managed to escape. Recaptured, he spent three frightful years in the Grossrosen and Buchenwald concentration camps, and was an inmate of Mauthausen when American troops liberated the camp and freed him on May 5, 1945.

Needless to say, I did not find Bormann either in the hospital or anywhere in Asunción. But if he was not in Paraguay, as Dr. Nogues so convincingly insisted, where was he?

I didn't know then, but I was on the eve of answering this question positively at long last.

Chapter Four

Big Break in Buenos Aires: The S.I.D.E. Dossier

At 11:30 P.M. on April 12, 1972, in Santa Clara, a suburb of Lima, the capital of Peru, an army of 150 hand-picked policemen laid siege to a fortresslike compound across the street from a busy Texaco filling station. Behind the thick walls that surrounded the enclave lived Lima's most controversial resident, posing as a humble chicken farmer and insisting that he was doing nothing more sinister than raising poultry in his stronghold.

He was, in fact, a sixty-six-year-old German named Friedrich Schwend, a man of mystery, although the most dramatic phase of his checkered career had been exposed in several books. A swaggering SS colonel during World War II, Schwend had been the key man in Operation Bernhard, concealing a fantastic Nazi scheme to counterfeit the notes of the Bank of England and flood the world with the fake currency. The idea was to undermine Britain's economic base in its war effort by destroying the pound sterling in the international marketplace.

Schwend had fled to South America after the war, and though he was wanted in Italy, where he had been sentenced *in absentia* to a long prison term for complicity in the murder of one of his associates in Bernhard, he succeeded in establishing himself in Peru and amassing a fortune through obscure deals, as counterfeit as the banknotes he once peddled. As we will see later, he used Lima as his power base for his transactions, which ranged from Peru through the whole of Latin America, all the way to Germany and even Israel; and also for the fiscal management of the big Nazi colony in South America, acting as the self-appointed minister of finance of a sort of Fourth Reich in exile.

But he understood how to remain unmolested by the Peruvian authorities, mainly by cooperating on a top level with both the secret police and the Army's intelligence service. If his house was now about to be raided and Schwend was to be arrested, it was not to apprehend him for extradition to Italy; not for anything he had done as the wholesale distributor of counterfeit money in World War II; not for his shabby deals in the postwar world. Now, in the spring of 1972, the slippery ex-Nazi was a prime suspect in a sensational murder case—the killing of a fishing magnate named Luis (Lucho) Banchero Rossi, one of the richest men in Peru, on New Year's Day.

The raid had been arranged by Dr. José Antonio Santos Chichizola, a Lima lawyer acting as the *ad hoc* investigating magistrate of the Banchero case. He was hoping to uncover evidence that would firmly link Freddy Schwend to the tycoon's murder.

Dr. Santos was personally leading the raid, moving quickly behind the policemen as soon as they broke into the fortified compound. There were several buildings in the enclave behind those formidable walls, among them the big house in which Schwend lived with his second wife, the former Hedda Neuhold, and a smaller house for his sister-in-law, Frau Martha Neuhold, herself a former high-ranking officer in the SS, now calling herself Señora Moretti.

When Dr. Santos rushed into the big house, he found Schwend in his study, frantically tearing up sheets of paper which he was grabbing from a big filing cabinet. Schwend was placed under arrest, and his house was searched, but a quick examination of his files revealed nothing to incriminate him in the murder of Lucho Banchero.

During the search Dr. Santos became intrigued when he discovered that Schwend had *two* stoves in the kitchen of his house. On a hunch, he ordered a couple of policemen to move the stoves and was startled to find a trapdoor in the floor where one of them had stood. He lifted it eagerly and saw a row of steps leading down to a cellar, where he then came upon a vast collection of papers neatly tied together in bundles, weighing 150 pounds. It turned out to be the complete record of Schwend's transactions both as a general wheeler-dealer and the fiscal wizard of Nazism in South America.

Dr. Santos then entered the house of Schwend's sister-in-law, hoping to discover more such papers there. In a room lined with bookshelves, he examined the volumes and found that one was a dummy, concealing a smaller book between its covers. It turned out to be an alphabetical register containing the names and addresses of every important Nazi in South America, including certain fugitives whose very presence there was unknown and several who were believed to have died during the last days of the war in Germany.

In August 1972, word was flashed to me from Lima, describing the raid on the Schwend compound and advising me about the documents Dr. Santos had impounded there. My contact informed me that the Schwend papers supplied positive proof at last that Bormann was alive.

I took the next plane to Lima, hoping to obtain from Dr. Santos the evidence I had so strenuously but vainly sought, but he himself had no use for, if only because it had no relevance to his own investigation of the Banchero murder case. But Dr. Santos evaded me, probably because, as I was told, he himself was planning to market his Bormann material, expecting to realize a million dollars by selling it to the highest bidder.

In spite of the lawyer's refusal to aid me in my research, I succeeded in gaining access to several sets of crucial documents in the Santos collection as it then was. One was a bulging folder of correspondence, including an exchange of letters between Schwend and Bormann, dealing with some money matters involving the purchase of a huge estate near Valdivia in Chile. Another, patently even more important, was the address book found in Frau Neuhold-Moretti's library. The latter contained not only Bormann's various addresses on his wanderings, but also his different aliases and a list of certain passwords and identification codes he insisted on using in his written contacts with his Nazi friends and other associates.

The so-called Santos papers* thus supplied the first *absolutely conclusive* evidence that Bormann had not died in Berlin on his

* They are no longer supposed to be in the care of Dr. Santos. When he concluded the Banchero investigation (with an ambiguous report that confused rather than clarified the murky case) and returned to his law practice, he was obliged to hand them over to his successor, Judge Luis Carnero Checa, who now shares their custody with the *fiscal* (prosecutor), an energetic elderly lady named Naves. The papers represent an interesting problem to the Peruvian authorities. Most of them are in German, and neither Santos nor Carnero had funds to hire an interpreter, translate the documents into Spanish, and find out what they contained. I was shown the bulk of the impounded files under somewhat melodramatic circumstances (surreptitiously in a seemingly deserted house near the race tracks in Lima) and am satisfied that I was the only German-speaking person who ever had access to this real-life Odessa file.

flight from the Führerbunker in May 1945, but managed somehow to escape to South America, where, according to the explicit entries in Schwend's address book, he moved constantly from one country to another under five different aliases. The little black book showed that, at various times, he had lived in Argentina, Brazil, Paraguay, Bolivia and Chile, and visited Peru from time to time, occasionally and ironically sometimes using a couple of Jewish-sounding names.

My search now revived and intensified, I flew to São Paulo from Lima, for consultation with my friends, who had been joined in the meantime by an official of DOPS, called the F.B.I. of Brazil, with direct access to his agency's Bormann file. My arrival coincided with the smashing of a ring of narcotics peddlers that operated in Latin America from its home base in Paraguay and the arrest in São Paulo of two Germans—ex-Nazis, at that—who represented the ring in Brazil. The two drug-pushers were held incommunicado in a safe house. The Brazilian authorities planned to use them as bait, hoping to procure additional information through them as long as their downfall could be kept a secret from their associates who remained at large.

Their interrogation then yielded an unexpected bonus. Broken by what is called "intensive interrogation," a euphemism for the torture practiced by law-enforcement agents throughout South America, the men divulged all they knew about the dope ring, and then volunteered, probably to ingratiate themselves with their interrogators and take themselves off the hook, some additional secret information. They exposed the Nazi underworld in Paraguay with its tentacles to other South American countries. Yet their revelations, of which I was given a transcript, proved somewhat disappointing. The bulk of the intelligence concerned Dr. Mengele, in whom my interest was limited and of whose activities my knowledge was virtually complete. Although the name of Martin Bormann cropped up occasionally in their statements, they professed to have little information about him.

On Mengele, however, they were most specific. They had given their interrogators a list of highly classified documents which, they said, could be recovered, not only from the secret archives of the Paraguayan police, but also from those of the security organs of Argentina, where Dr. Mengele had lived before a botched-up abortion, in the course of which his patient died, had forced him to flee the country. The roster of these seemingly important confidential papers listed the numbers under which they had been filed in the secret services and would make their finding relatively simple. The Brazilians were successful in procuring the Mengele papers from the Paraguayan archives. But all their efforts to obtain the Argentine documents had failed.

This was the situation when I showed up in São Paulo. My friends gave me the list and suggested that I go to Buenos Aires and, using methods I had learned during my years in American intelligence organizations, try to come by the papers, some of which they knew had been on file in Coordinación Federal.

I welcomed the proposition, for more reasons than one. Although I was not as keenly interested in Mengele as in Bormann, I hoped to find significant clues that would aid my search for the missing Reichsleiter. During the past seven months, I had been in Brazil several times, in Paraguay twice, also in Bolivia, Peru and Chile. But foolishly, as it turned out, I neglected Argentina. In the meantime, I had come to the conclusion that the key to the solution of the Bormann mystery was not in the places I had been to, but in Buenos Aires. I had been making my own arrangements in Argentina to develop contacts who would help me in gaining access to files in which I was convinced I would find invaluable leads to, if not the definitive solution of, my problem.

I corresponded with a man who had spent eleven years in the secret service of the Buenos Aires Provincial Police. He professed to have vast and intimate personal knowledge of the activities of the Nazis in Argentina from the years when their surveillance was one of his duties. He also assured me that he had ways and means to infiltrate the secret services and procure the documentary evidence I needed, through close connections he maintained with his former colleagues and key officials in several intelligence and security organizations. The latter included the old Coordinación Federal, the Policía Federal and the División de Asuntos Extranjeros, the bureau responsible for aliens in Argentina.

Among his live contacts, he informed me, was a distinguished federal judge involved in the Mengele case when the doctor's extradition was demanded by the German authorities; a commissioner of the Buenos Aires police; several secret agents closely connected with the festering Nazi problem in Argentina; and the political secretaries of various former Argentine Presidents. He also told me that he could, if need be, penetrate the intelligence services of the

Army, Navy and Air Force, especially important since among officers of these agencies were numerous reactionaries who protected the Nazis in Argentina from "molestation" by the other security organs which had no such ax to grind.

The man, whom I will call B. F. Singer, for reasons which will soon become obvious, had superb credentials. Still in his early forties, he had experience that seemed second to none as an intelligence officer and police investigator. During his long tenure in the intelligence division of the Buenos Aires Provincial Police, Singer perfected the methodology of criminal investigation by introducing to Argentina the most modern means of electronic surveillance.

Now he was associated in his project with another former agent, whom I will call Hugo Marchetti, an intrepid young man who had an international reputation as a police investigator and whose exploits had once been featured in the Latin American edition of *Life* magazine. Known to insiders by his nickname of Perro de Casa ("Watchdog"), Marchetti used to be the executive organ of Singer's intelligence efforts. They formed a formidable team.

Now I alerted Singer to my coming and arrived in the teeming capital city of Argentina on September 10. I was accompanied by my wife, Liesel, who had been my courageous and indefatigable partner in this search. I also took with me a reel of microfilm, with a thousand pages of documents from the captured archives of the German secret service from World War II. They concerned Nazi espionage agents who had been active in Argentina between 1935 and 1945, and also contained delicate intelligence about many important and influential Argentine nationals who had aided them in their activities. I hoped to make a deal, if possible, by exchanging this roll of microfilm with its significant indiscretions for documents I was anxious to acquire about the postwar activities of these people and the men who had come to Argentina after the war.

Singer captivated me at first sight. A tall, slim, wiry, very good-looking young chain smoker of American cigarettes, with sartorial elegance and innate charismatic charm, he turned out to be enormously well informed. He was in absolute control of the connections which he had boasted about in our correspondence.

He appeared to be eager to help me without any mercenary motives. "I am a Jew," he told me, "with a historic interest in helping you solve your problem. You have only one reason for your efforts, to write a book. But I have six million reasons—the six million Jews killed by Hitler."

Marchetti was deceptive in his appearance and manners. A short, somewhat fleshy, bullish-looking young man in his late thirties, with a big round head in which flickered his enormous eyes, he was dapper in his double-breasted blue blazer and gray-flannel pants, and exquisite in his highly developed good taste for fine food and the best of wines, as room service was soon to discover. He was smooth and suave, speaking in a low voice, contemplating every sentence carefully. He treated me with extravagant courtesy that often seemed obsequious.

Yet this debonair, soft-spoken, polite young man had been the ruthless cop the criminals and Nazis of Buenos Aires used to dread most. Beneath his polished, affable exterior was the real Marchetti. He had a record of thirty-nine killings in his law-enforcement career, five of which he still has to explain and justify to the authorities, who took a dim view of his quick-triggered method of solving cases. In his private life, Singer reassured me, Hugo could not hurt a fly. But as a cop he was a killer. No case he had been assigned to remained open, but few had any prisoners left alive to be tried in the courts. His records included the killing of three Nazis in Ezeiza, the full story of which is an important part of this narrative and will be related in its proper place.

I handed my new friends the list I had been given in São Paulo, and they assured me promptly that they would have no difficulty in "procuring" the documents whose filing numbers it contained. I was amazed the next morning when Singer and Marchetti arrived, delivering into my hands every paper on the list.

I spent half the night trying to read them in my faltering Spanish, only to find that they were the rehash of documents I already had and which, in fact, had been in the public domain ever since Herbert John published them in *Der Spiegel* a decade before. My respect for the astuteness of the Brazilian secret service received a severe jolt. And my hopes of finding anything new and important in the files of the Argentine secret service dimmed considerably. But Singer waved away my misgivings with an irate gesture.

"This is *basura,*" he said, using one of his favorite expletives, which means "garbage" in English. "It's good only for stupid, gullible Brazilians who let themselves be conned by those Nazi drug-pushers. Here," he added, reaching down into his trousers, "I have something for you that nobody else has."

He pulled out a pink folder and handed it to me. "I am giving you," he said solemnly, "a *sample* of the documents I am able to procure—and this in addition to the *secret* file of the Mengele case." With that, he retrieved the folder and opened it, picking out the documents it contained and explaining them one by one. For the first time in my nine-month search I had in my hands apparently unimpeachable evidence that Bormann had survived the war and escaped to South America.

But were the documents really incontrovertible? I was consistently warned that these Latins were past masters in producing documents on any matter, even of the greatest sensitivity, by the relatively simple method of forging them. How could I be sure that the documents Singer was giving me were authentic? I saw no reason to conceal my misgivings.

"What assurance do I have," I asked darkly, "that these documents are genuine?"

Singer responded with the condescending, slightly contemptuous smile which he let play on his lips whenever I dared question his integrity or veracity. "They *are* genuine," he said in a low key. "You will have *every* opportunity to confirm their authenticity. Tonight I'll take you to the private showing of a great Argentinian motion picture which a friend of mine directed in 1941. It's nice to see such a fine movie that has lost none of its beauty with age. But that's not why I'm taking you to see it. It's a cover. I have arranged for you to meet some of my friends who work at Coordinación Federal. Moreover, I'll introduce you to several of the special agents who prepared these documents in the first place and whose signatures appear on them, but who are no longer on active service and need no subterfuge to meet you."

That night, in the House of Culture, I had a double feature of thrills. I saw *La Guerra Gaucho,* one of the greatest films ever made, the Argentine equivalent of D. W. Griffith's *Birth of a Nation.* And I met Juan José Velasco.

Our meeting was carefully staged as a casual, coincidental encounter. It lasted but a minute or two. But what Velasco told me in that brief span put me on my toes. "I am pleased to meet you, László," he said with an impish grin, calling me by the Hungarian version of my first name. "I know all about your fine work in the American Office of Naval Intelligence during the Second World War."

After the performance, Singer took me to the Michelangelo, a cavernous cabaret, which was starring Estelle Ravel, the great chanteuse, in a performance that included an unforgettable rendering of the stirring song from the film *Sacco and Vanzetti.* He wanted me to meet another of his "contacts-in-place," a high-ranking official of the Policía Federal. On the way to the nightclub, I asked Singer, "How come that Velasco called me 'László' and knew about my wartime work in Naval Intelligence?"

"Oh," he said casually, "he looked you up in the files. We cannot afford to do business with amateurs."

"Who is this Velasco anyway?" I asked.

"He is a special agent in Coordinación Federal," Singer said, "fairly high-ranking—as a matter of fact, he's the number-eight man in the agency. We are friends from my own years in the service. We worked together on some very interesting cases, like Che Guevara, you know him, no? But that is not why he agreed to work with us. For one thing, he is fed up that the Nazis are still allowed to infest Argentina after all these years. For another, I told him about your microfilms and he is very interested in them. His beat includes the surveillance of our own native reactionaries, you see, and he hopes to get some new leads from your material."

That same night, back in my hotel, Singer explained the procedure they would follow to get copies of the documents for me. "These are originals," he said, pointing to the ones I had. "They must be back in the files tomorrow morning. In the future, you'll get *true* copies of the originals which you will be able to keep.

"Velasco, of course, has easy access to the files. He needs to refer to them all the time, in the course of his current investigations. Whenever he needs a document in a case he handles, he himself pulls it out of the files, has a copy of it made in an office on the second floor, where the agency has a Xerox machine, then returns the original to its folder and keeps the copy. He'll mix the documents we think are of interest to you with the papers he himself will need, and have them copied with the rest. He won't be able to handle too many documents at any one time, without attracting the suspicion of the technician on the second floor. So it may be some time before we can let you have all the documents you need. They will be delivered in batches of five or so at a time. The ones you got today are the first shipment. You'll get another bunch tomorrow."

He looked at his wrist watch. It was quarter past four in the morning. "As a matter of fact," Singer said, "I better go home and catch some sleep. Our friend is in his office right now, collecting some of the material. I have an appointment with him at ten A.M., when he'll hand over to me the second shipment. I'll bring it to you immediately."

At ten o'clock the next morning Singer was sitting at a table in the crowded Florida Garden Café, almost next door to my hotel, when promptly at the prearranged time, Velasco arrived, carrying a copy of *Siete Días,* a popular weekly illustrated magazine, under his arm. He joined Singer for a hearty breakfast, then left, forgetting the magazine on his chair. Singer paid the check, picked up the magazine, and came over to me for what turned out to be our most memorable session.

It was on this morning of September 15 that he pulled from Velasco's abandoned *Siete Días* two documents—both captioned "Martin Bormann"—that clinched the case.

The first was the summary of the Bormann file kept by the Federal Police, attached to which were copies of the full reports submitted by the agents. The second appeared to be even more important. Beneath the words *"Estrictamente Secreto y Confidencial,"* stamped in blue ink at the top of the page of its cover sheet, it bore the inscription:

Secretaría de Informaciones de Estado
Dependiente de la Presidencia de la Nación
Central Nacional de Inteligencia
Informe Especial No. 3/63
MARTIN BORMANN

The copy I had before me was log-numbered "6384" and marked *"Ejemplar No. 6."* Obviously only six copies had been made of the document, and this seemed to be one of two apparently retained in the files of Coordinación Federal. As the distribution stamp on the sheet indicated, the other copies had been forwarded to four of the topmost officials in the government, including the President of the Republic.

By this time, I was familiar with the structure of Argentina's intelligence establishment and realized that this was the key document in the folder, a report of the utmost importance and sensitivity. It originated, as the cover sheet showed, at S.I.D.E. (as the Secretaría de Informaciones de Estado was usually called by its initials), Argentina's equivalent of our Central Intelligence Agency which, like the C.I.A., is the intelligence arm of the President himself.

Stapled to the cover sheet were four closely typed pages, containing a summary of all the information the Argentine authorities had available about Martin Bormann.

Both the compendium of the Federal Police and the S.I.D.E. summary stated categorically that Bormann, far from having died on his flight from the Führerbunker, had managed to make his way to Argentina and establish himself there safely and comfortably behind a smokescreen provided by Argentine authorities during the presidency of Colonel Juan Domingo Perón, whom Bormann himself later described as *unser grosser Gönner*, "our great benefactor."

Under the caption "*Asuntos Martin Bormann*," the S.I.D.E. summary began as follows:

> Born in the city of Halberstadt, province of Magdeburg, Germany. He was chief of the Chancellery of the Nazi Party. The International War Crimes Tribunal [sic] of Nuremberg sentenced him to death *in absentia*. He had several sons, among them a Jesuit, who, in 1945, disseminated the news that his father had died. This was a lie designed to interfere with the search for the missing criminal. [Bormann's] birth was registered as the year 1900. He was regarded as Adolf Hitler's right-hand man and was mentioned, at the end of the war, as his successor.
>
> As other escapees like him, [Bormann] entered Argentina in 1948, having sailed from Genoa on a second-class ticket, with false documents issued by the Vatican. They were obtained for him by an organization called La Esclusa, which was instrumental in aiding the escape of dozens of refugees.

As the summary continued page after page, it described year by year and step by step Bormann's every move, first in Argentina, then in other countries of South America. It ended with the report of an agent named Mather, who had spotted Bormann, in the company of "several of his Party comrades," in the ABC beer hall at 500 Calle Lavelle, in San Carlos de Bariloche, "on several occasions in 1961."

The summary of the Federal Police corroborated these data by stating in its first paragraph under a "mug shot" of Martin Bormann:

> National Socialist German politician, born 1900 in the city of Halberstadt, province of Magdeburg. Chief of the Chancellery of the National Socialist Party. The Nuremberg war crimes tribunal condemned him to death in his absence. After the fall

> of the Third Reich, in common with other refugees, he entered our national territory in a clandestine manner, coming from Genoa, Italy, in 1948, disguised as a Jesuit priest, and traveling with false identity documents.

It went on to present what the document called "the chronology of the case," covering the period between 1948 and 1961. The last entry described an evening Bormann, using the alias "Bauer," had spent in the Ali Baba bar in Asunción, Paraguay, in the company of his friend Dr. Josef Mengele.

There was a direct link between these two key documents, a kind of personal connection that enhanced the appearance of their authenticity and accuracy. The S.I.D.E. summary had been written in 1963 by a colonel named Alberto Samuel Caceres, who was then director of Coordinación Federal and whose jurisdiction included the alien control office. He prepared the three-thousand-word compendium for the information and "eyes only" of José Mario Guido, former head of the Senate, who had succeeded Dr. Arturo Frondizi to the presidency on March 29, 1962, in the wake of a bloodless military coup. It was one of several summary reports Colonel Caceres had compiled for the provisional President to familiarize him with security matters which the President of the Republic was entitled to have and needed to know.

Colonel (later Major General) Caceres survived in various offices several Presidents as the top security chief of Argentina. At this time in 1972 he was chief of the Federal Police, the agency where the second Bormann compendium was compiled. He, therefore, symbolized in his person the authenticity of these crucial documents and the accuracy of the information they contained, one prepared by himself, the other compiled by the agency he headed.

Considerable additional primary documentation—including more than a thousand pages of original papers—was subsequently obtained from official archives in Argentina, Paraguay, Chile, Bolivia, Brazil and Peru. But this was the high point of Singer's brokerage.

For all practical purposes, it then seemed, the great search was over. The mystery of Martin Bormann's postwar fate was solved at last. His survival was attested, under their seal, by his hosts who had allowed him, a hunted criminal doomed to die on the gallows, to enter their country, and who then hid the famous fugitive even as the whole world was looking for him. Achilles absent was Achilles still.

In all his life, the tremendous outsider, Bormann shunned the limelight. Now, though, he sought to evade it more than ever, he could not escape it any more. His first odyssey ended when his Argentine-bound tramp ship put down anchor in Buenos Aires harbor a quarter century before. Now his new odyssey was about to begin—born to wander, cursed to stay.

PART TWO

Every Man for Himself

Chapter Five

Appointment in Byzantium

Adolf Hitler committed suicide on April 30, 1945. His bunker was overcrowded with the remains of the Nazi leadership in Berlin, among them Martin Bormann, Goebbels and his whole family (except his stepson), Generals Hans Krebs and Wilhelm Burgdorf, and Eva Braun, Hitler's long-time mistress. He dictated his last will and testament. He married Eva Braun. Then, obviously filled with self-pity while summoning courage for his final scene, he toured the bunker, bidding goodbye to all. What made this dramatic leave-taking unique was that nobody made even the slightest effort to deter their beloved Führer from his decision to kill himself.

Hands were warmly shaken. Gifts were dispensed, accompanied by vials and pills of cyanide. Tears were shed. Then Hitler dragged himself to his quarters, where Eva Braun was waiting, followed only by his valet, a big SS man named Heinz Linge. "You must break out," Hitler told Linge as he stopped at the door to the passage from which he would enter the living room and shook Linge's hands, "with one of the groups."

"My Führer," Linge asked, "what would be the point?"

"You must live," Hitler replied, "for the sake of my successor."

These were the last words anyone heard him utter.

A few minutes later, with the limp body of his wife at his side, Adolf Hitler was dead. Seized by a fleeting panic, Linge raced up the long staircase, as if trying to seek the daylight, but he was greeted with shells from Russian guns whistling around his ears. Retracing his steps, he returned to the door behind which his Führer had gone, opened it a crack and saw Hitler slumped in the right-hand corner of the settee. Somehow Linge did not dare to enter the death chamber alone. He summoned Bormann, and they went in together to make the necessary burial arrangements. The bodies were carried out of the bunker and, soaked in gasoline, were burned on an improvised funeral pyre amidst the rubble outside.

It was three-thirty in the afternoon.

All the others in the bunker, with Dr. Goebbels and General Krebs at their head, waited in their tiny quarters. When Linge brought the sad news, there was what amounted to a sigh of relief. Whether they admitted it or not, even to themselves, Hitler had become a liability. Now they were free to act on their own.

It was natural for Heinz Linge to call Martin Bormann to accompany him into the room where Hitler and his wife lay dead. In the final analysis, the Reichsleiter was only another servant of the Führer, and not his deputy, as his predecessor, the pathetic Rudolf Hess, was called.

In the case of Hess, the title carried none of the powers it implied. When Hess flew to Scotland in the late spring of 1941, as the carrier pigeon of an inane peace plan, even the title lapsed. The Hess bureau, which, in fact, was the Führer's secretariat and his liaison office with the Party, was purged ruthlessly. Its sole survivor was Bormann, until then Hess's chief of staff and the indefatigable bureaucrat who did all the work for his indolent and neurotic chief.*

Two days after that Saturday evening, May 10, 1941, when Hess had vanished and before the British announcement of his arrival in Scotland, the news that her husband had supposedly crashed into the North Sea and was missing was broken to his wife, Ilse, at Harlaching, while she and members of Hess's staff were watching a movie at the Deputy Führer's private projection room. Refusing to believe the bad news, she put in a top-priority call to Obersalzberg to find out what had really happened. After a long

* Clad in a superbly tailored new uniform, wearing a gold wrist watch and a gold wrist compass, and carrying medication for his weak heart and gall-bladder ailment, Hess took off from Augsburg in a new type of reconnaissance plane. Even as the world waited for Winston Churchill to explain the mystery of his flight, it was evident that Hess, frustrated by his eclipse at home caused by the Führer's preoccupation with the war, was motivated by a fanatical desire "to serve Hitler by negotiating a peace agreement with Britain." Certain documents I found in the Boston University Library indicate that he had some reason to assume that Churchill might be interested in talking peace with him. But the information on which Hess acted harked back to December 1940. In the meantime, Churchill had been advised by his Intelligence Service that Hitler would attack the U.S.S.R. in June, and the Prime Minister lost all interest in making peace with Hitler.

delay and some wire-pulling, she managed to get through to Bormann, who assured her that he himself was completely in the dark.

Ilse Hess was initially convinced that her husband had been liquidated and assumed that Bormann's intrigues had caused his "execution."

It is unlikely that Bormann intrigued against Hess at court, although he was openly contemptuous of him. It was always clearly evident that Bormann's overriding allegiance belonged not to Hess but to the Party and, above all, to the Führer.

Hitler knew that the efficiency of the Hess bureau was Bormann's doing and he trusted Hess's hard-working, loyal subordinate. But he revamped the bureau and reduced its new chief's authority while leaving him all his own and Hess's former responsibilities. The fictitious position of "Deputy Führer" was abolished. Bormann was appointed head of the *Parteikanzlei,* the Party's administration, a huge and complex directorate, more managerial than political in its functions and orientation.

Bormann's title was Reichsleiter, the equivalent of minister in the dual government of the Third Reich.* There were in the end forty-three gauleiters, thirteen Reichsleiters, and eleven others in leadership jobs on the highest echelons like Arthur Axmann, the Reich Youth leader, and Dr. Leonardo Conti, the Party-oriented Surgeon General.

Nominally, Bormann was only one member of this chosen group of sixty-seven bosses. But Bormann, of course, had far greater power and wielded broader influence than his colleagues, acquiring the reputation from his increasing closeness to Hitler of being Hitler's gray eminence.

Bormann held the reins of the Party; he dispensed patronage; he supervised and frequently disciplined the gauleiters; and he saw to it that the Party remained paramount in the life of the state, the nation, and the citizens. As Hitler's spokesman, he ruled, governed and commanded the Party, and bent all, from Reichsleiter and gauleiter down to the most humble *Parteigenosse,* to Hitler's will, which he equated with his own. But his rule was by no means absolute.

* On March 30, 1945, when the Party had a life expectancy of only thirty-nine days, its top administrative hierarchy consisted of sixty-seven positions held by as many individuals (many of whom, like Goebbels, Himmler, Wilhelm Frick, Dr. Otto Thierack and Ernst Bohle, also held top jobs in the government).

For his own part, Bormann was satisfied with what he had. Although he would sometimes issue orders and make arrangements in the Führer's name on his own initiative and authority without the Führer's knowledge, most of the time he functioned as the Führer's chief comptroller and appointments secretary.

"Bormann," said Gerhard Klopfer, a Silesian-born lawyer who was secretary of state of the *Parteikanzlei,* "regarded as gospel everything that came from the Führer, then passed on Hitler's ideas in an exaggerated form. He often issued orders to carry out certain things merely on the assumption that they represented Hitler's ideas or wish." Klopfer inferred that Bormann was the real power behind major decisions and wicked acts which he then attributed to Hitler. "He told us again and again," Klopfer said, "that we [at the *Parteikanzlei*] were the executive organ of the Führer, solely of the Führer. He repeatedly assured us that everything he did or said had been cleared with and approved by the Führer."*

Like most of his top colleagues, Bormann rose to his position from a middle-class background. He was the son of a former trumpeter in a military band who became a postal clerk after his retirement from the Army. He was an agronomist by training, one of the small men who had grown big under Hitler—the onetime poultry farmers, tavern keepers, petty officials, army sergeants and used-car dealers, who were the first to rally around Hitler during the twenties.

Bormann differed from them in that he never sought the limelight. He enjoyed his prerogatives and power to the utmost, but he never arrogated to himself anything that belonged to Hitler, nor abused the confidence his Führer reposed in him. This was the secret of his durability. Yet, because he was the bearer of Hitler's arbitrary decisions, his peers, who envied him, made him responsible for what, in their most secret hearts, they resented in Hitler.

He was loathed within the hierarchy. Even his friend Heinrich Himmler (whom he called Uncle Heinrich) felt his own position as chief of the SS threatened by Bormann.

Rudolf Hess, his original mentor, who at first liked Bormann

* Although Klopfer was the number-two man in the *Parteikanzlei,* the chief administrative center of the Nazi Party, and its *de facto* boss in Bormann's perennial absence from the Führerbau and Pullach, its headquarters; and although he represented Bormann at the so-called Wannsee Conference of January 20, 1942, at which the *modus operandi* of the "Final Solution," the extirpation of millions of Jews, was settled, the former Gruppenführer (SS No. 272,227) was never charged or tried after the war. At the age of sixty-eight, he enjoys both his health and his freedom in a lucrative practice as an attorney at Ulm, his clients including many prominent German firms of today.

and was initially responsible for his meteoric career in the Party administration, eventually thought of him with derision and contempt. In Hess's voluminous correspondence with his wife, Ilse, in which he referred to Goethe thirty-two times, he mentioned Bormann only once, and even then so obscurely that a footnote had to identify Bormann. In a letter from England, dated September 4, 1943, answering a note from his wife about Bormann's rapid rise at Hitler's side, Hess wrote that the news so surprised and upset him that he paced his cell in unbridled anger for days afterward. "As far as I am concerned," he wrote, "[my departure] created a vacuum—one that will remain a vacuum forever."

It was Ilse Hess, in a letter to her husband in Spandau, who mentioned a piece of truly grandiose gossip that had been rampant in Hitler's inner circle (and endured until 1959) and explained to some the reason for Bormann's closeness to Hitler. According to this legend, Bormann's eldest son (called Krönzi by his godparents, the Hess couple) was not, as Ilse put it, "the child of Papa Bo" (meaning Bormann), but the illegitimate offspring of Hitler, from an affair he had with a young woman identified only as Uschi.

It was true, Ilse wrote to her husband at Spandau on February 5, 1959 (because Hess himself was inclined to believe the rumor), that Martin Junior was prematurely born, under circumstances still shrouded in some mystery. But she was certain that the boy (by then a missionary) was the child of Martin Bormann and his wife Gerda. "The rumor," she wrote, "is *hirnverbrannter Quatsch* [idiotic nonsense]. If anyone knows the truth, it's certainly me, for at that time I was close to both couples."*

At Hitler's court, however, the gossip was accepted as gospel truth. Men like Speer and Bormann's other sworn enemies were persuaded that the Reichsleiter's willingness to take his Führer's child as his own was the major source of his hold over Hitler.

Probably Bormann was hated most by his wife's parents, Walter Buch, the son of a judge and former Prussian army officer, who

* A variation on the same gossip identified a former nun named Pia as the mother of Hitler's child, who was then adopted, so to speak, by the Bormanns and presented as their own son Martin. This Pia was so infatuated with Hitler (called by some females *"der schöne Adolf"*—the handsome Adolf—during those years) that she followed him on his ill-fated march on the Feldherrnhalle in 1923, left her religious order, and bore a mysterious child. The boy was brought up at the expense of the Party, from a special top-secret fund administered by Bormann. The mother was given a job in the editorial department of the *Völkischer Beobachter.* It is possible that Hitler was the father of Pia's child. But it is certain that the boy was not taken in by the Bormanns as a favor to the Führer and presented as their own firstborn.

became the chief justice of the Nazi Party's system of tribal courts, and his wife, Hildegarde. The latter invariably referred to her daughter's husband as "that swine." Major Buch concluded that his son-in-law had gone mad in office.

"Was Bormann really such a terrible man?" he was asked during his interrogation in 1947.

"I rather think," he replied, "that he had become insane."

"Was he always like that?" he was asked, and he answered:

"No. I thought Hitler too was a lunatic," explaining with a colorful parable what he meant. "When they became drunk with power, their gears somehow failed. I have often experienced that uncouth people who lacked proper education could not function properly in the rarefied air [of their high offices]. Let me make a comparison. I liked to spend time in high mountain chains. To begin with, it is hard to endure the thin air up there. There are people it makes dizzy. This was somehow the case with these fellows. Hitler and his cohorts could not stand the air of their high altitude. It made them dizzy."*

Bormann bridled his ambition and never tried to usurp his superiors' jobs or seize their power. The ascent to his ultimately formidable position was gradual, aided by events and circumstances over which he had no control. His position in the hierarchy was clearly defined and strictly circumscribed. At the very end, Goebbels was given the chancellorship, but Bormann was left in his old position as the Party boss, with a more glittering title but with his power and influence unchanged.

Basing my assessment of the private man on frank interviews with his many foes and few friends, and on his own voluminous writings (some of which are amazingly candid and revealing), I disagree

* The Buchs broke with their son-in-law in 1942, supposedly because they disapproved of what today would be called an open marriage, the Reichsleiter philandering wildly with the wholehearted approval of his wife. When on October 29, 1944, Gerda phoned her husband to tell him that her mother had died, Bormann sent her a strange letter of condolence. "Please give my sympathy to your father," he wrote, "you can do it better than I could in a letter. Your mother wasn't so close to me—I say it quite frankly—as your grandmother, whom I loved very much." He sent off the letter at 10:30 P.M., then celebrated his mother-in-law's death at a raucous birthday party given for General Fegelein, Himmler's representative of the Führer's headquarters (see page 121). Testimony on file in the Prosecutor's office in Frankfurt quotes Major Buch's second wife, the widow of a dentist, as having been told by her husband that, according to reliable information he had, Bormann had not died in 1945 but was alive somewhere in South America. "*Nun lebt das Schwein doch* [the swine is alive after all]" was the way Frau Buch quoted her husband (who had committed suicide in the meantime). No efforts were made by the Frankfurt authorities to verify the story by interviewing Frau Buch.

with the familiar characterization of Martin Bormann as a brute—an uncouth, uneducated bully and inveterate intriguer—or as a man driven by a cold calculating ambition. I am also inclined to dismiss the widespread notion, nurtured by some survivors of Hitler's court and by historians who took their cues from those same self-serving men, that Bormann was "Hitler's Mephistopheles" (Speer), the "Brown Eminence" (Schwerin von Krosigk), "Hitler's *alter ego* . . . the most powerful, the least public, and the most mysterious of all the Nazi leaders" (Trevor-Roper).

When Major Buch was asked after the war why he thought everyone spoke so harshly of his missing son-in-law, he simply said, "Because they think he is dead." On the other hand, Hitler allegedly said, "I know he is brutal, but what he undertakes he finishes. I can rely absolutely on that. With his ruthlessness and brutality he always sees that my orders are carried out."

This statement, quoted by his friend Heinrich Hoffmann, for all its derogatory undertone, accurately describes Bormann's position at the Führer's side. As early as 1941, Hitler conceded that he had become bored with the details of the Party's business and had "totally lost sight of the organizations of the Party." This was why Bormann, a superb organization man, became so indispensable to him. "Bormann's recommendations," Hitler once said, "are so precisely worked out that I need only say yes or no. With him I dispatch in ten minutes a pile of papers over which others would take hours of my time. When I tell him to remind me in six months' time of this or that business, I can be sure that he will do so."

While he functioned as the Fuhrer's personal secretary and, indeed, as his trustee—for all of Hitler's real-estate holdings in Germany and Austria were registered in Bormann's name, and title to many of his valuable possessions, including his works of art and his priceless rare-coin collection, was held by him—Bormann regarded Hitler's confidence as a sacred trust, and he was incapable of violating it. This was the mainspring of the "ruthlessness and brutality" with which he executed his master's orders.

If he was a mystery man, as Trevor-Roper and others have called him, it was by the very nature of his dual position in the Nazi hierarchy. In addition, he had an innate passion for anonymity and deliberately avoided publicity.*

* "I am merely anxious," he once wrote in a note he penned for himself, "that we should not expose ourselves to any reproach and should have no cause to reproach ourselves. . . . Precisely because I occupy a position of trust with the Führer

Some time in the late summer of 1943, a book about the Third Reich's innumerable orders and medals was issued, and Bormann was sent a complimentary copy of the richly illustrated catalogue. It so disgusted him that he did not even want to look at it. "It may well be," he wrote afterward, "that the Führer is forced to reckon with the vanity of his fellow countrymen and so to slap orders and the like all over them. As for me, I have all my life been content with my own inner satisfaction and that of the Führer. . . . Since I've always openly expressed my distaste for orders and medals, and so on, I have been spared accordingly."

He went on musing about fame and fortune. "Orders and so forth are no more a standard by which to measure genuine achievements," he wrote, "than so-called popularity. [Dr. Robert] Ley (chief Party organizer and head of the German Labor Front), for instance, is well known to the masses, while I have deliberately avoided this type of notoriety. I am accomplishing more, considerably more, but while my instructions only reach the men of the leadership, [Ley's] writings directly reach the whole population."*

He was the least "public" among the Nazi leaders, but his features were not unknown. He appeared in photographs, usually with the Führer, as hundreds of pictures in the collection of the court photographer Heinrich Hoffmann and in Nazi newspapers and magazines attest. Both his administrative appointments as Rudolf Hess's successor at the head of the Party chancery in May 1941, and as Hitler's personal secretary in April 1943 were announced in the press and publicized.

Although he professed to shun the trappings of power, Bormann never curbed his masculine vanity. He had an enormous wardrobe and wore his custom-made suits and uniforms quite well. His favorite attire, a combination Reichsleiter's uniform and riding clothes, consisted of the reddish-brown service dress tunic, with the embroidered golden insignia of his rank on its collar flaps and the gold-braided red armband with the huge black swastika in a white circle, and tight breeches and highly polished riding boots (of which he had over forty pairs).

---

and am the chief of the *Parteikanzlei,* I have to remain above any possible reproach. This is all the more important as there are some people who would be delighted to make much of it if I or my family were to give them reason for criticism."

* In an informal last will and testament, Bormann specified that "if ever there is a memorial ceremony after my death, there must under no circumstances be a cheap exhibition of cushions with rows of medals and so on."

Let us now see in a few vignettes how powerful the man whom Trevor-Roper called "the most powerful . . . of all the Nazi leaders" really was. His true power was revealed during the final weeks of the Third Reich. On January 5, 1945, for example, yearning for the companionship of his wife, who was living in the tenuous safety of their chalet in the Obersalzberg, and also for a brief respite from the chaos of the Führer's environment, Bormann planned to visit her in Munich. By then the city was accessible only by car on the badly damaged Autobahn or by courier planes, if one did not want to spend days making the trip by train. But, as it turned out, "the most powerful Nazi leader" lacked the power to obtain a seat on any of the planes flying between Berlin and Munich, and he had no car of his own mechanically fit for what had become a ten- to twelve-hour drive.

He borrowed the battered BMW of General Hermann Fegelein, only to find that the automobile was in even worse condition than his own. In the end, after some wire-pulling with Hitler's help, he did succeed in getting away in another borrowed car for almost three weeks.

On February 3, his Berlin headquarters in the Wilhelmstrasse area was hit by a blockbuster during an American raid. Bormann described what was left of the Party chancery building as "a sorry sight."

It was from this makeshift office, while railing bitterly about conditions "resembling the worst phase of the Seven Years War," that he wrote one of the most revealing thoughts he would ever confide to his wife: "To you I can write frankly and tell you how very unpleasant—indeed, if I am completely honest, how desperate—the situation really is." And then, a few days later: "The situation is so deplorably bad that one has to expect the worst."*

Shortly, the Party chancery disintegrated so completely that Bormann found himself evicted from it altogether and could no longer "take refuge" even in its badly damaged air-raid shelter. He had to commute daily between Berlin and Zossen, the fortified garrison city housing the headquarters of the Army General Staff, some twenty miles from the Wilhelmstrasse, to have a place to sleep.

* His wife solicitously expressed the hope that he would not catch a cold before the windows were put in. But by then, Bormann had "a real bad cough," remarking plaintively that he couldn't remember when last he had a cold.

But it was only toward the end, after Zossen had been evacuated and Bormann had no other place to go, that he was allowed to take up full residence in Hitler's bunker. Even then, he was allotted only a couple of cubbyholes for himself and his small staff in what used to be a storage room located on the floor *above* the Führer's own shelter, with its priceless paintings and Persian rugs.

Bormann visited the lower floor regularly to present his daily reports to Hitler. Apart from these briefings, he had little direct contact with Hitler, who busied himself, as far as his ebbing strength permitted, almost entirely with the war.

Bormann did attend some of the *Lagebesprechungen* (situation conferences) usually held twice a day, around noon and very late at night, but he made himself as inconspicuous as possible. Most of the time, he was represented by Standartenführer Wilhelm Zander, his military aide, who stood by to supply necessary Party data.

If he was ignored, slighted or ostracized, Bormann did not seem to care. Whenever he had ideas or plans beyond the matters involving the Party, he asked men like Field Marshal Wilhelm Keitel and General Burgdorf to submit them to Hitler as their own. He remained the anonymous bureaucrat. He was vehement on only one subject: the urgency of moving to Bavaria.

On April 19, a day of decision, when Hitler's professional staff was debating the impending doom, Bormann was busy arranging the hurried trip of Eva Braun from Munich back to Berlin, as any personal secretary would for his boss.

Thus, we see that Bormann had his way when he spoke and acted with the Füher's direct authority. But when it came to making arrangements for himself, even if only for a bed in which he could spend a night after his own sleeping quarters had been destroyed, this omnipotent Nazi proved almost powerless.

Much has been made of Bormann's rivalry with other top Nazis, especially with Goebbels, Göring, Himmler and Speer. More often than not, these rivalries were only figments in the minds of his alleged adversaries. Bormann had better opportunity than most to observe and assess these men as they really were, not as they strove to appear, cringing and subservient in their personal encounters with the Führer.

He saw Goebbels as a poseur, the victim of his own propaganda, whose warped romanticism, devious mind and glib eloquence masked a "dimension of evil that [was] hard to rival." In Göring he detested the Reichsmarschall's ostentatious style of living and his "unbureaucratic methods," which in the end contributed materially to the Luftwaffe's doom. Speer he cut down to size, recognizing in him the opportunist and liar, whose principles could always be bent to personal advantage.

Although his attitude toward Himmler was more ambiguous, by no stretch of the imagination could they be called rivals. Bormann's candid letters to his wife reveal a friendship based on mutual confidence, unmarred by competition. It was to Bormann that Himmler complained whenever he felt slighted by Hitler; and it was from Bormann that he expected to gain an improved position at court.

On January 16, 1943, Bormann thus confided to his wife:

> As I have already told you, H[einrich] H[immler]'s visit today was no sheer joy; he is deeply hurt, and obviously not only today or since yesterday. The Chief treats him unjustly—he mentioned specific instances of recent years—the unworthy are treated so much better, are even given decorations. But H.H. is good only to assemble divisions, etc. He waved aside all my objections: I said, *yes*, the Chief has the right to be unjust once in a while.

Himmler trusted Bormann even in the face of intrigues at his own court, where one of the Reichsführer's aides, Gottlob Berger, went out of his way to drive a wedge between the two men. In one of his espionage reports to Himmler, Berger even hinted that Bormann might be a Soviet spy—as General Gehlen was to claim so many years later.

Extremely frugal in his personal needs, Bormann applied the same trait to his official business, and became a competent economist, whose shrewd transactions and strict regime kept the Party in the black and made Hitler, whose fiscal agent and business manager he also was, a very wealthy man.* Later he used these same talents

* It was Bormann who hit upon the idea of making a specially bound edition of Hitler's *Mein Kampf* a compulsory gift to newlyweds, for which the communities had to pay. It would be statistically possible to establish how much money the wholesale distribution of the Nazi bible added to Hitler's private wealth, by counting the number of weddings in Germany after the introduction of the gift (by a formal order issued by Bormann), and establish how many young people had to pay tribute to their Führer through the communal purchase of his unread book. Under Bormann's astute management, Hitler's private income was variously estimated at 1.5 million the lowest and 6 million marks the highest, his actual income somewhere between these two figures, year after year.

to enrich the Party in a conglomerate with covert holdings in the Krupp empire, and with a cut of the legendary Thyssen fortune.

Bormann managed the enormous hoard of money and valuables his *Parteikanzlei* was extorting from big business and industry, huge slush funds so secret that the very fact of their existence was withheld from Franz X. Schwarz, the chancellor of the Party's official exchequer. He doled out lavish endowments with which Hitler rewarded (or bribed) his ministers and generals. But he himself scrupulously refrained from taking advantage of Hitler's largesse. The Bormanns lived within their means, on a relatively modest salary for the head of a big household, without many of the fringe benefits lesser lights in the Party enjoyed.

He longed to own a house of his own or a country home, especially after the summer of 1943, when Hitler decreed that on the death of a Reichsminister or a Reichsleiter the widow would not be permitted to retain her dead husband's official residence. The Bormanns occupied a house on the compound of the *Parteikanzlei* in Pullach and a chalet in the Obersalzberg, but owned no home of their own. They had their eyes on several pieces of real estate—one called the Bergle, another a cottage in the Black Forest, and a homestead in Krumbeck. But Bormann had no savings to buy any of these places, and he was reluctant to ask Hitler for a loan.*

Even as friendly a witness as François Genoud, the Swiss Nazi sympathizer who claims to be the rightful custodian of Bormann's papers, ventured the opinion that "the reputation of Martin Bormann is not flattering to his character." He added, however, and I am inclined to agree with him, that the former Reichsleiter was "a simple and uncomplicated [man], at times even . . . naïve."

Naïve or not, Martin Bormann loved life. Beneath the placid exterior was a man who valued his comfort and pleasures. As his world was crumbling about him, he gave poignant expression to what seemed to be his philosophy of life. "I would like to muddle on through life," he wrote to his wife on February 19, 1945, "together with you, as many years as possible, and in peace. . . . Oh, wouldn't that be lovely!"†

* In the end, he managed to acquire a small estate in Mecklenburg, in the hope, as he told his wife, that the Führer would reward him with a bigger one after the war.

† On that same day, in one of his frenzied attempts at self-preservation, he issued strict orders placing the Gau of Salzburg and Obersalzberg out of bounds to all refugees. He forbade even gauleiters and their families to seek a safe haven in Salzburg, Berchtesgaden, Reichenhall and Trautstein. He did not want to clutter up the region to which he fervently hoped Hitler would retreat and he himself would be able to escape when Berlin fell.

Bormann was homely even as a slim young man in his twenties. His sallow-skinned face was round and fleshy with prominent cheekbones, broad nostrils, squinting little eyes. When he became plumper and more shapeless—an ugly little man far too fat for his height—his sex appeal, never pronounced, vanished altogether. "Dr. Goebbels exuded sexual charm," remarked the handsome wife of a journalist, who moved in his circle at the Führer's court, "but Bormann had no attraction for women at all—at least not for me." But pretty women had enormous attraction for Bormann. "His sexual appetite was well-nigh insatiable," one of his confidants told me with a bemused, approving smile. "He and his wife were perfectly attuned to each other sexually. But she was pregnant most of the time, and he was rarely with her even when she was not, so he got rid of his temptations by yielding to them."

His much-advertised affair with Manya Behrens, a young actress, flattered his ego, but Bormann was in love with the famous motion-picture star Magda Schneider and even used his rank to bring her to his bed, wooing her brazenly and brashly. Although he bragged to his cronies that he "had little Magda in my arms," he never actually succeeded in seducing her. His sexual successes were with less important people—mostly with the younger secretaries on his staff, who could not avoid or would not resist his advances.

He was a "fanny pincher," one of his former secretaries told me, still amused by the memory. It was a familiar and funny sight, she said, to watch "the little fat man" standing behind Fräulein L. or Fräulein U. (two of his special favorites among the younger crop of typists) as they were transmitting his messages on the teletype. Bormann was "playing with them"—fondling their breasts with a hand slipped under their blouses or working his fingers upward under their skirts—while the flustered girls tried to concentrate on doing their job.

Yet he never let pleasure interfere with business. "He slept with his secretaries," an associate who was especially close to him told me in Stuttgart, "but that didn't prevent him from kicking them in the ass with his heavily booted foot when they were slow on the teletype, misunderstood a dictation, or made some clerical error that upset this man, whose boiling point was quite low, but only with people below him. He was rough and tough with his staff, even with girls who had just left his bed."

"He was a family man," Genoud wrote nevertheless in his introduction to a volume of Bormann's correspondence with his wife, "who adored his wife and was devoted to his nine children." As his letters to Gerda showed, he was genuinely devoted to her. But he was no family man. He rarely saw his family together and paid little attention to his growing children. Whenever he could take time out for vacation, he would meet his wife somewhere without the children who, he said, would only spoil their fun. His many letters to Gerda never ceased to attest his love. But they rarely as much as inquired about any of the children—were they well or ill, how were they doing at home or in school—as one would expect from a doting father.

His reputation as a heavy drinker was not deserved. He drank, but only toward the end could he be seen inebriated more often than sober. Yet, at Eva Braun's birthday party in the bunker on February 6, 1945 (the day after Silesia and East Prussia had to be written off as lost), when bottle after bottle of Moët et Chandon champagne flowed to the few invited guests and Evi, as Fräulein Braun was called, would complain petulantly about the lack of a good dancing partner, Bormann himself did not empty a single glass. He anticipated that Hitler would summon him during the night. At three in the morning the call came. "The Führer had a long talk with me," Bormann wrote later, "so it was just as well that I was completely sober."

Bormann's background was plebeian. He had had some formal schooling (he dropped out of *Realgymnasium* in his sophomore year), but he received his real education in the anti-Semitic and paramilitary organizations that mushroomed in Germany after 1918.

After a few years managing an estate, when he became an outdoor enthusiast and daredevil horseback rider, Bormann at last found his mission as a full-time professional Nazi. He began his meteoric career in the Party as a junior press officer in Thuringia, occasionally contributing articles to the *Nationalsozialist*, a propaganda journal. From then on he fancied that he had talent as a writer. Though Genoud was inclined to depreciate his style—he described Bormann's language as unpolished and his vocabulary as limited—official papers and letters that Bormann dictated to his battery of secretaries at the rate of more than a hundred each day show that he could write crisply, lucidly and, at times, quite attractively.

Bormann became an avid reader with a wide and rather erratic range in his literary taste. Probably he was the only high-level Nazi who had waded through the whole of *Das Kapital* and had sampled some of Lenin's books. But what he really devoured was trashy fiction produced by Nazi literati. His favorite book was *Der Herr Kortuem,* a popular novel by the best-selling author Kurt Kluge. When he first read it, and found that the author was dead, Bormann drove to the cemetery in Berlin-Nicholassee, where Kluge was buried, and placed a wreath on the grave. (Incidentally, the book is still in print, selling well, a minor classic.)

He accumulated an extensive personal library and would take some of his favorite books with him wherever he went. When the evacuation of Berlin seemed imminent, he did not even bother to pack up his personal belongings, but he did have his library crated and sent to a safe place, virtually the only possession that he had in Berlin that he was anxious to salvage from the holocaust.

His small circle of close friends included a number of writers and artists, among them the sculptor Arno Breker, the film director Leni Riefenstahl, and Frau Gerdy Troost, an interior decorator who was the widow of Professor Paul Ludwig Troost, Hitler's architect. He felt comfortable in their company and was eager, while things were going well, to promote their works and then, when the great crisis developed, to protect them from destruction.*

Dr. Heinrich Heim, one of Bormann's closest confidants, was his "court intellectual"; he helped him in the choice of his reading matter and in the selection of works of art which he was forever buying for Hitler, and he served as his liaison with writers, artists and actors—"the Bohemian set," as he called them. A lawyer by profession, Heim gained entry into Nazism's inner sanctum by having defended Hitler in courts during the bad old days.

However, all these extra-curricular preoccupations were marginal. Martin Bormann's chief interest was life itself. Now, "in these grave times," as he put it, when he regarded "anyone who still grants that we have a chance" as an incurable optimist, his whole being was dominated by what had become his basic creed:

"I have no premonition of death; on the contrary, my burning desire is to live."

* During "the panic," as he himself called it, caused by the Red Army's crossing of the Oder at Wriezen in January 1945, Bormann still found time to rush to the aid of the Brekers, whose home was at Jäckelsbruch in the Red Army's path. He sent trucks to evacuate the sculptor's giant statues from his threatened studio. Breker specialized in monumental nudes. He "did" Gerda Bormann and also Eva Braun, who did not quite like herself in Breker's marble.

Chapter Six

Ambush of Doubts and Dreams

Shortly after four o'clock in the afternoon of April 30, 1945, the spring sky above Berlin was leaden with heavy clouds, the ground was still wet from the rains of recent days, the air was chilled by a raw breeze. Standing under the thick concrete roof of the porch at the rear entrance to the Führerbunker in Berlin, Martin Bormann watched as the gasoline-soaked bodies of Adolf Hitler and his wife, Eva Braun, were slowly consumed by the flames of an improvised pyre. He had retired to the porch to seek protection from Russian shells, which were finding their mark in the Chancellery compound. By coincidence, the artillery barrage had started just when the burial began, the shelling providing funereal accompaniment for this otherwise silent ritual.

Bormann was surrounded on the porch by Dr. Goebbels, General Wilhelm Burgdorf, Hans Günsche and Heinz Linge. Erich Kempka was standing by with jerrycans filled with gasoline to be added, from time to time, to the funeral pyre, whose fire was to cremate the bodies.

After a few moments, when the first big column of black smoke subsided and the bodies began to catch fire, the stench became unbearable. The six mourners on the porch snapped to attention, stiffly gave the Hitler salute, then withdrew to the safety of their shelter, from which, it seemed, not only Hitler but also his memory had abruptly departed. As a simple SS guard, who had secretly observed the scene from a window in the new Chancellery building, later complained, "It was sad that nobody seemed to care about the poor Führer or worry about his body. As far as they were concerned, it was good riddance."

Bormann never returned to the site, but inquired from time to time how the cremation was going. At 6:30 P.M., he was told that the bodies were still burning. The flesh was gone from the lower parts of the corpses and the shinbones of Hitler's legs had become visible. But the fire could not reduce them to ashes. At eleven o'clock Bormann instructed SS General Johann Rattenhuber, commandant of the Führer's bodyguard, to bury the charred bodies in the unmarked shallow grave of a crater and cover them with the rubble created by the bombardment.

When Bormann returned to the bunker, he went straight down to the lower floor. He sent for Else Krüger, his secretary, to dictate a carefully worded message to Grand Admiral Karl Doenitz at Plön, the man Hitler had designated in his will as the new chief of state. Fräulein Krüger was unaware of the funeral that had just taken place. But she was quick to find out.

As Bormann sat down to dictate, he reached into his pocket and pulled out a pack of cigarettes, then lit one, smoking it with sensuous puffs, watching the smoke with fond eyes as it curled over his head. Nobody had been allowed to smoke in the bunker while Hitler was alive. Fräulein Krüger knew instantly that the Führer was gone—the symbolism of the pale smoke coming from Bormann's lips and through his nostrils was unmistakable. It was the end of an era, going up in the smoke of Bormann's cigarette.

He was a different man. Gone was the diffidence that kept him, like a prince consort bound by protocol, always behind Hitler, never at his side. This, now, was *his* domain, and he could barely hide his impatience to get out of it.

There were problems ahead—enormous problems, a whole sweep of history yet to come—but some of his biggest ones were already behind him. He had solved them one by one and step by step, assuring by intricate maneuvers that when the end came, and whatever arrangements Hitler would make for succession, he would emerge at the top, his power uncontested by men who had priorities and claims stronger than his.

This supreme realist had anticipated the end of Hitler's rule. Like a doting son making arrangements for an aged father, Bormann had built his plans around the Führer. Watching that pyre, he felt a heavy burden lifting from his mind and soul. He no longer felt bound by the pious, unswerving allegiance that had tied him almost physically to Hitler, depriving him of every last shred of individualism in thought and action. Only a few weeks earlier he had written that his "unshakable faith in ultimate victory" was founded "in a very large measure on the fact that [the Führer] exists."

But Hitler, who once bitterly castigated as a coward a general who committed suicide when his front collapsed, had quit in what Bormann regarded as a cowardly desertion. Now his "unshakable faith" was itself shaken, not merely by the fact that Hitler no longer "existed," but even more by the manner of his death. His devotion to Hitler was suddenly replaced by a keenly felt resentment. For the first time he was close to loathing the man he had loved and admired for so long. He never left Hitler; Hitler had left him. He never betrayed Hitler; Hitler had betrayed him.

It was exactly two years before, in April 1943, that Bormann had become *Sekretär des Führers* (the Führer's secretary). The dictionary definition describes a secretary as a "person employed by another to assist him in correspondence, literary work, getting information, and other confidential matters, often private or unpaid, especially a person acting as secretary to prominent politician for the sake of experience." Bormann did all that and much more. He used those two years to serve Hitler diligently and make himself indispensable.

He was completely subservient, but by no means blinded by his subservience. Bormann realized that if he wanted to remain Sekretär des Führers, he would never be permitted to contradict or disagree with Hitler. He hid his own perspicacity, suppressed his sometimes superior knowledge of events, withheld information and data, and repressed his ruthless streak of realism.

That did not mean that he had never entertained doubts or seen the world exactly as Hitler had seen it. Bormann's appointment to the Secretariat was made in the wake of the massive Russian counteroffensive in the Don region on January 31, 1943, which culminated in the Stalingrad disaster. The situation was aggravated by the Allies' victories in Morocco and Algeria, and by Field Marshal Erwin Rommel's humiliating defeats in North Africa. Rommel's failure was of limited strategic importance, but Stalingrad was a clear warning of disaster. Hitler had regarded the Donets Basin, with its vast natural resources, as the basic precondition of his ultimate victory, if only because he thought its coal would be needed to sustain Germany's war effort. When the Führer had to consent to the evacuation of the Donets Basin, he minimized the significance of the withdrawal. What had been vital when he had it was unimportant now that he had lost it.

Bormann was incapable of this kind of rationalization, yet he followed his master on his fateful path of self-deception. He did nothing to convince Hitler of the real dangers of the situation, though he had the means to do so. One of the collateral functions of Himmler's domestic secret service was to observe the mood of the people, monitor their morale, and distill a nationwide opinion sampling, the so-called *Stimmungsberichte* (mood reports). A branch of the Security Service under the personal supervision of SS General Otto Ohlendorf, its chief, had confidential agents planted in all walks of life to report on "how the situation stood."

Exceptional care was taken to insure the objectivity and accuracy of these reports. "It's no concern of ours," Ohlendorf once said, "whether the man who makes the report is a member of the Party, or whether he's a German or a foreigner. Our only interest is the accuracy of his information," so that, he said, "a mosaic of impressions becomes a valid survey of the entire Reich."

Reading them in retrospect, one is amazed to find how correctly a majority of Germans assessed the situation in spite of the propaganda. It also was astounding how accurately and courageously the monitors dared to report antagonisms and doubts.

As long as things went well, Himmler circulated copies of these top-secret reports to Göring, Goebbels, Dr. Hans Heinrich Lammers, the head of the Reich Chancellery, and to Bormann. From time to time, Bormann would present a summary of the reports to the Führer, typed up in large letters because of Hitler's myopia, which he was too vain to acknowledge by wearing glasses. But after Stalingrad, the general tone of the *Stimmungsberichte* gradually deteriorated. "The popular attitude to the war is characterized by growing pessimism," wrote Sturmbannführer Rudolf Eckardt, chief of the Security Service in Schwerin, on June 6, 1944. "It must be admitted that by and large the people are depressed because they don't know what the future holds." Eckardt's "admission" was echoed in all the other reports, their unmistakable message bluntly spelled out by the Leipzig chief of the Security Service, who wrote on December 8: "Increasing number of individuals, including members of the Party, now earnestly doubt that the war can still be won."

With nothing but bad news pouring in, Himmler cut the distribution list so drastically that in the end he was the only person who read them. However, Bormann missed nothing when they stopped coming. He had a similar reporting system of his own, which he had inherited from Rudolf Hess. As far back as December 21, 1934, Hess had ordered the gauleiters to send a monthly *Stimmungsbericht* to him. The order was reinforced by Bormann in 1938, when he ordered the gauleiters to send him their reports "by teletype, regularly every Saturday evening."

The reports he was now receiving from the gauleiters were also remarkable for their objectivity and bluntness. Since mid-1944, they reflected the psychological unrest that was becoming widespread in war-weary Germany.

Hitler may have deluded himself that the morale of the German people remained undamaged by the disaster of Stalingrad, the reverses in the Battle of the Atlantic, and the gradual encroachment of the Allies on *Festung Europa* (Fortress Europe). But Bormann had no such delusions.

Had he presented these reports or even the summaries to Hitler, the Führer might have accepted the gravity of the situation realistically. But nobody in his entourage even dared to raise the specter of defeat, and Bormann knew better than most that Hitler had the habit of exorcising bad tidings by punishing their bearers. Only good news was shown to Hitler. "The Führer," Ohlendorf once told Felix Kersten, Himmler's magic-fingered physical therapist, "and high officials in the Party and the government ought to know about every measure's effect without regarding this as a personal attack on them. . . . But Bormann always keeps [bad news] from the Führer. This is absolutely fatal, since these reports deal with the home front, for which the Party is responsible."

By the end of 1944, the reports resounded with a shrill pitch of doom, but Hitler remained oblivious. He made a desperate last effort to turn the tide with "Operation Watch on the Rhine," the Ardennes offensive, ordering Field Marshal Gerd von Rundstedt to "regain the initiative in the West with an attack that is certain to result in another Dunkirk."

On December 10, 1944, Hitler moved into Adlerhorst, the luxurious command post in the Ziegenberg near Bad Nauheim, which had been built for him in 1940 for the campaign in the West, but had never been occupied. Bormann, of course, accompanied him, only to find that Hitler had no use for him. Totally absorbed in the battle, the Führer surrounded himself with his military advisers, rarely finding time for Bormann. Assigned quarters at some distance from Hitler's, and virtually excluded from the military councils, Bormann, for the first time in his exalted job, was separated from his master.

The last five-month period of Bormann's career was a slow-motion replica of Hitler's last ten days. What the Führer rushed at the end, the meticulous Bormann planned gradually, his arrangements slowed by the exasperating uncertainties created by Hitler's erratic decisions.

This period began hopefully enough. Bormann was caught up at first in the exhilaration that swept the Adlerhorst during the early days of the Battle of the Bulge. He busied himself as usual, running the Party by remote control, using the Telex machine so much that a quipster, aware of his frustration in this gold-braided military environment, promoted him to "Field Marshal of Teletype."

He spent most of his time relaxing rather than working, going on picnics or outings to the beauty spots of the Goat Mountain, and attending the raucous parties given by SS General Hermann Fegelein, the playboy of the Führer headquarters, whose rambunctious good cheer moved even the dour General Alfred Jodl to dance vigorously and to flirt all night with his partner, a pretty noncommissioned officer in communications.

With idle hours still left to fill, Bormann occupied himself with such trivia as the special footpaths for pedestrians which he planned to construct throughout the Berchtesgaden district after the war.

He eventually asked Hitler for permission to leave Adlerhorst on a brief vacation. He wanted to spend some time alone with his wife, leaving the children behind. Bormann was forever complaining that they prevented him from relaxing on the rare occasions when he could rest. The Bormanns met in Munich in January of 1945 and stayed for a couple of weeks in seclusion.

On the sixteenth, Hitler abandoned the Adlerhorst and moved to Berlin, where Bormann joined him ten days later. The situation he now found at the Führer's headquarters came as a shock, reminding him of "the very worst phase of the Seven Years War." Defeat in the Battle of the Bulge and bad news from the U-boats in the Atlantic shook his confidence in the Wehrmacht's ability to save the day after all. "Our troops show signs of disintegration" was the way he put it in the utmost privacy of his correspondence with his wife.

Unlike Hitler, who settled down for a protracted stay in the Reich Chancellery compound, Bormann found Berlin stifling. He began to ship out his belongings, sending most of his custom-made breeches and highly polished brown riding boots to Ausweichquartier Nord in Stolpe, another command post in the north, which Hitler never used but Bormann occasionally visited.

His apprehension about staying in Berlin reached near-panic proportions on January 31. Hitler had made his last speech to the people the day before, brimming with confidence and defiance. Whatever effects it had were nullified by the events of the next morning. Two Soviet "fronts" reached the River Oder at Frankfurt and established bridgeheads on the strategic west bank of the river. The news from General Theodor Busse, whose Ninth Army was supposed to prevent the Soviet breakthrough but failed, arrived in Berlin in the morning. It so unnerved Bormann that he decided to awaken Hitler, who was sleeping late as usual. Also as usual, Hitler received the bad news with equanimity. He assured Bormann that the forces in the threatened area would hold and turn the tide. This was sheer nonsense, for he knew that General Busse's army had been stripped of urgently needed guns and armor for the sake of other fronts.

It was the events of January 31 that convinced Bormann that Berlin had become untenable and the sooner Hitler left it the better it would be for all concerned. His campaign to move to the south now began in earnest and continued unabated, even when Marshal Georgi Zhukov refrained from exploiting the breakthrough for a direct attack on Berlin.

This was also the beginning of a fateful clash with Goebbels. While Bormann was imploring Hitler to move to the *Alpenfestung* (Alpine fortress) around Berchtesgaden, Goebbels was using his enormous powers of persuasion to impress Hitler with the advantages of remaining in Berlin. An unmatched propagandist to the bitter end, Goebbels cited the symbolic significance of the Führer's valiant stand in the capital, whose fate he regarded as by no means sealed. These inane heroics appealed to Hitler far more than Bormann's common sense. From this date on, Bormann's influence on Hitler gradually waned.

Bormann fretted for two weeks. Then, on February 18, his

nerve cracked under the chaos and he asked Hitler to let him go to Stolpe for a few days to regain his strength. Hitler consented, imploring him to drive with care. Bormann was anxious to examine Stolpe as a headquarters for Hitler himself, as well as to escape from the confusion and danger of Berlin, where it was becoming increasingly difficult for the Führer to exercise control and command. He even went so far as to consult General Rattenhuber about assigning a special detachment of the bodyguard troops to Stolpe in preparation for Hitler's move. In the end, however, Stolpe had to be ruled out. It had inadequate communication facilities—not even a properly functioning teletype. Hitler would have been isolated there at a time when his constant and rapid liaison with the Wehrmacht had become imperative.

The absence of a teletype also eliminated Stolpe for Bormann. He decided to get the rest he craved at Zossen, the strongly fortified headquarters of the Army high command, only twenty miles from Berlin. At Zossen he acted like a vacationer, going to the sauna bath daily, getting massaged, and relaxing as much as possible. The holiday did him a lot of good. While the day before his departure he told his wife in a frenzied letter that he could no longer "endure the Wilhelmstrasse" where the noise was "tearing my nerves apart," a single day at Zossen seemed to have calmed his fraying nerves. It was from there, refreshed and reassured, that he wrote to his wife: "I have no premonition of death; on the contrary, my burning desire is to live."

But he continued to lobby for the move to Berchtesgaden. In order to secure it for the exclusive use of the Führer, he closed the area to all refugees, banning even gauleiters and their families. And he asked Frau Troost, the widow of Hitler's chief architect and herself a gifted interior decorator who had designed the Berghof, to make Hitler's house attractive and comfortable for his coming since all the paintings and bric-a-brac had been removed to the safety of air-raid shelters.

February 24 was the twenty-fifth anniversary of the proclamation of the Party's twenty-five-point program, and Bormann celebrated the event with an eloquently worded reminder of the importance of the day, which he sent to the gauleiters. But his sense of proportion was such that he issued orders that no reference be made to the anniversary in the press and no public celebration of the anniversary be held.

In the meantime, he commuted between Zossen and Berlin, but only when it was safe to make the trip. On February 26, for example, when over a thousand planes of the Eighth U.S. Air Force dropped more than 2,800 tons of bombs on Berlin, Bormann preferred to sit out the raid in Zossen, watching the fires from a distance.

All this time he faithfully repeated Hitler's variations on the theme of ultimate victory. He duly forwarded to the Wehrmacht high command the Führer's order to "intensify the political education of the troops," adding his own footnote that the soldiers must be "imbued with a spirit of fanaticism." He himself then issued a new slogan—"Victory at any cost"—whose ambiguity somehow reflected his hidden doubts.

He was not making any headway with his campaign for the move to Berchtesgaden, but he refused to give up. His hope that Hitler would leave in the end gained impetus during a seemingly endless nocturnal situation conference that lasted into the early hours of March 24.

Colonel Nikolaus von Below, one of his adjutants who represented the Luftwaffe in the Führerbunker, brazenly broke into the discussion. "Could we," he asked, "save on the smokescreening of the Obersalzberg when you, my Führer, aren't there? It is now the practice to smokescreen it at every approach of enemy planes, and that consumes too much of the hard-to-get chemicals."

Hitler seemed to be taken aback. "Yes," he shot back, "but then, of course, everything will be lost, one must realize that. It is one of the last places of evasion we have left. Nothing can happen to the bunker there, and I don't care about my house. But the facilities will all be destroyed. If one of these days Zossen here were to be pounded into dust, where would we go? A heavy raid on Zossen and it is finished. Probably much of it is already in shambles."

"It is still usable," General Burgdorf chimed in. "The houses are still in one piece, and there are enough barracks undamaged. But, of course, if the barracks were to be destroyed, the last possibility of going there would be gone." Then he added, somewhat sheepishly for he suddenly realized that he should have reported this before, that there was still a place in Greater Berlin to which Hitler could move. It was a big bunker the Luftwaffe had built two years before at its old training center in Wannsee, with an impregnable shelter underground.

Hitler was stunned. "This," he said angrily, "had been concealed from me." But then he dismissed it from his mind. The Führerbunker was safe for the time being, he said, even from aerial bombs up to 2,000 pounds. But what if it became untenable on the ground? He ended the discussion by ordering the smokescreen continued at Obersalzberg. It was his last resort.

While biding his time, Bormann devoted his attention to urgent problems, devising sensible solutions for them in the face of the rapidly deteriorating situation. He issued an order to pick wild plants of all kinds in the woods to improve the food situation. In defiance of Hitler's opposition to abortion, he permitted them to be performed on women who could prove that they had been raped by soldiers of the Red Army. He was busy, as ever.

March 31 produced another major crisis, and Bormann again reacted to it with near-panic. Troops of the Third Ukrainian Front were racing through Hungary, moving irresistibly on Vienna. Their offensive posed a threat to Austria, especially since General Eisenhower was also regrouping his forces in the south for a massive attack in the same direction to prevent the Germans from ensconcing themselves in a huge redoubt in the Alps.

Although the Red Army began to lay siege to Vienna on April 5, Bormann anticipated it by almost a week. He made arrangements to remove his family. In an urgent signal, he instructed Gauleiter Franz Hofer of the Tyrol to go to the aid of his wife immediately and arrange for the removal of his family to a safer place. "The situation is so deplorably bad," he wrote to his wife, explaining the emergency, "that one has to expect the worst."

In a single day, on April 2, he wrote three letters to Frau Gerda, one in the morning, another at 9:30 P.M., the third shortly before midnight. The first two were full of forebodings, telling his wife in almost hysterical sentences that the deterioration of the situation in Austria was making it necessary for her and the children to flee to the Tyrol.

It was the second day of Easter, and the serenity of the holiday then somehow soothed his nerves. For the first time in the bunker, he turned on the radio and listened to some music, popular songs like "You're So Good to Me" and "You Are My Sunshine" that calmed him down. In his last letter, his hysteria was gone. He apologized to Gerda almost abjectly for his earlier fit of panic. Perhaps things were not really as bad as he thought, he wrote.

"We must just wait and see what happens," he added. "But the worst thing of all is the despair that has gripped all—civilians and soldiers alike—which amounts to the feeling that 'there is no sense in resisting any more.' . . . According to a report which just came in, at 10:30 P.M., a thousand [enemy] vehicles, of which 3–400 are armored, are in the vicinity of Meiningen. How miserable are the resources we have to oppose them!" It was the last letter preserved of this strange correspondence. He ended it by asking Gerda to "keep well and strong and brave, Mummy mine."

Clearly his festering doubts were gaining the upper hand. A little over a year before, Stalingrad had disturbed him, but it made hardly a dent in his faith in the Führer's "genius and rocklike determination"—which, he said, were "superhuman, for so many things fail to go according to plan when he is not there."

Although his panic was gone, at least for the moment, he did not rescind his order to Gauleiter Hofer to aid his family. Moreover, he asked Dr. Helmut von Hummel, his confidant and personal agent in Berchtesgaden, to whom he had entrusted the welfare of his wife and children, to report to him in Berlin and arrange for measures to be taken when even Berchtesgaden would become untenable.

Nothing in the ominous development of the war would have justified Bormann's relaxation of his misgivings. Indeed, they became aggravated while Dr. von Hummel was with him in Berlin, after a situation conference on April 4. He attended it, self-effacing as always, listening mutely as Keitel, Jodl, Doenitz and Himmler discussed with General Gotthard Henrici and Colonel Hans-Georg Eismann, his operations officer, a collateral problem of Vienna's plight.

In a desperate move to bolster the city's defenses, the Führer had ordered a Panzer division and two of Henrici's divisions out of the line defending Berlin, and moved them to Vienna and Prague to intercept the Russian armies. Henrici and Eismann rushed to the Führerbunker to protest, but found Hitler, his bloodshot eyes hidden behind dark sunglasses, in one of his explosive moods. He dismissed Henrici's objections out of hand, in words that reflected his growing lack of realism. Vienna and Prague were in critical need of help, Berlin was not. "This city is subject only to minor side attacks," he said. "The major assault will be on Vienna and Prague."

After the conference, Bormann took Colonel Eismann to one side and asked him what he really thought of the situation and whether he agreed with the Führer that Berlin was merely a secondary objective of the Russians. With the Red Army deployed only thirty-eight miles from the capital, Eismann regarded Hitler's reasoning as sheer madness. But Bormann cautiously reverted to repeating Hitler's delusions.

"You shouldn't worry so much," he told the flabbergasted colonel, slapping him on the back with clumsy geniality. "The Führer is sure to come through with the reinforcements you need." Listening to Bormann, Eismann had the eerie feeling that General Henrici and himself were the only sane people in the room.

Actually, Bormann was not sure at all that any reinforcements could still be conjured up, even with Hitler's magic wand. And he was firmly convinced that Berlin was the goal of Marshal Zhukov's onslaught. He did not quite succeed in fooling Eismann with his spurious confidence. By this time, he had lost some of his old equanimity. While Goebbels never ceased to radiate resolute confidence, Bormann appeared troubled behind his coarse grin and back-slapping joviality.

His inner thoughts became easy to read on his face, in his gestures, in the changed tone of his voice, even in his remarks. When he recalled his brief encounter with the Reichsleiter, Colonel Eismann thought he had detected this tension in Bormann. Another colonel, Theodor von Dufving, who later saw Goebbels and Bormann together in the bunker, noticed distinctly the unmistakable difference in the demeanor of the two men. "Goebbels was calm," he wrote after the war, "and spoke clearly and courteously. I did not get the impression that he was afraid, quite unlike Bormann and some others I saw in the Chancellery. As far as Bormann is concerned, I had the feeling he trembled for his life."

It was in this atmosphere of suspense that the Führer celebrated his fifty-sixth birthday on April 20. The situation was utterly devoid of any hope. At 9 A.M., the Army high command marked the Führer's birthday by evacuating its huge headquarters from Zossen and moving to Bavaria. American forces under Major General Wade Hampton Haislip spoiled the day with an Allied victory, the symbolism of which was keenly felt in the bunker. They captured Nuremberg, the site of Hitler's vainglorious Party rallies. Marshal Konstantin Rokossovski's Second White Russian Front moved out of its bridgeheads along the Lower Oder and was overrunning Pomerania and Mecklenburg.

In the consternation that swept the bunker, only Hitler and

Goebbels were still spreading their hypnotic cheer. When the news arrived at noon that the Oder front had collapsed, the Propaganda Minister exclaimed jubilantly: "So it's a fight for Berlin!" And Hitler said: "You'll see, the Russians will have their greatest defeat, the bloodiest hiding in their history, before the gates of Berlin."

Although nobody in the room dared to dissent, the sound of contradiction came from the outside. At 1:35 P.M., as if designed to add their own greetings to the celebration, the Russians opened up with a deafening barrage from the long-range guns of their Third Army, bombarding the inner city for the first time.

The bunker became overcrowded. From the still unoccupied parts of Germany, Hitler's cohorts flocked to the miserable concrete warren fifty feet below the shattered Chancellery to pay their homage. It was a fulsome celebration. None of those present, riddled with doubt and fear, dared to express his true feelings as he now offered his best wishes with the familiar servility. Himmler was fidgety. Even as he was reiterating his undying fealty to the Führer, he was preparing to keep a secret appointment at his estate in Hartzwalde, near Berlin, with a Swedish businessman named Norbert Masur, representing the World Jewish Congress, to negotiate the release of a thousand women from the Ravensbrück concentration camp.

Göring concluded that Hitler had outlived his usefulness. While wishing Hitler many happy returns, he was already thinking of replacing the Führer at the head of the regime, and preparing for his trip to Bavaria.

Albert Speer, the most obsequious among these glorified lackeys, was preparing to leave for Hamburg immediately after the celebration, for a meeting with Gauleiter Karl Otto Kaufmann, with whom he was plotting the overthrow of the regime and the mass arrest of its top leaders, with Bormann heading the roster. Speer had enlisted the aid of Dr. Gerhard Klopfer, the Reichsleiter's second in command at the Party Chancellery in Munich, for the abduction of Bormann. Klopfer was keeping him informed of Bormann's movements, and Speer was confident that he would succeed in maneuvering the Reichsleiter into a lethal trap.

Outwardly, however, all was serene. Hitler acknowledged the congratulations with feeble handshakes. Then, clad in a greatcoat with its collar turned up against the raw April weather, he left the bunker for the last time alive, to pin Iron Crosses on the chests of a group of boys whom Reich Youth Leader Arthur Axmann had brought to the compound to be decorated for their bravery in defending a bridge.

Martin Bormann was unaware of Speer's plot to capture him, but he did not simulate confidence in ultimate victory. When the day of this dismal party was over, he wrote in his diary: "Today is the Führer's birthday. Unhappily the situation is anything but festive. An advance group has orders to fly off to Salzburg."

The last sentence reflected what he thought was Hitler's decision at last to leave Berlin and move to the Alps. The pendulum of the Führer's mood was swinging as before between elation and despair, between determination and resignation. What he let out about his plans and intentions during the day thus lent itself to different interpretations. Goebbels assumed from what he heard that Hitler had made up his mind to heed his advice and remain in Berlin. But Bormann preferred to conclude that the Führer would move to Berchtesgaden after all.

He left the party hurriedly to arrange the move, then supervised personally as trucks and planes were loaded for the trip. All the personnel under his jurisdiction were given marching orders. So certain was he that the great exodus would begin the next day that he sent six of the eight stenographers, whose job was to record every word Hitler spoke at the situation conferences and even at his dinner table, to Berchtesgaden, with orders to set up their offices at the Hotel Solekurbad while awaiting the Führer's arrival. The great load was lifted from his mind. But his elation was destined to be short-lived.

April 22, 1945, a Sunday, was the most critical day in the life of Martin Bormann. It began ominously enough. Stuttgart fell to the First French Army. Bremen was hit by 969 bombers of the R.A.F. The Second British Army stood at the gates of Hamburg, where Albert Speer was plotting the overthrow of Hitler and the kidnapping of Bormann.

But the Führer was undaunted. For thirty-six hours after his birthday celebration, he was buoyed by great expectations, convinced that Berlin was not lost after all. An able SS general, Felix Steiner, had been given command of a hastily improvised Panzer corps and was ordered to take it southeast in a bold maneuver to forestall the encirclement of the capital by cutting through the Soviet spearhead. Hitler had unbounded confidence in Steiner, who had managed to slow down the Red Army in Pomerania only a few weeks before. He was convinced that the general would accomplish the impossible.

On the twenty-second Hitler rose at what for him was an early hour, awakened by the din of the 9 A.M. Russian bombardment, then called the first of a series of situation conferences that would be held throughout the day. He appeared almost his old self at the noon session, expecting the good news from Steiner to arrive momentarily. As he saw it, the lifting of the siege was only a matter of hours.

He listened impatiently as General Hans Krebs, the Army chief of staff, made his routine opening report. It was the general's usual performance, attuned to Hitler's mood of the moment, magnifying the scattered tactical successes of platoons and battalions, minimizing or glossing over the reverses of divisions and armies. In Krebs's optimistic presentation, the battle was not going too badly, but then, Krebs, a weak opportunist, was the virtuoso of the silver lining.

It was too much for General Jodl. Irritated by Krebs's wishful thinking, he broke into his report to tell Hitler bluntly that Berlin was as good as surrounded. The Führer paled. "What is Steiner doing?" he asked, dumbfounded. Krebs had to admit the truth—Steiner was not doing well. He was still trying to organize his forces, he said, and a pitiful "corps" it was, consisting of only ten thousand men at best, fresh from defeat in Stettin and Danzig. What was worse, the vaunted Panzer "corps" could scrape up only a handful of battered tanks.

The scene that followed had no precedent in history. As Field Marshal Keitel recalled the historic incident during his interrogation, the Führer was in a state of total collapse. His head jerked, he swayed and began to breathe heavily. In a tight, hoarse voice he ordered everyone out of the room except his generals and Bormann. The rest stumbled over one another in their eagerness to get out. In the waiting room they stood in silent apprehension.

As soon as the door was closed, Hitler lunged to his feet, his left arm flopping. He shouted that he was surrounded by traitors and liars as he lurched back and forth, swinging his right arm wildly. All were too low, too mean to understand his great purpose, he screamed. He was the victim of corruption and cowardice, and now everyone had deserted him.

The generals absorbed the abuse in silence. Surprisingly and unexpectedly, Bormann, the only civilian in the group, who otherwise rarely intervened in such proceedings, now rose to their defense. But Hitler outdroned his intervention.

"He shouted something about Steiner," Keitel recalled, "and abruptly flopped into his chair. In anguish he said, 'the war is lost!' Then with a trembling voice he added that the Third Reich had ended in failure and all he could do now was die. His face turned white and his body shook spasmodically, as if torn by a violent stroke."

Bormann watched the frightening spectacle with incredulous eyes. Was this the Führer he so faithfully worshiped? Hitler just sat there, his jaw slackened, his body twitching, staring ahead with vacant eyes. In the stillness that followed the tantrum, Bormann realized instinctively that the abiding faith he had had in Hitler's miraculous powers would thenceforth be misplaced. Now it was he who pleaded with Hitler to have faith. "If you lose faith, my Führer," he said, "then everything is lost."

As Keitel, Jodl and Burgdorf echoed his words, Bormann pleaded with the Führer to leave for Berchtesgaden at once. Why Berchtesgaden when the whole of High Bavaria with the Obersalzberg in its center was in jeopardy? Keitel and Jodl, the technicians whose imagination was narrowed to their jobs, preferred the area because it had the facilities which Hitler needed to exercise control and command. But Bormann had broader ideas. He realized that while it offered no guarantee of survival, it had advantages Berlin did not have.

It was the giant hub of the beautiful, rugged highland with its wide valleys and towering peaks, trails fanning from it to the Alps, the enormous mountain system forming a huge arc from the Mediterranean and Adriatic coasts through Switzerland to Austria and Bavaria. It was an ideal place for prolonged defense against superior strength, and the defenders could, when they decided it was necessary, withdraw into the mountain range for continued, effective resistance. In Bormann's calculations time was important.

Contrary to the belief, shared by Hitler himself, that there would be no haven in the world to which the Führer could go, Bormann assumed that two countries might grant him asylum. From his Alpine fortress, Bormann thought, Hitler could move to Spain in transit, and eventually go to South America, where Juan Perón's

Argentina beckoned most promisingly. He had made arrangements on an enormous scale for the move, shipping a vast treasure to Buenos Aires in a secret deal with Perón.

Now he realized his efforts were in vain. For once, the Führer proved more realistic than his supreme realist. Hitler concluded that while his courtiers might be able to escape to safe havens, he himself would have no place to hide.

Shaking his head, Hitler said in a voice that was barely audible: "You're free to go, but I will never leave Berlin." He then summoned Goebbels, the absent architect of his decision. When the Propaganda Minister rushed over from his own shelter across the street, Hitler invited him to move into the bunker with his wife and children, and remain at his side to the end.

Watching the arrival of the Goebbels family, each child clutching the single toy he was allowed to bring, Bormann knew that he had lost his big gamble. The frenzied scene dissolved. Keitel and Jodl took leave of Hitler, who had regained his composure and solicitously ordered a couple of picnic baskets with sandwiches and wine for the departing generals. Krebs and Burgdorf refused to leave the bunker, and Bormann announced with uncharacteristic bathos that he too would stay. The Führerbunker, never a happy place, took on the air of a mortuary between funerals.

When the bizarre situation conference was over, Bormann went with Goebbels, Krebs and Burgdorf into another room to discuss their own future. Prodded by Goebbels, who was almost cheerful, they shook hands on a suicide pact with grim solemnity. Then they parted. Goebbels joined his family in their new quarters. Krebs and Burgdorf left to get drunk. Only Bormann went off briskly to attend to the business of the new situation.

The Bormann who walked out of the room was a changed man. The old spell was broken. He had agreed to the suicide pact only because it was unavoidable. He did not have the slightest intention of killing himself. His new mission in life was survival.

Chapter Seven

The Reichsleiter Vanishes

On April 20, during Hitler's gloomy birthday party, Martin Bormann observed the well-wishers with cynical eyes, assessing the scope of their treason. In the case of Albert Speer he had no doubts. A few months before, Bormann had proscribed the evacuation of the families of high Nazi functionaries from the war zones, branding their removal an act of defeatism punishable by death. That the order was taken seriously became painfully evident even in the bunker. In early April it was discovered that Dr. Karl Brandt, one of Hitler's chief surgeons, had moved his family to the relative safety of Thuringia. Although Brandt was the veteran among the Führer's doctors, he was sentenced to death by a court-martial appointed by Hitler himself.

At the birthday party, Hitler inquired solicitously where the families of his cohorts were, and Speer glibly told him that his wife and children were staying with a friend on an estate near Berlin. But Bormann knew that Speer was lying. On April 6, in defiance of the order he had sent his family to a safe haven in Holstein.

Himmler impressed Bormann as a broken man, living in terror. Foreign Minister Joachim von Ribbentrop was of no consequence. He was too stupid to plot even his own salvation. It was only Göring who puzzled Bormann.

The Reichsmarschall blew into the Führerbunker like a tornado, clad in a brand-new khaki uniform obviously tailored, as one observer remarked, with an eye to the future, for it made him look like an American general. From the moment of his arrival to his somewhat sheepish departure (subdued because he announced that he for one was moving to the south), Göring dominated the proceedings, if only by his bulk, which was even more conspicuous in the crammed quarters of the bunker.

His power and influence were waning in proportion to the failure of his Luftwaffe, but the Reichsmarschall did not seem to care. Grown enormously rich and increasingly indolent, he was the one man in the Third Reich who appeared to have everything. Bormann loathed him, and not only because he detested his sybaritic life style, ostentation and eccentricities. When, after the flight of Rudolf Hess to Scotland, Bormann became the leading candidate for his post at the head of the Reich Chancellery, Göring rushed to Hitler in a blunt attempt to forestall his appointment. Bormann never forgot and rarely forgave such insults though he could do little to harm the Reichsmarschall beyond petty pinpricks. Nominally at least, he was still the number-two man in the Third Reich, under the decree of June 29, 1941, in which Hitler named him his deputy while he lived and his successor in the event of his death.

Annoyed by Göring's innate *joi de vivre,* Bormann watched him with added misgivings. The Reichsmarschall was in fact thinking more and more that only surrender could stave off Germany's total destruction, and he fancied that he would be more acceptable than Hitler to negotiate it with the Allies. It disturbed Bormann when he found that Hitler himself had similar thoughts. Once recently in a discussion, when the likelihood of a negotiated end of the war was mentioned, Hitler remarked pensively, "Göring could do that better than I."

Yet only two days after the birthday party, Bormann himself seemed to be thinking along those lines. In the wake of Hitler's tantrum on the twenty-second, he apparently concluded that Göring should take over. During the afternoon of that fateful day, in ironclad secrecy, Bormann radioed a message to Göring at the Obersalzberg, advising him that the Führer had "suffered a nervous breakdown." Then, implying that the proposition came from Hitler, he suggested that Göring take over the government.

The message startled the Reichsmarschall. It also made him suspicious. He could not imagine that Bormann would ever be a party to such an invitation. He mentioned the radiogram only to his caretaker, withholding it from his aides. He was afraid of making a fool of himself by discussing its implications with the more sophisticated members of his entourage.

The message was genuine. It had been sent by Bormann. But it marked Bormann's opening move in a maneuver, not to aid in the elevation of the Reichsmarschall, but to bring about his elimination.

Although officially Göring was still the heir presumptive, Himmler and Goebbels were moving relentlessly in on his seniority. Bormann was not conspicuous in the field of contestants. Nobody—not Hitler, not even Bormann himself—ever considered the chief ward heeler of the Third Reich a candidate. But the rapid disintegration of the leadership created a novel situation that nobody could have anticipated.

Bormann now gave free vent to the ambition he had carefully bridled so long as Hitler was around. Convinced that he alone remained steadfastly loyal to the Führer, he now envisaged himself as his only possible successor. Completely dedicated as he was to Hitler's ideas and principles, he regarded himself as more capable than anyone else of ensuring the continuity of his ideology.

Having no time to lose, he then and there began to plot for this new eventuality. The men who until now sat firmly above him now became his equals and rivals. Like a crack marksman aiming at moving targets, he picked out those he would shoot down.

In the last analysis, only three dangerous competitors were left in the race—Göring, Goebbels and Himmler. Goebbels presented no problem. Bormann knew that the Propaganda Minister was resolved to perish in the bunker at Hitler's side and was already drafting his last will and testament. He dismissed Himmler with a new contempt. The Reichsführer was by now a thoroughly discredited man. He failed dismally when Hitler made him commander in chief of the Army, first in the West, then in the East, in positions that he, during his more equable days, eagerly coveted. Nobody in his right mind would take seriously the stillborn war lord as the new commander in chief of the Wehrmacht.

That left only Göring to deal with. For all his reduced status at court, the Reichsmarschall was still a formidable adversary.

The radio message of April 22, so contrived as to induce Göring to show his hand, was the opening gambit in this intricate game. At first it appeared to be too obvious a trap for Göring to fall into obligingly. But the morning after, on the twenty-third, General Karl Koller, chief of staff of the Luftwaffe, arrived at the Obersalzberg with a firsthand account of the Führer's collapse, just as Bormann had described it in his message. Koller now urged Göring to put forward his claim. From then on the Reichsmarschall acted exactly as Bormann shrewdly anticipated he would.

Back in the bunker, Bormann waited with bated breath for Göring's reaction to his message. It arrived in the early afternoon of April 23 and was rushed to Bormann. The telegram signaled Göring's inevitable doom. "My Führer," it read in part, "is it your wish, in view of your decision to stay in Berlin, that I take over complete control of the Reich, in accordance with the decree of June 29, 1941? If no answer has been received by 10 P.M. I shall have to assume that you have been deprived of your freedom of action, and I will consider the terms of your decree as being in force and act for the good of our people and Fatherland."

Hitler was closeted with Speer when Göring's telegram arrived, but Bormann, in his impatience, barged in on them. It did not seem to upset Hitler. If anything, he gave the impression that it might not be such a bad idea after all to abdicate his powers to the Reichsmarschall. That he was corrupt and a drug addict, he knew. But, he said, Göring "could negotiate the capitulation, it doesn't matter who does."

Bormann, however, moved deftly to ignite the fuse in Göring's telegram. "My Führer," he said indignantly, "the Reichsmarschall demands an answer by ten o'clock tonight. This is tantamount to an ultimatum if not, in fact, to high treason."

Hitler's mood changed abruptly, but he still refused to heed Bormann, who now suggested that the Reichsmarschall be arrested and shot. In the end he merely instructed his irate secretary to draft an answer to the telegram reprimanding the Reichsmarschall, suggesting that he resign, in which case his treasonable action would be forgiven.

In Bormann's final draft, which was eventually put on the air, the message emerged far more ominously. "Your action represents high treason," it read, "against the Führer and National Socialism. The penalty for treason is death. But in view of your earlier services to the Party, the Führer will not inflict this supreme penalty if you resign all your offices. Answer yes or no." He signed it himself.

As an afterthought he then fired off a second telegram, since he realized that his first, in fact, left the Reichsmarschall the heir presumptive. For greater emphasis he now signed Hitler's name to the telegram, which read: "Decree of 6.29.41 is rescinded by my special instruction. My freedom of action undisputed. I forbid any move by you in the direction indicated by you."

Then it seemed that Hitler would ruin his game after all. Late at night, after he had discussed the case with Goebbels and some of his other confidants, the Führer himself drafted a third telegram in which he rejected Göring's "assumption" that he was too feeble to act for himself. He said nothing about treason and the death penalty. In fact, in its general tone the message was defensive and almost conciliatory.

Now Bormann had to take matters into his own hands if he was to save his plot. Earlier, when he talked over the matter with General Krebs, he regarded Göring's downfall as an accomplished fact. But now he was not so sure that he was right. He decided to kill Göring by remote control. Without consulting Hitler or so much as hinting to him what he was doing, he radioed Standartenführer Frank, the commandant of the SS guards at the Obersalzberg, to arrest the Reichsmarschall for high treason and shoot him. Then he sat back to contemplate how he would explain the "unfortunate misunderstanding" to the Führer.

The SS colonel balked. He tried to solve his problem by visiting Göring at his house, advising him of the charges, then placing a pistol with a single bullet in it on the night table. He quickly left, hoping that the Reichsmarschall would get the message.

Göring understood it all right, but he refused to act. At half past nine in the morning of April 25, he was a bit alarmed but still very much alive when the SS commandant called again, accompanied by a detachment of his men to see what had happened. Now it seemed Göring's moment of truth was at hand. Just as the SS men drew their guns, however, the air-raid alarm was sounded. It was 10 A.M. A swarm of American bombers swept over the mountain, dropping their bombs on the edge of the Führer area. Then a second wave showered blockbusters on the Obersalzberg, destroying Göring's chalet. The raid was perfectly timed. Everyone in the room upstairs, Göring with them, had fled in panic. There was no more talk of execution in the shelter.

Thus was Bormann's well-laid plan staved off by the raid. Then it seemed that it would be foiled altogether when a detachment of Luftwaffe soldiers liberated their commander in chief. Bormann was forced to change the direction of his attack. He harangued Hitler about Göring's enormous treachery, and saw him weakening under the barrage of the charges. He then realized that he would have nothing more to fear from Göring as a rival when he heard Hitler say to General Robert von Greim, commandant of the Luftwaffe at Munich, who had been ordered to fly to Berlin and report to the bunker, "I called you because the Reichsmarschall has deserted me and betrayed the Fatherland. He made contact with the enemy behind my back. I hereby name you his successor and commander in chief of the Luftwaffe with the rank of field marshal."

In the meantime, Bormann was busy with preparations for his departure from the bunker as soon as Hitler was out of the way. When the Führer collapsed on April 22, he realized that he had only a few weeks, perhaps only a few days, to organize his escape. In great secrecy he arranged for an armored scout car to stand by to take him out of Berlin and, if possible, to Berchtesgaden, to which, he was confident, a safe passage might still be found. Holed up as he was in the bunker with hardly any means of communication to the outside world, he could not do much more than that either for himself or for his family.

His wife and children were still in Berchtesgaden, except for his oldest boy, Martin Adolf. Since 1940, the youngster (rumored to be Hitler's offspring) had been at an exclusive boarding school for the sons of Nazi leaders at Feldafing on Starnberg Lake. Unbeknown to Bormann, he was about to be moved to Steinach near the Brenner Pass, out of the enemy's way. It was the eleventh hour, and not only in Berlin.

On April 24, Bormann summoned Dr. Helmut von Hummel to Berlin to aid him in making his dispositions. In the table of organization of the Party Chancellery, Hummel was listed as the head of Group III B in charge of social and economic affairs. Even today, practicing law in Munich, he insists that he was only a humble functionary in the Party bureaucracy in a post to which Bormann appointed him in 1942, and was never close to the Reichsleiter. In truth, Helmut, as he was called by the Bormann family, was Bormann's chief lieutenant and most trusted confidant, who managed both his business and his private affairs.

Meeting with von Hummel, Bormann asked him to ready Ligaret and other secluded log cabins on the Ofneralm and on the east slope of the High Göll, and stock them with food, water and all that a man in hiding or on the run might need. Strategically placed east of Berchtesgaden on the way to Salzburg and points beyond on the Austrian side of the border, they might come in handy should he himself be forced to take to the mountains, or as way stations on a flight out of Germany if all else failed.

Instead of rescinding it, Bormann had merely suspended his order of March 31 to Gauleiter Hofer to arrange a place where his family could go in an emergency. Now he told von Hummel to get in touch with Hofer in Innsbruck, and also with Gauleiter Gustav Adolf Scheel in Salzburg, and expedite things so that his family could be moved right away. He gave his aide a set of false papers made out to "Bergmann," the name under which the family would live in exile. Remembering a number of war orphans he had evacuated to the Berchtesgaden district from the war zones, where his wife and her sister cared for them, Bormann now instructed von Hummel to transfer them with his family and treat them as if they were his own children.

On his return to Berchtesgaden, the faithful Helmut helped the family and the orphans pack up, then saw them off in a convoy of cars and trucks, escorted by a detachment of SS guards, going to the village of Silva near Gardenia in the Dolomites in the South Tirol, where Gauleiter Hofer had found a little house for them. Included in the convoy were a couple of trucks loaded with Bormann's private archives. It was his practice to ship to his wife in Berchtesgaden his secret papers for safekeeping with an eye on posterity. He had collected significant documents of his own regime, volumes of his diary with its blunt entries, and many of Hitler's most confidential papers, which he did not feel safe to entrust to the custody of the Party archives in Munich. Frau Gerda kept the collection in a huge Kieselguhr-insulated safe in one of the air-raid shelters.

Now Gauleiter Hofer took charge of the papers. But unlike the family, which arrived safely in Silva, the trucks with the documents were lost. Some of the papers eventually wound up with François Genoud in Switzerland, but most of them are still missing.

Dr. von Hummel then sent a couple of SS men to Steinach and had young Martin Adolf brought to Berchtesgaden. But by the time the boy arrived, the family was gone. He was sent to Salzburg, where Gauleiter Scheel was to look after him. Scheel turned him over to an SS transport company that took him in a roundabout way to Weissenbach, Austria, and left him with a farmer named Nikolaus Hohenwarter, for whom he then worked, until September 1947.

Just before the family left Berchtesgaden on April 29, Bormann managed to get through to his wife on the telephone and asked her to do exactly as Helmut would tell her. He tried to sound calm and confident, assuring Gerda that they would meet again. As for himself, he said, he had a scout car waiting to take him out of Berlin to a safe place from which he would contact her as soon as possible.

It was a momentous day, the twenty-ninth. Although Bormann had triumphed over his last remaining rival three days before, a fatal blow was now dealt to his aspirations by Hitler himself in one of his last acts. On this Sunday, the Russians were only some five hundred yards from the Führerbunker. Yet strange as it may seem, it was not their objective. They were storming the nearly deserted Reichstag building nearby, defended by a handful of desperate Volkssturm men, because the Russians thought it was the seat of Hitler and his government.

In the seclusion of the Führerbunker, unnerved by the din of the battle, whose sound the thick walls and earthworks could not keep out, Hitler was spending the whole morning and the early afternoon dictating his last will and testament to Frau Gertrud Junge, one of his secretaries, from notes he had jotted down the night before. At 3 P.M., when Frau Junge returned with the transcript, Bormann, Goebbels, Krebs and Burgdorf were summoned to the Führer's inner sanctum, and Hitler read it to them. Written on his personal stationery, it consisted of two parts—a six-page preamble called "My Political Testament," and a four-page implementation, captioned "Second Part of the Political Testament."

It was the opening paragraph of this second part that startled and stunned Bormann. The Führer read Göring and Himmler out of the Party and stripped them of all their ranks, titles and positions. He made Goebbels and Bormann members of a new cabinet of fourteen ministers, all of them old Party hacks. But he named an outsider, Grand Admiral Karl Doenitz, who was not even a member of the Party, his successor as Reich President and commander in chief of the Wehrmacht.

It was four o'clock in the afternoon. Hitler signed three copies of the document, then asked Goebbels, Bormann, Krebs and Burgdorf to witness each. It was a shocking, humiliating blow. In all his conspiracy, Bormann never for a moment thought of Doenitz as Hitler's possible successor. Yet now the admiral loomed up suddenly and enormously as his arch rival in a struggle for which he was neither forewarned nor properly armed.

With the Führer dead, the testament was in force. What this meant to those he left behind was put into words by a lowly sergeant named Tornow, the keeper of Hitler's kennel. He had been called into the lower floor of the Führerbunker by Professor Werner Haase, one of Hitler's court physicians, to assist him in the execution of one of the Führer's last wishes—administering poison to Blondi, his favorite dog. Tornow led the bitch into the toilet, forced its mouth open, allowing Dr. Haase to reach into it and crush an ampule of potassium cyanide with a pair of pliers. The sergeant then shot Blondi's pups, the dogs of Eva Braun and of Frau Gerda Daranowski Christian, one of Hitler's secretaries. Then in a frenzy he rushed from the bunker to the new Chancellery building, shrieking hysterically: "The Führer is dead, every man for himself."

His cry echoed in the minds of all who heard it. It sounded eloquently what Bormann was thinking. At 6:07 P.M. on April 30, when the Führer had been smoldering in the yard for more than two hours, he sent Admiral Doenitz, the new chief of state, a cryptic message, advising him only that the Führer had designated him "his successor in the place of the former Reichsmarschall." He left it to the admiral to puzzle out what that meant.

In the light of the next morning, Bormann saw that the situation had changed again. If he had had no prospect of extricating himself from his fateful predicament as long as Hitler was alive, he now gained a glimmer of hope from his death. May 1, his first day without the Führer, was probably the busiest day in Bormann's life. At 7:40 A.M. he sent Doenitz a second telegram, telling the admiral that "the testament was in force."

He was still thinking of other tangents of action before letting Doenitz know the full implications of the situation and committing himself to his new leader. Hitler had been a liability during his last ten days. But now he had performed a final service by committing suicide, enabling Bormann to make an attempt at bargaining with the Russians for a safe-conduct in exchange for the surrender of Berlin.

With the melancholy acquiescence of Dr. Goebbels, he sent General Krebs, who spoke Russian fluently from his days as military attaché in Moscow, with a white flag to General Vasili I. Chuikov, the commander of the Red Army elements which were battering Berlin's defenses. Krebs returned to the bunker around noon, not quite empty-handed, it seemed. General Chuikov had told him that the decision was up to the Kremlin and the answer from Moscow would be communicated to the Germans as soon as it arrived. Goebbels, who did not regard the Russians' decision as having any bearing on his own fate, asked Colonel Dufving, who had been to Chuikov with Krebs, whether there was a chance that the Russians would consent to a truce. "I don't think so," Dufving replied. "They kept insisting on immediate surrender."

Bormann now knew that the die had been cast. Nothing more could delay the inevitable. At 2:46 P.M., in his third message to Doenitz, he finally confided to the admiral that the Führer was dead. As far as he himself was concerned, he had clearly indicated that he had no intention of perishing in the bunker. He told the admiral that he had sent him a copy of Hitler's testament and that he would try to reach him, suggesting that no public announcement be made of the Führer's death, pending his arrival at Doenitz's headquarters.

The line to Doenitz, virtually the only link to what was left of the Wehrmacht, was operated by a mobile radio station that the Navy had in beleaguered Berlin, one of several such units that Doenitz had set up at strategic points in anticipation of the breakdown of his ground communications. The network functioned with astounding efficiency. Bormann's first message reached Doenitz within half an hour, the third in thirty-two minutes. Only the second took a little longer, but even that was in the admiral's hands within three hours.

Doenitz was startled and confused by the cryptic messages, but he had no reason to question their authenticity. For one thing, they moved in a special cipher his chief cryptographer had devised for this eventuality and which was now used for the first time. For another, its keys were known only at the sending and receiving ends of the transmission. But it was an exasperatingly one-sided communication; the admiral refrained from acknowledging receipt of the messages, and thus Bormann could not know what the admiral was doing or what he was up to. As far as he knew, the communications went to Plön, a small lakeside town in Schleswig-Holstein, Doenitz's next-to-last headquarters.

Just when Bormann was preparing to go to Plön, Doenitz was forced to evacuate the town. Unexpectedly, the Allies had opened an offensive in his direction, and its unchecked progress threatened to make his position untenable. By 4 P.M. on May 2, when Bormann would be on his way to Plön, the armor of the British prong of the drive reached Lübeck, only twenty-five miles to the southeast, bypassing Doenitz even as an American column was moving northward to his west in the direction of the Kiel Canal.

Trapped in the pincer, Doenitz had to look for another place. Traveling in his five-ton armored Mercedes-Benz limousine, a gift from the Führer in happier days, his nocturnal passage slowed by incessant strafing by Allied fighter planes, he arrived in Flensburg, an old port city on the Baltic famous for its rum and smoked eel, at 3 A.M. There he set up his headquarters in the command post of a U-boat flotilla.

It hardly mattered that Bormann knew nothing of this. His journey to Plön, or wherever he would find Doenitz, was fraught with danger, and not only from the Allies. The admiral, who was determined to have nothing to do with the shadow government Hitler had foisted on him in his testament, had decided to arrest Bormann if he ever appeared at his headquarters.

By the time Bormann sent Doenitz his third message, the bunker was in a turmoil. "People kept running to and fro," Colonel Dufving wrote. "Helplessness and panic could be read everywhere." In the end, only Goebbels and his wife and Krebs and Burgdorf followed their Führer into death by committing suicide in the bunker. The Goebbels children died from lethal injections administered to them in their sleep by the same Professor Haase who had killed Blondi. He was a crippled, mortally ill man who had decided to stay in the bunker and let fate overtake him.

Bound by the suicide pact, Bormann waited for Goebbels to have himself and his family exterminated. Then he stood by as Krebs and Burgdorf, almost unconscious from too much cognac, committed suicide. That was that. With none of his partners left alive to claim the forfeit, he chose to live.

It was the evening of May 1. Even as the corpses were still smoldering in their shallow, rubble-covered graves outside, Bormann was making arrangements to get out as quickly as possible. He was now more determined than ever to make the trip to Admiral Doenitz.

Time was essential. He summoned General Rattenhuber, commandant of the bunker's security service (who had also vowed to commit suicide but then chose to live), and together they organized their exit. The scout car Bormann had ordered to stand by was nowhere to be found. Its driver had taken off in it to save his own skin. The scant information Rattenhuber had about the outside world was enough, however, to plan at least the first leg of their escape. He had reason to believe that four of the other big bunkers in Berlin were still holding out—one in the Zoo; another in the

Olympic Stadium; a four-tiered third, the luxurious maze the Luftwaffe had built for Göring, in Wannsee; and a fourth at Humboldthain in a working-class district in North Berlin. And Bormann knew of a fifth, in the Kurfürstenstrasse, to which he had been tipped off by Heinrich Müller, the Gestapo chief.

But first they had to get out of the Führerbunker. They would have to make a dash to the subway entrance at the Hotel Kaiserhof on the other side of Wilhelm Platz, then move underground as far as they could in the meandering tunnel until they reached a spot where they could emerge safely.

The exodus was organized in several groups. Leaving with one of them was thirty-year-old Else Krüger, a handsome, plucky woman who had been one of Bormann's secretaries since 1942 and was now the last to remain with him in the bunker. Just before she left, the Reichsleiter shook her hand warmly and said, almost choking up, "Well, then, *auf Wiedersehen.* It no longer makes much sense, but I'll try to break out, though I cannot be sure that I'll make it."

Bormann himself left at 11 P.M. with General Rattenhuber and Colonel Högl, the latter's deputy, followed by a large group of miscellaneous escapees that included some of the highest functionaries in the bunker. Among them were Dr. Werner Naumann, who had been named the new Propaganda Minister in Hitler's will; Reich Youth Leader Arthur Axmann; Colonel Hans Baur, the Führer's longtime personal pilot, and Major Beetz, his copilot; Ambassador Walter Hewel, the Foreign Ministry's liaison to Hitler; Captain Günther Schwägermann, Goebbels' aide-de-camp; Dr. Ludwig Stumpfegger, one of Hitler's physicians; SS Major Heinz Linge, his valet; and General Wilhelm Möhnke, commandant of the Führer's personal bodyguard.

With the exception of Högl, Beetz and Dr. Stumpfegger, they made good their escape and lived to prosper in postwar Germany. "We know exactly," wrote Erich Kuby, "how all these men got out of the Chancellery; we also know that many others who stayed with their Führer to the last survived the fall of the Third Reich." With the death of Goebbels, Krebs and Burgdorf, the Chancellery ceased to be the center of events in Berlin. "Bormann," Kuby wrote, "the only Nazi top brass left, was concerned solely with saving his own skin."

General Rattenhuber, Bormann's original companion, made it

alone to the Humboldthain bunker. Högl, his deputy, was mortally wounded en route and had to be abandoned. At Humboldthain, Rattenhuber told Fräulein Krüger, who had arrived in the bunker before him, that upon reaching the Friedrichstrasse, they emerged from the subway, commandeered a car and drove northward in the direction of the Charité hospital, hoping to make it to the Maikäfer Barracks. But when Rattenhuber was wounded in the leg by a sniper's bullet, Bormann had abandoned him to his fate. Rattenhuber ventured the opinion that Bormann must have been killed somewhere on his flight, which he continued alone.

Then others came forward with the claim that Bormann died in Berlin. The chauffeur Kempka produced the most unlikely story, which he changed several times in the retelling. According to a composite account pieced together from his various testimonies, he had reached the Friedrichstrasse ahead of Bormann and took refuge in the Admirals Palast, a music hall at the Weidendammer Bridge over the Spree. Looking out a window, Kempka said, he saw a row of tanks rolling onto the bridge, and recognized Bormann walking on the left side of the lead tank, either followed or preceded by Dr. Naumann.

Just then, a salvo from a bazooka hit the tank and blew it up. The flash of the explosion blinded Kempka, yet he insisted that he *saw* Bormann perish in the blast, together with others, including Naumann. It was a good story, but somehow it went too far. For Kempka was looking out of a window which was some two hundred feet, if not more, from the scene of the explosion; he was watching a procession whose contours were barely visible in the predawn darkness; and yet he claims he saw the aftermath of the blast although he had been blinded by it.

Others at the scene poduced contradictory versions of the same incident. Linge and Baur stated that Bormann was killed but admitted that "the scene was confused" and that they themselves never saw his body. On the other hand, an officer of the bodyguard named Harry Mengershausen declared firmly that Bormann was not killed in the blast. According to him, he was *riding* in a tank, and not *walking* at its side as Kempka said; and it was not his tank at all that was blown up.

To be sure, both Bormann and Naumann vanished from the Weidendammer Bridge on this early morning of May 2, but as far as Naumann was concerned, not as completely as Kempka thought.

In 1950, Naumann was found in Düsseldorf, running a lucrative business in partnership with an old friend named Herbert Lucht.

Bormann's survival was then confirmed by Arthur Axmann, the one-armed leader of the Hitler Youth, but he gave the Reichsleiter only an hour or so to live afterward. He too managed to escape from the bunker and make it from Berlin all the way to Bavaria. But he was captured in the late fall of 1945 after six months of hiding in the mountains with a group of diehard youngsters with whom he planned to continue the war after the surrender. Unlike Naumann, he was effusive and eloquent in offering his version of Bormann's fate, further contradicting Kempka's story. Axmann said he had broken off from the group at the Friedrichstrasse and made his way to the Lehrter railroad station alone. En route, he claimed, he came upon Bormann's lifeless body at a spot where the Invalidenstrasse crossed the railroad tracks. It showed no signs of injury from the explosion of the tank, nor any marks of violence. Bormann was just lying there on his back, his limp body illuminated by the fires of the doomed city.

It seemed, however, that Bormann must have gotten up after Axmann had left, for SS Major Joachim Tiburtius, who also fled from the bunker with the same group, bumped into him later at a hotel in nearby Moabit. "We pushed on together," Tiburtius said, "toward the Schiffbauerdamm and the Albrechtstrasse. Then I finally lost sight of him. But he had as good a chance to escape as I had."

Chapter Eight

The Birth of the Bormann Legend

When Martin Bormann vanished from sight in the early hours of May 2, nobody seemed unduly interested in finding him, dead or alive. It was not until early September 1945 that a first organized effort was made to look for him, but even then the search, as far as it went, was tied to an effort to investigate the circumstances of Hitler's death. Brigadier Dick Goldsmith White, one of Britain's veteran counterespionage chiefs who had been made comptroller of British security in defeated Germany, conceived the idea of solving what was still the mystery of Hitler's death. He invited his friend Hugh Trevor-Roper, the young Oxford historian, who was a major in British Intelligence, to conduct the inquiry.

The Russians, who had captured the Führerbunker and were holding it, seemed to be doing nothing to clear up the mystery. So inadequate and incompetent was the Russians' coverage of the Hitler compound in Berlin that when Trevor-Roper was permitted to visit it four months after V-E Day, he found the Führer's appointment book still on Hitler's desk.

A month before Trevor-Roper had been called in to conduct his inquiry, the victorious Four Powers had set the wheels of retribution in motion. On August 8, meeting in London, they appointed an International Military Tribunal to try the *major* war criminals, as they were called, in Nuremberg. The city was chosen for the historic trial because it used to be the site of Hitler's Party rallies.

The Tribunal held its opening session on October 18 in Berlin, to receive the bill of indictment which had been drawn up by an international collegium of prosecutors headed by Justice Robert H. Jackson of the United States Supreme Court.

Unlike Hermann Göring, Joachim von Ribbentrop, Field Marshal Wilhelm Keitel and their colleagues who were in Allied custody, and unlike Hitler, Goebbels and Himmler, who were known to be dead, Bormann was, as Trevor-Roper put it, "suspended in limbo." He could not be produced either alive or dead. Nevertheless, the prosecution decided to charge him since, as the bill of indictment phrased it, "no convincing evidence of Bormann's death is available." The Tribunal accepted the indictment and, invoking Article 12 of its statutes, decided to try him in his absence.

This was a momentous decision, contributing materially to the rise of the Bormann mythology. Its very beginning was spectacular. Noting that "one of the accused, Martin Bormann, cannot be found," the Tribunal issued an order that the missing man be informed of his indictment by broadcasting and advertising a public notice that read:

> Martin Bormann is accused of having committed crimes against the peace, war crimes, and crimes against humanity, as charged in a bill of indictment submitted to this Court.
>
> The bill of indictment is on display and can be examined in the Court Building in Nuremberg.
>
> In the event that Martin Bormann appears, he has the right to defend himself either in person or by counsel.
>
> In the event that he does not present himself, it is possible to proceed against him in his absence. The trial will begin on November 20, 1945, in the Court Building in Nuremberg, Germany. Should he be found guilty, his sentence will be carried out without any further proceedings and according to the decisions of the Control Council for Germany, as soon as he is apprehended.

The task of notifying Bormann of his indictment was assigned to Major William Hurlstone Hortin, a British officer with the Allied Control Council and serving as the secretary of the Tribunal in Berlin. Major Hortin thus became destined to play, in the proper performance of his official duties, a significant part in the birth of the Bormann saga. As a matter of fact, if any individual can be singled out as the architect of the Reichsleiter's postwar notoriety, Hortin must be regarded as that man. His efforts ended once and for all Bormann's cherished obscurity and planted the seeds of the ensuing mystery.

Major Hortin went about his mission on an elaborate scale. He had 200,000 copies of the Tribunal's notice printed and posted in all four zones of occupied Germany. Between October 20 and November 1, he had the notice broadcast four times each week on the radio and published in newspapers in Berlin, Halberstadt and Mecklenburg.

Bormann was suddenly propelled into full public view. When the campaign was over, he was still at large, but he had become a macabre and romantic figure as the world's most-wanted fugitive, firmly implanted in the minds of people as the one henchman of the dead Führer who was smart enough to escape.

He was one of four defendants who were absent from the dock at the Tribunal's opening session. Robert Ley, the labor tsar and organization chief of the Nazi regime, had committed suicide seventeen days before; the industrialist Gustav Krupp von Bohlen und Halbach was at his castle in Austria, too ill to stand trial; and Dr. Ernst Kaltenbrunner, general manager of Hitler's terror machine, had suffered a mild stroke and had to be hospitalized briefly. But nobody knew what happened to Bormann or where he was.

His name came up in the proceedings for the first time on November 22, with the presentation of a document from 1941 in which he referred to God as "the so-called dear Lord," and described the ideology of Nazism as far superior to the teachings of Christianity. During the rest of the trial, he remained relatively inconspicuous, and not just by his physical absence. He was mentioned on few occasions, and the references to him were mostly ephemeral. In the huge index of the proceedings, references to Hitler took up twenty-nine columns, those to Göring fifteen columns, those to Keitel fourteen columns. But the Bormann case took up only four columns, some entries repeated several times. The question of his death was mentioned only eight times.

The entire court—judges, prosecutors and defense attorneys—was keenly conscious of the anomaly created by Bormann's absence, especially in Nuremberg of all places. The old city was famed for an adage of medieval burghers: "Never hang a man you don't hold."

Since nothing was heard from Bormann and nobody came forward to defend him, the Tribunal appointed Dr. Friedrich Bergold, a distinguished Nuremberg lawyer devoid of any Nazi taint, to serve as Bormann's counsel. He joined the battery of forty defense attorneys (among them Dr. Robert Servatius, who was to defend

Adolf Eichmann in Jerusalem in 1961) during their final strategy conference in the afternoon of November 19, the day of his appointment and the eve of the opening of the trial. He was bewildered by his assignment and baffled by his task. He was ignorant of the case. He had no time even to peruse the bill under which his client had been indicted, charged with monstrous crimes against peace and mankind. He was totally unfamiliar with the purported evidence contained in a slim folder of documents.

In his confusion, Dr. Bergold first sought to persuade the Tribunal to postpone the whole trial for a week at least, to afford him time for the study of his client's case. In the end, however, he refrained from presenting a motion that he knew would be futile. But he asked for and was given time to prepare his defense.

It was, therefore, only months later, on May 7, 1946, that Lord Justice Lawrence, president of the Tribunal, asked Dr. Bergold whether he was ready with his presentation, only to be told that the attorney was not. He had all the documents he needed, the Justice admonished him, but Bergold was not sure.

"In view of the fact that I have to develop the information I need by my own efforts," Dr. Bergold said, "and since I have to research the case in books, I cannot yet say whether these are all the documents I will need." He asked for more time to prepare the defense, and he proposed to consult two of the Reichsleiter's former secretaries in the hope that they might be able to enlighten him about his absentee client.

At last, on June 10, Dr. Bergold was ready. The day in Nuremberg was galvanized by an offhand remark of General R. A. Rudenko, the chief prosecutor. "We don't know that Bormann is dead," he had said. "All we know is that he is absent from the dock." The statement was quickly construed to mean that Bormann was alive. The cavernous Court Building was abuzz with rumors that the Russians were holding him and would produce him later in the day.

After the brief flurry of excitement stirred up by Rudenko's remark, everything that followed seemed anticlimactic. Bormann was not produced, for the simple reason that the Russians did not have him. And Dr. Bergold's long-awaited presentation sounded hollow. He listlessly described his documentation as "meager," and tried to show that Bormann was "merely a humble private secretary" who could not have "played the legendary role that is now attributed to him after the collapse."

This, however, was not the fundamental theme of Dr. Bergold's defense. What he now set out to show was that Bormann was dead. His problem was how to support his assertion. It was not easy. "The defendant Bormann is not present," he said. "His co-workers are not at my disposal."

With this cryptic statement Dr. Bergold implied that what he found himself confronted with was a plot to *withhold* from him information—any data at all—that he could use in the development of his defense, especially information that would prove conclusively that his client was either dead or alive. A conspiracy appeared to be brewing around Bormann, to shield and conceal him, to prevent accusers and defenders alike from coming to grips with his case.

All Dr. Bergold was able to produce in support of his contention was the inchoate affidavit of Else Krüger, one of Bormann's secretaries, who had stayed with her boss in the bunker virtually to the end. It stated that she had "heard" General Rattenhuber "speculating" on the morning of May 2 that Bormann might have been killed.

She proved a ghostly and feeble witness, and nobody else came forward to harden Bergold's argument. In fact, he had three witnesses, Bergold said, to attest to Bormann's demise firsthand. But where were they? He did not know. If they really existed at all, they were beyond his reach. The chauffeur Kempka, who said he had seen Bormann blown up with the tank on the Weidendammer Bridge, was in an American internment camp. General Rattenhuber, who left the bunker with Bormann and was said to have been present at the explosion, was alleged to have been captured by the Russians. Frau Christian, another secretary in the bunker, could not be found.

"At first," Bergold complained, "she was interned in Camp Oberursel. When she was given a short leave of absence from the camp, she used the opportunity to disappear. As a result," the hapless lawyer conceded, "aside from the Krüger affidavit I have no evidence to support my claim."*

Frau Christian's disappearance seemed to be no accident, but rather part of an elaborate conspiracy to cover up Bormann's trail. His second in command at the head of the Party Chancellery, Dr.

* Kempka did testify on July 3, 1946. But when he was questioned by two justices of the Tribunal, he gave such vague and contradictory answers that his testimony was curtly dismissed by both prosecution and defense.

Gerhard Klopfer, pleaded ignorance of anything and everything. Arthur Axmann, the Hitler Youth leader who had been captured a few months before, suddenly vanished again. Dr. Werner Naumann, Goebbels' deputy and another inmate of the bunker, who was supposed to have been behind Bormann when the tank exploded, had disappeared without a trace. Wilhelm Zander, Bormann's military aide and representative with the OKW, evaporated like his former chief. Dr. Helmut von Hummel, the mystery-shrouded manager of Bormann's fiscal empire and the man most likely to shed light on Bormann's fate, could not be found anywhere.

On July 22, 1946, it was Dr. Bergold's turn to plead his client's cause before the Tribunal. At the outset of his address, he exclaimed: "During the halcyon days of the National Socialist regime, the accused lived in the shadows. He remained shadowy throughout this trial. And in all probability he is even now among the 'Shadows,' as the dead were called in antiquity." He pictured Bormann as a sinister Orpheus wandering in some Nazi Hades.

"Throughout these protracted proceedings," he said, "the figure of Bormann as well as his activities was shrouded in the same darkness in which the accused, by his innate disposition, always preferred to live." Dr. Bergold concluded his address with the emphatic pleas that the Tribunal either terminate the case against Bormann on the ground of "his established death" or suspend the proceedings until he himself could be heard submitting his vindication in person.

The Tribunal dismissed the motions out of hand. "There is no convincing evidence," its verdict read, "that Bormann is dead, and, therefore, the Tribunal decided to convict him *in absentia.*"

On the afternoon of October 1, 1946, the two rows of the dock were empty. "Amidst breathless tension," as young Dr. Viktor Baron von der Lippe, Admiral Erich Räder's attorney, noted in his diary, the accused were escorted into the courtroom singly, each left standing at the door only long enough to hear his sentence read.

Baron Konstantin von Neurath, the former Foreign Minister and "Protector" of Czechoslovakia, was the last of the accused to be brought into the courtroom. Then its door remained closed. Nobody was escorted to the threshold as Lord Justice Lawrence read the final paragraph in a list of nineteen sentences. Bormann was found guilty on two of the four counts of the indictment.

The symbolism of this gripping act was overwhelming. Martin Bormann, whose vague shadow hovered over this unprecedented trial, a dead man according to his defense counsel, was sentenced to death by hanging.

The verdict was no rebuff to Dr. Bergold. It was rather the carefully considered rejection of his desperate claim that Bormann was dead. It was exactly 3:37 P.M. in Nuremberg. The long trial was over. On the authority of the High Tribunal, Martin Bormann's postwar fate had been decided.

But if Bormann was alive, as the Tribunal had just ruled, where was he? And wherever he was, how did he get there?

PART THREE

Broken and Scattered

Chapter Nine

The Flight into Oblivion

> Martin Bormann succeeded in escaping from the Reich Chancellery and . . . for some time thereafter lived in Schleswig-Holstein, where he attempted to contact Grand Admiral Karl Doenitz. There is reason to believe that he did join him briefly and was then helped by the admiral to cross the border into Denmark. We believe that Bormann stayed for some time in the Danish royal castle at Graasten, which is not far from the town of Sönderborg. An SS military hospital during World War II, the castle later became the hideout of many high-ranking Nazi leaders. The man who hid them and Bormann was a certain Heyde.

Until the spring of 1973, this was what came closest to an official German account of Martin Bormann's postwar fate. It was offered in 1965 by Dr. Fritz Bauer, General State Attorney of Hesse, the undisputed dean of the Bormann hunters and, until his untimely death, the world's best-informed man on the fugitive Reichsleiter.

Dr. Bauer pieced together his account of the first leg of Bormann's wanderings from a number of clues supplied by sources he regarded as reliable. Most important among these sources was an anti-Nazi journalist named Heinrich Lienau, who insisted that he had been with Bormann for hours in a train heading for Flensburg, Lienau's native city. This was in June 1945, after his release from the Sachsenhausen concentration camp. Although Lienau lost him there, others came forward to give information about Bormann's furtive progress in the north.

A Copenhagen physician named Preuss had been approached

by a Nazi friend "asking for money to get Martin Bormann out of Denmark." Dr. Bauer also had evidence about a Nazi cell of refugees close to the German-Danish border which Bormann had allegedly founded and headed. Last but not least, in Simon Wiesenthal's account of Bormann's eventual escape to Italy en route to South America, the long journey was said to have begun in Schleswig-Holstein.*

My own search produced an interesting clue in the Argentine documents. In Buenos Aires I was tipped off that Perón had maintained a special bureau in Copenhagen after the war to aid the escape of Nazis by a roundabout route. It was managed by a mysterious Scarlet Pimpernel attached to the Argentine legation in Denmark. Going though Danish records of the period, I found that an Argentine national posing as a diplomat had been ousted by the Danes on December 6, 1947, when they discovered that he had been "smuggling Nazis out of Denmark to South America." The evidence on which the Danes acted was conclusive. Prominent on a list found in the bogus diplomat's dossier of the Nazis he allegedly had aided was the name of Martin Bormann.

But how did Bormann make his way to that royal castle in Denmark after his escape from the bunker? Tracing his route back to the Weidendammer Bridge—for there is no reason to doubt that he managed to get that far—the escape suddenly dissolved there like a movie scene and faded into another. Colonel Högl, the odd man of the trio with the group, was killed in the bazooka incident, leaving Bormann and Rattenhuber to make the rest of the trip alone. If Erich Kempka really did observe what happened, it was probably Högl whom he saw falling and dying.

At this point the tale bursts into many fragments like shrapnel. According to the various versions, Bormann was clad for the flight in his Reichsleiter's uniform, over which he wore the leather greatcoat of an SS Obergruppenführer (lieutenant general). Somewhere

* A couple of less trustworthy witnesses also placed Bormann in Schleswig-Holstein at one time or another in 1945. Shortly after Dr. Bauer published his account of Bormann's escape, Roland Gray came forward with his claim that he had smuggled Bormann into Denmark for a fee of £3,000 and had killed him when the Reichsleiter tried to cheat him out of the money by running away on the safe side of the border. Erich Karl Wiedwald asserted that he had escorted Bormann from Schleswig-Holstein all the way to South America via Italy, afterward confessed under cross-examination by Judge von Glasenapp that he had invented the tale to "shake down" the London *Sunday Times,* which featured his story under the byline of Anthony Terry, its Bonn correspondent. Wiedwald later published the weird concoction in a book.

along the route, he was supposed to have changed into civilian clothes, discarding the greatcoat, which was later found and identified as his from a "diary" found in one of its pockets.

Since this is a composite story, put together from bits offered by some Nazis and a couple of Red Army officers, it is not surprising that no two versions conform. As a general named Telegin recalled it, the greatcoat had been found without Bormann in or near it, and his diary had been discovered nearby during the clean-up of the streets days after the battle. A colonel named Smyslov knew nothing about any leather greatcoat, but insisted that the diary had been found not in the street, but intact in the Führerbunker, with the entry in Bormann's handwriting "*Ausbruchsversuch*" ("breakout attempt").

In fact, the coat was found by a French slave laborer in Heyde Street, near the Solex carburetor factory, and was handed over to an air raid warden at the plant. The Frenchman was allowed to keep the coat. But the "diary," as it was called, found its way to the Red Army Kommandantur in Karlshorst.

It was not a diary in the usual sense of the word but a little pocket calendar in which Bormann jotted down notes, appointments and addresses. The entries covered the period between January 1 and May 1, 1945. "The day begins, the second time, with artillery barrage," he thus noted on April 29; then recorded Hitler's marriage and, eventually, his suicide on the 30th. It contained little to shed light on Bormann's escape, except his famous last word and a hand-drawn map, presumably of the route he hoped to be able to follow.

According to the most plausible version of this part of Bormann's escape offered by Rattenhuber (some of it during his captivity in the U.S.S.R., some after his return, both appropriately colored), he and Bormann commandeered a stray vehicle and continued up the Friedrichstrasse, until Rattenhuber too was disabled when hit by a Russian shell fragment. Bormann, who could not risk staying with him, at this point discarded the greatcoat (and removed the telltale Party insignia from the collar of his tunic, the simple alteration turning his uniform into what was not much different from a brown civilian suit). He turned west briefly, and was going in the direction of the marshaling yards of the Lehrter railroad station (or, according to another version, the Alpendorf, the old exhibition grounds in the same area off the Invalidenstrasse) when near the Atlas Hotel, still not far from the Weidendammer Bridge, he encountered Major Joachim Tiburtius, a straggler from the SS Nordland Division.

Tiburtius, the leader of another group of escapees from the Reich Chancellery, had seen Bormann walking at the side of the tank when it was blown up. Together they now groped their way along the Schiffbauerdamm along the Spree, then parted in the Albrechtstrasse.

By then Bormann knew exactly where he was heading. In his planning of the escape, he had found out about yet another bunker in Berlin into which he could move until an opportunity offered itself to continue his flight. Another supreme realist had prepared that hideout for himself—Adolf Otto Eichmann, then the still-anonymous butcher of millions of Jews.

Anticipating the end, Eichmann had reinforced a shelter under the cellar of his own organization at 116 Kurfürstenstrasse, used as a communications center of the Gestapo since 1944. He equipped it with a generator and a ventilating system, and stocked it with enough water, food and kerosene to last for weeks. When, in March 1945, Eichmann fled to Austria on the first leg of his own journey to Argentina, he revealed his hideout to Dr. Kaltenbrunner, the scar-faced Austrian who headed the enormous apparatus of death of which the Eichmann bureau was part. In the critical moment, however, Kaltenbrunner left Berlin to be with his mistress in Altaussee when she would be giving birth to their child.

Kaltenbrunner appointed Heinrich Müller, chief of the Gestapo, to act as his deputy in Berlin and his representative in the Führerbunker, and revealed to him the secret of Eichmann's shelter. By then Gestapo headquarters in the Prinz Albrechtstrasse had been bombed out, and Müller moved into Eichmann's lair. On one of his daily visits to the Führerbunker, Müller told Bormann about Eichmann's shelter and invited him to join him there. When he left Tiburtius, Bormann remembered the invitation and he reached the shelter without a hitch. There he found Müller with a friend named Scholz, waiting for rescuers to come for them.

When they arrived they took Müller and Scholz southward. But Bormann, who had his date with Admiral Doenitz in the north, was given the green uniform of a forest warden for the trip to Schleswig-Holstein and was then left to his own resources to make the trip as best he could.

It had taken Bormann the better part of a month to work his

passage north, and it was on his way there that he met Lienau. It was already early June, therefore, when, at the town of Lüneburg, he caught a slow train to Flensburg. According to Lienau, Bormann arrived at the station in some style, driven in an ambulance of the International Red Cross. He then boarded the train in which Lienau was a passenger and they traveled "in the evil-smelling wagon facing each other in uneasy silence for nearly three hours until they reached the border town of Flensburg [the crossing point to Denmark]."

On their arrival, Lienau alerted a couple of passing British soldiers, but by the time they acted, it was too late. Bormann quickly jumped on another train moving out of the station before they could stop him. Even in his isolation en route, he must have known that Admiral Doenitz had been arrested by the British on May 23 together with members of his cabinet, all of them shipped to the Bad Mondorf internment camp in Luxembourg. The admiral's twenty-day government was over. The collapse of the Third Reich was complete.

Bormann was heading for Denmark, where several hastily organized rescue groups were already active in arranging the transfer of Nazi refugees to safer havens. From Bormann's point of view, two in particular were most important. One—a short-range outlet—was an underground railroad run by a small band of mercenaries behind the blind of the International Red Cross. They would be able to take him to Bavaria and smuggle him out of Germany. The long-range outlet was that Argentine mission operating under a diplomatic cover, paving the escapees' way to South America.

It was headed by one Carlos Pineyro, accredited as an attaché at the Argentine legation in Copenhagen, but actually Juan Perón's personal agent to aid the Nazis at large. Bormann had urgent reason to contact Perón. The vast treasure he had sent out of Germany in 1944 and 1945, and the bulk of the deposits which he had cornered abroad, were in Argentine banks, four of his friends acting as trustees until he himself would be able to take control of the funds. But Pineyro proved uncooperative in Bormann's case, for reasons which the Reichsleiter learned only later, when he was pinned down for over two years in northern Italy.

Bormann was able to move with relative impunity until October 17, when the efforts of Major Hortin to notify him of his indictment before the International Military Tribunal ended his obscurity.

His picture was posted all over Germany, with his description supplied by the American Counter Intelligence Corps. It read:

> *Born* 1900. *Height:* 1.60 to 1.70 m [Bormann's real height is hard to estimate because of his very stocky build]. *Build:* very broad shoulders, stocky, slightly knock-kneed. *Hair:* thin strands of dark-brown hair beginning to turn gray, slightly bald in the center. *Face:* bloated complexion, pale, almost Chinese yellow. Probably duelling scar(s) on left cheek. *Eyes:* dark blue or gray. *Beard:* none. *Voice:* deep. *Glasses:* none. *Marked physical peculiarities:* bull-neck, knock-kneed walk. *Speech:* Hoch-Deutsch. *Foreign Language:* none. *Costume:* when out of uniform normally affected to dark-gray or salt-and-pepper business suit, single-breasted, felt hat with brim turned down.

This warrant for his arrest was published in the newspapers and broadcast on the radio every day for weeks. Yet it was around this period that Bormann, wanted and hunted, undertook the perilous journey to the south across the whole of occupied Germany. It was obvious that he was living in Denmark on borrowed time. More important, he was anxious to join his family in the South Tirol, especially since word had gotten to him that his wife was desperately ill. As long as she would stay in Selva, in the Dolomites, he hoped it would be reasonably safe to visit her.

But while he was plotting the trip, Frau Gerda's condition deteriorated so badly that she had to be moved to a hospital. The Italian doctor who was treating her at the village went down to the beautiful Alpine city of Merano and called on Major J. P. Adlam, of the British Medical Corps, the officer commanding "W" Hospital, which he had opened in what had been Italian Army barracks to house the remaining German sick and wounded in South Tirol. The doctor told Major Adlam that he wished to hand over to the British a woman he had reason to believe was the wife of Martin Bormann. She needed hospitalization, he said, for what he had diagnosed as abdominal cancer.

Major Adlam immediately contacted the general commanding that part of northern Italy (known as the Number Two District) and was gratified to hear him say: "You are to take Schuppler [a German doctor who was the senior surgeon at the hospital] up to Gardenia with an ambulance and seek out Frau Bormann and tell her that the British Army does not make war on women or children.

You are to offer her the opportunity of being admitted to your hospital for the treatment that her own doctor is unable to provide. Make it plain to her that there is no compulsion. It is up to her to accept it or reject it. If she refuses, provide what assistance you can to her own doctor and then leave her be."

A few days later, Major Adlam and Dr. Schuppler made the journey to Selva in the major's beautiful captured black Mercedes sedan, followed by a German military ambulance. Arriving in the secluded village, they sought out the Italian Carabinieri officer and the mayor, and told them what their errand was. The Italians were frightened, and they protested vehemently that there was no "Frau Bormann" living in the town. However, when Dr. Schuppler told the Italians that they had come at the invitation of her own doctor, they relented and showed the two physicians where a "Frau Bergmann" was staying. There they were met by her sister, who asked them to wait while she went upstairs to tell Frau Gerda about the visitors. It was obvious to the doctors that she was very ill. She became almost hysterical when Dr. Schuppler told her in German that they had come to take her to the hospital in Merano.

"You are arresting me," she screamed. "It is a trick. You are putting me in a concentration camp. What will happen to my children?" As she spoke in good English, Major Adlam tried to calm her down. "The British Army does not make war on women and children," he said, repeating the general's words. "I am to tell you that there is no compulsion. I hope you accept the offer in your own interest but you may refuse if you wish."

"My children," she kept repeating, "who is to care for them?"

Major Adlam soothed her by pointing out that if she entered the hospital for treatment, she would be able to come back to look after them when she was better. Her sister then reassured Gerda that she would take care of the children in her absence and begged her to go. Frau Bormann cried with despair for a few minutes, then said: "I will go, I think that it is for the best." Dr. Schuppler went for the ambulance and two strong young ambulance drivers took her down on a stretcher. At the last moment, she asked to be permitted to take along her expensive, beautiful sable coat. Colonel Adlam carried it down, then placed it over her for extra warmth.

"I found her to be an extremely nice woman," Dr. Adlam told me in Bishopstoke, Hampshire, where he is now medical director of the Manor House Nursing Home. "It was difficult for me to understand that Bormann had sent her a number of German war orphans to look after with her own children in the comparative safety of the Dolomites. It seemed so out of character for him. She insisted that she had not heard from her husband in all those months. Had he been in the vicinity he could have paid her a visit in disguise. He could have got past the guards easily. There were few of us British. The Germans were running the hospital themselves. Although there were thousands of prisoners in the area, we had to use them to clear up the many Wehrmacht installations, and they could come and go as they pleased. That applied even to a celebrity like Bormann.

"Nazi officials," he went on, "were hiding in the villages near Merano. I came across a number of them in a large sanatorium, where they were masquerading as patients. Later I heard that they had escaped to Venezuela. Years afterwards, my former German secretary wrote to me from Caracas that she had seen many high-ranking Nazis living there. It would have been simple for Bormann to get away with them."

In the meantime, arrangements had been made with a group of young Austrians working for the Red Cross to smuggle Bormann out of Schleswig-Holstein and take him south with a transport of Austrian prisoners of war who were being repatriated from Allied camps in Germany and France. The deal was made by a woman, a former noncommissioned officer in the women's auxiliary corps of the Wehrmacht, who had become Bormann's steady companion in exile. She gave the men a huge diamond ring and a valuable brooch, and they took her and Bormann (who was wearing a small mustache and dark glasses) through Germany to the Austrian border.

It was already cold in the mountains. The small party, now moving on foot, was getting into snowdrifts often ten feet high. Near the border, their escort deposited them in one of the log cabins Dr. von Hummel had prepared for Bormann in April, and there they were welcomed by a friend of Bormann's, a photographer named Hoppe.

Then a young mountain guide named Hanno Bernhard took over for the last leg of the journey. He escorted them through woods, on snow-covered, icebound trails through the Resia Pass, almost five thousand feet up, at the springhead of the Adige river near the Liechtenstein border, to the gate of one of the monasteries on the Italian side of the South Tyrol. Bernhard stayed long enough to see Bormann ring the bell and an elderly monk open the gate.

Bormann removed a paper from a pocket of his pants into which it had been sewed and handed it to the friar, who took it inside. Returning after a few minutes, he invited the pair in.

By the time Bormann made it down from the mountains to the vicinity of Merano with the help of his new friends the monks, Frau Gerda was in coma with terminal cancer. In his hideout, Bormann was kept informed about her worsening condition, but he never dared to visit her in the hospital, although it was rumored that it would have been quite safe. For a few weeks after her arrival in Merano, plainclothes security men and uniformed sentries were posted all around the hospital in the expectation that Bormann might pay his wife a last visit. But, as the story went, General George S. Patton, Jr., then commanding the Fifteenth U.S. Army in Bad Tölz, heard of the arrangements and called off the guards. "Let the poor woman die in peace," he is supposed to have said. The watch was called off.*

In the hospital, Frau Bormann was "very content," as Major Adlam put it. His German medical staff was extremely competent. But in spite of all their skill and attention, her condition took a turn for the worse in early March of 1946. She died on the twenty-second and was buried in Merano. By then, it seemed, the Catholic Church had taken over the care of Bormann's private affairs. The Reverend Theodor Schmitz, an Army chaplain who was, in fact, a prisoner of war, became the guardian of eight of his children. Father Bruno Klingenmayer and the Rev. Franz Wimmer adopted young Martin Adolf. Then, aided by Archbishop Andreas Rohracher of Salzburg, paved his way to the priesthood at a seminary in Ingolstadt.

After his wife's death, wearing clerical garb and using the name of Luigi Bogliolo, presumably a native of Trieste, Bormann moved to Bolzano, a large city and the capital of the province, where he hoped to submerge more easily. He stayed there for over two years, under his false name, but he behaved rather strangely for a most-wanted war criminal. He could often be seen in town, and was in

* On the basis of my familiarity with General Patton's diary and the records of his Third and Fifteenth Armies in Germany, I am certain that this story (repeated in McGovern's Bormann book) is apocryphal. It was conjured up from secondhand information (at best) by a young man named Alexander Raskin, a Belgian who had been liberated from a Nazi labor camp by the Americans and given a job at the Munich office of the Counter Intelligence Corps. When a report of Frau Bormann's condition became known, Raskin later asserted, a C.I.C. officer supposedly of Patton's staff allegedly told him that "the general feels the woman should be left to die in peace."

fact spotted by several people, including a woman named Frau Thalheimer.

She knew Bormann well from Munich, where he had been a patient of her husband, a physician. One day on the Via Leonardo da Vinci in Bolzano, she ran into Bormann, casually dressed in an open-neck shirt and leather shorts. It was a brief encounter. Bormann, recognizing the woman even as she had recognized him, took to his heels and vanished into a house into which Frau Thalheimer dared not follow.

This was but one of such "accidents." But it convinced Bormann that his stay in Bolzano was dangerous, even though he was safely ensconced behind the walls of a friendly Franciscan monastery. He moved heaven and earth to expedite his departure to Argentina, where that hoard of money and gold was waiting for him.

It took some time and considerable string-pulling to get all he needed. In the end it was only with the help of the Vatican, where the Nazi refugees had a friend in the person of Bishop Alois Hudal, that Bormann could embark on the more exciting and rewarding years of his long exile.

Chapter Ten

"Many Roads Lead to Rome"

". . . the true story of the Church in Germany is not an unrelieved epic of faith and courage; it is to a large extent a sad tale of betrayal, timidity and unbelief. Even amongst those most faithful to the gospel, there were 'none righteous, no not one.'"

—A. C. COCHRANE, in *The Church's Confession Under Hitler*

Colonel Hans Ulrich Rudel flew 2,350 missions against the enemy and was the Luftwaffe's ace of aces in World War II. The young Silesian continued to fly the most hazardous combat missions even after he had lost a leg, and Hitler, whose favorite soldier he was, ordered him grounded to "preserve him as a shining example to the youth of Germany."

Rudel received ample rewards from the grateful regime. Since the Wehrmacht did not have an order high enough to do justice to the exploits of this superhero, Hitler created a decoration especially for him. It took eleven German words (fifteen in English translation) just to describe it—"Golden Oak Wreath with Swords and Diamonds to the Knight's Cross of the Iron Cross."

His closeness to the Führer and his special place under the Nazi sun turned Rudel into more of a zealot than Hitler himself. The politically naïve young man absorbed the clichés of Nazism like a sponge and developed an antipathy, which became a consummate loathing, toward the Roman Catholic Church.

Then shortly after the war, his ingrained antagonism changed into grudging respect and, eventually, grateful admiration. He discovered that the Church, which had fared so badly under the Nazis, was going out of its way to aid its former persecutors. During one of his intermittent escapes from the French P.O.W. hospital in Fürth, on a train trip between Munich and Immenstadt, Rudel shared a coach car with a score of virile-looking young men, all of them clad in what he called "the black uniform" of the Catholic Church. Most of the time they seemed to be engrossed in the reading of the New Testament or were whispering to themselves the Divine Office of the day from their breviaries.

They turned out to be students of a Jesuit seminary en route to a monastery in Austria. They were shepherded by a bony-faced, stern old Jesuit with a large cross hanging from his neck on a silver chain. When the old priest had to leave the car briefly, leaving the young men alone with Rudel, they swarmed around the hero, whom they had recognized, and confided that they were, in fact, Luftwaffe and SS officers. They were going into hiding with the help of the Jesuits to escape capture and incarceration in a prisoner-of-war camp.

This was Rudel's first of many encounters with the rescue work of the Church. He experienced so many more such incidents during the next few years that whenever he had to give hope to the weaker-hearted among his comrades-on-the-run, he reassured them: "You need not despair! There are still many roads that lead to Rome."

Rudel, who was not considered a war criminal and was never a fugitive from justice, did not need the protection of the Church. Whatever persecution he claimed he had to endure existed merely in his imagination. But as soon as he regained his freedom, in April 1946, he plunged into the organization of rescue work for the less fortunate of his comrades. Filled with an insatiable hatred for the victors, his mind poisoned by Nazism, he assembled almost single-handed the most far-reaching and best-financed of the rescue groups, which he called Kameradenwerk.

Much romantic nonsense has been written about a great number of post-Nazi groups going by such names as Lock Gates, The Spider, HIAG, Silent Help, Brotherhood and ODESSA, supposedly aiding Nazi criminals to evade retribution and to sustain themselves in exile. Some of them existed in name only; others were groups of wayward adventurers who operated briefly and spasmodically during the chaotic postwar months, then faded into oblivion, accomplishing little.

Only The Spider attained importance after the war, mainly in South America. Thanks to its access to Martin Bormann's treasure, it had substantial funds, which it first husbanded judiciously by meager disbursements to the needy and then built into enormous assets through wise investments. Publicized as the largest and most insidious of these groups, ODESSA was actually little more than a shadowy consortium of a handful of freelancers and never amounted to much in the Nazi underground.

On the testimony of Colonel Rudel himself, who candidly divulged both the scope and the scale of its activities, the Kameradenwerk was in fact what ODESSA was represented to be. It was financed lavishly from funds that Rudel, an unscrupulous fanatic, "procured" from his many friends among German financiers and industrialists. Eagerly adjusting themselves to the postwar realities of the great German boom, they were apprehensive lest their enormously profitable comeback be jeopardized if a rebuffed Rudel exposed the taint of their Nazi past.

Colonel Rudel is thus singularly important in the amorphous Fourth Reich. He is the man who keeps the Kameradenwerk functioning, aiding the fugitives and, more important, keeping alive the spirit of Nazism. His outspoken book, defiantly called *Trotzdem (In Spite of It)*, is the bible of the diehards, described by its publishers as "a monument for all who did their duty to Germany to the end." An obstinate bigot with some charm and undeniable organizing talent, the fifty-nine-year-old native of Konradwaldau now lives in Austria after years of self-imposed exile in Argentina.*

Yet, in spite of Rudel's undiminished zeal and great administrative ability, not even the Kameradenwerk could have accomplished what it did without the outside help it received from a most unexpected quarter. None of the rescue groups, in fact, had the vast organization and the enormous resources of the one agency that, in the end, took care of more Nazis than all the others combined—the refugee bureau of the Vatican.

* A brief item in the Buenos Aires newspaper *Crónica* revealed that, as far as the Nazis in Argentina were concerned, things had returned to normal, so to speak, with Juan Perón's election to the presidency. On March 1, 1974, Colonel Rudel was also back in Argentina and, accompanied by his old friend and Nazi comrade Kurt Tank, another Peron protégé from way back, was received "in a long audience" by the President. It is frightening to think that nothing has changed in three decades and that the Nazis, well represented by Rudel and his enduring Kameradenwerk, enjoy Peron's protection as much in today's supposedly changed world as they did in the chaotic wake of Hitler's collapse.

Rudel himself is the first to admit this. Twenty-five years after the war, this erstwhile enemy of the Roman Catholic Church said bluntly at his headquarters in Kufstein:

"One may otherwise view Catholicism as he wishes. But what during those years the Church, especially certain towering personalities within the Church, undertook to save the best of our nation, often from certain death, must never be forgotten! And this aid was given not only to members of the faith, nor was it abused to catch the souls of the non-Catholics who benefited from it. It was given completely without ulterior motives, solely for the sake of the men thus saved. In Rome itself, the transit point of the escape routes, tremendously much was done. With its own immense resources, the Church helped very many of us to go overseas. In this manner, in quiet and secrecy, the demented victors' mad craving for revenge and retribution could be effectively countermanded."

Rudel's own Kameradenwerk relied heavily on help from the Church. Some of his most effective undercover agents in Germany were Catholic functionaries, among them a Sister Elisabeth, a nun in Landsberg, the jail where Hitler wrote *Mein Kamp*f and which now was an Allied prison for war criminals awaiting trial. While Rudel himself was managing things from Argentina, the European center of his network was in Rome, where two of his former comrades, Herbert Bauer and Ernst Niermann, and another plucky woman who worked as a secretary in the Vatican represented him at the Church's refugee bureau.

The eager participation of the Church, Rudel remarked, was in sharp contrast to the general posture of the Italian people, who loathed the Nazis and viewed their coddling by the Vatican with grave misgivings. But the Church remained undaunted and persevered in this elaborate rescue work until the last of the refugees was assured of a safe haven, as late as fifteen years after the war.

In an ironic twist, during one of his missions to Paraguay only a few years ago, Colonel Rudel had an opportunity to learn how the world had changed. Posing as the representative of Siemens, the great German electronics concern (which, in fact, was one of his chief financial backers), he was in Asunción with his old swagger, pursuing his "rescue work" where he thought his influence reached to the highest echelons.

At a diplomatic reception given by President General Alfredo Stroessner, reputed to be the best friend the Nazis had in South

America, Rudel was seated beside a vivacious middle-aged man who spoke German fluently with a pronounced Viennese accent. The two engaged in animated conversation, Rudel finding himself captivated by the charm and wit of his fellow guest. "My name is Rudel," he introduced himself. "Are you, sir, the ambassador of Austria?"

"No," the man shot back, smacking his lips. "My name is Benjamin Varon. I am the ambassador of Israel."

Rudel's face darkened, his eyes became fiercer. Then he jumped up and dashed out of the room, obviously unappreciative of the subtle joke of General Stroessner's chief of protocol, who had seated him next to the popular envoy of the people he loathed so atavistically.

The incident went far to show how members of the Fourth Reich like Rudel continue to be steadfast in their cult of Nazism. Toward the Jews he remains unforgiving, but his old hatred of the Roman Catholic Church has been replaced by appreciation and esteem.

Martin Bormann went through a similar metamorphosis, although on much broader lines. He became the highest-ranking survivor of the Nazi hierarchy to benefit from the Vatican's extraordinary help. Even before he himself arrived in Italy, his wife and children had already been cared for by kindly priests, quick and only too willing to forget that the head of the family was the leader of the Nazis' crusade against the Church.

In his only full-scale literary effort (a manuscript that unfortunately has not survived), Bormann described Catholicism as a pernicious and decadent hangover and hailed Nazism as the Great New Church that would endure for much longer than "the Roman edifice of hypocrisy" it was destined to replace. The center of the Party's anti-Catholic campaign was Group III D of Bormann's bureau, its true activities concealed behind its formal designation as "Miscellaneous Matters." In fact, it was the Kirchen-Dezernat (Church Office) of the Party Chancellery. Six of its ten subsections engaged exclusively in the conduct of this campaign. One of them was designed to promote "the expeditious transfer of priests to other professions." Bormann, obsessed with the idea that the Church could be destroyed virtually overnight through the liquidation of the priesthood, decreed that "every clergyman who resigned his office and, preferably, withdrew from the Church," was to be given a government job. In this, as in most of his philosophy, Bormann echoed Hitler, who envisaged the final solution of the Church problem in a scene of the future. "The final state must be," he said in one of his flippant table talks, "in the pulpit, a senile officiant; facing him, a few sinister old women, as *ga-ga* and as poor in spirit as anyone could wish."

Until 1943, the Kirchen-Dezernat was headed by Dr. Ludwig Wemmer, a young Swabian lawyer, one of the talented quasi-intellectual careerists who hired themselves out to the Nazis in their eagerness to climb high in this vast bureaucracy of opportunists. A man of innate charm, Wemmer knew well how to ingratiate himself with Bormann. He became one of his favorites, the Reichsleiter addressing him affectionately as "*Bürscherl*" which meant "my little lad" in the Swabian dialect. Bormann liked Wemmer's efficacious but subtle management of the campaign; it was designed, he concluded, to avoid provoking resentment at home and adverse reaction abroad.

In 1943, a drastic change occurred in Germany's relations with the Vatican. As described by Ambassador Diego von Bergen and Counselor Ernst Menshausen of the mission at the Holy See, there existed a great reservoir of good will in the Vatican toward Nazi Germany, especially since the invasion of the Soviet Union. The fountainhead of this circumspect friendship was Archbishop Constantini, the powerful secretary of the Congregation of the Propagation of the Faith, who, in an outspoken speech, hailed "the brave soldiers" fighting "Satan's deputies" in Russia.

"We wish," the Archbishop said, "with our whole hearts that this battle may bring us the final victory and the fall of Bolshevism, which aims at revolution and negation."

As Menshausen pointed out, such a blunt statement was enormously significant, "because it could not possibly have been made without the consent of the Holy Father." Moreover, the counselor added, "one is assured time and again" that "in his heart . . . Pius XII stands on the side of the Axis Powers." His sympathies were manifested in "demonstrations of the Italian clergy and numerous articles in the Catholic press all over Italy" which Menshausen attributed to directives approved if not actually issued by the Pope himself.

However, the Holy Father held back in his praise and support of Germany because he was disheartened by the rampant anticlerical measures of the Nazis. He, therefore, "preferred to remain silent" —but even so, the ambassador insisted, the Pope's silence was "the best proof that he would like to avoid everything that could injure Germany."

Under this incipient tension, Ambassador von Bergen, an old-line diplomat and devout Catholic, was suddenly recalled at the urging of Heinrich Himmler, who was receiving nothing but derogatory reports about the envoy from his chief representative in Rome. Appointed in his place was Ernst Baron von Weizsäcker, a sixty-one-year-old former naval officer who rose to high rank in the Foreign Ministry as Under-Secretary of State under Joachim von Ribbentrop. The appointment, though a device to get rid of the Baron, was welcomed by Weizsäcker himself. He was yearning for a pleasant job after his hectic five years at the Foreign Ministry, where he had to sanction many an "operation" he found hard to stomach.

Bormann regarded the German diplomatic mission at the Holy See as the pivot on which the Church could be unhinged. At first he was annoyed by the appointment of Weizsäcker, a member of the traditional aristocracy who was "correct" but obviously lukewarm in his attitude toward Nazism and who hardly had any contact with him. But then the appointment gave him an opportunity to exploit the change of envoys for his own ends. He persuaded Hitler to send to the Vatican with Weizsäcker "a reliable National Socialist" to serve directly under the ambassador as his gray eminence. He chose for the job his *Bürscherl.* Replaced by Kurt Krüger at the head of the Kirchen-Dezernat, Dr. Wemmer was sent to the Holy See with the rank of minister.

In the Vatican, the affable, astute Wemmer remained true to his methods, conducting his business with the same sly duplicity that had characterized his regime in Munich. So nimble, in fact, was his strategy that it fooled even some of the shrewdest members of the Vatican Secretariat of State. After the war, they outdid each other in testifying in Wemmer's behalf when his denazification needed such persuasive and respectable character witnesses.

Under Wemmer's influence, Bormann gradually mellowed in his hostility to the Church and changed the orientation of his crusade. As Germany's situation deteriorated, he even envisaged some kind of accommodation between Catholicism and Nazism. He came to regard the Pope as a potential ally, who could be bent to serve the interests of the Nazis either in victory or, even more important, in defeat. It was in this changing atmosphere that Dr. Wemmer moved to the Vatican to act as the manipulator of Bormann's budding new long-range policy of fence-mending.

At about the time of his arrival in the summer of 1943, after repeated bombings of military targets in the Eternal City by the

Twelfth U.S. Air Force, the Italian government proclaimed Rome an open city. Despite this move, Italy was shaken to its foundations by tremendous events. Mussolini had been overthrown on July 25 and was succeeded by Marshal Pietro Badoglio. The Allies had conquered Sicily in July, then moved to the mainland at Salerno on September 9. The day after, the Germans occupied Rome and most of Italy.

Then in January 1944, the Allies landed near Anzio and Nettuno in the rear of the Germans, in what was designed as a leap-frogging move on the march to Rome. But the Germans quickly improvised a new front and frustrated the grand design, delaying the fall of the Eternal City.

In the meantime, now watched by Weizsäcker and Wemmer, the Holy See pursued its old game of equivocation. When the Germans occupied Rome on September 10, 1943, eight thousand Jews were trapped in the city, and Heinrich Himmler ordered SS Obersturmbannführer Hubert Kappler, "the butcher of the Ardeatine Caves," who, as the new SS chief, held the power of life and death in the city, to round them up and deport them to Auschwitz. All eyes were now on the Vatican, even the Germans expecting that the Holy Father would protest this challenge to his humanitarian mission.

The Roman clergy rushed to the aid of the threatened Jews. Religious orders opened their doors to the hunted people, so that on October 18, the day of the roundup, only 1,259 Jews could be caught and sent to Auschwitz. The others escaped into hiding, many of them finding shelter in monasteries and convents.

But the Holy Father remained silent. "The Pope," Ambassador von Weizsäcker reported to Berlin on October 28, "although reportedly beseeched by all sides, has not allowed himself to be drawn into any statement condemning the deportation of the Jews from Rome. Even though he has to take into consideration that this attitude will be held against him by our adversaries and seized upon by Protestant circles in Anglo-Saxon countries for propagandistic purposes against Catholicism, he has also in this delicate matter done everything in order not to burden relations with the German government and German agencies in Rome."

The only expression of disapproval was an ambiguous article in *Osservatore Romano* on October 25, presenting a communiqué about "the benevolent attitude of the Pope," presumably toward the unfortunate Jews. But the communiqué "was so richly embroidered and unclear," as Baron von Weizsäcker phrased it, that "very few people would read into it a special reference to the Jewish question." As far as the possibility of a Papal protest was concerned, Weizsäcker assured Berlin that it could be regarded safely as "liquidated."*

This inertia in the face of savage provocation was "typical," as Leon Poliakov put it in his pioneering study of the Final Solution, "of Pius XII, who never renounced the 1933 concordat with Hitler, and who denounced the National-Socialist system only after the surrender of Germany." Deplorable as the Pope's inaction was, it was made worse by the fact that it was motivated by sheer physical fear. The Vatican within occupied Rome was at the mercy of the Germans. From September 10, 1943, to June 4, 1944, Hitler could have done with the Pope as he pleased. As a matter of fact, only the last-minute intervention of the German ambassador to the Quirinal on a flight to Hitler's headquarters in East Prussia averted the occupation of Vatican City, where the Führer intended to keep the Pope in virtual internment. "For the Pope," Gerhard Reitlinger remarked, "to court such a fate meant sacrificing the advantages of his diplomatic immunity. What the value of that immunity was in terms of human lives is another matter."†

All this was grist for Bormann's mill. Dr. Wemmer kept him posted on these developments in the Vatican, with emphasis on the Pope's attitude. It seemed—to the Nazis at any rate—that Bormann's

* After the war, Father Killion, the Vatican's official observer at the International Refugee Organization, claimed that "His Holiness Pius XII gave asylum within the Vatican City to 3,000 people who were not of his own faith during the occupation of Rome by an enemy power." In actual fact, the number of Jewish refugees hidden in Vatican City was a few dozen. However, thousands—probably even more than the 3,000 mentioned by Father Killion—found refuge in monasteries and convents, and other Catholic institutions.

† "Pius XII," wrote Domenico Cardinal Tardini, the late Pope's former undersecretary of state, in his famous biography of the Pontiff (Vatican City, 1960, p. 59), "was by nature meek and almost timid. He was not born with the temperament of a fighter. In this he was different from his great predecessor." According to a volume of documents published by the Vatican on April 26, 1974, Pope Pius XII "knew already in 1941 of the [Nazis'] drive on [the] Jews," but refrained from doing anything because he "had to be cautious to avoid Nazis reprisals against the church." An unsigned preface to the volume remarks that the Pope, "as was his custom, shunned condemnations and did not denounce anyone by pointing a finger." In December 1942, a Jewish group sent an urgent plea from London beseeching the Pope to intervene to save the Jews in Eastern Europe from annihilation. A note by Monsignor Giovanni Montini attached to the plea recorded an instruction from Pius XII to "give possibly some verbal reply to the senders of this and similar telegrams, 'The Holy See will do what it can.' " But nothing in fact was undertaken by the Pope, and much of the rescue work of the Holy See had to be carried out behind his back.

bizarre notion of a Nazi-Vatican covenant had a solid foundation in the Holy Father's prevarication.

With Wemmer's effective help, but sharing his ideas with nobody else, Bomann pursued his new policy. Outwardly, however, he persisted in his apparently uncompromising hostility to the Church—anything else would have run counter to the Führer's ingrained principles, and Bormann realized he could not afford that.

In February 1944, while the Anglo-American forces were still stalemated on the Anzio beachhead, the Allied high command met at Caserta to plan the drive on Rome. The final details of the push were ironed out on May 1, and D Day for the offensive was set for the eleventh. At 11 P.M. on that day, the drive opened with a tremendous artillery bombardment on the Germans' "Gustav Line," under the cover of which the Fifth U.S. Army jumped off. It was followed by the British 13th Corps, which crossed the Rapido river in force. The fall of Rome—with Vatican City within its boundaries—was now only a matter of weeks if not days.

Bormann as usual anticipated events. He had realized by late April that the Allies' move on Rome was imminent. By then the possibility of cooperation with the Vatican had crystallized in his mind. While Hitler had once toyed with the idea of interning the Holy Father within the walls of a German-occupied Vatican City, Bormann devised a plan that would have brought the Pope into the German camp by his own decision. He decided that the Pope, whose indifference to Kappler's butchery and whose hostility to the Bolsheviks he mistook for pro-German sympathies, must be kept out of the hands of the Allies by moving him to a neutral spot where he could aid the Germans in their growing predicament. He raised the fantastic plan with Dr. Wemmer and instructed him to "persuade" the Holy Father to leave Vatican City ahead of the arrival of the Allies and establish the Holy See in the Principality of Liechtenstein.

Wemmer regarded the idea as insane, but he went through the motions of promoting it. As the plot developed, however, it lost its benign features. Instead of merely coaxing the Pope to Liechtenstein, Wemmer now received orders to force the issue if the Holy Father balked. Arrangements were to be made in ironclad secrecy to abduct him and move him forcibly to the little principality. Once in Vaduz, confronted with accomplished facts, His Holiness would have no choice but to accept Bormann's scheme.

Wemmer did nothing to "persuade" the Pope, and as little as

possible to advance the kidnap plot. But at a critical stage of the conspiracy, control of the operation slipped out of his reluctant hands. In late May, when the drive on Rome bogged down in indecisive fighting around Monte Passignano and on the Pico-Pontecorvo line seventy miles south of the city, Wemmer invited to his home Sturmbannführer Karl Seehofer, Kappler's second in command in Rome, to discuss the plan. He chose Seehofer rather than his boss, because he hoped that he would be able to sabotage the plot with Seehofer's help.

Awed by the responsibility stemming from his mere knowledge of the plot, Seehofer did not dare to keep the secret to himself. No sooner did he leave Wemmer than he called Kappler and told him all he had just heard. Kappler immediately sent a message to Himmler in Berlin, asking for instructions. This was the first that Himmler heard of the plot, so he flashed a top-priority signal to Kappler asking for details. Then a bombshell hit the plot that was supposedly known to only those five men—Bormann, Wemmer, Himmler, Kappler and Seehofer. While the telegrams moved back and forth between Rome and Berlin, the full story of the Nazi scheme to "kidnap the Pope" suddenly appeared in Allied and neutral newspapers.

Wemmer's first reaction to the exposé was relief. He correctly assumed that this would kill the absurd venture. But he was also stunned, as were Kappler and Seehofer. They could not imagine how their secret coud have leaked to the whole world.

By then, however, there was a plot within the plot, the result of one of the great unsung espionage coups of World War II. Obersturmbannführer Kappler got his first clue to the mystery the morning after the publication of the story. One of his aides, an SS officer named Koch (not to be confused with the notorious Pietro Koch, a sadist who was another member of his staff), did not report for work. When they looked for him, he was nowhere to be found. Was he the source of the leak?

It so happened that Koch, a farsighted man already bent on his own salvation, was in touch with MI.6, the British Secret Intelligence Service, and had informed his contact in Rome of Kappler's plot. The intelligence was flashed to London, where Winston Churchill himself decided to stave off the abduction of His Holiness simply by publicizing the plan.

When the stories appeared in the world press, the plot was

hastily abandoned, Wemmer insisting that Seehofer had misunderstood him and blaming Kappler's indiscretion for the embarrassing commotion. Koch defected to the British, taking with him copies of the telegrams that had passed between Rome and Berlin, documenting the stillborn enterprise down to its most minute operational details.

The absurd plot thus ended as a one-day newspaper sensation, producing only a brief period of increased vigilance by the Vatican's Swiss Guards. Wemmer himself had never taken it seriously. If anything, he himself had tried to thwart it by calculated indiscretion. His skillful and polished spadework at the Holy See explains what mystified Bormann's biographers. They could never understand why he accepted the aid of the very Church that he had for so long rejected with such consummate contempt. This in fact was what he actually planned and hoped for as he watched his efforts at rapprochement with the Vatican apparently moving to fruition, thanks to the invaluable work of the brilliant young Wemmer.

However, it does not explain why priests like Father Schmitz and Father Wimmer—even prelates like Archbishop Rohracher and, indeed, the Vatican apparatus on the level of Monsignor Giovanni Montini, then Deputy Secretary of State (and today, of course, Pope Paul VI)—were willing to cooperate with Bormann. It was done on purely humanitarian grounds, as in the case of Frau Gerda's relations with Father Schmitz; in the noble process of saving a soul, as in the case of Father Wimmer, who brought young Martin Adolf into the Church; and in the mystery-shrouded area of high politics, as in the case of Martin Bormann himself.

Bormann was by no means the only high-ranking Nazi among the fugitives who could thank the Vatican for making good their escape and reaching safe haven in South America. Actually, critical though it proved in the spring of 1948, the aid Bormann eventually received from the Church was modest by comparison with the support given others.

Bormann's companion in escape was, as may be recalled, Gestapo chief Heinrich Müller, with whom he shared the Eichmann shelter in the Kurfürstenstrasse until they parted in early May 1945. We have followed Bormann to Italy on his tortuous journey via Schleswig-Holstein and Denmark. Müller, accompanied by his friend Hans Scholz and a member of the Security Service remembered only by his last name of Heiden, went south, then vanished without a trace.

Jochen von Lang, the *Stern* reporter who developed the tale of Bormann's death, informed me at one point in my search that he also knew what had happened to Müller. "He fell into Russian hands," he said firmly, "and died in captivity in the Soviet Union. The Russians are about to announce his death momentarily." As of this writing, the Russians have made no such announcement. When recently questioned in Moscow by Judge von Glasenapp about Müller, the official in charge of the search for war criminals professed to know nothing of his fate.

Jochen von Lang was not the only one to proclaim Müller dead. A tombstone on Grave Number 1 in the first row of Division 6 in the Kreuzberg garrison church cemetery in Berlin (with a fondly tended rosebush) bore silent but eloquent witness to his demise: "In memory of our dear father, Heinrich Müller, born April 28, 1900, died in the Berlin fighting, May 17, 1945." His death was recorded formally by his children in the Berlin Registrar's office on December 5, 1945.

The grave remained undisturbed until September 1963. Then, however, the German authorities, acting on a tip, ordered it dug up to ascertain with bureaucratic finality whether the body buried there was really Müller's. In the grave, the searchers discovered an assortment of bones that turned out to be the remains of three anonymous corpses. Close examination then revealed that none of them was Müller's.

Then only, eighteen years after his disappearance, began the search for the former Gestapo chief. It was conducted haphazardly, with limited means, in the halfhearted manner that characterizes all such German investigations. It produced no results. The second-most-wanted Nazi fugitive was never tracked down—not, that is, until I found him living near Córdoba in northern Argentina, managing the estate of an Italian millionaire, under the pseudonym of Herzog.

Müller never had the popular appeal that Bormann had. During his lifetime, despite his crucial job, he was little known in Germany and virtually unknown abroad. He was not a prominent Nazi —he became a Party member in 1938, and even then only because his high position made membership compulsory.

Born in 1900 (the year also of Bormann's birth), Müller was a hard worker all his life, starting as an aircraft mechanic at the age of fourteen. After a year's military service in World War I (for which he volunteered when he was seventeen), he joined the Munich Police Department in 1919 as a probationary assistant. He advanced slowly until 1934, when he was named an inspector in the criminal division of the Bavarian Political Police.

Although politically he was close to the People's Party and had no affiliation with the Nazis, the talented and industrious young criminologist was taken into the SS in 1934 and transferred to Gestapo headquarters in Berlin. From then on his career was meteoric—Sturmbannführer, Standartenführer, Oberführer and Brigadeführer in rapid succession; then Gruppenführer in 1941. By that time he had been chief of Amt IV, the Gestapo, for two years.

As the head of the Gestapo, Müller was a mixture of competent criminologist, chief inquisitor and lord high executioner—a medieval character grafted onto the twentieth century. More than most—more than Eichmann (who, after all, was only his subordinate), certainly more than Bormann—Heinrich Müller had ample reason to vanish. The master of torture and death himself, he was certain to be executed when caught. He was wanted after the war on two vastly different counts, both by the victors and by the Nazi avengers. The Nazis had him on their own blacklist for treason. He was suspected of having been a Soviet agent since 1944, feeding intelligence to the Russians on a hidden radio.

Müller was no Soviet agent, even as Bormann was none. If there was anything that smacked of disloyalty to Führer and Third Reich, it was his innate defeatism. Müller never took anything for granted—neither victory nor defeat.

As early as 1942 he was assuming the worst. Using the technical apparatus of the Gestapo, he prepared for himself a set of false documents, from birth certificate to driver's license, including a passport. Filled with forebodings in the first dismal winter of the Russian campaign, he prepared this collection of bogus documents. He wanted to be sure that he would be prepared for any eventuality.

He had an eager young junior assistant, Oscar Liedtke, tall, blond, blue-eyed, full of vim and the patriotic spirit. He was Müller's "*Bürscherl,*" assured of a comfortable job in the Gruppenführer's office while other men of his age fought and froze in Russia. One day in early 1942, no longer able to stand the shame of his exemption, he asked Müller to release him, then volunteered for combat service on the eastern front. Only four months after his departure word came that he had died in action in the Battle of Kerch. It was a great personal blow to Müller; it dampened his elation at the resounding victory in which the Germans bagged 284 Red Army tanks, 1,397 guns and nearly 170,000 prisoners.

He had Liedtke's personal papers which the youth had left in his custody. Then an idea flashed through his mind. Oscar was dead. But he could take on his identity. Though the boy was eighteen years his junior, it did not matter. The papers were appropriately retouched. Müller's photograph went into Liedtke's passport and the birth date was changed. He took home the folder with the doctored documents and placed it in his private safe. He had it with him on April 29, 1945, when he was last seen alive, leaving the Führerbunker on his way back to his office on Kurfürstenstrasse, where he now occupied Adolf Eichmann's supershelter.

Müller left Berlin on May 17, going west on the first leg of his escape. Clad in the uniform of an army private and carrying the dead Liedtke's papers, he walked most of the way with his two companions, Heiden and Scholz, in tow. They traveled lightly. Müller, in fact, carried only a small suitcase, but it was filled with American dollar bills. Their first mishap occurred on the third day. Heiden was arrested at a British checkpoint near Kassel. But Müller and Scholz were passed on. It then took them two weeks to reach Munich, the first stop on their original itinerary.

Three days later they crossed into Austria near Mittenwald, the last village on the Bavarian side of the border, passing Kaltenbrunn, a hamlet that gave its name to his colleague Ernst Kaltenbrunner, who headed the Main Security Office (of which his Gestapo was part) and was destined to die on the gallows in Nuremberg a little over a year later. Passing through the beautiful Alpine highland dotted with groups of maples and beeches, Müller and Scholz headed for a safe house on Fallmerayerstrasse in Innsbruck on the Austrian side of the border, where another officer of the defunct Security Service, a man named Walter Brunner, was awaiting them.

They were still on their own, making their way furtively, avoiding Allied control stations, helped only by Brunner, who operated a one-man rescue service aiding Gestapo men to escape. He sneaked them through villages off the beaten path, hid them on secluded farms, and then hired for them a young mountain guide for the most difficult stage of the long journey, the crossing into Italy. The guide was to take them over the Brenner Pass to Albergo Lupo, an inn on the Italian side of the border. It was run by a German agent as a stop for refugees in transit.

By then the forty-five-year-old sedentary Müller, who walked with a limp and was suffering from fatigue, could take it no longer. The approach to the Brenner proved too much for him, and Müller had to return to Innsbruck. As a last resort, Brunner called on the "Phantom of the Mountain" for help. He was Rudolf Blass, who had earned his nickname by being the ace among Austria's mountain guides.

Blass chose the route on which Hanno Bernhard would guide Martin Bormann across the border a few months later. Moving from Nauders, the village which also became Bormann's last stop in Austria, through the Resia Pass, Müller reached Merano without a further hitch. There he was taken over by a man named Wolf, representing his friend Friedrich Schwend, the supersalesman of the bogus pound sterling bills which the Gestapo counterfeited wholesale during the war.

From there on, Müller traveled in style, no longer left to his own resources. Wolf drove him to Rome in Schwend's Mercedes and deposited him at Collegio Croatto on Piazza Colonna, a seminary of Yugoslav priests who were adherents of Ante Pavelic, the deposed Nazi dictator of Croatia. After a few days at the Collegio, Father Mihailovic, superior of the seminary, took the former Gestapo chief to Grottaferrata to see the Titular Bishop of Aela, rector of the German Istituto Santa Maria dell'Anima, and one of the closest friends of Pope Pius XII, whose Adjutant at the Throne he was. Contact was thus made with the Vatican rescue mission, which, in the person of Bishop Alois Hudal, assumed responsibility for Heinrich Müller's welfare from then on.

Today Bishop Hudal lies buried in Rome's Campo Santo Teutonico cemetery, his grave never bereft of flowers. But in 1945, he was the chief impresario of the Vatican's rescue efforts aiding these fugitives. By the time of Müller's visit, in the summer of 1945, the mission had already handled hundreds of them who had made it to Rome, including Hans Ulrich Rudel. He had arrived shortly before Müller, and was already "processed" for the trip to Argentina.

Others, even as Müller himself, had to be sheltered pending the completion of the arrangements for their departure. No questions were asked, no credentials had to be presented. Any name given was accepted. All a man needed was to ask, and help was given promptly and generously. This proved a complex and delicate task involving calculated risks. The Allied dragnet was out. Search parties of the security forces were combing Rome, picking up a fugitive Nazi here, a Fascist in hiding there, the Anglo-American teams working from lists of suspects with thousands of names on them.

But the names on the list were the *real* names of the fugitives, who had long discarded them and had even changed the aliases under which they had set out on their stealthy journeys. Müller, for example, started on his trip using Liedtke's papers. Now that he was pinned down in Rome pending his transfer to South America, he thought it safer to change his identity again. He was given papers made out to a Pole named Jan Belinski, born in Lodz on March 20, 1902. His companion, Scholz, had become a Yugoslav named Dusko Stepanovic. The refugees' counterfeit identification cards were supplied by Bishop Hudal's organization, which also arranged for a series of hideouts whenever a fugitive had to move to escape arrest.

Bishop Alois Hudal is the mystery man of the great conspiracy that aided as many as 50,000 Nazis, if not more, to make the transition into a new life after the war. He is mentioned only in passing even in the best books about the aftermath. Michael Bar-Zohar described him as a "German Archbishop" (although he was neither a German nor an *arch*bishop) and characterized him as "a loyal friend to the Nazis." According to Simon Wiesenthal, he was a Slovenian by birth, close to Archbishop Stepinac of Croatia, the notorious Nazi prelate of Zagreb who himself was a refugee. Hudal was always mentioned only in passing and in tantalizingly brief references. Presented like a ghost hovering over this enormous enterprise, he was called variously "an angel of mercy" and "the Nazis' Scarlet Pimpernel."

No report on the aftermath can afford to ignore this controversial prelate. With industry and energy belying his sixty years, and with a zeal that never ceased to amaze the desperate men he helped, he masterminded the escape of thousands of war criminals and thus laid the foundations for a Fourth Reich. This is the first full attempt at bringing into sharp focus the enigmatic, ascetic, brilliant bishop who understood only too well how to remain the most shadowy figure in this republic of wandering shadows.

Chapter Eleven

Bishop Hudal's Underground Railroad

On October 16, 1943, the Most Reverend Alois Hudal, "senior German-speaking bishop abroad," sent a letter to Major General Rainer Stahel of the Luftwaffe, who had been, since September 10, the town commandant of Rome. He had just been informed, Hudal wrote, "by a high Vatican source in the immediate circle of the Holy Father" that, on orders from Berlin, arrangements were being completed to "begin the arrest of Jews of Italian nationality." He appealed to General Stahel—whose "political insight and greatness of heart" he hailed as certain to "go down in the history of Rome"—to order "the immediate cessation of these arrests."

This was the same prelate who, only twenty-one months later, received Heinrich Müller in his chamber at the palatial seat of the Istituto Santa Maria dell'Anima and discussed with the former Gestapo chief the urgent problems of asylum for Nazi criminals flocking into Rome.

It would be pleasant to say that what impelled Bishop Hudal to aid the Nazis in 1945 was the same overriding good will toward all men that animated him in his effort to save the Jews of Rome in 1943. Unfortunately, his motivations in the two cases were quite different. Hudal was no friend of the Jews. He was a friend of the Nazis. It was his known sympathy with and closeness to the German authorities in Rome that had induced "the high Vatican source" —actually the Reverend Robert Leiber, a dedicated anti-Nazi German Jesuit who was the Pope's principal personal aide and confidant —to enlist Hudal's aid. He agreed to intervene with the presumably more reasonable military authorities in Rome, not as a generous humanitarian mission, but as a measure which he regarded as politic. In his letter to Stahel, Hudal pointed out that he undertook the plea "in the interest of the good relations which have existed until now between the Vatican and the German high command"; and because he "feared" that "otherwise the Pope [will] have to make an open stand which will serve the anti-German propaganda as a weapon against us."

Things did not work out as Hudal was led to expect. General Stahel not only failed to heed his plea, but also made three companies of his own military police units available to the SS authorities in Rome to round up the Jews. Although, as Ambassador von Weizsäcker reported to Berlin, "the College of Cardinals was shocked in particular because the event had taken place practically under the windows of the Pope," the Pontiff did not make "an open stand." Bishop Hudal on his part undertook nothing more for the hapless Jews. He was rather relieved that his fear proved unfounded—the Vatican's relations with Germany did not suffer, certainly not on the level of the Holy Father, as a result of the anti-Jewish measures. The Pope remained silent even when, on March 24, 1944, Obersturmbannführer Hubert Kappler ordered the shooting of 335 Italian hostages in the Ardeatine Caves, among them 57 Jews thrown in at random. By then, Hudal found no need either to plead or to protest.

While Father Leiber and other German priests in Rome—among them Monsignor Johannes Schönhöffer, of Propaganda Fides, Rector Ivo Zeiger, of the Collegium Germanicum, and Father Augustin Maier, a professor at the Benedictine University of San Anselmo—intensified their anti-Nazi activities at the Vatican at great peril to themselves, Bishop Hudal became the spiritual director of a band of pro-Nazi clerics in Rome. He aligned himself with Giovanni Prezioso, a rabidly anti-Semitic former priest who edited *La Vita Italiana,* a Jew-baiting newspaper patterned on *Der Stürmer,* and was "in touch" with a mystery-shrouded Benedictine monk, Prior Hermann Keller, who showed up in Rome from time to time to spy on the Vatican for the SD (the Sicherheitsdienst), the Nazi secret intelligence service, whose paid undercover agent he was throughout the war.

Heinrich Müller's audience with Hudal yielded substantial dividends, both for the former Gestapo chief personally and for other Nazis of his ilk who followed him to Rome. Since the Yugoslav monks who sheltered him were already overcrowded with fugitive Nazis from Croatia, they asked Müller to move. Bishop Hudal found quarters for him, first at the Teutonicum, a monastery within the walls of Vatican City, and then at the Anima on Via da Tolentino.

Müller stayed there only until the end of the year. Aside from Bormann, who had made it to northern Italy, he was the highest-ranking Nazi criminal hidden in Rome. It was feared that his presence, if it became known, might fatally jeopardize the rescue work. With a refugee passport of the International Red Cross, he boarded an Argentine ship in Naples, presumably going only as far as Barcelona in Spain. Then, traveling in stages the stops of which remain shrouded in secrecy, he finally reached South America in 1950, using a Vatican refugee passport and wearing clerical garb.

With the help of his friend Freddy Schwend, he settled in Peru and went into the insurance business, working for an unsuspecting Swiss named Hans Rosa. We will meet him again, a chastised, frightened man, moving frantically to Bolivia during the panic among the fugitives after the abduction of Adolf Eichmann in 1960.

As Müller left Rome, others arrived. By then, the brisk traffic of these wandering Nazis moved smoothly on a vast and well-financed underground railroad that Bishop Hudal had built behind the staid façade of the Anima.

Who was this odd cleric who fancied himself an incarnation of Thomas Aquinas, the sainted Dominican, whose rational approach to theology he sought to emulate? What made him engage in his freakish philanthropy, which he regarded as faithful service to the Church?

It was a warped interpretation of Thomist doctrines that brought Hudal into the Nazi orbit. It had nothing in common with the neo-Thomism of Jacques Maritain and Étienne Gilson, although Hudal also strove to apply the principles of Saint Thomas Aquinas to modern economic, social and political problems. Even as his great idol reconciled Aristotelian philosophy and Christian belief, Hudal hoped to bring to terms Christian principles and Nazi ideology for a purely utilitarian political purpose. Hudal expected to forge the accommodation as a powerful weapon in the Church's struggle with "godless Marxism." He began the difficult mission on May 1, 1933, by "explaining" Nazism and trying to make it palatable to the Church. He ended it after the war by "helping Martin Bormann, Adolf Eichmann, Gauleiter Reiner of Steyr, and many more high Nazi functionaries to escape retribution for their criminal acts."

Because of his intense pan-German commitment, it is believed that Alois Hudal was born somewhere in southern Germany. The Styrian province of Austria also claims him as a native son. We know only the date of his birth—May 31, 1885—but not the place. When he first came into focus, he had already been ordained (in 1908) and had been graduated from the University of Graz, in Austria, with doctorates in theology and philosophy. At the age of thirty-four he was professor of Old Testament and Oriental languages at his alma mater.

Restive by nature and a compulsive doer, the diminutive priest branched out in different directions within the huge framework of the Church, becoming Procurator General of the Order of German Knights and member of the Consistorial Councils of several dioceses. In 1923, he was called to Rome to become coadjutant of the Istituto Santa Maria dell'Anima, a German-endowed higher institution dedicated to the indoctrination of a new generation of priests.

His long friendship with Eugenio Pacelli began in 1924, when the future Pope Pius XII, then the Papal Nuncio in Germany, recommended Hudal for the rectorate, the office he held for twenty-eight years, until his retirement in 1952. Hudal drew from his great friend's unrelenting opposition to "atheistic Communism" the inspiration for his own mission; and he was stimulated in his work by Pacelli's predilection for and skill in secret diplomacy. It was, in turn, the Cardinal, when he was back in Rome as Secretary of State, who obtained for Hudal the titular bishopric of Aela and personally officiated at his consecration.

Bishop Hudal was a prolific author, his many books reflecting the diversity of his interests and didactic mind. His *Introduction to the Old Testament* is still used as basic text in many Catholic institutions of higher learning. *Missa papalis,* another of his major works, is widely regarded as one of the most profound studies of the liturgy of the papal Mass.

His obituary, which appeared in the Catholic press on May 14, 1963, the morning after his death in the Roman clinic Villa Stuart from cancer of the liver, presented him as a prodigious scholar, an activist of enormous faith and diligence, a humanitarian and self-effacing innovator whose influence was strongly felt at Vatican II. Nowhere mentioned was the fact that, unknown as he was in wider circles because his vow of anonymity best suited his goals and methods, he was probably the most controversial prelate of the modern Church for his two-pronged excursion into temporal matters. He chose to lead, deep under cover, the Church's most determined and ambitious campaign against Marxism, called "Action Hudal." What made him such a disputatious figure, however, was his apostatic espousal of Nazism, whose mythology and postulates he accepted as compatible with Catholic doctrine and ideology.

Hudal was drawn to Nazism by two magnetic attractions. He recognized in the Nazis formidable allies in the fight against Marxism; and, as a devout pan-Germanist, he regarded Hitler as a latter-day Charlemagne, the guarantor of a modern replica of the Holy Roman Empire.

The scope of "Action Hudal" (the name Adolf Hitler coined for the bishop's work) was enormous and complex, and it was a miracle that a single man could cope with its conflicting theories and realities. Aside from its being one of the motivating factors in Hudal's Nazi orientation, its review is beyond the scope of this book. However, his bold rapprochement with the Nazis is relevant to the understanding of his postwar rescue work—which, rightly or wrongly, is equated with the Vatican's generous aid to the Nazi fugitives. Other forces too were at work in the Holy See in creating this unholy alliance. But none was more important and effective than the frail bishop's decisive contribution to the rescue effort as more and more fugitives were helped to exchange their brown shirts for black cassocks.

Dr. Hudal's baptism of fire in his covenant with Nazism took place on May 1, 1933, only three months after Hitler's ascent to power. In celebration of May Day on the pagan Nazi pattern he opened the auditorium of the Anima and played host to seven hundred invited members of the German colony in Rome. In the audience were not only the Bishop of Aachen and the German ambassadors to the Vatican and the Quirinal, but also the top-ranking Nazis of Rome—leaders of the Party, the SA and the Hitler Youth.

"In this fateful hour," Hudal told them in his welcoming speech, "we German Catholics abroad greet the New German Reich, founded on loyalty to Christ and Fatherland. . . . The glorious past of the German nation is resuscitated. The more the un-German elements, which in the days of turmoil dishonored our soldiers and disgraced all that was great and sacred in our military system, vanish from public life, the mightier will be our national spirit, the exalted sense of German unity in language and culture. We set ourselves up against misunderstood pacifism, whose slogans seek to shackle us forever and which forge demeaning peace treaties, determined to regain for the youth of Germany the right to bear arms as the highest value of masculine virtue."

He concluded his impassioned speech with the cry of Arminius at the Teutoburg Forest: "German unity is my strength, my strength is German might."

Hudal then spent the next two years in formulating the bible of this rapprochement, and published it on July 11, 1936, a date he described as "the day of reconciliation between Germany and Austria."

"This book," the dedication read, "written with the blood of my heart, is consecrated to the inner peace of our German people." Its purpose was spelled out in the introduction. "The present volume," he wrote, "is an attempt at erecting a path to the appreciation of National Socialism from the Christian point of view."

In his 239-page book, called *The Foundations of National Socialism*, Bishop Hudal adopted all the eccentricities and aberrations of Nazi mythology, espousing its racist theories and, in Chapter III, endorsing its devastating negation of the Jews. Aside from his public appearance in 1933 and the publication of his extraordinary manifesto in 1936, Hudal preferred to remain in the background, using elaborate cloak-and-dagger methods in promoting his aims assiduously.

As long as Luigi Cardinal Maglione was Secretary of State, Bishop Hudal's political link with the Vatican was the Holy Father himself. How far Pope Pius XII shared his approval of Nazism is an open question. Dr. Riccardo Galeazzi-Lisi, the Pontiff's physician, asserted that in a conversation with him the Holy Father described Nazism as "far more dangerous" than Communism. However Father Leiber, the wise Jesuit who was the Pope's closest confidant, disputed the doctor's claim.

"If Pius XII," Leiber wrote, "ever spoke at all to his physician about the two systems, the doctor woefully misunderstood him. Despite the grave conflicts with National Socialism, Cardinal Pacelli never doubted that Communism represented the far more fatal danger. Many witnesses are alive who could testify to this." After the Allied occupation of Rome in June 1944, Father Leiber added, when high-ranking British and American officers and statesmen called on the Pontiff, the Holy Father never missed an opportunity to warn them: "To be sure, Hitler and National Socialism are what they are. But they offer themselves as a passing phenomenon, soon to be over. You must never overlook that we have ahead of us the immensely more difficult and perilous task of the showdown with Communism."

This, indeed, was Hudal's entrée to the highest echelon of the Holy See. After Cardinal Maglione's death in 1944, he was no longer dependent on the infrequent and, by necessity, tenuous contact with the Pope himself. Hudal then acquired a friend in the Secretariat of State, which Pius XII split between two prosecretaries—Monsignor Domenico Tardini, a brilliant administrator but, as Bruno Wüstenberg shrewdly described him, "a sheltered Roman ignorant of the ways of the world," and the much younger and more sophisticated Monsignor Giovanni Battista Montini, who shared the Pope's diplomatic talent and aversion to Communism.

In this order of things, Monsignor Montini headed Section II of the Secretariat, in charge of the day-to-day conduct of the Holy See's international affairs. More important in this context, Montini had under his supervision the Vatican bureau that issued the refugee travel documents and the Caritas Internationalis, the Church's international welfare organization, which was at this time (and for some years after the war) one of the main charitable institutions aiding the fugitive Nazis.*

In the immediate wake of the war, the passport office and Caritas blossomed out as the busiest offices in the Vatican bureaucracy. They were used, if not abused, by Bishop Hudal in his effort to aid the Nazi fugitives. Hudal himself characterized his work as the natural obligation of the priest to help those in need, regardless of their origin and creed, their background and political past. He rejected the charge that he was motivated by his Nazi sympathies. Although his pro-Nazi orientation is indisputable, this, in the final analysis, was not the entire reason for the aid he gave even to murderers like Heinrich Müller and, as we shall see, Obersturmbannführer Walter Rauff, former general manager of the gassing vans.

* Caritas Internationalis is not officially an agency of the Curia. Even today it is not listed in the *Annuario Pontifico,* the official register of the Holy See. In reality, as Hieronymus points out, it *is* an organ of the Curia subject to the direct supervision of the Secretariat of State. Even in 1949, branches of the Caritas were aiding Nazi fugitives in their escape to Argentina, as Dr. Hans Hefelmann, one of the accused at the Euthanasia Trial, testified in Limburg in 1964, when he described in detail how the Vienna branch of the organization supplied both the travel documents and the money he needed to make it to Argentina.

Hudal's lavish charity stemmed from his basic preoccupation with his clandestine anti-Communist crusade. The bishop had come to reconcile himself to the destruction of Hitler, made inevitable, as he saw it, by the Führer's unbridled lust for power and aggrandizement. As a matter of fact, Hudal wrote off Hitler when he concluded that, in his war with the *Abendländer* (England, France and eventually the United States), the Führer had gone too far.

At the same time, he considered the total destruction of Nazism a catastrophe, for it would shatter the most dependable and effective bulwark against Communism. He was not bent on saving the Nazi regime, nor was he attempting to perpetuate the system in a neo-Nazi structure in exile. He was determined, however, to save as much of it as was possible and advisable, broken and scattered as it would be, to continue the fight, henceforth throughout the world, with the rescued Nazis taking up positions in the front line of the struggle.

Bishop Hudal thus moved with all his prodigious energy and ingenuity to aid the individual Nazis. In the process, the supply of false identities became a primary and urgent concern. Various organizations, including the International Red Cross and established refugee agencies, chipped in, providing travel documents to applicants who registered under false names and whose vital statistics were accepted without any proof asked. There was recourse to the nearly ten thousand blank Argentine passports and identity certificates Colonel Perón had put into Nazi hands even before the collapse. Also available, by the hundreds, were fake credentials and forgeries from the collection of the German secret-service combine, the Gestapo, the SD and the Abwehr.

Most important and most easily accessible to Hudal and his aides was the Holy See as an authentication center. As a rule, the Vatican had two kinds of travel documents. Under the Lateran Treaty of 1929, a bureau of Monsignor Montini's section of the Secretariat of State issued *regular* passports to the approximately one thousand citizens of the sovereign state of Vatican City and, for that matter, to any priest, of whatever nationality, who traveled on the business of the Curia Romana. Also under Monsignor Montini, the Refugee Bureau (which was a truly catholic charitable organization in that it cared for all sorts of "runaways" marooned in Rome, without regard for their nationality or creed) issued "identity certificates." They were patterned after the so-called Nansen passes named for Dr. Fridtjof Nansen, the great Norwegian explorer and humanitarian, who was instrumental in the establishment of a High Commission of Refugees by the League of Nations in 1921 and functioned as its director until his death in 1930.

Now in 1945, on Bishop Hudal's intervention, with the Pope's explicit permission, Monsignor Montini authorized a radical change in the routine of both offices. A limited number of regular Vatican passports was given to a handful of "important" Nazis who took on clerical guise to become eligible for these most coveted of travel documents. It is a matter of record that thirteen of the top Nazis—among them Martin Bormann—reached South America disguised as Catholic priests on *regular* Vatican passports made out to Spanish-sounding aliases chosen for them. Such a passport was found among the impounded papers of Friedrich Schwend in Lima. He kept it as a souvenir, together with an assortment of other bogus documents he used on his later travels.

The Refugee Bureau issued "identity certificates" to "stateless and displaced persons," actually by the hundreds week after week, to Nazi fugitives from all over Europe who managed to reach one or another of the Catholic sanctuaries. The certificates carried limited authority; their acceptance was optional. But in this case, between 1945 and 1950, they were invariably good for at least two countries—Syria and Argentina. Their authorities regarded the Vatican's "identity certificates" as proof that their bearers were what may be called bona fide Nazi refugees seeking what these countries regarded as political asylum.

It seems that the Vatican authorities of today are uneasy about their predecessors' indiscriminate generosity, which benefited even people with prior guilt of the murder of thousands. They are, moreover, embarrassed by the fact that the Monsignor Montini, under whose authority this wholesale aid was given, is the Pope today. I felt their acute predicament keenly when I visited the Vatican in the summer of 1972 to clear up this matter and found very little cooperation at the Secretariat of State. Monsignor Sebastiani, speaking for His Eminence Jean Cardinal Villot, the Secretary of State, stated emphatically that whatever happened "under those difficult circumstances," it was a matter of "Christian love of fellow men which made it incumbent upon the giver of charity to impute good motives when possible."

Monsignor Sebastiani cited the New Testament—1 Corinthians

13:4—with a shrug and a sigh. "Charity suffereth long," he said, "and is kind." Professor Federico Alessandrini, a layman, who is the official spokesman of the Holy See,* confirmed that thousands of identity certificates had been issued "to help the helpless" in the immediate wake of the war. He acknowledged that "some of the people who received them might have been Nazi fugitives." He even went so far as to concede that "probably Martin Bormann was one of the beneficiaries." Did not Peter say that charity shall cover the multitude of sins? At the same time, Auxiliary Bishop Johann Neuhäusler of Munich conceded that Catholic refugee organizations (not further identified) had been instrumental in helping the escape of Bormann, but denied that he had been given any financial aid—which, the bishop said, he could well do without.

Next to authentication (which, thanks to Bishop Hudal's intervention, presented only a temporary problem at the outset), the funding of the operation was of more lasting concern. A substantial sum of money was needed to take care of the refugees in Italy and then to start them off on a new life in the countries for which they were heading. According to Bernardino Nogano, head of the Vatican Treasury, the Holy See's contribution from its own exchequer was negligible, as was that of the other Catholic welfare organizations. It was, in fact, one of the sources of Bishop Hudal's strength that he had "independent means" with which to finance the underground railroad.

So tight was the management of his funds and so closely held was the secret of their origin that it proved most difficult to obtain even telltale clues to their sources and disbursements. In the spring of 1963, the curtain was somewhat lifted when the Italian authorities in Milan detained a prosperous international dealer in steel on a tip from Vienna that he might be a wanted Nazi criminal. The man turned out to be Dr. Erich Rajakowitsch, alias Erico Raja, originally a lawyer in Bishop Hudal's home town of Graz, and the son-in-law of Dr. Anton Rintelen, Governor of Styria and Austrian

* One of the best-known Catholic journalists in Italy, Alessandrini was deputy editor-in-chief of *Osservatore Romano* before summoned to the Vatican to take over the press office (founded in 1966) from its first head, Monsignor Fausto Vallainc, a diminutive, rather flexible native of the Aosta Valley. It is a delicate and largely ephemeral job, frustrating both to its holder and to the people he is supposed to serve. "In spite of their best intentions," wrote Hieronymus, "and their understanding of the needs of news-hungry journalists neither Vallainc nor Alessandrini could be truly effective as spokesmen. They functioned as best they could with patience and humility, for which Vallainc was rewarded with a bishopric."

ambassador to Italy, known as "King Anton" for his dominant role in reactionary Austrian politics.

During the war, SS Hauptsturmführer Rajakowitsch represented Adolf Eichmann's Section IV B-4 (the executive organ of the "Final Solution") at the headquarters of Brigadeführer Wilhelm Harster in Holland. He was personally responsible for the deportation of over 100,000 Dutch Jews, most of whom perished in various extermination camps.

In 1945, he escaped to Italy with his family, also taking along his wife's lover, another Eichmann liaison officer charged with the murder of thousands of Jews in Yugoslavia. Rajakowitsch found his way to Bishop Hudal in Rome, who put up the family (including the boyfriend) in one of the hospitable monasteries, then arranged their trip to Argentina. Rajakowitsch remained there unmolested until 1955,* when the fall of President Perón uprooted the Nazis and caused many of them to move again. He adopted the name Erico Raja and, using an Italian passport bought in the black market, returned to Italy, going first to Trieste, then settling in Milan. There he went into business on such a large scale that, by 1963, his private fortune was estimated at four million dollars (much of it in transactions with Iron Curtain countries). He owned several apartment buildings and villas, in Italy and Switzerland, a "dream house," as it was called, on Lake Lugano in Switzerland, and a 3,000-acre estate in Mexico.

But when the Italians caught up with him, the investigation of his affairs produced an interesting aside. "It appears impossible," the Italians surmised in their final report of the case when Rajakowitsch was expelled, "that the accused could have amassed his enormous fortune by his overt business activities." It was suggested that his business was merely a cover and "his arrest probably yielded up one of the secret custodians of the missing SS treasure."

Trying to escape retribution in Austria, Rajakowitsch fled, first to Switzerland, then to Germany. But he was promptly expelled from both countries, and had no place to go but Vienna, where he claimed he had been promised immunity if he surrendered voluntarily. Nevertheless, he was arrested on arrival. During the trial his association with Eichmann and his part in the Final Solution were

* Rajakowitsch's "sojourn" in Argentina became known during the interrogation of Eichmann in Jerusalem, and through independent sources Wiesenthal had in Buenos Aires and Milan.

attested by a key witness from Holland, Aron Sijes, a research fellow at the official Dutch Institute for the Documentation of World War II. Given a scandalously light sentence, two and a half years, Rajakowitsch was at large again in 1966, free to sue Simon Wiesenthal for slander, a Spanish magazine for libel (losing both lawsuits), and to publish a handsomely produced book in an attempt to vindicate himself with a gross distortion of the facts.

At the time of his arrest in Vienna on April 17, 1963, a well-informed Austrian newspaper of Graz wrote about the wider ramifications of the Rajakowitsch case:

> After the collapse of the Third Reich, [Bishop] Hudal played a prominent role in organizing the escape of Nazi leaders overseas, mainly to Argentina. Hudal thus aided the flight of Eichmann, of Martin Bormann, Hitler's deputy . . . and of Rajakowitsch.
>
> Dr. Rajakowitsch was one of the persons who had the power of attorney for the disposition of the enormous funds in money and valuables, on deposit in secret accounts with Swiss banks for Nazi leaders. It was capital gained from the so-called immigration tax (*Reichfluchtssteuer*) which every Jew who left Germany and Austria had to pay, as well as sums which accrued from the ransom paid to the SS to obtain the release of certain individual Jews.

The Italians, and subsequently the Austrians, thus revived one of the most intriguing mysteries of the aftermath—the disappearance of the tremendous hoard of valuables the Nazis' Main Security Office had on deposit in the Reichsbank. Although the so-called "SS treasure" is often dismissed as nothing but a myth, it is by no means the product of imagination. There *was* an SS treasure. And it *is* missing.

Valuables worth hundreds of millions of Reichsmark were taken from the victims, mostly Jews. The loot was sent to Obergruppenführer Oswald Pohl, a former petty officer of the Navy who became economic tsar of the Main Security Office. He later testified (with pedantic thoroughness, to the last penny) that his office in Berlin had received the following "shipments" from only two of the concentration camps, those at Auschwitz and Lublin:

Gold and foreign currencies valued at	RM	178,745,960.59
German currency amounting to	RM	4,500,000.00
Diamonds and jewelry valued at	RM	43,000,000.00
Precious metals valued at	RM	9,000,000.00

The method of collecting the gold, for instance, was described by Obersturmbannführer Rudolf Höss, commandant of the Auschwitz camp: "After a few [of the early] transports, Eichmann brought an order from Reichsführer Himmler, instructing us to remove the gold teeth from the corpses, and to cut off the long hair of the women who had been gassed . . . Gold teeth were melted down into bars. Later a special workshop, employing forty prisoners, was set up in Crematorium III to melt down the gold."

According to Höss, the *daily* yield was 24 pounds of gold (or, as it measured, 385.5 troy ounces). What was not stolen at the camps was sent to the Reichsbank, where Senior Vice-President Emil Johann Rudolf Puhl and a clerk named Albert Thoms had custody of the loot.

In another part of his testimony Höss stated: "There was [at Auschwitz] a special division for valuables which were handled by experts. The same applied to money. Valuables came mainly from Western Jews who owned precious stones worth millions, valuable watches of gold and platinum crusted with diamonds, diamond rings, coral chains and necklaces. There was money from every country in the world—worth millions. Often we found hundreds of thousands on a person, usually in thousand-dollar bills.

"When the sorting was completed after each bigger [search] action, the valuables such as money were put into suitcases, loaded on trucks and sent to the SS Economic Administration which was headed by Obergruppenführer Pohl. From there they went to the German Reichsbank, which had a special department storing the valuables taken from the Jews."

When the end came, the accumulated treasure was gone. Neither Puhl nor Thoms could account for it or give a satisfactory explanation for its disappearance. After the war, on the assumption that it had been buried under the rocks of the Alpine redoubt, a treasure hunt reminiscent of the gold rush of Klondike days was unleashed, both the Allied authorities and private entrepreneurs going all out to find the "SS treasure."

Mountains and lakes of the rugged region were thoroughly searched. One lake yielded a number of crates containing millions of the counterfeit bills the Nazis printed during the war. Divers then brought up more crates from another lake, filled with the secret documents of the Security Service. But the treasure that had vanished from the Reichsbank vaults was nowhere to be found. There was but one spot, Lake Töplitz in Austria, that remained untouched. Although certain signs indicated that it might conceal a part of the treasure, the Austrian government, for reasons never satisfactorily explained, placed it out of bounds for treasure hunters and declared that "it would not be in the public interest" to undertake an official search by the authorities.

The Italians, Germans and Austrians suspected that Rajakowitsch had in his custody a portion of this missing treasure. They assumed that he had used some of it in his own business ventures and, probably as the trustee of an invisible Nazi syndicate, invested some of it in the real estate to which he held title. But what happened to the bulk of the treasure he supposedly handled? Was he not a protégé of Bishop Hudal, who was, moreover, a close friend of Dr. Rintelen, Rajakowitsch's father-in-law? The authorities conjectured that most of the funds had been made available to the bishop to finance the underground railroad.

In early 1963, Bishop Hudal was linked to the missing treasure in a long, well-informed article that appeared in a Graz newspaper. The publication of the report then prompted one of the Austrian investigators to write: "The suspicion long held by the authorities is now raised publicly for the first time. Valuables of gruesome origin, and worth millions, have vanished without a trace. Other millions of mysterious origin showed up in the possession of former leaders of the Nazi Party and the SS. Even more bloodstained money is now said to have been spent on an obscure rescue mission of which a high Vatican official was reputed to be the leader.

"Where is the blood-soaked treasure of the SS? Unless Bishop Hudal is willing to shed light on the sources of his funds, it will not be possible in the future to suppress the suspicion that the SS treasure, or a substantial part of it, had wound up in his hands and had been used by him in aiding the escape and rehabilitation of the [Nazi] fugitives."

Attempts to question Hudal about his relations with Dr. Rajakowitsch proved impossible. When the case broke on April 18, 1963, the bishop was in the hospital with terminal cancer. He died less than a month later. The secret was buried with him in his Roman grave.

My own investigations in Rome, Vienna and Graz tend to absolve Bishop Hudal of major complicity in this gigantic financial maneuver. Contrary to widespread assertions, his underground railroad was run on a shoestring. No fees were charged, of course, by the monasteries and convents which boarded and fed the fugitives in Italy. Their supply of travel documents cost next to nothing. The only expenses incurred were the fares the fugitives had to pay for their trips across the South Atlantic. These relatively small sums were available to the bishop from funds of undeniably mysterious origin, not ruling out the possibility that part of them did stem from the missing treasure.

Many of the fugitives had money of their own to take care of themselves. Henrich Müller, for example, arrived in Rome with a suitcase full of American dollar bills. It proved enough to sustain him for years in Europe and pay for his trip to South America in 1950. Others, like Raja, also possessed the money they needed to finance their escape. As documents found in Lima in 1972 tend to prove rather conclusively the bulk of the money the bishop needed was placed at his disposal by an obscure benefactor in Switzerland. He was in fact a financier named Friedrich "Freddy" Merser, partner of Friedrich Schwend in Operation Bernhard. The money came from the hoard Schwend had amassed in Swiss accounts from the revenue produced by the exchange of the counterfeit pounds for hard currencies.

Irrespective of what it cost, the rescue work of Bishop Hudal was a vast and enormously complex operation, what with guiding thousands of fugitives through the tight security network that the Allies had thrown over Italy. Hudal's Vatican cover was of enormous help, of course, especially since the Allied authorities in Rome went out of their way to accommodate the Holy See and let nothing disturb their friendly relations with the Pontiff.

Even so, the fugitives represented a liability in these relations. Bishop Hudal thus had to be doubly cautious and dexterous in his management of the underground railroad, to outwit the Allies and soothe if not hoodwink the Vatican at the same time.

The bold rescue operation involving Walter Rauff, the foreman of the gassing vans in which 97,000 Jews perished, stands out in sharpest focus to illustrate the difficulties of the enterprise. It was the boldest such venture, saving the skin of a most-wanted Nazi criminal, until Martin Bormann's carefully plotted departure for Argentina in 1948.

Chapter Twelve

"In the Name of Christian Charity"

Obersturmbannführer Walter Rauff, the very model of an SS bureaucrat, who reached his exalted station in the Main Security Office by sticking to his desk and letting sleeping dogs lie, was drawn into the Final Solution by a fluke. But once he was in it, he could not extricate himself from one of its most gruesome outrages. As chief of the Security Service's immense motor pool, he was a glorified mechanic whose major concern involved the procuring of spare parts and gasoline to keep his cars and trucks running. He wound up as one of the most-wanted of the Nazi criminals, charged with the murder of 97,000 Jews, mostly women and children.

From then on, he had to struggle on three continents, a harried, desperate man—all this as the unexpected result of an inspection trip of Himmler to Minsk in July 1941, when the Reichsführer chanced to watch a group of Jews shot down by one of his murder squads. Since Himmler had never seen such a massacre before, he asked Brigadeführer Artur Nebe, commandant of Task Force B exterminating the Jews in Byelorussia, to demonstrate one for him. A hundred Jews were hurriedly rounded up and herded to the place of execution. They were ordered to remove their clothing and kneel down at the edge of a ditch. Then they were shot from behind by a firing squad, the men and two women falling forward into the ditch.

The spectacle made Himmler sick to his stomach. It did not help any when Erich von dem Bach-Zalewsky, commandant of another murder squad, remonstrated with him: "Look into the eyes of these soldiers," he cried. "How jolted and nauseated they are! These men are *finished* for the rest of their lives."

Himmler had heard the same complaints from other commandants of his murderous task forces. Brigadeführer Otto Ohlendorf, an honor graduate of two universities, who had been made the commanding officer of one of the task forces as a punishment for his indolence at a desk job, told the Reichsführer that he had discontinued shooting Jews with a bullet to the base of the brain. "It was too cruel," he said, "unbearably hard on both the soldiers and their victims." Bach-Zalewsky asked in an emotional outburst, "What kind of men are we begetting here? Either neurotics or savages!"

In Minsk, Himmler pulled himself together and made a little speech to the visibly shaken men of the firing squad; he conceded that they had to perform "a repulsive duty" and said that he himself was "appalled by this bloody business." But it had to be done and somebody had to do it! When he returned to Berlin, however, he issued an order to "devise a different method of killing that would be more humane." The result was the construction of gas vans. Designed by a Dr. Becker and called "*Saurers*" after the Berlin factory that made most of them, they were covered trucks camouflaged as house trailers with little curtained windows on each side similar to those in peasant houses. The victims were driven in them to the burial grounds and "put to sleep" en route by diverting the lethal exhaust gas of the engines into the interior of the trucks.

Since they were vehicles, their management was assigned to the motor pool of the Main Security Office. And since Walter Rauff was its chief, he suddenly found himself in charge of the gassing vans. But Rauff had nothing but complaints about them. The gassing left the victims with "distorted faces and covered with excrement." The SS men, Dr. Becker reported to him, who had to unload the corpses were as shaken by the experience as were their comrades from the firing squads. The gas vans did not eliminate "the psychological problems of the killings." Disliked by the men and their commanders alike, they were kept in service nevertheless, although sparingly used. By the end of the war, only 97,000 of the millions liquidated died in these vans. But when it was all over, Walter Rauff found himself saddled with the responsibility for their murder.

He himself never saw a van in operation. But his involvement in what was called "mobile killing operations" convinced Rauff that he would be treated as a first-degree criminal, tried and undoubtedly sentenced to death. In a last-minute effort to free himself from this frightful responsibility, he asked to be transferred to Italy. It did not help. He was captured by the Americans on April 30, 1945, just eight days before V-E Day. He spent the next twenty months in a P.O.W. camp in Rimini, trying desperately to conceal his secret from his British and American interrogators.

It worked for some time. But as the questioning became increasingly pointed and the interrogators were getting closer to the truth, the ordeal wore him down. In December 1946, when he realized that he was about to break, he escaped from the camp and made his way to Naples. "There," he later wrote, "a Catholic priest helped me get to Rome, and I stayed in various monasteries for the next eighteen months."

His escape was a coup for the Hudal organizations. Rauff's departure from the camp was aided by two priests who had been sent to Rimini to help him when his pleas reached Rome. Then other priests smuggled him out of Naples and took him to Rome, where it was much easier to submerge in the maze of friendly monasteries. At one time, Rauff taught French and arithmetic in an orphanage on Via Pia run by nuns. He was lonely. His wife and children were left behind in East Germany, and he yearned for them. The "priests" came to his aid again. "With [their] help," he wrote, "they were able to join me in Rome."

In 1948, his friends secured a contract for him with the Syrian government as technical adviser to the secret police and chief bodyguard of the President. He moved to Damascus, but did not feel safe in Syria. The State of Israel had just come into being, its avengers were too close for comfort. In 1949, the underground railroad arranged his transfer to Ecuador, after which he settled in Chile. He is still there, still harried and frightened, but at last legally under his own name. The Supreme Court of Chile has ruled that since his crimes, as listed in a West German request for his extradition submitted in 1962, were "essentially political in nature," Rauff could not be extradited. The ruling was upheld in 1973 by the late President Salvador Allende.

While the Nazis were being shipped out of Italy one after another—Müller going to Spain in transit to South America (where he arrived only in 1950), others sent straight to Argentina and Ecuador or to Syria and Egypt—Martin Bormann was fretting in his monastery hideout in Bolzano. He was puzzled by the delay that kept him pinned down. Under death sentence by the International Military Tribunal, he had more urgent reasons than his fellow fugitives to move. He had a vast treasure waiting for him in Argentina, in the care of four friends who were serving as his trustees pending his arrival.

This treasure was the ultimate proof of Bormann's supreme realism. In late 1943 or early 1944, when he had found out about a supersecret hoard stored in a special compartment of the Reichsbank's main vault, he recognized it as the means of solving one of the problems of his survival after the war.

Beginning in August 1942 and continuing until late 1944, a vast assortment of valuables were delivered in increasingly massive quantities to the Reichsbank in Berlin. The deliveries, which eventually totaled seventy-seven shipments, were made in automobiles, small vans and, occasionally, in trucks, as the quantities required. At the Reichsbank, where a special account was opened for these "deposits" under the fictitious name of "Max Heiliger," only five officials were privy to this secret—President Walter Funk, Senior Vice-President Emil Puhl, Chief Cashier Kropf, Director Fromknecht, and the man who personally handled the shipments, Senior Clerk Albert Thoms.

Despite strict orders from President Funk to shroud this transaction in strict secrecy, they assumed at the outset that this was legitimate *Beute*, part of the booty captured by the Wehrmacht in the course of military operations. But then certain unmistakable signs made them suspicious.

The official supervising the deliveries, named Melmer, claimed that he represented what he vaguely and variously described as an economic branch of the Wehrmacht and an office of Reichsmarschall Göring, although he wore civilian clothes at all times. It soon appeared, however, that he was an SS man, a functionary of the Main Security Office's economic division. Besides, the cars and the trucks which delivered the goods were driven and guarded by men in SS uniform. Some of the crates and suitcases bore in block letters the names of the places where they originated, like "Auschwitz" and "Lublin." "The incoming quantities of gold teeth," Thoms stated, "grew by leaps and bounds, as did other valuables. Once we received twelve kilos of pearls in a single shipment. I've never seen such a mass of sparkling baubles in all my life." As the shipments increased, Thoms needed up to thirty men to aid him in the sorting of the valuables and in their repacking in the special pouches of the Reichsbank.

Included in this hoard were, among other items, millions in gold marks, pounds sterling, dollars and Swiss francs, 3,500 ounces of platinum, over 550,000 ounces of gold, and 4,638 carats in diamonds and other precious stones, as well as hundreds of pieces of works of art.

This ghoulish hoard was coming, exactly as the Reichsbank officials surmised, from the extermination camps via the Main Security Office, which was the clearing house of this loot. There only Dr. Ernst Kaltenbrunner, Obergruppenführer Oswald Pohl and one of his aides knew of the exact nature of this treasure.*

But no secret could be kept from Bormann. When he became convinced that "everything was lost," he decided to help himself to at least a portion of this treasure. Through Dr. Helmut von Hummel, head of his own economic division, he instructed Vice-President Puhl to surrender some of the crates and pouches, explaining vaguely that their contents would be sold to aid in meeting the Party's expenses. In reality, he had decided to send these valuables out of the country to be waiting for him when they might be needed.†

The shipments were sporadic to begin with. But as the situation in Germany deteriorated, Bormann ordered them speeded up and

* "The accumulation in crates," wrote Professor Kempner, "of gold teeth, dentures with gold fillings, jewelry, watches, valuables and coins was one of the most repugnant by-products of the extermination of the Jews. In Galicia [Poland] alone, gold coins weighing nearly 100,000 kg were taken from Jews already by the middle of 1943. . . . By the end of 1943, Oswald Pohl's [bureau] 'inherited' 180 million Reichsmarks from murdered Jews in the Lublin district [of Poland] alone."

† One of Bormann's last recorded messages from the Führerbunker was sent on April 22, 1945, a cryptic message to Dr. von Hummel that read: "Agree proposed transfer overseas." Lev Bezymenski, the foremost Russian Bormann hunter who discovered a copy of the message among the abandoned papers of the Reich Chancellery, regarded this document as conclusive proof that the funds had been sent to South America and Bormann eventually followed them there. However, the German authorities in charge of the case discounted Bezymenski's theory. They pointed out that the German original of Bormann's message approved the transfer to Übersee, which translates into "overseas," to be sure, but was in reality the name of a whistle stop on the Munich-Salzburg railroad line, a small resort famous for its peasant theater and festivals on the Chiem Lake. I found, however, that the entire Traunstein region, in which Übersee was located, had come under Allied attack by then. Since Bormann was well informed of the military situation in his own district in Bavaria, it was unlikely that he would have approved any transfer to a place that was certain to fall into Allied hands momentarily. "Helmut von Hummel probably knows the answer to the Bormann puzzle," Bezymenski wrote. But Dr. von Hummel, who now practices law in Munich, prefers to keep exasperatingly quiet when it is a matter of Bormann. He refused to talk to me even as he declined to be interviewed by Bezymenski. "I have never seen [Bormann] since the spring of 1945," he told the Soviet journalist; and he added, "Look, I never talked badly about Herr Bormann while he was alive. It would be incorrect on my part to do it now."

increased in volume, until the transaction became a vast enterprise with its own code name, Aktion Feuerland, "Operation Land of Fire."*

Up to June 1944, heavily guarded armored trucks carried the consignments across Germany and France to ports in southern Spain, where U-boats were standing by in hidden bases near Cadiz to take on Bormann's precious cargo. In Spain, General Wilhelm Faupel, a former ambassador and head of the Latin-American Institute, and now stationed in Madrid with a diplomatic cover, managed the operation. He was aided by Captain Dietrich Niebuhr, who had been the Abwehr chief in Buenos Aires posing as the naval attaché until he was expelled in 1941 for espionage activities so brazen that they upset even the pro-Nazi government of Argentina; and by Gottfried Sandstede, another old Argentine hand ousted from Buenos Aires when it was discovered that he was not what he claimed to be, the innocent press attaché of the German embassy. Captain Niebuhr supervised the transfer of the shipments to the U-boats, which then left their hideouts and sailed to Argentina.

After D Day in 1944, the overland route to Spain became blocked. Bormann then issued orders to continue Aktion Feuerland by air. Earlier, on May 22, two weeks before the Allied landings in Normandy, General Faupel had written in this connection to one of his agents in Berlin:

"Reichsleiter Bormann, who has received two reports from von Leute and the Argentine General Pistarini, insists that the shipments to Buenos Aires be resumed forthwith. Ask General [Adolf] Galland [a Luftwaffe ace experienced with long-range Condor planes] to place two aircraft at our disposal, solely for flying at night, and to inform [Colonel Hans Ulrich] Rudel and Hanna Reitsch. The bearer of this letter and Kuster must start preparations at once. Köhn must come [to Madrid] with the first available plane to help [Gottfried] Sandstede, who has been ordered to report to me tomorrow."†

* The transaction was named "Land of Fire" after the archipelago of Tierra del Fuego at the southern extremity of Argentina and Chile, the area to which some of the shipments were originally consigned.

† Only a relatively small portion of the SS treasure was impounded by Bormann and sent overseas in the course of Aktion Feuerland. Much of it is still missing. Some of it was found by the Allies and taken from salt mines in Thuringia, where many of the Reichsbank crates were hidden, before the Russians got there under the demarcation agreement with the Western Allies. "In the immediate wake of the war," wrote Dr. Kempner, "the sight of the crates with the gold teeth shocked me as much as did the emaciated bodies of Eichmann's victims. The crates, transferred from the Reichs-

The clandestine traffic did not escape the attention of either the Allied or the Argentine authorities. The virtually complete record of this operation, which is enormously important because it laid the foundation for the economic structure of Bormann's postwar world, is preserved, not only in the archives of Coordinación Federal in Buenos Aires, but also in the files of the F.B.I. and the British Admiralty. The latter's Division of Naval Intelligence assumed that the U-boats engaged in this traffic were on regular operational cruises, using hidden bases in Argentina to refuel. But the Argentine authorities knew better.

The man in Argentina who knew most about the secret mission of the U-boats was Niceforo Alarcón, an astute special investigator of the Argentine Navy's Intelligence Service. The Navy's interest in the matter was twofold. For one thing, the operation involved the movement of warships, which every naval intelligence office regards as its primary object of surveillance. For another, despite the pro-Nazi sympathies of a cabal of senior naval officers led by Admiral Leon Scasso, the promoters of the scheme were army officers, and the Argentine naval intelligence was habitually more interested in what was going on behind the scenes in its own army than in foreign navies.

On April 18, 1945, Agent Alarcón submitted a report, captioned "German Disembarkation at San Clemente del Tuyu," to the Ministry of the Navy (a copy of which was logged in under number CF-OP-2315 at the Coordinación Federal). Brief as it was, the report gave an insight into the operation, pinpointing two of its principals. One was Ludwig Freude, described as "an agent of the Third Reich." Alarcón had succeeded in planting on Freude one of his informers, called "Natalio" in the report. Natalio ascertained that Freude "had made extensive deposits in various banks" in the name of the other key figure in the plot, "the well-known radio and stage actress Maria Eva Duarte Iburguren."

Natalio learned from Freude himself that, on February 7, 1945, "a U-boat of Admiral Doenitz's submarine fleet" had arrived at a secluded spot in Samborombón Bay off Punta Norte near the village

---

bank [in Berlin] and hidden elsewhere, were [found] and shipped by the U.S. Army to the vaults of the Reichsbank [branch] in Frankfurt." Dr. Kempner assumes that this portion of the SS treasure eventually wound up with the U.S. Treasury. There were, it seems, very scant records of these transactions kept by the Allies, probably because a considerable portion of the treasure was stolen a second time—by Allied personnel—after the war.

of San Clemente del Tuyu, 150 miles south of Buenos Aires. According to what Freude told Natalio, the U-boat had brought "shipment No. 1744" to Argentina, consisting of an unspecified number of crates and bags "containing," as Alarcón wrote in his report to the Navy Ministry, "a 'treasure' designed to help the rebuilding of the Nazi empire."

Subsequent investigations revealed that the containers, labeled *Geheime Reichssache* ("top secret"), had been brought ashore from the U-boat in rubber dinghies, were loaded on trucks and taken to a ranch in Patagonia owned by a German named Lahousen, arriving on the night of March 28–29. The documents included in the shipment were left at the ranch. But the "treasure" was sent on to Buenos Aires to Freude, who deposited it in the vaults of four banks —the Banco Aleman, the Banco Alemán Transatlántico, the Banco Germánico and the Banco Tornquist—all of it in the name of Señorita Duarte.

Freude and Eva were members of the syndicate that handled Operation Land of Fire at the Argentine end—Freude for General Faupel, another member, Ricardo von Leute, as Bormann's personal representative. The syndicate had two other partners, Dr. Heinrich Dörge and Ricardo Staudt. Indicative of the size of the "treasure" they handled was the deposit in the Banco Alemano alone. It required seven of its largest safes, their keys held by Ricardo von Leute. Already by early 1944, the seven safes were filled with gold and silver, valued at 115 million pesos.

It was a star-studded cast that managed Operation Land of Fire in Buenos Aires. Heinrich Dörge, a former aide of Dr. Hjalmar Schacht, the Nazis' financial wizard, had come to Argentina in the thirties as a representative of German banking interests, then stayed to become consultant of the Central Bank of Argentina and one of the paymasters of German spies. Ricardo von Leute, Bormann's comptroller, was an officer (*gerente*) of the Banco Aleman Transatlántico and was reputed to be "a financial genius." Ricardo Staudt was general manager of the huge Lahousen ranch and a senior member of the German contingent of espionage agents in southern Argentina.*

* Staudt was labeled the number-two Nazi in Argentina in the *Blue Book* of the U.S. Department of State issued in 1946 about pro-German activities of the Perón crowd during World War II. Staudt managed what was tantamount to a conglomerate of industrial and agricultural properties, and was the first to make a deal with American big business after the war.

Head of the syndicate was the ebullient, ubiquitous "Ludovico" —Rudolf Eugen Ludwig Freude, a lieutenant in the Argentine Naval Reserve, the Nazis' not-too-secret agent in Buenos Aires whose broad assignments covered both political and economic matters. He was the German ambassador without portfolio ranking *de facto* above Edmund Baron von Thermann, the officially accredited envoy, who had to take orders from him.

Freude was drawn into Operation Land of Fire in the spring of 1943, when Bormann sent General Faupel and Gottfried Sandstede to Buenos Aires to arrange for the receipt and storing of the shipments. Traveling in a U-boat from Cadiz, Spain, through the Anglo-American blockade, Faupel and Sandstede arrived in Buenos Aires on Sunday, May 2, and immediately contacted Freude in the German Evangelical church on Calle Esmeralda.

This was the beginning of a partnership that had its ups and downs, and ended tragically for Freude ten years later. But between 1943 and 1953 he was riding high, probably the most important and influential German in Argentina, which was becoming increasingly corrupted by the Peróns.

His power stemmed from his friendship with the lady mentioned twice in Alarcón's report. Eva Duarte—today called "the Little Madonna" and almost canonized in Argentina (although the Holy See refused to make it official)—was a third-rate young actress of questionable reputation until 1941, when she met the handsome son of a farmer from the pampas town of Lobos, a forty-six-year-old colonel named Juan Domingo Perón. She became the mistress of the politically supercharged, dynamic officer (whose wife had died three years before) and then his partner in the wild schemes her ambitious lover was already hatching. Spellbound by the Nazis and Fascists from his tour of duty in Europe in the late thirties and early forties ("our future lies in an inflexible dictatorship patterned on Germany," he once declared), Perón was a founder of a cabal of reactionary colonels called G.O.U. (Group of United Officers). With the help of Evita's superb brain, he soon became its leader.

On her part, Eva had use for politics only so far as it served her greed. Freude had known her from her days when she was a popular fixture of the Buenos Aires *demimonde*. Recognizing her sudden usefulness in politics, Freude made an alliance with Evita that endured trickeries and vicissitudes for years. He loaded her down with exquisite jewelry shipped to him from Germany in the diplomatic pouch from the store of priceless gems stolen from the Jews, like the $30,000 diamond necklace he gave her in November 1944.

In return, Señorita Duarte rendered services that sometimes had all the melodrama of espionage fiction. When Gottfried Sandstede was unmasked by British Intelligence as a Nazi spy in 1941, and his arrest was demanded by London, he holed up in the extraterritoriality of the German embassy until August 19. Then, however, orders arrived from Berlin to send Sandstede to Spain, where he was urgently needed. Passage was booked for him on the plane to Rio de Janeiro, his first stop on the perilous wartime journey. But Freude was tipped off by his contacts in Policía Federal that plans had been made to arrest Sandstede at Quilmes airport.

He managed to make the trip smoothly, thanks to the help Freude solicited from Evita. "Fräulein Duarte," Captain Niebuhr, then still the naval attaché in Buenos Aires, reported to Faupel on August 26, "came through magnificently. She brought to the Embassy a coat and a cap of our friend Colonel Perón, and thus clad in the uniform of an officer of the Argentine General Staff, Party Comrade Sandstede, accompanied by Fräulein Duarte, passed through the barrier the police had set up, driven in an official sedan of the Ministry of War. He reached the airport in the nick of time and departed as planned without any incident."

Now, in early 1943, as a charter member of the Freude syndicate, Fräulein Duarte lent her name to the transaction. As the "treasure" continued to pour in, all of it went into the vaults under her name. She also became a silent partner in four dummy corporations Freude had set up (with capital totaling four and a half million pesos) to conceal the source of the incoming money in various currencies.

In another facet of the operation, Freude asked General Friedrich Wolff, who had become military and naval attaché in 1943, to find secluded spots on the long Argentine coastline where the U-boats could berth and unload. Wolff commissioned one of his agents, Otto Albert Seidlitz, manager of the Mitropa Travel Bureau, to reconnoiter the coast from Punta Norte all the way to Cabo San Diego, 1,500 miles away. Seidlitz's point of departure in his search was a number of big estates along the Atlantic owned by Germans, among them a friend of General Wolff's who owned a big ranch near Mar del Sur, which then became the first snug harbor of the U-boats on these secret missions.

Within months Seidlitz created a network of hidden bases in

what became an elaborate maritime organization servicing the traffic. Aside from the clandestine ports, dotting the coast from San Clemente del Tuyu in the north to the little Bay of San Sebastian down in Patagonia, Freude also established two radio stations—at Tandil and Bella Vista—to guide the U-boats on their approach.

The submarines arrived at intervals of six to eight weeks throughout 1943 and 1944, keeping up the flow of the "treasure." The last two arrived on July 23 and 29, 1945, weeks after V-E Day, in the Bay of San Sebastian near Ricardo Staudt's *estancia* in Patagonia. Freude sent two German sailors, Dettelmann and Schulz, stranded in Argentina from the scuttled pocket battleship *Graf Spee,* to help in the unloading of the cargo.

By then, of course, the Third Reich was a shambles. But Freude and his syndicate remained in business, and Perón's meteoric career was just beginning. In 1945, still a few steps from the pinnacle of power, he was grabbing one high position after another, becoming either successively or simultaneously Minister of Labor, Minister of War, Minister of Welfare and Vice-President. On October 21, Perón and Evita were wed secretly in a civil ceremony. Four months later, when the bridegroom was elected President of the Republic, the bride became the First Lady of Argentina.

They were united, not merely in wedded bliss, but in a flourishing business partnership in which the Bormann treasure was looming largest. In a complicated maneuver, Perón and Evita now moved cunningly to gain control of the Nazi hoard. Shortly after the U-boat's arrival off San Clemente del Tuyu, Argentina declared war against Germany. It was the last of the Latin American countries to fall in line. Although the Bormann treasure had been deposited in Evita's name, the four trustees still maintained a measure of control over it.

In a two-pronged drive, Perón first appointed himself alien-property custodian, on the theory that the Bormann treasure could be declared "enemy property" and confiscated. Then the members of the syndicate found themselves in trouble. Freude was "investigated" on a number of charges, including espionage and fraud. He had no illusions about the consequences of the change in the Peróns' attitude toward him.

On September 6, 1946, however, it was officially announced that "the investigation of Ludwig Freude had been terminated by presidential decree." Freude had bought a lease on his life, at a high price. While not completely renouncing his share in the hidden fortune, he agreed to take a back seat in its administration, assigning the dominant part in its control to "the Little Madonna, Mother of the Poor." The other partners in the shaken syndicate promptly followed suit.

Bormann was making a nuisance of himself, badgering Perón to expedite his departure for Argentina. But the Peróns did not seem to be in any great hurry to welcome him. It was not until 1947 that they agreed to his coming, and even then it took almost another year before he finally arrived.

In Martin Bormann's postwar career, the period between the fall of 1945 and the spring of 1948 remains blank. American Intelligence in Germany, Austria and Italy never relaxed their interest in the fugitive Reichsleiter, but their numerous investigations yielded only a meager account of empty boxes. In most cases, instead of getting any closer to the clarification of the mystery, they compounded it.

The most competent investigation—with inconclusive but interesting results—was conducted by two officers of the Military Intelligence Service Center of United States Forces European Theater, Lieutenants Peter K. Heimann and Ernest Block. When Bormann's former driver, Matthias Rehrl, was interrogated in the P.O.W. cage of the Third U.S. Army in August 1945, he said that he had driven the car that took Frau Bormann to northern Italy in April, and ventured to remark that the Reichsleiter himself might have joined her there.

In early April 1945, Lieutenants Heimann and Block picked up this lead and decided to track it down. They motored to the Gardenia Valley, where Rehrl said he had left Frau Bormann, and were directed to Selva, a village nestled in the Dolomites, the place, in fact, to which Dr. von Hummel and Gauleiter Hofer had evacuated Bormann's family almost a year before. When they reached the house pointed out to them as the Bormann residence, they found it deserted. By then, of course, Gerda had died and been buried at the Heldenfriedhof (Army Memorial Cemetery) in Merano.

Her children had been picked up by Father Theodor Schmitz, the German Army Catholic chaplain, who had befriended her in the hospital and become her confidant during the few months she had left. After her death, Father Schmitz found foster homes for the children in and around Brunico in Italy. The oldest daughter, Eike

Ilse Renate, was fifteen years old, the youngest, a boy named Volker, not yet three. Nothing was heard from sixteen-year-old Martin Adolf, the couple's eldest son.

As for Bormann himself, the search produced nothing positive. "Local residents reported," Lieutenants Heimann and Block wrote in their compassionate account of the search, "no strange German had ever visited the Bormann house." Father Schmitz told them that, as far as he knew, there had been no communication between the couple, and Gerda had died in the belief that her husband was dead.

But the C.I.C. refused to give up. On October, 1947, an agent named Blankenship, who was one of Bormann's case officers, was asked to follow a lead obtained from a seamstress named Sonnenschein at a place called Hindelang. According to her story, Bormann was no longer in the Soviet Zone of Germany but was hiding in the vicinity of Bad Oberdorf-Hindelang, supposedly in a cowherd's hut on the Zipfelalm or the Hohe Iselar, two rugged mountains in the area.

The most intriguing part of the story dealt with Frau Bormann. Frau Sonnenschein said that she was working as a receptionist in the office of Dr. Hermann Arntz in Bad Oberdorf. Blankenship's answer, dated October 28, 1947, was marked "Investigation came to its logical conclusion," a euphemism for having yielded no corroboration of Frau Sonnenschein's story. And no wonder. Bormann was nowhere near the Zipfelalm and Frau Gerda had been dead for a year and a half.

At the same time, First Lieutenant Arnold J. Lapiner of the C.I.C. Detachment of the 301st Military Intelligence Company came up with a hairdresser who asserted that Bormann and his wife were at a place called Weiden in Bavaria. They were hidden by a baroness named Elsa von Wollank, a lady active in the flourishing black market and hostess to "many secret visitors who must be Nazi bigshots." Lieutenant Lapiner was puzzled. "General impression gained by this investigator is," he wrote, "that there is something definitely queer going on here and further checking is warranted."

The wheels began turning again. A rather elaborate investigation was made, its tentacles extending from Weiden all the way to 30 Lyckallee in Berlin-Charlottenburg, where the baroness was eventually located. No trace of Bormann was found, of course. But, as Lieutenant Lapiner suggested, probably only because the wily baroness had "a pat story" and was "interrogation wise."

The wild-goose chase went on into 1949 and even 1950. On July 11, 1949, Special Agent Robert C. McCormack of the indefatigable C.I.C. stumbled upon a felon named Theo Dirks, who tried to buy his way out of the St. Georgen prison in Bayreuth by revealing where Bormann was. Dirks claimed that he had been a member of a courier system used by Bormann to send letters to his wife, then allegedly living in a place called Neustadt. The correspondence harked back to the summer of 1947—more than a year after Gerda's death.

In late 1950, the American intelligence network in Germany was still floundering in its Bormann search. On October 23, Major David Huncoon of the 66th C.I.C. Detachment received the copy of an intercepted letter sent from 4 Dominikanergasse in Würzburg signed "Martin Bormann." It was addressed to—of all people—Secretary of State Dean Acheson. One of the major's subordinates, Erich W. Isenstaed, hired a couple of handwriting experts in Munich to examine the signature. When they brought in their verdict that it "compared exactly with existing genuine Bormann signatures," C.I.C. agents were sent to the address in Würzburg to pick up Bormann. They found living there only a man named Ernst Stein Krauss, who readily admitted that he had forged Bormann's signature under the letter in an attempt to get some money for it from a Munich magazine, *Echo der Woche*.

The elaborate C.I.A. investigation of the early fifties, conducted by James McGovern for Walter Houk, then the C.I.A. station chief in Berlin, produced only a set of assumptions, one invalidating the other. Taken together, they left the case more confused than ever.

My own investigations of this period did not fare much better. I did find a couple of eyewitnesses—an electrician who claimed to have known Bormann in Pullach and an Italian journalist who had met him at the Führer's headquarters in East Prussia in the summer of 1944—both of whom insisted that they had seen him in Bolzano after the war. But neither their credentials nor their recollections satisfied me.

Even so, it seems to be established with reasonable certainty that Bormann spent most of this period at Bolzano. In his deposition of August 2, 1971, in which he recounted his experience with Frau Thalheimer, Professor Trevor-Roper said, "Frau Thalheimer stated that it was probability bordering on certainty that the man she saw [in Bolzano] was Bormann. If it had been a look-alike, it cannot be explained why the man should have been so frightened." As for Frau Thalheimer's trustworthiness, Trevor-Roper said, "As a witness, she gave the impression of being competent, judicious and reliable. Her story seemed to me plausible. It did not conflict with any other known facts."

It is possible and, indeed, probable that Bormann, gregarious by nature, refused to be pinned down in his Italian hideout, and moved about to take care of the complicated affairs of his exile. It is reasonable to believe that he had been in Rome several times, and also in Spain, where he had been spotted by other witnesses. A fairly reliable informant of the 1948 F.B.I. investigation, Juan Serrino of Quilmes, Argentina, even asserted that Bormann had been in Argentina during this period on a visit prior to his immigration in the spring of 1948.

Wherever he was and whatever he was doing during these empty years, he was never close to the "treasure" awaiting him in Buenos Aires, for the simple reason that, at this time, the Peróns had no use for him in Argentina. They still assumed that they could gain possession of the entire hoard more expeditiously without Bormann messing up things. They proved to be in error. Under the ironclad terms Freude had arranged for the deposits in the banks, no disposition of the "treasure" could be made in Bormann's absence and without his personal participation in its disposal or distribution. By the end of 1947, it became obvious to Perón and Evita that it would be impossible in the long run to bar Bormann permanently from Argentina.

It was at this point that Evita Perón took matters into her hands. In the summer of 1947, it was announced in Buenos Aires that she would make a good-will trip to Europe, visiting Portugal, Spain, Monaco, France, Switzerland and Italy. Britain was conspicuous by its absence from her itinerary. This was strictly a business trip, in fact, and whatever good will it was to produce would accrue mainly to the Peróns.

Eva had neither any intention of nor any chance of success in doing business with the British. They would naturally take a dim view of any expedition to smuggle Bormann out of Europe so that his treasure could be split up at last.

In Europe, Señora Perón conducted major business transactions behind the scenes as she moved from one city to another—in Lisbon, in Madrid, twice in Geneva, in Lucerne and Zurich, in Paris, Avila and, finally, in Rome, where at last she disposed of the Bormann matter.

How she went about doing it and what she accomplished were spelled out in a report submitted to the Argentine Central Intelligence Bureau by the Reverend Egidio Esparza. Father Egidio was a brilliant and fiery Catholic priest in the forefront of the spreading opposition to Juan Perón.

Evita had died of cancer in 1952, and left to his own resources, without recourse to his blond wife's brilliant brain, the dictator stumbled from one blunder into another. El Líder, as Perón was called, had taken on the Roman Catholic Church in the growing coalition of his enemies, antagonizing the clergy with a number of anti-Catholic measures. He ended religious instruction in the schools, introduced a divorce law, and was planning to legalize prostitution. He also alienated the clergy when gossip linked him romantically with a fourteen-year-old girl as Evita's successor in his bed.

Father Egidio was a Church activist who enlisted in the anti-Perón crusade as an intelligence agent. Through superb connections reaching deep into Perón's own circle, and even better, by penetrating the conspiratorial pro-Peronist faction at the Vatican, he succeeded in assembling considerable inside information about the man he personally regarded as unfit to be the President of the Republic.

Egidio worked for A.I.C.A., the Catholic intelligence service, which was, for all practical purposes, another branch of Coordinación Federal. It was so well-informed, reliable and dependable that the secular intelligence agencies, which found it difficult to infiltrate the Church, abandoned the coverage of Perón's relations with the Vatican to A.I.C.A., placing the highest reliability rating (A-1) on reports they received from the Reverend Father Andres Canale, another activist priest, who was its chief.

At the time Father Egidio submitted his report, Father Andres was in Rome on one of his frequent intelligence-gathering missions at the Vatican. Father Egidio was acting chief of the agency in Canale's absence, and this, in the eyes of Coordinación Federal, added another dimension of reliability to what in fact was the summary of relevant intelligence on file in A.I.C.A. When I reviewed the report with the competent authorities in Buenos Aires in 1972, they assured me that it was still regarded as the last word in the mystery of Martin Bormann's coming to Argentina. It had been corroborated by intelligence submitted by other informants and by information obtained from independent sources regarded as reliable.

In view of the highly sensitive nature of Father Egidio's candid disclosures, I prefer not to paraphrase his report. I reprint the original version in verbatim translation, including one or two minor errors, like the reference to Monsignor Montini by the first name José although, in fact, it was Giovanni.

This, then, was Father Egidio's report:

Intelligence Headquarters. Re: Martin Bormann.

> Around 1947, the department of the Vatican's Secretariat of State helping displaced persons was under the direction of Monsignor José [*sic*] Montini, whose assistant in providing travel documents for refugees was an Argentinian priest, named Silva. It was the latter who was the link between the Bishop of Genoa, Monsignor Guiseppe Siri, the wife of the president of the Republic of Argentina, Señora Maria Duarte Ibarguren [*sic*] de Perón, and former deputy fuehrer Martin Bormann. The main interview took place in Rapallo, in the vicinity of the city of Genoa.
>
> According to confidential information, neither Bishop Siri nor Father Silva was in the beginning aware that the man involved was Martin Bormann. Señora Perón had introduced him as a distant relative of her family—a philosopher of Jewish-Italian descent, named Luigi Boglilio.
>
> Bishop Siri came to be suspicious because Boglilio spoke a harsh kind of Italian, like someone from Trieste, with a German accent. But on July 10, 1947, Señora Perón, accompanied by two Italian generals—Graziani and Cassiani—as well as Commendatore Giovanni Maggio, put pressure on the bishop to collaborate in concealing the identity of Bormann who had to embark for South America as soon as possible.
>
> The bishop agreed, stressing that he did so in the name of Christian charity, and not because he shared the ideas of those "friends" who were interceding on Bormann's behalf. But he did advise that Bormann should not pass himself off as an Italian, since he not only did not speak the language, but when he tried to make himself understood in it, he "shattered the eardrums of anyone listening to him."
>
> From that moment Bormann assumed his new identity of Eliezer Goldstein, the name appearing on the new papers with which he embarked at Genoa in the *Giovanna C* during the first half of 1948.

Chapter Thirteen

Alias Eliezer Goldstein—Halcyon Days in Argentina

Martin Bormann arrived in Argentina on a Monday morning, May 17, 1948, aboard the steamer *Giovanna C*, out of Genoa, Italy. Wearing what resembled the garb of a Jesuit, he entered Argentina on a Vatican passport identifying him as the Reverend Juan Gomez.

The document on which he traveled had been given him only for the trip. It was not one of the "identity certificates" that the Refugee Bureau of the Holy See was issuing to stateless persons. It was, rather, a *regular* Vatican passport, made out on February 16, 1948, by the Secretariat of State, and it bore the printed facsimile of the Pope's signature in his capacity as the sovereign head of the Vatican state.

Bormann was welcomed at the pier by Ludwig Freude and General Juan Batista Sosa Molina, the Minister of War, representing President Perón. The choice of Molina as Perón's proxy was a pointed reminder of the past and an emphatic portent of the future. When the general was still one of the conspiratorial colonels, he was Freude's main contact in the Argentine Army and the Nazis' best friend. Now he was at the peak of his career as the President's closest confidant. General Molina whisked Bormann in his official limousine to a house at 120 Calle Salta in San Martin, an elegant residential district of Buenos Aires, and deposited him there in the care of friends.

A few weeks later, after his Vatican passport had been discarded, Bormann registered at the Apostolic Nunciature in Buenos Aires as a stateless person and was issued "Identity Certificate No. 073,909." He gave his profession as a geologist and stated that he was born on August 20, 1901, in Piotrkow, near Warsaw, in Poland, the son of Abraham and his wife Maria Esther Sadrinas, originally a native of Argentina. The name under which he registered was the one chosen for him at the Rapallo conference in the fall of 1947 and was ironic, not merely because it sounded like a typically Jewish name. It was somehow appropriate, whether or not it had been chosen deliberately with an eye on the fortune he was coming to collect. It was *Goldstein*—Eliezer Goldstein.

On the strength of the Nunciature's identity certificate, Bormann was given the mandatory *cédula identidad*—No. 1,361,642—by the Policía Federal. He then applied for a residence permit at the Immigration Office of the Ministry of the Interior, whose head, Angel Gabriel Berlanghi, was another of his guardians in President Perón's cabinet.

On October 12, 1948, he was given the coveted "blue stamp" granting him permission to remain in Argentina permanently. Martin Bormann had come to stay.

I have the paper recording these facts, an authentic copy of the document still on file at the Immigration Office. A reproduction of the original can be found in the Document section.

Read in conjunction with the document prepared by A.I.C.A., the Catholic Information Agency of Argentina, over the signature of Father Egidio Esparza (see page 215), which described in detail the background of Bormann's escapade, it provides the historic clue that he did not perish on his flight from the Führerbunker at dawn on May 2, 1945.* Father Egidio's report established beyond doubt that the name "Eliezer Goldstein" on the Vatican's identity certificate was, indeed, the cynically chosen alias under which Martin Bormann was to register with the Papal Nuncio in Buenos Aires after discarding the Vatican passport made out to Juan Gomez, on which he crossed the Atlantic, "in the guise of a Jesuit priest."

The fee Borman had to pay for admission into Argentina was enormous. At the time of his entry, the gold alone amounted to

* The copy of Bormann's registration sheet was one of the documents I presented in Frankfurt to Wilhelm Metzner, Chief Procurator at the Oberlandesgericht in charge of the Bormann search conducted by the State of Hesse. Another document I left with him and his man Richter, the sole official actually conducting the hunt, was Father Egidio's report. They chose to ignore them in their final determination of the case, which did not result in the court order they sought declaring Bormann dead, but canceled the warrant for his arrest, setting him free as far as the Germans are concerned.

$8,476,440, aside from other valuables estimated at many more millions. At today's market price, the gold is worth as much as $32,694,840.

The gold, with which Bormann's road to Argentina was paved, now became the first item on the agenda of his conference with the Peróns held shortly after his arrival in Buenos Aires. It must have been a lively confrontation, with the negotiating parties embroiled in a bitter, tough bargaining. The issue was how much of the Nazi treasure the Peróns would keep and how much Bormann and his partners would be allowed to retain.

In the end, according to Father Egidio Esparza's report (and other documents corroborating it), Perón "surrendered" to Bormann only one quarter of the total hoard of platinum, gold, silver, precious stones and hard currencies, including millions of dollars' worth of gold certificates. Seventy-five percent of the loot was held back by the Peróns, who explained to the Reichsleiter that Evita needed the "treasure" for her extensive charity work.

The Peróns conducted the negotiations from a position of apparent strength. Most of the gold, which formed a substantial part of the "treasure," that Freude had deposited in the four Buenos Aires banks under Evita's name was no longer in Argentina. It had been taken to Europe in 1947 by Señora Perón who, according to information that became available to the Argentine government after Perón's downfall in 1955, deposited gold then valued at $800 million in numbered accounts in various banks in Zurich and Geneva. But part of the gold was left behind, and it was this fraction of the "treasure" the Peróns held out as bait during the negotiations.

According to Father Egidio's accounting, "Juan Domingo Perón surrendered to Deputy Führer Bormann one quarter of the following valuables:"

- 187,692,400 gold marks.
- 17,576,386 U.S. dollars.
- 4,632,500 pounds sterling.
- 24,976,442 Swiss francs.
- 8,370,000 Dutch florins.
- 17,280,009 Belgian francs.
- 54,968,000 French francs.
- 87 kilograms of Platinum.
- 2,511 kilograms of gold.
- 4,638 carats diamonds and other precious stones.

Most of Father Egidio's information reflected classified reports on file at the Intelligence Service of the Argentine Navy, the agency in Buenos Aires that was initially and most directly interested in the Bormann treasure, since most of it had reached Argentina by sea. On September 1, 1970, a partial account of this hidden wealth and the Peróns' share in the Bormann treasure appeared in *Le Figaro* of Paris, based on the A.I.C.A. reports of which the French Secret Service had obtained copies and "leaked" their contents to Alain Pujol, the paper's specialist in Nazi fugitives.*

If it seemed a bad deal for Bormann, he could well afford it. For one thing, what he was left with still amounted to an enormous fortune. For another, the farsighted Freude had not put the entire "treasure" into one basket. A considerable portion was invested in gilt-edged South American enterprises and blue-chip Argentine stocks and bonds.

On July 23, 1946, Senators Silvano Santander and Julio Busaniche introduced a resolution in the Argentine Chamber of Deputies that a five-man committee be set up to investigate what they called anti-Argentinian activities—Comisión Investigadora de Actividades Antiargentinas, as it was formally to be called. The establishment of such a commission was pigeonholed by the *Poder Ejecutivo*—that is, President Perón. Nevertheless, an investigation was held with prolonged public hearings, directed by Senator Santander, one of the most courageous and determined anti-Nazis in the Western Hemisphere.

A mass of documents was available (still maintained intact by the late Senator's son at a presumably safe hiding place), both from the German archives captured by the Allies and Russians in 1945 and from domestic Argentine intelligence sources. Santander also had access to the files of the unquestionably best-informed and most-aggressive Allied intelligence service in South America, man-

* Two years later, *Le Figaro's* story with additional data from the files of A.I.C.A. and naval intelligence also surfaced in Argentina, at a time when Perón first began negotiating the terms of his possible return with the junta of Lieutenant General Alejandro A. Lanusse. According to the September 14, 1972, issue of *Última Clava*, the newsletter close to naval intelligence, the so-called "Swiss account" (also called "the numbered account of Zurich"), in which the Peróns had deposited some of the yield from the Bormann treasure, figured prominently in these negotiations. The inference was that the junta had been offered a cut of the idle treasure in Switzerland in exchange for letting Perón return to power in Argentina. If this was what ultimately happened, it was an ironic case of history repeating itself. Now it was Perón who had to pay a price for his admission, and he paid it in part from the admission fee he had received from Bormann.

aged by William Stephenson, a diminutive Canadian millionaire and amateur spy master, who headed the British Secret Intelligence Service in the Western Hemisphere during World War II. Additional unimpeachable documentation came from the files of Spruille Braden, a mining engineer turned diplomat, who was the American ambassador in Argentina and served subsequently in the State Department as Assistant Secretary of State for American Republics Affairs.

Drawing on this primary evidence, Senator Santander revealed in 1946 that what we now call the Bormann treasure had been invested by the Freude syndicate (to the tune of between 400 million and a billion pesos) in 175 financial, commercial and industrial enterprises, seventeen agricultural concerns (like the Lahousen ranch in Patagonia, which received 80 million pesos), and 149 other miscellaneous companies. This was confirmed by Carlos Arogue, president of the Argentine Alien Property Administration, before Perón arrogated his powers to himself as a step toward gaining possession of the "treasure." These investments laid the foundation for an economic empire which gained tremendous impetus from Bormann's arrival. Under his management it became a major factor in the economic life of South America.

Although generally unrecognized as such, Bormann was in fact a financial wizard. It was his astute management of a Nazi Party welfare fund in 1928–32 that first brought him to the attention of Franz Xavier Schwarz, the Party's stern and tight-fisted treasurer. It caused him to recommend the frugal young man to Rudolf Hess to bring order into the chaotic fiscal affairs of the Party bureaucracy, then badly mismanaged by the erratic Hess, who had no interest in such matters.

Aside from heading the Party chancery and acting as Hitler's secretary, Bormann also served his Führer as the confidential manager of his personal finances. Bormann's astute management made Hitler a very rich man. But much of the Führer's holdings was kept in Bormann's name. A Denazification Court at Linz, Austria, which looked into Bormann's finances after the war, found that he held title to practically all real estate belonging to Hitler. These holdings included the house in Braunau where Hitler was born, the cottage of Hitler's parents at Leonding near Linz, and the whole enormous complex at Obersalzberg consisting of eighty-seven different buildings, which the Court, in 1946, valued at over two million marks.*

The handful of insiders who knew this aspect of Bormann's hidden talents called him, with infinite contempt, "Jew Süss," after a legendary medieval German Shylock in the service of unbusinesslike feudal princes, immortalized by Lion Feuchtwanger's historical novel. During his postwar interrogation, Schwarz drew a sharp distinction between his administration of the Party treasury and Bormann's management of the Party chancery's financial affairs.

Insisting that he always "tried to keep the financial administration of the Party on an honest basis," the seventy-year-old ex-treasurer readily conceded that "the Palace Guard was rotten to the core." Its venality stemmed from Hitler's notion that corrupt followers were innately loyal to their leader, and kept suborning his minions with bribes and grants, which he dispensed through Bormann. Describing the Reichsleiter as "a man with a lust for power," Schwarz said that "Bormann was a sinister force in the chancery, more responsible than any single person for the whole corruption among the higher ranks of the Party."

When he remonstrated with Bormann for his "easy attitude regarding the administration of funds," the Reichsleiter gruffly rebuked him, claiming that "this was the way the Führer wanted it." Once "in a tart letter," the Reichsleiter warned him to "keep his nose out of matters which were none of his business." Whatever he did, he wrote, was "the Führer's will."

Bormann had a couple of "smart cookies," as he referred to them, at his beck and call, bright young men who took care of the day-to-day administration of this secret exchequer. His first "undersecretary of finance," so to speak, was Helmut Friedrichs, nominally

* Much of this real estate was acquired under duress, Bormann forcing the original owners to sell at nominal prices, in several cases for one mark per square meter when the actual value of the property was hundreds of marks per square meter. Bormann made the offers to "buy" in personal letters offering terms which left the owners scandalized but without alternatives. Those few who, like one hotel proprietor (reputed to be an anti-Nazi), refused to succumb to the intimidation were arrested and their property was confiscated. Others who proved difficult had their properties condemned. The real value of this estate was demonstrated after the war, when a tiny part of it was sold by the State of Bavaria to a hotel concern for 10 million Bundesmarks, or $4 million. The former owners of the more or less stolen properties, victims of Bormann's shrewd management of Hitler's estate, are trying to recover their houses or lands, but run into insurmountable difficulties. The region is now nominally owned by the Bavarian State, but its real owner continues to be the United States, which regards it as an Army Recreational Area.

the head of the chancery's Section II, which was concerned with the internal affairs of the Party. Actually he was Bormann's right-hand man for all executive functions, including the administration of the various slush funds. Friedrichs was succeeded by the enigmatic Helmut von Hummel.*

The secrecy in which this activity was shrouded, even amid the morbid confidentiality Bormann insisted upon in all matters, was illustrated by an incident in 1943. The chief accountant of the enormous secret funds, a man named Karl Winkler, was dismissed by Bormann for reasons never revealed. When Schwarz tried to hire Winkler for his own treasury, Bormann vetoed his employment and ordered the man into one of the most exposed task forces on the eastern front, where he was promptly and conveniently killed in action.†

Friedrichs and Hummel were mere bureaucrats. The actual management of the chancery funds was held tightly by Bormann himself. He alone had the authority to make disbursements from one of the capital stocks of the Party chancery, what was called "Funds for General Purposes," granting generous stipends to deserving Party leaders and victorious generals. He also managed the vast blackmail operation, called "Hitler Bounty of the German Industry." With the industrialist Gustav Krupp von Bohlen und

* Dr. von Hummel vanished with Bormann after the collapse, and remained at large until May 21, 1946, when his wife persuaded him to surrender to the Austrian authorities in Salzburg. Recovered from him was a collection of old coins, allegedly belonging to Hitler and valued at $5 million, with which, an American Military Government spokesman said, "the Germans intended to finance a last-ditch fight in the Bavarian redoubt." In actual fact, the coin collection was the "Treasure of Kremsmünster," so called because it had been looted (on Bormann's instructions) from the Kremsmünster and other Austrian monasteries. The treasure was administered by the Party chancery's secret exchequer, and Bormann had appointed Dr. von Hummel its custodian. Dr. von Hummel told Lieutenant Walter Horn, art-intelligence investigator for the American Military Government, "how, under orders from Bormann, he had spirited the treasure to the Tyrol to finance continued Geman resistance." Aside from his statement to Lieutenant Horn during his shock interrogation, Dr. von Hummel proved to be the most discreet and taciturn of all former Nazis in brief captivity. Released by the Austrians and permitted to return to the practice of law, the former SS major and Bormann confidant still refuses to divulge any part of his vast store of inside information involving Bormann's secret fiscal empire and postwar fate.

† After the dismissal of Winkler, an official of the Party chancery named Zeller was entrusted with the bookkeeping of Bormann's secret exchequer. Apparently he did not please Bormann either, for he wrote to his wife on February 4, 1945: "We have a thoroughly unsatisfactory and inefficient administrative service! I kept Winkler far too long, and his successor, Zeller, is full of vague plans and ideas; he has surrounded himself with a lot of nincompoops, instead of getting a few truly efficient men. It really is a great source of worry." By then, it seems in retrospect, it was too late to worry. At any rate, much of the secret funds had been disposed of by Helmut von Hummel, leaving little if anything for Herr Zeller to handle.

Halbach serving as Bormann's stooge, the "Hitler Bounty" squeezed from industrialists enormous "voluntary contributions" to the Party's secret exchequer. Moreover, Bormann had the final say in the allocation of tremendous sums collected penny by penny from all Germans for Winter Relief. He alone knew how much money was thus amassed and he alone had the privilege of disposing of it.

This is an important aspect of Bormann's career, if only because his fiscal wizardry was shrewdly projected to the future, even during the heyday of the Third Reich. Several of the funds he managed made substantial contributions to the postwar treasure, which Bormann was to control with the same cunning that characterized his management of the Party's various stockpiles.

The so-called "Hitler Bounty," for example, became a major source of Bormann's fortune in exile. He compelled some of the big industrial concerns to transfer to the Party certain assets they had abroad, especially in Switzerland and South America. For the sake of appearance, these "contributions" were left on the donors' account in foreign banks. But Bormann had power of attorney to gain possession of them at will. Now in Argentina, he moved promptly to collect these funds and transfer them to the various holding companies he had set up as clearinghouses for his scattered assets and investments.

Also waiting for him in Argentina were two vast sums of money he had acquired during the war and could now take over *de facto* as well. One was a substantial part of the fortune the Thyssen family had in Argentina. The other was the secret share the Nazi Party had acquired in the Krupp empire.

Dr. Fritz Thyssen of Mühlheim, chairman of the powerful United Steel Works, had the dubious distinction of having been the first tycoon among the Nazi Party's early angels to give Hitler 100,000 gold marks in one lump sum, a fantastic donation in 1923 when the Führer had little to give in return. Fascinated by the man's "astonishing intelligence" and "miraculous political intuition, devoid of all moral sense," Thyssen openly joined the Party in 1931 and remained Hitler's most generous supporter in the Ruhr during "the years of struggle and waiting." But he was gradually alienated when the man he supported so lavishly as a rabble-rouser became the Chancellor. Assuming that the million marks he ultimately donated to the Party gave him the right to speak out bluntly, he wrote Hitler a bitter letter in 1940, reflecting his disillusionment. Hitler in his fashion seized upon the opportunity to repay the debt. He had the tycoon arrested and taken to a concentration camp. He would have been put to death there, but Bormann was quick to spot an opportunity to make some money by intervening on Thyssen's behalf.

A deal was made, as usual, and it proved a good one for all concerned. It paid off for Thyssen twice—first when Bormann arranged his release from the concentration camp and safe departure for Switzerland; and then, in 1942, when Thyssen was recaptured in his villa on the Riviera and returned to a concentration camp. He was maltreated there, to be sure, but saved from death because word was passed down that he enjoyed the Reichsleiter's protection. Bormann received an unspecified ransom in return—rumored to be a sum between one million and three million dollars—payable at his call either in Switzerland or in Argentina, where Thyssen's daughter lived, married to an Austro-Hungarian nobleman named Zichy.

No opportunity apparently presented itself to collect in Switzerland. But now, in Argentina, Bormann put in his claim. He was paid in full, thanks to the efforts of the young Bolivian lawyer Alfonso Finot, who persuaded the Perón regime to release the Thyssen fortune impounded by the Alien Property Custodian, his intervention aided materially by the fact that in pleading the case of the Thyssens he was also representing Bormann's interests.

The Krupp deal was vast and considerably more complex. The Krupp dynasty of Essen, whose enormous fortune was rapidly multiplying during the Third Reich, was anxious to keep "the industrial part of the estate" in the family, as stipulated by Alfred Krupp in 1882, passing on the ownership in a so-called fideicommissum, or "inheritance by entail," to a single heir. Under an act of 1920, however, this would have been impossible. Determined either to bypass the law or to change it, Dr. Gustav Krupp von Bohlen und Halbach (a former junior diplomat who had become a Krupp in 1906 by marrying Bertha Antoinette, Alfred's daughter) approached the man he thought would be most effective in pleading their case at Hitler's court. The idea was to coax from the Führer a new law under which the line of succession could be maintained and, in this case, the firm could pass on to the eldest son, Alfried, a devout Nazi and SS man.

Gustav concentrated on Martin Bormann, obviously the ideal go-between. On August 10, 1942, contact was established when Alfried called on Bormann in great secrecy at the Wolfsschanze, in the Führer's headquarters in East Prussia, and acquainted him with the contours of the scheme. It was then spelled out in detail by

The Führer as Bormann last saw him in the bunker in April 1945.

Young Bormann, on the way to marry Gerda Buch, accompanied to the wedding in style by best man Adolf Hitler.

HITLER'S SHADOW

Bormann with Hitler and Foreign Minister Joachim von Ribbentrop during a stroll in the garden of the Reich Chancellery.

A rare picture of Martin Bormann at the beginning of his meteoric career in the Nazi Party, at the age of thirty-three.

This photo of the relaxed and jovial Bormann was allegedly taken in Bolzano, Italy, during his first year in exile.

THE FUGITIVE

The deserted hacienda in the jungle of eastern Paraguay, the mysterious "District X" near the Brazilian border, where Bormann lived briefly in the 1950s.

Posing as a lay member of the Redemptorist Order in Bolivia, Bormann officiated at the wedding of German friends in La Paz under the alias of Brother Augustin von Lange (from the Bormann File of the Bolivian Ministry of the Interior, enlarged from an 8-mm film taken during the ceremonies).

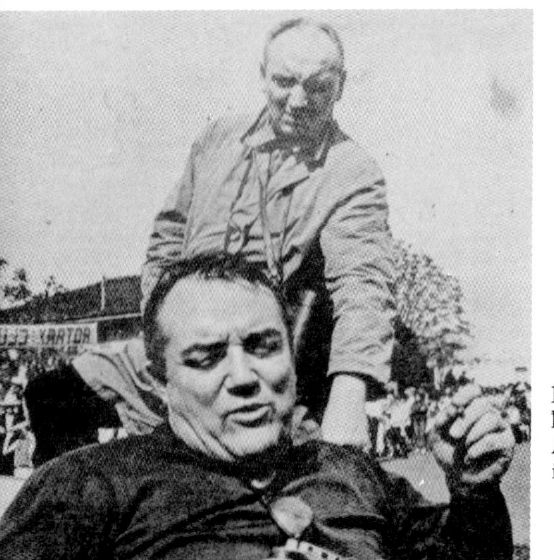

Bormann in Bolivia: with his friend Adolf Hundhammer (the man with camera) at a county fair in Apolo in 1958 (from the Bormann File of the Bolivian Ministry of the Interior).

THE SEARCH

Attorney General Dr. Fritz Bauer of the State of Hesse, whose indefatigable search for Bormann and Mengele was terminated by his sudden death in the summer of 1968.

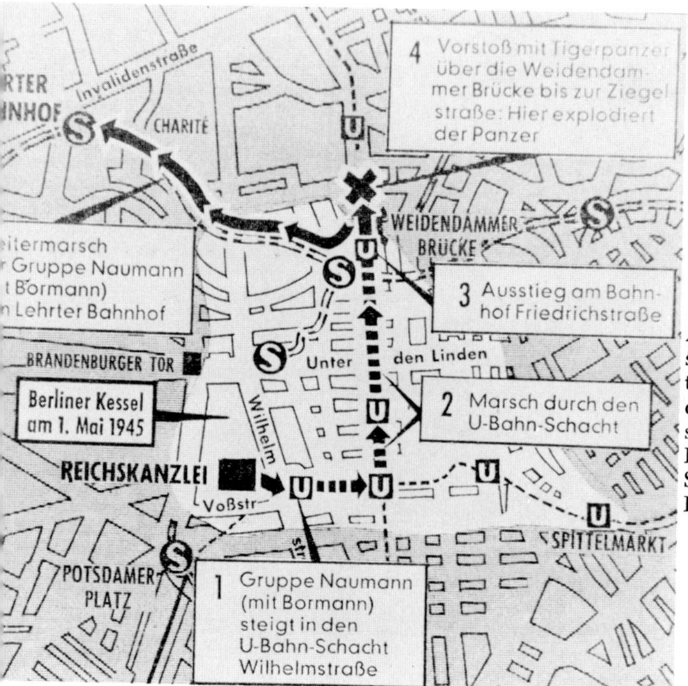

A German artist's sketch tracing the stations of Bormann's escape from the Führerbunker during the night of May 1–2, 1945. His route is shown by the dotted line from the Reich Chancellery to the Lehrter Station via the Weidendammer Bridge.

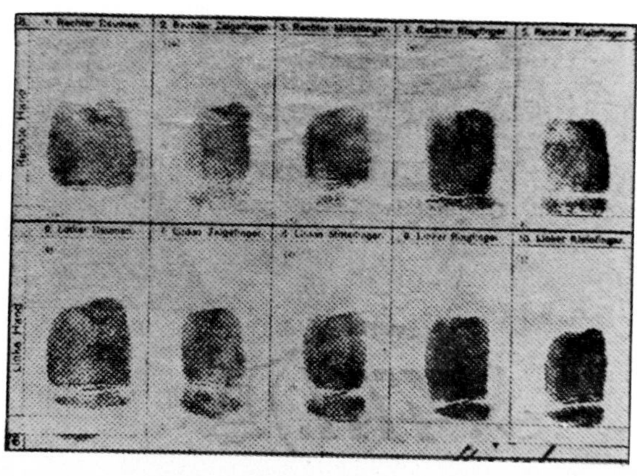

A set of Bormann's fingerprints, taken when charged with the murder of a political opponent in 1922, and found accidentally in the files of a Bavarian police station. Until recently, copies of the prints were on deposit at all German diplomatic missions abroad, to facilitate and expedite Bormann's identification when apprehended under the warrant issued in 1960 for his arrest.

Prosecutors Wilhelm Metzner and Joachim Richter (center and right), assistants of Dr. Bauer, digging for Bormann's remains in Berlin in 1965. They failed to find any sign that he had died in the area 20 years before.

Skulls said to be Bormann's. Supposedly, they were discovered accidentally in 1972 by construction workers at the exact spot where no trace of Bormann's remains could be found during the prosecutors' elaborate dig seven years before.

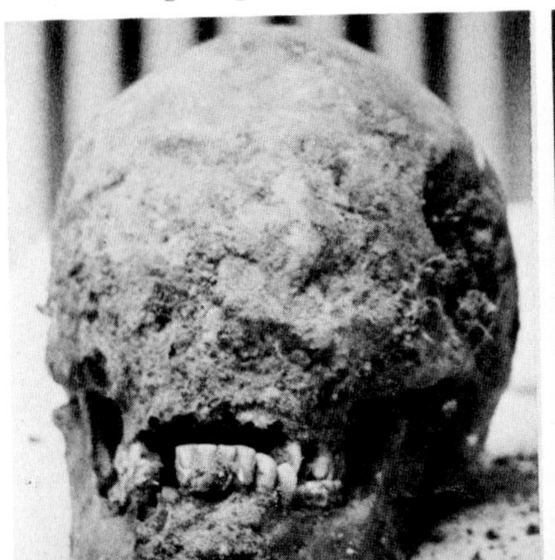

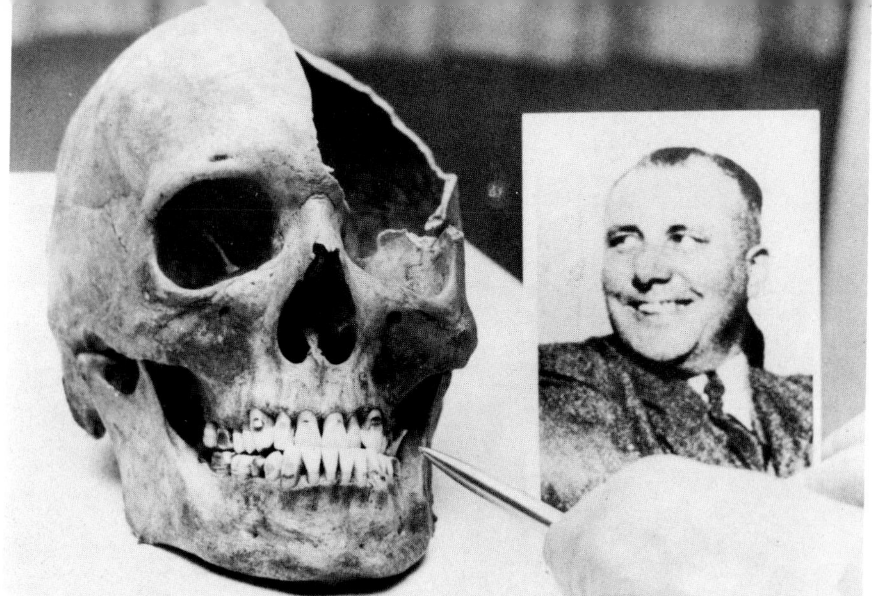

Note of the evolution of the skulls in the hands of the prosecutors and medical examiners.

Bormann's dental structure, reconstructed from memory by the late Dr. Hugo Blaschke, his former dentist.

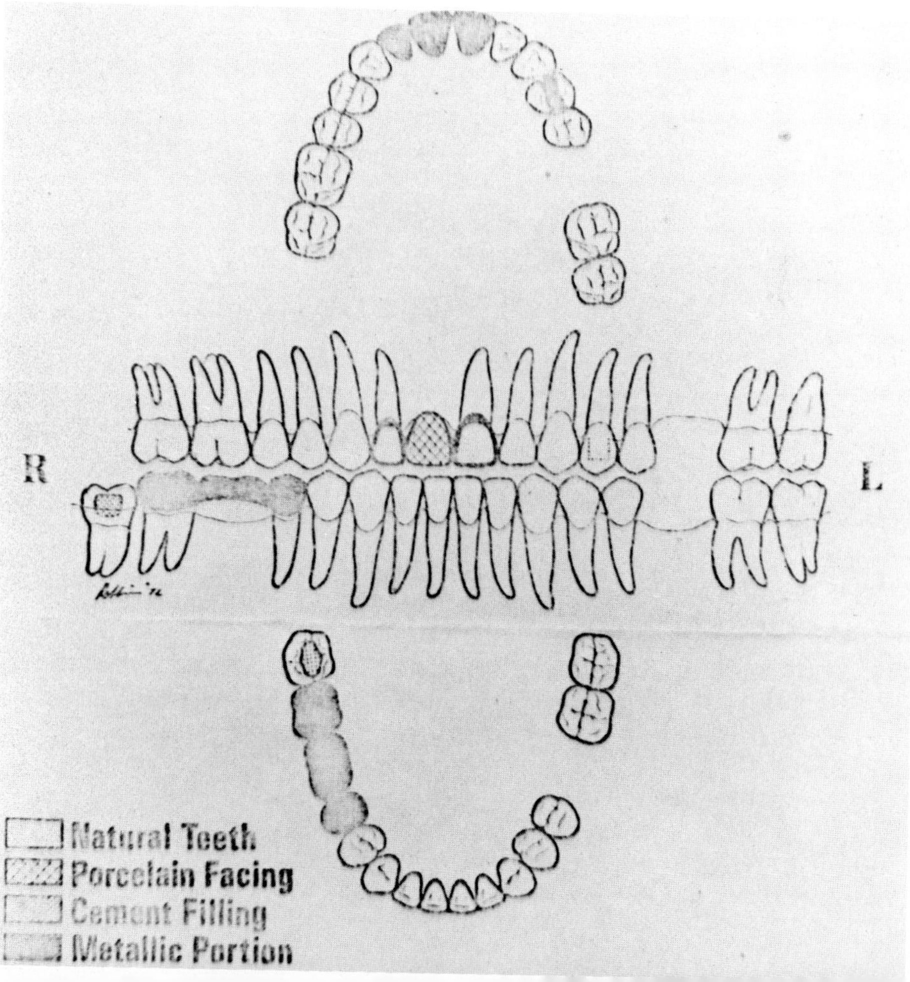

R

L

Natural Teeth

Porcelain Facing

Cement Filling

Metallic Portion

A ROGUES' GALLERY

Dr. Mengele in action—a very rare picture, showing him selecting victims for the gas chambers from among newcomers at the Birkenau railroad ramp near Auschwitz.

Sixteen years later—police photograph of Mengele, taken in Buenos Aires during his brief detention in 1959.

Mengele's fingerprints, on file at the Argentine Federal Police and the secret police (DOPS) of Brazil.

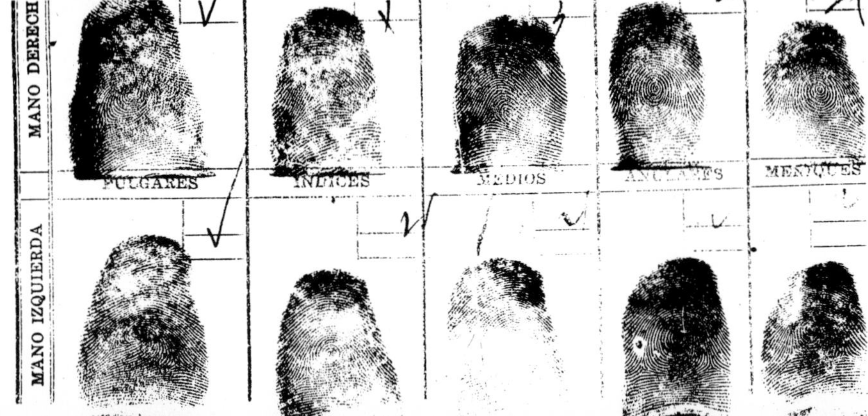

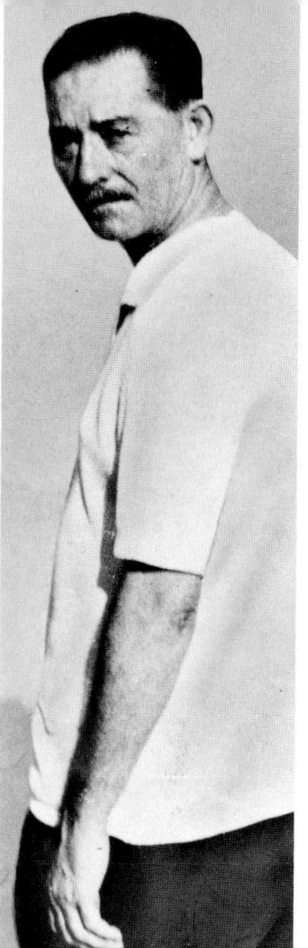

Mengele in 1971—startled by the photographer Adolpho Chandler of Brazil, who ambushed him at his hideout in Paraguay.

Mengele's house in Paraguay.

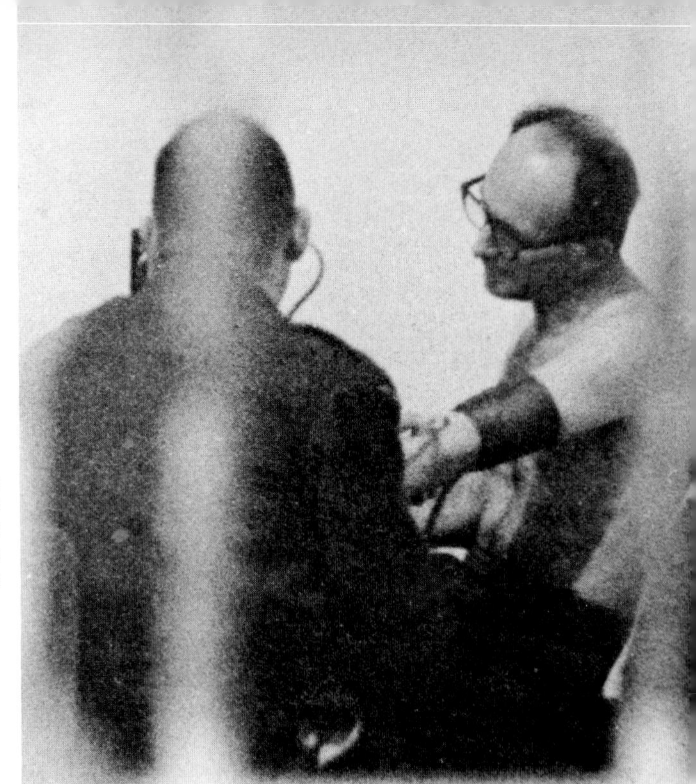

First picture of Eichmann in Israel, his blood pressure taken immediately upon his arrival in Jerusalem, twelve days after his abduction in May 1960.

Eichmann's house on Calle Garibaldi in San Fernando, Buenos Aires, beflagged to commemorate an anniversary of his execution in Jerusalem. Son Horst can be seen in the yard.

ILUSTRACION PERUANA
Caretas
Nº 451 – Enero 31 – Febrero 10 Precio 20 soles
Foto en color: Leoncio Mariscal/
En blanco y negro: France-Presse
¡EXPLOSIVO!
CASO BANCHERO
BARBIE (LYON, 1944)
ALTMANN
(LIMA, 1972)
CAZANDO
A UN
VERDUGO

The scoop that shook Bolivia and France—the exposure of Klaus Altmann as the war criminal Klaus Barbie, wanted for murder in Lyons, on the front page of *Caretas* magazine of Lima, Peru.

The heavily fortified entrance to Altmann's house in Choclacaya, near Lima, Peru, where he stayed as "Freddy" Schwend's guest and associate during the mysterious murder of fishing tycoon Luis Banchero Rossi, in the villa across the street (on New Year's Day in 1972).

During happier days. SS Colonel Friedrich Schwend, Hitler's official counterfeiter, at his palatial home in Italy in 1943, with his second wife, Hedda, and his daughter Erika.

Schwend in Lima, on the day of his arrest by Judge Santos Chichizola.

Franz Paul Stangl, former commandant of the Treblinka extermination camp, on the eve of his extradition to Germany by Brazil.

Rolf Günther, one of Eichmann's top aides, who vanished in the chaotic wake of the war and is still "missing."

Colonel Hans Ulrich Rudel, Luftwaffe ace, with Adolf Hitler, whose favorite soldier he was to the bitter end. This picture was taken in 1945.

Rudel, head of the Nazi rescue organization *Kameradenwerk,* with President Perón of Argentina, in the Casa Rosada in 1948. He was with Perón again on March 1, 1974 (!) after an absence of nineteen years, caused by the Argentine dictator's enforced exile.

Herbert Cukurs, the "butcher of Riga," in São Paulo in Brazil, a few days before his departure for the murder trap in Montevideo.

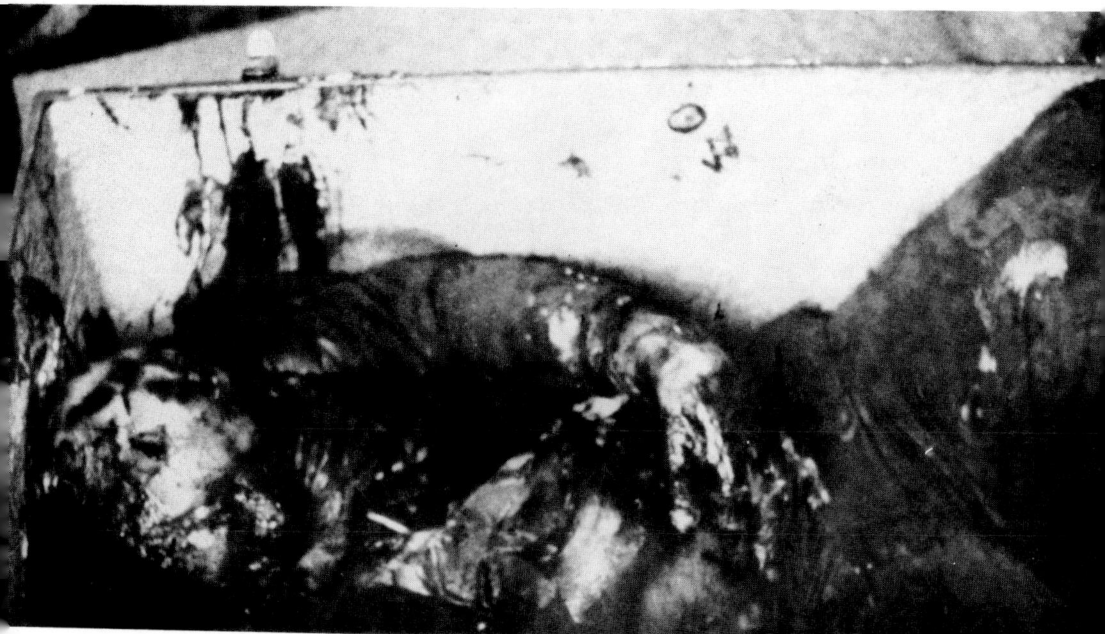

Cukurs' battered body in the trunk in which the Jewish "avengers" placed him after his "execution."

The man calling himself "Anton Kunzle," charged by the Montevideo police with complicity, as chief of the murder squad, in Cukurs' assassination.

THE RISE OF THE NEW REICH

Each year the Nazis of South America pick a beauty queen. This young lady was "Miss Nazi" in 1968.

Franz Pfeiffer (center), organizer of one of the most active and obnoxious neo-Nazi groups in South America, photographed at his headquarters in Santiago de Chile.

The second generation—young Chileans of German origin organized in a neo-Nazi organization in Santiago, whose membership is said to be growing by leaps and bounds during the right-wing military dictatorship.

Bormann's residence in Paraguay today.

12 OCT 948

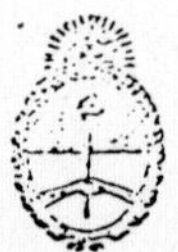

PODER EJECUTIVO NACIONAL
MINISTERIO DEL INTERIOR
DIRECCION NACIONAL DE MIGRACIONES

REPUBLICA ARGENTINA — 12 OCT 948 — ENTRADA PERMANENTE

DATOS PERSONALES
Nombres ELIEZER
Apellidos GOLDSTEIN
Fecha nacimiento 20 de Agosto de 1901
Lugar PIOTRKOFF – Polonia –
Nacionalidad POLACA Profesión GEOLOGO
Domicilio real SALTA Nº 130 San Martín Pcía. Bs. As.
Domicilio comercial

DOCUMENTACION
Cédula Identidad Nº 1.361.642 Policía Federal
Libreta Enrolamiento Nº
Libreta Cívica Nº
Pasaporte Nº Oficina Personas Perdidas — Vaticano.- Nº 073.909 de Nunciatura Apostólica en Bs. As.
Afiliado Nº
Otros

DATOS DE LA FAMILIA
Estado Civil SOLTERO Nupcias
Nombre del Cónyuge
Padre ABRAHAM GOLDSTEIN Vive NO
Madre MARIA ESTHER SADRINAS. Vive NO.
Hijos

Copy of Martin Bormann's registration at the National Immigration Directorate of Argentina, under the name of "Eliezer Goldstein," given him at the Rapallo conference (see next document, paragraph 3, line 12, identifying "Goldstein" as Bormann, and page 217 of text).

COPIA FIEL

†

Central de Inteligencia
MARTIN BORMANN

AGENCIA INFORMATIVA CATOLICA ARGENTINA

Hacia 1947, la organización de ayuda a las personas perdidas dependiente de la Secretaría de Estado del Vaticano, era dirigida por monseñor JOSE MONTINI, secundado en la tarea de proveer de documentación a los refugiados producidos por la S.G.M. por el sacerdote argentino de apellido SILVA, quien efectuó los enlaces pertinentes entre MONTINI, el Obispo de Génova monseñor JOSE SIRI, la esposa del entonces Presidente de la República Argentina, Sra. MARIA EVA DUARTE IBARGUREN de PERON y el ex vice furher MARTIN BORMAN. La entrevista principal se produjo en la Ciudad de Génova en el barrio elegante de RAPALLO.

Según información confidencial, en un primer momento ni el Obispo SIRI ni el cura SILVA tenian conocimiento que su interlocutor era MARTIN BORMAN, pues EVA DUARTE lo había presentado como " il mio bicondo cattivello ", según ella pariente lejano de su familia, de profesión filósofo, de ascendencia judeo - italiana, de nombre LUIGGI BOGLIOLO.

El obispo SIRI entro en sospechas porque BOGLIOLO se expresaba en un italiano duro, triestino, con inflexión alemana. Pero el 10 de Julio de 1947 EVA DUARTE, en compañia de los Generales Italianos GRAZIANI y CASSIANI y el comendatore GIOVANNI MAGGIO, presionan a SIRI para que colabore en cubrir con su presencia la personalidad de BORMAN que debe ser embarcado lo antes posible para Argentina. El Obispo accede aclarando que lo hace impulsado por su sentimiento de caridad cristiana y no porque comulgue con las ideas de los " amigos " que interceden por BORMAN, pero aconseja que no se haga pasar por italiano, pues BORMAN no solo no habla ese idioma sino que cuando pretende hacerse entender en él, lo destroza y destroza los timpanos de quien lo escucha; allí nace entonces la nueva personalidad de Martin BORMAN, quien comienza a llamarse ELIEZER GOLDSTEIN, a tal nombre esta la nueva documentación y con ella se embarca en Génova en el GIOVANNA "C" en el primer semestre de 1948.

Hacia el segundo semestre de 1948 ya esta en Buenos Aires, en casa de unos amigos genoveses, en la casa de la calle Salta Nº 120 de la Ciudad de San Martín, Pcia. Bs.As.

JUAN DOMINGO PERON SOSA, hace entrega al Vice fuhrer MARTIN BORMAN, la cuarta parte de los siguientes bienes:

Father Egidio's intelligence report about the circumstances of Bormann's migration to Argentina in 1948 (for translation of the text, see page 215), identifying "Eliezer Goldstein" as Bormann's alias. Bishop Siri is now a cardinal at the Curia in Rome. Monsignor Montini's first name should read "Juan" (Giovanni) instead of "José" (Giuseppe), a mistake by Egidio.

Central de Inteligencia
MARTIN BORMANN

COPIA F.E.

En marcos oro	187.692.400,=
En dólares	17.576.386,=
En libras esterlinas	4.632.500,=
En francos suizos	24.976.442,=
En florines holandeses	8.379.000,=
En francos belgas	17.280.009,=
En francos franceses	54.968.000,=
En platino Kg.	87,=
En oro Kg.	2.511,=
En Diamantes y Brillantes Kilates	4.638,=

Rdo.Padre EGIDIO ESPARZA

JEFE ACCIDENTAL A.I.C.A.

Father Egidio's confidential report to Coordinación Federal, giving the breakdown of the Nazi treasure smuggled to Argentina, one quarter of which the Peróns "surrendered" to Bormann.

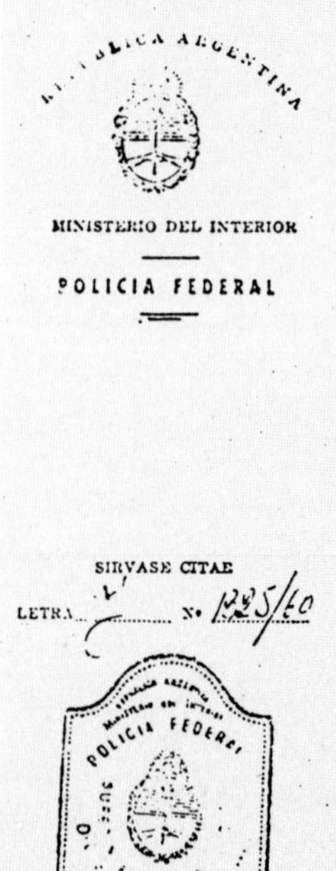

REPUBLICA ARGENTINA

MINISTERIO DEL INTERIOR

POLICIA FEDERAL

SIRVASE CITAR

LETRA ... N° 1225/60

ADOLF OTTO EICHMANN

Teniente Coronel de las Tropas de·Asalto del Tercer Reich,nació en Palestina en el año 1906 pero paso su niñez y adolecencia en la Ciudad de Linz,Austria.Fué condenado a muerte en rebeldía por el Tribunal internacional de NUrenberg.Igual que otros fugitivos nazis,entro al País en forma clandestina,utilizando los favores del Vaticano,logro embarcar con destino a Bs.As.en el vapor GIOVANNA C.que efectuaba la travesía regular NAPOLES – BUENOS AIRES,bajo la cobertura de RICARDO KLEMENT de profesión mécanico,nacido en BOLZANO,Italia,de origen alemán;desembarcó en Bs.As. a mediados de Julio de 1950.

Cover sheet of Adolf Eichmann's master file at the Policía Federal in Buenos Aires, the first paragraph detailing the record of his move from Italy to Argentina ("using the favors of the Vatican") in July 1950.

MINISTERIO DEL INTERIOR

POLICIA FEDERAL

MARTIN BORMANN

SIRVASE CITAR

NOTA.............. Nº ....

Político nazi alemán, nacido en el año 1900 en la Ciudad de Halberstadt, Pcí de Magdeburgo – Alemania. Jefe de la Cancillería del Partido Nacionalsocialista. El Tribunal de Crímenes de Guerra de NOremberg lo condenó a muerte en rebeldía. Junto con otros prófugos del derrumbe del Tercer Reich, ingresó a territorio nacional en forma clandestina, disfrazado de sacerdote jesuita, procedente de Genova – Italia, con documentos de identidad falsos, alrededor del año 1948.

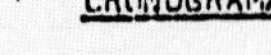

CRONOGRAMA DEL CASO

1948.–

BORMANN es visto e identificado en la Capital Federal. (Informe del Dr. PINO FREZZA, médico italiano que conoció a BORMANN en ocación de la visita del DUCE del que era acompañante.– S.I.R.Nº 0318).

BORMANN, contacta con un ex Oficial del Ejército Alemán en la cervecería " ABC " de la calle Lavalle al 500 de la Capital Federal.–S.I.R. 01319. JUAN FELISIAK).

1951.–

BORMANN se desplaza a la Ciudad de PARANA E.R. donde es entrevistado nuevamente por el Ingeniero JUAN FELICIAK, en un viaje relámpago que el último de los citados efectua a la Pcía. de Entre Rios, por eso entonces BORMANN se ocultaba mezclandose con la nutrida colonia de alemanes, croatas y polacos.

En el mismo año paso a Brasil, existiendo versiones que lo ubicaban dicandose en la impenetrable selva del area del Matto Grosso.

En su paso por la Argentina utilizó diversos pseudónimos, destacand

Cover sheet of Martin Bormann's master file at the Federal Police in Buenos Aires. Note that it is identical with the Eichmann file. Translation of the key first paragraph is on page 95. The file contains a year-by-year record of his movements and activities in South America going back to 1948. *"Chronology of the Case,"* the caption of the summary reads. "*1948:* Bormann is seen and identified in the Federal Capital (Buenos Aires). Report of Dr. Pino Frezza, Italian physician who met Bormann on the occasion of the visit of the Duce whom he [had] accompanied [to Germany]. SIRN/60318—Bormann makes contact with an ex-officer of the German Army in the ABC beer hall at 500 Lavalle Street in the Federal Capital. SIRN/01219 (*Juan Felisiak*).—1951: Bormann moves to the city of Paraná . . ."

CONFIDENCIAL y SECRETO

entre otros el de JUAN GOMEZ,bajo cuya cobertura,en 1948,MARTIN BORMANN recibió el grueso del tesoro que componían las reservas financieras del DEUTSCHE BANK,cuyo último poseedor LUDWIG FREUDE,murio envenenado.Otras coberturas fueron: JOSE PEREZ,ELIEZER GOLDSTEIN y BAUER.- Informe S.I.R.N° 01320.- Sr.TADEO KARLIKOSKY.

MARTIN BORMANN,tuvo varios hijos,uno de ellos,se ordenó sacerdote católico en la temida Compañia de Jesús (jesuitas) y fúe el que más ayudo a su progenitor en su permanente fuga,llegando incluso a admitir publicamente que creía que su padre había muerto en 1945,mentira cuidadosamente planeada con el único fin de interferir en la busqueda del criminal de guerra.

1952 :

Se tiene conocimiento que pese a que BORMANN tenía su recidencia más o menos fija entre el Estado de Matto Grosso y el Estado de Santa Catalina en los EE.UU. del Brasil,efectuaba viajes sumamente rapidos a disparesy diversas localidades,por ejemplo:

..Paraguay,Valdivia en Chile,Bariloche y Ascochinga,en la Argentina;en este último lugar,zona serrana de la Pcia. de Córdoba,contactaba con el comando central de la Organización ARAÑA,institución nacida en un lejano campo de prisioneros aliado,donde los recluidos alemanes se conjuraron para protegerse y ayudarse,unos con otros,en todo el mundo y mantener y resucitar el "ideal" Nacionalsocialista.

1953/54/55 y 56:

En este último año es identificado por una mujer en SAO PAULO,Brasil.Visita una vez Bariloche.

1957:

Continua en Brasil y restringe sus desplazamientos a la Argentina por que en ese año comienzan a penetrar agentes de Cdos. israelíes en el último de los Países citados,en busca de los criminales de guerra que han perdido el apoyo y la hegemonia anterior.-

1958/59:

Se lo ubica a MARTIN BORMAN, en una granja solitaria cerca de la localidad de CURITIBA- Brasil

1961:

En este año, bajo el seudonimo de BAUER, concurrió al parecer con Mengele, al Night Club " ALI BABA" en Asunción del Paraguay.

Su rastro se pierde en éntre la zona denominada Suiza Chilena, comprendida entre el Oceano Pacifico y la frontera argentina y el area imaginaria de Valdivia en Chile y Bariloche en Argentina.

Excerpts from the Argentine Federal Police summary sheets, with data about Bormann's movements and activities in South America: ". . . Passing through Argentina, he used various pseudonyms, among which the name 'Juan Gomez' was especially conspicuous. Under this cover, Bormann took possession of the bulk of the treasure from the reserves of the Deutsche Bank, whose last owner, Ludwig Freude, had been poisoned. Other aliases [of Bormann] included José Perez, Eliezer Goldstein and [Ricardo] Bauer. Report SIRN 01320 (Tadeo Karlikowski) . . . *1952:* It is known that while Bormann was a resident of the United States of Brazil, living in the states of Mato Grosso and Santa Catarina, he also took quick trips to such diverse places as Paraguay, Valdivia in Chile, Bariloche and Ascochinga in Argentina. In the last named location, in the province of Cordoba, he was in touch with the central command of the *Araña* (Spider) organization, an organization [designed] to sustain and revive the National-Socialist ideology. . . *1958–1959:* Bormann is located in an isolated farm near Curitiba, Brazil . . . *1961:* Using the alias Bauer, Bormann meets Mengele in the Ali Baba nightclub in Asunción, Paraguay. . . . His trace is lost after moving to the area known as the Chilean Switzerland, located between the Pacific Ocean and the Argentine border, in the regions of Valdivia in Chile and Bariloche in Argentina."

- 122 -

am Samstagnachmittag Vieles , was aus unserer großen Zeit Rang und Namen hatte zu zwanglosen Gesprächen oder auch zu harten politischen Diskussionen bei denen es oft an herber Kritik an Taten und Entscheidungen unserer nationalsozialistischen Führung nicht fehlte.

Page 122 of the manuscript of Martin Bormann's unpublished memoirs, authenticated by his signature at the top right of each page.

IV. Ausland.

Waren Sie im Ausland ? .... wo ? .... wie lange ? ....

In welcher Eigenschaft ? (Kaufm. Farmer. Angest. usw.) ....

Waren Sie in ehemaligen deutschen Kolonien ? .... wie lange ? ....

In welcher Eigenschaft ? (Kaufm. Farmer, Angest.)oder (Beamter, Soldat) ....

....

Unterschrift: 9. 3. 37.

Dienstgrad:

Martin Bormann's characteristic signature under his application for membership in the SS in 1937 (from the Berlin Document Center).

Persönlicher Stab Reichsführer-SS
Schriftgutverwaltung
Akt. Nr. Geh./ 62/5

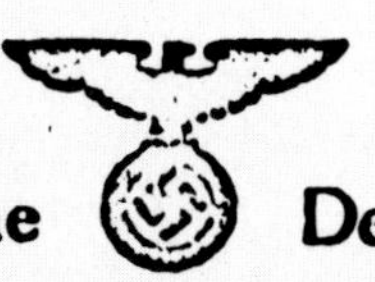

Nationalsozialistische Deutsche Arbeiterpartei

Partei-Kanzlei

Der Leiter der Partei-Kanzlei

Führerhauptquartier, den 11.7.1943

Geheim

Rundschreiben Nr. 33/43 g.

Betrifft: Behandlung der Judenfrage.

Note Bormann's charactisic signature on a document from the Führer's headquarters at right below stamped "*Geheim*" (Secret), and compare with #6.

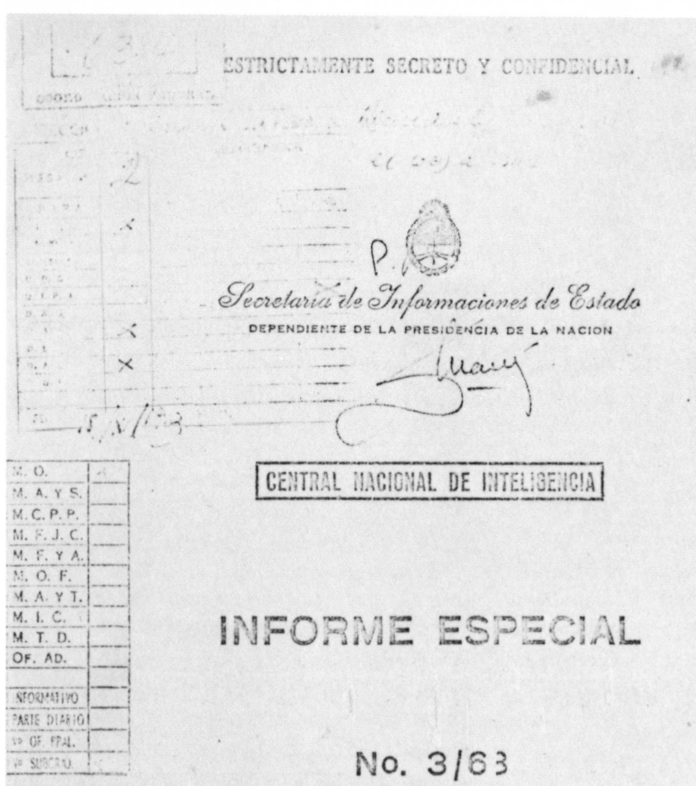
ESTRICTAMENTE SECRETO Y CONFIDENCIAL

Secretaría de Informaciones de Estado

DEPENDIENTE DE LA PRESIDENCIA DE LA NACION

CENTRAL NACIONAL DE INTELIGENCIA

M. O.
M. A. Y S.
M. C. P. P.
M. F. J. C.
M. F. Y A.
M. O. F.
M. A. Y T.
M. I. C.
M. T. D.
OF. AD.

INFORME ESPECIAL

No. 3/63

Cover sheet of the Martin Bormann File at S.I.D.E., the Argentine President's secret service (see page 94). The following is Colonel Caceres' summary account of Bormann's consultation of Dr. Otto Biss in Asunción (see pages 245–46), contained on page 3 of his secret report to the President: "Accompanied by Mengele, Bormann moved to Asunción, Paraguay. Since he was ill, and his condition was deteriorating it became necessary to call a physician, Dr. Otto Biss, residing in that city. He recognized Bormann and Mengele. Dr. Biss observed that Bormann, who had a scar on his forehead, suffered from momentary gastritis, but otherwise enjoyed good health."

en razon de que M.BORMANN, se encontraba enfermo y su estado al parecer se agravó a tal punto que debieron llamar un médico, el Dr. OTTO BISS, residente de esa ciu dad, quien reconoció a M.BORMANN, y a MENGELE. Que el Dr. BISS, observó que M. BOR MANN, tenía una cicatriz en la frente y que salvo esa pasajera gastritis, gozaba de buena salud. Asi mismo se pudo establecer que MENGELE, se encontraba en PARAGUAY muy bien protegido por el coronel ARGANA S, que controlaba todo el contrabando de ASUNCION A SAO PAULOZ, que se hacía por via aerea con algunos pilotos alemanes que habían s ido ex-miembros de la aviación alemana. En el año 1961, M. BORMANN se des plazó desde el MATTO GROSSO, a la zona del "ELDORADO" (Misiones) Argentina, y a la ciudad de IGUAZU, parando en la casa de un ex-SS, tres dias escasamentue, pues nunca se estacionaba en un lugar mucho tiempo, ya que no confiaba en nadie y ge neralmente andaba solo, muy pocas veces acompañado. Que durante los años subsiguion tes aparentemente se habría perdido el rastro de M. BORMANN, aunque siempre se te nían noticias de J. MENGELE en PARAGUAY que por otra parte desarrollaba intensas actividades y segun los informantes la situación de M.BORMANN , era distinta pues contando con grandes c ntidades de dinero invertido en muchas empresas no tenía nin guna necesidad de trabajar sino cuidar en el peor de los casos de sus intereses in vertidos y continuar alentando la ideología nazi y a sus adeptos. Todos los que tuvieron oportunidad de conocerlo estan contestes en q ue se trataba de un hombre sumamente astuto, habil y muy resue lto. Era evident e que desde la captura del otro criminal EICHMANN, la actividad de los grupos clandestinos judios había recru decido y sus movimientos se habian intensificado con respecto a los años ant eriores Es así que a principios del año 1964, fué nuevamente detectado en la zona de Villa BALLESTER, en una cerveceria muy frecuentada por alemanes y en una forma diriamos insolita ya que el informante T. KARLIKOWS KI, conocido estafador, con la venta de monedas supuestamente de oro, viajaba en forma permanentepor los paises limitrofes y así pudo saber que J.MENGELE s e hallaba bien protegido por un coronel ARGANAS del Ejercito Paraguayo y desarrollaba tareas en la venta de maquinas agricolas y asi pudo saber que M. BORMANN, hacía tiempo que no se le veía. Pero fué un día in

(5)

DIRECCION COORDINACION FEDERAL F. 2-68-8000-5-70

ESTRICTAMENTE CONFIDENCIAL Y SECRETO

CF " " Nº Buenos Aires, 16 de febrero de 1968

MEMORANDO

Para: CENTRAL DE INTELIGENCIA

Producido por: DIVISION DE ASUNTOS EXTRANJEROS

ASUNTO: Vigilancia y desplazamiento de personas extranjeras

Llevo a conocimiento de Ud., que de acuerdo a las instrucciones impartidas en su oportunidad se ha recibido en esta el informe del agente afectado al S.I.R. RODRIGUEZ, quien al tomar contacto con el informante ZUCCA RELLI, este le indicó que tenía un informe de suma importancia, ya que al tomar contacto con su amigo medico el Dr. Francisco Urbistondo, con consultorio en Arenales y Pueyrredon, este le indicó que había recibido en su consultorio una persona presa al parecer de un ataque que el Dr. URBISTONDO, diagnosticó como colico hepatico, de urgente atención, suministrandole SERTAL inyectable, aconsejandole reposo y cuidado en las comidas. El individuo en cuestión venía acompañado de un hombre aspecto aleman. Que su enfermo no hablaba casi el español, era bajo mas bien calvo, representando mas de 65 años, y tenia una cicatriz da frente, haciendo el que lo acompañaba, de traductor. Que luego de estar cerca de una hora el enfermo dijo llamarse RICARDO BAUER y luego de haberse repuesto se retiró de inmediato con su acompañante que era un joven alto y bien vestidos ambos. Que el informante ZUCCA RELLI, comentó el suceso al agente RODRIGUEZ, quien de inmediato con ZUCCARELLI, se dirigió al consultorio del médico, exhibiendole RODRIGUEZ dos fotografías una era de MENGELE y la otra la de BORMANN y fué que cuando vió esta ultima el Dr. URBISTONDO, respondió que esa era la fisonomía de su enfermo auque mas envejecido. Agregó el médico que no le llamaó la atención en ningún momento la entrada en su consultorio de esas personas, pero ahora recuerda que el enfermo le dijo que sufría de Gastritis y se tomaba el estomago y que venía de BRASIL viajando hacia el sur. Que en un bar de las inmediaciones se había sentido descompuesto y por ello reclamó un medico y una persona le indicó el de su casa.

Surveillance report of Bormann's consultation of Dr. Urbistondo (see page 411), the chief of the Division of Alien Affairs, reporting to Coordinación Federal on February 18, 1968: "I beg to call to your attention that, in accordance with his instructions, Special Agent Rodriguez has contacted the informant Zucca Relli [sic], who had very important information to impart. He had learned from his friend Dr. Francisco Urbistondo, whose offices are at the corner of Arenales and Pueyrredon Streets, that a person apparently suffering from an attack of what the doctor diagnosed as hepatic colic had visited him seeking relief. He was given an injection of Sertal and was advised to rest and watch his diet. The person in question was accompanied by a German-looking man. The patient spoke little Spanish, was short, balding, about 65 years old, and had a scar on his forehead. His companion acted as interpreter. The patient said that his name was Ricardo Bauer. After some rest, the patient and his tall young companion, both well-dressed, departed. When informant Zuccarelli related the event to Agent Rodriguez, the latter, accompanied by Zuccarelli, immediately visited the doctor at his office, and showed him two photographs, one of Mengele, the other of Bormann. When Dr. Urbistondo saw the second picture, he recognized that it was the photograph of the patient he had treated, although somewhat older than shown in the picture. The doctor added that although at that time he did not take special note of this event, he now recalled that the patient said he was suffering from gastritis. Holding his stomach, he added that he had come from Brazil, en route to the south [of Argentina]. He was seized by the attack in a nearby restaurant and sought the doctor's help at the recommendation of someone."

Supreme Court of the United States
Washington, D.C.

June 16, 1948.

The President,
The White House,
Washington, D. C.

My dear Mr. President:

After the telephone conversation in which you authorised me to ask Mr. Hoover to consider means to verify the report that Martin Bormann, convicted in absentia and sentenced to death at Nurnberg, is now a fugitive in the Argentine, Mr. Hoover immediately arranged a preliminary interview with my informant and, from other data available here, has furnished me a complete report.

In summary, the situation is this: The information that Bormann is in the Argentine came to me through John F. Griffiths, not known to me but formerly employed in the cultural department of the American Embassy at Buenos Aires. He had differences with the present Argentine government and was expelled from the country. He is well informed, but the F. B. I. reports that, in the opinion of many, he is not particularly responsible. He was not, however, trying to sell his information or seeking a reward and he has no apparent motive in this matter.

COPY

Another key document from Bormann's F.B.I. file, Justice Jackson's letter to President Truman (see page 49).

August 3, 1948 PERSONAL AND CONFIDENTIAL

Honorable Robert H. Jackson
Associate Justice of the
Supreme Court of the United States
Washington, D. C.

My dear Mr. Justice:

You will recall that an intensive search has been made for Martin Bormann, a German war criminal, and that at the present time inquiries are being made in Uruguay and Argentina looking toward the location of this man.

It may be of interest in this connection to you that recently a member of the British Intelligence, stationed in Italy, has informed a representative of this Bureau that it is an undisputed fact that subject Bormann's wife died in Southern Tyrol and that she is buried in or near Bolsano, Venezia, Italy, and that the exact position of her grave is presumably known to Intelligence Authorities in that district. Further information furnished was to the effect that Bormann has three children, and that these children were seen by this member of the British Intelligence in Bolzano in February 1948. Information was also given that the true identity of the children is generally known to all residents in the Bolsano district and presumably to the Intelligence Authorities there.

The Scotlant Yard Inspector in question stated that he believes the subject is alive and that he is hiding in Southern Tyrol, which is exceedingly rugged country and very suitable for being used as a hide-out. The Italian Police Officials in that part of the country are reported to be very corrupt and uncooperative.

This information is being brought to your attention as a matter of interest and you will be informed of further developments in this case.

With expressions of my highest esteem and best regards,

Sincerely yours,

J. Edgar Hoover's letter (see page 58) concerning information the Bureau had received from Scotland Yard (from Martin Bormann's file in the Federal Bureau of Investigation).

DIRECCION COORDINACION FEDERAL CF " OP " N° 2315

COPIA FIEL MEMORANDO

Para información de: MINISTERIO DE MARINA	Producido por: CENTRAL DE REUNION Bs. As., 18 de ABRIL de 1945.

ASUNTO: DESEMBARCO ALEMAN EN SAN CLEMENTE DEL TUYU - BAIRES.

Por intermedio de nuestros agentes que controlan el operar de LUDWIG FREUDE, agente del Tercer Reich, se sabe que ha hecho cuantiosos depositos en diversos bancos de plaza, a nombre de la conocida actriz de radio-teatro, MARIA EVA DUARTE IBARGUREN.

FREUDE comentó a " NATALIO " que el 7 de Febrero pxmo. ppdo. un U - boot (Submarino de la flota del Almirante DOENITZ) efectuó el transporte N° 1744 trayendo un " Tesoro " a la ARGENTINA, que ayudara a reconstruir el imperio NAZI en el mundo.

Investigaciones posteriores han permitido saber que los bultos desembarcados fueron consignados a la ESTANCIA LAHUSEN, caratulados " GEHEIME REICHSSAGE " y arribados en diversos camiones en la noche del 28 al 29 de Marzo del cte.

Los depositos han sido efectuados en el Bco. ALEMAN,

F. 2852

//////////////////

Report of the Naval Intelligence Division on the arrival of Nazi submarines ferrying the Bormann loot from Germany to Argentina via Spain (see page 205).

DIRECCION COORDINACION FEDERAL CF " OP " N° 2315/2

COPIA FIEL MEMORANDO

Para información de: Continuación:	Producido por: Bs. As., de de 19

ASUNTO: Bco. Transatlantico Alemán, Bco. Germanico y Bco. Tornquist. Todos a nombre de la dama ya mencionada precedentemente.

Se continua investigando.

Nicéforo Alarcón
Oficial Principal

Supervising the furtive surveillance of the incoming treasure-laden U-boats was Inspector Niceforo Alarcón of Naval Intelligence, whose activities and reports to the Ministry of the Navy are described on page 205.

Amtsgericht 22 Freiburg im Breisgau, den 5. Juni 1959

Aktenzeichen:

22 Gs 77/59

NE

Haftbefehl

Der deutsche Staatsangehörige Doktor der Philosophie und Doktor der Medizin

Josef Mengele,

geboren am 16. März 1911 in Günzburg, Regierungsbezirk Schwaben, Land Bayern, Bundesrepublik Deutschland, früher wohnhaft gewesen in Freiburg im Breisgau, Sonnhalde Nummer 87, im Jahre 1954 wohnhaft gewesen in Buenos Aires/Argentinien, Sarmiento 1875 Olivos, jetzt wohnhaft in Virrey Ortiz 970 Vicente López - FCNCBM Pcia. de Buenos Aires, Sohn des Fabrikbesitzers Karl Mengele in Günzburg und dessen Ehefrau Walburga Mengele geborene Hupfauer,

ist wegen dringenden Verdachts des vollendeten und versuchten Mordes in Untersuchungshaft zu nehmen.

Part of Dr. Mengele's seven-page, ten-count bill of indictment for murder and attempted murder. English text of opening paragraph and excerpts from charges on page 273.

Amtsgericht Freiburg Freiburg im Breisgau, den 11. März 1960

Aktenzeichen:

22 Gs 77/59

4

An das
Justizministerium
der Republik

Argentinien

Betrifft: Auslieferung des deutschen Staatsangehörigen Doktor Josef Mengele aus Argentinien nach Deutschland

Die argentinischen Behörden werden gebeten, den Verfolgten Doktor Josef Mengele zur Strafverfolgung wegen der ihm im Haftbefehl des Amtsgerichts Freiburg im Breisgau vom 5. Juni 1959 zur Last gelegten Straftaten in die Bundesrepublik Deutschland auszuliefern.

West German government's original petition for Mengele's extradition, as received by Argentine authorities in 1960, at a time when Mengele was no longer in Argentina.

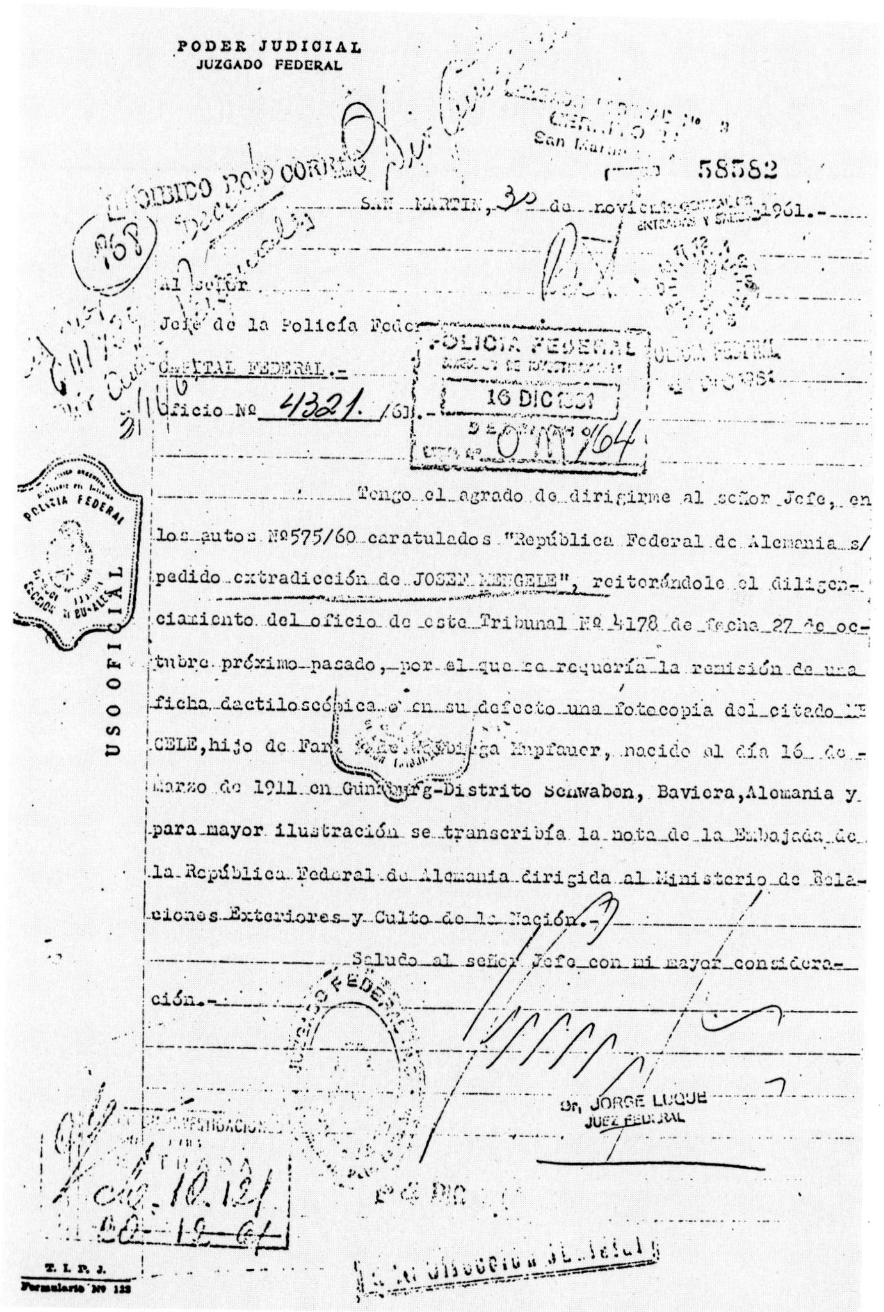

PODER JUDICIAL
JUZGADO FEDERAL

RECIBIDO POR CORREO

58582

SAN MARTIN, 30 de noviembre 1961.-

Al señor
Jefe de la Policía Federal
CAPITAL FEDERAL.-

POLICIA FEDERAL
16 DIC 1961

Oficio Nº 4321/61.-

Tengo el agrado de dirigirme al señor Jefe, en los autos Nº575/60 caratulados "República Federal de Alemania s/ pedido extradición de JOSEF MENGELE", reiterándole el diligenciamiento del oficio de este Tribunal Nº 4178 de fecha 27 de octubre próximo pasado, por el que se requería la remisión de una ficha dactiloscópica o en su defecto una fotocopia del citado MENGELE, hijo de Kar[illegible]burga Hupfauer, nacido el día 16 de marzo de 1911 en Gun[illegible]urg-Distrito Schwaben, Baviera, Alemania y para mayor ilustración se transcribía la nota de la Embajada de la República Federal de Alemania dirigida al Ministerio de Relaciones Exteriores y Culto de la Nación.-

Saludo al señor Jefe con mi mayor consideración.-

Dr. JORGE LUQUE
JUEZ FEDERAL

USO OFICIAL

T. I. P. J.
Formulario Nº 123

Argentine Federal Judge Dr. Jorge Luque's warrant for Mengele's arrest, issued on November 30, 1961, with request for his fingerprints.

Jonny:

alles diesmal grosser Bheibenhonig

Kartoffeln restlos verloren, mussten zahlen

um frei sein zu kännen. Ric und ich sind

vorläufig wegen gefahr nicht zu Hause.

Hoffe sehr dass sonst nichts passiert.

Freddy.

"Freddy" Schwend's hastily typewritten warning to his accomplice Altmann-Barbie (code named "Jonny"), impounded by Judge Santos in Lima during 1972 raid on Schwend's fortress-home (see page 86). "This time," it read, "all is big shit. Potatoes [money] lost, had to pay to stay at large. Ric and I temporarily absent from home, on account of danger [of arrest]. Hope nothing else will happen." Signed "Freddy."

POLICLINICA CIANCAGLINI

Director: Dr. ALFONSO P. CIANCAGLINI
Sub-Director: Dr. FRANCISCO P. CIANCAGLINI

ITUZAINGO 134/138 - T. E. 743-0961
SAN ISIDRO

//material de estudio radiográfico,electrocardiograma y análisis varios como para hubicar el mejor resultado del enfermo,y los que me trajo cuando realicé el primer injerto(quedando en mi poder nada más que dos radiografías).

La filiación de este enfermo según sus datos personales dice llamarse Ricardo Bauer,de aparente orígen germánico(dice que lo recomendaron del paraguay y que el es de la colonia alemana de Entre Rios,aunque en San Isidro acusa domicilio transitorio en la calle Presidente Uriburo Nº701-Pcia de Bs.As.)de contitución Pícnica,cuello grueso,acusaba 65 años aunque aparentaba más de 70,desarrollo muscular normal,esquleto fuerte,tenía una prótesis dentaria que no se descubría muy fácil,hablaba un castellano co acento alemanizado,piel blanca,ojos claros con profundidad en su mirada,sonreía de costado con facilidad hablando lo estrictamente necesario,deja ver en su frente una ligera cicatriz cruzando su frente en diagonal,camina como si hubiese existido un espasmo cerebral(el enfermo lo niega).Al ser interrogado el paciente porqué quería un injerto general,respondió que ultimamente su estado general era cada vez más bajo,que además hacían unos años que se sentía impotente sexxual(dice que

A portion of a report from the clinic of Dr. Ciancaglini, in which the doctor describes a visit to his office in San Isidro of Ricardo Bauer (Martin Bormann):

"The description of this ill man, according to his personal records, says that his name is Ricardo Bauer, and that he is apparently of German origin. (He says that he was recommended to come here in Paraguay, and that he is from the German colony of Entre Ríos. In San Isidro his temporary residence is in Presidente Uriburu Street, number 701.) He was of squat appearance, thick-necked, with a strong, muscular build, and had false teeth, although they were hard to detect. He spoke Castilian with a German accent, his skin was white, he had a deep look in his eyes, he smiled easily and spoke only when necessary. A scar went diagonally across his forehead, and he walked as if he had suffered a stroke (but he denied this)."

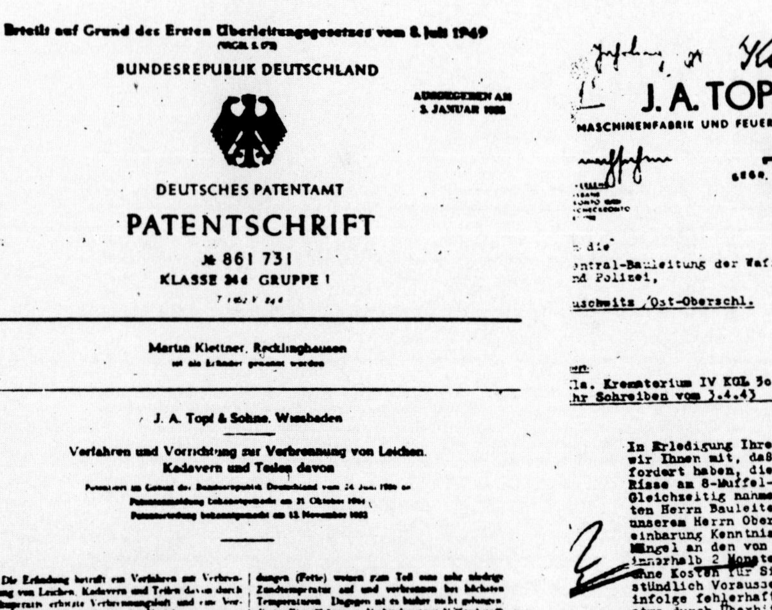

Erteilt auf Grund des Ersten Überleitungsgesetzes vom 8. Juli 1949

BUNDESREPUBLIK DEUTSCHLAND

AUSGEGEBEN AM 5. JANUAR 1953

DEUTSCHES PATENTAMT

PATENTSCHRIFT

№ 861 731

KLASSE 24d GRUPPE 1

Martin Klettner, Recklinghausen
ist als Erfinder genannt worden

J. A. Topf & Söhne, Wiesbaden

Verfahren und Vorrichtung zur Verbrennung von Leichen, Kadavern und Teilen davon

J. A. TOPF & SÖHNE

MASCHINENFABRIK UND FEUERUNGSTECHNISCHE BAUUNTERNEHMUNG

Eingang: 12. APR. 1943

An die
Zentral-Bauleitung der Waffen-SS und Polizei,
Auschwitz /Ost-Oberschl.

ERFURT

Betr.: Krematorium IV KGL 30 b,
Ihr Schreiben vom 3.4.43

Bftgb.Nr. 26419/43/JA/Lo.

In Erledigung Ihres oben angeführten Schreibens teil[en] wir Ihnen mit, daß wir unseren Polier, Herrn Koch, a[uf]gefordert haben, die angeblich in letzter Zeit entstan[denen] Risse am 8-Muffel-Ofen im Krematorium IV zu beseiti[gen]. Gleichzeitig nahmen wir von der zwischen Ihrem sehr [geehr]ten Herrn Bauleiter Sturmbannführer B i s c h o f f [und] unserem Herrn Oberingenieur P r ü f e r getroffene[n Ver]einbarung Kenntnis, nach welcher wir die auftretende[n] Mängel an den von uns errichteten Einäscherungsöfen, innerhalb 2 Monaten nach Inbetriebnahme der Öfen auf[treten,] ohne Kosten für Sie beseitigen. Hierbei ist selbstv[er]ständlich Voraussetzung, daß die evtl. aufgetretenen infolge fehlerhafter Ausführung entstanden sind und etwa durch Überhitzung der Öfen bezw. durch Abstoßen inneren Ausmauerung durch die Schürgeräte usw.

Wie bereits eingangs erwähnt, haben wir unserem Po[lier] Koch Anweisung gegeben, die jetzt eingetretenen Sch[äden] zu beseitigen, was in der Zwischenzeit wohl erfolgt

Stets gern für Sie beschäftigt, empfehlen wir uns I[hnen] bestens

Heil Hitler!

No end to the Final Solution. In January 1953, eight years after the war, the Erfurt-Wiesbaden firm of J. S. Topf & Sons received patent No. 861,731 in West Germany for the crematoria which it supplied to and serviced at the extermination camps in 1943. The typewritten letter at right, addressed to the SS administration in Auschwitz, closed with the words, "Always pleased to be working for you, etc."

Gustav in a long letter on November 11, 1942. "We have," he wrote to the Reichsleiter, "to find an entirely new way" with regard to safeguarding the Krupp firm for the future, by "creating new legislation."

Bormann liked old Gustav. He was his contact at the head of the "Hitler Bounty." Now he set him up as his dupe, recognizing that what was good for the Krupps would be eminently profitable for the Party. He would push through the new legislation and let the Krupps have what they wanted—for a price. They would have to take in the Party as a silent partner, assigning to it some of their assets abroad and sharing their ownership of vast real-estate holdings they had in South America. It promised to be an immensely lucrative (and, as it turned out, farsighted) deal, and Bormann agreed to promote it with all his energy and influence.

Explaining to Hitler the immense advantages that would accrue to them from "the new legislation," he obtained the Führer's permission in principle to turn Krupp into "an absolute industrial monarchy." On December 12, in a letter he sent to Essen with Helmut von Hummel, Bormann informed Bohlen that the deal was set. "The Führer wishes," he wrote, "a 'Lex Krupp' entirely designed for the preservation of the Krupp family enterprise."

Despite their sins and snobbery, the Krupps, a dour, decadent dynasty of cannon makers, appealed to martial sovereigns like Napoleon, the Kaiser and the Führer. In this weird mutual-admiration society, the results could be measured in hundreds of millions. Hitler on his part had a fancy for foppish, clannish old "Taffy," as Gustav Krupp von Bohlen und Halbach was called by his intimates. Was he not an ardent Nazi and the major solicitor of funds for the Party's secret exchequer? Hitler rewarded him with lavish contracts until the Krupp concern became the most prosperous cog in the industrial war machine. Now he was ready to give Taffy what he so ardently wanted, the Lex Krupp.

It took some time to iron things out. The Party's share in the mammoth deal had to be specified and agreed upon. The Krupps acquiesced eagerly to Bormann's terms, especially since he was not proposing to encroach upon anything they had in Germany and demanded no share in the control of the firm. The "Führer's wish" became a *Verordnung* ("directive") on November 12, 1943, and then law when the Lex Krupp was published in the official journal a few days later.

Now, five years later in Argentina, when he was *the* Party, even as Louis XIV was *the* state, Bormann claimed the spoils. His share included considerable liquid assets the Krupps had in Argentine banks and part ownership of a huge *estancia* in the Province of Salta, the Rancho Grande. It was owned outright by the family, regarded as private property that was outside the "industrial part of the estate."*

The Krupps rarely if ever visited the ranch, which covered some 800,000 acres; it was too far, too wild, too exotic. It was administered for the absentee owners by an estate manager from an office at 311 Corrientes in Buenos Aires. But now it suddenly acquired a new landlord, who staked out his claim and indicated that he intended to move in.

The Rancho Grande thus became one of Bormann's homes in exile, an ideal place in which to hide. "It is so big," I was told by Alejandro Raffaele, the police commissioner of Salta Province, "so remote, so inaccessible that locating Bormann there, even if we wanted to, would be like finding a needle in a haystack. We know whenever he is at the ranch. But we never make even an attempt at looking for him. He can live there peacefully, concealed by the dense jungle of chanar bushes, thick algarrobas and tala trees, with the wild guanacos and the other skunks that inhabit this rugged region."

Settled in Argentina—where he lived mostly in or around Buenos Aires in the sumptuous villas of friends or business associates, or in the mountainous resort region of Bariloche, which reminded him of his beloved Bavaria—Martin Bormann embarked on a new life at the age of only forty-eight. He assembled a new entourage of "smart cookies" to take care of his needs and to front for him in the management of his business. His arrival in Buenos Aires brought to Argentina a new Führer and established a definite hierarchy in the huge colony of Nazi exiles who were making the most of President Perón's furtive hospitality. Colonel Rudel was there,

* This almost mythical "ranch"—actually the largest single agricultural property in South America—is the conglomerate of five huge ranches in and around Salta. It was wholly owned by the Krupps until 1967. Then, however, for mysterious reasons, it was given corporate entity and anonymity, with no more Krupp apparent in its ownership and management. However, it continues to be called "the Krupp Ranch" by the inhabitants of the region, who see members of the shadowy family coming and going in this remote part of Argentina. It should not be confused with the Ampascachi ranch of a daughter of Gustav Krupp von Bohlen und Halbach who refused steadfastly to have anything to do with the fugitive Reichsleiter. In Salta, Bormann also stayed at the Victoria Plaza Hotel, registering under various names, mostly as Ricardo Bauer. He last stayed at the hotel in April or May 1972. See also p. 420.

as was Colonel Otto Skorzeny, the scar-faced Austrian swashbuckler who had kidnaped the Duce from the custody of his jailers after his downfall in the summer of 1943.

There were many more, too numerous to mention, the small fry by the thousands, but also prominent personalities of the defunct Third Reich, diplomats, politicians, writers, physicians, scientists, all of them bearing—some of them with a morbid pride—the mark of Cain. Bormann became their undisputed leader, a kind of Nazi Godfather in exile, administering the complex affairs and tending to the welfare of his vast "family" with an iron hand.

He enjoyed the generous patronage of President Perón, who drew a tight curtain of secrecy around his sheltered guest. So far, indeed, did this protection go that Perón insisted on keeping all documents referring to Bormann in Argentina in his personal safe. They were found and became available to Coordinación Federal only in 1956, almost a year after Perón's fall.

But if Bormann's relationship with Perón was stabilized, a new controversy suddenly flared up, confronting him with a serious challenge to his control of the "treasure." Bormann did not covet it for himself. Extremely frugal in his own needs and parsimonious in the management of the funds, he projected his own thriftiness to those who looked to him for financial aid. He doled out mere pittances to the indigent Nazis and cut off altogether the "*Nassauers*," as he referred to the "freeloaders" who expected to live entirely on his munificence.

His miserly economizing amid the growing affluence of his regime caused a lot of grumbling among the fugitives, who thought they had a rightful share in the treasure. But while the rank and file merely champed at the bit and groused, the old syndicate asserted itself brazenly as a determined claimant to a share. Ludwig Freude and his three partners demanded to be paid off, and then—dissatisfied with what Bormann offered—began to contest his dictatorial regime.

The calm of Bormann's exile during these first few years was marred by intrigue and bickering. Something had to be done to settle the accounts once and for all. The feuds increased in intensity as the settlement dragged on and Bormann remained adamant in his refusal to "take care" of his former trustees. They ended only with the deaths of the men who dared to question his interpretation of the leadership principle.

Heinrich Dörge was the first to go. In 1949, only a little over a year after Bormann's arrival in Argentina, his body was found in a Buenos Aires street. Although the Policía Federal conducted an inquiry, the results were never made public.

Then in December 1950, Ricardo von Leute was also found dead. His murder is still unsolved. Next it was Ricardo Staudt's turn. He too died mysteriously, a few months after Leute's murder.

Freude was now the only member of the old syndicate still alive. A sturdy gut-fighter and master of intrigue, he outlasted his late partners for another year. But in 1952 he was found dead in his house in Buenos Aires, an empty cup on the table in front of him. He had drunk poisoned coffee.

After that, Martin Bormann had no more rivals to contest his rule. The brief period that followed Freude's death and preceded Perón's downfall became his best years in Argentina—comfortable, pleasant, undisturbed. He moved about freely in Buenos Aires, and vacationed around San Carlos de Bariloche (where the local German residents, who knew who he was, erected a protective shield around him and still do whenever he shows up in the area). Or he enjoyed the rustic seclusion of the Rancho Grande, spending his mornings at his favorite pastime, gardening.

The life he led was best described by Bormann himself in the memoirs he began jotting down in the early sixties and on which he continues to work even today.

> After the horrors of the war [he wrote in his typical unadorned style] and the adventures of our flight to South America by way of several countries, Buenos Aires with its tranquil and elegant suburbs of villas was the ideal place where we, the so-called "heavies" [*schwere Fälle*], could unwind at last. Much more than today, the German colony was then split into two "hostile factions." One group consisted of people who had come to Argentina before the great war—before 1938, that is—mostly Jews and our political opponents. In the other group were we, the hunted since 1945. There were, of course, newcomers in between who had immigrated to Argentina for economic reasons and were preoccupied solely with their own welfare. They had nothing in common with us and, therefore, nothing more need to be said about them.
>
> Both groups had their stanch friends lined up even prior to their arrival, people who were comfortably well off and could well afford to aid materially our comrades in need. Among the wealthy families well disposed to our group and sympathetic to

the National Socialist ideology were the Hertigs, the Freudes, the Staudts, the Haases and many others. Not only did they stand by with monetary help, but they also opened their homes to us, so that very soon a lively social life developed.

Unforgettable for me are the parties in the hospitable home of the Haase family, which had moved to Argentina from Paraguay only shortly before our own arrival. At first they lived in Munro, but later built a big house in Florida near the Pan-American Highway, complete with a beautiful garden and swimming pool. Regularly each Saturday afternoon, many of us who used to be men of prominence and rank during the great days assembled in genial get-togethers, to engage in casual chitchat but also in heated discussions that often included harsh criticism of the deeds and decisions of our National Socialist leadership.

Among the guests at the Haases' were such famous soldiers as Rudel, Galland, Baumbach, Niedenführ and Kramer. Also artists like Professor Ritter, who conceived and directed some of the best motion pictures made during the war, and Peter Kreuder, the noted pianist and popular composer of hit songs. The political scientists and historians gathered around Professor Johannes von Leers. Mingling among them in hermetical incognito were we the "heavies," Eichmann, Mengele and myself.

Eichmann called himself Klement, Mengele went by the name of Dr. Gregor, and my pseudonym was Richard Bauer. Nobody seemed to know who I really was, not even Eichmann—who, like myself, refrained from submitting to plastic surgery—even though I remembered him from several meetings in Berlin. Mengele was then politically a complete nonentity. It was only later that he became notorious, after his identity was disclosed and his deeds advertised in sensationalistic exposés by Simon Wiesenthal. At any rate, he did not expect yet that he would have to live out his life in hiding. Undoubtedly Eichmann also still hoped that he could remain undetected. I will come back later to the shameless incident of his kidnaping by an Israeli commando group during the regime of President Frondizi and the implications of the case under international law.

These were years dominated by our great benefactor, Juan Domingo Perón. The elite in our group served him well and faithfully as military and scientific advisers. Others succeeded in establishing themselves firmly in the private sector, like Stertzinger, the former Reich Commissioner for Water Supplies, who founded the firm Capri in Buenos Aires and was busy conducting interesting hydrological studies in Argentina. Dr. Holler, the former Reich Commissioner for the glass industry, was back in his old metier, active in the same field now in Buenos Aires.

While Mengele plunged eagerly into the social whirl, Eichmann and I preferred to live quietly and in seclusion, for obvious reasons. Our political inspiration was Professor von Leers whose journal, *Der Weg*, published and printed in Florida, was the mouthpiece of our group. The growth of the German national consciousness of our colony could be measured in the steadily increasing circulation of his journal, not a few copies of which found their way into our subjugated and shackled homeland. Von Leers stood up with incomparable courage for our National Socialist legacy of ideas, exposing the lies of the international press, and presenting the true background of the conflict that was moving rapidly toward a showdown between the West and the East.*

For all the inconveniences that compelled Bormann to shroud himself in his "incognito" and live in seclusion, there appeared to be not a cloud on the horizon to darken the idyllic comfort and contentment of his exile. But the days of his good life in Argentina were numbered, not because he himself had anything to fear from pursuers. It was his "great benefactor" who was riding for a fall.

* This representative excerpt is my translation of the part of Bormann's memoirs which Dr. Alfonso Finot of Bolivia, his literary representative, placed at my disposal during our meeting in Lima, Peru, in February 1973, at the time when I was invited by him, on Bormann's behalf, to edit the manuscript for publication. Each page featured Bormann's initial at the top and his right thumbprint at the bottom.

Chapter Fourteen

Exit Perón—The First Crisis

As the man who fell from the skyscraper said upon passing the third floor, so far I'm doing fine.

—Juan Domingo Perón on June 17, 1955, the morning after he suppressed a rebellion of air force and naval officers.

On the evening of June 27, 1952, in Buenos Aires, a party of three solemn-faced men was ushered through a back door in the Ministry of Labor building to the improvised chapel in the round, columned auditorium on the second floor. A torrential rain was drenching the long line of weeping mourners, shuffling in an unbroken line since the day before to view the body of Eva Maria Duarte de Perón, lying in state in a glass-topped white mahogany casket.

The little group of privileged mourners was escorted to the orchid-covered bier, where the stocky, middle-aged man who was obviously the object of this special attention stepped forward and stood silently for a single minute with head bowed facing the coffin. Then he turned, left as he came, and vanished with his companions into the hushed city, which looked more like a village after dark, with all amusement places shut down, advertising signs and the lights of the shop windows turned off, the street lamps draped in black crepe.

Nobody recognized the quick-stepping mourner—that was how he had wanted it, for he was Martin Bormann. Accompanied by his secretary and the young son of his host, he had come to pay his respects to the woman who had been instrumental in paving his way to this haven.

Was this the end of an era? Bormann could not know, and perhaps he did not care to contemplate what the death of his beautiful blond sponsor portended for his own future. For all his prominence in the Third Reich and unique station among the Nazi fugitives, he was not accorded any special honors or attention in Argentina. His relations with the Peróns were correct but distant. They guarded the secrecy of his presence in the country and assured his personal safety. But they kept him at arm's length, even as they treated the thousands of fugitives who enjoyed Argentine hospitality by the grace of El Lider.

The year of Eva Perón's death—as dramatic and unpredictable as was everything she had done in her life—saw what struck many of us as a sudden rebirth of Nazism, and not only in South America. In Germany, the possibility of such a revival was darkly conceded by U.S. High Commissioner John J. McCloy, in his report for the last quarter of 1952. "The all-prevailing power of the National Socialist regime has left many former officials with a longing for power," he wrote, adding that "the undercurrent of extreme nationalism might form a combination willing again to set Germany off on another disastrous adventure."

His warning was emphasized by the results of local elections in the State of Lower Saxony. Parties that openly labeled themselves right-wing nationalists—a euphemism for National Socialist—received almost two million votes. Wilhelm Schepmann, a notorious SA leader, became the first prominent Nazi to win elective office since the war. General Kurt von Manteuffel, a famed Panzer commander running on a rightist ticket, was also elected.

Schepmann was supported by Otto Ernst Remer, a young major in 1944 whose quick intervention had foiled the coup of July 20 and who was promoted to general by the grateful Führer for his part in avenging the attempt on his life. Remer's own Reich Party had been outlawed the year before. But its members, most of them former officers of the Waffen SS, banded together in a number of splinter groups that brought out the vote for Schepmann and the others running on thinly camouflaged neo-Nazi platforms. An even more alarming sign of what McCloy regarded as "the pattern of the revival of Nazism" was a rally with all the familiar Nazi trimmings. The Hitler-type keynote speech by former Luftwaffe General Bernhard Ramcke, whose last-ditch defense of "fortress" Brest was hailed as "a great National Socialist feat," brought down the crowded house.

Even in London, the times had an ominous undertone in a quaint incident that marred the annual Armistice Day ceremony at the Cenotaph in Whitehall. The solemn silence that followed the laying of the wreath by Queen Elizabeth was broken by a man who shouted, "Heil Hitler." In the United States, the New Orleans police scooped out a "Nazi Storm Trooper Club," complete with swastika, photographs of Hitler, a cache of hidden arms and a program of violence. Its leader announced at his arrest: "I have information that *der Führer* is still alive in Argentina and I am going to join him there."

Argentina, of course, was the hotbed of Nazism and Fascism in exile. The country was swarming with fugitives, many of them holding positions of influence in government. The noisy and powerful colony of fugitives was not confined to Germans. Led by Vittorio Mussolini, the Duce's son who had built a multimillion-dollar economic empire since his arrival in April 1947, Italian Fascists occupied key positions in the country's industrial life and wielded considerable influence on public opinion. They even had their own "Bormann"—Carlo Scorza, Mussolini's right-hand man when he was general secretary of the Fascist Party in Italy. He had been tried *in absentia* after the war by a court in Pistoia and sentenced to thirty years' imprisonment for participation in the murder of the Monarchist leader Giovanni Amendola. Scorza too escaped on the monastery route and, using a false Vatican passport made out in the name of "Dr. Camilo Sirtori," entered Argentina, where he was now publishing the magazine *Historium*.

Dino Grandi, the former Italian Foreign Minister, was posing as a Portuguese lawyer named Domenico Galli; and old Cesare Maria de Vecchi, last of Mussolini's original Quadrumvirs, lived as a lay brother in a Franciscan monastery. Among the lesser-known personalities of a defunct era were the Fascist industrialist Benito Sternoni (who later became, perhaps unknowingly, one of the employers of Adolf Eichmann) and the financier Dr. Grimaldi. They were busy constructing conglomerates from the base of four lucrative holding companies, including the Argentine representative of Fiat.

The crudest among the fugitives were the Croatian Nazis,

whose murderous Poglavnik Ante Pavelic also enjoyed Perón's hospitality until he was shot in the street by an irate Yugoslav; and the Hungarians, whose neo-Nazism was the shrillest. Even ethnically authentic quislings received refuge in this hospitable land, including two of Norway's top war criminals, Finn Stoern, the former ambassador to Berlin, and Dr. Arne Hoeygard, a physician charged with conducting Nazi-type "medical" experiments. They arrived mysteriously in Buenos Aires by small motorboat in March 1949 and were permitted to join the Norwegian colony of at least six other wanted Nazi criminals (who had come apparently from nowhere in a small craft in July 1948) although their immigration status was conceded to be "wholly irregular."

The German Nazis were not only the most numerous, but also the noisiest and most powerful. At this time, it seemed, they decided to reassert themselves publicly in a brazen neo-Nazi campaign organized by Dr. Goebbels' onetime secretary, a man calling himself Wilfred von Oven. Seizing upon the showing of the American motion picture *The Desert Fox* about Field Marshal Erwin Rommel, Oven, writing in *Freie Presse*, the mouthpiece of the neo-Nazi movement, attacked "the patently false if not criminal" policies of the United States. The article was designed as the opening salvo in a brash campaign to swing Argentina's 200,000 Germans (of whom only 70,000 were citizens) to the Nazi way of thinking. The most disturbing aspect of the intracolony struggle was that Dr. Hermann Terdenge, the West German ambassador who was a close associate of Chancellor Konrad Adenauer, was loath to disassociate himself from the boisterous neo-Nazi group.

Unlike Ambassador Terdenge, Martin Bormann frowned on such demonstrations. He could move about as he pleased, with apparent impunity, going out in Buenos Aires, traveling to Bariloche on holidays, checking into hotels and participating in convivial beer-drinking parties at the *Stammtische* of friends. He was using different aliases—Ricardo Bauer most of the time, but also Juan Gomez and José Perez, even Eliezer Goldstein on occasions, because he thought it was an excellent "cover" to keep Jewish pursuers away. But with what he had at stake, he preferred to lay low and avoid anything like Wilfred von Oven's rantings. It focused attention on the Nazis in exile, and Bormann was apprehensive lest too much publicity and too close scrutiny expose him in the end.

He may or may not have been aware of it, but he was, in fact, not just another face in the crowd. We know now that he was watched closely, by agents of the Policía Federal and of the Division of Alien Affairs, whose interest in Bormann was academic but keen. They knew that Bormann was untouchable, thanks to the protection of the country's Chief Executive. Bormann could not be molested or arrested. But he could be watched and a record of his movements could be kept.

There was an undercurrent of domestic politics in his surveillance. It was undertaken exactly because of Perón's interest in him. The flamboyant President was riding high. But he was accumulating enemies in powerful circles who were becoming increasingly displeased with his free-wheeling, demagogic regime. Elements in the armed forces were restive, and so was the top leadership of the police, the very people who alone had the means to topple him. Two high police officials in particular, Brigadier General Arturo Bertollo of Policía Federal and Colonel José F. Velasco, chief of the Buenos Aires Provincial Police, were not exactly gunning for Perón, but they thought it wise to keep a record of his aberrations and put him on notice that he was by no means as infallible and inviolable as he fancied himself.

The surveillance of Bormann—a reflection of Bertollo and Velasco's growing disillusionment with El Lider—was their groping for the soft spot in the dictator's armor. They tolerated the watch on Bormann, although they should have called it off if they had been playing the Perón game.

The surveillance produced two sets of results. One consisted of direct observations by special agents, among them three in particular, Raneri, Chamado and Verri, who specialized in Bormann. The other consisted of data supplied by informants, not a simple task, for the former Reichsleiter was a wily and elusive quarry. A meticulous planner and iron-fisted manager of his affairs, he was running his life with the same efficiency and circumspect organization that had characterized his regime at the head of the Party chancery with over seven hundred employees under him.

Nothing in his life was haphazard, nothing was left to chance. He never used public transportation, such as trains, buses or planes. He invariably traveled in hired cars, driven by his bodyguard, a German-speaking Chilean of Irish descent named O'Higgins, or by his secretary, a tall, blond, youngish man called Jiménez, whose parentage was Mexican and German.

Bormann never touched anything with bare hands, for fear that he might leave his fingerprints. He would put on a pair of rubber gloves even to lift a glass of beer in his favorite hangouts, such as the ABC Bar on Calle Lavalle or a beer garden in Bariloche.

He would loudly announce his destination at each departure point. One of the surveillance reports, Number 4378/S.I.R., prepared by Special Agent Pinto of the Posadas branch of the Intelligence Service, said: "Martin Bormann has just left Eldorado," a town in northern Argentina on the Paraguayan border, "giving instructions to his driver to take him to Córdoba. However, I succeeded in trailing him and found that he was heading for Encarnación in Paraguay, for a meeting with Dr. Josef Mengele. . . ."

According to the stream of surveillance reports covering this period between 1948 and 1955, Bormann spent most of his time in Buenos Aires, living as the guest of friends in sumptuous villas in Vicente Lopez and Florida, elegant residential districts of the Argentine capital. Frequently he would go to Bariloche on holidays. In 1951, he was spotted in Oberá, a town in Misiones Territory near the Paraguayan border, where he was making extensive investments in the region's thriving lumber industry. He was also trailed to the city of Paraná, where he "arrived by boat coming directly from Buenos Aires in the company of a German-looking woman." He was seen with her in a coffee shop on the main square "holding firmly to a large attaché case bulging with papers," and was shadowed until he left the city "in a black Chevrolet sedan."

Apparently this was when he first became determined to break with the past and embark on a new beginning. It was 1952, his fourth year in Argentina. At fifty-two, although troubled by a stomach ailment, he was in the prime of life. Something had to be done to put an end to his aimless existence and change his foundering republic of vagabonds into a tight organization.

What happened was described in another intelligence report, dated October 14, 1952, from the police commissioner of the Córdoba region to the chief of the Division of Alien Affairs. According to information gathered by special agents Raneri, Chamado, Mega and Pinto, the Nazis had held an emergency conference at a place called Ascochinga in the Serrana Zone of Córdoba Province, high in the Cerro Negro, on a secluded *estancia* owned by a mysterious Nazi refugee who had come to Argentina by submarine during the last days of the war. From all over South America, leaders of the scattered Nazi colonies flocked to the conference to review the situation, their own as well as that of Nazism in exile.

Bormann was said to be displeased with such a convention of fugitives. These dissatisfied Nazis, foot-loose in the Western Hemisphere, had started to complicate his relationship with President Perón. The further he could keep from his sponging followers, who referred to him as "the Führer," the closer he could be in touch with his money. He preferred, therefore, to remain in Buenos Aires and run the meeting in the Black Mountain from a distance.

The Bormann specialists among the agents of the Argentine security services had been alerted to the conclave and infiltrated the council. The Argentine authorities thus found out that the major issue at this emergency meeting was an organization called Die Spinne, referred to as La Araña in Mega's and other reports.

Founded in 1948 in an Allied P.O.W. camp at Glasenbach, Germany, by a few fanatical SS prisoners, it soon spread its web all over Germany and then the world. "Web" is the appropriate word for it, for *die Spinne* means "the Spider."

Heading the organization in Europe was a former SS general named Paul Hausser. He obtained the funds he needed by blackmailing major German firms harboring former Nazis. However, in South America Die Spinne expected to be financed entirely from Bormann's enormous funds.

As reported by agents Raneri and Chamado, Bormann acted as "coordinator among the German colonies of Paraguay, Argentina and Brazil . . . through his control of the organization known as La Araña, and thanks to his access to large quantities of money, gold, valuables and works of art."

It is known, and not only from this report, that that meeting in October 1952 sounded the death knell of La Araña as an organization capable of financing and sustaining the indigent fugitives in South America.

Bormann had different plans for the spider's web. Instead of using it as a rescue organization, as intended by Hausser, he decided to transform it into the base on which a financial empire could be built. The subsequent story of La Araña is spelled out clearly in Argentine, Brazilian and Paraguayan intelligence reports.

It gradually lost its ideological and charitable character, and became a hard-headed business organization controlled by Bormann through various fronts, including reputable businessmen who were not necessarily aware of the identity of their silent partner.

Less than a year after the Ascochinga conference, the conversion of The Spider into an investment concern became visible, as special agents Chamado and Raneri stated in a report dated March 18, 1953. When they next spotted Bormann, he was in São Paulo, Brazil, on a brief business trip, supposedly discussing with "former Nazi comrades the possibility of investing in an electrification project that they were promoting."

The last report of this period was dated April 22, 1955. Prepared by Special Agent Mega, the Bormann specialist of the Córdoba Provincial Police, it was forwarded to the Division of Alien Affairs, where all such tracers were then pigeonholed as long as Perón was in the Casa Rosada. This is the verbatim translation of Mega's interesting report, reprinted in full because it sheds light on Bormann's way of life and movements in his gold-plated exile.

> Subject: *Surveillance of the movements of foreigners.* I beg to bring to your attention that agents of the S.I., sector Córdoba, have submitted an important report which I forward for your information and evaluation.
>
> Summoned by a hotel proprietor named Galvan, Agent Mega went to Mina Clavero, where Galvan testified as follows:
>
> About six days ago, three guests booked into his hotel—one a rather short, balding man with a round face, about 66 years old, who signed the registry as José Perez and gave his profession as businessman.
>
> He was accompanied by two younger men, one calling himself Luis Jiménez, a Spaniard, 38 years old, tall, blond, with blue eyes, and the other Armando Zavalia, a 42-year-old Mexican, on the heavy side.
>
> Galvan noted that the above-named persons spoke German, especially since the man who called himself Perez could hardly speak Spanish. He appeared to be the chief or employer of the other two.
>
> Most talkative and friendly of the three was Jiménez, who dealt with Galvan since he could speak fluent Spanish.
>
> When Galvan had to make a trip to Rio Zabalos, Jiménez asked permission to accompany him.
>
> They traveled together to the place where Jiménez went to the tavern called Caballito Blanco, frequented by many Germans. Jiménez spoke to some of them in fluent German.
>
> According to Galvan, Jiménez exchanged documents with two other Germans at the inn and received a report from them. Back at the hotel, Galvan found that Perez had remained in his room most of the time.

> One morning he had breakfast very early and although he himself cannot speak German, he noted they mentioned Bariloche, Valdivia, Miguelets, São Paulo and other places in their conversation.
>
> On the fourth day of the trio's stay in Galvan's hotel, Perez fell ill and Jiménez asked Galvan to go to a pharmacy to buy some drugs called Pepsamar and Buscapina.
>
> When he returned with the medicine, Perez asked for a glass of milk in broken Spanish and Galvan then overheard Jiménez say to him: "*Jawohl, Herr Borman*" [*sic*].
>
> This intrigued Galvan. He thenceforth kept a close watch on the trio and immediately tried to get in touch with Agent Mega in Córdoba to alert him to the presence of these suspicious people.
>
> By the time Agent Mega arrived in Mina Clavero, they had left the hotel without saying where they were going. Nevertheless, Agent Mega immediately proceeded to Rio Zabalos and, accompanied by Galvan, placed the Caballito Blanco Inn under surveillance. He succeeded in establishing that the man Jiménez called Bormann and his companions had gone to Bariloche.

The chief of the Córdoba branch concluded the report with the words: "I await instructions." There is no record to show they were ever given.

Even while he was still vacationing in Bariloche, when the delightful resort was at its wintery best, events in Buenos Aires must have alerted Bormann to the inescapable reality that his "great benefactor" was in serious trouble. Since his own fate was tied to Perón's future, he was suddenly confronted with an acute crisis of his own, the first in his exile.

As a dictator, Perón proved such a flop that, as one of his bitter critics put it, he couldn't even make the trains run on time. By mid-1955 it was evident that El Lider had gone too far. On a single day, June 16, he suffered two body blows delivered by a strange coalition of his exasperated enemies. Riots of Catholics had erupted four days before, when Peronista thugs tried to break up celebrations of Corpus Christi, which Perón had outlawed as a national holiday. The President reacted on the fifteenth by ordering the deportation of two monsignori whom he accused of inciting and leading the riotings. The Vatican hit back hard the next day with a sweeping excommunication order *lata sententia* ("in a broad sense"), without a hearing, because "Perón's crimes were obvious."

Simultaneously he was attacked from an unexpected quarter. His army of 100,000 men was controlled by corrupt officers abjectly loyal to him. But dissident elements in the Air Force and the Navy launched a rebellion against what turned out to be impossible odds. Perón had deprived all military units he could not trust of arms, munitions, tanks and trucks, even of motor fuel. The Air Force, which he regarded as the least reliable, was given planes but no bombs. Curiously enough, Perón had no such qualms about the Navy and let its air arm keep its bombs.

On the sixteenth the bombs he had left in the hands of the Naval Air Force fell "like the clap of doom" on the Casa Rosada, killing 360 on the Plaza de Mayo. But Perón was not there. At the approach of the planes, he had fled to the neighboring Army Ministry. What he himself called his "luck of the devil" saved him. The rebellion was a fiasco. The weather was bad and the ceiling was so low that the pilots had to release their bombs at an altitude from which they would not go off. Besides, most of the Navy's bargain-basement bombs were duds. The scattered army elements which were to join the uprising were caught off balance. But the units in Buenos Aires, whose officers were tied to Perón by bonds of self-interest, stood firm and saved the day for their Lider.

It was not the first revolt that had failed. In 1951, General Menendez had staged a brave but unsuccessful coup. Its failure led to the collapse of a conspiracy by General Eduardo Lonardi, who was dismissed from the Army and imprisoned for almost a year. Military chiefs like Lonardi thought that uprisings must always start in Buenos Aires. But a rebellion unleashed by Colonel Suarez in 1952 convinced them that it was "impossible to keep any military revolt that was begun in Buenos Aires alive long enough to mobilize the rest of the country."

By this time in 1955, the dissident military chiefs with Lonardi among them had learned this lesson. Exactly three months after the aborted uprising of June, the provincial garrison of Córdoba, 800 safe miles from Buenos Aires, rose in revolt and took over the old Spanish-aristocratic, devoutly Catholic city. Other garrisons, inspired by Lonardi and led by General Pedro Eugenio Aramburu, commanding the troops at Curuzú-Cuatiá, now followed suit. All this, however, was not enough. The issue was decided by Admiral Isaac Rojas, who led the entire Navy into the rebellion.

When the old United States cruiser *Phoenix*, now the *General*

Belgrano, Admiral Rojas' flagship, sailed into Buenos Aires harbor with its 8-inch guns at the ready, Perón exclaimed: "Dammit, this fool Rojas is the sort of man who's likely to shoot." With that he scrambled for refuge at the Paraguayan embassy, then asked the Lonardi-led victorious junta to grant him safe passage to Asunción on a gunboat President Stroessner of Paraguay had solicitously sent for him. "We never expected Perón to prove such a coward," General Pedro Aramburu said afterward. "If he had taken the field against us, the revolution would have been crushed."

Lonardi and Rojas became the new President and Vice-President of Argentina. For the next two months it appeared that Martin Bormann had nothing to fear from the new regime. Reactionary elements soon captured Lonardi and sold him a policy of appeasing the Peronistas-*sans*-Perón in the hope of re-forming them into a right-wing political party. Other revolutionary leaders watched this drift in rising dismay. One Sunday afternoon they rose again, this time against Lonardi. Again with the help of Rojas, they eased him out and installed Aramburu, a gravely formal, frugal, somewhat gloomy fifty-four-year-old graduate of Argentina's Prussian-style Military Academy, as the Provisional President. "Ours was a revolution," he said, "against the dictatorial state system. We fought for the right to live."

His first job was what he called the "de-Peronization of Argentina." Much of the policy was aimed directly at the refugee dictator now living in accustomed splendor in Asunción in the palatial home of Ricardo Gayol, a rich Argentine merchant. It took some time to uncover all the evidence of the monumental malfeasance of the deposed dictator, who had even dipped into the country's gold and foreign-exchange reserves, a fabulous $1.6 billion piled up during and after the war. His loot in dollars alone, the auditors found, totaled $500 million.

Aramburu's sleuths then discovered Perón's sumptuous hideout in a kind of Führerbunker of his own, its floor covered with bearskin rugs, accommodating several mirror-lined bedrooms and boudoirs for his trysts, replete with gold-plated phones. The most important discovery in the shelter was a huge safe filled with Perón's personal papers and secret state documents, which included data about his deals with the Nazis and details of Martin Bormann's seven-year sojourn in Argentina. What until then was the best-kept secret in the world now became known to General Aramburu and a handful of his closest associates. It was not a matter the general regarded with pride. In his eyes, it was not merely proof of Perón's opportunism and depravity but the shame of the Argentine nation as well. It was now Aramburu who put a tight lid on the Bormann papers, ordering them sealed and transferred to the most confidential archives of Coordinación Federal—where I found them sixteen years later.

Bormann followed events without any illusions. He did not expect Perón to make a comeback and was not misled by the defiance of millions of Peronistas who continued to clamor for their hero, their sentiment expressed in the graffito: "*Ladrón o no ladrón, queremos a Perón!* [Thief or no thief, we want Perón!]" But Bormann realized that the halcyon days of his exile were over. The question was, where to go and how to arrange a new system of protection.

In late 1955, when the direction in which General Aramburu was moving became unmistakably clear, Bormann left Argentina. Still calling himself Eliezer Goldstein, the name on his Vatican identity certificate, he moved to Brazil. There he was an almost conspicuous figure, according to intelligence reports, not only in the remote regions of the Mato Grosso, but also in the most prurient nightclubs of São Paulo whose accommodating ladies held a special appeal for a man known for his masculine prowess.

By the late fifties, Bormann began planning a drastic change to end his precarious exile in Brazil, where protection was becoming increasingly difficult to buy. The indolent life of more or less aimless wanderings did not suit him; and accustomed to style and comfort, he was becoming disenchanted with the primitive living conditions of the underdeveloped Far West of the country. A man of action, he had enough of the sinecure and tired of his role of paterfamilias of the fugitive Nazis, who accepted his paramountcy mainly because he was succoring so many of them with occasional handouts.

Bolivia was one of the safe countries where he had friends and economic roots. He had stock in satellite firms of his big holding company and was silent partner in a number of other commercial firms.

Among his friends in Bolivia, his relations with a photographer calling himself Huber—but who was in fact Adolf Hundhammer, a former member of the Leibstandarte, Hitler's bodyguard regiment—were mostly convivial and social. But others were strategically placed and had the kinds of contacts he needed to establish himself with the security he enjoyed in Argentina. Among them were Honorary Consul Oscar Obrist, the Swiss owner of the foundry Fundición Vulkan in La Paz, and his son-in-law, Heinz Aschbacher.

Most important among them was a sharp entrepreneur known as Klaus Altmann, president of a prosperous shipping company and partner of Freddy Schwend in numerous shady enterprises. He was still safe both in Bolivia and in Peru, because nobody knew yet that he was really Klaus Barbie, the "Butcher of Lyons," wanted by the French government for the outrages he had perpetrated as a Gestapo bully during the war. In La Paz, Altmann had powerful friends on the highest echelons and was able to line up for Bormann a new set of influential protectors, among them Admiral Alcibiado Ruiz, commander in chief of the Bolivian Navy, Minister of the Interior Alberto Taborga, Colonel Carlos Souza, commandant of the First Military District at Curlo, and even Archbishop Abel Antezana of La Paz.

Bormann moved to Bolivia using his favorite alias of Eliezer Goldstein and lived at first, incredible though it may sound, in the home of a Jewish travel agent and money-changer, himself a notorious character in La Paz and Santa Cruz. When, however, his host found out who his guest was, he asked Bormann to leave, and "Eliezer Goldstein" ceased to exist. Bormann then spent thousands of dollars to buy a *complete* new identity for himself, supported by all the documents a man usually assembles in his lifetime—birth certificate, school report cards, vaccination certificates, military passbook, marriage license and certificate, driver's license, passport, membership cards in clubs and fraternal societies. They were all genuine when originally issued, belonging to a real person named José Perez, born in Bolivia in 1901.

Bormann even acquired in the lot José's death certificate (which, of course, he had no use for as yet). Perez had died in 1956, but his posthumous dossier was supposed to give Bormann the sense of security he was forever seeking. However, the documents were not as foolproof as he wished. They presented a Spanish-speaking Bolivian, a far cry from this newcomer who, for all his years in South America, had never mastered Spanish with anything even remotely resembling fluency.

He now underwent a drastic metamorphosis, the psychological mainsprings of which were strange and bold. He became a mongrel

Catholic priest, patterned on the deaconry of the Primitive Church. Then, recommended by Archbishop Antezana, whose support was solicited for him by his friends Altmann and Schwend, he moved into the monastery of the Orden dos Redentoristas, on Calle Camasho, a Catholic order of German monks dedicated to—of all things—the deliverance from sin and damnation by the atonement of Christ.

Now he adopted the name Augustin von der Lange-Lenbach, calling himself Father Augustin. There was an amusing footnote to Bormann's choice of his latest pseudonym. He picked it from Goethe's ribald play *Götz von Berlichingen,* in the opening scene of which a character declares: "They call me Friar Augustin von Lange, though my name is Brother Martin."

The Reverend Maximo Leutenegger, father superior of the Redemptorists, recalls Brother Augustin distinctly, but with somewhat less than fond memories. "He was a very strange person," he told me. "Although he insisted on performing the functions of a priest, and once even celebrated Mass in the Cathedral of San Juan de Dios, it was obvious that he did not care much for the Church. His conduct was anything but pastoral, as he flitted in and out of the monastery, wearing ordinary clothes as often as clerical garb. But he had come with the recommendation of the Archbishop and we had to give him shelter."

The rich order had vast holdings in Bolivia, monasteries at San Borja Covendo and Ixiamas, and a home for itinerant priests at Rurrenabaque, which had been renovated only a couple of years before. Irked if not scandalized by Brother Augustin's temporal escapades, Father Maximo ordered him to leave the monastery in La Paz, but agreed when Bormann asked to be permitted to move to the home in Rurrenabaque, where he then lived for two years on and off.

This was probably the most bizarre period of Bormann's exile. His power and influence were sharply curtailed. His investments in Bolivia were modest compared with the huge holdings he had to leave behind in Argentina. He compensated for giving up the high life by indulging in what was to become his favorite pastime of not only posing but also actually functioning as a Catholic priest.

To one of his landlords in Bolivia, who doubted his clerical credentials, he explained: "Actually, I am an ex-officer of the Wehrmacht, and though I have never been formally ordained, I have special dispensation from the Vatican to perform the functions of an auxiliary priest."

Whether he actually succeeded in convincing himself of the fantasy, he acted out his delusion. He thus participated in several Catholic sacraments of baptisms, weddings and funerals. He was a familiar figure in his priestly garb at the chapel of the convent of German nuns in La Paz and in the town of Apolo, eighty miles north of the capital, where he once appeared in the company of Archbishop Antezana.

Pitting his clerical image against his earlier hatred of the Church, it may be difficult to understand Bormann's seemingly enthusiastic embrace of Catholicism. But it can be explained. After Perón's downfall, he never enjoyed the official protection of a chief of state. Whatever safeguards he had in Brazil, Paraguay, Bolivia, Peru, and eventually Chile had to be bought for hard cash, suborning not only the native authorities but also the chiefs of Interpol in La Paz and Santiago, themselves natives and, therefore, susceptible to bribes.

What with the quick turnover of regimes in the countries he was forced to spend his exile from exile, Bormann could never be sure whether the people he had on his payroll today would still be in power tomorrow. He, therefore, went to considerable lengths during these years to deepen his masquerade with grotesque subterfuges. This was why he spent thousands of dollars on the useless Perez dossier, and why he felt safer in his priestly guise, the lay brother of an order of German monks, with his German pseudonym borrowed from Goethe. Like the cynical alias "Goldstein," which was supposed to afford him protection from Jewish avengers, the clerical disguise was his idea of added safety. Who could suspect Martin Bormann behind the impressive façade of Father Augustin? The distance he was thus putting between the present and his past was enormous. The guise was so incompatible with his well-known opposition to the Church that it promised by itself to throw his enemies off his scent.

During his stay in Bolivia Bormann made several forays into Paraguay, showing up in Asunción to meet his friend Dr. Josef Mengele, but also visiting Encarnación and other places in the south, closer to the rich lumber region where he continued to control substantial investments. It was on one of these visits that a flare-up of his abdominal pains exposed him to Dr. Otto Biss, a distinguished physician who practiced at 877 Eligio Ayala in Asunción.

"One evening in 1959," Dr. Biss later stated in an interview, "I don't remember the exact date, a woman came to my house, long after sunset. I had never seen her before. She asked me to go with her at once to see a man who was dangerously ill. I agreed, as any doctor would, and got into the woman's car. She drove some distance, out to a suburb of Asunción, to a house almost in darkness.

"We went inside. A man who looked very ill was lying on a large bed. As soon as we stepped into this bedroom, another man came out of an adjoining room, and I gathered he was a doctor. I examined the sick man and spoke to him in German, but he wouldn't answer in that or any other European language I know. He insisted on bad Spanish. So I found it rather difficult to get any help from him in establishing the nature of his illness. The other doctor realized this, and bending over the sick man he said, 'You may speak German.' And to my great surprise the man then spoke in fluent German."

Dr. Biss examined the patient. The man had no cancer, as he apparently thought, nor was he in any danger of expiring. "He was merely suffering from gastritis," Dr. Biss said, referring back to his medical charts, "and his general condition was good."

Even the mystery of the patient's identity was quickly cleared up. "A few days later," Dr. Biss said, "a friend of mine came to see me, in great excitement. He told me that he had met the woman who had come for me, and that she had confided to him that the man I had seen professionally was Martin Bormann. I got hold of some photos of Hitler's right-hand man at once. There was no possible doubt. The man I had seen was older than the man in the photograph, but it was the same man. He was certainly Martin Bormann."

The "other doctor" at Bormann's bedside was later identified as Josef Mengele.

During my two stops in Paraguay, I made a special effort to check out and elaborate on Dr. Biss's account of his house call. In all the many-pronged searches for Bormann, he was by far the most reputable among the witnesses in South America, and his positive identification of the former Reichsleiter was generally regarded as irrefutable. I, therefore, examined his credentials and took considerable pains to illuminate the dark areas left in his testimony.

Dr. Biss was a Hungarian by birth, the graduate of the best universities and medical schools in Central Europe whose diplomas decorated the walls of his waiting room. He emigrated to South America in 1936, winding up in Paraguay, where he took out citizenship and settled down to a lucrative practice of medicine. While Dr. Biss was a converted Jew, his brother a businessman in Asunción, was a prominent member of the country's colony of 804 Jews.

Dr. Biss was highly respected as a physician, and despite the notoriety which his fortuitous involvement in the Bormann case brought him, retained the respect and trust of both his colleagues and his fellow citizens. By the time I reached him in Asunción, thirteen years after the event, he was living in retirement outside the capital. The telephone listed in his name was answered by a woman who professed to know nothing about him. However, with the help of friends and by the coincidence that he shared a cleaning woman with an acquaintance of mine, I was able to locate him at Piribebuy, a resort town not far from Asunción, and obtain a more rounded version of his statements and dispositions.

I also gained access to certain intelligence reports which filled in the gaps in Dr. Biss's account and succeeded in identifying the entire cast of characters in the drama. To begin with, the woman who had come to fetch him at 877 Eligio Ayala and drove him to a house which, in fact, was in Villa Mora borough of Asunción, was a widow named Señora Casaccia, the housekeeper of a White-Russian naval officer, Nicholas Stepanov, now serving in the Paraguayan Navy with the rank of commander. Stepanov's involvement stemmed from his friendship with Alexander von Eckstein, head of the Nazi Party in Paraguay during World War II, and one of the two witnesses at Dr. Mengele's naturalization a short time before the incident.

Dr. Biss had been recommended to Mengele, who himself was still a stranger in Asunción, by a medical student named Bertilotti. Mengele then asked Eckstein to send someone inconspicuous to fetch Dr. Biss, and this was how the widow Casaccia was chosen. She could betray nothing by her sheer ignorance of the facts behind her errand.

On the basis of this follow-up investigation, I have no reason to doubt Dr. Biss's integrity and competence as a witness, or question his conclusion that the patient he treated was Martin Bormann.

Bormann vanished from Asunción as quietly as he had arrived, and returned to Bolivia, where he put down roots and tried to live what he himself later called "a normal life." But since his hurried departure from Argentina in the wake of the downfall of his "great benefactor," five years had gone by. They were spent in risky hide-

and-seek in different countries under various aliases. Whatever his disguise, it was wearing thin. More and more people, especially in Paraguay and Bolivia, penetrated the masquerade. Even today, more than a decade later, one meets scores of them in Asunción, La Paz, and even in Lima, who recall him, not by any of the aliases he used, but plainly and positively as *the* Martin Bormann they themselves met socially or on business, and whose true identity was only a thinly veiled secret even then.

By 1960, condemned to perpetual exile, Bormann could feel it weighing him down more than the distant death sentence of Nuremberg. Never a man to feed on dreams, he viewed his passage realistically. Each day's escape merely meant tomorrow's confusion. Then the bombshell burst in the midst of his growing insecurity. On May 23, 1960, Prime Minister David Ben-Gurion went before the Knesset and announced to the world that Israeli commandos had captured Adolf Otto Eichmann.

PART FOUR

Trouble in the Fourth Reich

Chapter Fifteen

The Abduction of Adolf Eichmann—The Second Crisis

Adolf Otto Eichmann spent almost ten of his fugitive years in Argentina. It was borrowed time. He had arrived in Argentina in July 1950, hoping at last, after five uncertain years of hiding in Germany and Italy, to live out his life with a new identity. When he landed in Buenos Aires, Eichmann was confident that nobody would find him in this far-off haven, where so many other Nazis lived and prospered.

As it was, his presence became known already two years after his arrival. From then on, until his capture in 1960, he was stalked without a moment's pause—and not by the enemies he feared most. The well-deserved credit for the historic feat of finding him is given to a small band of Israelis who located him after a relentless search that lasted for fifteen years. It needed massive initiative, ingenuity and courage to capture him in an alien land, many thousands of miles from their home base, and smuggle him to Jerusalem to stand trial at last. But the Israelis were not alone in their quest.

A sheaf of documents in the Eichmann dossier kept in the secret archives of Coordinación Federal, and the testimony of eyewitnesses, show conclusively that at least some of the credit must go to the Argentine authorities. In particular, six functionaries of the Argentine security services made contributions to Eichmann's downfall; without those contributions his finding and capture would have been much more difficult if not indeed impossible.

The Argentine officials who participated in Operation Intercambio, as the clandestine campaign against Eichmann was called in Buenos Aires, were Commander Jorge Alberto Messina, director general of Coordinación Federal in 1959–60; Commissioner Luis Hector Herrera, chief of the regional police at Vera in the Province of Santa Fe; Inspectors Hector Rodriguez Morgado and Osvaldo Randuni, as well as special agents Raneri and Machado of the alien police. Most of all, in the final analysis, credit is due to President Arturo Frondizi, under whose orders they operated.*

In 1945, Adolf Eichmann had such a record of crimes that he was even quicker than Bormann to sense that he had to move fast if he was to save his life. In February 1945, he left his plush lair in Berlin, which he no longer regarded as safe. He moved out of the beleaguered capital, going to Prague with an aide named Josef Weisel, to consult Hans Günther, a suave young murderer who represented him in what was then called the Protectorate of Bohemia and Moravia.

But Günther was no help. His gloom and constant talk of suicide drove Eichmann out of the city. He made his way to the redoubt of refugees at Altaussee, high in the Austrian Alps, where he knew the chief of the Main Security Office, Ernst Kaltenbrunner, was hidden. Eichmann was not welcome. The last man he saw at Altaussee was Dr. Wilhelm Höttl, the young Austrian who was Kaltenbrunner's spy master in Hungary, where he had "worked" with Eichmann in 1944. Höttl told me a quarter century later:

> Eichmann burst in on us like a Typhoid Mary, the personification of all the crimes that were now haunting Kaltenbrunner and his cohorts, the apocalyptic memento of their own sins. Kaltenbrunner in particular did not want to be reminded of the past, which Eichmann symbolized. He told him to get the hell out of Altaussee, as fast as he could. Like a beaten dog with his tail between his legs, Eichmann went away, wearing the uniform of a Luftwaffe corporal, carrying a bundle of all his worldly goods as he *walked* on the high mountain road westward in the direction of Bad Ischl. Somehow the air became cleaner when he left.

* As for the claimants on the fringes of this coup, they were entirely uninvolved or were mere extras in the drama. "I tracked Adolf Eichmann down," Tuvia Friedman claimed in 1961, although in reality he had played, as Moshe Pearlman stated unequivocally, no part in the operation and was never so much as consulted by the persons who planned and carried it out. To be sure, Friedman and Simon Wiesenthal were cogs in the big machine that ground down the fugitive. They kept alive interest in Eichmann and, as Raphael Bashev wrote in *Maariv* about Friedman, "wove him into our consciousness and would not let us forget him, even during our most joyous moments."

A couple of American soldiers patrolling the road stopped him, but Eichmann, whose name was then still unknown and whose features appeared on none of the wanted lists, talked himself out. He told the Americans that his name was Barth and that he was only a *kleiner Mann,* a little man, trying to make it to Linz where he lived.

Then he ran into another patrol, led by a nice young American lieutenant in a jeep. This time his glib explanation was not accepted at face value. They took him to a camp for SS officers at Weiden for a closer look. There he quickly concocted a *curriculum vitae* that held up miraculously through various interrogations in camps at Ansbach and Oberdachstetten. If anything, his encounter with the second group of Americans had aided his escape. When they challenged him on the road, he was exhausted by his ordeal and reconciled to whatever fate was in store for him. The lieutenant in the jeep asked him what his name was, and he replied wearily, "Adolf Otto Eichmann." But then he saw the lieutenant putting "Otto Eckmann" down on his pad and he knew that he was safe again.

It was as "Otto Eckmann" that they checked him into the Oberdachstetten prison camp. The good-natured Americans who interrogated him believed him when he said he was a native of Breslau, a former lieutenant in the 22nd Cavalry Division. They never asked him why he had called himself "Barth" or to explain why he was wearing a Luftwaffe uniform with the stripes of a corporal.

He was safe, he thought, but only until January 3, 1945. On that day the International Military Tribunal in Nuremberg heard a witness named Dieter Wisliczeny, himself a doomed man brought in handcuffs from Slovakia, where he was awaiting trial. Wisliczeny had been one of Eichmann's best friends, and Eichmann had named his third son, Dieter, after him.* The two men had worked together in Greece, Slovakia and Hungary. In Nuremberg, however, Eichmann's old friend became his worst enemy; Wisliczeny tried to mitigate his own crimes by unloading all blame on the father of his godchild.

He named Eichmann as the head of Section IV B-4, the office

* At this time the Eichmanns had three sons, Klaus, Horst and Dieter. Later, in Argentina, a fourth son was born to the couple calling themselves Klement, and was named Francisco in gratitude for the help Eichmann had been given by the Franciscans on his way to Argentina, away from retribution.

in Heinrich Müller's Gestapo that handled the Jewish question in the Main Security Office. "Eichmann," he said, "had special authority directly from Müller. He was responsible for the so-called solution of the Jewish problem in Germany and all the occupied countries." Prodded by Lieutenant Colonel Smith W. Brookhart, Jr., the American prosecutor presenting the case, Wisliczeny then spelled out what "the so-called solution" actually meant:

"It was what was called the *final* solution, in other words, the systematic extermination of the Jewish people." He told the Tribunal that when he saw his friend for the last time, in February 1945, Eichmann, who once hinted that he might commit suicide, added with a grin, "I will jump into my grave laughing, extraordinarily pleased that I have the death of five million people on my conscience."

The morning after Wisliczeny's testimony, Eichmann was big news. His famous last words had turned him into a ghoulish celebrity. He read in the papers what his friend had said and realized instantly that the "relaxed routine" of his gentle imprisonment might not last much longer. By this time "they" were looking for him—not only those naïve Americans but a group of Jews from Palestine. They could track him down and expose him to the Americans any minute. Two days later, on January 5, 1946, he escaped from the camp, then submerged in Germany for three long years, until late 1949, reemerging under the new alias of Otto Heninger. He was aided in his wanderings by a petty government official in Prien, a forest warden in Lüneburg Heath, and by other pro-Nazis who felt duty-bound, and indeed privileged, to hide such fugitives.

Eichmann's years in Germany illustrate how easy it really was, even for a fugitive hunted for mass murder by a coalition of pursuers, to go undetected, despite his notoriety, which was fast growing into infamy. His name had become the synonym for Nazi butchery. Yet Eichmann was not found.

With the help of one of the rescue groups, he made it to Italy in 1950, first going all the way to Rome. From there the Hudal organization sent him to Genoa, where a Franciscan monk offered him the better protection of his monastery. It was not a matter of Christian charity that motivated Brother Hyacinth. Eichmann's true identity was known to him. He was familiar with his monstrous crimes, the confessed murder of five million Jews, give or take a million. He wrote to the Refugee Bureau in the Vatican and applied for a pass for Eichmann, inventing the alias for him that was to become his name henceforth: Richard Klement. Born 1911 in Bolzano, of German parentage; mechanic by profession. Every entry in the application was false, including the date of his birth. Brother Hyacinth made Eichmann five years younger than he actually was.

The refugee pass arrived in the first week of June. Three weeks later, Richard Klement boarded a ship in an Italian port, and in the middle of July he arrived in Buenos Aires. He was safe at last.

As the files of the Argentine Federal Police recorded it, "Like other similar Nazi fugitives, he entered our country clandestinely utilizing the favors of the Vatican." He was given his identity card by the Buenos Aires police on August 3, 1950—Number 1,378,538. When he moved on to Tucumán on April 13, 1952, he was issued a residency permit by the local police, Number 0341952. Later still, another I.D. card was given him under Number 3,456,789.

Now utilizing the protection of Martin Bormann and, in the final analysis, that of Juan Perón, he established himself in his new life with a set of credentials made out in the name of Klement.

Although according to Bormann they had met in Berlin, Eichmann supposedly did not recognize him and knew the former Reichsleiter only as Richard Bauer, one of the aliases he used in Argentina. The fiction was maintained for a while, though it was obvious to one and all that "Bauer" was the Führer of the colony. The big decisions were made by him, and he was the one who dispensed the doles that enabled the indigents among the refugees to eke out a living.

When they met in Buenos Aires upon Eichmann's arrival, the newcomer asked his mentor how he would be able to sustain himself without independent means. As subsequent correspondence between the two, copies of which I have seen, clearly indicates, Eichmann expected that Bormann would provide the money he needed.

Stingy by nature, despite his enormous wealth, Bormann told Eichmann that while he would aid him occasionally, the mechanic would have to earn his own keep.

Now "Bauer" helped "Klement" to get settled, out of gratitude for what Eichmann had done for him. It was, after all, the availability of the Eichmann shelter during the Battle of Berlin that had permitted Bormann to get away. In Buenos Aires, he put him up at a boardinghouse in Vicente López frequented by these newcomers and owned by a Nazi named Jurmann, got temporary jobs for him in and around the capital and then recommended him to his friend Karl Stertzinger, who used to be the Third Reich's commissioner of water supplies, for employment as a surveyor with Capri. Called Compañía Argentina para Realizaciones in full, Stertzinger's firm had a contract with the Argentine government to construct water works in Tucumán, a city some seven hundred miles northwest of Buenos Aires.

By then it was 1952. The year was important in Eichmann's life for more reasons than his move to Tucumán in the first steady job he had since his arrival. For one thing, he felt safe and comfortable enough to ask his wife, Vera, who claimed she had not heard from him for seven years and believed that he had died in April 1945, to join him with their three children. For another, it was in that fateful year that the Argentine authorities, operating independently of Perón's policies in these matters, discovered that Ricardo Klement was, in fact, the wanted war criminal Adolf Eichmann. On his "bio-sheet" Number 1325, the original of which is still on file in Buenos Aires, 1952 is the first entry. It reads: "Continuing to call himself Ricardo Klement, he becomes a topographer in the Province of San Miguel del Tucumán."

From then on, Eichmann never again succeeded in evading the surveillance of the Argentine authorities. Among the various entries, one exposes him in 1953 as the manager of a goat farm, a somewhat demeaning job, which Bormann obtained for him with the help of his friend the tycoon Benito Sternoni, described in one of the intelligence reports as "a former member of Benito Mussolini's Black Shirts who was associated with well-known members of the organization La Araña in Argentina."

The employment lasted only for eight or nine months, and then Eichmann was back in Buenos Aires looking for a job. Bormann got it for him with the Mercedes-Benz plant at Suarez on the outskirts of the capital, and this time it was to last. Starting as a mechanic, Eichmann worked himself up to foreman in the seven years he was with the factory. He and his family moved into an apartment on Calle Chacabuco in the La Lucila section of Vicente Lopez.

None of his moves escaped the vigilance of the Argentinians. He was tracked almost continuously, even after Perón's downfall when Eichmann panicked with the rest of the fugitives and, for a short while, thought it advisable to tighten his security by adopting a set of different aliases. He called himself variously Nicolas Krumey, Rodolfo Adverse and Rodolfo Spee during this period of emergency, but remained Ricardo Klement both on Calle Chacabuco and at the Mercedes-Benz plant. Unlike Bormann, who left Argentina in a hurry, Eichmann remained satisfied that he had nothing to fear from the new regime of General Aramburu. He was totally unaware that a new threat loomed up from a quarter he thought he had succeeded in shaking off.

In 1957, a man arrived in Buenos Aires looking for Eichmann. He was a lone agent of the Israeli Secret Service on what seemed even to him a wild-goose chase. The Israelis' interest in Eichmann was not the steady, burning, purposeful preoccupation it is generally believed to have been. "It would be incorrect," wrote Moshe Pearlman, "to presume, as many now have done, that there was a continuous hunt every day, week and month of the fifteen years between his escape and his capture. . . . There would be a burst of activity when a tip seemed hopeful, followed by long periods of inaction when the lead turned out to be false. It is this, perhaps," Pearlman added, "which makes the capture even more impressive. Once it was established that there was a good chance that a man in Argentina living as Ricardo Klement was in fact Adolf Eichmann, there was nothing halfhearted or amateurish about the chase, the kidnap and the ultimate arrival of the prisoner in an Israeli jail. But before that time, there was only sporadic sniffing around to find the trail."

The chase began in 1945, when the establishment of Israel was still almost three years away. David Ben-Gurion was not yet the prime minister of a sovereign state but merely "the head of the Jews in Palestine," when he assembled a team of battle-seasoned young men in his office at the headquarters of the Jewish Agency in Tel Aviv and gave them a double mission. They were to go to liberated Europe to aid the Jews in getting to Palestine through the British embargo on immigration. That was not all. "Many of the Nazis have been caught," he told them, "and will soon be tried at Nuremberg. But many have escaped. Some are probably dead. But others are alive, hiding in the funk holes of Berlin and Vienna, Munich and Bratislava, or in the forests of Germany, Austria and Slovakia. Go out and get them, but strictly in collaboration with the Allied intelligence agencies."

A single name was mentioned by Ben-Gurion at the closed-door meeting. "Adolf Eichmann," he said, "that's the man who *must* be brought to justice if he is still alive."

The search for Eichmann was placed at the top of Ben-Gurion's list, but it became only a part-time job. It was conducted from an office on Frankgasse in Vienna by a brilliant young hunter who called himself Arthur Pier. He emerged into prominence later as Asher Ben Natan, Director General of Israel's Ministry of Defense, known to millions of readers around the world as the hero of *Exodus*. In 1946, he was far too busy with his double mission to devote much time and energy to the search for Eichmann. The man was gone—lost in the shuffle—perhaps dead. Even if he was living, he was a mystery man. Not a photograph of his could be found to aid in the search.* Much of the effort was amateurish, hit or miss. Only one of Pier's agents stayed with the job for any length of time, a handsome young Polish Jew named Manus Diamant, who had the brains the task needed and the added advantage of "looking German."

Manus was the perfect infiltrator. He succeeded in befriending Eichmann's family, and went to bed with Eichmann's former mistress, a plain-looking thirty-five-year-old woman named Maria Masenbacher. Between trysts, he managed to "procure" a snapshot of her lover from a scrapbook. But Frau Eichmann was quite persuasive when she told him that her husband was dead and Manus was inclined to believe her. After all, he concluded, there was no firm proof that he was alive. It was this, Moshe Pearlman thought, that did much to take the heart out of the hunt. "I am certain in my own mind," he wrote, "that, from then on, the search for Eichmann became less spirited."

A promising tip was received in 1957, and Isser "Little Isser" Harel, chief of the Israeli Central Intelligence and Security Agency, sent a man to Argentina to check it out, but found no clue. On the other hand, his search did not escape the attention of the Argentine authorities.

A policy decision had to be made at the highest echelons of the government as to how to deal with the problem the case presented.

The decision reached is spelled out in secret document Number 0095/2, which reads as follows:

> The Alien Control Office of the Coordinación Federal has detected the presence of Israeli commandos in the Republic of

* Actually, Eichmann's photographs (passport size) were in Allied hands, included in the captured archives of the RSHA, the SS main office, and on file at Nuremberg, numbered No. 2259. The complete dossier of Eichmann, together with a set of these photographs, can be consulted at the Centre de Documentation Juive Contemporaine in Paris. In the chaos and confusion of those hectic postwar years, when Eichmann himself succeeded easily in outwitting the Allied authorities, it is not surprising that his pictures escaped attention and had to be procured the hard way.

Argentina. But on orders received from higher quarters, it refrains from acting against them, except to keep the situation under control.

Although the Argentine authorities could have helped the Israeli agent to his elusive quarry, or on the other hand could have thrown him out, they decided instead to remain neutral.

Then, in 1958, Arturo Frondizi was elected President and, in his official capacity, became aware of the presence in his country of one of the worst criminals of the Nazi regime. One of his first acts was to issue secret and personal orders to the security organs to intensify the surveillance of Eichmann with a view toward "an early disposition" of the case.

On August 2, 1959, all branches of his Coordinación Federal were instructed by Commander Jorge Messina, the director general, to maintain the watch. In a message to all his agents involved in the surveillance, Messina identified the man calling himself "Ricardo Klement" as Adolf Otto Eichmann and issued strict orders not to let him out of sight.

On September 9, Messina followed up his initial wire with letters to his subordinates, which read:

> I bring to your attention that in accordance with orders of the President, we are continuing the surveillance and vigilance over Adolf Otto Eichmann's movements, using the alias Ricardo Klement.
>
> He has been seen with another important Nazi, in the vicinity of Da Gallereta, Department Vera in the Province of Santa Fe. The description of the other man corresponds to that of Josef Mengele, information about whom as being present at the ranch has been received by Inspectors Hector Rodriguez [Morgado] and Osvaldo Randuni, who have been commissioned to observe the movements and activities of foreigners in the national territory.

At the same time, the enterprise was given a cover name—Operation Interchange—to conceal its nature even from people inside the service who would betray it to their Nazi paymasters.

The first agency to act on the Frondizi order was the Provincial Police of Santa Fe, headed by Inspector Luis Hector Herrera, in the city of Vera.

His report was dated August 30, 1959, a few months before the arrival of the Israeli task force in Argentina. On that date, Inspector Herrera reported to Commander Messina as follows:

> Subject: Operation Interchange.
>
> In accordance with confidential and secret instructions from the President concerning the movement of certain Nazi elements within our nation, it is my duty to inform you that a person called Señor Ricardo Klement, C.I. 3,456,789 has arrived at this locality, but his real identity is known to be the one that corresponds to the person cited in your S.I. secret report of last month.
>
> The person named Klement is lodged at the Casa Campo with other foreigners in this locality. It was difficult to identify the others in view of the reticence of the management of the farm, consisting of persons of German origin.
>
> This branch contacted Inspector Randuni of the Federal Police, who then arrived here accompanied by a person later identified as Sandor Fekete. Inspector Randuni, seeking the cooperation of this branch, informed me that he had come to observe the actions of the aforementioned Klement.

From then on, the story appears to be a comparatively simple one. On May 23, 1960, Prime Minister David Ben-Gurion announced to the Israeli Knesset, that Adolf Eichmann, head of the Gestapo's Jewish Extermination Department, had been captured.

When it became clear from Israeli statements that Eichmann had been kidnaped in Argentina and taken to Israel, the Argentine government lodged a protest.

On June 15, Argentina requested and got an urgent meeting of the Security Council of the United Nations, because of the "violation of the sovereign rights of the Argentine Republic," resulting from the "illicit and clandestine transfer" of Eichmann to Israel.

The commotion, which resulted in the expulsion of the Israeli ambassador, seems contrived in the light of the story spelled out in the Argentine government's own secret papers, which, one assumes, tell the truth without regard for diplomatic exigencies and the complex considerations of international relations. The documents show that much of the protestation was a smokescreen undoubtedly designed to obscure the crucial undercover part Argentinians themselves had played in the coup.

I do not question the integrity and sincerity of the officials who issued the denials and raised the objections. As is common in all governments, the overt departments rarely know what the covert agencies are doing. The sheltered diplomats of the Foreign Ministry in Buenos Aires and of the Argentine mission at the United Nations were quite properly scandalized because of their ignorance of the facts and, therefore, were convincing when they conveyed their own honest belief that the Israelis alone had perpetrated the outrage on Argentine soil.

President Frondizi did nothing to mitigate their indignation and discourage their protestation. It is possible, as he now insists, that the secret services misread his policies in this delicate matter and misinterpreted his instructions, upsetting the delicate balance in their zeal. However, the reports abound in explicit references to the President as he was hovering over the proceedings, stating unequivocally and repeatedly that everything they did—or failed to do, arresting the kidnapers, for example—was on "the orders of the presidency."

According to the documents, when Eichmann returned from Vera and resumed his job in the Mercedes-Benz plant, special agents Raneri and Machado were assigned by top-secret presidential orders to keep Eichmann under the closest round-the-clock surveillance.

Their assignment was to watch Eichmann's residence and to shadow him in all his movements. Inspector Raneri personally trailed him to his work each morning and, as he wrote in his report dated May 11, 1960, "accompanied him as usual home in the bus sitting right behind the man."

At the same time, according to information given me by Dr. Horacio A. Perillo, a top presidential aide at that time, Frondizi informed the German government that Eichmann had been located. Frondizi allegedly offered to deliver him to the Germans, but the response of the Bonn government was negative.

However, the information had become known to a high official within the German judicial system, the late Dr. Fritz Bauer, Procurator General of the State of Hesse in Frankfurt. Dedicated both professionally and emotionally to the prosecution of the fugitive Nazis, Dr. Bauer was shocked by the decision of the German government to pigeonhole the information from Argentina. It was unimpeachable, based on the surveillance of the man Klement whom the Division of Alien Affairs had identified as Adolf Eichmann. Since he himself was not allowed to pursue the matter, Bauer leaked the information to a friend in the Israeli Ministry of Justice, who forwarded it promptly to Ben-Gurion. The Prime Minister called in Isser Harel and ordered him to use "the entire apparatus of the secret service if need be."

By a curious coincidence, another tip reached Israel almost simultaneously, from a Jewish merchant in South America who made frequent visits to Argentina. The informant alerted Jerusalem that a man named Ricardo Klement, who worked at the Mercedes-Benz plant in Suarez, might be Adolf Eichmann. He could not be sure. But this Klement was married to a woman who frankly conceded that she was "once the wife of Adolf Eichmann." She continued to call herself Vera Liebl de Eichmann instead of using the name of the man who was supposed to be her *second* husband. The sons of the couple, Klaus, Horst and Dieter, also went by the name of Eichmann.

Intelligence Chief Harel coaxed permission from Prime Minister Ben-Gurion to fly to South America at once to check out what he regarded as "the hottest leads in fifteen years." He met the informant in Montevideo. Then, impressed, he went to Buenos Aires, where he organized a team to aid him in verification.

Back in Jerusalem in September 1959, Harel was getting encouraging news from his friends. Everything they could find out about Klement indicated that he was Eichmann. The abduction plans matured after that. A task force of three seasoned secret agents was assembled (the Argentinians later called it the "Blue Falcons," with romantic gallantry) and was sent to Buenos Aires, where the trio was augmented by a half dozen trusted local volunteers. They were to do the menial work—like "casing" places or driving getaway cars—but the climactic job of the kidnaping would be handled by the three Israelis.

The task force flew in early in December 1959, and immediately began shadowing Klement at Vicente Lopez and trailing him to and from his place of work in Suarez. In January, however, the Eichmanns disturbed the Israelis' plans. They moved from their apartment in La Lucila to San Fernando, a dreary, dusty, deserted suburb, and settled down in a little one-story brick house on Calle Garibaldi off the much-traveled San Fernando highway.

The Argentine detectives had no difficulty in following them. But as far as the Israelis were concerned, the trail was suddenly lost. It was picked up soon again, when one of the trio located Klement in his house in San Fernando after trailing him on the long bus ride from his place of work at Suarez.

This interval illustrates the relationship between the two efforts, and the difficulties confronting the Israelis despite the up-to-the-minute, comprehensive knowledge of the Argentinians. It also explains why the Israelis so resent it when credit is given to the Argentine agents for their share in Eichmann's downfall.

Immediately after the arrival of the Israeli task force, orders came from the Casa Rosada to observe their movements, adding the crucial proviso that Argentine intelligence "must not interfere with their activities." This, then, became the guideline for the extent of the "cooperation."

The Argentine authorities were never in direct communication with the Israelis. Their help consisted in leaving the Israelis alone. If it had been left to the Argentinians, Eichmann could still be Ricardo Klement and live in Argentina watched but unmolested. They were interested in the man but not in "the final solution" of the case.

In their reports, the Argentine agents tended to aggrandize and embellish their own passive role in the coup, chiefly by minimizing the part played by the Israelis and by casting aspersions on their competence. Inspector Morgado, leader of the "Eichmann commando," was openly derogatory when talking to me about "the quality of the men" Israel had assigned to capture Eichmann. According to Morgado, whose remarks were echoed by Inspector Machado, the Israeli agents conducted themselves far too conspicuously for their own good. They "lived it up" in the Alvear Palace, the best hotel in town. Morgado and his colleagues had to spend almost as much time on shielding them as on the surveillance of Eichmann. If they had not saved the "Blue Falcons" from their own mistakes—"which were numerous"—Eichmann would have been alerted to them and would have slipped through the noose tightening around him.

This was not borne out by Moshe Pearlman and Gideon Hausner, who wrote the most authoritative and authentic accounts of Eichmann's capture, and it was denied indignantly by the Israelis. "The Israeli task force," wrote Ya'acov Caroz in one of the rebuttals (itself not without errors), "did not carry Israeli passports, and it was impossible to identify them as Israeli citizens. Only a few of them stayed in hotels, and then only for part of their time in Argentina. And there was never more than one Israeli agent at a given hotel, so that it is hard to see how they could have made themselves conspicuous."

But if there are asperity and resentment today, there was none in 1960. Since the information that the Argentine agents had was not made available to the Israelis—Frondizi's instructions did not stretch that far—the task force from Jerusalem had to shift for itself. This was precision work, with no margin for error. Above all, the Israelis could not afford to kidnap the wrong man. But as of March 20, they were not yet absolutely certain that Klement was Eichmann.

The next day, however, the decisive clue was obtained. The Israeli agent whose assignment was to watch Klement at the Mercedes-Benz plant saw him coming through the gate as usual, but his daily routine was slightly changed for once. Before boarding the bus to San Fernando, the man stopped at a flower stand and bought a modest bouquet.

The day was March 21, the thirty-fifth anniversary of the Eichmanns' wedding. Recalling the significance of the date, the agent had no more doubts. Klement *was* Eichmann. Those flowers gave him away. It was a day of triumph, which the task force celebrated with a message to Jerusalem. "*Ha'ish hu ha'ish,*" it read in Hebrew—"The man is the man."

Then another hitch developed with a sudden flare-up of worldwide interest in the fugitive. Tuvia Friedman, a free-lance Nazi hunter of Haifa, who was pestering the Israeli authorities with tips about Eichmann which invariably proved to be false alarms, now announced with considerable fanfare that Eichmann was hiding in Kuwait, an oil-rich sheikdom on the Arabian Peninsula. Friedman's information was patently spurious. It had come to him from Dr. Erwin Schule, then head of the Nazi war crimes center in Ludwigsburg, who claimed to have obtained the tip from another fugitive, the Grand Mufti of Jerusalem.

Schule was later unmasked as a former Nazi, himself on the wanted list, and he was fired. Whether or not his misleading information concealed an ulterior motive, Friedman's announcement was disastrously timed and fraught with danger. The Israelis knew, of course, that Eichmann was not in Kuwait. But they were alarmed that Friedman's hoax, which revived interest in the Nazi criminal just when it was imperative to keep silent about him, might jeopardize the operation. It might cause Eichmann to deepen his cover or even to escape to a place where he would be difficult, if not impossible, to find.

Friedman's "bombshell" added an unexpected and unwelcome suspense to the chase, but only for a week or so. The Israelis (and, for that matter, the Argentinians) on the Eichmann trail satisfied themselves that Eichmann had been unaware of this development when they saw that he continued the routine of his exile.

D Day was now set for May 11. This was to be *the* day at last.

I quote verbatim from the report of Agent Raneri to the Argentinian Minister of the Interior, his eyewitness account of the abduction:

> The siren sounds at 7 P.M. at the Mercedes-Benz plant. Among the last ones to leave is Ricardo Klement. He boards the bus. I am sitting behind him as on all other afternoons, but he doesn't seem to notice that he is being watched.
>
> He gets off at his usual corner and walks toward his home. Suddenly, a big black car arrives at high speed and stops about a meter behind him, giving the impression that it had lost its way. But suddenly four persons jump out of the car. In the twilight I couldn't see who they were or of what sex. They scuffle before they subdue him and put him into the car.
>
> The undersigned jumped on a motorcycle parked at a prearranged spot and followed the kidnapers to a farm in the locality of Florencio Varela, Province of Buenos Aires.*

Two days later, Inspector Machado was commissioned "by direct order of the President of the Republic" to take personal charge of what was left to be done. For a whole week, he and his colleagues closely observed the house in Florencio Varela where Eichmann was held. Then, on the twentieth, they watched him being transported by limousine to the international airport at Ezeiza.

It was during these days that the Argentinian authorities made their most valuable contribution to the success of the operation. At the house, they looked on idly, letting the Israelis do as they pleased with their prisoner. At the airport, Machado replaced the regular immigration personnel with his own agents, instructing them to let

* It was an astounding report. What Raneri witnessed in San Fernando was the perpetration of a brazen crime, the kidnaping that he, as an officer of the law, would have been duty-bound to prevent. He did nothing to interfere, in accordance with President Frondizi's order not to intervene in the "operation" of the Israelis.

the special party pass without incident. No questions were asked, therefore, when Eichmann, clad in a dressing gown, was taken to the plane on a stretcher carried by two of his kidnapers. He was in a coma, drugged by a doctored cup of coffee. As the report of this phase of the operation stated: "By superior orders, Inspector Machado facilitated the entrance of the Israeli commandos to the airport."

According to the log of the Argentine secret service, the plane, marked 4-X-AGE, a Bristol-Britannia, left Ezeiza for Israeli via West Africa on May 20, with the heavily sedated Adolf Eichmann on board. It was the chartered El Al aircraft that had brought a delegation of distinguished Israelis to Buenos Aires to attend Argentina's 150th anniversary celebrations. Its schedule had been specially arranged by Yehuda Shimoni, a senior official of El Al at its New York office, to be standing by until Eichmann was ready for the trip to Jerusalem.

When the plane took off, the case was closed for Machado and his colleagues, except for a summary report prepared for the Minister of the Interior by Principal Official Miguel Angel Fornari.

> On the day of Eichmann's capture [he wrote] the Israeli commando team, called the special brigade of Blue Falcons, cabled in cipher to Prime Minister Ben-Gurion: "The beast is chained." Thus the commandant of the Israeli plane, Yehuda Shimoni, was able to take with him his prisoner, in satisfactory execution of the orders issued by the President of the Argentine nation and your Ministry.

The Israelis' own account of the abduction, published on December 11, 1972, in an effort to discredit my articles based on the Argentine documents, differed in some minor details from the record presented in the various intelligence reports. Thus, it was claimed that two cars were used for the abduction, and the "cars were moving, not standing." In actual fact, three cars were used, and all three were standing. Also, the Israelis said, nitpicking, "Eichmann was not taken to a farm but to another sort of place."

As it was, Agent Raneri was able to observe only what Pearlman in his account called "the kidnap car." He could not possibly see the back-up cars, including the one in which the agent who was the lookout in Suarez preceded Eichmann's bus to the stop in San Fernando by some twenty minutes. It was parked about forty yards from the bus stop, while the third car, held in reserve, was completely out of sight. The kidnap car had arrived at 6:15 P.M., and rolled to a stop midway between Calle Garibaldi and the bus stop at the curb of the main San Fernando highway. To account for its presence where no cars were usually parked, its hood was raised, with one of the agents bending over the engine.

As far as the "farm" was concerned, Raneri called it *granja* in his report. The word translates into "grange, farm, farmhouse," to be sure, but also into "country house" or "a house in the country," which Eichmann's destination actually was. The phrase *ir de granja* means "to go to the country for recreation."

Inside that *granja* on the evening of May 11, 1960, the leader of the task force asked his prisoner: "Who are you?"

The man replied instantly, almost eagerly: "*Ich bin* Adolf Eichmann." A quarter century earlier the young American lieutenant in Austria had heard him wrongly and thus gave Eichmann his long lease on life. This time there was no misunderstanding. "I *am* Adolf Eichmann," the man said with a slight shrug. "I know. I'm in the hands of Israelis."*

* In the aftermath of my Eichmann article in November 1972, a private secretary of Dr. Arturo Frondizi denied that the former President ever played the part the Argentine documents specifically ascribed to him. But Dr. Frondizi himself failed to follow up the denial with a statement he promised to issue in this matter. On January 26, 1973, in a statement given to my representative, attorney Guillermo Macia Rey of Buenos Aires, Señor Orestes Frondizi, acting as spokesman for his brother, conceded that the former President had been in the process of aligning himself with Perón at the time of my revelations and had the denial issued because my article proved embarrassing to him in that it threatened to annul his budding rapprochement with Perón.

Chapter Sixteen

The Eichmann Jinx

Oscar Liedtke first heard of Adolf Eichmann's bad luck on the morning of May 24, 1960, when he arrived at Hans Rosa's in Lima, where he worked as an insurance salesman. Nobody in the office knew that he was Heinrich Müller, former chief of the Gestapo, but they suspected that he was not "Oscar Liedtke" either. Müller could not hide his past entirely, and he "sort of conceded," as Rosa put it, that he was once "a big shot" in the Third Reich and had reason to live in exile under an assumed name. His employer and associates left it at that. He was a hard and conscientious worker at his humdrum job, easy to get along with. "He wouldn't hurt a fly," Rosa said. Nor was Müller the only Nazi in Lima, anyway, whose past no longer intruded on the new life they led.

This morning the worldwide excitement the Israelis' brazen *coup de main* had whipped up also engulfed the Rosa office. Eichmann was the sole topic of the conversation. When his colleagues noticed that Liedtke was unusually pale and fidgety, one of them slapped him on the back and told him, "Oscar, you'll be next!"

It was said in jest, of course. The others joined in the laughter and chimed in, teasing him with variations on the same joke, but it was obvious from Liedtke's reaction that he did not think it at all funny. His mood darkened visibly as the day wore on. When it was time to close the shop, the man who left the Rosa office near Plaza San Martin was not Oscar Liedtke. It was Heinrich Müller all over again who had been running since April 29, 1945.

He did not go straight home as was his custom but took a *colectivo* to Santa Clara, the suburb where Friedrich Schwend had his fortified compound. His friend Fritz, who had been instrumental in paving Müller's way to Lima and put him up in his house during the first few months of his stay, was the only man in Peru who knew his true identity. Now Müller needed help again, even if only an opportunity to talk things over man to man with someone who was in on his secret.

Müller was closeted with Schwend for hours. It was past ten o'clock that night when he arrived home to his Peruvian wife and children. He appeared worn out as he waved them away, went straight to his den upstairs and locked himself in. Alone with his problem, apparently not reassured by his session with Schwend, he toyed with the idea of killing himself. Taking his Luger out of the drawer, he placed it on a little table in front of the sofa on which he spent part of the night.

It was still there when his wife went looking for him in the morning and found the door to the den no longer locked. Müller was gone, and so was "Oscar Liedtke"—forever. By this time, driving his Volkswagen at breakneck speed on the road south to Arequipa, Müller was nearing the Bolivian border at the crossing point of Charaña. He had no exit visa, but it was only a matter of a few thousand soles to get out of Peru. He entered Bolivia on the new passport Schwend had given him the night before as a parting gift. It was made out in the name of Schreiker.

After that, Müller's trail was lost, except for a small bundle of letters Dr. Santos Chichizola found in Schwend's filing cabinet when he raided the compound twelve years later. They were from someone who signed himself with the letter "H" but wrote on the envelope "H. Schreiker" as the sender, the stamp canceled at La Paz. On each sheet under the "H" the habitually precise Schwend penciled in "Heinrich Müller," probably because he had so many aliases to remember that he wanted to be sure he had this one right.

Müller was also listed in the little address book of Nazis which Dr. Santos confiscated from Schwend's sister-in-law. There under "H. Müller" was the notation: "He now uses the name Herzog, lives near Córdoba in Argentina, managing a rabbit farm." He is still there.

Walter Rauff read the news of Eichmann's abduction on his way to his office at Goldmann-Jannsen, a firm of importers in downtown Santiago de Chile. When he left Syria in 1949, he went first to Ecuador, where a job was waiting for him in Quito with the German firm of Compañía Bayer. It was too modest for his background and talents, and Ecuador seemed to him a dead end. So, in October 1958 he moved again, accepting an invitation from the Sara Braun Company to manage its branch at Punta Arenas, the southernmost city of the world where Chilean territory extends across to the Atlantic entrance to the Magellan Strait.

The work was interesting, the salary only fair, but it was enough to support him and his wife and pay for the education of his two growing sons in a Chilean military academy. Punta Arenas, this curious 130-year-old city of some 30,000 inhabitants behind God's back, was attractive. But it was what its name said, a sandy spot, with few trees in the streets and hardly a blade of grass anywhere. The surrounding country was barren and bleak, and the climate was wearing Rauff down—overcast skies, constant changes from fair to foul weather, fog, mists, high winds, and rain, rain, rain. When he could no longer bear it, Rauff returned to Santiago. Now he was sorry he had made the move.

The scattered Nazis throughout South America were badly jolted by Eichmann's fate. The question foremost in their minds was the one that bothered Müller: Who will be next? They saw Israeli agents lurking behind every tree, waiting in ambush around corners ready to strike. But none was more frightened than Walter Rauff. He slept with a shotgun beside him in bed, had two ferocious German shepherds on a leash wherever he went, locked his doors day and night, and stopped seeing people. He yearned for Punta Arenas, so distant—from everywhere. Not even the far-ranging Jewish avengers would range that far.

Rauff felt especially vulnerable in Santiago. It was only an hour's flight from Buenos Aires or Montevideo, where Jewish avengers had been spotted by his friends, who had formed vigilante groups to protect themselves. But where to go? In his panic, Rauff thought seriously of returning to Germany. Facing a court, if it came to it, on his own home grounds was by far preferable to standing in the dock in Jerusalem. But he dismissed the idea and returned to the relative safety of Fernando de Magellan's vast archipelago at the southern extremity of the subcontinent whose myriad islands, channels and fjordlike inlets offered many excellent places to hide.

He was there in 1964 when the West German government sent

Chile a request for his extradition. His case went through the judicial instances all the way up to the Supreme Court, which rejected the Germans' request on grounds of insufficient evidence and ruled also that the charges had expired under the statute of limitations. Rauff is still at Punta Arenas, managing a little fishery, a frightened, wilted old man of sixty-seven, in total seclusion, friendless by choice. His wife had died, and his sons live in Germany. Except for the companionship of his two shepherd dogs, Rauff is alone with the memory of the 97,000 Jews his gassing vans had so efficiently killed.

There were a number of other "*prominente*," as Bormann called them in his notes on the incident, the so-called "celebrities" among the fugitive Nazis who had reason to be apprehensive in the wake of Eichmann's abduction—Franz Paul Stangl, for example, former commandant of the Treblinka extermination camp, and Herbert Cukurs, the liquidator of the Latvian Jews, both of whom had escaped to Brazil; and a couple of bloodstained diplomats, Franz Rademacher and Karl Otto Klingenfuss, who had served as Eichmann's contacts in the Foreign Ministry handling the international ramifications of the Final Solution. Stangl and Cukurs were thick-witted louts. They belonged to the uncouth horde of the brutalized Nazi proletariat who were mere instruments of terror, personifications of what Hannah Arendt called "the banality of evil." Just as they could not sense the dismal horror of their crimes when they committed them, they could not even now appreciate properly the full threat of retribution that followed them into exile.

Rademacher and Klingenfuss were of a different breed. They were members of the intelligentsia, highly trained professionals with status in society. Yet these sophisticated, supposedly civilized diplomats had involved themselves with direct participation in mass murder. Rademacher had participated personally in the liquidation of the Belgrade ghetto in 1941 and arranged the deportation of the Belgian Jews a year later. So callous was he in the performance of his "duties" that when he went to Belgrade he wrote "liquidation of Jews" in the voucher of his travel expenses as the purpose of his trip.

Wanted as one of the signatories of the infamous Wannsee protocol and as Eichmann's man in the Foreign Ministry, Rademacher had managed to remain at large for seven years after the war, avoiding trial because he was needed as a witness, and avoiding giving evidence because he was awaiting trial. In the meantime, he had a pleasant job as private secretary to Philip Reemtsma, the cigarette tycoon, who himself was tainted with an ugly Nazi past. The German authorities got around to Rademacher in 1952, and he was sentenced to three years and five months by a Nuremberg court in a farcical trial. While his appeal was pending, he jumped bail and made his way to Argentina, where he joined his companion in the Foreign Ministry, Legation Secretary Karl Otto Klingenfuss.

When Klingenfuss was sought by the Americans for questioning in 1949, the French authorities, for whom he worked as a translator, refused to surrender him. But alerted by the sudden American interest in him, Klingenfuss fled to Argentina. Although he was charged with complicity in the deportation of thousands of Jews from Italy, Croatia and Bulgaria, and with the gruesome part he had played in the tragic sinking of the death ship *Struma*, in which 677 Rumanian Jews drowned, the Argentine authorities refused even to consider his extradition when, in 1958, the Germans requested it. This quartet—Stangl, Cukurs, Rademacher, Klingenfuss—were free in Brazil and Argentina when the Israelis struck. Finding themselves briefly in the spotlight, they stayed away from their usual haunts and concealed themselves behind hastily chosen aliases. It soon became evident that for the time being they were lost in the shuffle.

Nobody knows exactly when, where and how Dr. Josef Mengele first heard of the kidnaping of Eichmann. When the news broke, he was on the run. He already was the living symbol of the worst of Nazi crimes, a man more loathed than Martin Bormann, sought by Germans and Jews alike.

Mengele was one of scores of SS physicians detailed to the extermination camps, a handful of them to cure the sick, most of them to kill. With the rank of Haupsturmführer, he belonged to the hand-picked contingent of black-uniformed doctors who received the incoming inmates at the railroad station, where they were herded down the ramps like cattle driven to the slaughterhouse. His job was to decide at whim who would be spared for forced labor and who would die in the gas chamber.

A long bill of indictment drawn up on June 5, 1959, in Freiburg, by Judge Robert Müller of Court No. 22, singled Mengele out as indubitably the cruelest among the murderous doctors, and a warrant was issued for his arrest. "The German national," its opening paragraph read,

> Doctor of Philosophy and Doctor of Medicine *Josef Mengele,* born March 16, 1911, in Günzburg, District of Swabia, Land of Bavaria, West Germany, formerly residing at 87 Sonnhalde in Freiburg . . . the son of manufacturer Karl Mengele and his wife Walburga Mengele nee Hupfauer, is to be taken into custody on emphatic suspicion of murder and attempted murder.

The warrant listed seventeen counts of premeditated murder, some of which needed the skill of the surgeon and the depravity of a homicidal maniac to perpetrate. The specific charges included these:

> The accused killed the newborn baby of Frau Sussmann of Vienna 19, Sieveringstrasse 107, by throwing the infant into an open fire before the eyes of the mother.
>
> The accused killed a 14-year-old girl by splitting her head with a cleaver or dagger, her death occurring after excruciating pain.
>
> He injected pain-causing solutions into the eyes of infants as a result of which they died. . . .
>
> He killed several twins of Gypsy parentage, either with his own hands, or by mixing lethal poison into their food; he murdered these children for the purpose of conducting specious medical studies on their bodies during their autopsies.

Mengele submerged easily in Germany after the war, living comfortably on a generous allowance from his rich father*—until witnesses came forward to pick him out of the faceless mass of escaped murderers. Then he fled, going to Argentina via Austria,

*The name "Mengele" is a household word in many countries for it is the trademark of the high-quality agricultural machinery manufactured by the family firm in Günzburg. It is an eerie sight when traveling in Germany to see the name made notorious by this scion of the family emblazoned in raised metal letters on innumerable tractors and all sorts of implements. Dr. Mengele is a very silent partner in the prosperous firm, whose branches abroad include one in Argentina and another in Paraguay, both managed by his brother, who also operates a parquet factory. This substantial economic base aids Dr. Mengele materially in sustaining himself in exile, showing that the ready availability of substantial funds, as in the case of Bormann, is the best guarantor of survival as a fugitive.

Italy and Spain, arriving in Buenos Aires in 1954 on a passport made out in his own name, his tedious passage financed from the ample family funds. He first came into focus on October 27, 1956, when the Argentine authorities issued to him the mandatory *cédula,* No. 3,940,484. It did not do justice to this trim, tidy, tall, good-looking man who tried, in his morbid vanity, to appear beautiful. "Height: 174 cm [5 feet 10 inches]," his description on the *cédula* read: "Straight forehead, light-brown eyes, straight nose, medium mouth, prominent chin, medium ears, distinct lobes." He also carefully cultivated his dapper little mustache; his light-brown eyes were forever roving.

It was only after his arrival that he thought it wise to conceal himself by adopting a string of bogus names. In the files of Interpol in Paris, which contain the only complete record of the Mengele case, is one of the longest rosters of aliases ever used by any criminal. First calling himself Gregor Schklastro without adding the honorific of his two doctorates, he changed to *Dr.* Helmut Gregor-Gregori. On his subsequent escapades he used ten other pseudonyms, each adapted to what the occasion required—Fausto Rindon, José Aspiazu, S. Alvez, Edler Friedrich von Breitenbach, Walter Hasek, Lars Ballstroem, Heinz Stobert, Franz Fischer, Stanislas Prosky, and Karl Geuske.

Once he was allegedly buried in a mock funeral in Paraguay, with the name Cirillo Flores Chavez inscribed on the wooden cross on his grave—until it was found out that Mengele was alive and well, as was Señor Flores, whose good name had been expropriated for this occasion. In 1964, Interpol made public the list of his various aliases, conceding that one of the reasons Mengele's whereabouts were so difficult to ascertain was his trick of changing his name so frequently.

A decade had gone by since the end of the war, but as of 1956, nothing was done in Germany to investigate his case or indict him, despite the damning evidence piling up in the hands of the magistrates investigating war crimes. Mengele had lawyers in Germany who monitored the situation, and they advised him that he seemed to have been filed and forgotten. The reassuring news restored his complacency. He felt so safe in Argentina that he returned to the practice of medicine under his own name.

Starting out modestly at 1875 Calle Sarmiento in the Buenos Aires suburb of Olivos, he moved to a house at 970 Virrey Ortiz in the elegant Vicente Lopez district, where he established himself in style. The killer of so many infants in Auschwitz-Birkenau between May 1943 and April 1945 was now making an excellent living as the abortionist most in demand in Buenos Aires.

An "accident" happened in 1958, when a young woman died on the operating table in his surgery. Mengele was arrested but was held only briefly. Two hours after his booking, a friend arrived at the police station with a "bundle" and Mengele was allowed to "escape." He left Buenos Aires, abandoning his wife, Martha, and young son to their own resources. Traveling with a valid German passport in his own name, he entered Paraguay on October 2 on a visitor's visa allowing him to stay for ninety days. On January 1, 1959, the eve of its expiration, he disappeared from Asunción, going to his favorite haunts in Bariloche, where he then spent four uneasy months.

San Carlos de Bariloche was the popular resort of all the Nazis who flocked to the enchanting mountain region either to relax or to hide. It was in Bariloche that the Argentine authorities found Eichmann during one of his carefree vacations (destined to be the last) and started the chase that ended in his capture. It is in Bariloche where Bormann feels most at home, walking about in greasy leather pants held up by garishly embroidered suspenders, wearing a rakish Tirolese hat, as if he were still hiking in the mountains around his beloved Berchtesgaden.

The place is German in all but name. It was first settled by Don Carlos Wiederhold, an entrepreneur of German descent, to expand his thriving forestry business. Coming from Chile with a group of German lumberjacks, he built the first house on the shore of Nahuel Huapí on January 5, 1895. He and a company called Huber Aliches developed the region, which is still populated by Germans—the descendants of the early settlers and newcomers. Named Bariloche in 1909 and renamed San Carlos de Bariloche in 1924 (after Wiederhold), the city is the hub of South America's most popular tourist region; its mountains and lakes surpass the best of Switzerland in scenic beauty.

Here the Andes are more rugged than the Alps, the lakes more glimmering, their colors more vivid. Although tourism lends a cosmopolitan atmosphere to this enchanted region of three million acres of forest teeming with wildlife, it is dominated by the Germans, among whom live numerous Nazis, many of them in the hotel business. It is probably the most densely populated Nazi enclave in the world. Long before the coming of Bormann and Mengele, Theodore Roosevelt (in 1914) and General John J. Pershing (in 1925) visited Bariloche. General Dwight D. Eisenhower was the guest of President Pedro Aramburu in the Llao-Llao, a rambling rustic establishment at the foot of Cerro López.

Towering over the whole region is the well-nigh inaccessible 6,810-foot Tronador Peak. But the favorite of Bormann and Mengele is Cerro Catedral, 5,742 feet high, only thirteen miles from San Carlos de Bariloche by road, 6.5 miles of which are paved and open all year round. Aside from its natural beauty, Bormann and Mengele are enamored of the region because it reminds them of the Bavarian highlands and visit frequently to relax, to hide and to plot.

It was during his restive sojourn in Bariloche that Mengele decided to stabilize his life in South America. He returned to Asunción and hired Dr. Cesar Augusto Sanabria, a young real-estate lawyer, who took on the case as a special favor to a friend, to file his application for citizenship. While his case was pending at the Naturalization Office of the Ministry of the Interior, he traveled a bit in Brazil, visiting a friend at Doña Ema in the State of Santa Catarina, then returned to Bariloche. The case of his botched-up abortion obviously had been forgotten.

Mengele stayed until October 23, when he reentered Paraguay, now on an immigration visa, and he was naturalized a week later in a quiet ceremony attended only by Dr. Sanabria and two of his sponsors, Alexander von Eckstein, leader of the Nazis in Paraguay, and a man named Werner Jung. He was issued citizenship paper No. 293,348 and a work permit. His address in Asunción was the house in Villa Mora where, only a few weeks later, Dr. Biss would make his famous house call to minister to the indigestion of Martin Bormann.

There was nothing irregular about these proceedings. Mengele was not yet a wanted criminal, and so he was not ineligible for Paraguayan citizenship. The Argentine authorities had issued no warrant for his arrest. Although his warrant had been prepared in Freiburg, five months before, the German government made no effort to circulate it among the authorities of the countries where Mengele was known to be living.

He was a fugitive nevertheless. Thanks to the dedicated efforts of Hermann Langbein, a Viennese of Mengele's own generation who had fought with the International Brigade during the Spanish Civil War and had spent two years in Auschwitz as a political prisoner, Mengele was no longer a nonentity. His notoriety was growing as more and more witnesses came forward to attest to his crimes.

The crescendo of publicity around Mengele was growing. The man was elusive, to be sure, but his monstrous crimes were there for all to see. Unlike Eichmann, who succeeded in evading the limelight until the remorseless moment of truth, Mengele was tangible game. It was a matter of public record that he was alive in South America, commuting between transparent hideouts, always a step ahead of his pursuers, with an uncanny penchant for squeezing out of the tightest situations. He was drawing upon himself the curiosity of newspaper reporters and the wrath of avengers.

At this point, the long-dormant pursuit of war criminals intensified even as it narrowed down to two parallel tracks—the search for Eichmann moving on one with its final momentum, the search for Mengele suddenly picking up new impetus. Eichmann had been identified, and his remaining days at large were numbered, even if he himself was oblivious of the imminence of his downfall. It was different with Mengele. Gregarious by nature, and peripatetic in his habits, he was setting himself up as a target, difficult and fast moving, but a target nevertheless. But he could not be found. Unlike the placid Eichmann, whose innate bureaucratic ingenuity failed him when his own life was in the balance, Mengele managed his exile with intelligence and cunning. Eichmann fell into the trap helplessly. Mengele knew how to evade all pitfalls, leaving nothing to chance.

The chase, the stage for which was set in June 1959 in Freiburg with the drawing up of the warrant for his arrest, began rather tentatively, and then only five months later. On November 13, the German embassy in Asunción asked the Paraguayan Ministry of the Interior to permit Counselor Winfried Engemann to "examine the Mengele dossier, even if only for a few hours." The request was a diplomatic sequel to the investigation Judge Müller had begun. The data was needed to implement the warrant for his arrest preparatory to a possible request for his extradition.

While the German judiciary was pursuing the case with bureaucratic leisureliness, Interpol suddenly appeared on the scene. The German authorities had forwarded the warrant to its headquarters in Paris. On November 18, Interpol petitioned the Naturalization Section of the Paraguayan Interior Ministry to make available Dr. Mengele's so-called "Record Card" to its Paris headquarters and also its branch office in Buenos Aires.

Mengele did not remain unaware of this sudden multiple interest in him. An Asunción police official, who had been hired by Alexander von Eckstein to report any untoward development in the case, had tipped him off that only five days after Counselor Engemann had been permitted to examine his dossier, a copy of his record was sent to Interpol in Paris and Buenos Aires.

With the possibility of extradition to Germany or apprehension by Interpol suddenly looming up, Mengele thought it advisable to vanish from Asunción. As so often before, he moved to his favorite hideout, a Nazi-managed hotel near San Carlos de Bariloche. What he did not know yet was that he was leaving the frying pan for the fire. Almost exactly on that day when the Israeli task force arrived in Buenos Aires to arrange the abduction of Adolf Eichmann, a shadowy group of young men reached Argentina, not to kidnap Mengele, but to kill him. But while the so-called Blue Falcons of the Eichmann hunt knew exactly where to look for their quarry, the commando team was operating in the dark. It had kept Mengele under surveillance in Paraguay, but called it off, it seemed, when one of the young men shadowing him was found near Eldorado with his throat slashed. Before another sentry could be assigned to his trail, Mengele vanished.

Guarded by Paraguayan police officers whom he and his younger brother, who was operating a family-owned woodworking plant in the region, had suborned, and warned by his own spies, Mengele discovered the tail and cut it off. The young man had come closer to killing him than any of the previous hunters. Mengele drew the logical conclusion from the incident—it was time to move again. He first went to Santa Catarina in Brazil, where he appeared to be settling down for a long stay on the secluded estate of Dr. Alexander Lénárd, his friend at Doña Ema, whose home was always available to him when he needed a safe house.

When he felt reassured that his pursuers had lost him, Mengele went back to Bariloche. He took a room in a chalet twelve miles from the center of the town, nestled picturesquely on the rugged southern slope of Cerro Catedral, at an altitude of almost three thousand feet, but far below the towering Tronador peak. He chose the alias Franz Fischer for his stay here.

This promised to be an exceptionally pleasant sojourn in the mountains. Not only was the weather fine and the place unusually delightful, but both were enhanced by the presence of another guest at the chalet. A couple of weeks after Mengele's arrival, a handsome blond woman checked in under the name of Nora Aldot, giving Frankfurt as the place and 1911 as the year of her birth when registering. Not young, to be sure, but she was extremely attractive, charming and vivacious. She passed for a German, which she actually was by birth, and was quickly befriended by the Nazis, who then passed her on to Mengele.

Franz, as Mengele was introduced, and Nora, as she called herself, became inseparable, holding hands in the lobby, going on long walks on the trails, sipping coffee in the *Konditorei* and having drinks in the bar. There seemed to be no reason to suspect Nora's interest in the handsome Franz, but Mengele always played it safe. After lunch on February 12, 1960, he took his new girl friend on a long hike up the Cerro Catedral. While they were gone, one of his bodyguards entered the woman's room at the chalet, just to make absolutely certain that she was from Frankfurt as she claimed.

When the man came out of the room, he summoned Mengele's other bodyguard in some excitement, then the pair left the chalet in great haste, looking for the couple They found them standing at a precipice looking up to the majestic snow-capped peaks, obviously lost in taking in the breathtaking view. What happened next has never been explained satisfactorily, but only the three men returned from the hike. When they reached the café on the road back to Bariloche, one of them rushed in shouting in Spanish with a heavy German accent: "A terrible accident! The woman who was with us fell off the cliff!"

A search party of mountain guides, vacationing skiers and local peasants immediately went to the spot where Nora disappeared, but it was not until the fifteenth that her body was found, apparently the victim of an accident. Perhaps she was. Yet Nora was destined never to come back from this hike. Mengele's man who searched her room had come upon her secret, and it tolled her inevitable doom. In a false bottom of her suitcase, the man found her travel papers—an Israeli passport, No. 160,697, made out in the name of Nourit Eddad, a native of Frankfurt, resident of Tel Aviv, a secretary by profession.

The visas in her passport showed that she had spent some time in Cologne as an employee of the Israeli purchasing mission, and that she entered Argentina as recently as late 1959. "She was very beautiful and very good," one of her relatives said of Nourit when her death became known in Israel. She was also very brave. A year after her death, the Argentine authorities added a footnote to her case before closing it with the label "accidental death," for lack of evidence that she had been murdered. According to the report, she was a member of the Israeli Secret Service and arrived in Bariloche "with a group of Israelis who went to stay at a different hotel from hers." The Argentine police refrained from speculating as to why she had gone to Bariloche. Was she there to "finger" Mengele? And the Israelis in those other hotels? Had they come to kill him?

The Israelis are still reluctant to divulge the whole story of Eichmann's abduction and refuse to identify the members of the task force sent to collect him, except by their cover names of Dov, Yigal and Gad. They keep resolutely silent about the second team, refusing even to acknowledge that its members were Israelis. But Bar-Zohar had no doubt. "When Prime Minister Ben-Gurion had given the green light," he wrote, "for Operation Eichmann, he had also set Operation Mengele in motion. While one group of them went after Eichmann, another began looking for the 'Angel of Death.'"

It would have been logical to send Nora to set up Mengele for the kill. They correctly gauged the soft spot in his armor, his weakness for the opposite sex. A strange man would never have had a chance to get through to him and observe the routine of his daily movements from such close quarters. A pretty woman could, and Nora did.

Nobody died in the search for Eichmann. But Nora was the fourth known casualty of the hunt for Mengele. The protective wall he had built around himself could be pierced. But nobody who pierced it lived.

The case of "Nora Aldot" was soon overshadowed and the death of Nourit Eddad was quickly avenged by the capture of Eichmann. The Israelis now had the prize they had come to get, and they decided to call a halt to the Mengele hunt. For one thing, the Israeli government, smarting under the violent reaction throughout South America to Eichmann's abduction, which manifested itself in sporadic outbreaks of anti-Semitic demonstrations unchecked by the police, was disinclined to aggravate the situation with another tres-pass on Argentine sovereignty. For another, it was abundantly evident that Mengele was too well protected and too smart, a much more difficult prey to bag than Eichmann. The mystery-shrouded Israeli team was recalled, its group of local helpers was disbanded.* Israel never again made even an attempt to interfere with Mengele's exile.

But the chase was by no means abandoned with the departure of the Israelis. Indeed, it became intensified. The Germans now took over where the Israelis left off, but they preferred to work strictly within the confines of the law.

* Although the State of Israel is no longer officially active in the search for and apprehension of Nazi criminals still at large in South America, the Jewish pursuit of these marked men is by no means dormant. Groups of unforgiving and adventurous young Jews exist in Brazil and Argentina, to keep after them as best they can, in pursuits that are more romantic than effective. Dr. Mengele remains their chief target, and he is acutely aware of the threat they represent to his life. This is why he continues to live furtively, using ever-different aliases on his travels. But, as we shall see, he is not impossible to find.

Chapter Seventeen

The Search for Dr. Mengele

The record of the judicial chase after Dr. Josef Mengele is a mixture of commendable industry and deplorable inefficiency. For reasons best known to themselves, the Germans chose for some time to ignore the information that Mengele had moved to Paraguay and become a citizen of that country in 1959. Their efforts to find Mengele was concentrated on Argentina, where, they professed to believe, he still lived.

His extradition was a matter of foreign affairs, and diplomatic protocol had to be observed. Judge Robert Müller needed more than nine months—until March 11, 1960—to cut all red tape before he could begin the process of submitting Mengele's arrest warrant to the Argentine authorities. Then it took forty-eight days to have the warrant notarized by Alberto A. Maddoni, Argentine consul in Munich, and fifty-two days more to forward the document to Buenos Aires. It had to be channeled through the Foreign Ministry in Bonn to the German embassy in Buenos Aires, which then presented it to the Ministry of Foreign and Religious Affairs of the Republic of Argentina.

In the Ministry, the case was assigned to Assistant Secretary Angel M. Centano. The German motion called for a policy decision on the highest level, by President José Maria Guido of the Senate. On June 28, 1960, President Guido signed a decree directing the Procurator General of the Republic to begin extradition proceedings by assigning the matter to a federal judge competent to handle the case.

Assistant Secretary Centano then forwarded the papers to

Judge Dr. Raul Horacio Rios Centeno of Federal Court No. 1 in San Martin in Buenos Aires Province, only to be told that Judge Centeno had no jurisdiction in the matter. The case was then transferred to Federal Judge Dr. Jorge Luque of District Court No. 3. Today, almost fifteen years later, he is still struggling with the solution of an obviously unsolvable problem.

By his erudition, personality and creed, Judge Luque was eminently qualified to come to grips with the Mengele case. The scion of an old and wealthy Spanish family of Córdoba, he had been appointed to the bench by President Aramburu in 1956, when the corrupt Peronist judiciary was undergoing a purge, its venal judges replaced by those whose integrity and belief in democracy were beyond doubt.

Dr. Luque regarded the assignment as a challenge. Appalled by the gruesome crimes cited in Judge Müller's brief, he resolved to bring Mengele to justice and see to it that he would be sent to Germany. On June 30, when he was given the case, he ordered the chief of police in the San Martin district to arrest Mengele. The German application included a number of addresses where Mengele was supposed to reside. Judge Luque instructed the chief of police to proceed at once to 968 Calle Vertiz in Olivos, one of the addresses listed by the Germans, take Mengele into custody, and report to him forthwith the outcome of his mission.

Commissioner Primitivo Gonzalez acted promptly, but his report to Luque, sent the next day, was most disappointing. All he could tell the judge was that Calle Vertiz had no No. 968 and that a man named José Mengele was totally unknown in the neighborhood. When the man could not be found at the first address submitted by the Germans, Judge Luque asked the police commissioner at the suburb of Boulogne to try other places Judge Müller had listed. Commissioner Fernando Dingreville complied with the request promptly, sending his detectives to 1875 Calle Sarmiento in Olivos and to 1015 Calle Merano in Vicente Lopez, where the Germans indicated Mengele might be found.

At the first address, the detectives encountered a sixty-year-old widow named Bertha Pantz, who assured them that she never so much as heard of a doctor named Mengele. At the second address a bewildered German couple insisted that, as far as they knew, Dr. Mengele had never lived in that house.

By his own efforts, Commissioner Dingreville then dug up another address, at 1969 Calle Monasterio, where he had reason to believe Mengele might live. There his sleuths found a forty-year-old German named Heinrich Quasten, and this time it seemed that the detectives had hit pay dirt. Although Quasten claimed that Mengele had never lived at that address, he readily admitted that he knew the doctor, and advised the officers to go to 1074 Calle 5 de Julio, where he was certain they would find the man they were looking for.

This was the address of the boardinghouse where Bormann had put up Eichmann when he first arrived in Argentina. Señora Bergilde Jurmann, owner of the *pension,* stated categorically that Mengele had never been one of her boarders and professed to know nothing about his whereabouts. She conceded, however, that she was in touch with Mengele's wife, Martha, and his sixteen-year-old son, Karl Heinz, who visited her from time to time. Where they lived she did not know. Efforts to locate them proved futile.*

Within a single week the search for Mengele that had begun so promisingly ended without yielding a single clue. On July 6, Senior Inspector Luis Acerbo sent a brief note to Judge Luque, advising him that the police were abandoning the hunt in view of the fact that none of the addresses the Germans had supplied produced positive results.

Dr. Luque refused to give up. He obtained photographs of Dr. Mengele and circulated them to every police delegation within a radius of 150 miles. Then he wrote to Rear Admiral Ezequiel N. Vega, the country's senior policeman at the head of Policía Federal, requesting him to use his nationwide apparatus to locate Mengele. But another hitch developed. Admiral Vega asked Dr. Luque somewhat testily on what authority did he presume to impose such a task on Policía Federal.

It took Luque six weeks to secure the proper authorization from the Criminal Court to satisfy Admiral Vega. On October 14, 1960, at last, a search warrant was issued by round-robin telegram to all units of Policía Federal throughout Argentina, ordering the arrest of Mengele when and if found. Although he continued to commute as usual between Paraguay and Argentina, visiting San Carlos de Bariloche at frequent intervals, he was never found, much less arrested.

* It later developed that Mengele's family also had left Buenos Aires for an unknown destination to begin with, eventually turning up in Merano, Italy, where they still live, Martha now divorced from her husband.

On March 3, 1961, the German embassy again intervened in the search. Dr. Kopp, chief of the embassy's consular section, sent to Judge Luque what he regarded as a positive lead. It was a communication from one Señora Silvia Caballero de Costa, dated February 21, sent from Santiago del Estero, Argentina's oldest city, founded in 1553. In her letter the Señora stated rather convincingly that Dr. Mengele was still in Argentina after all, living in her ancient city on a false name, engaged to marry a rich young lady who was his sole means of support. Dr. Luque immediately forwarded the letter to Commissioner Vicente Victor Fimiani, chief of the La Plata police district where Santiago del Estero is situated.

Commissioner Fimiani's agents then spent two and a half months running down the tip and returned with a romantic story that was more reminiscent of the plot of *Romeo and Juliet* than the melodrama of Josef Mengele. They contacted Señora Caballero de Costa at her home on Avenida Alvear, and found that she was a simple, almost illiterate middle-aged woman who was totally unfamiliar with the Mengele case and far too uneducated to have been able to write the denunciatory letter. Her interrogation led the detectives to the sumptuous villa of a wealthy merchant named Manuel Tevez, and he confessed that he had written the letter, using Señora Carmen's name and address to conceal his authorship.

He turned out to be a brokenhearted father, upset because his beautiful young daughter Alicia was in love with and secretly engaged to a doctor he suspected was José Mengele. He hoped he would be able to end Alicia's affair with the unworthy German by exposing him, having him arrested, and kicked out of the country. The man Tevez thought was Mengele turned out to be an international adventurer, and a physician of sorts, with a long criminal record. But aside from this superficial similarity, and their common weakness for beautiful young women, nothing in the vital statistics and careers of the two men matched. The "doctor" Señor Tevez denounced as Mengele was an imposter named Willy Delaney, a New Yorker by birth who had come to Argentina from Chile in 1933, running away from a string of felonies, the full record of which was on file at the La Plata police department. Delaney was a bogus practitioner of medicine, while Mengele was a genuine physician; he was a native American who had been living in Argentina for twenty-seven years while Mengele was a German who had spent less than five years in the country; and Delaney was rather too old as well—he was in his seventies, whereas Mengele had just turned fifty. Nothing in his physical appearance even remotely resembled the fugitive Nazi whom Alicia's distraught father had taken him for.

The Delaney file was closed on May 11, 1961. Only nineteen days later, the Mengele case was wide open again. Another note was received from the German embassy at the Argentine Foreign Ministry, seeking "clarification of unconfirmed reports" that Mengele had been arrested on March 21 in a house on Avenida San Martin in Coronel Suarez, and was being held incommunicado by the police.

The embassy's note was forwarded to Judge Luque, who was astonished by the information it contained. This was the first he had heard of Mengele's alleged arrest. Despite all his round-robins and scattered search warrants, nobody in the Argentine police had bothered to inform him of this sensational break in the case. It was just as well. The man who was picked up by Inspector David M. E. Pedemonte of the La Plata police at Coronel Suarez was a wayward German named Lothar Hermann.

There seemed to have been no valid reason to take him for Mengele. But now that the intervention of the German embassy turned Hermann's arrest into an international incident, as well as into a heated jurisdictional dispute between the judge and the police, something had to be done. The obvious thing was to establish promptly and positively whether Hermann was really Mengele. The Germans suggested that they be provided with Lothar's fingerprints to facilitate their own conclusive determination of the case. This struck the Argentine authorities as a good idea.

It took weeks to procure the fingerprints through devious channels. So it was only on July 24, four months after his arrest, that Hermann was exonerated. Inspector Pedemonte conceded that "the examination of fingerprints shows that this was a case of mistaken identity and that Lothar Hermann is not José Mengele."

In his exasperation, Judge Luque turned to Interpol for help. Could they let him know what the international status of the case was and where Mengele was supposed to be? It was only three years later, on May 19, 1964, that a reply was received from Commissioner Augustin A. J. Lafont, the Interpol chief of Buenos Aires. In a three-line note Lafont informed Luque that, as far as Interpol knew, "Dr. Mengele was not in Brazil."

Luque shot back an angry note telling Lafont that he was keenly interested to find out not where Mengele was *not*, but where he *was*. He demanded that Interpol go after him with all its prodigious resources, and arrest him wherever he happened to be.

It is generally believed that Interpol is active in the pursuit of Nazi fugitives, an impression enhanced by the fact that at one time Israel was effectively represented on its executive board by one of its supercops, Yossef Nahamias, Inspector General of the Tel Aviv Police. It is true that Interpol maintains dossiers on fugitive Nazis, including a bulging one on Mengele and a rather thin one on Bormann.* But the basic purpose and clearly defined functions of Interpol more or less exclude it from too close preoccupation with Nazis on the run.

According to the very first article of its statutes,

> The purpose of the International Police Organization is to ensure and officially promote the growth of the greatest possible mutual assistance between all criminal police authorities *within the limits of the laws existing in the different states,* to establish and develop all institutions likely to contribute to an efficient repression of common-law crimes and offenses to *the strict exclusion of all matters having a political, religious or racial character.* [Italics mine, L.F.]

The borderline between "common-law crimes" and "matters of a political character" has never been clearly drawn for Interpol as far as the Nazis were concerned. This leaves a gaping loophole in Interpol, which is ingeniously exploited by the fugitive Nazis themselves. Certain forces within Interpol never cease to remind its Secretary General that his job is to aid in the detection of drug-pushers, the forgers of Picassos and other swindlers in the international crime market. They caution him subtly not to show too much zeal in looking for any of the Nazis at large, especially in countries which frown upon a too broad interpretation of the Interpol's sometimes deliberately ambiguous statutes.

* I myself had an opportunity to examine the Bormann dossier that is kept at the Buenos Aires office of Interpol. It turned out to be a slim folder, containing mainly inconclusive correspondence, rather than any substantive information obtained by original independent detective work. The only visual identification of the Reichsleiter included in the folder was the photostat of an old Heinrich Hoffmann picture, copied from an Argentine newspaper. The dossier was important to me nevertheless, if only because it categorically confirmed that Bormann had lived in Argentina.

Moreover, the local commissioners of Interpol are natives of the countries through which people like Bormann and Mengele move. They are susceptible to the usual influences (bribes and similar "pressures") that make the vaunted international police organization woefully ineffectual in South America.*

At any rate, Judge Luque's intervention produced no results.

Nothing happened for about a year. Then in the summer of 1965, the uneasy calm that enveloped Mengele from time to time was shattered. Twelve young Jews in Brazil banded together to make a try at kidnaping the doctor. The group moved to Pôrto Mendes, on the Brazilian side of the Paraná river, while two of them crossed the stream, to reconnoiter the terrain. They were next seen with their throats cut from ear to ear, floating down the river, their arms outstretched as if crucified.

The death of the ill-fated "avengers" did not remain unavenged. Mengele's chief protector at that time was a Paraguayan officer named Colonel Arganas, who also headed one of the country's major smuggling syndicates. Two months after the murder of the two "avengers," a plane in which Colonel Arganas was flying on an inspection tour in the company of Commissioner Bartolomi of the Argentine Federal Police, crashed in southern Paraguay. The authorities in Asunción tried to hush up the accident. But the Argentine government insisted that an investigation be made to establish the cause of Bartolomi's death.

According to telegram Number 015 from the Formosa Branch of Argentine Federal Police to the Ministry of the Interior in Buenos Aires, the investigation produced the startling evidence that Colonel Arganas' plane had been sabotaged—by the ten young Jews left over from the brave dozen who set out to capture Mengele.

For three long years afterward, all was quiet on the Mengele front. Dr. Luque's efforts had ground to a tentative halt. The persistent judge knew that his quarry continued to challenge fate by

* At least two Interpol chiefs stationed in South America had to be dismissed summarily for blatant corruption. One was so "influenced" that he refused to act in the extradition case of Klaus Altmann-Barbie, even when the Peruvian government lodged a complaint with Interpol headquarters in Paris, pointing out that the case involved "common-law crimes" (the smuggling of currency and suspicion of murder) and not Barbie's Nazi past in France.

setting foot on Argentine soil from time to time. Luque had photographs and fingerprints distributed to all frontier posts with orders to arrest Mengele on sight, and to notify him at once of his detection. He had his home telephone number posted at every checkpoint along the border, so that he could be called day or night, weekdays or holidays, the moment Mengele was caught. Of course, he never received that call.

Suddenly it seemed that Mengele's moment of truth was at hand at last. In the summer of 1968, a secret agent of the Paraná state police in Brazil—an Austrian-born soldier of fortune calling himself "Dr. Erico," whom we will meet later again under his real name, Erich Erdstein—embarked on a crusade against the elusive doctor. He was aware of Dr. Luque's abiding interest in Mengele. With the approval of Dr. Luiz Alberto Machado and Commissioner Wilfredo Piloto, his superiors in Curitiba, and in collaboration with Dr. Hector Shée, a high-ranking police official in Santa Catarina, the state swarming with former Nazis, Erico developed an intricate plot to catch Mengele in an inescapable trap. The idea was to intercept the doctor on one of his frequent trips to Brazil, then abduct him to Puerto Iguassú, the frontier town on the Argentine side of the border where the Alto Paraná separates Brazil, Argentina and Paraguay. Arrangements were made with Commander Roberto Figueredo, chief of the frontier police at Puerto Iguassú, to "receive" Mengele and "forward" him to Dr. Luque in Buenos Aires.

Then, in June, Erico received word from one of his double-agents (a former Nazi who kept in touch with his old comrades but was leaking information about them to the Paraná police for a fee) that Mengele was back in Brazil, somewhere near Rio do Sul in Santa Catarina. According to the informer, he was staying with Dr. Alexander Lénárd, a Hungarian-born pharmacist-physician and a nationally known figure in Brazil. Thanks to his consummate knowledge of the life and music of Johann Sebastian Bach, he had won the top prize in a quiz show patterned after our own ill-fated "$64,000 Question."

It was not Bach's music that tied Mengele to Lénárd. The doctor's housekeeper on his estate in Doña Ema near Rio Grande do Sul was a Natalie Klein, a former nurse at Auschwitz-Birkenau, where she had served on Mengele's staff.

It would have been the smart thing to do in a situation like this to drop everything, rush to Doña Ema, and storm the Lénárd villa, where Dr. Mengele would be caught. But Erico, a flamboyant detective, not too subtle in his methods, was in no hurry. He was determined to squeeze the last bit of drama out of "the historic operation," and also to make a little money on the side.

Before going to Doña Ema for Mengele, he went to Rio de Janeiro where, he now insists, he made a fatal mistake. He shared his big secret with Dr. Uwe Kästner, the official at the German embassy who was supposed to keep watch on the Nazis, and with the correspondent of one of Germany's leading newspapers, to whom he sold "the story of the century." Erico then stopped off in Curitiba to make yet another deal, this one with Francisco Camargo, star reporter of Paraná's biggest newspaper.

By the time Erico got to Doña Ema and stormed the Lénárd villa, Mengele was gone—tipped off, Erico swore, by the German correspondent who pretended to be interested in the big story but was in fact just one of the many Nazi spies at large in Brazil. Erico remained hot on Mengele's trail, charting the doctor's progress northward in the Lénárds' sleek little Simca automobile. He caught up with him a few weeks later, on September 13, 1968—a fateful date in Erico's life and a memorable one for Mengele as well, for Erico insists that he killed Josef Mengele that day.

This is his own story, jotted down for me:

> From the Argentine border to the banks of the Alto Paraná, I had all my agents looking for Mengele. I did not have to wait long. A schoolteacher from Marechal Rondon who was working for me signaled that something very strange was going on in his town. Tension. Strangers coming and going between Rondon and Pôrto Mendes. Spare parts of a forty-h.p. outboard motor shipped in from Argentina.
>
> It was immediately evident to me that all these feverish preparations were being made for Mengele, the only bigtime Nazi still left in Brazil, to get him across the river. I took two of my best agents and my young son, Erico Jorge, to Pôrto Mendes, laying the trap for Mengele. He arrived as expected, accompanied by one Walter Bernhardt, a former sailor from the scuttled pocket battleship *Graf Spee*, who was to ferry him to Paraguay, and another man who later turned out to be Heinrich Müller, the former chief of the Gestapo.
>
> We pounced on the three men, handcuffed them, and rushed them to my car parked at the roadside. We drove a little way north, to the boat I had chartered to take Mengele to Argentina.

It was four o'clock in the morning when we passed Foz do Iguassú. An Argentine patrol boat was to rendezvous with us one mile downstream to take us all into Puerto Iguassú, where Commander Figueredo was waiting with his men to take Mengele over from us and ship him to Buenos Aires.

Then the shooting started. A long, antiquated Paraguayan gunboat, with fifteen soldiers aboard, had come out of the darkness. We had been betrayed! The gunboat slipped alongside us, the soldiers boarded our boat and tried to take Mengele away. Instinctively I drew my .38. My son Jorge had his .32 out. We opened up almost simultaneously. I hit Mengele twice in the chest and saw him going down, head first, into the water.

At that instant, the Argentine patrol boat pulled up. We were embroiled, it was obvious, in a grave international incident on a river which marks the frontiers of three countries. The Paraguayans fished Mengele's body out of the water, took the wounded Müller on board, and sailed off, as fast as their old junk-heap could make it, in the direction of Puerto Presidente Stroessner. My son and I boarded the Argentine patrol boat and put into Puerto Iguassú. The boat I had chartered returned to Foz in Brazil. The morning broke calm. The hunt was over.

It was a good story; it later appeared, embellished with a blow-by-blow description of the chase and the battle, in a number of reputable European newspapers and magazines. As for Erico, the killing of Mengele, he later told me, was the crowning achievement of his career as a Nazi hunter, his greatest claim to fame. But later when I tracked down Dr. Mengele and found that he had miraculously survived his murder, I confronted Erico with my discovery. He merely shrugged his shoulders and said, perhaps in jest, "I guess I must have killed the wrong man."*

As far as Judge Luque is concerned, he is still waiting for Erico to deliver on their deal. The distinguished judge's diligent search is

* During my visit to Marechal Rondon and Pôrto Mendes four years later, I was able to establish that the killing of Mengele, as claimed by Erico, was a monumental mishap of mistaken identity. It seems Mengele had been tipped off at Doña Ema, even as Erico assumed it, but instead of escaping northward on Brazilian soil, he motored west and returned to Paraguay immediately. The group Erico then mistook for the Mengele party was a trio of Brazilian construction workers en route to Paraguay to smuggle a cargo of American cigarettes and Scotch whisky into Brazil. One of them was actually killed, another wounded. The incident terminated Erico's career as a policeman in Brazil, regrettably, at that, for as we will see, he could be an effective Nazi hunter and was instrumental in ridding the State of Paraná of many dangerous Nazis. For his encounter with Martin Bormann in Foz do Iguassú, see page 402.

a textbook example to illustrate the futility of official pursuits of the fugitive Nazis by the staid judiciary. Aside from the fact that they bog down in legalistic red tape, giving the wanted men every opportunity of escaping, the search proved especially frustrating in Mengele's case. The Germans had sent the Argentinians on a wild-goose chase. When they originally submitted the warrant with the motion for Mengele's extradition, they knew full well that he was no longer in Argentina.

The Germans misled Judge Luque with a number of addresses in and around Buenos Aires where they must have been reasonably certain that Mengele would not be found. If the German authorities had deliberately conspired to forestall the detention and extradition of Mengele, while giving the impression that they were seriously interested in his apprehension, they could not have chosen shrewder strategy and better tactics.

The old warrant of 1959 and the 1960 request for Mengele's extradition are still in effect, but only insofar as Judge Jorge Luque is concerned. The Germans' "search" now proceeds on a different tangent, in accordance with Resolution No. 4 Js 340/68, signed by Judge Schneider of the Land Court of Frankfurt, to which the case had been transferred.

Dated April 26, 1968, the Resolution takes us back to where we came in. It enumerates Mengele's crimes in a rehash of Judge Müller's bill of particulars. But it does not order his arrest. It merely stipulates that "in view of the state of the case [*Sachverhalt*], a judicial preliminary investigation is hereby initiated under Paragraph 184 StPO."

Called *Voruntersuchung* in the nomenclature of the German judiciary system, and conducted by a magistrate of inquiry who is expected to gather evidence in a criminal case, it is a *preliminary* investigation, nothing more or less. In Mengele's case, it is concerned solely with a past every incriminating detail of which is already abundantly on the record.

In 1969, Judge Schneider abandoned the preliminary investigation to Judge von Glasenapp, with Joachim Richter representing the State Prosecutor in the proceedings. Judge von Glasenapp has spent four years on the preliminary investigation, traveling on three continents interrogating witnesses. He has gone through more than two hundred of them, but he is still on the road, now in Los Angeles, then in Warsaw, now in London, then in Tel Aviv, piling up reams of legal sheets which add nothing new to what we already know.

Neither Schneider nor Glasenapp was ever in South America. They have tacit instructions from the Foreign Ministry in Bonn to stay away from Paraguay, which Mengele is pleased to call his adopted country.

Dr. Mengele is indubitably the worst of all Nazi murderers to remain at large. He may be a hunted and frightened man, but he does not have to worry about being delivered into German hands.

In answer to an inquiry from Professor Cz. Pilichowski, director of the Warsaw Commission of Inquiry into Hitlerite Crimes in Poland, Joachim Richter of the State of Hesse spelled out the true status of the case.

On August 31, 1973, he wrote:

> The extradition of Mengele had been attempted from several South American states prior to the initiation of the preliminary investigation. In a note to the Federal Ministry of Justice dated May 9, 1968, the Foreign Ministry of the Federal Republic has taken the position that an extradition of the accused is impossible as long as he possesses Paraguayan citizenship. Mengele has been naturalized in Paraguay by decree No. 809 of the Supreme Court of Paraguay. The Paraguayan authorities intimated in reponse to repeated interventions of the diplomatic mission of the Federal Republic that they would regard any further motions for extradition as an unwarranted interference with the internal affairs of their country.

The preliminary investigation continues unabated.

> The authorities of the Federal Republic [Richter wrote] are meanwhile of the opinion that this situation redounding to the advantage of the accused may not necessarily be of a permanent nature. The conduct of the preliminary investigation rests on this assumption, and is to be considered a form of preparatory assembly of evidence.

The first substantial claim of success the official investigators put forward appeared in November 1973, after Judge von Glasenapp and Procurator Richter visited Warsaw to review the Mengele situation with Professor Pilichowski in his office on Ujazdawskie Street. Already in his letter of August 31, arranging the visit, Richter told the Poles in no uncertain terms:

"1. Josef Mengele is still alive.

"2. According to information on file here, the accused resides in Paraguay, in the city of Pedro J. Caballero, in the Province of Amambay, which is located near the Brazilian border."

When the two German emissaries were back in Frankfurt, the Poles announced with some fanfare that Dr. Mengele had been found. They repeated what Glasenapp and Richter had told Dr. Pilichowski, but presented it as their own original discovery, claiming credit for one of the great scoops in the history of the Mengele hunt. Not to be outdone, the Germans then announced that it was they, and not the Poles, who had discovered Mengele's residence in Paraguay. Setting the record straight, they even managed to get their scoop into *The New York Times* with a four-column headline on October 25, 1973: "Auschwitz Doctor Said to Be in Paraguay."

> West German justice officials said in Bonn yesterday [wrote *The Times*] that Dr. Josef Mengele, the Nazi physician sought for the last 22 years for alleged mass murders in the Auschwitz concentration camp during World War II, was believed to have been located in a remote village in Paraguay. Mengele, known as "the angel of death," was reported to be in the village of Pedro Caballero, near the Brazilian frontier, in the province of Amambay.

This was a strange contest. The same Procurator Richter, who refused even to consider my evidence in his *Endlösung* ("final solution") of the Bormann problem, was now using what, in fact, was my data to score his international scoop and claim the credit. On my second visit to Paraguay in the summer of 1972, with the help of what could be called mutual acquaintances, I succeeded in locating Dr. Mengele, and announced my discovery on December 1, in the fifth article of the Bormann series.

"At the time of this writing," I stated, "[Mengele may be found] at the Paraguayan town of Pedro Juan Caballero, in the remote Amambay Province bordering on Brazil. The place is well hidden by a dense jungle to the west and the Amambay mountain range to the east." Although Mengele was using the name Dr. Nadich, I added, everybody in town knew him and who he was. I then presented directions for getting to Pedro Caballero from Asunción, for anyone who cared to make the trip as I did, on the complex and primitive Paraguayan roads.

I elaborated on this brief description of Mengele's hideout during my two sessions with Procurators Metzner and Richter in Frankfurt; and I presented my voluminous Mengele documentation (including the complete record of Judge Luque's efforts in authentic copies of the original documents) to Judge von Glasenapp, who made it part of his own record.

In the meantime, Dr. Mengele enjoys unrestricted freedom. Unlike Bormann, whose stubborn spirit continues to haunt this remote country, Dr. Mengele is very real in Paraguay. His presence is keenly felt, attested as it is by numerous eyewitnesses in Asunción, where he shows up from time to time to visit friends, take care of some private business, or do his shopping.

He is a well-nigh familiar figure downtown and can be seen at mealtimes at the rambling German restaurant behind the Guarani Hotel (whose Jewish owner, President Stroessner's most vociferous booster in town, does not seem to be bothered by the record of this guest). The handful of officials who know profess ignorance of his exact whereabouts—this in a country where the police are aware of the presence and movements of every soul, friend or foe, citizen or alien. He is allowed to do as he pleases, and his protectors cultivate an aura of menace about him, giving the impression that it is dangerous if not fatal to pursue him or even to get too close to him.

Dr. Sanabria, the young lawyer who handled his naturalization, is still around—not as young as he used to be, but still in touch with "the Doctor," and representing him whenever Mengele needs an attorney.* Some of the local Jews who smuggled reports to Wiesenthal or kept the Yad Vashem in Jerusalem posted—or were merely indiscreet in showing their irritation about the freedom Mengele was enjoying in the country—found it advisable to leave Paraguay for their own good.

But at least two witnesses of the past remain in Asunción to confirm his presence in the most positive terms. They are Esther Abramovici and Sonia Tauber, former inmates of Birkenau (Esther, whose husband now represents the Bulova watch company in Paraguay, was then Number 29457). They were very pretty girls in their early teens and somehow survived the holocaust by working in the

* By an ironic coincidence, Dr. Sanabria represented the owner of a palatial villa on Avenida Marescal López in Asunción in a transaction with the Israeli Embassy which, in 1968, leased the property as the ambassador's residence. The Israelis found the attorney outspokenly anti-Nazi, completely untainted by his professional relationship with his notorious client.

laundry. They are overcome by a strange feeling of nausea whenever they see *den schönen Doktor* ("the beautiful doctor") pass by outside, even stopping to inspect the display in the window of Casa Inolvidable, the Abramovicis' thriving variety shop in the Estrella.

Now in his sixties, Mengele is not as "beautiful" as he used to be. His pitch-black, immaculately groomed hair is now graying and cropped in a crewcut. His little mustache has been trimmed. His face, well-shaped and still memorable, is no longer as striking as it once was. Those eyes, once so naturally seductive, have become steely from suspicion and fear. They are small now and squinting, looking at the world with perennial mistrust.

Mengele is aware of Dr. Luque's consuming and relentless interest in him, and he realizes that he virtually alone is left among those Nazis still marked for death. He suffers from his fate; his loneliness is bearing down on him. When confronted, he blossoms out as a compulsive talker, seizing the occasion to discuss two favorite topics. The first is his special research into the genetics of twins—a research that he pursued in Birkenau with frightful results on his human guinea pigs. The other is what he calls his "Big Mistake" in life. He regrets that he went on the run when he did instead of staying in Germany to face the music. He points out that he was only one of scores of "Auschwitz Doctors." Yet he has been singled out as the worst of them all, the epitome of butchery in the guise of medicine and science, and became one of the world's most hunted men, second only to Bormann.

"Had I remained in Germany," he said, "I would have been sentenced to a few years in prison as were my colleagues—like [Dr. Franz Bernhard] Lucas, the dentists [Willi] Frank and [Willi Ludwig] Schatz, or that pharmacist from Rumania, what was his name? Yes, yes, Viktor Capesius! By now I would be back in my profession in twin research, for frankly I prefer it to the practice of medicine." He is effusive in professing a feeling of guilt and will say again and again that he cannot rationally account even to himself for his deeds during those "terrible years" in Birkenau.

He cites several instances where his "compassion" saved the lives of inmates, as in the case of a pregnant woman he spotted on her way to the gas chamber. "I put her in the hospital instead, pending her delivery," he said. "When the baby was born I even sent her flowers." But he does not pretend to know what became of mother and child in the end.

He shrugs off or brushes aside references to his main job, which was to select people for the death chamber rather than rescue them from it. And he seems to have forgotten that awful occasion when inmates at the camp complained of lice in one of the barracks for which he had the medical responsibility. He listened to their plea, then ordered the barracks fumigated—killing both lice and people.

Even as I was writing this, an item in several South American newspapers averred that a band of those perennial avengers managed at last to corner and liquidate him. According to this latest story, Mengele had been lured across the Paraná into Brazil, and was mowed down with a burst fired from an Israeli-made machine gun by a single assailant, as he was climbing ashore from his boat.

I myself was privy to a budding plot in whose murky background the indefatigable Judge Luque played an obscure role. In the early spring of 1973, he suddenly revived the dormant case of Mengele's extradition and asked the authorities to assign four detectives to his legal staff, for, as he put it, he had reason to believe that Mengele would show up in Argentina before the end of the month of April.

The plot was based on presumably reliable intelligence that Mengele was planning to visit his brother in Encarnación, coming by boat from Pedro Caballero. The plan was to buy off the Argentine skipper of the river boat on which he would be traveling. Instead of stopping at Encarnación, he was to take his boat straight down the river until it reached Argentine waters. There Luque's detectives would board it and take Mengele into custody. The idea was to kidnap Mengele and deliver him into Judge Luque's court.

He was scheduled to arrive on April 23. But the day came and went, and nothing happened. The plot failed, probably because the skipper refused to go along with the plan, or perhaps because Mengele got wind of it and made the trip to Encarnación by another, safer route. He did show up in Encarnación when expected, and was even reported to have gone to Lisbon, Portugal, from there, by way of Rio de Janeiro, to attend to some family business. Never short of funds or of connections, he has the means to come and go as he pleases; and he is a hard man to lure into a trap.

Yet his alleged death in that ambush in Brazil intrigued the

German authorities, who decided to attempt a special inquiry to find out what really happened. An opportunity then presented itself to conduct a discreet investigation in Asunción. When President Stroessner visited Germany in the summer of 1973, he was given only a lukewarm reception by Bonn, but was well received by the jovial Bavarians in Munich. So pleased was he with the warmth of his welcome—his forebears had gone to Paraguay from those parts—that he invited Alfons Goppel, the Minister President of Bavaria, to visit him in Asunción.

The Germans seized upon the invitation to probe the Mengele matter. President Goppel was encouraged to make the trip and was asked to find out what he could about Mengele—whether he was dead or alive. Herr Goppel carried out his mission with a combination of diplomatic tact and Bavarian cunning, never raising the issue directly in any of his conversations or popping the question bluntly. But at a reception given in his honor, he buttonholed the Minister of Justice and asked him casually how good old Dr. Mengele was getting on.

"Mengele?" the Minister asked wide-eyed. "I'm afraid I don't know what you mean. I don't think I've ever heard of the man."

President Goppel thought it advisable to change the subject.*

* In February 1974, Alois Mengele, head of the family and managing director of the great manufacturing concern, died suddenly, necessitating a reorganization of the family's holdings and the top management of the firm. On the assumption that Dr. Josef Mengele, the family black sheep who was deeply devoted to his younger brother, might risk a return to Germany to attend Alois' burial, the Mengele homes in Günzburg and the funeral itself were closely observed by detectives, assigned to the surveillance at the request of Judge von Glasenapp. At the same time, the family's telephones were tapped, anticipating that Mengele would call from Paraguay. He did not attend the funeral, but called several times, the intercepts providing important clues about his whereabouts and immediate plans. Shortly afterward, Dr. Mengele left his hideout in Paraguay and, traveling under one of his aliases, went to Acapulco in Mexico for clandestine meetings with his late brother's daughter and her husband, to discuss family and business matters that had become acute because of the unexpected demise of Alois. At the time of this writing (in May 1974), Dr. Mengele is still believed to be in Mexico. However, he is expected to return to Paraguay, the country whose legal citizen he is and where he enjoys foolproof protection. According to Judge von Glasenapp, however, he might move to a country "closer to where the action is," now that he is the only Mengele left of the triumvirate of brothers who fell heir to the fortune built by Karl Mengele, founder of the "dynasty." As Judge von Glasenapp put it, "the Doctor is as unpredictable as ever." On the other hand, the inescapable fact of his life is that there are not many places left to him to hide in.

Chapter Eighteen

Bormann Dies Again

Adolf Eichmann's capture left the Nazis in South America in a turmoil that never quite subsided. The frenzy of Müller and Rauff's panic was not matched by the anxiety of the others, but those others too were seized with the jitters. The Eichmann affair was dragging on and on, culminating in the quaint trial in Jerusalem. Though the tumult reached Eichmann in his glass booth only faintly through earphones, it resounded stridently throughout the world and made these Nazis, who heard it live, very, very nervous.

Franz Paul Stangl, former commandant of the Treblinka death camp who had the murder of 700,000 Jews on his conscience, had been safe in Brazil since 1951. He worked as a senior technician at the huge Volkswagen plant in São Paulo, where many fugitives like him had wrested jobs from Friedrich Wilhelm Schultz-Wenk, a brilliant forty-six-year-old former architect of Hamburg, who was now president of Volkswagen do Brasil. Schultz-Wenk was eminently respectable, with a remarkable record of achievement. Promptly denazified by the British after the war, he was now a Brazilian citizen, a civic leader in São Paulo and a Knight of Malta although he was a Protestant. But his tolerance of so many Nazis at Volkswagen fed the rumors that he was covering up some stain in his own past.

Herbert Cukurs, the "butcher of Riga," who on horseback personally directed the liquidation of 30,000 Baltic Jews in 1941, shooting scores of them himself, had moved to Brazil with his wife and three children in 1946. An aviator by profession, he worked on and off for Lufthansa in Rio de Janeiro and rented out little glass-bottomed boats to sightseers at the beautiful lagoon of Rodrigo de

Freitas in Ipanema. While Stangl faced the future with such fatalism that he did not bother even to change his name, Cukurs tried desperately to erase traces of his past. He hoped that nobody who knew him in Riga would recognize him so far from Latvia and expose the crimes he committed off the beaten path of Nazi atrocities.

He was harassed nevertheless, so much so at times that he thought it advisable to leave Rio and move to São Paulo, where he operated an air taxi service with a couple of rickety Piper Cubs. When Eichmann was captured, he panicked. Going to the police and protesting his innocence, he asked for protection to escape Eichmann's fate. It worked for a while. But his number came up five years later in Montevideo when, as we shall see, his mutilated body was found in an abandoned Volkswagen.

Klaus Barbie in La Paz and Friedrich Schwend in Lima were probably the only ones who showed no signs of apprehension. Barbie's cover as Klaus Altmann was holding up, and his protection was firmer than ever, encouraging him in the expectation that his powerful friends in the Bolivian government would keep him out of harm's way. But he hired a bodyguard, for not even the close friendship of Bolivia's chief admiral could prevent a stray assassin from shooting him in an unguarded moment.

The ever-ingenious and totally unscrupulous Freddy Schwend had nothing to fear from the Jews or, for that matter, from the Germans. He was wanted only in Italy, and the Italians did not seem to be interested in getting him back. Even so, Eichmann's capture persuaded him to make certain arrangements. He concluded a working alliance with the secret services in both Germanys, adding their clandestine protection to what he already enjoyed in Peru through his connections with P.I.P., the secret police, and the army's intelligence service.

He even enlisted Jewish help to bolster his security. His confiscated files showed that while he was fronting for Bormann, was working closely with Rauff in the development of a neo-Nazi movement, was one of Colonel Hans Ulrich Rudel's fund raisers for the Kameradenwerk, and represented several Nazi rescue groups in South America, he was also cultivating the friendship of and was doing business with a number of Jews, like Moises Wolfsohn in Buenos Aires, Hans Strauss in Santa Cruz, a certain Spitz in Paris, a man named Reichwein in Zurich. Among his impounded letters Judge Santos Chichizola found a brisk correspondence with Colonel

Otto Skorzeny in Madrid, emphatic in its protestation of his unshakable Nazi allegiance; but also with Dr. Ohrenstein, the chief rabbi of Munich, just as emphatic in its expression of his pro-Jewish sentiments.

To top it all, he founded a Jewish paper organization with apparently worldwide tentacles. Called Jewish-Orthodox Community, it was nominally managed by one Gideon Ryner, himself a shadowy character, who had his "headquarters" in a small office at 18 Hans Sachs Strasse in Bonn. In a brazen maneuver designed to shield Schwend, who was always prepared to sacrifice friend or foe on the altar of his own interests, the spurious Community denounced fugitive Nazis, picking out only men against whom Schwend bore some personal grudge. He also used the phony organization as a character witness for himself. His stooge Ryner in Bonn and a Miss Jeanette Moulin, who signed herself as the Public Relations Officer of the Jewish Community, would write to the authorities vouching for him whenever Schwend needed some testimonials to get himself off the hooks on which he was forever prone to get caught.

It was a strange switch. There were a few so-called honorary Aryans in the Third Reich, hand-picked Jews exempted from the harsh racial laws for services rendered, several of them designated as such in decrees signed by Hitler himself. But Schwend probably was the only Nazi ever to become an honorary Jew.

In his clerical seclusion in Bolivia, Martin Bormann seemed to be aloof and confident when the abduction of Eichmann threatened to make his own safety a burning issue. He had never cared for Eichmann, whom he regarded as an indolent freeloader and whose inept behavior in exile filled him with forebodings. Bormann responded to Eichmann's capture with indignation, complaining pompously that the abduction was a gross violation of international law. He then professed to be disgusted with the spectacle of Eichmann's trial, which he described to friends as a typical example of Jewish showmanship.

He once wrote a letter to Eichmann in jail, a very brief and condescending note, consisting of only two one-syllable German words, "*Mut, mut* [Courage, courage]." But he signed it "Martin" with his characteristic calligraphy of the exaggerated big "M." When the Israeli authorities intercepted the letter, they called in experts to examine the note. They were unanimous in concluding that it was in the handwriting of Martin Bormann.

When, however, the trial dragged on and a cavalcade of witnesses laid before the world the whole incredible depravity of the Hitler regime, Bormann too became uneasy. An elaborate effort was then made to enhance the Reichsleiter's security.

Bormann was in Lima in October 1962, staying near Schwend's compound in a delightful resort of luxurious bungalows. They were built on the steep slope of a sandy hill greening with lush vegetation, the ground made fertile with a system of irrigation learned from the Incas. The bungalows, arranged in three tiers, provided an ideal hideout with all the comforts and amenities of a deluxe hotel. They could be reached only by a little cable funicular with a stationary engine below, its solitary car climbing slowly up and down.

Bormann occupied one of the northernmost and most secluded cottages on the third tier, accessible only by a branch line of the funicular. It assured absolute privacy, and afforded an excellent opportunity for observing the approach of visitors. The unwelcome among them and suspicious strangers could be easily stopped on the way up and sent down again by remote control.

Shortly after his return to Bolivia, on December 7, newspapers in South America published a sensational story emanating from Lima. It was Bormann's obituary notice written in such specific terms and including so many detailed facts that it sounded most convincing. Implying that he had indeed survived the war and succeeded in escaping to South America, the article reported:

> Martin Bormann died on February 15, 1959, in Asunción, the capital of Paraguay. He breathed his last in a house owned by a Paraguayan of German origin, Bernard Jung. A local priest was at his bedside. The cause of death was cancer of the stomach, and a death certificate to this effect was signed by a physician in Asunción, Dr. Otto Biss. The burial took place in the little cemetery of Itá near Asunción.

The priest was left anonymous and Bernard Jung refused to comment. But Dr. Biss's name was spelled out, probably to lend authenticity to the story. This proved to be a mistake, for the doctor denied promptly and indignantly that he had any part to play in the incident. "I never declared Bormann's death," he said, "never diagnosed cancer and, of course, never signed his death certificate."

The categorical nature of Dr. Biss's denial ignited the imagination of a brilliant foreign correspondent stationed in Lima who had the special distinction of knowing more about the Nazis at large in South America than any journalist on this particular beat. Herbert John, himself a German, was a roving reporter for a Hamburg newsmagazine and the author of many a scoop about the Nazi diaspora. He sensed intuitively that something was fishy, as he put it, about Bormann's death in 1959 and the announcement made almost three years later. John suspected that the announcement of Bormann's death was one of the favorite devices of fugitives—to have themselves declared dead and then become resurrected in a different identity.

He flew to Asunción, then motored to Itá, where he confronted the sole official of the little cemetery, Daniel, the village drunk, who functioned as caretaker, registrar of death and gravedigger. Daniel had never heard of Bormann and was positive that in 1959 he had buried nobody he did not know. He remembered, however, that in late November 1962, a "tall, blond German" stranger had inquired whether any foreigner had ever been buried in his cemetery. The only one Daniel could recall was an Indian from Argentina, and the book of dead in his ramshackle office bore him out. He found the entry, harking back to 1948, recording the death and burial of one Juan Emilio Hermocilla, interred in grave No. G-3, a cemetery plot for two persons. He was still there.

Daniel refused to exhume the body, but accepted a small bundle of guaraníes John offered him "for the information," then obligingly left the cemetery to get drunk. With the help of the taxi driver who had driven him to Itá, John dug up the body, and what he found bore out his doubts. He could not tell, of course, whether the skeleton was that of Hermocilla, but he was positive that it was not Bormann's. He found in the grave the tiny hat of an obviously little old man. There was not a single tooth in the skull, and no trace of a coffin in the grave. The dead man must have been so poor that his family could not afford a casket and had to inter him in a crate or soap box, which disintegrated into dust over the years.

Back in Asunción, Bernard Jung could not be found. It then developed that he had moved to Spain, where he refused to either confirm or deny that it was his house, as the newspaper accounts claimed, where Bormann was supposed to have died. Dr. Biss reiterated that he had never signed any death certificate for Bormann.

"After it had become known," he said, "that I had once treated him, a couple of Germans called on me with the suggestion that I declare him dead, simply because he isn't dead. All this furor about his 'death' just goes to prove that he's still alive."

I have reason to believe that the hoax was Schwend's brainchild. He himself told me in Lima that he had had "something to do with it," conceding only that he had "innocently participated" in the dissemination of the story of Bormann's death, but only "to get rid of an obnoxious French journalist who pestered me for details."

If it was his idea, Schwend could not claim that it was very original. Heinrich Müller had been declared dead, and so had Adolf Eichmann, in Bad Ischl in the spring of 1947, on the testimony of one Karl Lukas, who swore that he had been present when Eichmann died in Prague on April 28, 1945. As for Bormann, it was not the first time that his death was announced, nor would it be the last.

On January 30, 1954, the Berchtesgaden court ruled (on evidence which it refused to divulge) that Martin Bormann had "died at midnight on May 2, 1945." The ruling was for the purpose of settling his estate, which was then found to amount to $8,300, all that could be found. On July 24, 1954, Bormann was certified legally dead under Certificate No. 29,223 in the West Berlin Registrar's Office, where Müller was also so registered, only to find that he was conspicuous by his absence from his alleged grave in the Kreuzberg cemetery. Finally, the State Attorney of Hesse proclaimed peremptorily on April 13, 1973, that Martin Bormann was dead and petitioned the courts to endorse his decision to close the case.

Thus, in 1962, the report of his death turned out to be greatly exaggerated. But the Eichmann jinx was not yet over. The man himself was rapidly approaching his end. Sentence was passed in the Jerusalem District Court on December 15, 1961, and his appeal was dismissed on May 29, 1962. At 8 P.M. on May 31, Eichmann was notified that the President of Israel had refused to commute the sentence. He died at 11:58 P.M. on the improvised gallows in a second-floor room of the prison building. The mind that manipulated the death of millions changed little, if it changed at all. "The closer Eichmann came to execution," the Reverend William Hull, a Protestant clergyman who accompanied him to the gallows, said afterward, "the more defiant he became in rejecting Christianity."

His body was taken to a secret place, where it was cremated three hours later. In the predawn hours of June 1, a police boat took his ashes out to sea and Prison Commissioner Arieh Nir tossed the urn overboard. But Eichmann's ghost remained unlaid. It was still haunting the world—and Bormann, as it turned out—a year later.

In the early spring of 1963, a police informer called Freddy approached Lieutenant José (Ugo) Hugetti, his contact in the police at La Plata, with a proposition. Some of his friends in the underworld, Freddy told Ugo, had formed a gang that in the informer's description sounded like a takeoff on the Lavender Hill mob bossed by Alec Guinness in the hilarious motion picture. They were planning a series of burglaries and holdups, and needed explosives and guns. Would Ugo be interested in making a deal? When the young police officer indicated that he might be, Freddy suggested that he meet the gangsters, and a nocturnal rendezvous was arranged in a wooded area in Ezeiza.

Hugetti was a twenty-nine-year-old former army officer from Chaco, now serving in the criminal investigation division of the Buenos Aires Provincial Police with the rank of subinspector. He represented the brawn in an enormously lucrative partnership of crime-busting, whose brain was a legendary secret agent called "Saul." I. Z. Sztemberg was Saul's full name; he was a native of Poland, where he was born in a *stetl* near Lublin in 1933, and was brought to Argentina by his mother at the age of six. A university graduate with a master's degree in biology, Saul first went into business, then worked as a journalist until 1959, when he was made head of the intelligence division of the Buenos Aires Provincial Police, forming the partnership with Ugo.

Together they cracked some of the toughest cases in Argentina's annals of crime. They put an end to the career of Poncho Negro, the Argentine version of the "Boston Strangler," who terrorized Buenos Aires until Saul tracked him to his hideout, where Ugo mowed him down. The team became best known for their triumph over Loco Prieto, still remembered with misplaced nostalgia as "the greatest Argentine bandit of all times." When Saul's investigation set him up, Ugo killed him with a single bullet.

Obviously Freddy had made the pitch to the wrong persons. The two men were compulsive, incorruptible policemen. When he was invited into the deal with the mob, Ugo alerted Saul, and they then reported Freddy's proposition to their superior, Principal

Barcia, suggesting that they be permitted to feign interest and catch the criminals in their own trap. Barcia agreed and gave them a small arsenal of guns as bait.

Freddy set up the meeting in a little grove about half a mile from the Ezeiza international airport, and Ugo and Saul met five men whom they could tell apart in the darkness only by their voices. They quickly established that they were not the kind of men Freddy had described to them. They spoke German among themselves, and the conversation (which Saul, who spoke Yiddish, could understand) indicated that they belonged to a Nazi gang. Saul asked them a number of loaded questions, which they answered nervously, until one of the men had enough. "This is a trap!" he exclaimed. "These bastards are coppers!"

This was the cue for Saul and Ugo. They drew their guns, and the meeting turned into a shootout, both sides firing aimlessly into pitch blackness. At daybreak, accompanied by squad cars and bloodhounds, Sztemberg and Hugetti returned to the scene and found one of the men dead and another, some distance away, wounded. He was a clean-shaven, good-looking, well-dressed man in his middle twenties, looking as Hugetti put it, "like a playboy."

As it turned out, he was only slightly injured, and could be taken straight to the police station instead of a hospital. He behaved arrogantly during his questioning, giving a Spanish name that belied his blond Teutonic appearance. He did not get far with his shamming. Ugo grabbed his right arm, twisted it behind his back, grabbed the left arm and then holding both tightly together, forced him to fall to the ground, where he kicked him in the back and face.

"You can't do this to me," the man screamed, then added with some pride, perhaps to show that he was a sort of celebrity eligible for special consideration, "I am Dieter Eichmann, the son of Adolf Eichmann."

What at first looked like a simple criminal case now took on a different complexion. Tipped off by the escaped Germans, who obviously had friends in the right places, an army officer suddenly appeared at the police station, demanding that the prisoner be surrendered to S.I.M., the Military Intelligence Service, which he insisted was the proper agency to conduct the investigation. Principal Barcia refused to comply. "This man tried to bribe my officers, he said, "so this is an ordinary criminal matter. It has nothing to do with politics. The man is *our* prisoner and he will stay *here*."

Dieter remained in the custody of the police for eight days. He was interrogated in a soundproof, concrete-encrusted room in the cellar of an empty house near the station to make sure he wouldn't fall into the hands of his friends at Military Intelligence. He proved a hard nut to crack, insisting that he was ignorant of any Nazi conspiracy; all he and his friends were up to were those planned burglaries and perhaps the cracking of a safe or two. That was why they needed the equipment they expected to buy from Ugo.

"Okay, Dieter Eichmann," Saul told him in a low voice. Then, turning to Hugetti, he said, "I think this gentleman needs the *picana.*"

Dieter winced. He knew what the *picana* was—the dreaded torture instrument with which the police shocked confessions out of even the most hardened criminals. This was to be the third degree after all, the gamut of Hugetti's famed "intensive interrogation," which the crooks of Buenos Aires knew and dreaded. The big lamps were turned on, their blinding spotlights glaring into Dieter's bedazzled eyes. Then Hugetti plugged in the electric goad and put it to the boy's neck and hands to tease him with samples of the shock, but he endured the torment without flinching. He was ordered to undress, and Hugo ran the *picana* down his body to his testicles. Young Eichmann had stamina. It took part of the night before he finally caved in, whispering faintly, "Please don't hurt me any more. I will talk."

He was a member of a neo-Nazi group, he then confessed, which operated behind the blind of a Boy Scout camp in Ezeiza. He and his friends tried to obtain the explosives because they were planning to ambush and blow up a bus carrying forty children from a Hebrew school, "to commemorate May 31," Dieter said. It was the first anniversary of his father's execution.

Apart from getting the full story of the aborted outrage, the interrogation yielded a totally unexpected dividend. At one point Dieter dropped the name of Martin Bormann, almost casually, mentioning merely that his father had been "in touch" with the man he called "Uncle Martin." He signed a deposition declaring that "Martin Bormann was alive" and "was the leader of National Socialists in South America." For all practical purposes, the long-festering puzzle of Bormann's fate could have been resolved then and there, with the testimony of this eyewitness who asserted under oath that he had met Martin Bormann in Buenos Aires "several times between

1952 and 1959." But Saul and Ugo were criminal investigators. They were interested only in Dieter and his accomplices, not in Martin Bormann. They missed the clue when it first came up, and did not press the issue toward the definitive solution of the Bormann mystery.

But Bormann remained with them to haunt the case. Dieter's arrest produced another critical clue corroborating what he had said. Never before had the Eichmann house on Calle Garibaldi been searched, if only because the Argentinians did not want to do anything that would have connected them with the abduction of the head of the family. Now, however, the situation was different. Dieter's plot was clearly a criminal case and a warrant could properly be obtained for the search of Adolf Eichmann's old home where his wife and four sons still lived.

The search produced many interesting items, not all of which had value as evidence. Saul confiscated Eichmann's ceremonial SS pistol marked "Number 41," a goldplated, ornate gun with its owner's name engraved in it, a birthday gift from Reinhard Heydrich. It is now in a museum in Israel, donated by a collector who bought it for one thousand dollars. Nine years after the raid, in the home of one of the policemen who participated in it, I was served tea in a gold-green cup from a delicate set of Hutschenreuther porcelain, one of the finest kinds of earthenware with translucent glaze. It was another "exhibit" now adorning the home of a Buenos Aires cop as the souvenir of the memorable raid.

The pistol and the tea set were parts of the incidental loot. Far more important, the search uncovered Eichmann's papers, which had been lovingly preserved by his family. Among them Saul and Ugo found *three letters* from Bormann, addressed to "*Mein lieber Adolf.*" They were brief notes signed "Martin" with the unmistakable Bormann touch, the huge "M" drawn like the double hump of a Bactrian camel, the other letters of his first name scrawled on to it. In more formal correspondence he signed his name in full, scribbling the "Martin" illegibly with the big initial and spelling out "Bormann" letter by letter in his legible good hand. Even though he did not deem it necessary to sign his full name, and although the letters were typed on sheets of plain paper, the characteristic "M" in the three extant notes to Eichmann identified them as Bormann's.

Dated March 7, 1952, January 11, 1957, and March 3, 1957, the letters must have disappointed Eichmann when he received them, since they contained curt refusals to give him any more money. The third letter was a little longer than the other two, but even that consisted of only two paragraphs of three lines each. It reflected Bormann's irritation with Eichmann for his continued sponging on him. "You now have a decent job with an adequate salary," he wrote. "It is high time that you start relying on your own earnings and live within your means, instead of looking to me for charity."

Perhaps it was Bormann's stinginess that had caused their father such anguish; perhaps it was his uncanny ability to survive; perhaps it was his gradual withdrawal from the leadership of the Nazis in South America—whatever it was, the Eichmann boys intensely disliked "Onkel Martin." After the abduction of their father, both Klaus, the oldest son, and Dieter reached the point where they would no longer suppress their enmity and resentment. They gave away the big secret that every Nazi was duty-bound to preserve as a sacred trust.

In February 1961, two years before Dieter's arrest in Ezeiza, Horst Eichmann confided to Heinz Wolf that he had seen Bormann both in Buenos Aires and in San Carlos de Bariloche, and had "frequent conversations" with him. Then, five years later, in January 1966, his older brother Klaus published an open letter to Martin Bormann in the magazine *Quick*, of Munich, designed, as he put it, as a memorial to his father, who had been made the scapegoat for the crimes of others.

"I am waiting for you to give yourself up," Klaus addressed Bormann. "I am waiting for you to come forward for that part of the guilt for which you are responsible and for which my father stood in your place during the trial in Israel." He left no doubt that Bormann was at large. "You still live on," he wrote, "in your South American hideout. You rub your hands over every report of your death in Berlin in 1945."

Then, however, in an interview published in a Buenos Aires newspaper, Horst repudiated his older brother's anguished letter to Bormann. Far from repeating what he had told Dr. Bauer in 1961 (see p. 312) and what Dieter had confessed in 1963, Horst now voiced the opinion that Bormann had died in Berlin, after all. It was a desperate effort to protect Klaus. "When one lives in South America," Klaus said when asked to explain his brother's strange statement, "where there are still powerful Nazi groups, one must take into consideration that they might one day strike at anyone who makes things uncomfortable for them." It was obvious that Horst had been reached and that he understood the message.

Nobody ever followed up these leads, one way or another. The Eichmann brothers were allowed to retire into obscurity, as James McGovern so aptly phrased it, "along with their memories and whatever useful evidence they possessed." No effort was ever made by the proper authorities to ask Klaus Eichmann to present his evidence on the record. Horst's 1961 deposition to Dr. Bauer was never published in full. Dieter's testimony of 1963 is locked up in a safe of Military Intelligence in Buenos Aires.

With the son of Herbert Cukurs and the children of Franz Stangl, Klaus and Horst belong to the second generation of a nebulous Fourth Reich in South America, much younger men in whom the old flame continues to burn brightly. Klaus, in particular, and Gunnar Cukurs are traveling salesmen of their fathers' doctrines, their own ardor increased by their personal tragedies and the stigma they have to bear. From time to time they give venom-filled interviews to newspapers or appear on television in Argentina and Brazil, obviously seeking to avenge the violent end of their fathers with vicious attacks upon their executioners. There is not the faintest note of repentance in their tirades, no recognition of their parents' guilt, no sign that they have changed with the times.

In a sense, they are joined by Bormann's oldest son, who had become a missionary priest of the Jesuit Order after the war but left the Church abruptly, and vanished mysteriously in recent years. In the one interview he ever granted, to Edward R. F. Sheehan of the *Saturday Evening Post* in 1967, he said he was "almost completely sure" that his father was dead. "He died in Berlin," he said, "I think."

But when asked whether he would protect him if he were alive, and give him a place to hide, young Bormann replied firmly in the affirmative. "He is my father," he said. "In spite of everything he has done, he is my father. There is no law of man or God or of the Church which says I must deliver my own father to the hangman."*

Beyond the evidence thus presented by members of the second

* On April 25, 1971, Martin Bormann, Jr., made news when he was seriously injured in a traffic accident involving a U.S. Army vehicle near the Bavarian town of Amberg. On July 24, the 41-year-old Jesuit left the ministry and married a former nun. In December 1972, he sought employment as a teacher of religion at a public school in Mühldorf, Bavaria, but was turned down by the mayor, who regarded his parentage and name as a liability. He now lives in northern Germany, teaching under an assumed name.

generation, there was one witness whose testimony weighs heaviest in the balance. He was Adolf Eichmann himself. During his long pretrial examination in Jerusalem, he told Captain Avner W. Less, the young Berlin-born Israeli police officer who interrogated him for weeks, that Martin Bormann was alive. He said it bluntly, positively and voluntarily.

A significant clue to what Eichmann knew was dropped by Dr. Robert Servatius, his German defense attorney, on August 14, 1961, during the 114th session of the trial in Jerusalem. In his rebuttal of the prosecution's sweeping assertion that Eichmann was the principal culprit in the Final Solution, Dr. Servatius exclaimed:

> If the exposition of the Prosecutor regarding the intentions and character of the accused were right . . . the followers of Hitler could rejoice. Now we know: Hitler did not issue the murder order . . . Himmler, the "Jew-helper," had no reason to kill himself, Bormann can come out of hiding.

Dr. Servatius did not say that Bormann had died as did Himmler. He did not speak of Bormann in the past tense. He stated bluntly that Bormann could emerge from concealment, absolved of guilt, the threat of retribution removed from his head.

What Servatius said was based on what his client had told him—that Bormann was alive, hiding to escape Eichmann's fate. It echoed the theme of Klaus's open letter in *Quick* magazine, and Dieter's two sworn depositions. Vague as it was, the lawyer's statement that "*Bormann kann aus seinem Versteck herauskommen*" virtually declared that Bormann was alive, coming from the man who spoke for the man who knew.

Chapter Nineteen

Dr. Bauer Versus Bormann—The Third Crisis

A prosecutor does not build a dossier on a dead suspect.
—*The New York Times*
February 28, 1965

In late February 1961, a young seaman (who was born in Germany but grew up in Argentina) returned to his native land in a cargo ship coming from Buenos Aires. In his frantic efforts to escape attention, he traveled under an assumed name on a seaman's bill as member of the ship's crew, then fled the boat on a weekend pass for what he said would be a brief liberty in port. But he took the first train to Frankfurt to keep a date he had made by correspondence with a man he was anxious to meet.

If there was melodrama in the young man's arrangements, he had ample reason to conceal himself and his mission. He was Horst Eichmann, second son of the mystery-shrouded, closely guarded prisoner in Jerusalem. By the time Horst reached Frankfurt, Adolf Eichmann had been in the hands of Division 06—the bureau Israel had set up especially to handle this precious prisoner—for over nine months. But his trial was scheduled to begin only in April, and so, Horst was confident, there was still time to do something that might save his father.

He had no illusions that Eichmann could be kidnaped from the Israelis. A prison break was out of the question. Eichmann was held in a three-room jail improvised for him in an old police building that was now guarded by a detachment of the Frontier Police. Inside his barred suite he was watched day and night by a detail of hand-picked cops. There even were antiaircraft posts on and around the building. An attempt to rescue Eichmann was regarded as a distinct possibility, and the Israelis took no chances.

Yet Horst was convinced that he held a key that would unlock the door of his father's cell. This was why he risked the trip to Germany and his own life, to buy his father's freedom with the secret to which he was privy. The man he came to see in Frankfurt was Heinz Wolf, the senior prosecutor in the office of the State Attorney General, who specialized in the cases of Nazi criminals.

Horst Eichmann had a bold plan. He was making the trip to reveal to the Germans the Nazis' best-kept secret in South America —that Martin Bormann was alive and well. He himself knew it first-hand. He had seen Bormann several times, as a young boy in Buenos Aires and in Bariloche, where the Eichmanns vacationed with the Reichsleiter, and more recently in Brazil. Although Bormann used the name Ricardo Bauer, the Eichmann boys knew who he really was, and called him Uncle Martin.

Senior Prosecutor Wolf played an important part in young Eichmann's scheme. In exchange for the information about Bormann, Horst hoped to enlist the Germans in an effort to help his father. The issue of Eichmann's nationality was becoming a critical question in deciding his fate. Although he was born in Solingen, the famous old cutlery town on the Wupper in North Rhine-Westphalia, Adolf Eichmann was raised in Austria and lived in Argentina. The Israelis were anxious to establish with certainty "who could claim him," as it was put, the Germans, the Austrians or the Argentinians.

Actually, Eichmann remained a German citizen throughout his life and as such, his family concluded, he was entitled to the protection of his native land. As Dr. Servatius, his defense attorney, phrased it later, "The accused has the right to expect to be protected by his country. . . . He can still enter such a claim before the Administrative Court, and indeed he will."

No such complaint was ever made, probably because Chancellor Adenauer had announced that Germany had "definitely no intention" to "protect" Eichmann. Even so, considerable pressure was being brought to bear upon Bonn to do something, both by former Nazis who still had ways of pulling strings and even by people (some in the United States) whose behind-the-scenes intervention on Eichmann's behalf was surprising.

Horst was aware of these efforts, many of which originated in

South America. He was brought to believe that Martin Bormann, professing to have been scandalized by "Israel's wanton violation of international law," was behind them. This was one of the things he was eager to confide to Prosecutor Wolf—that Bormann was planning to come out of hiding and make a dramatic personal appearance "before an international forum" to defend Eichmann by "clarifying the Germans' treatment of the Jews between 1939 and 1945." He would show that all the decisions had been made on the highest echelon, and Adolf Eichmann was but a minor cog in the huge machine.

This line of defense appealed to young Eichmann, if only because he himself regarded his father in this light. To the son, the father was not "the giant shadow of death" or "the prince of darkness," as the Israeli prosecutors referred to him, nor the perpetrator of history's most hideous crime, "the murderer at the telephone" and "the administrator of genius," as Professor Trevor-Roper called him.

Horst saw the man he had thought for years was his stepfather in H. T. Webster's image as a sort of Caspar Milquetoast—a painfully timid man, apologetic and nonassertive, who seemed to be happiest when tending the vegetables in his little back-yard garden. With Spartan discipline imposed upon himself, his feelings were blurred and his emotions bridled, their occasional flare-up betrayed only by the nervous, spasmodic movements of his prominent Adam's apple.

Eichmann himself had an oddly twisted, schizophrenic view of his own place in the great Nazi order of things. During his halcyon days, he was always kept in the background, slow to advance and low in rank. One of the back-room boys, he was running "the complex apparatus" of the Final Solution from what Heinrich Müller, his chief, deliberately maintained as a seemingly minor section of his enormous Gestapo.

Eichmann was forever reminded that he was an upstart, an autodidact at best, a self-made slob in the company of colleagues who all had the coveted "Doktor" before their names—*Dr.* Kaltenbrunner, *Dr.* Wisliczeny, *Dr.* Höttl, *Dr.* Grell, *Dr.* Pütz, *Dr.* Mildner, even a Herr Professor *Dr.* Hirt. They were all his inferiors in power and influence. Yet they towered above him in their status in society.

Lowbrow as he was, and the charlatan as he seemed to be, the fact was that Eichmann held in his hands the ultimate power over the life or death of millions. Even while Reinhard Heydrich, the sinister genius who had conceived the Final Solution, was alive, it was little Eichmann, a mere Sturmbannführer, who had actual charge of the giant undertaking. Reichsmarschall Göring had been tricked into the signing of the letter of intent that Heydrich needed to cover himself by thus codifying the massacre of millions, with the obscure designation of the awesome project—*Endlösung,* or "Final Solution"—woven almost casually into the last sentence. But it was Eichmann who drafted that letter, and it was he who invented what was to become the most awesome term ever coined for any human endeavor in history.

When Heydrich was killed, Eichmann inherited the entire project. He alone was left to press forward the murderous scheme. Göring never again stopped to think—not, that is, until he was reminded in the dock in Nuremberg of the havoc he had wrought with his signature on Eichmann's fateful draft. Himmler, whom Heydrich shrewdly loaded down with the final responsibility for the *Endlösung,* was becoming sick to his stomach when he realized that he could not evade it in the end.

Bormann for one tried to muffle the whole frightful thing in his own mind, and shroud the enterprise in secrecy and silence. On July 11, 1943, he thus sent to the Reichsleiters and the gauleiters what was the only communication in which he dealt with the awkward question. "By order of the Führer," he wrote, "I advise you:

"In all public discussions of the Jewish question, all references to a future total solution [*Gesamtlösung,* as he called it, as distinguished from Eichmann's blunter phrase, *Endlösung*] must be avoided.

"It may be mentioned, however, that the Jews as a whole will be drawn into productive labor projects."

That was all—three brief paragraphs, a total of thirty-five words in the German original—getting the enormous enterprise off his chest and out of the way.

Eichmann alone was left to do the job and bear the responsibility. He did not care and did not mind. He had no ambition to become a public hero. He did not aspire to hobnob with the big shots—he never met the Führer, and he ran into Bormann only once during all the years of the Third Reich. He did not care to make his name a household word. He was comfortable among all the *Herr Doktors* in the adjoining offices, savoring to the hilt the power he wielded, aware that he had it because nobody else wanted his job or could have done it as well.

He hoped in his secret heart to make it up to Standartenführer, a full colonel, all a section chief could expect to become in the Gestapo's caste-conscious hierarchy. He never made it. He wound up a mere Obersturmbannführer. That was a low rank, measured by the enormous scope of his section. But it was high, considering that his modest breeding and lack of education had disqualified him from ever becoming a senior officer in the SS.

Now in Israeli hands, Eichmann no longer saw himself as the general manager of mass murder. He was only a little man—"the helpless victim of higher orders." His son was coming all the way from Buenos Aires with this message and to tell the Germans in strict confidence that Bormann himself would corroborate this view. The Reichsleiter was prepared to materialize at last, to place Eichmann's role in the proper perspective and to absolve him of the Jews' apocalyptic charge.

When Horst met Prosecutor Wolf on a Saturday, February 25, 1961, behind closed doors in a house on Arndtstrasse in Frankfurt, his message left the seasoned jurist stunned and incredulous, but not for reasons which Horst had anticipated. Eichmann? Wolf could not care less! He would not lift a finger to help him! He was interested in Bormann, the most elusive of all the fugitives, seeking exactly the kind of clue young Eichmann was now bringing.

Horst did not know, of course, that he chose for his intervention and was trying to enlist the help of the very people in Germany who were, in the final analysis, the original architects of his father's plight. It was Heinz Wolf's superior, State Attorney General Dr. Fritz Bauer, who had tipped off the Israeli Ministry of Justice that Adolf Eichmann was living in Argentina.

In a deposition and in a follow-up letter to Wolf, Horst Eichmann reiterated that Martin Bormann was alive. According to his unequivocal testimony—designed not to hurt Bormann, but to help his father—he had had "several conversations with Bormann, some quite recently, each lasting at least half an hour." Although Bormann was no longer residing in Argentina, Horst told Wolf, he still visited the country from time to time from residences in Brazil and Paraguay.

By this time in early 1961, the Bauer office had several folders literally bulging with all sorts of information about the missing

Bormann, some of it inane claptrap, some of it plausible. This, however, was the first firm evidence—a first clincher in what, in effect, was the campaign of a single angry man against the fugitive Nazis—or the case of Dr. Fritz Bauer versus Martin Bormann.

Years before the abduction of Adolf Eichmann, a seemingly minor event in West Germany had placed Martin Bormann in jeopardy. In 1956, Dr. Fritz Bauer, a fifty-two-year-old jurist who had spent the Hitler years in exile in Denmark and Sweden, was transferred from Braunschweig, where he headed the State Attorney's office in utter obscurity, to the limelight of Frankfurt to become Generalstaatsanwalt (Prosecutor General) of the State of Hesse.

Seven years before, Dr. Bauer had returned from Stockholm to the land of his birth, at the request of the German authorities, who were then trying to persuade the many former "non-Aryan" judges and prosecutors to come back and replace the Nazi-tainted officials who crowded the German judicial apparatus in all its branches. Few of them heeded the invitation. But Fritz Bauer returned eagerly, imbued with what he had come to regard as the mission of his life, the ferreting out and the prosecution of Nazi criminals. While still in exile, he had written a basic text about war criminals. It was used by the prosecution in Nuremberg as one of their chief guides through the labyrinth of this novel kind of international criminal justice.

With Bauer the Germans got back much more than they had bargained for—a selfless, dedicated crusader who proved both embarrassing and invaluable. At home, he was *unbequem* ("troublesome"), as his friend Robert Kempner put it, because he was, in the words of another friend, Bishop Lilje, of Sweden, "the first and foremost jurist in the Federal Republic who took seriously the systematic pursuit and prosecution of Nazi murderers." It was a task to which much lip service had been paid but was regarded as better left neglected. At the same time however, Dr. Bauer proved extremely useful as "an ambassador without portfolio," demonstrating to a skeptical world that the task of retribution was being executed sincerely and energetically in West Germany.

Dr. Bauer suffered from what he gradually came to regard as a misrepresentation of the true situation. He was saddened and eventually discouraged by the obvious fact that common criminals charged with simple homicide would be treated much more strictly and given far more severe sentences than the mass murderers of the Nazi era. As a legal philosopher, he considered the whole German system of judicial retribution as inadequate and hypocritical. He held that the real culprits were not the physical perpetrators of the horrendous crimes, not the brutalized guards and the drunken SS soldiers, the people in the extermination camps and behind the lines whose fingers pulled the triggers. "The real murderers," he once told an interviewer, "never bloodied their own hands, and now they are trying to use this as proof of their innocence." He complained to Dr. Kempner: "The periodic clean-out of an obnoxious red-light district in our cities is given much more serious attention and assigned more personnel than the penal purge and prosecution of the criminal Nazi regime."

When he arrived in Frankfurt in 1956 to take over the top job and was given the latitude he was seeking by the Hessian Minister of Justice, Dr. Johannes E. Strelitz, a fellow Social Democrat and congenital anti-Nazi, Fritz Bauer found nothing but suspicion and hostility awaiting him. He was mercurial and ebullient, using imagination and relentless initiative; he was ruthlessly and sometimes impetuously anti-Nazi. "When he first became our chief," said Senior Prosecutor Metzner, one of his closest associates, "we who had been employed in the office for years considered him an unknown quantity. We knew nothing about him. Our curiosity was compounded by certain misgivings that he might not be satisfied with the work we had been doing."

As a matter of fact, Bauer was not satisfied. He introduced new methods, a new spirit and drive into the office in which the prosecution of Nazi criminals had been handled in an indolent fashion. He imbued his staff with his own enthusiasm, made them work hard and follow up every lead. His monument became the marathon trial of the twenty-two Auschwitz guards and doctors which started in December 1963 and ended in August 1965. It shocked the world with its gruesome panorama of brutality, torture and savage murder, but also with the lenient sentences meted out by the court.

It was due largely to Bauer's dedication, initiative and unflagging industry that these men—and a relative handful of other mass murderers—had been brought to justice at all. His work earned for him the passionate hatred of former Nazis and neo-Nazis, the stricture of people who preferred to let bygones be bygones, and the hidden antagonism of certain members of his own staff. They regarded him as a do-gooder, an avenging Jew, a fire-eating old grouch who let his emotions run away with him when his head should have prevailed.

The Nazi fugitive who had more reason than all the rest to fear Dr. Bauer and do all he could to paralyze his anti-Nazi crusade was Martin Bormann. On Bauer's list of public enemies the former Reichsleiter was number 1. When he first arrived in Hesse he found that little had been done to track down the Nazi criminals in their hideouts and to bring to justice even those whose whereabouts were known. In particular, nothing at all had been undertaken to deal with the two worst criminals among the fugitives—Bormann and Dr. Josef Mengele. There were no bills of indictments drawn up, no search warrants out, no charges preferred against them—nobody in West or East Germany appeared to be interested in them.

The Allies had given up on the Nazis, even on those who had been sentenced to death *in absentia* by their own tribunals. The federal government in Bonn, which apparently inherited the job, abandoned it to the states. It was left to their own discretion to pick from among the blacklisted Nazis those in whose pursuit and prosecution they wanted to become involved. Dr. Bauer moved heaven and earth to get jurisdiction over Bormann and Mengele for Hesse.

The case of Mengele was no mystery. It had no loose ends. The nefarious doctor had spent some of the postwar years in Germany and left only when he thought it was becoming too dangerous. Even then, he left openly, under his own name, by his own means, emigrating rather than fleeing.

The case of Bormann was different. Was he dead or alive? As in the case of Eichmann, whose alleged demise he refused to believe, it was Simon Wiesenthal who first persuaded Dr. Bauer that Bormann had not perished in Berlin in May 1945, as was widely advertised by his partisans and even assumed inside Bauer's own office. Dr. Kempner supported Wiesenthal's argument, convinced as he was that Bormann had escaped. "As far as Martin Bormann's death is concerned," he wrote in his famous book about Eichmann in 1961, "there is no conclusive proof for me."

Fifteen years earlier, Kempner was instrumental in the decision of the Nuremberg prosecutors to refrain from accepting the tale of

Bormann's death at face value and dropping the case before the International Military Tribunal. He was coauthor of Bormann's bill of indictment that resulted in the death sentence of October 1, 1946.

Fritz Bauer was impressed by their arguments. The search for Bormann—neglected by both the Allies and the Germans, probably because they were afraid that they might find him—became a matter of genuine concern and urgency.*

From 1959 on, in fact, hot tips and warning signs had multiplied and convinced Bauer factually, and not merely emotionally, that Bormann had survived the war and was hiding somewhere. It was an exciting period, full of promise and rich in clues; but these proved difficult to harden. Now, however, the groping in the dark appeared to be over. If Dr. Bauer still needed any firmer proof to bolster his belief that Bormann was alive, young Eichmann's unqualified deposition now supplied it. But it also left him in a quandary. Bauer could not make up his mind how to act upon this most concrete and promising of all the leads he ever had.

A complicating factor was the upcoming trial in Jerusalem. With the Eichmann melodrama monopolizing world interest in fugitive Nazis, Bauer felt that his hands were tied. Moreover, Horst had told Wolf that he was risking his life with his revelations, and implored the prosecutor neither to publicize his testimony nor to act directly upon it in such a manner that "the Bormann people" would be enabled to trace the information to young Eichmann.

Dr. Bauer realized, moreover, that the search for Bormann could not be conducted behind closed doors. On the contrary, it had vast international ramifications. Obviously he could not pursue the matter without the help of the Bonn authorities. He was apprehensive, however, that certain people in Bonn, who had preferred to sit on the quasi-official information about Eichmann straight from the Presidential Palace in Buenos Aires, would pigeonhole the Bormann tip. He doubted that the Foreign Ministry, repeatedly rebuffed in previous inquiries, would aid him in approaching any of the South American countries where Bormann could have been living with a

* By singling out Dr. Bauer, I do not mean to cast aspersions on the sincerity, seriousness of purpose, integrity and industry of the handful of other German state attorneys and senior prosecutors involved in the pursuit and prosecution of Nazi criminals. Among them I found great humanitarians, driven by an inner revulsion and a lingering shame of Germany's Nazi past. By and large, however, the prosecution of criminal Nazis is coming to be widely regarded as a kind of séance in which the spirits of another era are conjured up by some *outré* hocus-pocus.

request through diplomatic channels to find, arrest and extradite him.

Dr. Bauer could not involve his own staff in the long-range adventure of an on-the-spot search, simply because they were neither permitted nor had the means to extend their investigations beyond Germany without the explicit approval of the Foreign Ministry. Yet Bauer was determined to do something, if only by creating a *fait accompli* that would force the issue.

He hit upon the idea of enlisting the aid of his friend and confidant Dr. Robert Kempner. His plan was to send Kempner "unofficially" to South America to check out young Eichmann's story and to ascertain, if possible, exactly where Bormann was. Then Kempner would either discreetly but directly intervene with the authorities where Bormann had his residence to cooperate in his arrest or force Bonn to act by exposing the case and using the pressure of aroused public opinion.

Just at this time, in 1961, Dr. Kempner (who lives in Lansdowne, Pennsylvania, but has a law practice in Germany, consisting mainly of cases against Nazi criminals) happened to be absent from his overseas base at Frankfurt. Bauer quickly traced him to a hotel in Bremen. There Dr. Kempner was surprised and somewhat annoyed when he heard stern knocking on the door of his room and found two local policemen bringing the ominous-sounding message that he immediately phone the Herr Generalstaatsanwalt in Frankfurt on a matter of the utmost urgency. When Kempner put in the call, Bauer asked him to return to Frankfurt directly to discuss with him a matter of overriding importance.

After careful consideration, however, Kempner advised Bauer against the exploratory trip. It would be impossible, he argued, to do anything behind Bonn's back. And the chances of enlisting the cooperation of the South Americans appeared to be dim, indeed. Instead of sending his friend, Bauer then used Simon Wiesenthal's local contacts in South America in his efforts to gain corroboration for Horst's sensational story. It was as a result of their independent rundown of the clues supplied by Horst Eichmann that Wiesenthal announced in no uncertain terms on March 29, 1961: "Martin Bormann is alive and is traveling unimpeded to and fro in South America."

If nothing else, the intervention of Horst Eichmann made Bauer conclude that the evidence was firm and sufficient at last to warrant what was called the reopening of the Bormann case. From Judge Opper of the Amtsgericht in Frankfurt, he obtained a formal warrant for Martin Bormann's arrest. Issued on June 6, 1961, the charges included murder. Accompanied by Bormann's authentic fingerprints (discovered in the files of a provincial police department from a case in which Bormann was charged with complicity in a political assassination), the warrant was then transmitted to Interpol and to every German diplomatic mission throughout the world.*

In the budding bout between Bauer and Bormann, the desperate plan to send Robert Kempner to South America in the hope that he might be able to collect the fugitive Reichsleiter demonstrated two things. First, it showed how seriously Bauer took Horst's deposition and how explicitly he believed the young man's sensational piece of intelligence. Second, it went far to show how frustrated Fritz Bauer was becoming in his efforts to get Bormann through regular, official government channels, either German or South American.

But no setback could dampen Bauer's zeal or daunt his determination to bring Nazi war criminals to justice. His creed was symbolized in the bronze which he, a lover of the arts, had left as his parting gift in Braunschweig to decorate the new Prosecutors Building. It was the statue of Justitia holding the familiar balance in her hand, but with a man in each of its scales. It was meant to express the fulcrum of his legal philosophy—it was man against man, the criterion of all things on earth. On the façade of the building he spelled out his credo in so many words. "The dignity of man," the inscription read, "is inviolable. To respect and protect it is the supreme duty of the executive power in every state."

The Kempner plan had to be abandoned. But the hunt was not given up.

* They were kept there until April 1973, when Dr. Bauer's successor persuaded a court (Strafsenat 3) in Frankfurt to invalidate with one stroke Dr. Bauer's lifework and place Bormann effectively in limbo by canceling the twelve-year-old arrest warrant.

PART FIVE

Contours of the Third World

Chapter Twenty

The Wayward Clues

It was Fritz Bauer's irate tip that sent the Israelis after Adolf Eichmann in Argentina. Now the Israelis returned the favor. Eichmann's pretrial interrogation by Captain Avner Less had been concluded. His recorded statement produced a transcript of 3,654 typewritten pages. Every page had been submitted to Eichmann for his corrections each of which he initialed. It was a startling document in which Eichmann unburdened himself, far more candidly and fully than at the trial.

Strange as it may seem, and probably indicative of the Israelis' attitude, Martin Bormann's name came up but once during the long trial, and then only when Dr. Servatius, Eichmann's lawyer, mentioned, significantly in the present tense, that "Bormann can come out of hiding," and had nothing to fear, if the contention that Eichmann was the sole villain of the Final Solution prevailed. But behind the scenes, in his informal conversations with Less and especially Servatius, Eichmann had referred repeatedly to the Reichsleiter as a man who was far more guilty, yet managed to escape retribution.

Dr. Bauer was given a record of these conversations. "Eichmann," he said after he had read them, "talked about Bormann all the time, in the manner of speaking of a living person."

It was a cautious, restrained statement in the light of what Bauer knew. There was specific intelligence available, even harder than the record of Eichmann's casual chitchat with Less and Servatius. It also stemmed from Eichmann, whose abduction had opened up a Pandora's box about a number of missing Nazis and their overseas odyssey. Both the Israelis and Bauer knew that Eichmann had "come clean" while he was still in hiding in Argentina. He had recounted in unvarnished detail the whole lurid inside story of the Final Solution, admitting almost with pride his own part in it and informing on its other chief protagonists.

He had completed his "confessions" barely a few weeks before his kidnaping in May 1960. They were brutally and, as it turned out, recklessly frank. According to a source that was aptly described as disreputable but unimpeachable, Eichmann had given away the whole show, disclosing that other marked Nazis like himself had in fact survived the war and describing the manner in which they had made their way to South America. Among these survivors he mentioned Heinrich Müller, his chief at the head of Amt IV, Rolf Günther, his own deputy at the Kurfürstenstrasse, Heinz Röthke, one of his top aides in France, and a number of others who were either believed to be dead or had been listed as missing.

He produced details of the Nazis' safe cantonment in friendly Argentina, describing, for instance, how Otto Skorzeny had found a berth in Buenos Aires amply supplied with Krupp money, and how Colonel Rudel, posing as the representative of Siemens, had cavorted with Perón as an honored guest in the Casa Rosada (see photograph section). Eichmann revealed that his chief collaborators in the Foreign Ministry—the bloodstained diplomats Rademacher, Wagner and Klingenfuss—had also sojourned in Argentina, living in their accustomed style without any visible means of income.*

He mentioned others, men as closely mired in the Final Solution as he was himself, but who had gained freedom and affluence at home, holding down well-paying, responsible jobs in government, business and industry. Among them he singled out Alfred Franz Six, an accomplice of the mass murderers (NSDAP No. 245,670/1930, SS No. 107,840/1935), who advanced from Sturmführer (major) in 1941 to Brigadeführer (major general) in 1944. Eichmann referred to Six as the man who descended lowest from his pedestal as a certified intellectual—a *Herr Professor,* at that, with a university background—to the depravity of the murder commandos in the

* Another Nazi diplomat, Dr. Ernst Günther Mohn (NSDAP No. 3,500,174/1935), former political boss of the Party in Peking and later assistant to Minister Otto Bene in the Netherlands, who was implicated in the liquidation of Dutch Jewry, also made it to Argentina, via Bolivia, but as ambassador of the Federal Republic in the 1960s.

U.S.S.R. (Vorkommando Moscow), then rose highest after the war as the confidant of the new Germany's economic masters.*

By far most important, Eichmann revealed that Martin Bormann, too, had managed to escape to Argentina. Living under the name of Ricardo Bauer, the former Reichsleiter was somewhere in South America.

Eichmann explained how it was conceivable for him and for the other fugitives to leave wives and children behind virtually destitute, in selfish efforts to save their own skin—how he himself, "in a state of shock," had made no provisions for his family, "unlike the so-called fancy Dans of the SS" and Bormann in particular. The latter, he said, had their families "securely wrapped in a very comfortable cocoon of foreign exchange and gold," with nest eggs abroad they had prepared before the collapse.

These remarks, calculatedly indiscreet, were all on tape and on paper, recorded in Eichmann's own voice and their transcript corrected and edited in Eichmann's own hand.

Called the Sassen tapes, after the man who made the recordings, they represent a sordid chapter by themselves in the postwar saga of Nazi fugitives. This Eichmann legacy—absolutely authentic and yet to be published in full—makes appalling reading. It damns Argentina as the most unscrupulous and corrupt of the host countries, where Nazi criminals could let down their roots virtually unmolested, irrespective of the regime in power.

Perón was gone in 1956, his coddling of the Nazi criminals condemned by his successors. Fearing the worst, Bormann had left the country for safer pastures. But his apprehension turned out to be unfounded. Only a year or so after Perón's downfall, life returned to normal for those Nazi refugees who chose to remain in Argentina.

Nazis who had been silenced by Perón's abrupt departure only eighteen months before suddenly regained their voices, which by 1957 resounded more stridently than ever. They now became the architects of a worldwide campaign designed to "expose as a hoax," as they put it, the story that six million Jews had perished in the

* On April 10, 1949, Six was sentenced to twenty years in prison by an American military tribunal, but his sentence was reduced to ten years in 1951 by General Thomas Handy. He was amnestied shortly afterward by U.S. High Commissioner John J. McCloy on the recommendation of his Clemency Board. In 1965, Dr. Six was publicity and advertising manager of Porsche-Diesel, a subsidiary of the huge Mannesmann Company, and was consultant of the Gehlen Organization "with special competence in Soviet matters."

murder camps, a claim, they said, invented by the Zionists to blackmail reparations from Germany for Israel and compensation for the scattered survivors of the holocaust. The leader of the new crusade was Colonel Rudel, head of the Kameradenwerk. He was aided by Eberhard Fritsche, former Hitler Youth leader in Argentina who was now editor of *Der Weg* (*The Way*), the Kameradenwerk's shrill anti-Semitic weekly, and two of its contributing editors, Guido Heimann and Wolfram Sievers. According to them, the crematoria were mere figments of Jewish propaganda!

Editor Fritsche asked his friend Eichmann to prepare "a detailed account" of the Final Solution to show that its alleged horrors had no foundation in fact. The paper Eichmann then prepared sparked an idea in the mind of another member of this consortium, a former SS officer of the Dutch Nazi movement. A journalist by profession, Willem Antonius Maria Sassen was a fugitive, even as Eichmann, from a death sentence in his native Holland.

"Let us write a book together," Sassen proposed to Eichmann, "to counter the enemy propaganda." In the collaboration, Eichmann was to supply the facts—*facts,* not the fiction Fritsche wanted. Sassen was to write the book under his own name, while Eichmann's part in the project would be kept a secret to be revealed only after his death. Sassen had no distorted impression of the fate of the Jews under the Nazis, nor was he letting himself be confused by the Rudel-Fritsche crowd's spurious propaganda. At the outset of the collaboration, he had no idea of the full extent of the murderous enterprise that Eichmann had managed. He was in for a surprise.

In 1957, exactly twenty-five years after he had first joined the Nazi Party, Eichmann agreed to embark on the project. Week after week, month after month, for almost three years, he met with Sassen behind closed doors and talked a blue streak, sometimes for hours in one take. This was to be no whitewash, like the paper for Fritsche, no apologia, no refutation of "Jewish lies." This was the ultimate rationalization of evil. "To sum it all up," he told Sassen in one of their sessions, "I must say that I regret nothing. . . . It would be too easy to pretend that I had turned suddenly from a Saul to a Paul. No," Eichmann said emphatically, "I must say truthfully that if we had killed all the ten million Jews that Himmler's statistician [Dr. Richard Korherr] had listed in 1933, I would say, 'Good, we have destroyed an enemy.' "

Sassen proved to be an exacting taskmaster and, as a professional writer, he knew what would sell a book. He urged Eichmann to tell it all, frequently coaxing him into blatant indiscretions. When Eichmann once thus blurted out an incident damaging to Rolf Günther, his former deputy and chief of the deportation apparatus (who was rumored to have committed suicide at an American internment camp in Ebensee in 1945), he quickly backtracked and admonished Sassen: "Don't put that into the book, for Pete's sake. Rolf is still alive!"* He was especially anxious to suppress all his unguarded and often jaundiced references to Bormann that slipped out of him during the interview.

When the project was interrupted in May 1960, Sassen had in his possession sixty-seven tapes with that many transcripts neatly kept in seventeen "Leitz" document binders, each containing from three to seven individually paginated transcripts. Eichmann had read the whole manuscript and made corrections and additions, some of them on the typewriter, others in his own handwriting. Transcripts 11 and 12, for example, had separate lists of numbered corrections. A whole page was added to Transcript 51, describing incidents which Eichmann apparently remembered after the taping. His additions were called *Bemerkungen am Rande* ("marginal notes") or marked as *Extrablatt* ("extra page"). The whole manuscript totaled 695 typewritten pages, about the size of this book.

For Eichmann, although this was a welcome catharsis, he sometimes regretted that he had gone along with Sassen's plan. The project was intended to be a long-range one, the book to be published either as a third-person narrative under Sassen's byline or probably only after Eichmann's death. For the time being, Eichmann had enjoined Sassen not to release any part of the text, nor even to publicize its existence, until he "had an opportunity of studying it and initialing each page," or unless he explicitly authorized Sassen to go ahead and publish. Eichmann made his corrections and added marginal notes and extra pages, but he steadfastly refused to initial even a single page, as a safeguard against unauthorized publication.

* Reitlinger listed Günther as dead, but Hilberg referred to him as missing, as did Tuvia Friedman in his roster of fugitive Nazis who will continue to burden "the world's conscience [until they] are found, arrested, tried and punished." There is every reason to believe that Rolf Günther is living under an assumed name unmolested, most probably in Argentina. His postwar success in evading retribution goes far to show how a smart fugitive could evade his hunters and live out his natural life unfound and unpunished.

When Eichmann was captured, Sassen no longer felt bound by their agreement. This was too good an opportunity to be missed by this Dutchman who was always hard up for cash. On September 10, 1960, about four months after Eichmann's abduction, Sassen revealed the existence of the manuscript in an interview in *La Razón*, a Buenos Aires daily. By then, it was in the hands of brokers abroad, peddling it to the highest bidder. World rights were then sold to Time Inc. in New York, and *Life* magazine published some 25,000 words from the 208,500 word manuscript, in two installments, on November 28 and December 5, 1960. The editors of *Life* were appalled by the unvarnished brutality and unrepentance of Eichmann's confessions, and they hesitated for some time before publishing their carefully selected excerpts. In the end, they printed them with an apologetic preface, calling their gruesome scoop "a major contribution to the history of a horrifyingly brutal era."

But Time Inc. was not the only client which succeeded in getting hold of the Sassen papers. The Israeli Secret Service had been tipped off to them even before they went on the market, and in a cloak-and-dagger operation that almost matched the melodrama of their author's abduction, succeeded in "procuring" a copy of what was then believed to be the entire manuscript. During the trial, almost a year after the Israelis had come into the possession of the document, Attorney General Gideon Hausner moved that the court admit the transcript as evidence, incontrovertible proof, as it promised to be, condemning Eichmann in his own words.

Eichmann objected frantically. Dr. Servatius emphatically contested the very authenticity of the document. By a two-to-one decision, the court ruled for Eichmann, admitting as evidence only the last folder, Number 17, in toto and bits and scraps from the other sixteen binders. Attorney General Hausner was especially rankled by the aspersions Servatius was casting on the authenticity of the document, in spite of the fact that experts had identified as many as eighty-four of the notes as definitely written by Eichmann.

By this time, the Israelis found out that the tapes themselves had been sent abroad and were, in fact, in the hands of the brokers who had sold the transcript to Time Inc. Now another clandestine race began, even while the long trial was dragging on. The Attorney General deliberately slowed down his cross-examination of Eichmann to gain time for buying the tapes. Approached by a go-between, whose connection with the Israelis was a deep secret, Sassen asked $20,000 for the tapes, and the Israeli government authorized the payment. In the eleventh hour, however, a hitch developed. Sassen categorically refused to sell unless the buyer gave a bonded assurance that the tapes would not be taken to Israel while the Eichmann case was before the courts.

It would have been a simple matter for agents who had managed to kidnap Eichmann himself to obtain the tapes under the counter and smuggle them to Israel. But Hausner vetoed their "acquisition" by any illicit means. "I did not wish," he wrote afterward, "any part of our evidence to be obtained by false pretense; so I instructed our people on an unconditional sale." Time was running out. Hausner was told that, according to the go-between, Sassen's condition to exclude Israel was irrevocable, even in the face of the painful prospect of losing a fortune. So the deal was off. The tapes were never played in court.

Today we know that Willem Sassen was holding back not only the sixty-two tapes which were in the hands of his brokers and were for sale, but five additional tapes the very existence of which was kept a secret. He also suppressed fifty-one pages from "the huge transcript of Eichmann's words" that he had sold to Time Inc.

In actual fact, Hausner's loss was not too serious. Even the fragments admitted in evidence proved devastating for Eichmann, and the court did not need the tapes to accept the partial transcript as fully authentic. But for Dr. Bauer's cause, the full transcript would have been invaluable—the missing link that he was seeking in the Bormann mystery, the corroboration and amplification of Horst Eichmann's deposition. On those five tapes which Sassen was withholding, Eichmann had recorded the sordid story of his own escape and presented his knowing account of Bormann's journey to Argentina, with explicit details of the Reichsleiter's first seven years in exile overseas.

When I learned what those missing tapes would divulge, I contacted Willem Sassen in Buenos Aires, hoping to be able to persuade him to part with them at last, at a reasonable price. He readily conceded that Bormann figured prominently both on the tapes and in his decision to withhold them, but refused categorically to surrender any of them or to let me as much as listen to the five mysterious tapes. "I know," he said ruefully, "how far I can stretch my luck."

He was, he told me quite bluntly, "afraid of the long arms of certain people" who might take a rather dim view of his indiscretion if he released the tapes "at this stage." He is still planning to publish the Eichmann book as a whole, including the material he keeps off the record—but, as he phrased it, "only after the death of either of us, Bormann's or mine."*

There was another flurry of excitement in 1962, when a Spaniard named Don Angel Alcazar de Velasco added his own story of Bormann's survival and escape to the growing dossier reposing in Bauer's office. According to Don Angel, Bormann had made good his escape from the Führerbunker, spent some time in Spain as guest of a certain Dr. Sanchez—actually Léon Degrelle, the Belgian Fascist leader in exile—and had gone to Argentina from there by submarine. Don Angel professed to have firsthand knowledge of this venture, for it was he himself, he claimed, who had escorted Bormann to Argentina as a favor to Degrelle and his Falangist friends.

Don Angel's sensational revelations were taken with a grain of salt, even by Dr. Bauer—but only because he must have been ignorant of the Spaniard's credentials. Although he appeared to be just one of the scores of crackpots who tried to grab headlines by muscling into the Bormann act, I have reason to believe that Don Angel was telling the truth. My discovery of the presumably lost archives of the Abwehr, the German military secret service, considerably added to Don Angel's stature as a credible witness. As far as I am concerned, his record lends credence to his story, and I am inclined to believe it virtually at face value.

I found that during World War II, Don Angel was "Guillermo," one of the strategically placed and trusted Spanish operatives of the Abwehr, which carried him under "V.312" in its supersecret roster of V men, or espionage agents. He had been sent to London in 1940, with the cover of a press attaché at the Spanish embassy, to manage the espionage ring of about a dozen like-minded Spaniards he himself had recruited for the German secret service. After the war, as

* I had an opportunity to read the other sixty-two transcripts and disagree with Dr. Hannah Arendt's characterization of the Sassen papers as "disorganized, rambling notes [Eichmann] made in preparation for the interview . . . which was tape-recorded and then rewritten by Sassen, with considerable embellishments." This was disputed angrily by Sassen himself. He assured me emphatically that the manuscript was the verbatim transcript of the tapes and that he himself never added a single word to Eichmann's spoken text.

member of the pro-Nazi faction of the Falange, he participated prominently in the operations of the underground railroad on which a number of prominent Nazi fugitives (including Heinrich Müller of the Gestapo and several generals of the Waffen SS) had been "sleuthed" to Argentina via Franco's Spain.

Although the key Argentine documents state that Bormann had gone to Buenos Aires in an Italian ship sailing from Genoa, I see no contradiction between the version of the documents and Don Angel's claim. I have strong reasons to believe that Bormann's arrival in Argentina in 1948 was not his first. Trustworthy witnesses, like the F.B.I.'s Juan Serrino (see page 46), the late Paul Hesslein, a former member of the Reichstag, where he used to meet Bormann and became familiar with him, and Count Hans Ulrich von Reichenbach, a German landowner in Chile with holdings near the Argentine border, insisted that they had seen Bormann ("Don Martin," in Señor Serrino's version) in Argentina *before* the 1948 date of his arrival recorded in the documents. Bormann may have made at least two "exploratory trips" to Argentina during what may be called his blue period in Italy, spending most of his time in Bolzano, but detouring from time to time to Seville and Salamanca in Spain, moving from monastery to monastery to Rome by way of Lake Garda, and going overseas.

The secret story of two German submarines as narrated in reports on file at the Naval Intelligence Division of the Argentine Admiralty explicitly confirm one such Bormann voyage, during which his landing in Patagonia was observed by an agent of the Division.

Chapter Twenty-One

The Strange Case of a Man Named Sawade

In the light of Horst Eichmann's deposition of February 1961, Dr. Fritz Bauer was convinced that the Bormann mystery was as good as solved. He had transferred Prosecutor Johannes Warlo from Wiesbaden to Frankfurt, with orders to devote himself exclusively to the processing of the Bormann case, the cracking of which, he told Warlo, now needed only another fortnight. "I think," Bauer confided to friends jubilantly, "we're on the threshold of a breakthrough in the Bormann matter."

Two years later, however, Prosecutor Warlo was still in Frankfurt processing the stubborn case. Bauer had been stymied at every step in his efforts to follow up the promising lead young Eichmann had handed him. In the meantime, the Bormann file in his office swelled to 1,300 pages filling eight big binders, and the telltale material was still pouring in. Most of it came from cranks who insisted they had seen the Reichsleiter in South America, but also in such far-apart places as Algeria and Australia, Egypt and the Soviet Union.

Among the chaff were some data that Bauer took seriously, since it corroborated, he thought, what Horst Eichmann had confided to Prosecutor Wolf. The former German politician who had known Bormann well from the cloakroom of the Reichstag, whose members they both were in the early thirties, stated positively that he had bumped into Bormann in the border region of Chile in an encounter that ended in mutual recognition.

More important was another story, which the Bauer office picked up secondhand. On July 30, 1960, in the wake of Eichmann's abduction, Frau Hildegarde Buch, Bormann's mother-in-law, told friends in Munich that a few days before, two strangers had visited her husband, the former chief judge of the Nazi Party's tribal courts, and were closeted with him for hours. "That night," Frau Buch had said, "when the men were gone, my husband told me in bed, 'So the swine is alive after all.' " The "swine," of course, was Bormann.

Efforts to find the woman and ask her to elaborate on her cryptic tale all failed, because, as I was told by one of Bauer's former associates, she had supposedly moved to America and the aide Bauer had commissioned to locate her in the States bungled the assignment. "We had our setbacks and disappointments," Bauer said, "but I firmly believe that our work was not in vain. The investigation continues unabated." His optimism did not seem to be justified. The mystery of the fugitive Bormann, who was now wanted by the Germans as well—on arrest warrant No. 931 Gs 4388/61, which Judge Opper had issued on June 6, 1961—seemed more opaque than ever.

Then, however, the big break that Dr. Bauer never ceased to hope would come his way sooner or later briefly flashed in sight. What now happened in Bauer's inner sanctum during an action-packed six-month period recalled the gangster melodramas that made big headlines in the United States two decades before. The part of the informer of Murder Inc., doomed by the mob because he had talked, was played by a Nazi-tainted, bloodstained ex-professor of neurology from Würzburg. The locale was Butzbach prison near Frankfurt instead of the Half-Moon Hotel in Coney Island. In other respects, however, the similarity between the two cases was uncanny. In the end, like the quixotic New York district attorney fighting windmills, Dr. Bauer was left high and dry just when he thought he was closest to clinching his biggest case.

By this time it was the summer of 1963. The Bauer bureau was busy with the case of four men charged with complicity in the murder of some 200,000 so-called "misfits" during the Third Reich. The Germans' belated prosecution harked back to, and was meant to supplement, the 1947 Allied trial of twenty-seven SS quacks and pseudoscientists, some of them charged with having conducted savage experiments with human guinea pigs, others charged with participation in one of the Nazi mass-murder schemes that was camouflaged as the euthanasia program.

In 1939, in one of his diabolical moods, Hitler personally

ordered Reichsleiter Philip Bouhler, a baby-faced SS killer, who headed his cabinet office (the *Führerkanzlei,* whose function ironically included the pardoning of common criminals and the commutation of death sentences in ordinary criminal cases), "to widen the authority of individual doctors to enable them . . . to administer a mercy death (*Gnadentod*) to incurably sick persons." What was made to sound like a humanitarian project was in fact a vast program to exterminate "the unfit," from retarded children to patients in terminal stages of illness, from lunatics to senile old people. In the Nazis' murder rampage, the euthanasia program became one of the major murder tools, killing superfluous foreign workers, Russian prisoners of war, political opponents. Eventually it was used as another method of liquidating the Jews.

By the time Dr. Bauer got around to the prosecution of the euthanasia case on his crowded agenda, many of the people connected with the program were beyond his reach. Bouhler had committed suicide. Victor Brack, the program's chief administrator (who, incidentally, also was instrumental in the installation of the gas chambers in the Polish death camps), had been hanged in Landsberg Prison on June 2, 1948. Executed with him were the two notorious Brandts—the physician Karl, who was one of Hitler's confidants and his veteran doctor, and the lawyer Rudolf, who was Himmler's chief aide—and Professor Dr. Karl Gebhardt, a prominent SS surgeon who was Himmler's personal doctor; Professor Joachim Mrugowsky, another superdoctor of the SS; and Hauptsturmführer Dr. Waldemar Hoven, one of the Dachau doctors. Their death was premature, so to speak. Only a couple of years later, Allied magnanimity would have freed them to resume their practice of medicine, as merciful German courts later allowed hundreds of their similarly incriminated colleagues to do.

Fritz Bauer succeeded nevertheless in rounding up four men missed by Judge Walter B. Beals's American court at Nuremberg in 1947. There was only one medical doctor in this quartet of ghouls, but he was among the biggest game Bauer had been stalking for some time. In 1965, as we have seen, Bauer thought he had enough reliable evidence on file to enable him to make a definitive statement about Bormann's postwar fate, even though he still had no direct lead to the man at that time. In a formal announcement Bauer stated unequivocally that Martin Bormann had survived. He went on to describe in specific detail how the Reichsleiter sneaked out of

Berlin and made good his escape by going north, where he found a temporary haven in a hospital in Denmark. Bauer pinpointed a German physician named Heyde, who aided Bormann during this first stage of his escape. The State Attorney General had the information from Heyde himself.

Professor Werner Heyde was one of the four men whose trial for mass murder Bauer was laboriously preparing in 1963. He was, in fact, a respected Bavarian neurologist before he fell in with the murderous Hitler crowd. Among all the spineless doctors of infamy in the Third Reich, Heyde probably sank deepest in the Nazi morass. What Mengele was in Auschwitz, Professor Heyde was to the euthanasia program.

The "mercy killing" of psychotics had been going on for some time, but the extension of the euthanasia program to Jews began tentatively only in the summer of 1941.Three hundred inmates of the Dachau concentration camp were then peremptorily shipped to the nearby Bernberg Institute, a home for the mentally retarded, where they were "put to sleep" with lethal injections. These ill-fated pioneers had been selected by a medical commission composed of Dr. Fritz Menncke, one of Dachau's resident physicians; the euthanasia expert Professor Nitsche; and Dr. Heyde. At that time he was head of the neurological clinic of Würzburg University's Medical School and superintendent of an SS hospital in the city. But recommended for the job by Bouhler as "a clean-cut, splendid individual" (*eine saubere, gediegene Persönlichkeit*), he found time to serve as "medical director" of Action T-4, as the euthanasia program was discreetly called, after the location of its administrative headquarters at Tiergarten Street 4 in Berlin.

Promoted energetically by Heyde (sometimes in the face of opposition by a handful of courageous colleagues appalled by the true scope of the program), the "mercy killing" of Jews became institutionalized by the end of 1941. After that, a traveling circus of four quack psychiatrists moved from camp to camp, going through the motion of selecting "emotionally disturbed inmates"—invariably Jews of perfectly sound mind—to be put to sleep in "charitable institutions" at Bernburg, Harthein, Sonnenstein, Hadamar, Eglfind-Harr, Andernach, Grafeneck, Brandenburg, and twenty-two other former "nursing homes" set aside for this freak show of the Final Solution. The "psychiatrists" did their job, sitting in the open, behind tables arranged for them in the camps. They chose the hapless Jews by sheer whimsy for the fatal injection or the lethal Luminal pill at one or another of the "hospitals" managed by a dummy organization called "Charitable Foundation for Institutional Care."

From the very outset of the program, Professor Heyde headed this itinerant four-man *Ärztekommission* ("commission of physicians"). Like a traveling salesman of death, he showed up in succession at Dachau, Sachsenhausen, Buchenwald, Mauthausen, Auschwitz, Flössenburg, Gross-Rosen, Neuengamme and Niederhagen, sending tens of thousands of Jews to their death for merely being Jews. Their "mercy killing" was meticulously justified—for bureaucratic order and the appearance of propriety had to prevail in this Teutonic bedlam—with falsified lunacy certificates called Form 14F3, signed by Heyde.

Assisting Heyde were three of his fellow accused on Bauer's calendar: Dr. Hans Hefelmann, an agronomist, and Dr. Gerhard Bohne, a lawyer, took care of the clerical chores of T-4; Friedrich Tillmann, the owner of a firm operating ambulances, served as Heyde's traffic manager in charge of transporting his victims from the concentration camps to the "nursing homes."

When, in April 1945, elements of the Seventh U.S. Army's 42nd Division neared Würzburg, Heyde hastily evacuated his hospital to a place that he recalled from his boyhood hikings in Schleswig-Holstein, just across the border in Danish Jutland. The region looms large in the Bormann saga, as a milestone on his wanderings in the immediate wake of his escape from Berlin. Although by the plebiscite of 1919 it was Danish territory, there were many diehard Nazis among its sizable German population. Heyde was heading for Sönderborg, a beautifully located border town on the sound, ravaged many times by war. It was across this much-contested border that Hitler's army marched into Denmark in April 1940.

On the road leading westward from Sönderborg was Graasten Castle, originally built in the fifteenth century but restored by King Christian, who used it as one of his summer residences. During the war, the Germans turned it into a hospital for the Waffen SS. Since it was but a few miles inside Denmark, with the German army of General Busch still apparently controlling the area, Heyde thought that it might be a safe place to retreat to and to stay at until things calmed down.

He took with him Hefelmann, Bohne and Tillmann, trying frantically to escape the Allied dragnet. Heyde in particular was high on the list of C.I.C. suspects, as one of the vilest among the fellows of Hitler's college of mad doctors.

The war was over, the Third Reich was a shambles. The Heyde hospital—which was in fact a hospice for Nazis on the run—endured for only a few weeks at Graasten. In late June (shortly after Bormann arrived at the castle) the Danes moved in on what was one of the last remnants of Himmler's defunct SS state. They closed down the hospital, but only after most of its German staff and its "patients," tipped off in the nick of time, managed to escape, with Bormann in the vanguard.

If Dr. Heyde and his closest associates were thus helped to escape retribution, it was because they had a secret that had to be protected at all cost. Because of their involvement in Bormann's escape, extra efforts were made by the Nazi rescue workers to keep them out of Allied hands. Tillmann, the ambulance tycoon, could thus vanish in thin air in Germany. Hefelmann and Bohne were spirited out of the country and shipped off to the safe haven of Argentina with the help of Bishop Hudal's underground railroad.

At first, Dr. Heyde was not so fortunate. The Danes caught up with him, took him into custody and delivered him to the British in Schleswig-Holstein. He was lodged in a prisoner-of-war camp in Gadeland (where, as it turned out, he struck up a couple of invaluable friendships), then moved to Frankfurt, where he was wanted as one of the "doctors of death" slated as defendants in the first of a new series of trials that the American military governor had instituted under a decree issued on October 25, 1946.

But when the trial opened on November 5 (with every single one of the doctors in the dock pleading not guilty), Professor Heyde was missing. The court was told that he had escaped en route to Nuremberg by jumping from the jeep in which a couple of American M.P.'s were taking him from Frankfurt.

For the next thirteen years, all attempts to find him failed. After the fall of Perón in 1955, which coincided with the transfer of the prosecution of the Nazi criminals to the German authorities, Hefelmann and Bohne decided that they would be safer at home than in Argentina. They returned to Germany and when they found that nobody was looking for them any longer (for Dr. Bauer was still far from hitting his stride) they resumed their normal lives, Hefelmann in agriculture and Dr. Bohne as a lawyer.

But there was no trace of Dr. Heyde. Although he was very much alive when last seen in Allied hands and was prominently mentioned as a fugitive in the most damning testimonies before Judge Beals's tribunal in Nuremberg, since the spring of 1945, when he left Würzburg in a hurry, he made no attempt to contact his family, who were left to shift for themselves in the city. When, then, his wife's search failed to find the father of her two children, Frau Erika Heyde had her husband declared dead. She even managed to wrangle for herself a pension as a war widow by presenting his death certificate to the gullible authorities of Würzburg.

But, of course, Heyde was not dead! Like Heinrich Müller and the other *Scheintote* ("seeming-dead") of the Nazi regime, he had merely abandoned his past, turned his back on his family, and assumed an entirely new identity. Two of his former fellow inmates in the British prison camp at Gadeland had in the meantime become the mayor and registrar respectively of the city of Plön. They issued to Heyde all the papers he needed to embark on his new life, made out to one Fritz Sawade, a former native of Saxony, whose name and vital statistics they took from the registry of the dead.

During those years in the immediate wake of the war, the province of Schleswig-Holstein was the ideal place in West Germany for fugitive Nazis to hide in. They were supported by the local authorities, denazified by the British but still pro-Nazi, and backed by a considerable segment of the populace. Heyde had no difficulty in submerging among them. Although the late Fritz Sawade had no degree whatever, he remedied that with the help of his new friends. Styling himself Dr. Sawade, he gave himself a diploma and returned to the lucrative practice of medicine. During his years on the run, he earned on the side over 300,000 marks (then worth $75,000, a very respectable sum) in addition to his regular income as a practicing neuropsychiatrist, by serving as medical officer of the city of Flensburg, an examiner working for an insurance company, psychiatric consultant to the Social Security Court and to the Schleswig-Holstein Krankenkasse, the equivalent of our Medicare organization. The officials who appointed Dr. Sawade to these well-paying posts did not consider it necessary to ask for his credentials or to examine his qualifications. They knew all the time who he really was.

Over the years, the kindly *Herr Doktor* came to be respected and liked by his fellow Flensburgers. His neighbors, who knew of his past only what he cared to tell them, commiserated with him for the terrible tragedy which, he said, had shattered his life. He told his new friends that his wife and two children had been murdered by the Russians during the advance on Berlin. Down south in Würzburg, his wife and children actually believed him to be dead. Like Bormann, who broke completely with his family when he embarked on his secret life in exile, Heyde never bothered to contact his wife and children during the fourteen long years he spent underground.

In 1954 it seemed briefly that his masquerade would be exposed. Professor Kreutzfeld, the head of a clinic for nervous disorders in Kiel, recognized him and formally notified Dr. Burech, chairman of the Regional Board of Physicians, that Dr. Fritz Sawade was in fact the fugitive wanted for the murder of 100,000 men, women and children. Dr. Burech waited five weeks before he replied in a brief note that the information was of no interest to the Board. Similarly, when the courts, before which Sawade appeared as a medical expert, were confidentially told that he was the "missing" Heyde, the judges refused to act upon the denunciations. In deliberate defiance of the law they had sworn to uphold, they knowingly prolonged the secret life of this wanted fugitive.

Another five years passed. Then, however, the police, acting on a hunch of Dr. Bauer's, called at Dr. Sawade's house in Flensburg. It was November 7, 1959. Sawade still had friends in high places. Alerted by them, he fled a couple of days before the arrival of the police. It was a foolish move, if only because his frenzied departure gave him away. Bauer now had the proof he needed that Heyde was alive after all, masquerading as Fritz Sawade. The dragnet was out. All the known escape routes of the Kameradenwerk and other Nazi rescue organizations—still very much active, fourteen years after the war—were placed under surveillance. A watch was kept at the airports, and all border checkpoints were notified. The manhunt proved too much for the fifty-nine-year-old man who had been a fugitive for fifteen years of his life. On November 19, Heyde gave himself up, prepared, as he told Dr. Bauer, "to face the music at last." Tipped off by him, Bauer rounded up Hefelmann, then Bohne, and eventually Tillmann as well.

The sinister forces that arranged the escape of these men fifteen years earlier now went into action again to hinder the course of justice. Orders arrived from overseas that under no circumstances must Heyde be left in Bauer's hands to stand trial. Arrangements were made behind the scenes to spring Heyde from the Limburg jail near Koblenz, where he was kept pending the trial, and to take him, as well as Gerhard Bohne, the other man who was privy to the secret of Bormann's brief stay at Graasten, quickly out of the country—to Argentina.

First Heyde vanished. Then Bohne, who was free on bail, also disappeared. Now another manhunt was on, but Bohne could not be found. He outwitted his pursuers and managed to make it back to Argentina, with the help of the very same people who had aided him during his flight in 1949. But Heyde was dispirited, tired of life in exile. He had come to peace with himself and was ready to pay the forfeit for his terrible wartime malpractice of medicine. Unwilling to cooperate in his own escape, he was easily caught. It was then learned that his jailers in Limburg had been in cahoots with his old Nazi friends and had aided his escape. He was, therefore, transferred to the maximum security of Butzbach prison near Frankfurt. It was from his cell there that he smuggled word to Dr. Bauer that he wanted to see him, alone and secretly.

Although the exact nature of their subsequent talk was known only to these two men, Bauer intimated afterward that Heyde was "singing." He had revealed that after the war, at that secluded hospital in Denmark, with Bohne and Tillmann's help, he had sheltered many prominent Nazis—among them Martin Bormann! The Reichsleiter, who had worked his way north in his futile attempt to see Admiral Doenitz, stayed at Graasten only a few days, while awaiting the arrival of the Red Cross team of young Austrians who then smuggled him south and out of the country. It was a fantastic break. Unexpectedly and unsolicited, Bauer had the key witness to prove that Bormann had survived the war.

A few days before the Heyde trial was to open in Limburg, the bizarre melodrama reached a stunning climax. On February 10, obviously proceeding on the strength of what Bauer had learned from Heyde and Tillmann, Chief Prosecutor Wilhelm Metzner announced officially that "despite allegations to the contrary, including the testimony of Hans Baur, Hitler's chief pilot, the office of the Attorney General of the State of Hesse continues to pursue its search for Martin Bormann in the factual belief that the head of the Party chancery of the N.S.D.A.P. had survived what certain witnesses described as his 'hour of death' on May 1, 1945."

Metzner then added emphatically: "The office of the Attorney

General in Frankfurt is satisfied that in the meantime it has come into possession of information that tends to prove that, at that time, Bormann was spared and got away with his life."

The cat was out of the bag. Metzner's statement was printed in the press on February 11 and was followed by a chain of startling events. On February 13, 1964, left unguarded in his cell, Heyde was found hanging from the radiator by his belt—dead. The day before, Tillmann fell to his death from an eighth-floor window in an office building in Cologne. The case that Bauer had pieced together so laboriously over a period of more than four years collapsed like a house of cards. The sudden mysterious death of its two protagonists was an even greater blow. Bauer's two key witnesses in the Bormann matter were lost.

Did Heyde commit suicide? Was it an accident when Tillmann fell out of that window in Cologne? Or was there foul play behind Heyde's strange death? Did Tillmann fall or was he pushed?

Colonels Rudel and Skorzeny could, I submit, shed light on these puzzling questions within the Bormann mystery, for it was the old organization that they had founded and maintained that was behind the plot. Bauer stated without qualification that Tillmann did not fall or jump—that in gangster fashion he was pushed out of the window in what was a premeditated effort to get him out of the way, as in the "suicide" of Jan Masaryk in Prague. How about Heyde? Bauer would not commit himself on the record beyond saying that "his suicide had been *provoked* by some people behind the scenes."

Members of his staff, whose work of almost five years had gone down the drain, were more outspoken. Although they were not taken into Bauer's confidence and did not know, therefore, that their chief was on the verge of solving the Bormann mystery with Heyde's help in open court, they charged bluntly that the deaths of the two men "were the result of a carefully plotted conspiracy."

"I suspect," one of Bauer's assistants told *The New York Times*, "there are many people who are desperately interested that their name and work during the Third Reich do not become public property. It is obvious that they are willing to go to any lengths to silence the men who would talk."

Murder or suicide, Heyde did not take his secret with him to the grave. He had shared it with Dr. Bauer, who could thus state categorically, with the ghosts of Heyde and Tillmann hovering over the scene:

> Martin Bormann succeeded in escaping from the Reich Chancellery [in 1945] . . . We believe that Bormann stayed for some time in the Danish royal castle at Graasten, which is not far from the town of Sönderborg. An SS military hospital during World War II, the castle later became the hideout of many high-ranking Nazi leaders. The man who hid them and Bormann was a certain Heyde.

Dr. Bauer's greatest—and, as it turned out, last—opportunity to explode the Bormann myth was gone. There was nothing more he could do. His evidence was dead and buried with Heyde and Tillmann.

The suicide of Heyde and the accident of Tillmann were never investigated by any government agency in Germany, although the Federal Republic has two giant secret services, patterned after our C.I.A. and F.B.I. respectively. They could (or, indeed, should) have been called in to use their fast, furtive facilities in an attempt at resolving the enigmatic death of two key figures in this great Nazi drama.

According to Michael Bar-Zohar, however, a foreign secret service (which he did not identify but obviously was that of Israel) undertook a post-mortem with Dr. Bauer's discreet assistance and concluded that both men had been killed. "I am quite sure," Bar-Zohar quoted the anonymous special agent in charge of the clandestine inquiry, "that Heyde did not commit suicide. Shortly before the trial was due to open, he agreed to give evidence for the prosecution, and to make various disclosures . . . So the Nazis had to prevent him from talking at all costs."

After his death, I learned, a quantity of sleeping pills was found in Heyde's cell. He could easily have used them to kill himself. As a matter of fact, the autopsy found "certain toxic chemicals" in his stomach, but the report did not elaborate on this crucial finding, nor was the matter pursued by the authorities.

> We looked into the circumstances of his death [the special agent went on] and came to the conclusion that members of Die Spinne or of some organization that has succeeded it managed

to get into Heyde's cell, aided and abetted by the prison staff, and then executed him.*

> Don't forget [the man said] that Heyde had provided Martin Bormann with a refuge at the hospital in Graasten Castle. If he had talked, he could have given evidence to prove that Bormann's death in Berlin was just a fake. The groups of ex-Nazis did all they could to protect Heyde and to make sure that he was not brought to trial. They warned him in time when the police went to arrest him. They even tried to arrange his escape from prison in August 1963. As soon as they heard that Heyde (and, for that matter, Tillmann) had decided to tell all [they] knew, in the hope of getting a lighter sentence, there was only one way out—they had to silence [them]. Heyde knew too much. The Nazis killed him to save themselves.

Dr. Bauer picked up the pieces of the broken case and on February 18, 1964, opened the long-overdue trial in the ancient city of Limburg in the Rhine Palatinate with Dr. Hans Hefelmann, the only remaining defendant, in the freshly painted dock. With two of the accused dead and a third a fugitive in Argentina, what promised to be a spectacular pageant of Nazi horrors failed to come near expectations. Then Hefelmann also fizzled out. On August 28, playing the familiar game, he told the court that he had had enough of his ordeal and "only immediate and lengthy hospitalization could save his life." Ten days later the court solemnly ruled that the man accused of having murdered 73,000 persons was, indeed, "physically and mentally unable to stand trial." The case was postponed indefinitely, never to be reopened.

But even as far as it went, the so-called Limburg case produced a sensational revelation in open court and a remarkable "first" in Germany's precarious relations with Argentina over the delicate issue of Nazi fugitives. The fact that Bauer's defendants were willing to "sing" and implicate people still protected by the long arms of the Kameradenwerk and The Spider became evident on the very first day of the trial. On February 18, 1964, Hefelmann described in explicit detail—the first and only time by any defendant in any

* Die Spinne was not dead by any means. Called La Araña (The Spider) in South America, it was the neo-Nazi refugee organization through which Bormann exercised some of his control of the movement and behind the façade of which he transacted many of his fiscal maneuvers. It remained independent of Rudel and Skorzeny's Kameradenwerk, but cooperated with it closely in operations resembling the liquidation of Dr. Heyde and poor Tillmann.

of these trials—how the Roman Catholic Church aided his escape.

Asked by the president of the court why he wanted to go to Argentina in the first place, Hefelmann, thin and graying, and looking much older than his fifty-seven years, said in a low voice: "I did not trust the justice of the people who occupied Germany." How did he manage to get to Argentina? He was smuggled out of Germany in 1948, Hefelmann confessed, by kindly people he met for the first time, and taken to Austria, where Caritas, the Roman Catholic welfare organization, obtained an Argentine visa for him. "The Church," as he put it, then arranged the rest of the trip via the monastery route and across the South Atlantic.* He named Archbishop Heinrich Wienken of Innsbruck as the man who sponsored his escape.

The other extraordinary offshoot of the case was what happened to Dr. Bohne. In 1949, when he first escaped to Argentina, he made it in style, "given," as he himself put it, "money and identity papers by officials of the regime of Juan Domingo Perón." When he returned furtively in August 1963, he was traveling on a passport belonging to another West German citizen and, although aided by the Kameradenwerk, had to go into hiding at once, for he was followed quickly by a diplomatic note from Bonn asking for his extradition.

Bohne was unfortunate in his timing, arriving during a period when the Argentine authorities were sincerely anxious to rid the country of the Nazis. What President Frondizi started in 1960, with his "acquiescence" to Eichmann's abduction, President Arturo Illia continued even more energetically. Under his guidance, Colonel Alberto Samuel Caceres, director general of Coordinación Federal, which included the Division of Alien Affairs, embarked on a purge that caused many of the Nazis to scatter.

On November 18, 1963, only three months after Bohne's arrival, Caceres issued Special Order No. CF-S01365 O.J.P. I will quote it

* Sixteen years had passed since the Church was leading the great Nazi rescue work, but the Vatican's response to Hefelmann's revelation was as feeble as ever. A functionary of Caritas International in Rome, described as "one of the prelates who aided postwar European refugees," ventured the opinion that Hefelmann must have used a fictitious name in getting help from Caritas, or else the Church, traditionally opposed to euthanasia, would not have aided the veteran Nazi charged with the "mercy killing" of thousands of innocent human beings. In actual fact, Hefelmann traveled under his own name. The Vatican had a copy of the suspect list of the Allies which carried him as one of the chief functionaries of the murderous euthanasia program.

in full, for it marked the only period in Argentina's recent history when Nazi and Fascist fugitives were in real jeopardy, and Bormann's own hide-and-seek also took a critical turn. The remarkable order read:

> From now on, the vigilance of all foreigners must be intensified, in particular of those elements of German nationality known to be Nazi or war criminals, persons for whom warrants of arrest are out or whose extradition has been requested.
>
> As concisely as possible, the activities of German colonies in our national territory must be reported. All agents must be instructed to this effect, and also briefed that all measures of vigilance and control, as well as contacts with confidential informants, other authorities, and the press, must be conducted in ironclad secrecy.
>
> The Central Intelligence Bureau will proceed immediately to assemble complete files containing information already on hand and to be obtained about all foreigners, regardless of nationality, known to be adherents of the Nazi ideology.
>
> Said files will be kept up to date, with reports received from the Alien Control Division and the branch offices of this agency throughout the country. Agents must be instructed to forward promptly all data procured by them.
>
> [Signed] ALBERTO SAMUEL CACERES, Dirección Coordinación Federal

Implementing this order, special Nazi-hunting squads were set up at the Posadas, Viedma, Córdoba, and Paraná branches of the agency, as well as in Buenos Aires. Together, they covered the part of Argentina that was known to harbor diehard Nazis and fugitives of the Third Reich.

Agent Pinto, stationed at the Posadas branch, was assigned to the wide-open region bordering on Paraguay and Brazil.

He was aided by Agent Correa of the office at Formosa. Agent Alvarez at Viedma was made responsible for surveillance in the Bariloche area.

Agent Mega of the Córdoba office covered northern Argentina.

Agents Chamado and Verri were sent to the strategic Paraná area with its constant traffic of Nazi fugitives.

The wretched Bohne, it seems, had been singled out as an example to deter others, and as the living proof that Argentina meant its sudden upsurge of anti-Nazism seriously. The whole apparatus of Coordinación Federal was mobilized to catch him. Living under a false name which he kept secret, and harbored by the men whose stake in his safety was the safeguarding of Bormann's great secret, Bohne was not easy to find. But, with the forces aligned against him, he had no chance. There was an opening through which Colonel Caceres expected to corner him. Bohne had a sister living in Belgrano, the elegant residential district of Buenos Aires, and on the assumption that he might visit her sooner or later, her home was placed under round-the-clock surveillance.

On February 26, 1964, a couple of blocks from his sister's house, while Bohne was actually on his way to call on her, special agents of Coordinación Federal intercepted him. Never before was Argentine bureaucracy made to work more expeditiously. On March 3, the case was assigned to Judge Leopoldo Isaurralde, who immediately started extradition proceedings. The very next day, President Illia personally signed a decree ordering the sixty-one-year-old Bohne deported to West Germany. But then the matter bogged down. The case dragged on for two and a half years. Finally, on November 11, 1966—almost exactly to the day three years and three months after his second coming—Bohne was put on a plane at Ezeiza airport and flown to Frankfurt in the custody of two German detectives.

This memorable event remains unique and historic to this day. *Bohne was, in all these well-nigh three decades, the one and only Nazi criminal of the estimated 40,000 to 50,000 fugitives who had found haven in Argentina ever to be extradited by that hospitable country.*

Extraordinary measures had to be undertaken to prevent him from being snatched back from the hands of the authorities and to forestall a riot of pro-Nazi elements understandably upset by his extradition. During this time policemen armed with submachine guns guarded the prison where Bohne spent more than two years while several Argentine courts considered the request for his extradition. On the day of his forced departure, the airport swarmed with policemen when the former Nazi official was driven in a truck straight to the aircraft aboard which the two German detectives were waiting for him.

Back in Germany a dozen hours later, he was lodged briefly in Butzbach prison. For all the money and time and energy the Germans had expended on getting him back, they could not hold him for any length of time. His lawyers appealed to the courts using the old standby, bad health, to obtain his release. It was granted promptly.

That was ten years ago. The man who was then described by his doctors as so ill that he had only a few months to live is still living in comfortable retirement near Frankfurt—still charged with complicity in the murder of 15,000 persons—on a pension he draws from the state as a former government official.

While the Limburg trial was dragging on with its sole wretched defendant in the dock, Martin Bormann remained the stellar attraction in the background of the never-ending Nazi hunt. In South America, the mercurial Schwend kept the mystery alive. He had taken on the job of covering up Bormann's trail by disseminating misleading information about the Reichsleiter—now asserting that he had died, then resurrecting him in different places, always far from the spot where Schwend well knew Bormann really was.

On February 4, 1964, almost coinciding with Heyde's and Tillmann's sudden death, Schwend planted a story in the newspaper *Correo* in Lima, which was then picked up by the press associations and reprinted throughout the world. According to his shrewdly phrased copy,

> the Israeli Secret Service had asked permission from P.I.P. [the Peruvian secret police] to let a team of its special agents cross surreptitiously into Chile via Peru on a supersecret mission—actually, as it was broadly hinted, to pick up Martin Bormann, whom the Israelis had found living in Arica, a city in northern Chile.

All this was pure eyewash, of course. The Israeli Secret Service was not involved in any such plot, and even if it had been, it would never have asked P.I.P.'s approval to invade Chile. It also goes without saying that Bormann was nowhere near Arica at this time; in fact, he was still in Bolivia. It was Schwend who had told P.I.P., whose regular paid informer he was, that an Israeli commando unit was in Peru planning to sneak into Chile to collect Bormann. Then, when his "secret intelligence" was on file at P.I.P., he turned around and leaked the story to *Correo*. The paper then obtained corroboration of the story from an unimpeachable source—P.I.P., of course.

Schwend also was behind another Bormann canard that followed a few weeks later, designed to compound the confusion caused by the Heyde and Tillman incidents. On March 19, a man calling himself Ricardo Bormann and claiming that he was the brother of Martin suddenly appeared in a police station near Santos in Brazil, and revealed that the missing Reichsleiter was living in the State of Mato Grosso in western Brazil. According to Delegado Francisco Peixoto, the head of the precinct, "the man made a good impression and seemed to know what he was talking about." He even had some credentials to lend weight to his story. He proved that he was a former SS man by showing the secret identification mark of the death-head brigade that Himmler had had tattooed in the armpit of every SS man.

But Bormann had only one brother and his name was Albert. Moreover, "little Bormann," as he was called although he was a head taller than brother Martin, was living quietly at this time in Germany, where his name and address were openly listed in the Munich telephone directory. Albert was a shadowy figure deep in the background of the Bormann saga. Two years younger than Martin and a bank clerk before he became a functionary of the Nazi Party (in which he rose to the rank of Gruppenführer, or lieutenant general, in the National Socialist Motor Corps), he briefly headed the *Führerkanzlei* at a time when the cabinet office was handling such humdrum chores as answering Hitler's fan mail, sending flowers to his lady friends on their birthdays, and seeing to it that the office was never short of paper clips. For some reason, the brothers did not get along, a fact that was not conducive to the advancement of "little Bormann" in the Party.

It was rumored, nevertheless, that Albert had rushed to his brother's side in his plight in 1945, and assisted his escape, allegedly flying him to Spain in a private plane. Albert steadfastly denies this. With nothing in his record to incriminate him, he was quickly denazified after the war and allowed to vanish from the limelight, retiring to his modest apartment on Liliestrasse in the Bavarian capital. Although he still refuses to discuss his brother, he leaves the door slightly open when he says: "When the time is ripe I'll talk about him. But not just yet!"

Obviously Ricardo was not Albert, and consequently could not have been Martin's brother. This was exactly how Schwend planned it when he sent the man—who turned out to be a demented ex-Nazi named Richard Rolnik—to baffle the police at São Vicente and whip up still another storm of headlines.

In May of 1965 there was another flurry of excitement when it was reported that the Reichsleiter suddenly appeared in person—not in South America, where he was generally believed to be hiding, but in Gävle, of all places, a teeming port city on the Gulf of Bothnia in Swedish Norrland. This time, it seemed, there could be no mistake about it; the man *was* Bormann!

Traveling north from Stockholm and Uppsala, the German-speaking, stocky stranger had been *recognized* by three of his fellow passengers on the bus, then positively *identified* by an excited gentleman who claimed that he had known Bormann in Berlin and was sure that the man in the bus was he. When the bus stopped at Furuvik, a small place en route, the Gävle police were notified by telephone, and the general alarm was sounded.

When the bus rolled to a stop in Gävle, the terminal was a beehive swarming with heavily armed uniformed police, aided by a detachment of plainclothesmen rushed down from Boden and agents of the secret police rushed up from Stockholm. The man was taken to police headquarters, quizzed for hours, then handed over to the laboratory technicians who probed his identity with all the known gimmickry of criminal investigation.

Well, in Gävle they still insist that the man was Bormann, even though those fussy detectives and crank fingerprint experts from Stockholm failed to make the identification *positive*. Didn't the man look exactly like Bormann? Didn't he behave strangely—exactly as Bormann would act when cornered at last? Didn't he fail to give a satisfactory explanation for his presence in Norrland, and never mind that he couldn't speak a word of Swedish? Most important, did he not vanish mysteriously without a trace, not merely from Gävle, but from Sweden, when he was allowed to go to the Hotel Grand Central on the Nygatan while his case was being further investigated, pending the arrival of certain data requested from Frankfurt?

It was at this stage of the big hunt that Jochen von Lang, *Stern* magazine's dogged Bormann specialist, decided to join the fast game.

Chapter Twenty-Two

Intermezzo in Berlin

Do you promise that your Detectives shall well and truly detect the Crimes presented to them, using those Wits which it shall please you to bestow upon them, and not placing reliance upon, nor making use of, Divine Revelation, Feminine Intuition, Mumbo-Jumbo, Jiggery-Pokery, Coincidence or the Act of God?

—The membership oath of the Detection Club of London, according to Dorothy L. Sayers (in *The Mind of the Maker*)

While all this was going on, Martin Bormann was burrowing ever deeper into his peripatetic exile, a weary, wayworn fugitive. Then suddenly it seemed that the mystery would be solved once and for all, one way or another—either proven that Bormann was alive (on the testimony of two of his closest associates) or established that he was dead (with the full weight of forensic evidence).

In what promised to be the home stretch of the long drive, the authorities were taking a back seat. The great and powerful *Stern* magazine of Hamburg, which had a respectable record of scoops involving the Nazis, was on the verge of proving (1) that Bormann was alive, and (2) that he was dead. It all depended on which one of two exposés in the process of being prepared in utmost secrecy by two opposing factions within the magazine would make it first into print.

Nothing that had happened since 1960, when he first initiated the search, softened Bauer's conviction that Bormann was alive. His search, which neither Schwend's nebulous efforts nor incidents like the Gävle encounter could force off the scent, remained in high gear. His accumulation of documents in the Bormann file of his Section VI, the special bureau in his office in charge of the pursuit and prosecution of Nazi criminals, had numbered eight big binders holding 1,300 pages of legal-size sheets. By now, the archive swelled to eleven binders, these hectic eighteen months adding 486 pages of new material to Bauer's collection of Bormanniana.

Inspired by him, the federal government had issued an appeal on November 20, 1964, to people everywhere in the world to furnish any information they had about crimes committed during the Third Reich. Three days later, Bauer followed Bonn's widely broadcast appeal with the announcement that a reward of 100,000 German marks (then worth $25,000 but valued at $40,000 at the current rate of exchange) would be paid to anyone who apprehended Bormann or supplied information leading to his arrest.

As rewards go in Germany, this was a huge sum. Prosecutor Metzner explained that Bormann rated such a high price (by contrast to Mengele, who had only 60,000 marks on his head) because the fugitive Reichsleiter was "protected by powerful secret organizations that shielded former Nazi leaders and aided them in their efforts to evade detection."*

Now, however, it seemed that more respectable advocates of the thesis that Bauer was wrong because Bormann was dead would force the ardent prosecutor to reverse himself for the first time in five years. Instead of searching for the live Bormann, they compelled him to dig for his bones. The man who was responsible for this sensational turn of events was Jochen von Lang, the controversial and enigmatic *Stern* reporter. He was, like Bauer, obsessed with the Bormann case. But his preoccupation with the elusive mystery predated the great prosecutor's systematic search by years.

In the Bormann game, Jochen von Lang looms large. He is one of its big-time gamblers, somewhat like the resolute regulars at Monte Carlo who stake all they have on breaking the bank. A strange Savonarola type, not unlike our image of a medieval monk, he is intense, aggressive, abrasive, high-strung, pigheaded, a chain

* The reward was withdrawn by Bauer's successor in the fall of 1973, when an attempt was made by the Hessian authorities to close the Bormann case. Incidentally, the high value Dr. Bauer had put on the apprehension of Bormann may also be gauged by the fact that the reward which he persuaded the Hessian Ministry of Justice to appropriate amounted to more than twice the total sum the search for Bormann cost Hesse between 1961 and 1973.

smoker and a fast talker with a condescending air of calculated mystery—an interesting figure! He behaves like a man who has no time to lose; and to be sure, he lives with a chronic gastrointestinal ailment which has caused him to lose most of his stomach.

Jochen von Lang explains his total involvement in the Bormann search differently at different times to different people. Certain only is the fact that he was not only in Berlin in April 1945, but in the Führerbunker during the last days of Hitler. Beyond that his stories are variations on this theme. To me he said that he was serving with a platoon of Hitler Youths defending a block or two near the Adolf Hitler Platz, and had been sent to the bunker by the commanding officer of the boys to pick up a batch of Iron Crosses to decorate these young heroes.

To Charles Whiting he said that he had been in Berlin when Bormann made the breakout. "I was a young soldier badly wounded in the East and I had been attached to Goebbels' Propaganda Ministry."

He made it out of the bunker, apparently with them and, of course, with Bormann, who had attached himself to the group that Dr. Naumann led. Later, he said, when he turned to journalism and joined *Stern,* he became interested in what he called *die grossen Bonzen* ("the big bosses"), especially Bormann. He had celebrated his twentieth birthday by trying to escape from Berlin. Exactly twenty years later, in 1965, at the age of forty, he was the foremost advocate of the thesis that where he had succeeded Bormann had failed.

According to others, he was not attached to the Propaganda Ministry as he told Whiting, but was in the Führerbunker as an aide of Arthur Axmann, the one-armed Hitler Youth leader.

Axmann, of course, was the sole claimant of the famous version of Bormann's end in the vicinity of the Lehrter Station. He and Günther August Wilhelm Schwägermann, an SS Hauptsturmführer, who was adjutant to Goebbels and had just burned the bodies of his boss and his wife and children in the courtyard of the Führerbunker, escaped from the bazooka blast on the Weidendammer Bridge. Joined by Bormann, the trio continued groping their way out of beleaguered Berlin until they split up near the station, each to go on by himself. Both Schwägermann and Axmann escaped safely from Berlin.

In his deposition, given later to his American interrogators in southern Germany, Schwägermann confirmed that the Reichsleiter had survived the incident on the bridge, and was still alive when they parted on their different ways in the direction of Old Moabit. Axmann, however, had a better story to tell. On his wanderings, he testified, in the neighborhood of the station, the dark dawn illuminated by the fires of the burning city, he had seen the limp body of the Reichsleiter stretched out on the ground. He was not alone. The compact Bormann was lying on his back beside a giant of a man whom Axmann, himself a habitué of the Führerbunker, recognized as Dr. Ludwig Stumpfegger, one of Hitler's physicians.

It was Axmann's fascinating story that ignited Jochen von Lang's imagination. "What [had] bothered me," he said, "was that none of the official investigators undertook to find witnesses who knew something about the last spot where Bormann had been seen alive. I found Axmann living in Berlin, at 80 Imchen Allee, and called on him. 'I am no doctor,' he told me, 'so I couldn't tell whether the Reichsleiter was dead or alive. He *looked* dead to me, but I couldn't *swear* that he was *really* dead.' "

The record becomes blurred at this point. When he escaped from Berlin on May 2, 1945, Axmann made his way to the mountains in the south. There in the makeshift redoubt he assembled a little ragamuffin army from the stragglers of the Hitler Youth force which he had led in the eleventh hour to die for the Führer. The war was officially over, but not for Axmann. He was planning to wage a guerrilla war with these young people against the Americans in Upper Bavaria.

The senseless heroics of this rabid Nazi could not last. He was captured before the year was out, and he was taken to an American prison camp in the Taunus, where he was interrogated by an officer who, unfortunately, was not too familiar with the background of his important young prisoner.* At the same time, Professor Trevor-Roper, who was then serving as a major in British Intelligence and

* Baldur von Schirach, his predecessor at the head of the Hitler Youth, wrote this about Axmann's phenomenal rise in the Nazi hierarchy: "I was thirty-three years old. It was time to relinquish the leadership of the German youth to a younger man. 'I recommend Arthur Axmann,' I told Hitler. Six years my junior, Axmann was Senior Regional Leader and head of the Social Bureau in the office of the Reich Youth Leader. He had formed the first squad of Hitler Youth in Wedding in the heart of Red Berlin, when he was only fifteen years old. A soldier at the front since the outbreak of the war, he was quickly promoted to noncommissioned officer." On August 2, 1940, the twenty-seven-year-old noncom became Reich Youth leader of the Nazi Party and Youth Leader of Greater Germany.

unquestionably was the most knowledgeable among the investigators the Allies had in the field, was probing "the last days of Hitler" and the circumstances of his death.

As soon as he learned that Axmann had been captured, he asked the American authorities for permission to interrogate the former Reich Youth leader. But either by some simple snafu, or more probably due to the rampant jealousies that kept the various Allied investigators separated to the detriment of historical truth, the Americans withheld Axmann from Trevor-Roper. However, the astute young British historian managed to obtain a transcript of Axmann's interrogation. It left him with an open mind.

In his famous book, which he wrote in the wake of the war, he referred to the Axmann testimony somewhat ambiguously in a footnote. "The account of the death of Bormann," he mused, "rests on the evidence of Axmann only; but since Axmann's account (apart from accidental errors in time) has proved accurate in other particulars, it is probably correct here also unless he is deliberately lying to protect Bormann. After consideration of all other evidence on the subject, I have decided to accept his statement as being at least consistent with all available information, although the evidence of a single witness can never be final."

Axmann remained the single witness for eighteen years. Between 1946 and 1964, while the controversy about Bormann was gaining impetus with every passing year, he kept mum. It was only after Jochen von Lang approached him in Berlin that he became *the* key witness in the fermenting concoction of Bormann's alleged death. Prodded by his friend, he came out of seclusion. Introduced by Lang, and vouching for everything he said, Axmann repeated his old story on September 11, 1962, to Joachim Richter, a rising new star among the working prosecutors in Dr. Fritz Bauer's office.

But, while this line of intelligence was hardening in Frankfurt, Trevor-Roper was developing doubts about Axmann's veracity. Several of the statements he had made in 1946 were shown to be no mere lapses of memory but outright inaccuracies and pure fabrications in part, quite obviously calculated to mislead the naïve young C.I.C. officer.

In his 1971 deposition to Judge von Glasenapp, Trevor-Roper thus added a footnote to his 1947 footnote. "I heard," he told the judge, "that Axmann [later] . . . retracted his testimony. I do not rule out the possibility that he had made up the story in the first place to cover Bormann's tracks."

But Jochen von Lang, it seems, never had any such doubts or qualms. He accepted Axmann's story at face value. "It was then"—after he had interviewed the former Reich Youth leader, that is—"when I began to look for Bormann myself."

The Lehrter Station loomed up enormously in all Bormann stories after that. When Schwägermann last saw Bormann there, the Reichsleiter was alone and alive. When Axmann had a last glimpse of him at the same spot, he was with Stumpfegger and both men were presumed to be dead.

There never was any mystery about Dr. Stumpfegger's fate. A letter had come to light that harked back to August 14, 1945. It was written to Stumpfegger's wife, Gertrud, at a sanatorium in Hohenlychen, and signed by a man named Berndt, who identified himself as the postmaster at the Lehrter Station. It read as follows:

> On May 8 this year a soldier was found by employees of this post office on the railroad bridge crossing Invalidenstrasse. . . . A military pass in his pocket identified him as Ludwig Stumpfegger. Assuming that the dead man was your husband, I am conveying this sad news to you with the expression of my condolence.
>
> Your husband was buried, together with other dead soldiers, on the grounds of the Alpendorf in Berlin NW 40, at 63 Invalidenstrasse. I am enclosing herewith a number of photographs found on the deceased. His military pass was subsequently destroyed.

A copy of this remarkable letter made it into one of the thirty-odd folders of Bormann papers which are now gathering dust on the shelves of Prosecutor Joachim Richter in what was once Dr. Bauer's office in Frankfurt. Nothing in the files indicates that the tantalizing clue it contained was ever thoroughly investigated. Who was the mysterious Berndt? Why was he never contacted and asked to elaborate on his letter? How was it to be explained that he mentioned the obscure doctor, but said nothing about Bormann, who was allegedly lying beside him and was presumably buried with him in the common grave of a number of otherwise unknown soldiers?

Moreover, according to *Der Spiegel,* Dr. Stumpfegger's mortal remains were never missing. "In actual fact," the newsmagazine wrote in its issue of February 14, 1964, clarifying some of the contrived contradictions that kept stubbornly confusing this phase of

Bormann's postwar fate, "the corpse of Stumpfecker [*sic*] was later found. But of Bormann, who was said to have been lying at his side, there was no trace."*

Then all of a sudden, after twenty years of hibernation, a number of people materialized in Jochen von Lang's séance to end Axmann's long solitude as the single witness to Bormann's death in Berlin. On May 3, 1965, a man named Herbert Seidel told Lang that "on May 4 or 5, 1945," when he was a boy of fourteen foraging for food in the freight yard of the Lehrter Station with a friend, he too saw "two dead bodies" on the left side of the railroad bridge. There were so many corpses all over that they no longer bothered the boy. He could not say, of course, "whether one of the dead bodies [he saw] was that of Bormann," if only because he had never heard of the man before and did not know how he looked. But though young Seidel had his reservations, Jochen von Lang had none. For the first time in his arduous search, he found somebody who bore out Axmann!

Even before the appearance of Seidel, a Czech named Jaroslav Dedic, who said he was one of the legion of slave laborers in Germany in 1945, wrote a letter to the Prague newspaper *Zemedelske Noviny,* asserting that he had directed a burial squad in May that worked for the Russians to get rid of the thousands of corpses that littered the ruins of Berlin. One of the bodies his squad interred, he now claimed, was recognized as that of Martin Bormann. How the anonymous Bormann was known to these foreign workers when, as Seidel had put it, "he was totally unknown to the [German] public," Dedic did not explain. Moreover, he claimed that Bormann's body had been found at some distance from the Invalidenstrasse, where Axmann and Seidel had come upon it, and was then buried in a cemetery in what in the meantime had become East Berlin.

Although Bauer's broad and energetic investigation had failed to turn up any such interesting witnesses, Jochen von Lang's private inquiry managed to conjure up one after another. He also succeeded in unearthing another man, who also said he had buried Bormann, even as Dedic claimed he did, although on a different date, at a different site, in a different grave. However, in this case there was

* If *Der Spiegel* was right, and Dr. Stumpfegger's remains had been found before, it remains to be explained how was it possible to find his skeleton *again* on December 7, 1972, as announced by the Prosecutor General's office in Frankfurt after my series of Bormann articles had just appeared.

a direct connection between Postmaster Berndt's long-overlooked letter and the new witness.

He was Albert Krumnow, a seventy-one-year-old invalid, "a fast-talking typical Berliner," as he was described, and a man remarkable for the uncanny sharpness of his memory at his age. Krumnow put the finishing touches to the growing momentum of Jochen von Lang's case. He identified himself as one of the mailmen of the burial detail Postmaster Berndt had mentioned in his 1945 letter to Frau Stumpfegger; he and two of his colleagues—a certain Wagenpfuhl and a man named Loose—"had been ordered by the Russians to bury the bodies which piled up outside the post office in the Lehrter Station." Wagenpfuhl and Loose could not be found. But Krumnow described how Wagenpfuhl had buried Stumpfegger and he himself had interred the other fellow, whom they did not recognize, but who, he thought, in the light of tutored hindsight, must have been Reichsleiter Bormann.

For reasons which neither Krumnow nor Lang ever bothered to clear up, the mailman had made special arrangements to mark exactly the spot where these two extra bodies had been buried apart from the other dead. In anticipation, perhaps, that somebody would come to claim them, or simply with extraordinary prescience, Krumnow buried Bormann beneath a little grove of silver poplars that he chose as a landmark by which he would later recall the burial spot.

There the case—as well as Bormann—rested for the time being.

Phenomenal as far as it went, but his homework still not quite finished, Jochen von Lang was biding his time before he would publish his sensational account of Bormann's last hours in Berlin. Then, however, it became known on the German magazine grapevine that two "independent sources," both in possession of "apparently unimpeachable proof," were about to come out with the story that Bormann was alive.

A couple of the Reichsleiter's closest intimates, Freddy Schwend in Lima and Klaus Barbie (alias Altmann) in La Paz, who shared with him life in exile in South America and were privy to some of his best-guarded secrets, were ready to betray him. For an honorarium of only five thousand dollars they had made a deal with *Quick* magazine of Munich, *Stern*'s biggest competitor on the German newsstands, to sell Bormann's inside story. They could furnish what they promised would be incontrovertible proof that the Reichsleiter was alive and as well as a fast-living man of his age could be under his circumstances.

As was common to every deal in which Freddy Schwend was involved, the transaction was hitting one snag after another. *Quick* was made to wait for the big story. The delay was caused mainly by Altmann-Barbie, who got cold feet in the eleventh hour and put pressure on friend Schwend to renege on the deal. Schwend, however, left the door open. In fact, he reopened negotiations with *Quick*, divulging additional checkable data to whet the magazine's appetite still more, then demanding that the fee be raised to ten thousand dollars, of which five thousand would be payable in advance.

The pending deal with *Quick* became known to a syndicate in Lima through a journalist-entrepreneur who, at that time, was one of Schwend's handful of confidants. Himself on the Bormann trail since the early sixties, with much original information from other sources in addition to the rich data that he had swiped from Schwend, the man was all set to stab the backstabbers in the back and trick them out of their scoop by selling their story to *Stern* magazine.

Obviously he could not do it without exposing himself as a double-crosser to his friend Schwend. He picked, therefore, a go-between in Hamburg who was unaware of what was going on behind-the-scenes. This middleman was a reporter named Wolfgang Bethke. Fronting for the fellow from Lima, he sold the Bormann story to *Stern* with the bait that, by buying it, they would beat the competition out of the scoop of the century.

At *Stern*, Bethke approached Dr. Gerd Bucerius, one of the publisher-owners, and proposed a deal. Bucerius, duly impressed with Bethke's data, agreed to buy, paying $75,000 for the story. But at this time, two powerful factions at *Stern* were locked in a frenzied feud—editor-in-chief Henri Nannen in one camp, Dr. Bucerius in the other. Without taking his chief editor into his confidence, Bucerius had the articles prepared by Bethke. The whole great journalistic adventure was to become public only when the magazine went to press with the first installment of the series. It was planned that only then would even Nannen find out that the Bormann mystery had been solved at last with the information pilfered from Schwend and Altmann under the noses of *Quick*.

Apparently the lid was not on tightly enough. Dr. Bucerius' top-secret scheme became known, unavoidably, to at least two other executives at *Stern.* In May 1965—the moment of truth—his first article, typeset and laid out, was yanked from issue Number 19 of the magazine.

What appeared instead was the story engineered by Jochen von Lang and approved by editor Nannen. Arthur Axmann searched his memories and wrote up the story of his experience that May dawn in 1945, in an article called "My Flight with Bormann." This became the opening salvo in the magazine's five-year campaign to bury Bormann. Axmann's piece proved that the man was dead, in terms as positive as Bethke's aborted story would have been in confirming that he was alive.

The fierce backstairs fights between *Quick* and *Stern,* between Bethke and Lang, between Bucerius and Nannen, and, in the final analysis, between the Schwend-Altmann cabal and the unsuspecting Bormann had their fallout in the office of Dr. Bauer. While the State Attorney General was wrapped up in fighting his quixotic battle, a major change occurred behind the scenes in his office. The decisive role in the bout shifted subtly (in fact although, of course, not in name) from Bauer to one of his aides, the enigmatic Joachim Richter.

A stocky little, perennially ailing man who, in fact, somewhat resembled Bormann in appearance, Richter was not openly rebelling against Bauer. He had nothing personally against his brilliant and humanitarian chief; in fact, he respected and admired him. But he vehemently disagreed with Bauer's unshakable conviction that Bormann was alive.

His doubts took shape in the early sixties, when Jochen von Lang, looking for an ally inside Bauer's office, first began to share with Richter the "evidence" he was collecting. Prosecutor Richter was, in the phrase of a colleague, "a typical Hessian."

A veteran of World War II, in which he somehow served in the Signal Corps as an interceptor monitoring the enemy's radio traffic (although he does not speak a word of English), he was now the prototype of the German bureaucrat, plodding, orderly, sullen, overbearing, and totally lacking in originality and imagination. He was a humorless man, easy to please and easy to irritate.

In his attitude on the Bormann case, as in every act of his official duties, he was never influenced by any ulterior motives. His personal and official integrity was immaculate, as was his inherent attitude toward the Nazis—he loathed them as much as did Bauer.

There could be no question that he was totally straightforward in reaching his conclusion that Bormann was dead. And once he had taken a position, he was difficult to unhinge or influence, even with facts. As a result, Richter seemed short-tempered with witnesses who professed to know that the Reichsleiter had survived. If not actually pigeonholing such information, Richter was apparently unenthusiastic over checking out the data and following up these leads. By contrast, he adopted every scrap of evidence that tended to show that Bormann was dead. He, therefore, eagerly embraced Jochen von Lang, who in Richter's opinion had the incontrovertible proof to make it stick. This is important to bear in mind, for this reason—between 1965 and 1973 (when Richter succeeded in discarding the Bormann case) he was the chief investigator of the case, and since December 13, 1971, the only German official in charge of it.

Whether Dr. Bauer suspected his aide's subconscious defection or was aware of Richter's subtle deviation from his set course, I do not profess to know. Suddenly, however, in this critical year of 1965, he found himself squeezed between the two factions, with an assistant in his own fold who, while not actually betraying him, was leaning, to say the least, toward the position taken by the Axmann consortium. After the airing of the Axmann version by *Stern*, Bauer had no choice. He accepted Richter's advice and decided to track down the information Jochen von Lang was funneling into his office in abundance through Joachim Richter.

If dig he must, dig he would! Bauer instructed Wilhelm Metzner, his senior prosecutor, and, of course, Richter to arrange one of the strangest archaeological ventures since the Hungarians' frantic search for Attila's mysterious grave at the bottom of the Danube. There were some problems, to be sure, but they presented no insurmountable obstacles to Richter, who was following the straight party line proposed by his friend and "unofficial assistant investigator" Jochen von Lang.

For one thing, in 1961, the Berlin Wall had gone up, crossing the very area in which Bormann might have been buried. The area, today as in the past, is tidy, with none of the hustle and bustle of railroad neighborhoods, quietly industrial and commercial in transit to a lower-middle-class neighborhood to the west. It was nothing but a heap of rubble in May 1945, and though the debris of the battle had been cleared away long ago, nothing can remove the dull air and stifling boredom that usually settles on the district through which the Invalidenstrasse runs from east to west. Whenever I visited it in the course of my own search or merely seeking local color, I could not help thinking that this spot in Berlin was the least likely locale for a historic event to take place. In fact, the only building in the whole area of about one square kilometer that lends an aura of mystery to the place and makes it somehow live up to its fame is the gray field-stone building that houses the West Berlin morgue.

The Wall complicated things somewhat. If it was true that Bormann had been interred in the cemetery east of it, as Dedic claimed, the dig needed the approval of the East Berlin authorities. And they were exasperatingly slow to respond to Bauer's application, even as the government of East Germany almost ostentatiously refused to become involved in this Bormann business.

In the meantime, however, Bauer's emissaries could proceed with the excavation in the small segment of West Berlin where Axmann, Seidel and Krumnow showed Jochen von Lang Bormann's point of departure. On July 19, 1965, Metzner and Richter, accompanied by Jochen von Lang and with the mailman-gravedigger in tow, arrived in Invalidenstrasse to reconnoiter the spot which old Krumnow, shrouded in anonymity, pointed out as Bormann's ossuary. The first thing they did was, of course, to look for those old poplars, now exactly twenty years older than on that grim May day in 1945. But there was none in sight; in fact, only two trees were left in the entire area. Krumnow was adamant. He distinctly remembered that little grove beneath which he had dug the shallow grave, so Richter went over to the park commission of the West Berlin municipality to inquire whether any vegetation had been removed in the area since 1945.

Sure enough, the well-kept records showed that Krumnow was right, but the place had been denuded of trees in 1961 when the Wall went up overnight. A little research and some conjecture then pinpointed the spot where the three poplars growing so firmly in Krumnow's memory must have stood.

Next morning, the twentieth, a sultry summer day, the exhumers moved to the spot, Metzner formally dressed, with jacket and tie, but Richter stripped for action in just white pants and shirt open at the collar. A cigarette was never absent from his lips or yellow-stained fingers; he was tense and fidgety, for he sincerely expected that the dig would lay to rest the bones of this contention.

It was a spectacular procession led by a bulldozer, followed by a combat team of laborers with spades and pickaxes, then Metzner, Richter, a medical examiner, an archaeologist with experience in digging for mummies in Egypt, policemen, reporters, photographers and rubbernecks. The contingent of *Stern* was headed by Jochen von Lang, who, like a war lord on the eve of a decisive battle, commanded a bevy of reporters and a special crew of cameramen at the ready. A tremendous spread was kept open for next week's issue of *Stern*, whose management, now reunited in purpose, had agreed to put up most of the not inconsiderable expenses of the dig.

Where the poplars once supposedly stood, the bulldozer tore a crater into the ground; then the workers descended into the pit and carefully began their spadework. The whole day's sweat yielded absolutely nothing. The dig was suspended at sundown, to be resumed the next morning.

The dig in the Invalidenstrasse received only minor attention from the world press—*The New York Times*, for instance, allotted only an inch and a half to the story of its Berlin correspondent, under a one-column 8-point headline, "Bormann's Body Sought." The next day, the *Times* recorded the anticlimax in nineteen words: "A new attempt to unravel the mystery of what happened to Martin Bormann, a Hitler aide, apparently has failed."

Writing to his paper in London, Neal Acheson was dramatic and caustic:

> On the wasteland beside the railway arches on a rainy Berlin afternoon, a blue police bulldozer rolls slowly back and forth. It roars and groans, and after each little charge brings up another hundredweight of yellow Prussian sand. Six or seven policemen in overalls shelter from the rain under two trees and lean on shovels. They are looking for the bones of Martin Bormann.
>
> Nothing has been found. Under a layer of ash the sand seems firm and undisturbed.

Jochen von Lang was stunned and dismayed. It was not that he was discouraged. He tried to give the impression that he himself did not expect too much from this first excavation. "Even if the bones had been discovered," he wrote with apparent detachment, "it would have been exceedingly difficult to identify them as those of Martin Bormann"—wise words, which returned to haunt him seven years later. What bothered him now in this summer of discontent was that he had lost face at *Stern.*

He pleaded for another appropriation to pursue the search by renting his own bulldozer to dig up the whole yard. And he complained that Richter had to break off the dig against his better judgment, on orders from Dr. Bauer. But editor Nannen, who was burned badly by the costly failure and was deeply embarrassed, thus losing a round in his running feud with Gerd Bucerius, had enough. "The great *Stern* hunt," wrote Charles Whiting, "for the missing Reichsleiter fizzled out ignominiously. Lang's personal hunt for Martin Bormann, which had started so long ago in those desperate days in May, 1945, was over."

But Whiting badly underrated the guts Jochen von Lang had still left in his emaciated, tortured body.

Dr. Bauer left no stone unturned to examine the last vestiges of the Axmann-Lang epic of Bormann's postwar fate. Without the fanfare of the stillborn exhumation farce in the Invalidenstrasse, he arranged for similar excavations in East Berlin's adjacent area. He had all the cemeteries in the district combed for a grave in which Bormann might be hiding. Nothing was found there either.

Richter went along with Jochen von Lang that the digs proved nothing. But no setback in his line of action could make him waver in his obtuse belief that Bormann was dead. At the same time, the events in Berlin on both sides of the Wall restored Bauer's faith in his own conclusion that Bormann was alive.

On December 5, satisfied that the Axmann line was humbug, Bauer called a press conference to make public for the first time Horst Eichmann's deposition, more than four years after it had been made at his office before Prosecutor Wolf. Prosecutor Metzner was photographed displaying the document in which the young man swore that Bormann was alive. In another press conference, in the spring of 1966, Bauer reiterated in no uncertain terms that, according to the mass of reliable information his office had on file, Bormann did not die in Berlin. As long as his remains could not be produced, he would continue his relentless search.

After the press conference, Bauer lay low. Nothing really happened to shake his confidence, but things were not going his way in his own office as far as the prosecution of the Nazi criminals was concerned, and the Bormann case was not the only one whose proper pursuit left much to be desired. Informants who had seen Richter with tips and clues complained—several of them in print—that the low-echelon prosecutor was arrogating to himself the power of decision in the handling of the Bormann matter. People whose information did not fit the pattern of his own thinking were brusquely dismissed. Leads that went contrary to his foregone conclusion were left unchecked. He seemed increasingly irritated with anyone who dared to say that, after all, Bormann might be alive.

At the same time, his alliance with Jochen von Lang, who was working quietly on his comeback from the debacle at the Lehrter Station, was sealed. As an insider who, in 1969–1971, had an opportunity to examine Richter's files of the case told me, "It was obvious that Richter was coming to lean increasingly on Jochen von Lang's assistance, until he was adapting the investigation exclusively to the *Stern* reporter's line of argument."

He channeled the people produced by Jochen von Lang to Judge von Glasenapp, the investigative magistrate in the Bormann and Mengele cases, and he urged his colleague to confine his inquiry to the interrogation of these individuals, referred to as the only witnesses who knew what they were talking about. Herr von Glasenapp heeded the suggestion and questioned every one of Jochen von Lang's contacts. He found most of them nebulous sources, none contributing anything materially valuable toward the solution of the problem, several of them apparently bent on confusing the issue.

During this period of uncertainty and discouragement, Bauer's flagging spirit was sustained by the unstinting help he was receiving from his friend Simon Wiesenthal. It was he, then, who in 1967, by a *coup de main* of his own, provided for Bauer the last piece of evidence against Bormann that the great prosecutor received in his lifetime.

In 1966, the former Polish architect turned avenger zeroed in on an Eichmann-type fugitive who, however, appeared to be merely a minor functionary of the Final Solution. He was Franz Paul Stangl, an obscure former Austrian policeman, who had joined the SS and moved up in Himmler's world—but just how far up nobody seemed to know for sure. Even Gerhard Reitlinger and Raul Hilberg, the two greatest chroniclers of the mass murder of the Jews, and keepers of remarkably complete and accurate rosters of all the men —living or dead, present or missing, prominent or subordinate—who had been enmeshed in the extermination program, missed this man Stangl. Hilberg omitted him altogether. Reitlinger picked him up once in passing, referring to him but obliquely in a brief footnote.

Yet Stangl was for several years the commandant of the Treblinka extermination camp, second only in horrors to the Auschwitz-Birkenau death factories, and a runner-up to them in the number of people who perished in its gas chambers. He was indeed the paragon of the industrious but self-effacing functionary who craved neither recognition nor publicity. He managed so well to remain in the shadows that while SS guards at Treblinka who served under him gained gruesome notoriety in the courts and headlines, while minor officials were tried and sent to jail for the crimes they perpetrated in Stangl's camp, Stangl himself remained unknown, untouched and unwanted.

In actual fact, his crime was comparable to Eichmann's and, in a sense, worse—he was a mass murderer in deed, not behind a desk or on the telephone. Treblinka was the pilot plant of the camp complex. Under Stangl's management, the gas chambers and other instruments of extermination were tested there before they were introduced to the other camps.

Even so, Stangl succeeded in escaping attention, by an innate manner that made him so inconspicuous and his character so deceptive that he was, in fact, lauded by some surviving inmates of Treblinka as a sort of humanitarian who must have been unaware of the atrocities his underlings had been perpetrating behind his back. By the end of the war, Stangl had the good fortune of no longer being the boss of Treblinka. He had been removed in 1943, because he even fooled his superiors with his humility. Although tens of thousands of Jews perished in his camp, his chiefs, misled by his mild exterior and soft sell, thought that he was too gentle for the job. This reputation earned for him, by some perverse reciprocity, gentle treatment in the Austrian prison camp in which he was kept after the war, pending the determination of his case.

He was made a trusty over the other prisoners, assigned to supervise details of inmates working on a road. So quiet and inconspicuous was Stangl that nobody really missed him when he disappeared one day—not plotting an intricate prison break, not conspiring with rescue groups to pave his way to freedom, but simply nonchalantly strolling away along the road which his fellow inmates were then blacktopping.

He moved to the Middle East, then to Brazil, like a shadow disappearing when the sun fades behind a cloud. At no time during his comfortable, casual escape did he find it necessary to change his name, undergo plastic surgery, or conceal himself by any means. It was as Franz Paul Stangl that he entered Brazil, settled in São Paulo, and obtained a well-paying job at the huge Volkswagen factory.

There was only one man anywhere in the world Stangl could not fool—Simon Wiesenthal. A mirage is not easy to pin down and it is not a simple matter to build a dossier on a cipher. Yet, before long, Wiesenthal had a fat folder about Stangl—the sworn testimonies of discerning eyewitnesses, incriminating documents bearing his signature, and the whole record of his way of running Treblinka. Wiesenthal began his search for Stangl quietly. He was anxious not to alert Stangl, who, easygoing if not careless, was satisfied that his quiet way of life was his best mask of concealment.

As it was eventually resolved, the Stangl case was important for three main reasons. First, it became Wiesenthal's triumph, a masterpiece of detection, a feat of perseverance. Second, it was the last major incident involving a prime Nazi criminal in the final determination of which the Israeli Secret Service played a significant part. Thirdly, it was the only case of a Nazi criminal seeking a haven in Brazil that ended in the fugitive's extradition to West Germany.

Chapter Twenty-Three

The Message from Brasilia

One of the traps which aided in the ensnaring of Franz Paul Stangl after twenty years on the run was a manila folder filed at an obscure American agency called the Berlin Document Center. It is probably the most arcane and, in a sense, the most sinister and powerful institution the United States has anywhere. How many Americans know even that it exists? It is tucked away in a rustic oasis in Berlin, in the part of the city's beautiful green belt the natives call Krumme Lanke, or Crooked Meadow.

Today, in the heart of West Berlin's American Zone, three decades after the war, the Krumme Lanke is still an enchanting spot with its lovely lakes, winding trails, dense greenery, only a subway ride from the center of the mutilated city.

Located in a *cul de sac* off the beaten path, called Cockchafer Alley, near quiet residential streets, the Document Center is a fortress camouflaged as a picnic ground. There is a faint aura of James Bond hovering over the place. Aboveground the visitor sees a villa-like edifice that could be the sumptuous home of a rich man with exquisite taste and a penchant for the good life. But the elegance of the mansion and the charm of the grounds are deceptive, as is everything that is visible to the naked eye at this strange site shrouded, it seems, in deliberate mystery.

Underground meander long corridors built of extra-thick, imperishable concrete, a maze of bending and twisting catacombs. During the Nazi regime, Marshal Göring kept his huge listening post manned by a small army of multilingual eavesdroppers in these casements. They monitored all the telephone talks at will, bugged inner sanctums, pierced the secrets of the diplomatic corps, cracked codes, compromised ciphers, and shattered the last vestiges of privacy in the Third Reich.

The Americans took over the place in 1945 and left it exactly as it was when Göring's snoopers occupied it. Soldiers with automatic rifles are still in the big sentry box at the barred gate topped with sharp spikes that opens into the electrically charged wire encircling the whole enclave. Entry is by special pass, which is difficult to obtain. Germans are not supposed to have access to the vast collection of rare items the Center houses, except via written applications, which may or may not be granted.

Down in those catacombs are the files of Martin Bormann—the complete archives of the Nazi Party which American troops captured intact in the spring of 1945. It is the inescapable, unerasable and embarrassing record of forty-four million Germans—a weird registry of some dead and the ominous roster of the living.

The Center is like the sword of Damocles hanging over these millions of Germans, the ultimate data bank about their checkered political past. A prominent German politician, who was a brave member of the anti-Nazi resistance movement and has nothing to fear from this collection, sincerely believes that the time has come to liquidate this frightful institution.

"The Berlin Document Center," he told me earnestly, "is the fundamental source of American power over Germany, something that is tantamount to the biggest subtle blackmail in history. Most of us have skeletons in our political closets, even if what still rattles is merely our often compulsory membership in the Party or one of its harmless branches like the Hitler Youth or the Federation of German Maidens. By holding these old files as a threat, somewhat in the aggressive manner of a lion tamer brandishing his forked iron rod, the Americans keep us in line and bend our politicians to their will. From the Berlin Document Center there is no place to hide."

The Americans use the Center wisely and with admirable discretion. When it was found that a senior minister of the cabinet, the coming man of the Free Democratic Party, who aimed at the number-two place in the Brandt administration, had a slim file in the Center recording his membership in the Party, the Americans, who know that the man was but a marginal Nazi and is today one of the sturdiest pillars of democracy in West Germany, quietly suppressed the file.

The Center is kept firmly in American hands. Its immense importance to the tranquillity of the world in the face of the drastic realignment of power is reflected in the fact that so many of the guilty of the Hitler era went unpunished. For every Nazi criminal who is known, a hundred remain shrouded in obscurity. For every Nazi criminal indicted, scores have been "overlooked."

Many of those who have thus been deliberately reprieved or unwittingly glossed over occupied some of the highest positions in postwar Germany, both West and East. A brilliant jurist who helped draft Hitler's lethal anti-Jewish laws survived his shame with his head held high to become one of West Germany's top-ranking civil servants. The man who presided over the vicious black propaganda of the Nazi "enlightenment" program, slandering and smearing the British and the Americans with endless electronic abuse, rose steadily in the politics of postwar Germany—in spite of his bulging folder at the Berlin Document Center.

Even one of the Federal Presidents had a "record." I do not know what the Center's files contained about Heinrich Lübke, charged during his presidency with the fact that he had worked in an architectural firm that designed the extermination camps and their gas chambers. But I know that when President Lübke was on a state visit in Argentina, the Coordinación Federal secretely arranged a clandestine meeting for him with one of the Nazi fugitives in Buenos Aires. Lübke needed the man as a character witness, to take him off the hook.

Even in the gallery of the famous and powerful, of statesmen, politicians and scarlet-striped generals, Franz Paul Stangl was not a minor figure. This little man, as he was wont to call himself, loomed enormously in the background of the holocaust as the commandant of the pilot plant in whose furnaces hundreds of thousands of Hitler's victims were turned into ashes. He was a monster like Eichmann and, for a while after the war, was saved by Eichmann. For years, Stangl was one of the beneficiaries of Eichmann's greatest contribution to the cause of Nazism in the postwar world, for it was Eichmann who drew most of the reprobation upon himself and thus averted attention from the "small fry" like Stangl, the men Simon Wiesenthal called "the murderers among us."

If anything, the Stangl case shows how a man charged with complicity in the murder of thousands could slip out of the noose and remain at large for twenty years, without ever bothering to change his name or do anything drastic to cover up his past, except to leave Germany at the right moment and move to Brazil. And his case goes far to demonstrate how helpless, powerless and spineless even decent and great nations can be when it is a matter of smashing and shattering the Fourth Reich in its foundations by gathering in the criminal remnants of the Nazi regime.

Franz Stangl had the dubious distinction of having been one of the two Nazi criminals, all told, who were retrieved from South America, and the only one extradited by Brazil. Even that was a fluke. It took three years just to prepare his case—altogether a quarter century to bring to trial one of the worst mass murderers in all history.

Here is the Stangl case in a nutshell as summarized by a German court on May 3, 1970, the day his trial opened before Presiding Judge Heinz Meven of the assizes at Düsseldorf, the great Alfred Spiess heading the prosecution, assisted by Josef Gnichwitz:

> In the criminal case against the *mechanic Franz Stangl* of São Paulo, Brazil.
>
> The accused Stangl was born March 26, 1908, in Altmünster, Austria, is married, and has never been convicted.
>
> Stangl was extradited by Brazil in this matter and has been lodged since his arrival in Germany on June 23, 1967, as a prisoner in remand, by virtue of the extradition warrant issued at the request of Examining Magistrate I by the Land Court of Düsseldorf, on March 17, 1967, Judge Dr. Erwin Hammes.
>
> The accused is charged with the murder by base motives, in a gruesome manner with malice aforethought, partly in complicity with others, of at least 400,000 persons at Treblinka, Poland, during the period beginning in August 1942 and ending in August 1943.

The enumeration of the charges and the manners of murder went on for ten pages. The only extenuation the court could find for Stangl was that he appeared to have been responsible for the death of "only" 400,000 persons out of 700,000 men, women and children exterminated at the Treblinka and Sobibor death camps during his tenure as commandant. Even the fact that 300,000 dead Jews were not charged to his account meant little in lightening his burden. Stangl had been transferred out of Treblinka in August 1943. By that time, well over half of all the Jews who perished in his camp were dead. This phenomenal record earned for Stangl the honorific of "Best Camp Commandant in Poland," and the War Merit Cross First Class with Swords, from his grateful government. He was promoted to Hauptsturmfürer (captain).

Yet it took twenty-five years to get him into court, and then only through a rare combination of circumstances that favored the hunters. In the end, however, it was a smart little behind-the-scenes plot, engineered by two irate young Jews in Rio, that *forced* the Brazilian government to extradite the man.

The chances are that fate would have allowed Hauptsturmführer Stangl to live out his natural life in middle-class comfort, a free man in Brazil, had it not been for Simon Wiesenthal. "For nearly sixteen years," he once wrote, "I had thought of Eichmann every day and night." Stangl preoccupied him for just as long, a remarkable proof of his perseverance and foresight. Eichmann was a name of infamy known all over the world. But who ever heard of the former Austrian cop who became one of the virtuosos of genocide?

Stangl understood better than most of his fellow Nazis in a similar predicament how to remain a minnow among the whales. In Reitlinger's classic account, a flamboyant sadist named Hirtreiter, a mere corporal at Treblinka, was given greater prominence than his boss Stangl. The poker-faced, callous killer was not considered important enough to rate even passing mention in the famous roster of 219 Nazis—from "Abetz" to "Zörner"—who "played responsible parts in the Final Solution, either on the administrative or on the executive side." Raul Hilberg passed him up altogether in *The Destruction of the European Jews*, the other definitive encyclopedia of these criminals.

Stangl was a past master of the incognito. Moreover, for years after his casual departure from the prison camp in Austria, nobody was looking for him in earnest, neither in Damascus, where he hid from 1948 to 1951, nor in São Paulo, which became his home town for a decade and a half afterward. His native Austria had two of the finest anti-Nazi diplomats stationed in Brazil—Chargé d'Affaires Ernst Illsinger in Rio and Brasilia, and Consul General Erwin Reiner von Harbach, a formidable "avenger" in his own right, at

Curitiba, capital of the State of Paraná, which was swarming with escaped Nazis. But neither of them had even an inkling that their infamous compatriot was in the country, in spite of the fact that Stangl, an Austrian citizen, had been sought as a fugitive since 1947 and had been on the Austrian government's most-wanted war-criminal list since 1962.

Thanks to his consummate skill at being inconspicuous, Stangl's long career in exile was mostly humdrum—a safe job at the Volkswagen plant; a pleasant home in Brooklyn, the quiet residential suburb of São Paulo; snug domesticity with his wife, four daughters, Brazilian son-in-law and little grandson; congenial friends to drink wine with and play cards with on Sundays—the good life. It was only the final phase of his stint as a fugitive that had high drama, and even the flurry of excitement was brief. After living quietly in Brazil for sixteen years, Franz Paul Stangl was exposed, arrested and extradited in 1967, all of that in just three months, three weeks and five days. It was by far the fastest disposition of such a case in all the history of Brazilian jurisprudence.

His fall was sudden, but it had been years in the making. He had a single enemy, a cousin-in-law who disliked him, and she was not a person to be dismissed lightly. On February 21, 1964, impressed by an interview Wiesenthal had given about his interest in the missing Nazis, she called and told him that if he happened to be looking for the Stangls, they were in Brazil. The morning after, by the strangest coincidence, a former Gestapo man approached Wiesenthal with a business proposition. For seven thousand dollars, he said, he would reveal to him where Franz Stangl lived and what he was doing for a living. Wiesenthal promised to pay when and if Stangl "was brought to justice." The Gestapo man took his word and told Wiesenthal that Stangl was working at the VW plant in São Paulo as a chief mechanic on the assembly line and was living nearby with his family.

For three years afterward, Wiesenthal, biding his time, collected whatever information he could get about Stangl, until he had filled two big dossiers about the unsuspecting fugitive. He knew from previous experience that no amount of prodding would move the Austrian bureaucrats and that his chances of catching Stangl with the help of the Brazilian police were dim. Then, however, a turn in Brazilian politics changed his prospects overnight. Wiesenthal was alerted by a friend in Rio that he could now bring about

Stangl's arrest, and probably even his extradition, if he acted with extra dispatch.

In early 1967, a change occurred in the State of São Paulo, and a new governor was voted into office. Roberto Abreu Sodré was a political maverick, an ardent liberal, a proven anti-Nazi, and a close friend of the Klabin clan, one of Brazil's most powerful Jewish families. The chief of the new governor's cabinet was Oscar Segal, a Klabin on his mother's side. This was the opportunity Wiesenthal had been waiting for. He shipped his Stangl dossiers to a go-between in Rio, a distinguished scholar, who was one of Governor Sodré's best friends.

Wiesenthal's plot came to a head on Monday, February 27, on the occasion of an official visit of Governor Sodré in Rio de Janeiro. The dossiers were already in Senhor Segal's hands. Then, at a session in one of Segal's residences on Rua Alemha, the professor was given an opportunity to present them to Governor Sodré. A humanitarian in the great Brazilian tradition, Sodré was appalled to find that a murderer like Stangl could find a haven in his state. Unorthodox in his methods, sincere in his convictions, firm in his principles, the governor was unmindful of the generally negative attitude of the federal government of right-wing generals to such matters with delicate international ramifications. He decided to strike at once on his own.

Once the decision was made, things moved rapidly. Governor Sodré personally telephoned the chief of police in São Paulo and ordered him, with all the authority at his command, to arrest *Paul* Stangl, as the man was registered with the authorities, using his middle instead of his first name.*

On February 28, Tuesday afternoon, policemen in mufti and

* What was part of Israel's last known involvement in the "capture" of a Nazi fugitive was described for me by Zevi Ghivelder, editorial director of *Manchete* magazine of Rio de Janeiro (who was also kind enough to check this account of the Stangl case for the accuracy of the facts as presented). "On the eve of Stangl's arrest," Senhor Ghivelder wrote, "I happened to be in São Paulo. A member of the Israeli diplomatic mission, a good friend of mine, visited me at my hotel, but refused to discuss the purpose of his errand *huis-clos*. As we then walked the streets of the city, he told me about the Stangl dossier which Governor Sodré had, but was apprehensive that the governor might not issue the order to arrest the man. 'If you don't hear from me by tomorrow noon,' he told me, 'then everything will be okay. Otherwise, I'll send you the material against Stangl and you'll have to see to it that it gets printed in the major newspapers of Brazil, because we hope that the publicity in the press and the pressure of public opinion will force the governor to act.' " Zevi was never called. "Two days later," he wrote, "I read in the papers that Sodré had acted on his own. Stangl had been arrested."

agents of DOPS (Department of Political and Social Order, actually Brazil's secret police patterned on the F.B.I.) discreetly surrounded the house in Brooklyn, waiting for Stangl. He was working overtime, and so it was late in the evening when he came home. He never had a chance even to bid farewell to his family. The policemen intercepted him as he was climbing out of his red Volkswagen and took him away "on a warrant," as it was put in the communiqué of his arrest, "issued at the request of the Austrian embassy."

The sudden involvement of the Austrians was the result of Wiesenthal's last-minute intervention, in a shrewd move to cover Governor Sodré. Obviously not even the governor could order the arrest of the worst war criminal solely on the strength of the evidence contained in the dossiers of a private party, even if the investigator happened to be Wiesenthal. The governor could act only if formally requested by the government of the country whose national Stangl was.

Word was flashed to Wiesenthal advising him of this hitch, and he acted promptly. Responsible as he had been for the inclusion of Stangl in the 1962 Austrian list of wanted war criminals, he now prevailed upon the Foreign Minister in Vienna to instruct the Austrian envoy in Rio by cable to demand that Stangl be arrested and extradited. The baffled diplomat did as he was told, and Stangl was duly taken into custody. But when Herr Illsinger was asked how the Austrian authorities had found out about Stangl in São Paulo, he said with *gemütlich* candor: "I don't have the faintest idea. All I know is that I received that cable from Vienna."

Governor Sodré was more explicit and, indeed, eloquent when making his official announcement of Stangl's capture. "The mass murderer Franz Paul Stangl," he said in a nocturnal press conference on March 1, "who made martyrs of the Austrian people and is responsible for the death of 700,000 Jews, had been detained by DOPS and transferred to federal authorities in the process of extradition." Senhor Sodré praised the police for "scoring a goal in apprehending one of the major war criminals still at large," ranking Stangl just behind Martin Bormann and Heinrich Müller on the list of the most-wanted Nazi fugitives.

Conceding only that his wartime job was merely to register the inmates at what he called "detention camps in Poland," Stangl protested indignantly and denied categorically any complicity in Nazi atrocities. So convincing was his protestation of innocence that the management of Volkswagen do Brasil, refusing to believe that this robotlike little mechanic could have been the commandant of a murder camp where hundreds of thousands of people perished, commissioned two of its lawyers to represent Stangl and see to it that he would be released forthwith. But the VW executives were quickly disabused. As soon as Governor Sodré acquainted them with the facts of the case, they hastily withdrew their legal aid and abandoned this ex-employee to his fate.*

Stangl was held incommunicado in São Paulo until the afternoon of March 2, when he was flown secretly by DOPS to Brasilia. He had become a federal case, and that meant trouble all around. For one thing Austria had no extradition treaty with Brazil. Under the international principle of reciprocity, however, it was possible to obtain Stangl's extradition by applying to the Brazilian Supreme Court within sixty days of the man's arrest. Unfortunately for the Austrians, they did not know much about Stangl's activities during the war beyond what Wiesenthal had in his dossiers, and that was not the kind of evidence which prosecutors used and judges needed to convict him.

The situation was improved somewhat when a quick appeal to the Berlin Document Center produced Stangl's fat dossier, containing his complete record in both the Nazi party and the SS. In the meantime, even without this evidence, the Stangl affair had become a *cause célèbre*, second only to Eichmann's case, almost exactly seven years after the historic kidnaping in Buenos Aires. The man nobody "wanted" even a few days before suddenly blossomed out as the most-coveted criminal in the world. In addition to Austria, Germany came forward; on March 17, 1967, the Land Court in Düsseldorf also applied for Stangl's extradition. Although the Germans had all the evidence needed on file at the Ludwigsburg center investigating Nazi crimes, the application submitted by the German embassy was so weak, so weasel-worded and so vague that, it seemed, the Supreme Court would have no choice but to let Stangl off the hook—for lack of evidence.

At this point, a third suitor, so to speak, suddenly appeared to

* The bulk of the evidence and the most damning charges against Stangl were contained in a book, *Hell in Sobibor*, published by Bloch Editores of Rio de Janeiro in 1966. It was written by Stanislaw Smazjner, a survivor of the Sobibor camp living in the State of Goias in Brazil. Later, Senhor Smazjner was a witness for the prosecution at Stangl's trial in Düsseldorf. In a surprising move, he offered a copy of his book to Stangl, who accepted it in the dock.

claim the prisoner. Since Stangl's crimes had been perpetrated on their soil, the Poles demanded that he be delivered into their hands. If the Austrians had no conclusive evidence, and if the Germans were, as it seemed, reluctant to produce what they had, the Poles were prepared to pour out all the frightful facts and figures about Stangl's reign of terror, not only at Treblinka, but also at the death camps of Sobibor and Belzec.

The case became extremely complicated. The Austrians began to regret that they had heeded Wiesenthal in the first place and stirred up this hornet's nest. The Germans seemed concerned that the trial of Stangl in Germany might revive ghastly memories which would better be left forgotten.

The Brazilian government itself was getting ever deeper into its own quandary. In the light of the developments, Governor Sobré's great humanitarian act now seemed to have been impetuous, threatening to embarrass the federal authorities.

Matters became further complicated by the arrival of a three-man delegation of jurists coming from Warsaw to pick up Stangl and take him with them to Poland. This high-powered team consisted of Prosecutor General Franciszek Rafalowski of Poland and Senior Prosecutors Ryshard Fijalkowski and Czeslov Limont. The evidence they brought with them, ready to submit to the Supreme Court, was overwhelming. By this time, the Austrians had retreated, satisfied to watch the match between the Poles and the Germans, with Stangl as the prize.

The sincerity of the judicial authorities of Düsseldorf, with Prosecutor General Alfred Spiess in the background, was beyond the shadow of doubt. But other forces seemed to be at work, trying to keep Stangl out of Spiess's hands. There was a sinister plan, hatched by certain elements among the remnants of the Nazi colony in Brazil, to silence Stangl by killing him in prison, then make the murder appear as a suicide. The man knew too much. He was familiar with the escape organizations which, in fact, had paved his way to Syria and Brazil. And he had firsthand knowledge that two of the major war criminals—Bormann and Müller—were in South America. Nothing would be left undone to prevent Stangl from getting into the hands of the enemy!

This, of course, was a desperate plot, unlikely to succeed. Stangl was heavily guarded at a secret place on the outskirts of Brasilia, and the federal authorities were doing everything they could to preserve the man for his fate. It was obviously not in the interest of Germany, the Brazilians thought, that Stangl should be extradited to Poland. Anything he would say in Polish hands would be grist for the mills of Communist propaganda.

In response to a confidential invitation from the Brazilian Ministry, a third German motion was presented. But now another hitch developed. The decision of the Supreme Court to extradite Stangl, made on June 7, had two strings attached: (1) the court that would try Stangl would have to stipulate the exact time he would have to serve instead of sentencing him to life imprisonment; and (2) after the completion of his term of imprisonment, Stangl was to be handed over to the Austrians, to be tried there for his complicity in the "mercy killing" of so-called patients at the Hartheim euthanasia institute.

These provisions could be interpreted as loopholes through which the Germans could, if they wished, extricate themselves; or as conditions unacceptable to the Poles without agreeing to an impingement of their sovereignty. It seemed to some that Stangl would escape retribution after all, when the governments that professed to be interested in him would reject the conditions of his extradition.

The Germans in particular appeared to be reluctant to agree to any restrictions placed on their jurisdiction or to having the terms of Stangl's conviction foisted upon them. Such a course—regarded as intolerable and unacceptable—would involve a commutation of the sentence by the Minister President of the State of North Rhine-Westphalia. The attitude of the Poles no longer mattered. The Supreme Court had ruled that Stangl was to be given back to Germany.

Still another party entered the controversy, in what, I believe, was the last provable intervention of the State of Israel in the fate of a Nazi criminal abroad. Whether or not he had the formal authority from his Foreign Ministry in Jerusalem, a counselor of the Israeli embassy in Rio de Janeiro, thought up a scheme to spread the rumor (nothing more, as he planned it) that Israeli commandos had arrived in Brazil and were standing by to abduct Stangl to Israel—unless, of course, his extradition was carried out promptly. Israel would not care whether he would be taken either to Germany or to Poland. This was June 15, exactly a week after the Supreme Court had handed down its decision with the loopholes.

The week had passed without any word from Germany. But

now on the sixteenth, the morning after, the German embassy received a top-priority cable from the Foreign Ministry in Bonn, advising the ambassador that the Minister President of North Rhine-Westphalia was pleased to accept the terms of Stangl's extradition, and that a detail of criminal inspectors was leaving Düsseldorf to collect the man.

On June 22, Stangl was handed over to the German detectives, and he was flown out of Brazil the next day. His trial, three years later, produced the inevitable life sentence. But before it could be commuted or Stangl could be forwarded to Austria, he died in prison, at the age of sixty.

A few weeks after Stangl's arrest, when the first fragments of his interrogation in Brasilia began leaking out, Simon Wiesenthal announced: "*Bormann ist doch am Leben* [Bormann is alive after all]." The papers picked up the statement from the wires of United Press International. It rated a five-line item in *Der Tagesspiegel* of Berlin, one of Germany's great dailies, under a little headline that ended in a question mark.

There was, of course, a cryptic connection between Stangl's capture and Wiesenthal's retread announcement. For Stangl had confirmed, from inside one of the best-informed Nazi groups in South America, that Bormann was "one of us," a fugitive like Eichmann and himself. The fact that Stangl was caught did not weaken the case that Bormann was at large. Stangl's fate was the exception. Bormann's ability to evade detection was the rule.

Wiesenthal had thought of Eichmann every day and night for sixteen years, as he once put it, and so did Tuvia Friedman in Haifa, Dr. Rückerl in Ludwigsburg, the assiduous scholars of the Yad Vashem in Jerusalem, the chiefs of the Israeli Secret Service, and Premier Ben-Gurion. But nobody else did. In the end, only these little men—as Eichmann and Stangl referred to themselves—got caught. They had no money and none of the means a fugitive needed to elude his pursuer. But even without an organization, without powerful protectors including chiefs of states, Eichmann still managed to endure in exile for fourteen years. It needed nineteen years to recapture Stangl.

Finding Stangl and patiently plotting his unmasking was the crowning achievement of Simon Wiesenthal. But bringing him to justice in Germany was a comparable coup, and the credit for that belonged entirely to Alfred Spiess. As chief prosecutor in Düsseldorf, to whom Franz Stangl was eventually consigned, Spiess was second only to Fritz Bauer and was perhaps his equal in zeal and skill when it came to the pursuit of Nazi criminals. Among his triumphs, the case of Franz Paul Stangl looms largest.

In all his life, Stangl shrouded himself in obscurity. In his death, "the murderer of at least 400,000 Jews" is completely forgotten. Unlike Eichmann's, in the District Court of Jerusalem, Stangl's in the assizes in Düsseldorf was not a show trial. It had no glass booth, no hidden microphones, no spotlights, no mob of journalists with such extra-special correspondents as Trevor-Roper, Telford Taylor and Hannah Arendt among them. The trial was the orderly culmination of an unspectacular chase.

And yet, I think, the conclusion of the Stangl case in that German court of Judge Meven was as significant and historic as was the drama of Eichmann's end. If another symbol was needed—for the symbolism of the Eichmann trial was unmistakable—the Stangl trial provided it. It was the second trial in Germany's own campaign of retribution, coming five years after the conclusion of Fritz Bauer's trial of the Auschwitz murderers. In both cases, it was not an alien court bringing a stranger to justice. It was Germans judging their own kin, confronting the shame of their own recent past. This was no retribution. It was expiation, something akin to exorcism.

But it was too much. To be sure, of about two thousand SS men posted at Auschwitz, only twenty-two had been chosen and charged with murder. Even *that* was too much. Hannah Arendt spoke of the monstrous deeds and grotesquely unrepentant, aggressive behavior of the defendants. And in his masterly report of the trial, Bernd Naumann of the *Frankfurter Allgemeine Zeitung* wrote, "For twenty months, a search for truth was conducted in the longest jury trial in German legal history. Neither the judges nor the jury found the truth—at any event, not the whole truth." The trial and the sentences were not expressions of the will to redress a historic guilt or teach a moral lesson. "They were not meant," Naumann wrote, "to map out the road that a cleansed people should henceforth take."

The chief judge cautioned the jury that it had not been chosen to sit in judgment over Germany's past. It was charged solely with establishing guilt, not with any regard or concern for morality, but strictly within the framework of the penal code. The purpose was to let justice triumph over the injustice of Auschwitz. It nearly broke Bauer's heart. One of his aides wryly told Dr. Arendt, "The majority of the German people do not want to conduct any more trials against Nazi criminals."*

Bauer's last overt act of intervention in the Bormann matter occurred on July 4, 1967, exactly eleven days after Stangl had arrived in Germany. A spokesman of the Supreme Court announced in Brasilia that the court had received a request from West Germany "for the preventive arrest and extradition of Hitler's former deputy, Martin Bormann." Observers in Brazil and elsewhere viewed this as "an indication that the West German authorities still believed the Nazi war criminal might be alive." The request was forwarded by the German embassy to the Brazilian Ministry of Justice, which also had an arrest and extradition request, as it was called, involving Josef Mengele which had been submitted a year before.†

Behind the communication to the Brazilians was Fritz Bauer, "the key figure," as the Reuters correspondent in Bonn described him, "in the hunt for Martin Bormann." When asked in Frankfurt what had prompted him to stir up the dead Bormann issue with his new request, Dr. Bauer shrugged off the inquiry. "Oh," he said, "it's merely routine, rather a reminder. We're lodging permanent requests for the arrest and extradition of Bormann, as well as other Nazi criminals, with almost all Latin-American countries." He was anxious to leave it at that. But when he was asked whether he still believed that Bormann was alive, he wrinkled his brow, squinted his eyes, and said in an almost indignant tone, "But of course, I do."

Bauer and Spiess were close professionally, their common interest in the Nazi criminals having forged a bond of friendship between them. It was natural for Spiess to alert Bauer to Stangl's coming, and to give him an opportunity to interrogate him about Bormann and Mengele. Stangl knew nothing about Mengele—except, he said, what he had read in the newspapers. But Bormann? Yes. He was around—always on the move, difficult to pin down, the big

* A little while later, another Auschwitz trial was held with a small handful of other defendants, but it was so poorly publicized and covered that it took Dr. Arendt some research to determine whether it was held at all. Even as I was writing this, in the spring of 1974, still another Auschwitz trial–of two defendants–was held in Frankfurt.

† At that time, the German request was accompanied by a sworn statement averring that Mengele was living on a small island in the Piquiri River near Cascavel in Paraná. But the Paraná state police said that they were unable to find him.

shot who no longer cared to keep in touch. Stangl was positive. Although he himself had never met Bormann, he knew others who had "bumped into him"—at Jimmy's in Copacabana, in Mato Grosso off the beaten path, once even in São Paulo.

This was the message from Brasilia.

Perhaps it had come too late. Perhaps it was too vague. Perhaps it added nothing to what was on file, except, perhaps, to bolster Bauer's belief in the face of all the skepticism around him.

If, aside from sending that "routine request" to Brazil, he acted upon Stangl's bit of spare evidence, it was a secret he was to take to the grave.

Chapter Twenty-Four

Contours of a Third World

In the summer of 1973, a German-American journal called *Die Brücke* (*The Bridge*), published by an organization called Friends of Germany, reacted to the extradition of Hermina Braunsteiner, the brutal Ravensbrück death-camp guard (who had made it to Maspeth, in New York City, by marrying a G.I. named Ryan), with righteous indignation. Not a word that she was sent back to Germany at the request of Chief Prosecutor Spiess to stand trial on a charge of murder.

> They say [*Die Brücke* wrote] that Mrs. Ryan forgot to mention on her citizenship application form that she once had been a camp official (had she really?), and THAT is undoubtedly a capital offense worthy of extradition and glasscage treatment, for our BUREAUCRACY is holy!
>
> This case serves to remind us to be most punctilious when filling out questionnaires. If you make a mistake, who knows? YOU TOO might end up in Poland.

In the same issue (which also campaigned to have Rudolf Hess released from Spandau), President Wilfried A. Kernbach, of Chicago, proudly announced that Alexi Erlanger of the Buffalo Chapter was heading a drive to bring two "famous German war heroes to the U.S.A. for a visit of our military institutions and our German community." One of the invited guests was Colonel Hans Ulrich Rudel. The other was Colonel Otto Skorzeny.

Germans elsewhere in the Hemisphere would come and go regularly, as long as their health permitted their personal management of the Kameradenwerk. If an "American" paper could rebel against the extradition of "the Long Island housewife," it should not be surprising that the Nazis throughout South America reacted violently, first, to the abduction of Eichmann, and then to the extradition of Stangl.

Already in 1959, they thought the time was propitious to reassert themselves. They crawled out of the woodwork, tentatively beginning the offensive early in the year, when a self-styled stormtrooper painted a huge swastika on a building in Düsseldorf, and the pitiful remnants of Germany's once thriving Jewish community in various localities were assaulted in the streets.

The campaign went into high gear in December, apparently in answer to an announcement on the fifth that West Germany was preparing twenty major trials of Nazi criminals. On the twenty-fifth, two thugs named Strunk and Schönen, allegedly belonging to Wilhelm Meinberg's neo-Nazi German Reich Party, smeared swastikas and anti-Jewish slogans on the Cologne synagogue, which Chancellor Konrad Adenauer had dedicated only a few months before. Others defaced a nearby memorial to the victims of Nazism.

The offensive quickly spread to other parts of Germany. Frightened old Jews were attacked near Frankfurt, Jewish cemeteries were vandalized in several places, and the swastika appeared triumphantly on walls throughout the Federal Republic. By the time the crisis came to a head with the kidnaping of Eichmann, a dozen neo-Nazi groups could be identified, going by defiant names like "Action Resistance" and "Viking." Their members greeted one another with a revised version of the Hitler salute, the three fingers of the right hand forming a *W* for *Widerstand,* or "resistance."

Each group had a storm troop of its own, engaged in a wave of what they called reprisals. They threw bombs at Israeli missions in Europe, overturned tombstones, and left their mark everywhere with noxious graffiti, including slogans like "Death to the Jews." One of the groups vowed to avenge Eichmann with the kidnaping of Isser Harel, the shadowy chief of the Israeli Secret Service. Another group planned to ambush Dr. Nahum Goldman, president of the Jewish World Congress, a conspicuous figure just then, cementing Israel's precarious relations with West Germany. In their megalomania, these people dreamed of a Fourth Reich in Germany and prepared for it with shadow governments, one of which had a Propaganda Minister, a truck driver in Hagen, named Günther Boldt, and a whole string of gauleiters.

It soon became evident, however, that their efforts were nebulous and their threats hollow. No strong leader appeared on the scene in the mold of Hitler to forge the diverse groups into a single organization. The great conspiracy petered out for lack of popular support. When they felt strong enough to call a convention of all neo-Nazi groups to be held in a beer hall in the Lüneburger Heath, only seven "delegates" showed up, and one of them was a police informer. In the wake of the fiasco, most of the groups returned into oblivion. The gauleiter of Berlin dissolved his "party" in disgust.

It was different in South America. The sudden upsurge of neo-Nazism produced fanatical young rowdies banded together in underground groups in alliance with local rabble-rousers like the Tacuara, a Fascist organization in Argentina, and the A.C.H.A. in Chile, to avenge Eichmann. They bombed synagogues and community centers, painted swastikas and anti-Jewish slogans on walls, beat up Jews (preferably children) and harassed them with threatening letters and phone calls. The Eichmann case unleashed anti-Jewish demonstrations in Colombia, where, already in 1950, students in Medellín, wearing swastika armbands and singing German war songs, held a memorial service for the war criminals executed at Nuremberg and Landsberg. Now Jewish homes and synagogues were daubed with swastikas in Bogotá.

In Uruguay, on the other side of the Rio de la Plata, "solidarity" with the Nazis of Argentina sparked vicious anti-Jewish attacks. A restaurant was machine-gunned, Molotov cocktails were hurled against Hebrew schools, a Jewish lad had his thighs branded with swastikas. In August 1962, the noted scholar Maximo Handel Blanc had a swastika slashed on his body after a group of Nazi thugs had beaten him unconscious in a street in Montevideo. The residence of the Israeli ambassador was bombed, and the walls of the capital were smeared with swastikas and the Hitlerite slogan "*Juden raus.*" Large crowds attended memorial services for Eichmann, with stormtroopers clad in brown shirts standing at stiff attention and giving the Hitler salute.

This phase of the campaign reached its climax the day after Eichmann's execution. A young Jewish woman named Graciella Narcissa Sirota, who was suspected of being the daughter of the owner of the house in Buenos Aires to which Eichmann was taken after his abduction, was kidnaped and tortured, with a swastika burned into her breast. Another innocent Jewish girl Mirta Penjerek, also linked to the Eichmann kidnaping, was found murdered.

Even the country considered the most liberal and tolerant in its attitude to race and religion was subjected to racist demonstrations and vandalism. In Brazil, Jewish cemeteries were desecrated in Curitiba and Pôrto Alegre, where Nazi minorities in the large German communities were densest and most arrogant. "These various incidents," wrote Dennis Eisenberg in his survey of the reemergence of Fascism, "may appear as mere pinpricks in the tumultuous growth of Latin America, but they are symptomatic of a deep discord in the body politic of the continent." The traditional forces of suppression and reaction—the landed aristocracy, the ruling urban classes, the military leaders and politicians with totalitarian orientation and dictatorial ambitions—were backed by many of the Nazis who fled from Europe after the war. "They and their supporters," wrote Eisenberg, "see in the confusion a chance to bring about the type of world which Hitler believed in and so nearly brought about."

Nowhere was the upsurge of Nazism more arrogant, ostentatious and, as it turned out, lasting than in Chile, thriving on a formidable power base, the country's large and powerful German community. "The Germans!" Oswaldo Pascual Gonzales of the Alien Police mused when telling me why he was not permitted to apply drastic measures to curb the Nazi-Fascist elements, even under the extreme leftist regime of the late Salvador Allende. "They are the best organized, closest knit, most efficient colony of foreign-born citizens and aliens in this country. They have a finger in every pie. Their power comes from the fact—and it is a fact—that they are the backbone of our economy, and they know it. In any emergency we may have, earthquakes, floods or whatnot, there would be total chaos in the land except for them. We have to treat them with kid gloves. They are the untouchables!"

In spite of its long tradition of independent and progressive thinking, the country spawns Fascism and Nazism. During World War II, the Nazis openly boasted that "Chile [was] a spring of strength for the German nation." After the war, Otto Skorzeny saw to it, from his vantage point in Perón's Buenos Aires, that Nazism remained alive and well in Chile. Skorzeny's local representatives built their own groups on native movements, like the A.C.H.A., an anti-Communist action group, and the mysterious Movimiento Pro-Chile, an underground conglomerate of jingos. They were aided by the large, energetic Arab community which perpetuated the anti-Jewish aspects of Nazism after the establishment of the State of Israel.

In 1963, the Nazis gained new strength from a political party that openly paraded its allegiance to Hitler (symbolized by the little mustache sported by the local Führer), and featured swastikas, stormtroopers in uniforms, and Nazi banners at its rallies. Headed by Franz Pfeiffer, the effeminate, slim young man with the Hitler mustache, it attracted ten thousand members within a year. In 1968, it made headlines by choosing a beauty queen called "Miss Nazi World"—a rather homely young lady, Señorita Porteña by name—in a widely advertised contest held in Valparaiso, to which Nazis from most South American countries sent candidates. They have a "secret tribunal" to try "the war crimes of the Allies," almost three decades after the war, and the atrocities they commit are described as "executions carried out by order of the Tribunal."

The flamboyant Pfeiffer party is only the tip of the iceberg. The real Nazi movement is centered in a brazen organization called Das Reich which, by its own claim, unites "all German ex-servicemen who fought in World War II." According to Bar-Zohar, the aim of Das Reich and similar organizations is not to set up a Nazi regime in Latin American countries or in Europe. "They are organizations," he wrote, "for mutual aid and defense against the law, with origins dating back to the Nuremberg trials. Their members include all the war criminals sentenced in their absence, not only leading Nazis and those who have become powerful in their countries of refuge, but also the little men, hotelkeepers, tradesmen, farmers, and the like. All have in common a determination never to serve the sentences awaiting them in Europe." Das Reich paid the substantial costs of Walter Rauff's defense when he was successfully fighting extradition.

The geographical centers of Nazism in Chile were in the area east of Valdivia, and in Parral, just south of Santiago. Located in the latter region is the weirdest Nazi encampment of the postwar world, housing a sect that combines Nazism and voodooism. Enormously rich from mysterious sources, it maintains a heavily fortified *estancia* called Colonia Dignidad. It is virtually extraterritorial, enjoying privileges and immunities otherwise reserved only for diplomats. It was to the hacienda of Colonia Dignidad, called "El Lavadero," eighteen miles from Parral, camouflaged as a "cultural and welfare society," that Martin Bormann would move when, fatigued by his restless life in exile, he sought a place where he could be at peace.

Neither the outbreak of riotous anti-Semitism in South America nor Argentina's violent reaction to the Eichmann incident deterred Israelis at long range and Jews at closer quarters from continuing the campaign against the Nazi criminals. By the mid-sixties, its center of gravity had shifted from Argentina to Brazil, the country that harbored Franz Stangl, to the man who had moved to the top of the avengers' blacklist. His name was Herbert Cukurs, and he lived openly, first in Rio de Janeiro, then, like Stangl, in São Paulo. At the Yad Vashem in Jerusalem, he had a file filling several folders. Prosecutors and judges in Hamburg were assembling evidence against him. A group of young men called him "the hangman of Riga."

Cukurs and Stangl are minor but interesting figures in the history of the Fourth Reich. They provide dramatic case histories—the Cukurs incident for the technique used in the blotting-out of a war criminal, the case of Stangl for the ability of a Nazi fugitive to cloak himself in utter obscurity and evade retribution for twenty years. What Stangl could do with his modest means in exile, Bormann could certainly do much better with his top-level protection, elaborate concealment apparatus and access to virtually unlimited funds.

By the time the avengers got around to dealing with Cukurs, the list of the most-wanted Nazi criminals had narrowed down to a handful of murderers still at large. Hans Biebow, the Lodz ghetto administrator, Paul Blobel, the SS manager of the Kiev massacre, Rudolf Franz Höss and Franz Hössler, the two commandants of Auschwitz, Franz Konrad, the liquidator of the Warsaw ghetto, Siegfried Seidl, commandant of Theresienstadt and Bergen-Belsen, and many of their colleagues had been caught, tried, sentenced to death and executed. Others, like the infamous Odilo Globocnik, organizer of the massacre called "Operation Reinhard," and Hans Höfle, his chief assistant, as well as Hermann Pütz, director of the Rowne massacre, Hans Prützmann, another butcher of Kiev, Dr. Heinz Thilo, one of the Auschwitz doctors, and Hans Bothmann, commandant of the notorious Chelmno death camp, had committed suicide.

Richard Glücks, inspector general of all death camps, was said to have died in captivity, although Simon Wiesenthal is steadfast in his refusal to believe it. A few remained in hiding for years—like Fritz Katzmann, organizer of the massacre of 400,000 Jews in East Galicia, who lived under the name of Bruno Albrecht in Darmstadt, where he died, never detected, in 1957. Werner Blankenberg, one of the managers of the Polish death camps and a high official in the euthanasia program, outwitted his pursuers by changing his name to Bielicke and moving to Stuttgart, where he died in the fifties.

The group of major Nazi criminals who vanished without a trace included Christian Wirth, supervising chief of the death camps in Poland, and Theodore Dannecker, the murderer of thousands of Jews in France, Italy and Bulgaria. These two fugitives are presumed to be dead, but Gerhard Reitlinger insisted that their postwar fate "warranted investigation."

Aside from Bormann, Müller and Mengele, of course, and after Eichmann's abduction, only Cukurs was left more or less in the open. Like Stangl, Cukurs found refuge in Brazil, but in all other respects they were different kinds of men, and this difference manifested itself in their careers in exile. Stangl was a mere face in the crowd. But Cukurs was brash, an extrovert, conspicuous in everything he did—he rode on horseback into Riga to supervise the massacre of Jews. He was killed under mysterious circumstances in Montevideo, Uruguay, on February 23, 1965, at a "business meeting" to which he had been lured from his home in São Paulo.

His death became known on the twenty-sixth, when a Montevideo newspaper received a cable from Bonn, Germany. "Herbert Cukurs," it read, "the murderer of thousands of Jews in Riga, was himself murdered two days ago in Uruguay by *Those Who Cannot Forget*. His body is inside the trunk of a Volkswagen, in the yard of a deserted house, at Columbia Street in Montevideo, near Carrasco Beach." The editor of the paper forwarded the cable to the police. A few hours later the Volkswagen bus was found, with the body in the trunk. Although the face was smashed by savage beating and was covered with dry blood, it was unmistakably the round face of Herbert Cukurs, distorted in a weird grimace. The murderer—or murderers—had come and gone, without leaving a clue or a trace.

Herbert Cukurs was a killer on a grand scale. "In November 1941," wrote Michal Miron, a Riga-born Jew who miraculously survived all the ghettos and camps, "I heard that Herbert Cukurs, a famous officer of the Latvian air force, was working hand in glove with the Nazis. A month later, I myself saw him, on horseback, in the Jewish quarter in the city. He had a gun in his right hand and was firing it indiscriminately, shooting the Jews down in the dust." Isaac Kram, another native of Riga, gave this sworn statement to the investigators of the Yad Vashem:

> In March 1942, when I was living in Ludza Street in the Jewish quarter [in Riga], I suddenly saw hundreds of people savagely chased and beaten by Nazi soldiers led by Herbert Cukurs. I was standing close to him when an old woman, who had been dumped into a truck, began shouting at the top of her voice, beseeching Cukurs to let her be put in another truck where she had spotted her daughter. Cukurs replied by killing the woman with a single shot fired with his big revolver. A few minutes later he shot and killed a small child just because he annoyed him standing in the street, and crying for his mother.

After the war, Cukurs moved to Brazil, bringing along his wife and three children. He first settled in Rio de Janeiro, investing his money in the tourist business—he rented out sightseeing boats on Rio's beautiful lakes. For four years, he lived in middle-class comfort, unrecognized. But then the Brazilians were tipped off to him, and his long road to that VW trunk in Montevideo began. Frightened, he moved to São Paulo. In May 1960, when Eichmann was kidnapped in Buenos Aires, Cukurs realized that he would be one of the next. He begged the police to protect him. He petitioned the President of Brazil to grant him Brazilian citizenship. And all the time, he protested his innocence.

But the Yad Vashem forwarded his dossier to Brazil. It contained incontrovertible evidence that Cukurs was personally responsible for the death of 30,000 Jews—out of a Jewish population of about 50,000 in Riga—during pogroms in 1941 and 1942, which he organized for the Germans. In the end, he had no place to hide.

In Brazil and Uruguay, where the unpleasant memories of riots and demonstrations in the wake of Eichmann's abduction were still simmering, efforts were made to absolve Israeli commandos—or, for that matter, Jews in general—of the assassination of Herbert Cukurs. "It is certain," wrote Zevi Ghivelder in a memorandum of the case he prepared for me,

> the Jews had nothing to do with the murder of Cukurs. For one thing, he lived in Brazil for twenty years without being harmed

by the Jews except in legal ways, like evidence given against him to the Ministry of Justice. For another thing, his executioners called themselves "Those Who Cannot Forget." An organization by this name never appeared anywhere in the world. In all probability it existed only in the imagination of those interested in the spearheading of anti-Semitism, such as former Nazis and neo-Nazis. Eichmann's trial demonstrated, not only to the people of Brazil and Uruguay, but to the whole world, that Israel's purpose is to judge war criminals, not to kill them.

Ghivelder ventured the opinion that Cukurs was assassinated by the Nazis themselves, probably to silence him. However, others insist that Cukurs was killed by Israeli agents in a series of operations that began in October 1964 as part of a new campaign to liquidate those Nazi criminals whom the proper authorities were not prepared to bring to justice.

The Cukurs operation was in fact the last such violent case of retribution involving Israelis, even if only indirectly.

The man who led the killers was identified as "a thickset man, bald, with plump features and a small groomed mustache." He always wore dark glasses, and he went by different names. The name under which he managed the liquidation of Herbert Cukurs was Anton Kunzle.

They first met in São Paulo in October 1964. Introducing himself as a businessman, Kunzle confided to Cukurs that his name was an alias, because he was "an ex-Nazi sought by Israeli commandos and the German police." But he had a deal to offer, and he had all the money the business needed, looking to Cukurs only for his experience as a former aviator and sightseeing-boat operator. How about opening a string of tourist agencies with offices in Buenos Aires and Santiago de Chile? And in Montevideo?

Cukurs went for the hook. "We old comrades better stick together," he told Kunzle. In January 1965, preparations were sufficiently advanced to warrant an exploratory trip, and Kunzle cabled Cukurs from Europe suggesting that they meet in Montevideo. In São Paulo, Cukurs felt relatively safe. He enjoyed the personal protection of Senhor Alcido Cintra Bueno Filho, a police officer. Now he went to see him at the station house, to get his advice. "Well, Alcido," he told his friend, "an important European businessman wants me to go to Montevideo. Do you think it's safe?"

"Don't go, Herbert," Bueno replied. "You're safe here, because I protect you. The moment you leave Brazil, you're on your own. Your enemies have not forgotten you!"

"It'll be all right," Cukurs said. "I trust the man. Besides, I have my faithful .22 pistol, and I'm still a crack shot."

Kunzle was not a hunted Nazi. Neither was he a member of the Israeli Secret Service, as it was later alleged. He was a Jew, traveling on mysterious errands around the world, on passport Number 920,195 issued by Austria. He was "in contact" with the Israelis who had arranged the abduction of Eichmann five years before, but he was "working" for "a private organization" whose members were free-lancing as Nazi hunters.

In this particular operation, his partner was a Jew who called himself Oswald Taussig, from Cukurs' native city of Riga, also traveling on an Austrian passport, Number 101,261, which had been issued in 1961. They sounded out their friends in Tel Aviv whether Israel would be willing to accept Cukurs if they delivered him in the Eichmann manner. No, the Israelis said, repeating the stock phrase, "One Eichmann case was enough." But, they said, Israel cannot, of course, prevent them from doing whatever they deemed proper, as it was put, in the matter of Herbert Cukurs. Now that the chips were down, Kunzle and Taussig had no choice. They had to kill Cukurs, for if they kidnaped him, they had no place to take him.

Montevideo was chosen for the showdown. Cukurs would be unprotected there, all alone in a strange city. Taussig arrived in the Uruguayan capital on February 11 and checked into the Norago Hotel, where he was assigned Room 302. About a week later he leased a green Volkswagen bus from the Sudamcar agency. He also rented a small villa, the Casa Cubertini on Calle Colombia, near the beach. Then he bought a big trunk—six feet long, eighteen inches wide—which he had delivered to the villa. Other members of the team drifted into Montevideo during the week. There were five of them altogether, including Kunzle, who flew in on February 15, and moved into Room 2112 in the Victoria Plaza, where he had made a reservation by cable from Rotterdam. He too rented a car, a black VW, from the Sudamcar agency.

By February 21, the trap was set. Cukurs arrived in Montevideo on the morning of the twenty-third and went straight to Room 1719 in the Victoria Plaza, which Kunzle had reserved for him. Kunzle told Cukurs that they would have to see the other partners, and he proposed a quiet villa close to the beach as the place of the meeting. Cukurs made no objection. The two went to the house on Calle Colombia in Kunzle's black Volkswagen.

It was a hot day. The street on which the villa stood, and the beach nearby were deserted. A green Volkswagen bus was standing some sixty yards from the Casa Cubertini to which Kunzle was taking Cukurs. The two stepped inside and at once four men waiting behind the door hurled themselves at the Latvian giant, firing their revolvers at him. Cukurs drew his gun and fired back. In the general scuffle, Kunzle got knocked on the head.

But Cukurs was dead. His body was placed in the trunk, then the Volkswagen bus was driven up to the villa, and the big trunk was put into it. That night, an Israeli cargo ship, the *Har-Rimon,* sailed out of Montevideo harbor. Kunzle and Taussig were sailing with her. Colonel Ventura Rodriguez, then chief of police in Montevideo, remembered the case well. "We made inquiries in São Paulo," he said, and conducted the most thorough investigation in Uruguay. They led us nowhere. The murderers were never traced."

When years later I exchanged notes with Zevi Ghivelder, receiving from him his account of the Cukurs murder in return for mine, he insisted that the man calling himself Anton Kunzle was not a Jew. "What's more," Zevi said, "I'm positive that he was not an Israeli agent."

How could he be so sure?

"Look," Ghivelder said earnestly. "I once traveled with him on a Varig flight from Lisbon to Rio. I was in economy, but this Kunzle was going first class." My friend looked at me with the triumphant expression of Sherlock Holmes when explaining the solution of a case to Dr. Watson. "You know how stingy the Israeli Secret Service is! No Israeli agent, even on the most important mission, was ever given an expense account that would have enabled him to travel first class."

What was the Reichsleiter doing while they were digging for him in Berlin, declaring him dead in Hamburg, filling more dossiers in Frankfurt? Despite the events surrounding Eichmann, Cukurs and Stangl, he was assured that he had nothing to fear. He was traveling as usual, even returning to Buenos Aires in 1966 and 1967, to attend meetings at which a worldwide movement was plotted—a Third World to be patterned after the Third Reich.

Bormann had been a member of the Reichstag, but he was

never a politician. He was a cog in the machine, a technician, an expert in his own metier. Even in South America where many of the Nazi exiles looked upon him as their Führer, politics failed to interest or attract him.

Now, however, he was drawn into this supersecret conspiracy that his South American friends called Tercer Mundo. As it was envisaged by its architects, it was to be the global successor to Hitler's New Order, the realization of Bishop Hudal's dream—a worldwide anti-Communist coalition of reactionary forces.

The secret archives of Coordinación Federal were bulging with highly classified documents bearing on this international conspiracy that was designed to unite the darkest forces of reaction and totalitarianism everywhere. Its tentacles ranged from the native Fascists of South America through the radical remnants of Nasser's revolution in Egypt to the pathetic gang of neo-Samurais in Japan. According to summary report "F" A No. 1285/70, dated April 12, 1970, which also contained the biographies and "mugshots" of men described as "the ideologues, the activists and the propagandists" of the conspiracy, the movement began during World War II—in 1943—with a brief "prerevolutionary period" of incubation. It grew out of a supersecret convention of Argentina's most reactionary and pro-Nazi elements, the Congress of National Recuperation, held the year before under the leadership of Alberto Capile and Roberto de Laferrere.

The congress issued an action program, proclaiming as its aim "the seizure of total power in Argentina" and the "ideological conquest of Latin America," in collaboration—as it was phrased in Article 3 of the original platform—with "the chiefs of National Socialism in Germany and the hierarchy of the Roman Catholic Church."

By 1944, Juan Domingo Perón was a charter member. He remained one of its leaders during the next eleven years, which witnessed the formation of a number of splinter groups around the central idea. With Perón's departure in 1955, a new supreme leader emerged in the person of Colonel Juan Francisco Guevara, who initiated the gradual paramilitarization of a wing of the movement, producing the Tacuara, "a terrorist organization on the Nazi pattern," as one of the reports to the Coordinación Federal described it, led by Alberto Ezcurra Uriburu, son of a former President of Argentina, Julio Menville and Patricio Errecalde Pueyrredon.

The *Sturm-und-Drang* culminated in the consolidation of all splinter groups in the Movimiento Sacerdote Para el Tercer Mundo ("Sacred Movement for a Third World") almost exactly as Bishop Hudal had envisaged it. The program of the movement was so ambitious, detailed and all-pervasive that it covered forty-five pages in print. Its caption read, "Our Objective: A New World."

In 1968, the Reverend Andres Canale, director of the Catholic Information Agency of Argentina, reported to Coordinación Federal that the Sacred Movement had major bases in Portugal, Spain, Italy and Belgium in Europe; in Libya, Algeria and Egypt in Africa; in Iraq, Jordan and Iran in Asia; in Taiwan and Japan in the Far East; and in Argentina, Paraguay, Bolivia, Peru and Venezuela in South America.

"The funds," Father Canale wrote, "required for the operation [of the movement] are provided from the hidden treasure of the Third Reich on deposit in Spain, Portugal and Italy, as well as in Paris, Monaco, Lucerne and Zurich; and from the exchequer of the Group Perón's $500,000,000. Additional revenue is derived from dividends paid by Mercedes-Benz of Stuttgart, on the portfolio of shares held for the Sacred Movement by Jorge Antonio."

Remarkable for the movement was the fact that although one of its heroes was Adolf Hitler and most of its roots were in Nazism, the Nazi remnants played a minor and insignificant part in its development. Germany was conspicuous by its absence from the countries where the Sacred Movement had a base of operations.

The reason for this stemmed mainly from the intellectual caliber of the new Nazi diaspora. Those prominent former Nazis (like Colonels Rudel and Skorzeny) who kept the faith and continued to promote Nazism in exile possessed little of the sophistication—and, indeed, the brains—needed to contribute anything to the growth of a movement founded on an abstract ideological premise. There was only a single Nazi ideologue still at large. He was Professor Dr. Johannes von Leers, a brilliant thinker of the Dr. Faustus school of German scholarship, a close friend of Juan Perón, a theoretician greatly admired by Martin Bormann. All others—including Bormann—were pragmatists and activists, both inexperienced in and ignorant of the complexities of politics.

The ideological dynasty to which Hitler had fallen heir ended with him. The only true ideologue who could perhaps have perpetuated Nazism after the fall was Goebbels, and he had eliminated himself. Only Martin Bormann was left, and if he was considered important by the leaders of the Sacred Movement, it was only because he was the most prominent Nazi still alive. In 1966, therefore, the Sacred Movement made overtures to him; and then, in 1968, he was formally invited to join the leadership.

A special session of the executive in South America was called to the Buenos Aires home of Colonel Guevara—who returned for the meeting from Bogotá, where he served as the Argentine ambassador—to initiate Bormann with a ceremony resembling the rites of the hated Masons. It proved a dismal fiasco.

Bormann arrived at the Guevara villa in the company of a visiting German general (who was in Argentina at the invitation of the Krupps on a hunting trip in Salta)—an officer who had the misfortune (doubly significant, as it turned out) of having fought in the Battle of Stalingrad on the losing side. Instead of getting down to the business on the agenda, Colonel Guevara, an avid student of military history, seized the opportunity of reviewing the battle, which, he said, was where Hitler had lost the war.

An acrimonious discussion ensued between the Argentine colonel and the German general. When in his unbridled excitement Guevara made the general personally responsible for the defeat at Stalingrad, Bormann jumped up and walked out of the meeting, followed by the bewildered general.

Bormann never again was involved in any way in the Sacred Movement, either by his own volition or by invitation. In fact, his brief association with the project was his only excursion into politics during his exile.

Chapter Twenty-Five

Can the Godfather Retire?

After six or seven exasperating years, the struggle between Fritz Bauer and Martin Bormann seemed to be petering out in a draw—Bauer never ceased to be convinced that Bormann was alive, and Bormann always succeeded in eluding Bauer. The prosecutor was getting discouraged. The summer of 1967 was the last time he received what he believed was positive proof that Bormann was in South America.

Then a new hunter appeared on the trail. He was not in Bauer's league by any means; he had none of the great prosecutor's professional qualifications, respectable official position, or integrity. But they had in common the initiative, the imagination and the energy that the pursuit needed, the stubborn concentration on the goal, and an abiding hatred of the Nazis. The new man had one big advantage over Bauer. He operated in Bormann's own backyard.

He was Dr. Erico, the sleuth we met before when he was chasing Mengele and killed somebody he thought was the doctor. His real name was Erich Erdstein and nothing in his background forecast the hazardous career of this extraordinary vagabond. The black-sheep scion of a wealthy Austrian-Jewish family, he had been shipped to South America in his twenties. A British agent in Uruguay during World War II, he then became the owner of a little espresso shop on a side street in Curitiba, Brazil.

At one point, however, he suddenly emerged as a supercop in the State of Paraná's complex police establishment. The exact nature of his job was difficult to ascertain. "I was a passionate cop," he once told me, "like some men are lovers or golfers, or like Patton was a soldier." In the police, he started out in the Section of Assault and Burglary in the Criminal Investigation Division, then became an interpreter (he spoke seven languages fluently). For some time, while stationed in the border zone, he specialized in narcotics smugglers who crossed into Brazil from Paraguay, and cut the traffic in half singlehandedly in a year. Then suddenly he became the hunter the Nazis dreaded most in all of western Brazil.

It happened unexpectedly and dramatically. A plainclothesman named Angelo Silvera picked up an out-of-town bum at the Rodoviaria, the bus terminal, for loitering, and it turned out that he was a German. Officer Silvera took him to Erico's coffee shop for interrogation, with the "doctor" acting as the interpreter. It developed that the bum was an executive of the Rio do Sul branch of the Banco Hollandes Unido. He had come to Curitiba after having a quarrel over Hitler with his brother-in-law, Dr. William Gimbala, a figure of some importance in Rio do Sul, who then ran him out of the town.

The brother-in-law was an ardent Nazi and a fugitive—in fact, one of Mengele's best friends and a kind of den master to a number of Third Reich survivors in Rio do Sul and Santa Catarina. In his despair, the man—whose name was Eugen Parries—stuffed his pockets with the bank's money and motored from town to town in his Volkswagen spending the stolen treasure on women and wine. By the time he got to Curitiba, his funds and his morale were low. He looked dazed and unkempt, and was suffering from a monumental hangover.

Talking to Erico in German refreshed him. He now regretted deeply that he had taken the bank's money. He was mortified that he was in the hands of the police, about to be extradited to Rio do Sul. "I am now only half ruined," he pleaded with Erico. "But if you put me in jail, I'll be destroyed for the rest of my life." He offered a deal. If Erico kept him out of prison, he would tell him all he knew about his brother-in-law's Nazi friends, dropping names like Franz Wenzler, Rolf Meissner, Franz Rybka, and then the big ones—Heinrich Müller, Mengele and Bormann!

The Parries offer intrigued Erico. He agreed to the deal. It was late at night. Instead of locking him up, Erico took the man to the Martin's Hotel, checked him into Room 33, left Officer Silvera in the corridor as a guard, and told the German he would pick him up at nine o'clock in the morning.

When he then knocked on the door at 9 A.M. and got no answer, Erico broke into the room and found Parries hanging by his suspenders from the brass bed—dead. It was obvious from the position in which he was found that he could not have committed suicide. Somebody must have killed him and hanged him on the bed. The night clerk was summoned and he said yes, at about 5 A.M. a couple of Germans checked into the hotel and he gave them Room 34, for they said they were friends of Parries, and wanted to be near him when he woke up. They must have left early, because their room was empty, the beds made, nothing disturbed. Nobody in the whole of Brazil was found by the names under which they had registered. Their I.D. cards were forgeries.

It was plainly a case of murder. One or another of the Nazi spies who used to hang around in Erico's coffee shop must have eavesdropped on the German's interrogation, tipped off the local Nazis, and they silenced Parries. That corpse in Room 33 abruptly changed Erdstein's whole professional life. Suddenly he lost all interest in the drug pushers, whisky smugglers and all the itinerant crooks who infested the wide-open border region with Paraguay. He became completely wrapped up in the Nazis. If he could not get their story from Parries, he would procure it in the field.

Erdstein was in his middle fifties, but looked twenty years younger, a slight man with a trim body. He had reddish hair and a pinched face, two tiny eyes sizzling with an inner fire. He was dapper, suave and glib, with an undercurrent of nervous energy, which he tried visibly to keep under control. He craved adventure and loved nothing more in his life—no woman, no child, no pleasure—than his gun, a black 7.65 special which a friend of his had captured from a German officer during World War II.

He brought to a job that required stubborn adherence to reality a lively romanticism. But he was a born fighter. Blessed with insatiable curiosity, he could instinctively penetrate to the hard core of even the murkiest matters. This made him a brilliant investigator, from whom few secrets could be concealed. He was indefatigable in his job, working around the clock if a case warranted it, often going for days without sleep.

Moreover, Erdstein had a unique qualification for his special assignment, an advantage that also became a bane. Of all the police agents engaged in the surveillance of the Nazis in the State of Paraná, he was the only one who could speak German and knew what Nazism was all about.

It was in 1966, when Parries was killed, that Erdstein's interest in the Nazis began. Within one year, roaming the Nazi-infested region between Marechal Rondon (see page 289) in the north to Rio Grande do Sul on Lake Patos in the south in his own jeep, Erdstein "covered" most of the fugitive Nazis, confining his offensive to a strategy of harassment, and it worked. All of a sudden, a number of the *Prominente*, the V.I.P.'s, among the fugitives hiding in western Brazil, decided to move out of Erico's territory. One of them went as far as Ecuador, others transferred to Bolivia and Peru, some went to Chile, but most of them moved to Paraguay—a kind of retribution in itself, for it is no pleasure to live out a life in that most underdeveloped country in South America.

One of his coups produced probably the quaintest story of a Nazi in exile, the arrest of Franz Xavier Rybka, a former associate of Freddy Schwend in counterfeiting English pounds and American twenty-dollar bills.

Erico now felt that he was ready to come to grips with the biggest game in anybody's Nazi hunt. But the number-one Nazi eluded him in a chase that ultimately resulted in the death of two of Erdstein's associates and in considerable injury to himself.

The first man to die in his search for Bormann was Major von Westernhagen, the German intelligence agent the Gehlen organization was said to have sent to Brazil. According to Erich, the first thing the major did upon his arrival in Rio was to contact him. "But he was killed," he said, "barely three hours after talking with me, on crowded Silveira Campos Street in Rio, at one o'clock in the afternoon, by four men jumping from a black Volkswagen. They pumped forty machine-gun bullets into him."

Only a few days later, he said, an ex-officer of the Free Polish forces of World War II named Pasternak was killed when the jeep in which he and Erdstein traveled to Ponta Grossa on a Bormann tip was blown up by a bomb that had been smuggled into the car. "I was severely injured," Erdstein added, pointing to some of the scars on his ruddy face, and impulsively taking off his shirt to show me marks of his old injuries. "Violence apparently was the only way the Bormann forces thought they could put an end to my investigation."

Then, however, came what seemed to be the big break. On a June day in 1968, two German-Jewish refugees, Moises Apfelbaum and Bruno Erntler, rushed into his office in Foz do Iguassú, and told him breathlessly that they had just seen Martin Bormann in the cafeteria of the bus station, having a beer.

"I thought they were crazy," Erdstein said, "but they insisted so much that I got into my car to see for myself."

He found an elderly man in a dark suit who resembled Bormann, sitting by himself in the cafeteria, with a beer bottle and a glass on the table in front of him. Three other men, obviously his bodyguards, were at the next table. "I had a sudden idea," Erdstein recalled. "From a jewelry shop next to the cafeteria, I called the owner of the bar by telephone and ordered him to change somehow the bottle and glass in front of the man with the dark suit, and keep them for me. From where I was standing just outside the cafeteria I could observe him doing so."

Before he could do anything more, the four men got up, left the cafeteria and boarded the bus to Guaíra, a city on the Brazilian side of the border. Erdstein commandeered a jeep and followed the bus, arriving in Guaíra ahead of it. When the bus came in, the four men were not on it. The driver told Erich that they had gotten off in Rondon, where a white Volkswagen had picked them up.

Combing the region for a couple of weeks, still hoping to find "Bormann," he came upon a man named Karl Kraft. The owner of a little boat called *Lambary,* he used to ferry people across the river from time to time. Kraft told him that two weeks before, he took the four men to Paraguay, including the one in the dark suit, whom his companions "treated with great respect, calling him 'Herr Bormann.' "

"I felt so miserable," Erdstein said as he recalled the incident, "that I almost became sick. I had had Martin Bormann in my hands and lost him. Karl Kraft showed me, from the Brazilian side of the river, where, on a small beach, he had landed Bormann on the Paraguayan side, and described how the party had been picked up by a Volkswagen bus, driving away on the narrow road leading into the jungle."

Despite his eloquence, his story sounded too good to be true. "Are you sure," I asked somewhat incredulously, "that the man in the dark suit was Bormann?"

"I'm positive," he shot back, obviously rankled by my doubt. "The bottle and the glass I recovered at the cafeteria were sent to the laboratories of the state police in Curitiba and the federal police in Rio to be examined for fingerprints. The test proved Apfelbaum and Erntler right. Five prints were taken from the bottle, four from the glass; apparently our man was one of those dainty drinkers who keep their pinky at an angle away from the glass. The prints were then compared with the ones of Bormann we had on file, and they matched. The man *was* Bormann, beyond the slightest shadow of a doubt!"

I was subsequently able in Foz do Iguassú, Curitiba and Rio de Janeiro to corroborate some of the details of Erdstein's tale from independent sources which I had every reason to regard as absolutely reliable and competent. I succeeded in locating Apfelbaum and Erntler in Foz, and they confirmed Erdstein's account of the alleged Bormann's appearance in and disappearance from the town, including their own part in the incident. Apfelbaum in particular insisted that he had seen Bormann several times in Germany, and again after the war in Asunción, and had recognized him positively at the bus station.

On a later trip that took me further north along the Paraná, I looked for and found Karl Kraft, a wrinkled old farmer still operating the rickety rowboat *Lambary* to ferry friend and foe across the river. He repeated to me his Bormann story exactly as he had told it to Erdstein.

In June 1968, his twentieth year in South American exile, Martin Bormann became sixty-eight years old. Feeling even older than his age, and fearing senility, he felt keenly the hardships of his long exile. He was weary of running, caught as he now was in the pincer of Bauer's search and Erdstein's hunt.

As it turned out, it was Bauer, not Bormann, who was living on borrowed time. And Erdstein, as fate would have it, had only three more months left in Brazil. But Bormann could not know what the future held. All he knew was that he was sick physically and tired mentally of the way he lived. He had enough!

Could the Godfather retire? Bormann thought he could!

But where to go to find the tranquillity he was seeking? Chile offered a number of enticements. It was the most modern of the South American countries as far as living conditions were concerned, the Switzerland of South America, with mountains whose scenic beauty matched that of his cherished Berchtesgadner Alps and beloved Bariloche. The decision of the Supreme Court in the case of Walter Rauff's extradition demonstrated that even a Nazi with proven complicity in the murder of almost 100,000 Jews had nothing to fear in Chile—Rauff certainly got a better deal than poor Stangl in Brazil and Dr. Bohne in Argentina. Chile, too, was off the beaten path of the Jewish marauders.

The ethnic atmosphere of the country was most congenial. Bormann no longer cared for his fellow Nazis, and he loathed, in fact, the Pfeiffer brand of neophyte Nazis. But he was impressed with the influence of the Germans in Chile; that influence predated the Nazi era and continued after Hitler was gone. He had some good friends among them: the enormously rich Hubasch family; a big financier named Loewenstein, and Mark Buechs, a well-to-do furniture manufacturer. Like others of his ilk, he preferred the company of the rich. While he did not mingle with the rank and file of the Nazi newcomers, he was close to a former SS colonel who was known as "the Baron," and who had made good in Chile as a trucking tycoon.

Most important, he was no stranger to the authorities. As a result, he was able to come and go as he pleased, thanks to long-standing "arrangements" he had made. Under the regime of Jorge Alessandri, he enjoyed the protection of Colonel Emilio Oelkers, the Director General of Investigations. Oelkers sold his services to all bidders, with Bormann at one end of the spectrum among his clients and the C.I.A. at the other. Later Inspector Hugo Villegas Garin, chief of the Policía Internacional, was on his payroll. True, Garin had to build a dossier about *el Gran Fugitivo* ("the Great Fugitive") for the record. But that was as far as he went. When the chips were down, it was Bormann who controlled Oelkers and Garin, not the other way round.

So Chile was chosen as the country to which he would retire at last. His flight from the peripatetic exile ushered in what he himself later called "the happiest years" of his life; and the story of those "happy years" was related to me by two exceptional sources. One was Inspector Oswaldo Pascual, Garin's successor at the head of the international police. The other was a brilliant former Argentine intelligence officer whose "territory" included Chile and whose professional interest extended to Bormann.

Unlike Garin, Pascual was a tower of integrity. Against his principles and better judgment, as it were, he continued the "arrangement" with Bormann nevertheless, simply because he realized he had no choice. Bormann's protection stemmed from much higher echelons. There was nothing Pascual could do on his own to detain the fugitive on Bauer's warrant or even to oust him as an undesirable alien. The Rauff case demonstrated only too clearly that Nazi criminals were given the status of political exiles in Chile. The sacrosanct South American doctrine of the inviolability of asylum was applied to them. If a "little man" like Rauff could claim such immunity and get away with it, Bormann could do the same on much firmer grounds. The arrest and extradition warrant (with the fingerprints sheet to be found in the Document section) which the Germans had sent to the Chilean Ministry of Justice charged Bormann with murder, to be sure. But the indictment was so vague and the evidence was so weak that nobody really expected the case to stand up in the Chilean Supreme Court.

According to the Bormann dossier at the Policía Internacional, to which I had authorized access in Santiago, Martin Bormann lived in Chile in a number of places until he settled down in a hacienda of his own at Petrohué in the far south near the Andes. The documents showed that he had first been spotted in Chile in 1956, in the immediate wake of Perón's ouster. At that time he was accompanied by an Italian Fascist named Giorgio Lizardo, also seeking a foothold somewhere outside Argentina, which had become too hot for the European fugitives. Already then, Bormann seemed to be closer to Peronist exiles—like Senator Sergio Monzon—and well-heeled Fascists—like Eduardo Cappini and Anselmo Gliossi—than to his own fellow Nazis. The only German in his circle at that time was a man named Zelewsky.

On later visits he stayed in Santiago in the house of Mark Buechs, his bachelor friend, or at the Loewenstein *estancia*, about sixty miles south of the capital. Using the pseudonym of Hans or Helmut Keller, he was also a guest at the Fernando Hubasch hacienda in Riachuelo, in the province of Osorno, as was attested by Abel Barria, the administrator of the Hubasch estate, in a sworn statement Pascual had on file.

Never a man to stand still, he commuted constantly between Petrohué and the heavily fortified German camp Colonia Dignidad, near Parral, also in Linares. Its owner, Fritz Schneider, an ex-Nazi who became the fanatical leader of a mystic sect in his exile, had thoughtfully installed an antiaircraft gun on the *estancia* to assure Bormann's safety from Jewish raiders who, Schneider feared, might come by helicopter for the snatch. From time to time, Bormann would visit Santiago, where he first used a big town house on Calle San Pablo owned by Buechs (but registered in the name of his nephew). Later he usually stayed at the apartment which he rented for the girl friend he found in Chile to make his contentment complete.

In the spring of 1966, my other informant, then chief of the intelligence division of the Buenos Aires Provincial Police known only by his cover name of Saul, was invited by the government of Ecuador to aid the political police in locating a notorious K.G.B. agent, Colonel Weiland. His mission accomplished (Weiland was found and expelled), Saul decided to make use of his stay in Quito by developing leads that might help him in his investigation of Nazis in the strategic province of Buenos Aires. One of the tips he picked up intrigued him especially, but he had an opportunity to follow it down only three years later. The clue was that Bormann, living in Chile, occasionally visited Santiago to see his mistress.

In early 1969, when Bormann was firmly settled in Chile, Saul had to go to Santiago on some business, and he decided to check out the old tip while he was in the Chilean capital. All he knew to begin with was that Bormann had this girl friend and that her first name was Maria. Now he hoped to find Maria, who in turn might lead him to Bormann. In Santiago, Saul established contact with his old friend Hugo Villegas Garin, then still chief of Policía Internacional.

Saul was startled to find that Garin was friendly with Maria and through her knew Bormann. By a strange coincidence Maria was also named Garin and lived in an apartment two blocks from Plaza Brasil, next door to a bordello, the Select Club. The madame was a Frenchwoman named Olivia, and they were on friendly terms. In fact, Bormann originally met Maria in Madame Olivia's house and set her up in a cozy apartment.

Saul, a dashing young *bon vivant,* decided to ensnare Maria and get information about Bormann. He especially hoped that she would allow him to visit what was in fact Martin Bormann's Santiago apartment and obtain the evidence needed to track down Bormann himself.

But Maria proved faithful to her lover. Although she allowed Saul to treat her to expensive outings at the Pollo Dorado and Bin

Ban Bum nightclub, she resisted all his efforts to get her into the bed reserved for Martin Bormann.

"This whole thing was pretty hard on me," Saul said later, "because this Maria was a rather plain and unattractive woman. In her late thirties but appearing older, she was always heavily made up, wearing simple cheap dresses, and without sex appeal.

"But she proved useful to me, nevertheless, because I did get a lot of information from her about Martin Bormann."

First, he found out that Bormann himself lived on a big farm south of Valdivia close to the Argentine border where a much-traveled mountain pass gave him access to Argentina. From time to time in scribbled postcards he would ask Maria to visit him at Colonia Dignidad, or alert her to his coming to Santiago.

An incident provoked by some of these postcards persuaded Saul, however, to drop the whole matter and stop chasing Bormann.

Some of these postcards fell into the hands of Inspector Garin and he tried to sell them in the flourishing market of Bormann memorabilia. No sooner had a contact been made in Brussels for the sale of this incontrovertible evidence of Bormann's survival than Inspector Garin was shot at on a Santiago street.

He escaped, unharmed. But the same afternoon, a telephone call warned him and he recognized the voice of Luis Jiménez, Bormann's secretary: "Next time you won't be missed." The same afternoon a courier appeared in his office with a scribbled note from Bormann himself, demanding the immediate return of the postcards.

Maria is the mother of the four children Bormann sired in exile. (He had ten children by his wife in Germany, nine of whom are still living.) According to what she told Saul, the apartment in Santiago was the only place in South America where Bormann could relax. He seemed to be genuinely grateful to her for providing this quiet domesticity in his otherwise harried life.

For Bormann those happy years in Chile ushered in what he hoped would be the calm sunset of his life. But to Nazism in South America his withdrawal was a heavy blow. Although he steadfastly refrained from being in fact the Führer his fellow fugitives (even including transients like Rudel and Skorzeny) wanted him to be, there was leadership in his mere presence. Alone among the fugitives, he had a certain style and dignity—some "class."

Now that he was serious about his retirement and broke all

ties except his social relations with Mengele and Schwend, Nazism in South America ceased to be a "movement" or a "force."

Leadership slipped to the two men who selfishly coveted it—to Freddy Schwend in Lima and to Klaus Barbie (calling himself Altmann) in La Paz. Before long it became a front for drug pushing, a cover for gunrunning, and a façade behind which Schwend and Altmann could conduct their big illicit currency speculations in countries in which strict laws sternly regulated the flow of all money.

Nazism in South America suffered a mortal blow on New Year's Day in 1972, when the Peruvian fishing and shipping tycoon Luis Banchero Rossi was murdered at his palatial home in a suburb of Lima. Although Banchero's half-witted gardener was promptly arrested and charged with the murder, two Nazi fugitives, Freddy Schwend and Klaus Barbie-Altmann, were rumored to be the masterminds behind the wanton act. Their motive was said to have been to gain control of some hidden millions Banchero allegedly kept abroad, to replenish the empty treasury of the neo-Nazi movement.

This one murder—in which, rightly or wrongly, Nazi fugitives became implicated—brought home to South Americans the base brutality of Hitlerism more immediately and dramatically than the remote massacre of millions of Jews. The rapid deterioration of Nazism into an international racket, now topped by the murder of a popular folk hero, destroyed whatever appeal or influence neo-Nazism still had in South America—except in Bolivia. Under the reactionary dictatorship of General Hugo Banzer Suárez, it remains the last haven of Nazism in the Western Hemisphere.*

* According to a cover-page headline in *Stern* magazine: "Bolivia is firmly in German hands." The article featured a number of wealthy and powerful Germans running Bolivia. However, it omitted any reference to the notorious Barbie whose influence is second to none in sustaining pro-Nazi sentiments in Bolivia. Because of men like Altmann and Schwend, Nazism remains a festering moral and an acute criminal problem. And judging by the role reactionary Germans play in Bolivia and Chile, it also represents a continuing political threat.

Chapter Twenty-Six

The Rejuvenation of Ricardo Bauer

It was oppressively hot on the February afternoon in 1972 when Martin Bormann returned to Buenos Aires, as he had been doing periodically since 1968, to attend to his affairs, both business and amorous. These furtive trips were not without hazards. But Bormann was able to sneak into the federal capital on one or another of the safe routes that his friends kept open for him. This time he came in style aboard a sleek white yacht that took him straight to a private jetty near the boat club in the elegant waterfront borough of Beccar.

Accompanied as always by Luis Jiménez, his Mexican secretary, and the faithful O'Higgins, his Chilean bodyguard, Bormann was met at the landing by a slim young man in a Pierre Cardin alpaca suit, then was driven to an elegant house on Calle José Evaristo Uriburu, where he was put up in a closely guarded apartment. I found out later that it was the bachelor flat of one of his friends, a kind of *pied à terre* in the city. It was placed at his disposal so that he could be close to the people he was coming to consult (see page 414).

Most of the time he visited Buenos Aires on business, because the city, where his postwar career as a tycoon began, was still the base of his fiscal operations and the center of his commercial interests. Other times he might drop in to keep a date with an interesting woman. Now, however, he had come to town on a different errand: to see a doctor.

This was not an especially pleasant and tranquil period in Bormann's life in exile. He was in the news again, and this time it was more than the usual flare-up of interest. In mid-March 1971, still another "Bormann"—the fourteenth, by official count—was spotted in South America. Arrested on the "evidence" printed in the Bogotá magazine *Siete Días*, which claimed it had "proof from a most reliable source," this Bormann turned out to be one Johannes Ehrmann, a German refugee in his seventies, who lived in the jungle in southern Colombia with his Indian wife and a daughter.

The toothless old man was destined to be the last such victim of Freddy Schwend, the magazine's "reliable source." It was he who had planted these bogus Bormanns at intervals, invariably far from the places where the real Bormann happened to be at any particular time. It was a gimmick, of course, designed to cover up the tracks of *el Gran Fugitivo*, as Bormann was called in the Latin countries in which he lived.

The trick was wearing thin and it was beginning to irritate Bormann. By this time he disliked anything that called attention to him, even if it was calculated to deepen the mystery and confuse his hunters.

If Schwend's latest revival of the old bluff annoyed him, something that was happening in Germany made him really angry. It became known in September 1971 that General Reinhard Gehlen, who was chief of the German secret service both during and after the Nazi regime, would claim in his forthcoming memoirs that Bormann had been a Soviet spy throughout the war. What the papers printed about the sensational charge made it seem that Gehlen had some inside information that he would be revealing for the first time. According to advance reports that made the Gehlen book the hottest literary property in years, the Reichsleiter had been radioing secret intelligence straight to the Kremlin directly from the Führer's headquarters on a clandestine wireless set that he allegedly operated to the bitter end.

Originally invented by one of Himmler's toadies, and revived by the most rabid opponents of Chancellor Willy Brandt's *Ostpolitik* (to demonstrate that even the most trusted aide of a chief executive could be a Soviet agent), the story was gaining circulation and respectability. It made Bormann absolutely livid with wrath. Frustrated as he was in his hiding to counter the malicious charge, he became, as always when provoked, violently sick to his stomach.

During the halcyon years of the Third Reich, when his big job kept him busy around the clock and gave him status, Bormann used to boast of the robust constitution that enabled him to be at the Führer's beck and call at all times, without missing a day because of illness. His life in exile was a monumental bore. Despite the comfort and even the luxury in which he lived, despite his erratic ways and the constant changes of scenery, he was like a supercharged engine left to run idle. It was not a simple matter for an erstwhile hustler to find himself suddenly a man without a job and, indeed, without a country to run.

When not on the move, Bormann's life was sedentary. Except for some horseback riding and his favorite pastime of gardening, he was not the outdoor type. Exasperated with the stifling monotony of his new existence, he developed an abdominal ailment causing him excruciating pain from time to time. The doctors he consulted diagnosed his condition variously as a duodenal ulcer, hepatic colic, gastritis, colitis, or a hiatus hernia. But the self-centered Bormann, who was unduly sensitive to the slightest discomfort of his body, was prone to magnify his indisposition. He was convinced that he was suffering from incipient cancer of the stomach.

His friend Mengele, who knew him better, of course, than any of his doctors, believed that Bormann's trouble was a psychosomatic condition caused by his nervous hypochondria. But whether his illness was psychogenic or purely physiological, his preoccupation with it was a genuine concern that made him reckless, threatening several times to become his undoing.

Thus, on a couple of occasions his identity could be established positively when his health deteriorated so abruptly that he sacrificed his security to obtain quick relief. During one of these acute medical emergencies in Asunción in 1959, when Dr. Otto Biss made the nocturnal house call described on page 245, a total stranger was thus admitted into Bormann's closely guarded inner sanctum.

Another such emergency occurred in the spring of 1968, during a visit to Buenos Aires. Stricken suddenly by the dread attack with unbearable pain while lunching incognito in a little restaurant, he demanded that his companions take him to a physician. The nearest they found was thirty-two-year-old Dr. Francisco Santos Urbistondo, whose office was at 1535 Calle Pueyrredon, just around the corner from the restaurant where Bormann had the seizure.

Dr. Urbistondo happened to be a specialist in plastic surgery, but Bormann felt too sick to be choosy—he demanded that the young surgeon do something to save his life. The doctor surmised that his spasm was what he called biliary colic, caused by a gallstone apparently forced through the narrow bile toward the intestine, and gave him a painkiller, the drug Serta-L. He advised rest and urged the patient to stick to a strict diet instead of eating the heavy *puchero* on which he had just lunched.

As was customary when Bormann was in Argentina, agents of the Alien Police shadowed him. This time too a couple of Bormann specialists—Inspector Rodriguez and Agent Zeffarelli—observed him as he was taken from the restaurant to the doctor. Immediately after he left the office, Rodriguez called on Dr. Urbistondo and showed him photographs from their rogue's gallery of fugitive Nazi criminals. Without hesitation, the surgeon picked out the picture of Martin Bormann as that of the patient he had just treated.

Now in 1972, it was again a visit to a doctor that aided—more conclusively than ever—the positive identification of Martin Bormann, not merely with old photographs but with new X-ray pictures and other data from his medical charts, such as his electrocardiogram and basal metabolism tests. This was a different kind of emergency. By February 1972, the recent flare-up of his gastrointestinal ailment had subsided somewhat, when Gehlen's assertion was exposed—even by Gehlen himself—as a politically inspired hoax. This time Bormann had come back to Buenos Aires to see a specialist because he was deeply troubled by the prospect of losing his sexual vigor.

It was especially distressing to him, since he had just become involved in a new liaison with Hannelore, an attractive and vivacious German-Chilean lady in her middle forties.

In all men, when the age of sixty-five is reached, some signs of senescence become obvious. Bormann was seventy-one years old at his last birthday. The stresses and strains of his hectic life had impaired the vitality of his tissues. His skin was becoming quite wrinkled, and his hair was falling out. His sunken eyes were developing a whitish-yellow area around the margins of the cornea, another sign of old age.

There were other symptoms of creeping senility. His once phenomenal memory was becoming sluggish—he found, more and more, that his mind was dwelling on incidents of long ago, while he was finding it increasingly difficult to recall what happened a week or even a couple of days before. All these signs of growing decrepitude vexed him, of course. But it was the obvious diminution of his sexual function that bothered him most. Age did not lessen his desire. But as Hannelore could tell best, it sharply reduced his masculine prowess.

A doctor in Paraguay suggested that he consult an Argentine specialist, the disciple of the late Dr. Niehans, the magical German-Swiss rejuvenator, whose patients had included Dr. Konrad Adenauer, W. Somerset Maugham, Pope Pius XII and the Duke of Windsor. The physician recommended was Professor Alfonso Pedro Ciancaglini, whose Policlinica Ciancaglini in San Isidro, a Buenos Aires suburb, was a mecca of elderly people seeking a second lease on life.

In Buenos Aires, Bormann found that Dr. Ciancaglini's credentials were first rate; he was a physician of high professional standing who could be trusted for both his skill and, equally important in this case, his discretion. A public-health expert of international reputation, Dr. Ciancaglini was born in Salta in 1916 and was graduated with high honors as a specialist in diseases of the blood at the Buenos Aires National University's School of Medicine in 1944. He pioneered blood transfusions in Argentina, taught hematology and hematotherapy at various medical schools, and was associated with the world-famous Professor Berotti in trail-blazing research on an anti-Rhesus serum to control the Rh factor. For several years chief of the blood-donor and transfusion center of the Argentine Red Cross, he served as the secretary general of the International Spastics Institute in the Republic of Argentina.

A full professor of hematotherapy, he became interested in geriatrics during his tour of duty as chief of special medicine at a San Isidro hospital, and began his practice in this field in 1968, at the clinics of APANE. At his own private Policlinica, he was associated with his brother, Dr. Francisco P. Ciancaglini, a gastroenterologist and specialist in cellular therapy.

His experience with Martin Bormann as a patient at the Policlinica Ciancaglini was spelled out in two sworn statements notarized by the Honorable Augustin I. Braschi and José Enrique Arnedo of the College of Notaries, and certified by Teodor J. Lopatkiewicz, the American consul in Buenos Aires. Both statements were dated January 23, 1973, only nine months after Bormann had been a patient at the Policlinica. Based on Professor Ciancaglini's records, notes and relevant charts on file at the clinic, the sworn statements were prepared specifically and exclusively for me.*

In the first document, Dr. Ciancaglini stated categorically that the celebrated patient he saw on four separate occasions, although registered under the name of Ricardo Bauer, was recognized positively by him from photographs as Martin Bormann. The second statement is a summary of the medical record of the incident. The following is based on the two sworn statements and repeated interviews with Dr. Ciancaglini.

Bormann drove to the Policlinica Ciancaglini at 134–138 Calle Ituzaingo in San Isidro on Monday afternoon, February 21, 1972, accompanied by Señora Hannelore von M., Jiménez and O'Higgins. The two men remained in the waiting room. But the woman, whom Dr. Ciancaglini described as a statuesque brunette of Germanic appearance, big-bosomed and firm-voiced, went with him into the doctor's office. She participated eagerly in this preliminary consultation, often answering questions for Bormann and, as the doctor put it, "obviously domineering him."

He was walking with a shuffling, short-stepped gait, which Dr. Ciancaglini attributed to a cerebral spasm, but the patient denied this. Mentioning briefly that he had been recommended to Professor Ciancaglini by a physician in Paraguay, he said that his name was Ricardo Bauer and that he lived in a German colony in Entre Ríos, the province in northeast Argentina bordering on Uruguay, where, in fact, Bormann had substantial forestry interests. He gave 701 Calle Presidente Uriburu as his temporary address in Buenos Aires.†

In his notes, Dr. Ciancaglini described the patient as "a man of obviously Germanic origin of pithecan constitution, with a thick neck, normal muscular development, stout skeleton, light-skinned,

* Professor Ciancaglini accepted no fee for this service, and even bore the expenses of the triple notarization. As he put it, he regarded this as his contribution to my work as the historian of the Bormann case, playing his part in the definitive clarification of the fugitive's postwar fate, even if it meant a possible violation of the confidential doctor-patient relationship.

† According to the Buenos Aires Directory of Streets, which lists the owners and residents house by house, this property in the residential district of Beccar is registered in the name of Arpad Thyssen de Zichy, an Austro-Hungarian nobleman who married one of the daughters of Fritz Thyssen (see page 223). For another locality where Bormann usually stays when in the Buenos Aires area, see page 432.

with bright eyes which had a penetrating look, a faint diagonal scar on his forehead, smiling easily but sidewise, with a dental prosthesis in his mouth that, however, was barely visible." Speaking Spanish with a heavy accent, and only when it was absolutely necessary, "Bauer" told the doctor that he was sixty-five years old. But the physician remarked in his notes: "The patient appeared to be in his seventies." Actually Bormann was only four months from his seventy-second birthday at the time of this first visit.

Asked why he was seeking Dr. Ciancaglini's help, the patient replied that he was troubled by his general condition, which he felt was deteriorating of late. When exerting himself in any way, he said, even if only climbing a few steps or puttering in his garden, he would tire easily. His mind was showing distinct signs of slowing down compared with its keenness even a year or two before. He did not smoke, nor did he drink, but his digestion had slowed markedly. He could no longer eat any of the seasoned sauces or condiments that he liked, without suffering intense discomfort afterward.

However, he seemed to be most concerned about his masculine prowess. He confided to Dr. Ciancaglini, with that sidewise smile of his, that he had abused his sexual powers during his younger years. Probably as a result of those excesses, he said, he had become impotent—not suddenly, as he put it, but gradually, over the past few years, until now, when he was so debilitated sexually that he was incapable of making love.

"Senescence," Professor Ciancaglini said, "is a gradual abatement of the body's physiological process, associated with a universal tendency to wasting and degeneration of the highly specialized cells, and their replacement to some degree by a lower form of tissue, usually of a fibrous nature. This process can be arrested by what we call cellular therapy. It is based on the recognition that it is possible to grow animal cells outside the parent body by providing correct conditions of life. We call this tissue culture. Tissues can be grafted into another body and can be kept alive indefinitely, certainly longer than the life of the animal from which they were originally taken."

Examining the patient, Dr. Ciancaglini found that his physiological functions were failing, to be sure, but not too drastically. "There were few of the acute or chronic symptoms which we find in senescence," the doctor said. "Some constitutional weakness, yes. But no degenerative diseases of the heart, no chronic poisoning from the kidneys, bowels or the liver, which are usually the great threats to normal old age. My patient's senile degeneration was most marked in the thickening and hardening of his arteries, especially in the brain. It produced a fairly constant blood pressure of 165 over 100, which was either symptomatic of or the result of his arteriosclerosis. His impotence was advanced and marked. In fact, he was obviously incapable of any functions involving sex."

Professor Ciancaglini suggested that the patient undergo a radical rejuvenation and rehabilitation process with cellular therapy, three grafting sessions to be held at intervals of one month, with a follow-up treatment later in the year. He then quoted $10,000 as his fee, to be paid in cash in American currency. Bormann looked at his companion, and when she nodded, he accepted the proposition, the schedule and the fee. The doctor then prescribed a strict dietary regime prior to the first grafting session, which he scheduled for early April, and asked "Bauer" to bring with him then whatever X-ray pictures, electrocardiograms and analytical records he had, to expedite the final diagnosis.*

The first grafting of ten tissues took place in Dr. Ciancaglini's office in early April as arranged. Hannelore was present throughout "the operation," holding the patient's hand affectionately and pleading with the doctor in her harsh, demanding voice, "Please don't make him suffer."

"The treatment went off well," Dr. Ciancaglini said. On this occasion, Bormann's lady friend turned over a down payment of $6,000 in American twenty-dollar bills, and agreed to call the clinic if any discomfort or complications developed. None did. By this time, Professor Ciancaglini knew who his patient was! Apparently Bormann was under surveillance as usual and had been trailed to the clinic in February, for shortly after the first visit, officers from both Military Intelligence and Seguridad Federal called on Dr. Ciancaglini at his office to question him about his patient. They brought along a set of photographs of Martin Bormann and from them, the doctor recognized the true identity of his patient readily

* Bormann later produced a set of X-ray photographs which, together with the rest of his medical charts, are still on file at the Policlinica Ciancaglini. I was assured that they would be made available to the German authorities to refute the false identification of the skull and bones found in Berlin on December 7, 1972. I conveyed Dr. Ciancaglini's offer to the authorities in Frankfurt, but nothing was undertaken to take advantage of his invaluabe data. In its stead, second- and third-hand "evidence" was used, such as the hearsay testimony of witnesses that, for example, Bormann once fell off a horse and fractured a leg.

although, as he told me, "he was now considerably older, of course, than at the time when the pictures were taken, and he was now leaner, almost drawn by comparison."

The drastic change in his appearance is an important issue in the recognition of Martin Bormann, for there is a marked difference between the man as he was and the man as he looks today. Agents of the Argentine secret service customarily carry the old photographs for identification purposes in case they happen to run into Bormann. They are blowups of his head, showing his forehead, eyes, nose, lips and bullish neck in separate pictures, and his face in profile and full-face, somewhat like mug shots.

I have a set of these "official photographs," but also several which I collected in South America to illustrate my story. Of three in particular I became reasonably certain that the man they showed was Martin Bormann. Two of the pictures were taken in 1955 and 1956 by agents of the Bolivian secret police. I had obtained them from an official of the Ministry of the Interior in La Paz. The third picture had been found in the files of Freddy Schwend when he was arrested in Lima on April 12, 1972. It came from Dr. Santos' collection of the captured documents. Bormann could be identified positively in at least one of these photographs. Taken by a Bolivian police officer who had trailed him to a Rotary Club luncheon during a county fair in Apolo, a city some 125 miles north of La Paz, it showed him leaving a tent where the lunch was held.

The Bormann etched on our mind is an undersized, corpulent man in his early forties, which was his age and image when the pictures we invariably see of him had been taken. We expect him to look older today, of course. But we assume that he is still thickset as we remember him from those old photographs.

Actually, Bormann had been muscular, lean, rather thin-faced, as his wedding pictures show him in 1929. It was only later, in the thirties, after he had become powerful, that he began putting on weight, until he became the lumpish man whose image endures. In 1953, however, he began to lose his excess poundage, probably because he cut back on his drinking (until he went on the wagon altogether) and adopted an ulcer diet.

The 1956 Bolivian photograph in my possession showed him as he was after he had lost considerable weight. He looked very much like the bridegroom in the wedding picture, only twenty-seven years older. Moreover, the picture had a check point that enabled me to verify it. Caught by the camera in front of Bormann was a round-faced, broad-shouldered man, with a wide grin on his face. With the help of the Bolivian functionary, I succeeded in identifying Bormann's companion as Adolf Hundhammer, a former member of Hitler's bodyguard who in the early fifties had emigrated to Bolivia, where he made good as a photographer. When Hundhammer was shown the photograph at my request, he identified the other man in the picture as "Augustin von Lange." This was the alias Bormann used when he lived in Bolivia in the middle fifties.

Now sixteen more years had been added to Bormann's age since Apolo in 1956, and the pictures the Argentine agents carried were at least thirty years old by 1972. Yet Dr. Ciancaglini had no difficulty in identifying Bormann from them, aided by the sharp eyes of the seasoned geriatrician, and the possession of additional scientific data.

He knew who "Ricardo Bauer" was when Martin Bormann showed up for his second treatment in May. He then came back for the final grafting of ten more tissues during a third session in July, at which time Hannelore gave the doctor the $4,000 still to be paid of the agreed fee. "Incidentally," Dr. Ciancaglini said, "I suspected right at the outset that he used the name of Ricardo Bauer as an alias. The fee was extremely high and my conditions were difficult to meet. I made them deliberately to see whether the pair would agree to them, and thereby give me a hint who they really were. They did not bat an eyelash and made that huge down payment. So I was not really surprised when I found out who my patient was."

After the third session Bormann felt better, and he eagerly agreed that he would return for another series of graftings either in late November or early December. But this visit in July was to be the last. "I never saw him again," Dr. Ciancaglini said.

Chapter Twenty-Seven

The Bormann Explosion

Back in the privacy of their huge Chilean hacienda, Señora Hannelore was complaining bitterly to anyone willing to listen that Professor Ciancaglini's intervention turned out to be a dismal flop, and that her man was badly in need of a second cycle of treatments. But when the time came to keep the appointment he had made at the Policlinica Ciancaglini in Buenos Aires for another round of cellular therapy, the quiet life of Martin Bormann was over. He was on the run again! Unexpectedly for him—but also for me—the story of his survival had broken wide open, creating a situation that was potentially as dangerous for him as it became awkward for me. For the revelation in the world press of my search for the fugitive Nazi leader not only unsettled me, but also uprooted Bormann.

In November 1972 the Bormann story broke, prematurely and incompletely, causing a worldwide sensation, which could not fail to alarm Bormann.

Events were piling up so fast that Bormann needed quiet and time to sort them out. He was in bad shape. The rejuvenation cure to which he had submitted earlier in the year had not yielded any of the hoped-for results. His decrepitude was progressing at a growing rate, and the obvious failure of the cellular therapy left him with a mild depression. Innately peevish and querulous, always quick to take offense, habitually suspicious, changeable in his affections, impatient of contradiction, impulsive and choleric, his petulant obstinacy was becoming more pronounced, his emotional responses were becoming less keen. In his condition, in which signs of senility were clearly manifest for the first time, he found it difficult to understand fully the impact of the onrushing developments on his fate and future.

He was planning to go to Buenos Aires again, ahead of the schedule of his second series of treatment, hoping—apparently against hope—that Professor Ciancaglini would perform the miracle even if it were to cost him another ten thousand dollars. On the previous occasion, he had gone to Buenos Aires via Paraguay, sailing through the provinces of Misiones, Corrientes and Entre Ríos, to the huge delta where the Paraná flows into the Río de la Plata. Now the plan was to enter Argentina from Chile via the Uspallata Pass, where the majestic range of the Andes drops to an altitude of 12,000 feet, then motor to Mendoza en route to the Rancho Grande, where he would make the final arrangements for the return trip to San Isidro.

According to the books of the Argentine border police, a man calling himself Ricardo Bauer—the familiar name by now—had entered the country from Chile on October 5, 1972. But in the words of Ramón Penafort, director of the Immigration Service in Mendoza, "some difficulties" then developed and "a lot of confusion ensued." What actually happened was this:

Just when Bormann crossed the border and reported in at the Las Cuevas check point (where he was entered in the manifest under the name of Ricardo Bauer), a young man with obviously forged papers was found loitering at the station. Bormann was quickly turned back, and the young man was taken into custody, never to be heard from again. The whole incident was hushed up on orders from the Ministry of the Interior in Buenos Aires. But today we know that it foreshadowed an event that was to take place a few weeks later. It indicated that certain uninvited people were trespassing on Ricardo Bauer's trail.

Even while I was in Montevideo, preparing to fly to London, and Bormann was back in Chile after the first false start on his second odyssey to San Isidro, a sudden emergency in northern Argentina alerted Bormann to the perils of his life. On November 18, when he was thought to be at Salta, an automobile driven at breakneck speed on Route 34 met with an accident in the town of Ampacaschi, about sixty miles south of the big Krupp estate.

Although an executive of Bracht S.A., the Buenos Aires firm

which represented some of the Krupp interests in South America, told *The New York Times* that the Krupps owned no land in Argentina, the fact is that two enormous ranches are controlled by them. The one at Ampacaschi, through which the car was passing when it crashed, is owned by a woman called Señora Burckhardt. But before her marriage to the man who is her second husband, she was Waldtraut Krupp von Bohlen und Halbach, the daughter of Hitler's most ardent fund raiser and sister of Alfried Krupp, to whom the Führer bestowed the industrial empire as a family fief. Waldtraut bought the *finca* in 1961, from the two and a half million dollars she received under the so-called Mehlem arrangement, which paid off members of the Krupp family in one of the reorganizations of the enormous but unwieldy industrial and financial octopus.

The other Krupp place in the area is the Establecimientos Rancho Grande, the well-nigh impenetrable wilderness covering scores of thousands of acres in Salta, Tucumán and Santiago del Estero, three of Argentina's remote northernmost provinces, owned sub rosa by Arndt von Bohlen und Halbach, an absentee landlord if there ever was one. The playboy son of the late Alfried Krupp by his "morganatic marriage," as the family viewed it, to Anneliese Bahr, a society beauty of Hamburg, he dropped the "Krupp" from his family name when he was "persuaded" to abdicate as the heir to one of the world's largest fortunes. Although he was left with some of the titles to a few of the family's overseas properties, he prefers the Riviera and the hangouts of the European jet set to this godforsaken region in Argentina. I was told he visited the Rancho Grande only once, in 1966, to hunt with invited guests. It was at the Rancho Grande that Bormann hid from time to time—a fact that was never any secret in the region where his arrivals became known promptly and whose inhabitants still call him *el Gran Fugitivo*.

From the smashed car at Ampacaschi, the police pulled a group of heavily armed young desperadoes, to whom Lieutenant Colonel Edgardo Lorca, chief of the Mendoza police, vaguely referred as "members of a terrorist group."

The subsequent investigation of the accident exposed the contours of a weird plot. According to the Argentine authorities, the crashed automobile was one of several cars carrying a "task force" heading north to raid the Krupp *finca*—but why? Except for Bormann, the enormous ranch had nothing to make it an enticing or plausible target for *Argentine* guerrillas. Who, really, were these "terrorists"? Could they have been members or remnants of one of the several native South American groups of Jewish desperadoes returning to the warpath? Was it possible, as it was actually suggested, that they were after the biggest game in the apparently never-ending hunt for fugitive Nazis?

If the Argentine authorities know the answers to these questions, they refuse to divulge them. But they confirmed (to Simon Muller, Mendoza correspondent of the Latin-Reuters News Agency, among others) that the "terrorists" they had intercepted as a result of the fortuitous accident were planning to "storm the *finca* in search of somebody." Whoever they were, and whatever they were after, the police took a serious view of the incident. The whole wild region was placed under siege. Federal agents and local police converged on the Rancho Grande—surrounding it, patrolling its outskirts in Salta, covering its main approaches, but, as usual, never actually entering it.

Bormann was not at the ranch (neither was Arndt, nor was Aunt Waldtraut at her *finca* in Ampacaschi). Word had been flashed to the "Führer" the moment those "terrorists" had been intercepted either to change his itinerary or to postpone his trip. It was into this extremely tense situation that the world press exploded its bombshell.

As the articles appeared in London one after another, copies of the *Daily Express* were flown to Buenos Aires each day, then sent by special messenger to a man in Salta. He had them translated into German, then took the translations to another man living in seclusion on a fortresslike *estancia* in southern Chile. The man in Salta was Captain Hans von Gerstein, one of Bormann's associates-at-large looking after his affairs in Argentina, and the recluse to whom he was taking the translations was Martin Bormann himself.

In Europe and the United States, where Bormann's postwar fate was a perennial mystery and everything connected with the fugitive had a touch of melodrama, the impact of the series was quite different from that in South America, where the revelation that he was alive was hardly news. Even the leaders of the Nazi diaspora made light of the whole business.

In Chile, Bormann's own reaction to the articles startled Hans von Gerstein. When the Great Fugitive read the German translation of the series, he found little that was wrong with it. But Herr von Gerstein refused either to join in his friend's unexpected approval of the articles or to share his ingrained equanimity.

A former regular officer of the German Army in World War II, and married to a well-to-do Chilean lady of German parentage with firm roots in Santiago, Captain von Gerstein was neither a bigoted Nazi nor a fugitive war criminal who had reason to hide. He was first spotted in Chile in the sixties, not because he was on anybody's wanted list, but because he had become one of Bormann's companions and, it seemed, his closest confidant in Chile.

In his self-imposed exile, Captain von Gerstein discarded his martial past and earned a living by managing the estates of rich absentee landlords. In the early sixties, he was the administrator of a huge *estancia* only sixty miles south of Santiago, owned by an enormously wealthy old German-Chilean named Loewenstein. When Loewenstein died and the estate was sold in 1965, Gerstein took over the management of another big estate farther south, not far from Valdivia in central Chile on the Pacific, the hub of the country's thriving German colony controlling the old city's modern tanneries, sugar refineries, shipyards, breweries, flour, lumber and steel mills.

During the peripatetic years of his exile, Bormann enjoyed Gerstein's hospitality as a transient guest in both places. In 1968, however, when his host moved to Salta, reputedly to become the senior chief of his cabinet and manager of his investments in northern Argentina, Bormann began his commuting, mostly inside Chile, between a hacienda that he had bought northeast of Valdivia close to the Argentine border, the heavily fortified German enclave at Parral, whose patron he had become, and his apartment in Santiago, the three places where we have encountered him before.

Unlike the other members of Bormann's immediate circle, Hans von Gerstein took a serious view of the series' possible implications. He was not worried that Bormann might personally suffer from the revelations, that he might be found, arrested and extradited, or that he might be tracked down and killed. What bothered him was the future of the economic edifice that had been built by Bormann and was still held together in good part by his name. It was, as Captain von Gerstein saw it, far more vulnerable and valuable than the decrepit Old Man.

Instead of waiting for the storm to subside, he decided to act.

He implored Bormann to call an emergency conference and then persuaded him to make whatever "adjustments" would be necessary in the control of the conglomerate. Gerstein insisted that Bormann be personally present. He needed his signature.

Gerstein took about three weeks to organize it. It was to be held in a deserted big house actually owned by one of Bormann's cronies in Santiago, a furniture manufacturer named Mark Buechs, although the property was registered in the name of Buechs's nephew. Located in the heart of the capital, it seemed ideally suited for the secret conclave. Built on a street corner with its façade fronting on a park, the house itself was behind a high wall with only one gate on Calle San Pablo through which admittance could be gained. Gerstein told Mark Buechs to tidy up the abandoned house and have it ready by not later than December 22.

Since most of the preparations and arrangements—and, in fact, the subsequent transactions—had to be made by telephone, the Chilean secret police's special bureau that was monitoring both interurban and international calls, under the direction of a good-looking, elegant blonde in her early thirties who called herself Señorita Erika van Sachs (and was, because of her vaunted connections with the American embassy, reputed to be a C.I.A. agent), thus found out about the impending conclave of the Nazis on Calle San Pablo and alerted Inspector Oswaldo Pascual Gonzales, chief of Policía Internacional, my own new source in the Bormann chase, and no friend of the fugitive.

Thanks to the details which Pascual culled from the intercepted telephone conversations, the Buechs house could be "cased and covered" several days in advance. By the date that Captain von Gerstein had set for the opening of the meeting, Pascual had the house watched around the clock by a small detachment of his agents, and two policemen on the San Pablo beat. Then, in the early morning of December 22, accompanied by two German-speaking aides (who were not members of his Policía Internacional but had been recruited by Pascual especially for this emergency), the inspector himself moved to Calle San Pablo. He established his lookout in the doorway of a house that was on the other side of the street exactly across from the strategic gate of the Buechs house, the vantage point from which he could observe all the comings and goings.

He did not have to wait long. In the early afternoon, on Captain von Gerstein's timetable, a car drove up to the gate, driven by a man Pascual recognized as O'Higgins, Bormann's rather gregarious Chilean bodyguard. Out of the car jumped another man familiar to the veteran inspector, Hans von Gerstein. O'Higgins and Gerstein then helped a shaky old man out of the sedan; he was the chairman of the board, Bormann himself. It was obvious that the man was ill. His emaciated face was ashen-gray and drawn, and he seemed to have aged much even since Pascual had last seen him in Santiago only a couple of months before. Now he needed all the help his escorts could muster to make even the few steps into the house. The strange trio disappeared behind the wall. But O'Higgins returned a few minutes later and drove away, not to be seen on Calle San Pablo until Christmas Eve, when his services were needed again.

Shortly after Bormann's arrival, coming on foot or in separate cars, the men Gerstein had summoned to the conference reached the house. Pascual could recognize old acquaintances among the newcomers, the identity of others he guessed from references to them in the intercepted telephone calls. First to arrive was a tall, rather distinguished-looking, elderly gentleman known to Inspector Pascual as a high-ranking SS officer during the war, now called "the Baron," a leader of the German community in Chile, where he amassed a fortune in the trucking business. Next to be admitted were three lawyers, obviously the key men at the conference, for its purpose apparently was to *negotiate* the future of the Bormann syndicate and put whatever changes had to be made in its structure in proper legal form and language. One of them was a frequent defender of the Nazis, whose deft handling of the Walter Rauff case had prevented the war criminal's extradition a few years before. The other attorney was also familiar to Pascual, but he knew him only by his last name of Deutsch. The third lawyer was a prominent member of the Santiago bar, a native Chilean who, as far as Inspector Pascual knew, never before had anything to do with the Nazis.

They were later joined by two more guests—a man named Appen, an old Chile hand of the German secret service who had been a radio spy in Valparaiso during World War II, and another former SS officer, Egbrecht von Oldershausen. He was, like Bormann himself, a fugitive from Allied justice. After them, only one other person was spotted entering the house, a man using the name Klaus Dobermann. He flew in from Montevideo by chartered plane on the second day of the conference, invited by Gerstein as an afterthought.

For the next forty-eight hours, the Buechs house off the quiet little park was a beehive. Couriers kept knocking on the guarded gate, leaving with the sentry large envelopes that arrived with every plane landing in Santiago from Montevideo, Buenos Aires, Rio, La Paz, Asunción and Lima. Bormann, Gerstein and attorney Deutsch never once left the house while the conference lasted. The others departed late at night, but returned early next morning for another day's long session.

The messages that passed to and fro on the wires did not remain secret. All the incoming and outgoing calls were duly monitored by Señorita van Sachs. According to what she later told Inspector Pascual, the recurring theme of all the long-distance discussions with members of the faceless syndicate scattered throughout South America (as far as Quito, Ecuador, and even Panama) was what lawyer Deutsch had bluntly told Dobermann before summoning him in Gerstein's name to come over from Montevideo: "We have to liquidate the business!"

Within weeks after the conference, while Captain von Gerstein was still in Santiago, now staying in the house of his father-in-law, all of Bormann's holdings in Chile, under whatever name they had been registered, were sold, including his hacienda in the south and his apartment in Santiago, to neither of which he ever returned. The syndicate's center of gravity shifted from Chile to Bolivia and to Argentina. Its leadership passed from Bormann, who was far too debilitated to retain the reins in the crisis, to the shrewd organizer of this emergency conference, Captain von Gerstein. For all practical purposes, the Godfather *was* retired!

As far as the Bormann fraternity was concerned, only two incidents marred the well-planned and cunningly organized conference. On December 24, obviously irked by the constant surveillance, and Inspector Pascual's unmistakable presence on the other side of Calle San Pablo, Gerstein ordered the guard to grab one of the police agents as he passed the gate and pull him into the house. The purpose of this "snatch" was to find out the purpose of the watch and how much of what was going on was becoming known to Pascual. But the ruse backfired. It gave Pascual the opportunity he hoped would come—to enter the house in this case, to retrieve his "kidnaped" agent.

Instead of going himself, Oswaldo Pascual decided to send in the two men who were with him on this vigil, if only because they were Germans and had the background knowledge needed to get an idea of what was happening in the Buechs house. They, in fact, succeeded in provoking a confrontation with Hans von Gerstein himself in the large entrance hall of the house. It produced little hard intelligence until the presence of Bormann became patently evident through a brief but loud dialogue Pascual's emissaries overheard in the lobby.

Obviously quite ill already when he first arrived, Bormann's condition must have deteriorated under the stress and strain of the negotiation, because a voice drifting down from an upstairs room urged him: "You need a doctor, Herr Bormann."

The plea was followed by an angry outburst. "I told you repeatedly that I don't want to see anybody while I'm here, not even a doctor, you hear me? Please, leave me alone!"

The voice had a furious pitch. It was plainly the voice of Bormann.

The conference ended on Christmas Eve. Just before sundown, O'Higgins, now accompanied by Luis Jiménez, returned with the car. Bormann was literally carried out of the house and placed gently on the rear seats. A minute later, Inspector Oswaldo Pascual of the Policía Internacional saw Captain Hans von Gerstein clicking his heels, raising his arm in an awkward greeting that could pass for a Hitler salute, then returning quickly into the house, as Bormann's car drove out of Calle San Pablo. Picking up speed, it vanished in the traffic of the rush hour moving around the edges of the park.

As it turned out, Martin Bormann was leaving Chile. But it was more than just abandoning still another country on his relentless wanderings. He was leaving behind an era in his exile.

Chapter Twenty-Eight

Alone on the Bormann Trail

It was at this stage that I saw Martin Bormann—*saw* him is the right word, because it would be too much to say that we *met*. This was the piteous end of the chase. I was now doing what I swore I would never do when I originally embarked on the hunt—using all I had and risking all I dared to meet the man face to face instead of leaving him as I found him—in the Argentine documents.

When Bormann left Santiago on the evening of December 24, 1972, at the conclusion of the conference that Hans von Gerstein had called, presumably to divide the legacy while the testator was still alive, Inspector Oswaldo Pascual of the Chilean International Police followed his trail out of the country—until he lost it. Bormann vanished again. He could not be traced to any of the places he had ever frequented. It was definite that he was neither in Asunción nor in La Paz, the two most likely cities he could have gone to. He was nowhere in Argentina, not in western Brazil, at none of the German colonies in South America whose members, in the past, would loyally raise a protective phalanx around him whenever he needed privacy or protection.

More than a month went by. There still was not a trace of Bormann. Then, however, on February 3, 1973, I received telephone calls from Bueno Aires and Lima, advising me that he had been located in southern Bolivia. Moreover, I was told, arrangements were being made for me to *see* him in person. There were "certain conditions" that needed to be discussed, and the circumstances of the meeting had to be clarified. However, I was told the terms could be explained to me only in a personal confrontation with his trusted representatives in a clandestine meeting at a place of my choice.

I chose Lima and arrived there the day after. Twelve days later, after having crossed frontiers illegally, violated air space in unauthorized flights in a chartered plane, and obviously risking my life in a foolish adventure, I was escorted to his bedside. This was the only opportunity I would have of seeing him, and his last chance of receiving me. He was a patient at a nursing home of the Redemptorist Order somewhere in southern Bolivia, and he was dying.

The clandestine journey to his bedside and the evading of frontier posts and customs guards (which was not as difficult as it sounds, for I was passing through smugglers' country) were conditions that had been imposed upon me by circumstances over which I had no control. The spot in Bolivia where Bormann was could not be reached from La Paz. The only approach to the godforsaken place was by a rickety old international railroad running up the San Francisco valley from Humahuaca in Argentina to its terminus at Tupiza fifty miles inside Bolivia. This rugged Andean country just east of the Cordillera Occidental has peaks that reach altitudes of 19,000 and 22,000 feet above sea level. It is in the rich Potosí Province, whose borderline is so undemarcated that even in 1962, Bolivia had to fight over it with Chile.

The convent where Bormann was held was on a high windswept plateau between mountain ranges and was accessible only from the south. For obvious reasons, I could not enter Argentina even in transit. The authorities there had threatened to charge me with espionage, for my temerity in procuring their Bormann dossier, and the lawyer I hired to represent me, Maitre Joaquín Rodriguez, strongly recommended that I stay away from the country, which was far more eager to catch me than it ever had been to get Bormann. I had no choice. I had to make the tortuous, dangerous, illicit trip partly by chartered air taxi, partly by car, and eventually on foot to the little convent where Bormann was supposed to be dying.

How was it possible for me to arrange the trip? In negotiations lasting for several days, at the Granja Azul, the delightful resort where Bormann usually stayed when visiting his friend Schwend during happier days, I made a tentative bid to buy Bormann's memoirs. At the negotiations I was flanked by Luis Carnejo, my lawyer, who had arranged the session during several trips to La Paz, and Señora Lala Fort, my friend and personal representative in Lima. Bormann was represented by two emissaries who had flown especially to the meeting, one from Bolivia, the other from Argentina.

So high was the quality of these emissaries, so impeccable were their credentials, and so straightforward was their manner of negotiation that I had no reason to question either their sincere good will or the authenticity of the transaction. One of the two envoys was Dr. Alfonso Finot, a distinguished Bolivian scholar well known also in the United States, high commissioner of cultural affairs in La Paz, with the title of deputy mayor. He did not know Bormann personally, but represented the syndicate which owned the part of Bormann's literary properties that his family in Italy had not mortgaged to François Genoud. The other delegate was Bormann's personal envoy, who had his power of attorney. (I am not at liberty to reveal his identity. Although obviously he had no qualms about representing Bormann, he was afraid that publicity about his relations might redound to his disadvantage in his country and damage him in his profession.)

After an all-night session of hard bargaining, I agreed to pay a $500,000 advance for the world rights to the memoirs, but I set two conditions. First, I was to be permitted to edit what struck me as an exceptionally dull and pedestrian manuscript, about one third of which I was permitted to read in its German original, in the presence of Dr. Finot. It dealt mostly with Bormann's rather monotonous life in exile and was entirely lacking in new information. Moreover, it was so lopsided that the historic years when he was Hitler's shadow were confined to eighty of the more than four hundred pages of manuscript. My second condition was that I must be given permission, *by Bormann personally,* to rewrite the whole manuscript, if necessary, and to add whatever original data or background information I deemed necessary to include, culled from *interviews with him* and his associates, and from the thousands of his papers, copies of which I had in my private collection of captured German documents.

The second condition was really a ruse. I was not truly interested in peddling his memoirs. It never was my intention to produce another big Nazi best-seller on the pattern of Albert Speer's recollections. I engaged in these negotiations, when the property was offered to me by a Bolivian attorney representing Finot, in the expectation that at one point Bormann himself would appear in the picture and I would thus be able to meet him face to face.

While Finot returned to La Paz to arrange things, Bormann's delegate left to consult his client. He returned two days later, bringing with him the acceptance of both my conditions. I was to be taken to his last retreat, to authenticate the memoirs and to prove that he was in fact Martin Bormann. We had no time to lose. He was alive, but barely so. As Dr. Finot phrased it gently, "The last effort to arrest his rapid debilitation by resorting to cellular therapy has failed. I'm afraid there is no hope that he'll be with us much longer."

The arrangements had been made for the trip. Partly by bribing our path through borders (out of Peru, into Bolivia and back into Peru), but mostly by simply avoiding the check points, we reached the spot in southwestern Bolivia near Tupiza where Bormann was. At the little hospital, which had only a dozen beds, and a single private room improvised for him, he had the excellent and dedicated care of four nursing sisters of the Redemptorists. When I was taken into his room for what we agreed would be a five-minute visit (with no questions asked and, certainly, no answers given), I saw a little old man in a big bed between freshly laundered sheets, his head propped up by three big downy pillows, looking at me with vacant eyes, mumbling words to himself, raising his voice only once, and then only to order us out of the room rather rudely. "Dammit," he said, not only with some emphasis, but with a vigor that astounded me, "don't you see I'm an old man? So why don't you let me die in peace?"

The impression I gained of Bormann was that he was not as sick as I was made to believe, but rather was a man in an advanced state of senility. It was the arteriosclerosis that Professor Ciancaglini had diagnosed almost exactly a year before, but much more pronounced than when the doctor had seen him. Outside, Sister Ursula, the kindly elderly nun who was his personal nurse, confirmed my lay diagnosis. "The trouble is not that he is *mortally* sick, because he isn't. The trouble is that he has lost his will to live."

After that I was left to my own resources to find my way back as best I could. I made it to Lima in forty-eight hours. When the morning after I was checked out at the beautiful new Jorge Chavez Airport, the immigration officer who stamped "*Salida*" into my passport had no inkling that this was not my first departure since my arrival on February 4, much less that I had *seen* Bormann when everybody—including my wife—thought I was enjoying myself at the Granja Azul in Peru.

Sister Ursula was right. Bormann's condition turned out to be psychosomatic, as usual. Contrary to the expectation of his worried friends, he did not die in that remote part of Bolivia. A few weeks after my hush-hush visit to Potosi Province, he was revived by the return of the Peronistas to power in Argentina. He recovered sufficiently, both physically and mentally, to move back to his adopted country (from which he fled posthaste in 1955) when the provincial dentist Campora, the absentee Perón's hapless stand-in, was elected what turned out to be the interim President of the Republic.

Accompanied by his girlfriend, he took up residence in the Victoria Plaza Hotel in Salta,* in northern Argentina, giving every-indication that he had come to stay. He lived in the city almost conspicuously, but still under the name of Ricardo Bauer. He and Hannelore were daily visitors at a variety shop owned by 30-year-old Olga de Juárez, mainly because one of Doña Olga's partners was a German and the Bormanns found that they could spend a genial time in the store each day conversing in their native tongue.

He was looking at real estate and was on the verge of buying a handsome whitewashed villa (for 25 million pesos in cash) from engineer Bernardo Ramón Biella when the electrifying news of Dr. Campora's resignation and Juan Perón's election reached him. He promptly cancelled the deal with Biella. Then, a week after Perón's triumphal return to the presidency, Bormann moved back to the Federal Capital, to a secluded place where he still lives at this writing, shielded by his friends and protected, now as before, by his "Great Benefactor."

He is spending his days in quiet and safe retirement (especially now that the warrant for his arrest has been lifted by the Germans) behind the walls of a big house in Buenos Aires Province. It is just north of the capital's huge San Isidro district, sealed off from the hustle and bustle of the city by high fences and dense bushes, and by its immense size. The enclave is parceled into several properties, each complete with its own swimming pool, tennis courts, manicured gardens, and garages. Situated on high grounds about 250 feet from the river, the urban estancia is accessible by boat via a private land-

* Bormann's sudden return to Salta was confirmed by Alfredo Serra and Ki Chil Bae, special correspondents and photographers of the magazine *Gente* (People). They interviewed Señora de Juárez and engineer Biella and obtained corroboration of Bormann's presence in the city from the personnel of the Victoria Plaza Hotel and from more than a dozen citizens with whom he was in personal contact, and who recognized Ricardo Bauer as Martin Bormann from a set of photographs Serra and Bae produced for them. His move to Buenos Aires Province was reported to me promptly by one of my intermediaries who, in the meantime, had become a troubleshooter and bodyguard attached to Bormann's entourage. At this writing in June 1974, he is still with him.

ing or on land through a heavily guarded gate. It is patrolled day and night by watchmen with dogs. Access to the place is definitely by invitation only.

Nearby are the palatial residences of such people as Baron de Zichy, an Austro-Hungarian nobleman married to one of the daughters of the late Fritz Thyssen, the German steel tycoon, and Theodor Victor Winterhalder, the 38-year-old scion of an immensely wealthy Argentine family of German stock, and president of the Rio-Mex Corporation whose headquarters are on the Corrientes in the city.

There Bormann lives.

It had never been my intention to track him down. When authoritative documents convinced me that he had survived—for how else would he have been able to enter Argentina in 1948?—I was satisfied that the Bormann mystery had been solved. The fact that I subsequently had the opportunity to see briefly the man I had every reason to believe was Martin Bormann was a kind of bonus.

My efforts to "authenticate" him foundered on his perfectly reasonable refusal to cooperate in his own unmasking. My repeated requests, via intermediaries trusted by both parties, that he submit to fingerprinting were rebuffed brusquely and indignantly; and why not? What incentives could I provide—or, for that matter, could anybody offer—to persuade him to drop his mask after these many years of concealment?

The request to permit me to record a brief interview was turned down (although recently Bormann agreed to a taped question-and-answer session, provided that my questions would be read to him by Señor Winterhalder in my absence). He steadfastly—and understandably, too—refuses to pose for pictures.

Most of the deliberations, conclusions and decision at the Nuremberg trials were based on *documentary* evidence. They produced death sentences despite the uniform "not guilty" pleas of the defendants, and in the almost total absence of anything resembling the formal investigation of ordinary crimes the police and prosecution invariably conduct before a case goes to trial. At Nuremberg, in the case against Martin Bormann, a single witness, Erich Kempka, was heard by the Tribunal in person, and his testimony was dismissed as ambiguous. Bormann was sentenced to death almost entirely on the evidence of documents—documents that had been hastily assembled and by no means covered his whole case. The documents submitted to the Tribunal to substantiate his presumed death were far less convincing, I submit, than the documents I have in my files substantiating his survival.

He comes to life in these documents, to be sure. But the only person in the world who could make Bormann's identification both simple and definitive would be Bormann himself.

The chances that he will ever participate in such an effort are dim.

There are an estimated minimum of fifty thousand Nazi criminals at large *outside* Germany—"the murderers among us," as Simon Wiesenthal called many of them. Several of them have been sentenced to death *in absentia*. Literally thousands of them are under indictment, charged with capital crimes. The extradition of scores if not hundreds had been explicitly demanded in all kinds of legal maneuvers by Germany, Poland, Yugoslavia, Norway and France.

But how many of these criminals have been actually extradited in over a quarter of a century this side of the Iron Curtain? The grand total is four—one by Argentina (Dr. Gerhard Bohne), one by Brazil (Franz Stangl), one by Ghana (Auschwitz doctor Horst Schumann), and one by the United States (Hermina Braunsteiner Ryan)—aside, that is, from the mass extradition to the U.S.S.R. of the Russians in World War II who fought with the Nazis under General Vlasov. Even when extradited, what happens to them? Vlasov and his cohorts were put to death promptly, of course. Stangl died in prison of natural causes. Mrs. Ryan is awaiting trial in a Düsseldorf prison. But Bohne and Schumann are living in comfortable retirement in Germany.

The possibility of official intervention is nothing but a pipe dream. When my articles appeared, in the fall of 1972, Dr. Robert M. W. Kempner, unquestionably the greatest living authority on the pursuit and punishment of Nazi criminals, examined my documentation and concluded that it was of the utmost importance. On December 5, 1972, the seventy-two-year-old jurist formally wrote to the American embassy in Bonn, also for transmission to the British, French and Soviet embassies, demanding that the United States reopen the Bormann case within the framework of the International Military Tribunal.

He received a reply by return mail (dated December 7, 1972) from the Honorable Martin J. Hillenbrand, the American ambassador in Germany. It read as follows:

> I have received your letter of December 5, 1972, in which you referred to recent news articles relating to the possibility that Martin Bormann may still be alive and living in South America. You expressed the view that an investigation should be initiated with a view to bringing Bormann to justice if he is still alive.
>
> As you will appreciate, it is difficult to comment on matters of this type solely on the basis of news articles. If Mr. Farago has available information which he believes establishes that Bormann is alive, it would appear appropriate for him to make it available to Department of State or Department of Defense authorities in Washington who will be in a position to evaluate the information and decide what action should be taken.

Although Ambassador Hillenbrand's letter was only a reply to one written by Professor Kempner, it remains to this day, the one and only *official* reaction to my documentary presentation of the Bormann case by any of the governments professing to be interested in the pursuit of Nazi criminals.

This book is my answer to Ambassador Hillenbrand's invitation.

Postscript

The Bones of Contention

In the late spring and early summer of 1974, certain major developments in Germany invalidated the so-called "final disposition" of the Bormann case by the State Attorney General of Hesse in Frankfurt. There were behind-the-scene activities that now raise grave doubts about the legality, propriety and finality of the proceedings.

Former associates of the late Professor Blaschke (who was also chief of the Dental Corps of the SS)—in particular two former dental examiners of the *Sicherheitsdienst* familiar with the Reichsleiter's teeth—expressed the opinion that the evidence used in the identification of the skull was circumstantial. In the opinion of these SS experts, the findings did not justify the assumption that the disputed skull was that of the missing Reichsleiter.

Yet the unilateral decision of the Hessian State Attorney General, unsupported by any clear-cut decision of the courts, was that the alleged remains of Bormann were to be delivered for burial to the surviving members of his family. This decision was in flagrant violation of the intent and decision of the United States, United Kingdom, France and the U.S.S.R., whose International Military Tribunal had sentenced Bormann to death *in absentia*. According to Wulf Schwarzwäller, the distinguished German biographer of Rudolf Hess, the Tribunal still exists, both formally and legally. None of the four governments that were signatories to the agreement establishing it had terminated the agreement by ever giving notice to this effect. "For all practical purposes," Schwarzwäller wrote, "the Tribunal could be reconvened tomorrow morning."

As stipulated by the original verdict, Bormann, if and when found and arrested, could present his defense in person. However, the rule governing the disposition of the remains of those sentenced to death and executed also applies to him. According to this rule, his bones must be cremated at a secret place at an undisclosed time, and the ashes scattered from a plane.

Although the Hessian authorities arbitrarily disregarded this standing instruction of the Allies, their decision to surrender the bones to the Bormann family hit another unexpected snag.

Advised by Dr. Anton Besold, former member of the Bundestag and the eminent Munich attorney who represents Bormann's seven surviving children in this matter, the family refused to recognize the remains as those of their father. They, therefore, categorically and irrevocably rejected the proposition of the Hessian authorities that they take possession of the skull and bone fragments and bury them at their convenience.

The reason for their startling decision was explained to me by Dr. Besold during an interview in his office on June 20, 1974.

"To say the least," he said, "we are skeptical that the skull and bone fragments, allegedly forming part of Martin Bormann's skeleton, are in fact the remains of the former Reichsleiter.

"Upon the most careful and conscientious examination of the documentation submitted to us by the Hessian State Attorney General as represented by Prosecutor Joachim Richter, we found gaping holes in the evidence (*Beweisführung*). We believe that Herr Richter, who was in sole charge of the matter prior to the final determination, has failed to prove his case.

"We pointed out that we had serious doubt that the remains offered to us were those of Martin Bormann. But Prosecutor Richter proved unable to give us ironclad assurance in support of his contention. He conceded that whatever proof he could offer was 'not one hundred per cent.' "

What irritated Dr. Besold most and made the Bormann family especially suspicious was Prosecutor Richter's stipulation that the remains must not be cremated or destroyed, but preserved intact, so as to be available at any time, as he put it, for possible future forensic study.

"Since Herr Richter thus indicated by himself," Dr. Besold concluded, "that there is doubt about the accuracy and finality of the present findings, I advised the members of the family to reject the State Attorney's offer. My recommendation was accepted unanimously by my clients. *They are naturally and understandably unwilling to care for the remains of a man who may or may not have been their father.*"

Acknowledgments

History was never as blatantly shown to be what Voltaire and Edward Gibbon called it, a register of human crimes, as in the hands of Adolf Hitler and his cohorts. This survey of their crimes, contemporary history presented in the French manner as *grand reportage,* learned but without pretense to formal scholarship, is part of the unending story of what happened in the wake of an event unprecedented in human history—the cold-blooded massacre of more than ten million persons. The premeditated murder on this vast scale was perpetrated by an estimated total of 100,000 depraved individuals, which averaged about one hundred murders per murderer.

After the fall of Hitler, the huge mystery of the Nazis' crimes dissolved into innumerable little mysteries—the *private* mysteries and miseries of men and women on the run. Resolved to escape recognition and retribution, they were using whatever means they could to conceal their past and themselves. It was, therefore, an unusually difficult task to grope one's way through such an unilluminated labyrinth. This indeed was the situation confronting me in my mission, and the enormous difficulties inherent in it undoubtedly left their mark in the deficiencies and inadequacies of the finished product.

However, I am satisfied that I have conducted my investigation diligently and conscientiously, applying as best I could the cumulative professional experience and savvy of fifty years as a reporter, foreign correspondent, editor, explorer, researcher and, last but not least, intelligence specialist and analyst. My research covered, as completely as possible, three big areas of sources: (1) published and unpublished documents; (2) personal investigation in the field and by correspondence; and (3) books and articles.

In the course of this investigation, I used up a passport and a half, twenty-one of their pages covered with ninety-one imprints of immigration officers or frontier guards recording my entries into and exits from their countries (except, again, the Germans, who do not stamp the passports they inspect). In South America, which was the fulcrum of my search, I visited Argentina, Bolivia, Brazil, Chile, Colombia, Ecuador, Paraguay, Peru and Uruguay, several of these countries several times. I virtually commuted between the United States and Germany while working on this book, and visited England, France, Austria, Holland, Denmark, Italy and Spain, seeking additional documentation of Nazi crimes and fugitives.

In all these countries, as well as at home, I had the help of people whose cooperation made my research a gratifying experience and the writing of this book possible. I am, like the good people of Vanity Fair, comfortably and thoroughly in debt to them. Before calling the roll, however, I must pay tribute to my wife, Liesel, and not merely because she suffered with wifely patience while her husband was toiling on a book. She was my courageous, indomitable and ingenious partner, accompanying me on most of my forays, even to countries the visit of which was both uncomfortable and dangerous. Dealing with faceless, unscrupulous, desperate people who necessarily inhabit this underworld of deceit and hidden refuge, her sense of proportion, her unerring judgment and practical approach proved invaluable in sustaining my own equilibrium and preventing me from falling into the pitfalls which dot the road of such research. I am grateful to my son John, whose logical mind, sense of history and pragmatism aided me in the evaluation of the research material and often of the sources which supplied it. He and Sharon, his lovely and erudite wife, were immensely helpful both during my two years of itinerant research and in the preparation of the final draft, separating the wheat from the chaff in the mass of data.

Before listing those who aided me in this endeavor in alphabetical order (and omitting some who requested me not to include them in this manifest of gratitude), I take pleasure in mentioning separately and especially the following friends, colleagues and authorities whose guidance and willingness to share with me their knowledge of the subject proved invaluable:

Professor Robert M. W. Kempner, unquestionably the greatest living authority on the criminal aspects of Nazism and the prosecution of Nazi criminals, was the tower whose beacon showed me the way, and the well at which I quenched my thirst. It is no figure of speech to say that without his unstinting, generous help and support this book could not have been written. I mention almost in the same breath, and with the same sense of gratitude, Judge Horst von Glasenapp, brilliant and brave magistrate at the Landgericht in Frankfurt, the special investigator of the Bormann and Mengele cases in Germany.

For the second time in a row, my inspiration was Professor H. R. Trevor-Roper, of Oxford University, the greatest student of the flotsam of Nazism, whose famous book *The Last Days of Hitler*, written in the immediate wake of World War II, endures as the most remarkable historic documentation of that weird era. He not only gave me important information about Martin Bormann which was otherwise not available, but kindly examined the new documentation I procured in South America, and pointed out what he called the "hard" and the "soft" areas of my evidence. His support in the darkest days of this project produced a debt I shall never be able to discharge.

In the development of additional documentation I was aided by Dr. Robert Wolfe, of the National Archives and Records Service, in Washington, D.C., and George Wagner, his erudite and indefatigable assistant; by Richard Bauer, acting director of the Berlin Document Center; by Professor Herbert Steiner, director of the Dokumentationsarchiv des österreichischen Widerstandes, in Vienna; and by Dr. Luis de Jong and A. H. Paape, of the Rijksinstituut voor Oorlogsdocumentatie, in Amsterdam.

Helping me through the maze and over the hurdles of my investigations beyond the call of mere friendship were my colleagues Zevi Ghivelder, executive director of *Manchete* magazine, Rio de Janeiro; Aron Neumann, chief editor of *Aonde Vamos*, Rio de Janeiro; Enrique Zileri Gibson, editor-in-chief of *Caretas* magazine, Lima; and Moises Rabinovici, assistant editor of *Jornal da Tarde*, São Paulo. They produced for me unexpected sources of exceptional importance to my quest, and allowed me free use of their publications' confidential files. I was also given permission to use without any restrictions the archives of *Der Tagesspiegel* in Berlin, *O Globo* and *Jornal do Brasil* in Rio de Janeiro, *Jornal do Paraná* in Curitiba, *Gazeta do Povo* in Curitiba, *O Estado do S. Paulo* in São Paulo, *Correo* of Lima, *ABC Color* of Asunción.

Two distinguished jurists courageously persisting in the pursuit of Nazi criminals, Federal Judge Dr. Jorge Luque of Argentina and Dr. Luis Carnero Checa of Peru, gave me access to their secret archives, including the complete files of the Mengele, Schwend and Altmann-Barbie cases.

I record with pride and gratitude that wherever I went in South America I was given the most generous and constructive help by the American diplomatic missions. I'm especially indebted to the Honorable Taylor G. Belcher, American ambassador to Peru, and Edward Wemple Clark, the deputy chief of mission; to the Honorable J. Raymond Ylitalo, former American ambassador to Paraguay; to Richard C. Wooton, public-affairs officer in Asunción, Alan Fisher, public-affairs officer in São Paulo, Eugene J. Friedman and Vytautas A. Dambrava, public-affairs officers in Buenos Aires, and to James J. Halsema, public-affairs officer in Santiago de Chile. I was also aided materially by Captain Archibald J. McEwan, U.S.N., former Naval attaché in Buenos Aires and Asunción, and later Defense attaché in Lima, and Lieutenant Colonel Fred Christman, Jr., Air attaché in Lima.

I would like to single out for special mention, with the assurance of my enduring gratitude, Hoyt Nicholas Ware, former public-affairs officer at our embassy in Peru. A veteran Associated Press correspondent in South America, he adopted me instantly from the moment I entered his office in Lima, and aided me throughout my quest with the enthusiasm and savvy left in abundance from his years as a newspaperman, seasoned with his long experience as a diplomat. I am especially in his debt for having given me his old files. They enabled me in particular to develop the Perón aspects of my story with greater depth, thanks to a plethora of background material.

Never-to-be-forgotten experiences were my long interviews with Ambassador Albert Chambon of France in Peru and former Ambassador Benjamin Varon of Israel in the Dominican Republic and Paraguay. It was their sensitive and sensible approach to the problem of Nazi criminals at large that crystallized my own orientation, and made the ground firmer under my feet during this pursuit. His Excellency Alberto Nogues, deputy foreign minister of Paraguay, opened up for my research his whole country without any restrictions.

I was helped generously, objectively and in the most constructive manner by several former members of Martin Bormann's staff, among whom I am permitted to mention only Dr. Ludwig Wemmer of Stuttgart and Ministerial Director Heinrich Heim (retired) of Munich. In my excursions into legal medicine, I consulted Prof. Wilton M. Krogman, former chairman, Department of Anthropology, University of Pennsylvania, the world-renowned specialist in skeletal identification; Dr. Milton Helpern, Chief Medical Examiner, City of New York; Dr. Lowell Levine, distinguished expert in forensic dentistry; and Dr. Jerome A. Zane of Columbia University's School of Dental and Oral Surgery. Their advice proved invaluable.

My profound thanks go to Senhor Marcelo Mroz of São Paulo, Señor I. Z. Sztemberg, José Hugetti and Juan José Velasco of Buenos Aires, for special services brilliantly and bravely rendered; and to my friends and colleagues Dr. Michael Bar-Zohar, David Irving and John Toland, for contributing to my research important documentation involving the Federal Bureau of Investigation, the Counter Intelligence Corps and the Yad Vashem, from their own vast collections of pertinent primary sources.

Although I was not personally in contact with them, I would like to mention in this special category Gerald Reitlinger, Raul Hilberg, Dr. Jacob Robinson, Hermann Langbein, Erich Kuby and Beate Klarsfeld, whose previous investigations and authoritative reports have aided me immeasurably with short cuts in my own efforts.

With apologies to those I omitted inadvertently, I am listing the following who were most active and instrumental in bringing this project to fruition with their aid:

Señora Esther Abramovici, Asunción, Paraguay
Major J. P. Adlam, British Army Medical Corps, Bishopstoke, Hampshire, England
Zwy Aldouby, New York, New York
Ozias Algauer, DOPS, Curitiba, Brazil
Irene Broese Alonso, Asunción, Paraguay
Delegado Priamo Amaral, Santa Catarina, Brazil
Dr. Ricardo Amorim, DOPS, São Paulo, Brazil
Colonel Osvaldo Biano, Foz do Iguassú, Brazil
Albert Bormann, Munich, Germany
Albert Brun, Agence France Presse, Lima, Peru
General Tomás Sánchez Bustamente, Buenos Aires, Argentina
Francisco Camargo, *O Estado do Paraná,* Curitiba, Brazil
Pablo Canabrava, Lima, Peru

Delegado Fausto Augusto Anselmo Cerri, Rio Grande do Sul, Brazil
Ireneo H. Cespedes G., Asunción, Paraguay
Adolfo Chandler, Rio de Janeiro, Brazil
Professor Alfonso Pedro Ciancaglini, San Isidro, Argentina
Sandro Colombo, correspondent of ANSA in South America
Major Luis Costa, in exile in Argentina
Robert G. Deindorfer, St. Kellems, Lower Slaughter, England
Lucas Demare, Buenos Aires, Argentina
Robin Denniston, London, England
Alberto Dines, editor, *Jornal do Brasil,* Rio de Janeiro, Brazil
Evaldo Diniz, editor, *Jornal da Tarde,* São Paulo, Brazil
Erich (Dr. Erico) Erdstein, Ottawa, Canada
Professor Alfonso Finot, La Paz, Bolivia
Eugene Fodor, Litchfield, Conn.
Rita G. de Frahne, Buenos Aires, Argentina
Professor Silvio Frondizi, Buenos Aires, Argentina
Augusto Gabaldoni F., Lima, Peru
Inspector Oswaldo Pascual Gonzalez, Santiago de Chile
James C. G. Greig, Glasgow, Scotland
N. Grisogono, LL.D., London, England
Gerardo Raimondo Hammer, Buenos Aires, Argentina
Erwin Rainer von Harbach, Consul General of Austria, Curitiba, Brazil
William Heath, Associated Press, Lima, Peru
Philip Inwald, M.B.E., M.D., London, England
Enrique Jara, editor-in-chief, Latin-Reuters, Buenos Aires, Argentina
Andor C. Klay, Department of State, Washington, D.C.
James Leasor, Salisbury, Wiltshire, England
Antonio Pascual Lledo, Asunción, Paraguay
Dr. Percy L. Loayza, Lima, Peru
Erhard Löcker, Vienna, Austria
J. B. M., Foz do Iguassú, Brazil
L. M., São Paulo, Brazil
B. M.-S., La Paz, Bolivia
James W. McGovern, New York, New York
Robert Mackie, U.S.I.S., Lima, Peru
Dr. Marcos Margulies, Rio de Janeiro, Brazil
Guillermo I. Martínez, United Press International, Lima, Peru
Dr. Werner Maser, Speyer, Germany
Dionicio F. Maza, Buenos Aires, Argentina
Zivota Melamed, Asunción, Paraguay

Iso Mittelmann, El Al, New York, New York
Rocco Moratibo, correspondent, *O Estado do S. Paulo,* Rome, Italy
Hector Rodríguez Morgado, Buenos Aires, Argentina
Gordon C. Mortensen, United States Mission, Berlin
Simon Muller, correspondent, Latin-Reuters, Mendoza, Argentina
J. H. Norman, A.I.C.A., Curitiba, Brazil
D. W. O'Brian, London, England
Betsy Zavella de Paron, La Paz, Bolivia
Ramón Penafort, Director of Immigration, Mendoza, Argentina
Francisco Cunha Pereira Filho, editor, *Gazeta do Povo,* Curitiba, Brazil
Rubens de Matos Pereira, Lima, Peru
Dr. Horacio A. Perillo, Buenos Aires, Argentina
Walfrido Piloto, Commissioner of Police, Curitiba, Brazil
Dr. Ivo Pitangui, Rio de Janeiro, Brazil
Ramão Gomes Portão, correspondent, *O Estado do S. Paulo,* Asunción
M. T. R., Foz do Iguassú, Brazil
S. C. de R., Quito, Ecuador
Comisario Alejandro Rafaelo, Salta, Argentina
Dr. Guillermo Macia Ray, Buenos Aires, Argentina
Patricio Ricketts Rey de Castro, editor, Lima, Peru
Hon. Carlos Serrate Reich, former minister, La Paz, Bolivia
Nilton Ribeiro, Rio de Janeiro, Brazil
Commandante Gerson de Mattes Ritz, Curitiba, Brazil
Jorge Rocha, correspondent, Latin-Reuters, Buenos Aires, Argentina
Jaime Rodríguez, CEDIBRA, Rio de Janeiro, Brazil
Dr. Joaquín Juan Rodríguez, Buenos Aires, Argentina
José Dionisio Rodríguez, Curitiba, Brazil
Colonel Ruidrejo, Buenos Aires, Argentina
Dr. Carlos Gonzalo de Saavedra, La Paz, Bolivia
Dr. Cesar Augusto Sanabria, Asunción, Paraguay
Comisario Dr. Hector Schée, Santa Catarina, Brazil
Alcidio Schwarzbrod, Marechal Candido Rondon, Brazil
Hon. Oscar Klabin Segall, Rio de Janeiro, Brazil
Dr. Rodolfo Siviero, Rome, Italy
Charles S. Spencer, U.S.I.S., Lima, Peru
R. Augusto Stellfeld, Curitiba, Brazil
Allan J. Stormont, Toronto, Canada
Señora Sonia Tauber, Asunción, Paraguay

Roberto Thompson, editor, *ABC Color,* Asunción, Paraguay
Kurt Tockus, Curitiba, Brazil
Gerd Tykocynsky, São Paulo, Brazil
Cesar Ugarte Salomon, Lima, Peru
Reverend Redemptus M. Valabek, O. Carmelite, Rome, Italy
René Villegas, correspondent, Latin-Reuters, La Paz, Bolivia
Professor Friedrich Vogl, Vienna, Austria
Mayor Werner Wanderer, Marechal Candido Rondon, Brazil
Theodor Victor Winterhalder, Buenos Aires, Argentina
Eric Winters, Marble Dale, Connecticut
Diana Zawluk, Asunción, Paraguay

In the pursuit of this project, from its conception to its fruition, I had on my side one of the most brilliant editors of the younger generation of British newspapermen, Stewart Steven, former diplomatic correspondent and foreign editor of the *Daily Express.* He and David Cairns, star cameraman of the *Express,* accompanied me on several of my research trips to South America. At the *Daily Express* itself, I was always enthusiastically and lavishly supported by Sir Max Aitken, the proprietor, and Ian McColl, the editor, and members of their staff, in particular Ian Brodie, Steven's successor as foreign editor, Andrew Fyall and Stanley Mays in the New York Bureau. My thanks go out to them, for their friendship, compassion and generosity that never faltered. I am also grateful to Michael James O'Neill, managing editor of the New York *Daily News,* for his interest and faith in this project.

Mere words are but empty expressions in thanking Michael Korda, editor-in-chief of Simon and Schuster, and Richard Snyder, his colleague as executive vice-president, whose contribution to this project far exceeded the cooperation an author usually receives from his editor and publisher. It needed vision to contract for this book, stamina to stay with it, and a sacrificial spirit bordering on philanthropy to see it through. Joan Sanger, who was in charge of editorial management and line-by-line editing, combined stern discipline and innate perfectionism with such consummate tact (if not compassion) that she stimulated my writing and expedited the completion of this book. Harriet Ripinsky made tight schedules bearable and agreeable, handling the production with cheerful, reassuring acquiescence and equanimity.

I thank Arthur Neuhauser, my editorial adviser since the days of the Patton biography, who was at my side with many of my literary efforts, including this one, and Maria Dever, my Madrid-born assistant, whose linguistic skill surmounted all barriers I found in my path. My friend Isabelle Bates was again at the typewriter day or night as needed—the most intelligent, dependable, and unselfish help an author can hope for and get.

Muito obrigado, Jipinho! My friend José Menezes Almeida of Foz do Iguassú, who probably saved my life when he dissuaded me from keeping a $10,000-baited date with "Alfredo," the Bolivian smuggler, who offered to take me to Martin Bormann. (And, incidentally, *muchas gracias* to "Alfredo" as well, for *not* taking me on that ride gangster-style when we bumped into each other in Asunción.)

During the difficult days of wholesale skepticism, when my morale badly needed bolstering, I was given exactly the kind of reassurance and encouragement I needed from Dr. Samuel Atkin and Edith Atkin, our oldest and best friends.

As always in the ups and downs of my professional pursuits and private life, I was supported by my friends and associates Maximilian Becker and Joel H. Weinberg. Max is a dream of a literary agent, and in my case, he is a dream come true. Joel's indomitable optimism buoyed me in moments of crises, and his skill as an attorney lifted us over all the obstacles blocking our path, including those we found in Buenos Aires when procuring and authenticating the Bormann and Eichmann documents.

All that is left for me to say is the passage of the general confession from the Book of Common Prayer: "We have left undone those things which we ought to have done; and we have done those things which we ought not to have done." For whatever was done or was left undone, I accept sole responsibility.

Notes on the South American Documentation

[Excerpted from the statement submitted by me to Senior Prosecutor Wilhelm Metzner and Prosecutor Joachim Richter, in Frankfurt, on January 10, 1973]

On April 12, 1972, in the course of a criminal investigation supposedly unrelated to the Nazis, Judge Dr. José Antonio Santos Chichizola of Lima [Peru], had come into possession of persuasive evidence that Bormann was alive in South America; was moving about with relative impunity; and was in touch from time to time with at least two of the men I was interested in—Dr. Josef Mengele in Paraguay and Friedrich Schwend in Peru.

Certain documents seized during a police raid on the house of Schwend fortified this assumption if not actually confirmed it. Thus, for example, a secret address book belonging to Schwend, but found hidden in the house of his sister-in-law—herself a former officer of the RSHA named Neuhold now called "Señora Moretti"—contained the name and apparently current address of Martin Bormann. Also found in Schwend's own home were several letters written by Bormann to Schwend, involving private and business matters.

This documentation is privileged but available. It is no longer part of the broader criminal investigation which [was] concluded a few weeks ago. Since, in the opinion of Dr. Santos, it has no bearing on the case and has no further relevance as far as his assignment was concerned, the impounded Schwend papers are sealed.

The Argentine Documentation

The situation changed radically on September 10, 1972, when, at the recommendation of certain Brazilian authorities with headquarters in São Paulo, I first extended my investigation to the Republic of Argentina.

Aided by two veteran Argentine police officials, one of whom had been employed in the Intelligence Division of the Buenos Aires Provincial Police for eleven years, I at last gained *physical access* to documentation of an official nature.

With the further help of two other experienced Argentine intelligence agents, I procured a great number of documents from the files of the following security and intelligence agencies:

Secretaría de Informaciones de Estado—Dependiente de la Presidencia de la Nación (S.I.D.E.) [State Intelligence Secretariat, a Division of the Presidency of the Nation]

Policía Federal [Federal Police]

Coordinación Federal (now called Seguridad Federal [Federal Security Agency])

Division de Asuntos Extranjeros [Division of Alien Affairs]

Central de Inteligencia [Center of Intelligence]

Ministerio del Interior [Ministry of the Interior]

Ministerio de Marina [Ministry of the Navy]

Dirección Nacional de Migraciones [National Directorate of Immigration]

Policía de la Provincia de Santa Fe [Police of the Province of Santa Fe]

In addition, I obtained a limited number of documents which originated with an organization called A.I.C.A. (for Agencia Informativa Catolica Argentina), on file at the Coordinación Federal. The latter documentation bore the signatures of the Rev. Father Andres Canale, chief of A.I.C.A., and the Rev. Father Egidio Esparza, its deputy chief

On December 29, 1972, I obtained additional and voluminous information from the archives of Juzgado Nacional de San Martin (the Federal Court of San Martin in the Province of Buenos Aires). The documents came from the files of Judges Dr. Raul Horacio Rios Centeno and Dr. Jorge Luque.

The documentation involved three individuals who, according to the papers, had spent years under Argentinian jurisdiction. Consequently considerable documentary material could be assembled about them in the course of their surveillance and investigation, the latter either directly related to their Nazi past or to other criminal activities on their part.

The three men were Adolf Otto Eichmann, Dr. Josef Mengele and Martin Bormann.

Two of the documents now in my possession in particular must be regarded as *key documents* containing definitive clues for the solution of the Bormann mystery. [See page 94.]

The Authenticity of the Documents

The documents explicitly, categorically and definitively assert that Bormann had survived the war and succeeded in making his way clandestinely to Argentina during the administration of former President Juan Domingo Perón.

Other documents trace the movements of Eichmann from 1952 to 1960, and those of Bormann from 1948 to 1970.

I have no reason to question the authenticity of these documents. The manner in which I acquired them; the sources from which they originated; and the physical appearance of the papers themselves combine to attest to their authoritative character and complete authenticity.

Moreover, I have in my possession an affidavit from one of my major contacts, who himself was the source of the two key documents, *stating unequivocally under oath that all the documents in my possession are genuine*—authentic copies of originals on file in the above-mentioned agencies.

Bases of My Contention That Bormann Survived the War

My contention that Bormann had survived the war and escaped to South America is based . . . on these official, authoritative and authentic documents.

I feel fully justified in my legitimate and logical assumption that *the pertinent Argentine authorities, directly involved in the matter, would not have stated in such categorical terms what seem to be the facts of the case if they had not had conclusive evidence at their disposal in support of their claims and statements.*

Broadening the Base of the Bormann Investigation

I would like to emphasize that I did not seek . . . Martin Bormann in South America.

All I claim is that I have in my possession authoritative and authentic documents directly from the files of the Argentine intelligence and police agencies which indicate in no uncertain terms that Martin Bormann has survived the war and succeeded in reaching a safe haven in Argentina, where he lived, protected and unmolested, from 1948 to 1955, and where he had been spotted as late as July 1969, and February–April, 1972.

Bibliography

THE BORMANN LITERATURE

Axmann, Arthur, "Meine Flucht mit Bormann," *Stern,* 1965, No. 19.

Bezymensky, Lev, *Auf den Spuren von Martin Bormann,* Zurich, 1965.

———, *Die letzten Notizen von Martin Bormann,* Stuttgart, 1974.

Bormann, Martin, *The Bormann Letters: The Private Correspondence Between Martin Bormann and His Wife, from January 1943 to April 1945,* ed. with introd. and notes by H. R. Trevor-Roper, London, 1954.

Bormann Documents in the National Archives and Records Service, Washington, D.C.; the Library of Congress, Washington, D.C.; Hoover Library, Stanford, Calif.; Berlin Document Center, Berlin.

Bormann Personalakten, in Berlin Document Center.

Bormann Vermerke: "Hitler's Secret Conversations," stenographic record made for Martin Bormann by Heinrich Heim, 1941–1944, tr. by Norman Cameron and R. H. Stevens, New York, 1953.

Borsdorff, Kurt, "Mit Reichsleiter Martin Bormann auf dem Obersalzberg," Collection Schumacher, Bundesarchiv Koblenz, May 1939.

Busse, Günter, *Behörden und Parteidiensstellen,* Bonn, 1939.

Davidson, Eugene, "The Party in Action and Theory: Martin Bormann," in *The Trial of the Germans,* New York, 1966, pp. 99–109.

Der Prozess gegen die Hauptkriegsverbrecher vor dem Internationalen Militärgerichtshof, Nürnberg, 14.Oktober 1945-1.Oktober 1946, 42 vols., Nürnberg, 1949, in vols. I, II, III, IV, V, VI, VII, VIII, IX, X, XI, XII, XIII, XIV, XVI, XVII, XIX, XX, XXI, XXII.

Ibid., Verteidigungs-Dokumente, XVI, 643; XVII, 288; XIX, 132, 135.

Fest, Joachim C., "Martin Bormann: Die braune Eminenz," in *Das Gesicht des Dritten Reiches,* Munich, 1963.

Gehlen, General Reinhard, *Der Dienst,* Main/Wiesbaden, 1971.

Genoud, François, *Libres Propos sur la Guerre et la Paix,* Paris, 1952.

Gray, Ronald, *I Killed Martin Bormann!* New York, 1972.

Kienast, E., *Der Grossdeutsche Reichstag,* with the biography of Martin Bormann as of November 1943, in his capacity as member of the Reichstag, Berlin, 1943.

Klopfer, Gerhard, *Personalakten,* in Berlin Document Center, including the table of organization of the Parteikanzlei as of May 1, 1944.

McGovern, James, *Martin Bormann,* New York, 1968.

Stevenson, William, *The Bormann Brotherhood,* New York, 1973.

Trevor-Roper, H. R., *The Testament of Adolf Hitler: The Hitler-Bormann Documents, February-April 1945,* London, 1961.

Wahl, K., *Er ist das deutsche Herz,* privately published, 1954.

Walkenhorst, N., Interview with former chief of personnel in the Parteikanzlei, Berlin Document Center.

Whiting, Charles, *The Hunt for Martin Bormann,* New York, 1973.

Wulf, Josef, *Martin Bormann: Hitlers Schatten,* Gütersloh, 1963.

DIARIES, MEMOIRS, PERSONAL NARRATIVES

Andrus, Col. Burton C., with Desmond Zwar, *I Was the Nuremberg Jailer,* New York, 1969.

Baur, Hans, *Ich flog die Mächtige der Erde,* Kempten, 1956; in English, *Hitler's Pilot,* London, 1958.

Bergk, Hellmuth, *Der Bunker am Zoo,* Rastatt, 1963.

Bernadotte, Count Folke, *The Curtain Falls,* New York, 1945.

Biddle, Francis, *In Brief Authority,* New York, 1962.

Biss, Andreas, *Der Stop der Endlösung: Kampf gegen Himmler und Eichmann in Budapest,* Stuttgart/Degerloch, 1966.

Boldt, Gerhard, *Die letzten Tage der Reichskanzlei,* Vienna, 1947; rev. ed. with an introd. by Ernst A. Hepp, 1964.

———, *Hitler: The Last Ten Days,* new tr. of 1964 ed., New York, 1973.

Braden, Spruille, *Diplomats and Demagogues,* New York, 1971.

Chambon, Albert, *81 490,* Paris, 1961.

Charles-Roux, François, *Huit ans au Vatican,* by the French ambassador at the Holy See, Paris, 1947.

Chuikov, Marshal Vasili I., *The Fall of Berlin,* tr. from the Russian by Ruth Kisch, foreword by Alistair Horne, New York, 1967.

Clay, General Lucius D., *Decision in Germany,* New York, 1950.

Degrelle, Léon, *Die verlorene Legion,* Stuttgart, 1952.

Diels, Rudolf, *Lucifer ante Portas,* Stuttgart, 1950.

Dietmar, Udo, *Häftling . . . X . . . in der Hölle auf Erden,* Weimar, 1946.

Dietrich, Otto, *12 Jahre mit Hitler,* Munich, 1955.

Doenitz, Grand Admiral Karl, *10 Jahre und 20 Tage,* Bonn, 1958.

DuBois, Josiah, *The Devil's Chest,* New York, 1951.

Fischer, Gerhard, *Die Irrlichter,* facsimile edition of the memoirs of a Nazi fugitive originally published in Chile, Braunschweig, 1961.

Frank, Hans, *Diaries,* Warsaw, 1957.

———, *Im Angesicht des Galgens,* Munich, 1953.

Friedman, Tuvia, *The Hunter,* New York, 1941.

Gilbert, Dr. G. M., *Nuremberg Diary,* New York, 1947.

Gisevius, Hans Bernd, *Bis zum bitteren Ende: Vom 30. Juni 1934 zum 20. Juli 1944,* Berlin, 1946; Engl. tr. *To the Bitter End,* London, 1948.

Goebbels, Joseph, *Tagebücher,* ed. by Louis P. Lochner, Garden City, N.Y., 1948; in German, Zurich, 1948.

———, *Vom Kaiserhof zur Reichskanzlei,* Munich, 1936.

Günther, Hans F. K., *Mein Eindruck von Adolf Hitler,* Pähl, 1969.

Hess, Ilse, ed., *Ein Schicksal in Briefen,* Leoni, 1971.

Hitler, Adolf, *Mein Kampf* (original published by Franz Eher Verlag in Munich, 1925, 1927), New York, 1939.

Hoffmann, Heinrich, *Hitler Was My Friend,* London, 1955.

Höss, Rudolf, *Kommandant in Auschwitz,* Frankfurt, 1958.

Hudal, Bishop Alois, *Die Grundlagen des Nationalsozialismus,* Graz, 1936.

Kardorff, Ursula von, *Berliner Aufzeichnungen,* Munich, 1964.

Keitel, Field Marshal Wilhelm, *The Memoirs of Field Marshal Keitel,* ed. with introd. by Walter Görlitz, tr. by David Irving, New York, 1966.

Kelly, Dr. Douglas M., *22 Cells in Nuremberg,* New York, 1947.

Kempka, Erich, *Ich habe Adolf Hitler verbrannt,* Munich, 1950.

Kersten, Felix, *The Kersten Memoirs,* tr. from the German by Constantine Fitzgibbon and James Oliver, with an introd. by H. R. Trevor-Roper, New York, 1957.

———, *Klerk en Beul,* Amsterdam, 1947.

———, *The Memoirs of Dr. Felix Kersten,* ed. by Herma Briffault, tr. by Dr. Ernst Morwitz, introd. by Konrad Heiden, Garden City, N.Y., 1947.

———, *Totenkopf und Treue: Himmler ohne Uniform,* Hamburg, 1953.

Koller, General Karl, *Der letzte Monat,* Mannheim, 1949.

Kordt, Erich, *Nicht aus den Akten: Die Wilhelmstrasse in Frieden und Krieg. Erlebnisse, Begegnungen und Eindrücke, 1928–1945,* Stuttgart, 1950.

Lengyel, Olga, *Five Chimneys,* Chicago, 1947.

Lingens-Reiner, Dr. Ella, *Prisoners of Fear,* introd. by Arturo Barca, London, 1948.

Lippe, Dr. Viktor Freiherr von der, *Nuernberger Tagebuchnotizen, November 1945 bis Oktober 1946,* Frankfurt, 1951.

Lösener, Dr. Bernhard, "Memoirs," in *Vierteljahreshefte für Zeitgeschichte,* July 1961.

Lüdde-Neurath, Commander Walter, *Die letzten Tage des Dritten Reiches,* Göttingen, 1951.

Maschmann, Melita, *Account Rendered,* London, 1964.

Mechanicus, Philip, *Year of Fear: A Jewish Prisoner Waits for Auschwitz,* tr. from the Dutch by Irene S. Gibbons, New York, 1964.

Meissner, Otto, *Staatssekretär unter Ebert, Hindenburg, Hitler,* Hamburg, 1950.

Oven, Wilfred von, *Mit Goebbels bis zum Ende,* Buenos Aires, 1949.

Perl, Dr. Gisela, *I Was a Doctor in Auschwitz,* New York, 1948.

Rauschning, Hermann, *The Voice of Destruction,* New York, 1940.

Ribbentrop, Joachim von, *Zwischen London und Moskau,* Leoni, 1953.

Rudel, Colonel Hans Ulrich, *Aus Krieg und Frieden,* Göttingen, 1954.

———, *Trotzdem: Kriegs und Nachkriegszeit,* Göttingen, 1970.

Schaeffer, Heinz, *U-977,* Wiesbaden, 1974.

Schellenberg, Walter, *Memoirs,* New York, 1962.

Schenck, Dr. Ernst Günther, *Ich sah Berlin sterben: Als Arzt in der Reichskanzlei,* Herford, 1970.
Schirach, Baldur von, *Ich glaubte an Hitler,* researched by Jochen von Lang, Hamburg, 1967.
Schmidt, Paul, *Statist auf diplomatischer Bühne, 1923–1945,* Bonn, 1949.
Schwerin von Krosigk, Lutz Count, *Es geschah in Deutschland,* Tübingen, 1951.
Skorzeny, Colonel Otto, *Lebe gefährlich,* Hennef, 1971.
———, *Wir kämpften, wir verloren: Deutsche Kommandos im 2. Weltkrieg,* Königswinter, 1973.
Speer, Albert, *Erinnerungen,* Berlin, 1969.
Spitzer, Jenny, *Ich war No. 10291: Tatsachenbericht einer Schreiberin der politischen Abteilung aus dem Konzentrationslager Auschwitz,* Zurich, n.d.
Steiner, General Felix, *Die Armee der Geaechteten,* Göttingen, 1963.
———, *Die Frewilligen: Idee und Opfergang,* Göttingen, 1958.
Strasser, Otto, *Mein Kampf: Eine politische Autobiographie,* with introduction by Gerhard Zwerenz, Frankfurt, 1969.
Studnitz, Hans Georg, *Als Berlin brannte,* Diary 1943–1945, Stuttgart, 1963.
Turkow, Jonas, *In the Struggle for Life,* Buenos Aires, 1949.
———, *It Happened This Way,* Buenos Aires, 1948.
Warlimont, General Walter, *Inside Hitler's Headquarters 1939–45,* New York, 1964.
Weidling, General H., "Der Endkampf in Berlin, 23.4. bis 2.5.1945," *Wehrwissenschaftliche Rundschau* (Potsdam, East Germany), Vols. 1-3, 1962.
Weizsäcker, Ernst Baron von, *Memoirs,* London, 1951.

SECONDARY SOURCES: BOOKS AND ARTICLES

Adam, Uwe Dietrich, *Judenpolitik im Dritten Reich,* Düsseldorf, 1972.
Adler, H. G., *Theresienstadt 1941–1945: Das Antlitz einer Zwangsgemeinschaft,* Tübingen, 1955.
Adolf, Walter, *Hirtenamt und Hitler-Diktatur,* Berlin, 1965.
American Jewish Committee, *The Eichmann Case in the American Press,* New York, 1963.
Anders, Karl, *Waren sie schuldig,* Nuremberg, 1948.
Appleman, John Alan, *Military Tribunals and International Crimes,* Indianapolis, Ind., 1954.
Arendt, Hannah, *Eichmann in Jerusalem: A Report on the Banality of Evil,* New York, 1963.
———, *Elemente und Ursprünge totaler Herrschaft,* Frankfurt, 1955.
Ascarelli, Attilio, *Le fosse Ardeatine,* Rome, 1945.
Asmussen, Dr. Hans, "Die Stuttgarter Erklärung," in *Die Wandlung* (Heidelberg), 1948, pp. 17–27.
Aziz, Philippe, *Au service de l'ennemi: La Gestapo française en province, 1940–1944,* Paris, 1972.
Barden, Hamilton T., *The Nuremberg Party Rallies, 1923–39,* London, 1967.

Bartoszewski, Wladislaw, *Vergossenes Blut uns verbrüdert: Über die Hilfe für Juden in Polen während der Okkupation,* Warsaw, 1970.

Bar-Zohar, Michael, *The Avengers,* tr. from the French by Len Ortzen, New York, 1967.

———, *The Hunt for German Scientists,* New York, 1969.

———, *Spies in the Promised Land: Iser Harel and the Israeli Secret Service,* tr. from the French [*J'ai risqué ma vie*] by Monroe Stearns, London, 1972.

Bernstein, Peretz F., *Jew-Hate as a Sociological Problem,* tr. from the German by David Saraph, New York, 1951.

Besgen, Achim, *Der stille Befehl: Medizinalrat Kersten, Himmler und das Dritte Reich,* Munich, 1960.

Bezymenski, Lev, *The Death of Adolf Hitler: Unknown Documents from Soviet Archives,* New York, 1968.

Boyle, Kay, "The People with Names," *The New Yorker,* September 8, 1950.

———, *The Smoking Mountain,* London, 1952.

Brand, Emmanuel, "The Handling of Nazi Criminals after World War II," in *Bitfutsoth Hagolah,* Jerusalem, 1965, pp. 18–27.

Braunbuch: Kriegs und Naziverbrecher in der Bundesrepublik—Staat, Wirtschaft, Armee, Verwaltung, Justic, Wissenschaft, [East] Berlin, 1965.

Bross, Werner, *Gespräche mit Hermann Göring während des nürnberger Prozesses,* Flensburg/Hamburg, 1950.

Broszat, Martin (ed.), *Studien zur Geschichte der Konzentrationslager,* a publication of the Institut für Zeitgeschichte, with contributions by Henning Timpke (Fühlsbuttel), Werner Johe (Neuengamme), Gisela Rabitsch (Mauthausen), Ino Arndt (Ravensbrück), Eberhart Kolb (Bergen-Belsen), Manfred Bornemann and Martin Broszat (Dora-Mittelbau), Stuttgart, 1970.

Buchheim, Hans, "Die höheren SS und Polizeiführer," *Vierteljahreshefte für Zeitgeschichte,* October 1963, pp. 362–91.

Bullock, Allan, *Hitler: A Study in Tyranny,* New York, 1954.

Burg, J. G., *Schuld und Schicksal,* Munich, 1963.

———, *Sündenböcke: Grossangriffe des Zionismus auf Papst Pius XII und auf die deutschen Regierungen,* Kalmbach/Munich, 1967, 1968.

Burk, Michall, *Das Tribunal,* a novel about the Nuremberg trial, Munich, 1973.

Cianfarra, Camille M., *The Vatican and the War,* New York, 1945.

Clark, Comer, *Eichmann,* London, 1962.

Conway, John S., *The Nazi Persecution of the Churches, 1933–45,* New York, 1948.

———, "Pius XII and the German Church: An Unpublished Gestapo Report," *Canadian Journal of History,* 1966, I, 1.

———, "The Silence of Pope Pius XII," *Review of Politics,* January 1965, pp. 105–31.

Crankshaw, Edward, *Gestapo,* London, 1956.

Dallin, Alexander, *German Rule in Russia, 1941–1945,* New York, 1957.

Davidson, Eugene, *The Trial of the Germans: An Account of the Twenty-Two Defendants Before the International Military Tribunal,* New York, 1966.

Delarue, Jacques, *Histoire de la Gestapo,* Paris, 1962.

Deutsch, Harold C., *The Conspiracy Against Hitler in the Twilight War,* Minneapolis, 1968.

Deutschkron, Inge, *Bonn und Jerusalem: The Strange Coalition,* Philadelphia, 1970.

Diehl-Thiele, Peter, *Partei und Staat im Dritten Reich: Untersuchungen zum Verhältnis von NSDAP und allgemeiner innerer Staatsverwaltung,* Munich, 1969.

Doman, Nicholas R., "The Nuremberg Trials," review of book by August von Knieriem (*q.v.*), *Columbia Law Review,* March 1960, pp. 412–23.

———, "Political Consequences of the Nuremberg Trial," *The Annals of the American Academy of Political and Social Science,* July 1946, pp. 81–90.

Donat, Alexander, *The Holocaust Kingdom,* London, 1965.

Döring, Hans-Joachim, *Die Zigeuner im nationalsozialistischen Staat,* Hamburg, 1964.

Dreetz, Höhn, "Die Zerstörung Berlins war von der Wehrmachtführung einkalkuliert," *Zeitschrift für Militärgeschichte,* 1965, vol. 2.

Eban, Abba, "Lessons of the Eichmann Trial," *The Jewish Spectator* (London), 1962, nos. 6/7.

"Eichmann Prozess in der deutschen öffentlichen Meinung," Frankfurt, 1961.

Eisenberg, Dennis, *The Re-emergence of Fascism,* South Brunswick, N.J./New York, 1967.

Engelmann, Bernt, *Krupp: Legenden und Wirklichkeit,* Munich, 1969.

Epstein, Klaus, "The Pope, the Church, and the Nazis," *Modern Age,* Winter 1964–65, pp. 83–94.

Ferguson, J. Halcro, *The Revolutions in Latin America,* London, 1963.

Fest, Joachim C., *Das Gesicht des Dritten Reiches,* Munich, 1963.

———, *Hitler: Eine Biographie,* Berlin, 1973.

Flechtheim, Ossip K., *Die deutschen Parteien seit 1945,* Berlin/Cologne, 1955.

Freund, Michael, "Hitler und der Papst. Kurie und Reich in den Jahren 1930 bis 1945," *Die Gegenwart,* 1956, pp. 237–42.

Friedlander, Saul, *Kurt Gerstein: The Ambiguity of God,* tr. from the French by Charles Fullman, New York, 1969.

———, *Pie XII and le IIIe Reich,* Paris, 1964.

Friedman, Filip, *Das andere Deutschland: Die Kirchen,* Berlin, 1960.

———, *This Was Oswiecim,* London, 1946.

Frischauer, Willy, *Himmler,* London, 1953.

Gilbert, Dr. G. M., *The Psychology of Dictatorship,* New York, 1950.

Giovanetti, Alberto, *Der Vatican und der Krieg,* Cologne, 1962.

Gisevius, Hans Bernd, *Adolf Hitler: Versuch einer Deutung,* Munich, 1963.

Goldar, Ernesto, *El Peronismo en la Literatura Argentina,* Buenos Aires, 1970.

Göppinger, Horst, *Die Verfolgung de Juristen juedischer Abstammung durch den Nationalsozialismus,* Villingen/Schwarzwald, 1963.

Görlitz, Walter, *Adolf Hitler,* Stuttgart, 1952.

———, *Die Waffen SS:* Das Dritte Reich, No. 5, Berlin, 1960.

Graubuch; Expansionspolitik und neo-Nazismus in Westdeutschland: Hintergründe, Ziele, Methoden, [East] Berlin, 1967.

Grenfell, [Captain] Russell, *Unconditional Hatred: German War Guilt and the Future of Europe,* New York, 1953.

Grossmann, Kurt R., *Die unbesungenen Helden: Menschen in Deutschlands dunkelsten Tagen,* Berlin, 1957.

———, "Wie hoch sind die juedischen Verluste?" *Rheinischer Merkur,* March 6, 1951.

Gunther, John, *Inside South America,* New York, 1967.

Hagen, Walter (pseud. of Dr. Wilhelm Höttl), *Die geheime Front,* Linz/Wien, 1950.

———, *Unternehmen Bernhard,* Wels, 1955.

Haupt, Werner, *Berlin 1945: Hitlers letzte Schlacht,* Rastatt, 1963.

Hausner, Gideon, *Justice in Jerusalem,* New York, 1966.

Hausser, [Colonel-General] Paul, *Waffen SS im Einsatz,* Göttingen, 1967.

Heiber, Helmut, *Adolf Hitler,* Berlin, 1960.

———, *Joseph Goebbels,* Berlin, 1962.

Heiden, Konrad, *Der Führer,* Boston, 1944.

Heimann, Guido, "Die Lüge von den sechs Millionen," in *Der Weg* (Buenos Aires), 1954, p. 479.

Henkys, Richard, *Die nationalsozialistischen Gewaltverbrechen,* Stuttgart/Berlin, 1964.

Herz, John H., "The Fiasco of Denazification in Germany," *Political Science Quarterly,* 1948, pp. 569–94.

Hesslein, Paul, Interview, *Le Figaro,* December 29, 1950.

Heydecker, Joe J., and Leeb, Johannes, *Der Nürnberger Prozess: Bilanz der 1000 Jahre,* n.p., 1960.

Hieronymus (pseudonym of two experts), *Vatikan intern: Alltag im kleinsten Staat der Welt–Der Apparat–Wie die Kirche herrscht und beherrscht wird–Der Papst,* Stuttgart, 1973.

Hilberg, Raul, *The Destruction of the European Jews,* fourth printing with a new postscript, Chicago, 1967.

Hill, Maris M., and Williams, L. Norman, *Auschwitz in England: A Record of a Libel Action,* foreword by Lord Denning, London, 1965.

Hochhuth, Rolf, *Der Stellvertreter,* with essays by Karl Jaspers, Walter Moschg and Erwin Piscator, Hamburg 1967[–1972].

Höhne, Heinz, *Der Orden unter dem Totenkopf,* Gütersloh, 1967.

Horbach, Michael, and Loehde, Wolfgang, *Geld wie Heu,* Hamburg, 1959.

Jackson, Robert H., *The Nuremberg Case,* New York, 1947.

Jacobsen, Hans Adolf (ed.), *Anatomie des SS-Staates,* with Helmut Krausnick, Hans Buchheim and Martin Broszat, Olten/Freiburg, 1965.

Jaspers, Karl, *The Question of German Guilt,* New York, 1948.

Jenke, Manfred, *Verschwörung von Rechts,* Berlin, 1961.

Karski, Jan, *Story of a Secret State,* Boston, 1944.

Katcher, Leo, *Post Mortem: The Jews in Germany Today,* New York, 1968.

Katz, Robert, *Death in Rome,* New York, 1967.

Kaul, F. *Ärzte in Auschwitz,* Berlin, 1968.

Kempner, Robert M. W., *Eichmann und Komplizen,* Zurich/Stuttgart/Wien, 1961.

———, "Kampf gegen die Kirche," *Der Monat* (Berlin), 1948, pp. 43–50.
———, *Das Urteil im Wilhelmstrassen-Prozess*, Schwäbisch-Gmüend, 1950.
Kent, George O., "Pius XII and Germany. Some Aspects of German-Vatican Relations, 1933-43," *American Historical Review*, 1964, pp. 59–78.
Kern, Erich, *Adolf Hitler*, a biography in 3 volumes, Oldendorf, 1971.
Kessler, Joseph, *Medizinalrat Kersten*, Berlin, 1963.
Kienast, E., *Der Grossdeutsche Reichstag*, November 1943.
Kintner, Earl W., ed., *The Hadamar Trial*, with a foreword by Robert H. Jackson, London, 1949.
Knieriem, August von, *The Nuremberg Trial*, with a preface by Max Rheinstein, Chicago, 1959.
Kogon Eugen, "Politik der Verschwörung," *Frankfurter Hefte*, 1948, pp. 323–24.
———, *Der SS-Staat: Das System der Deustchen Konzentrationslager*, Berlin, 1947; English ed. *The Theory and Practice of Hell*, London, 1951.
Kossoy, Edward, *Handbuch zum Entschädigungsverfahren*, Munich, 1957.
Kraus, Ota, and Kulka, Erich, *The Mills of Death: Auschwitz*, Jerusalem, 1960.
Krebs, Albert, *Tendenzen und Gestalten der NSDAP*, Stuttgart, 1959.
Kronika, Jacob, *Der Untergang Berlins*, Flensburg, 1946.
Kruuse, Jens, *War for an Afternoon*, tr. from the Danish by Carl Malmberg, New York, 1968.
Kuby, Erich, *Die Russen in Berlin*, Munich/Bern, 1965.
Kuperstein, Lieb, *The Fall of Struma*, Tel Aviv, 1944.
KZ: Bildbericht aus fünf Konzentrationslagern [Buchenwald, Belsen, Gardelegen, Nordhausem, Ohrdruf], published in 1945 by order of General Dwight D. Eisenhower by the Office of War Information.
Lampe, Friedrich Wilhelm, *Die Amtsträger der Partei*, Freiburg, 1940.
Lang, Jochen von, ed., *Adolf Hitler: Gesichter eines Dictators*, introd. by Joachim C. Fest, layout by Erich Priester, photographs by Heinrich Hoffmann, Hamburg, 1968.
Langbein, Hermann, *Auschwitz und die junge Generation: Zusammenfassung von Vorträgen an deutschen Schulen*, Vienna, 1966.
———, *Im Namen des deutschen Volkes: Eine Untersuchung der NS-Prozesse in Deutschland*, Vienna, 1963.
———, *Menschen in Auschwitz*, Vienna, 1972.
———, *Die Stärkeren: Ein Erblebsnisbericht aus Auschwitz*, Vienna, 1949.
———, with H. G. Adler and Dr. Ella Lingens-Reiner, *Auschwitz—Zeugnisse und Berichte*, Vienna, 1962.
Langer, Walter C., *The Mind of Adolf Hitler*, foreword by William L. Langer, afterword by Robert G. L. Waite, New York, 1972.
Lauterpacht, Sir Hersch, "The Law of Nature and the Punishment of War Crimes," *British Year Book of International Law*, 1944, pp. 56–95.
Leasor, James, *The Uninvited Envoy* [Rudolf Hess], New York, 1962.
———, "Pius XII," *Stimmen der Zeit*, 1958–59, pp. 81–100.
———, "Pius XII," *Theologisches Jahrbuch*, 1960, pp. 428–38.
Leiber, Robert, S. J., "Pius XII and the Third Reich," *Look* Magazine, May 17, 1966, pp. 36–50.

Lerner, Daniel, "The Nazi Elite," Palo Alto, Calif., 1951.
Levai, Jenoe, *Eichmann in Hungary,* Budapest, 1961.
Levi, Primo, *Se questo e un uomo,* Turin, 1958.
Levy, Claude, and Tillard, Paul, *Betrayal at Vel d'Hiv,* with a preface by Joseph Kessel, tr. from the French by Inea Bushnaq, New York, 1962.
Levy, Günther, *The Catholic Church and Nazi Germany,* New York, 1964.
———, "Pius XII, the Jews and the German Catholic Church," *Commentary,* February 1964.
Lezy, Alan, *Wanted: Nazi Criminals at Large,* Berkeley, Calif., 1962.
Lorrens Borras, José A., *Crimenes de Guerra,* 2nd ed., Barcelona, 1962.
Lükemann, Ulf, *Der Reichsschatzmeister de NSDAP,* Berlin, 1963.
Luna, Felix, *Dialogis con Frondizi,* Buenos Aires, 1963.
Lunau, Heinz, *The Germans on Trial,* New York, 1948.
Manchester, William, *The Arms of Krupp, 1587–1968,* Boston, 1964, 1965, 1968.
Manvell, Roger, and Fraenkel, Heinrich, *Heinrich Himmler,* New York, 1965.
———, *Hermann Goering,* New York 1962.
Maser, Dr. Werner, *Adolf Hitler, Legende, Mythos, Wirklichkeit,* Munich/Esslingen, 1971, 1972.
Meissner, Hans Otto, and Wilde, Harry, *Die Machtergreifung: Ein Bericht über die Technik des nationalsozialistischen Staatsstreichs,* Stuttgart, 1958.
Milano, Attilio, *Storia degli ebrei in Italia,* Turin, 1963.
Milward, Alan S., *The German Economy at War,* London, 1965.
Mitscherlich, Alexander, and Mielke, Friedrich, *Wissenschaft ohne Menschlichkeit,* Heidelberg, 1949, revised ed. 1960; American edition, *Doctors of Infamy,* tr. by Heinz Norden, New York, 1949; British edition, *The Death Doctors,* London, 1962.
Mit zweierlei Mass gemessen: SS- und Militaristen-Treffen erlaubt, Veranstaltung der Opfer des Nationalsozialismus verboten, Frankfurt, 1962.
Momigliano, Eucardio, *Storia tragica e grottesca de razzismo fascista,* Milan, 1946.
Morse, Arthur D., *While Six Million Died,* New York, 1968.
Mosely, Philip E., "The Occupation of Germany," in *The Kremlin and World Politics,* New York, 1960.
Mühlen, Norbert, *The Return of Germany,* Chicago, 1953.
Münzenberg, Willi, *Naziführer sehen dich an,* Paris, 1935.
Murh, Heinrich, "Die rechtliche Stellung des Stellvertreters des Führers," in *Deutsches Recht,* Berlin, 1935.
Naumann, Bernd, *Auschwitz: A Report on the Proceedings Against Karl Ludwig Mulka and Others Before the Court at Frankfurt,* tr. by Jean Steinberg, introductory essay by Hannah Arendt, New York, 1966.
Nellessen, Dr. Bernd, *Der Prozess von Jerusalem,* Düsseldorf, 1964.
Neuhäusler, Bishop Johann, *Kreuz und Hakenkreuz: Der Kampf der Nationalsozialisten gegen die katholische Kirche und der kirchliche Widerstand,* Munich, 1964.
Neumann, Franz, *Behemoth,* rev. ed., New York, 1944.

Neumann, Robert, and Koppel, Helga, *The Pictorial History of the Third Reich,* New York, 1971.

Noth Ernst Erich, *La tragédie de la jeunesse allemande,* Paris, 1934.

Nyiszli, Dr. Miklos, "Le SS-Obersturmführer Docteur Mengele," *Les Temps Modernes,* Paris, April-May, 1951.

Orb, Heinrich, *Nationalsozialismus: 12 Jahre Machtrausch,* Olten, 1945.

Padallero, Nazareno, *Portrait of Pius XII,* New York, 1957.

Parth, Wolfgang W., *Die letzten Tage,* [East] Berlin, 1946.

Pearlman, Moshe, *The Capture and Trial of Adolf Eichmann,* New York, 1963.

Perón, Eva, *Historia del Peronismo,* Buenos Aires, 1971.

Perón, Juan Domingo, *Condición Política,* Buenos Aires, 1970.

Phillips, Peter, *The Tragedy of Nazi Germany,* New York, 1969.

Phillips, Raymond, ed., *The Belsen Trial,* London, 1949.

Pirie, Anthony, *Operation Bernhard,* New York, 1962.

Pol, Heinz, *AO: Auslandsorganisation–Tatsachen aus Aktenberichten der 5. Kolonne,* Linz, 1945.

Poliakov, Leon, *La breviaire de la haine,* Paris, 1951.

———, *Harvest of Hate,* Syracuse, New York, 1954.

———, "The Vatican and the Jewish Question," *Commentary,* November 1950.

———, and Wulf, Jozef, *Das Dritte Reich und seine Denker,* Berlin-Grunewald, 1959.

———, *Das Dritte Reich und seine Diener,* Berlin-Grunewald, 1956.

Poltorak, A., and Saizev, J., *Nürnberg mahnt!* German tr. from the Russian by L. Steinmetz, Moscow, n.d.

Prittie, Terence, *Germany Divided: The Legacy of the Nazi Era,* Boston, 1960.

Pucetti, Roland, *The Death of the Führer,* New York, 1972, Hitler's death in a macabre novel.

Pulzer, Peter, G. J., *The Rise of Political Anti-Semitism in Germany and Austria,* New York, 1964.

Rassinier, Paul, *Le Mensonge d'Ulysse,* Paris, 1955.

———, *La Verdad Sobre el Proceso Eichmann,* Barcelona, 1961.

Recktenwald, Johann, *Woran hat Hitler gelitten,* Munich, 1963.

Rees, J. R., *The Case of Rudolf Hess: A Problem in Diagnosis and Forensic Psychiatry,* London, 1947.

Reitlinger, Gerald, *Die Endlösung,* Berlin, 1956.

———, *The Final Solution: The Attempt to Exterminate the Jews of Europe, 1939–1945,* South Brunswick, N.J./New York, 1953, 1961.

———, *House Built on Sand,* London, 1960.

———, *The SS: Alibi of a Nation,* London, 1956.

Reitsch, Hanna, "Account of Her Three Days in the Führerbunker," *News Chronicle* [London], December 28, 29, 31, 1945.

Repko, Erika von, *Justiz Dämmerung: Auftakt zum Dritten Reich,* Berlin, 1932.

Reynolds, Quentin, with Zwi Aldouby and Ephraim Katz, *Eichmann: Minister of Death,* London, 1961.

Robertson, Edwin H., *Christians Against Hitler,* London, 1962.

Robinson, Jacob, *And the Crooked Shall Be Made Straight,* New York, 1965.

Röhrs, Dr. H. D., *Hitlers Krankheit: Tatsache und Legende—Medizinische und psychische Grundlagen seines Zusammenbruchs,* Neckergemünd, 1966.

Rohwer, Jürgen, ed., *Die Versenkung der jüdischen Flüchtligstransporter Struma und Mefkure im Schwarzen Meer,* Frankfurt, 1964.

Röpke, Wilhelm, *Die deutsche Frage,* Erlenbach/Zürich, 1948; *The Solution of the German Problem,* New York, 1947.

Rousset, Dr. Jean, *Chez les barbares,* Lyon, 1947.

Roussy de Sales, Raoul, *Adolf Hitler: My New Order,* with introd. by Raymond Gram Swing, New York, 1941.

Roxan, David, and Wanstall, Ken, *The Rape of Art,* New York, 1965.

Ruge, Friedrich, "Doenitz, the last Führer," United States Naval Institute, *Proceedings,* October 1954, pp. 1157ff.

Russell, Lord, of Liverpool, *The Scourge of the Swastika,* London, 1954.

Ryan, Cornelius, *The Last Battle,* New York, 1966.

Salgado, J. A. Cesar, *O caso Eichmann a luz da moral e do direito,* São Paulo, Brazil, 1961.

Salvetti, Gualterio, *Las SS matan todavia: El tesoro del lago de Toeplitz,* (Spanish, from the Italian), Barcelona, 1970.

Samuels, Gertrude, "Wanted: 1000 Nazis Still at Large," *The New York Times Magazine,* February 28, 1965, pp. 27, 96–98.

Santander, Silvano, *El Gran Proceso,* Buenos Aires, 1961.

———, *Técnica de una Traición: Juan D. Perón y Evita Duarte, Agentes del Nazismo en la Argentina,* 2nd ed., Montevideo, 1953.

Sassen, Willem Antonius Maria, Interview, *La Razón,* September 12, 1960.

Scharf, A., *The British Press and the Holocaust,* Jerusalem, Yad Vashem Studies No. 5.

Schickert, Klaus, *Die Judenfrage in Ungarn: Jüdische Assimilation und antisemitische Bewegung im 19. und 20. Jahrhundert,* 2nd rev. ed., Essen, 1937.

Schilling, Karl, *Die Rechtsprechung der Nürnberger Tribunale,* Bonn, 1962.

Schmidt-Pauli, Edgar von, *Die Männer um Hitler,* Berlin, 1932, 1935.

Schnabel, Reimund, *Macht ohne Moral: Eine Dokumentation über die SS,* Frankfurt, 1957.

Schoen, Dezsoe, *A jeruzsalemi per,* Jerusalem, 1962.

Scholz, Arno, *Berlin im Würgegriff,* Berlin, 1953.

Schönberner, Gerhard, *Der gelbe Stern: Die Judenverfolgung in Europa, 1933 bis 1945,* Hamburg, 1960.

Schüle, Erwin, "Die Justiz der Bundesrepublik und die Sühne nationalsozialistischen Unrechts," *Vierteljahreshefte für Zeitgeschichte,* 1961, pp. 440–43.

Schultz, Joachim, *Die letzten dreissig Tage,* Stuttgart, 1951.

Schwarz, Hans, *Brennpunkt FQH: Menschen und Masstäbe im Führerhauptquartier,* Buenos Aires, 1950.

Schwarzwäller, Wulf, *Rudolf Hess—Der Mann in Spandau,* Vienna, 1974.

Schweitzer, Arthur, *Big Business in the Third Reich,* London, 1964.

Seabury, Paul, *The Wilhelmstrasse: A Study of German Diplomats under the Nazi Regime,* Berkeley, Calif., 1954.

Semmler, Rudolf, *Goebbels: The Man Next to Hitler,* London, 1947.

Seraphim, Prof. Peter Heinz, *Bevölkerungs- und wirtschaftspolitische Probleme einer Europäischen Gesamtlösung der Judenfrage,* Munich, 1941.

Servatius, Dr. Robert, *Adolf Eichmann: Plädoyer,* Harrach, 1961.

Sheehan, Edward R. F., "In the Forest of Fear," *Saturday Evening Post,* August 12, 1967.

Shirer, William, *Rise and Fall of the Third Reich,* New York, 1960.

Siegler, Heinrich, ed., *The Reunification and Security of Germany,* Bonn, 1957.

Sievers, Wolfram, "Die Endlösung der Judenfrage," *Der Weg, 1957,* p. 235.

Smith, Jean E., *The Defense of Berlin,* Baltimore, 1963.

Smoydzin, Werner, *Hitler lebt,* Pfaffenhofen/Ilm, 1966.

Stein, George H., *The Waffen SS: Hitler's Elite Guard at War, 1939–1945,* Ithaca, N.Y., 1966.

Steiner, Jean François, *Treblinka,* tr. by Helen Weaver, with a preface by Simone de Beauvoir, New York, 1967.

Steinert, Marlin G., *Die 23 Tage der Regierung Doenitz,* Düsseldorf/Vienna, 1967; in English, *The Final Collapse of Germany,* tr. by Richard Barry, New York, 1969.

Suhl, Yuri, *They Fought Back: The Story of the Jewish Resistance in Europe,* 2nd printing, New York, 1967.

Summa Inquira [on the question of the Pope's silence], Hamburg, n.d.

Tardini, Domenico Cardinal, *Pio XII,* Vatican City, 1960.

Tauber, Kurt, *Beyond Eagle and Swastika: German Nationalism Since 1945,* Middletown, Conn., 1967.

Taylor, Telford, "Faces of Justice in Jerusalem," *The Spectator* (London), January 5, 1962, pp. 9–10; also April 21, May 28, 1961.

———, *Sword and Swastika: Generals and Nazis in the Third Reich,* New York, 1952.

Toland, John, *The Last 100 Days,* New York, 1960.

Trevor-Roper, H. R., Introduction to *The Kersten Memoirs,* New York, 1957, pp. 9–21.

———, *The Last Days of Hitler,* London, 1947.

———, "The Mind of Adolph Hitler," introductory essay in *Hitler's Secret Conversations,* New York, 1953.

———, "On the Eichmann Trail," *Sunday Times* (London), April 23, 1961.

Vasconsellos, V. N., *Lecciones de historia Paraguaya,* Asunción, 1970.

Veale, F. P. J., *El Crimen de Nuremberg,* Barcelona, 1954.

Vernant, Jacques, *The Refugee in the Post-War World,* New Haven, Conn., 1953.

Vogt, Hannah, *The Burden of Guilt: A Short History of Germany 1914–1945,* American ed. of *Schuld oder Verhaengnis? Zwölf Fragen an Deutschlands jüngste Vergangenheit,* tr. by Herbert A. Strauss, New York, 1964, with introd. by Prof. Gordon A. Craig.

Waite, Robert G. L., *Vanguard of Nazism: The Free Corps Movement in Post-War Germany, 1918–1923,* Cambridge, Mass., 1952.

Wallenberg, Hans, *Report on Democratic Institutions in Germany,* New York, 1956.

Warmbrunn, Werner, *The Dutch under the German Occupation,* Stanford, Calif., n.d.

Weinreich, Max, *Hitler's Professors,* New York, 1946.

Weiss, John, *Nazis and Fascists in Europe, 1918–1945,* Chicago, 1969, articles from Germany and Italy by correspondents of *The New York Times.*

Wellers, Dr. Georges, *De Drancy à Auschwitz,* Paris, 1946.

Werth, Alexander, *France 1940–1955,* London, 1956.

Wheeler-Bennett, [Sir] John W., *The Nemesis of Power: The German Army in Politics, 1918–1945,* New York, 1953.

Whiting, Charles, *Hitler's Werewolves: The Story of the Nazi Resistance Movement 1944–1945,* New York, 1972.

Wiener, Jan G., *The Assassination of Heydrich,* New York, 1969.

Wiesenthal, Simon, with Joseph Wechsberg, *The Murderers Among Us,* New York, 1967.

———, ed., *Angriff auf das Dokumentationszentrum des B*[*und*] *J*[*üdischer*] *V*[*erfolgter des*] *N*[*aziregimes*] *und Simon Wiesenthal und die Reaktion aus aller Welt,* Vienna, 1970.

Wighton, Charles, *Heydrich,* London, 1962.

Wilmowsky, Tilo Freiherr von, *Krupp Verurteilt: Legende und Justizirrtum,* Düsseldorf, 1962.

Wolf, Jeanette, *Sadismus oder Wahnsinn: Erlebnisse in den deutschen Konzentrationslagern im Osten,* Grenz, 1946.

Wright, Lord, "Natural Law and International Law," in *Interpretations of Modern Legal Philosophies,* Oxford, 1947, pp. 794–807.

———, "Nuremberg," [by the chairman, United Nations War Crimes Commission], *Obiter Dicta, Toronto University Students' Law Journal,* Fall, 1947.

———, "War Crimes Under International Law," *Law Quarterly Review,* January, 1946.

Wulf, Jozef, ed., *Das Dritte Reich: Eine Schriftenreihe,* Berlin-Grunewald, 1960.

———, *Heinrich Himmler,* Berlin-Grunewald, 1963.

Wykes, Alan, *Goebbels,* New York, 1973.

Zahn, Gordon, *The German Catholics and Hitler's War,* New York, 1962.

Zipfel, Friedrich, *Gestapo und Sicherheitsdienst,* Berlin, 1960.

Zoller, A., *Hitler Privat,* Düsseldorf, 1949.

Index